Overthrowing Geography

Overthrowing Geography

Jaffa, Tel Aviv, and the Struggle for Palestine, 1880–1948

MARK LeVINE

University of California Press

BERKELEY   LOS ANGELES   LONDON

University of California Press
Berkeley and Los Angeles, California

University of California Press, Ltd.
London, England

© 2005 by The Regents of the University of California

Library of Congress Cataloging-in-Publication Data

LeVine, Mark, 1966–.
    Overthrowing Geography : Jaffa, Tel Aviv, and the struggle for
Palestine, 1880–1948 / Mark LeVine.
        p.   cm.
    Includes bibliographical references and index.
    ISBN 978-0-520-24371-2 (pbk. : alk. paper)
    1. Tel Aviv (Israel)—History—20th century.   2. Jaffa (Tel Aviv,
Israel)—History—20th century.   3. Jews—Colonization—Palestine—
History—20th century.   4. Palestine—Ethnic relations   5. Tel Aviv
(Israel)—In literature   6. Jaffa (Tel Aviv, Israel)—In literature.   7. City
planning—Israel—Tel Aviv.   8. Cities and towns—Israel—History.
9. Architecture—Israel.   I. Title: Jaffa, Tel Aviv, and the struggle for
Palestine, 1880–1948.   II. Title.

DS110.T357L42   2005
956.94′8—dc22   2004008779

Manufactured in the United States of America
13   12   11   10   09   08
10   9   8   7   6   5   4   3   2

This book is dedicated to ... .
Dr. H. Burton LeVine and Blanche LeVine, for their
moral and personal example and unswerving faith and
support; to my wife, Lola, for her endless love and
patience; and to my son, Alessandro, for his
spirit and inspiration.

7/18/16

There is a certain amount of life that just
needs to be accepted. Accept it, you dont have
a proper family, you just don't. Expect to
not be seen, because you aren't. Thats it. Its
no more complicated than that.
Some will say this is simply pessisism? Is it?
It is it optimism to accept that one has a happy
supporting family when one in fact does? No! Its
reality? We just have a preoccupation w/ positivity
that is beyond logic. Its downright psychologically
unhealthy. Oh well I understand. There is just
simply nothing I can do. That simply means
I have to support myself. Its either that or not
survive. Luckily I-hah is really supportive. love her.

Reading is a good coping skill. But I basically drank beer last night to avoid dealing with my feelings. Maybe not avoid but there was nothing I could do about my feelings. So I gave up.

They my last name is bedivan. So actually my name is Noler rave bedivan. Maybe I am just meant to be a wanderer w/ no ~~tool~~ home. Its more than obvious that I do not belong anywhere.

8/1/16

You know reading this know, I don't know that I feel all that different. It seems that I have been accepted by most of the family, but I don't feel connected to I-tlsn anymore. I guess I feel like a nomad emotionally, like I get my needs met for a short period, then I have to move to take care of myself. That doesn't mean finding new people, more like I have to find new ways of taking care of myself. I-tlsn dealt w/ things in a culturally appropriate way: avoid it/ignore the problem. I think what got me was the lack of space to do anything different; her ignoring the situation was intensely painful. But the thing is, if I cant get my needs met soon I am gonna lose my mind.

Contents

asleep deal w/o dealing w/ my emotions is probably the shittest feeling in the world. This happened even when we are alone in bed. To be fair, we were arguing earlier that day. But it became very clear that I just needed to suck it up. And in fact thats exactly what Judy yelled at me. Suck it up. The other statement was, "this is Taiwan". Makes sense, people change based on context; maybe thats one of my faults. But the answer "this is Taiwan" is not good enough. Who knows, maybe I am just completely wrong and cant see reality. That is certainly a strong possibility. Would not be the first time someone told me that. But I was right about relationships in the past. Maybe I am right here too. Judy wants it all. She doesn't want to budge to make room for me, but she wants me to suck it up. Maybe there is something she hasnt dealt w/ in her family. Who knows. All I know is that I am scared of her know too. Thats probably the worst feeling in the world, or at least one of them. Well, supposedly I only have more day to go. I dont know, maybe not w/ this typhoon. Always some shit. Judy has a correct point in just I am extremely sensitive, put that on the list.

Illustrations

Tables

Acknowledgments

I would like to thank the many teachers, mentors, colleagues, readers, and advisers who have helped in my intellectual development. These include Fr. Charles Bradley at John Vitale of Paterson Catholic Regional High School in Paterson, New Jersey, who started me on the long journey for which this book is the first milestone; and Murray Lichtenstein, Ron Long, Barbara Sproul, and Gail Tirana of the Religion and Hebrew Programs at Hunter College, City University of New York, for preparing me for the rigors of graduate research.

During my nine years at New York University, I had the privilege to study with a number of superlative scholars. I would like to thank my master's thesis advisers, Samira Haj and Norman Finkelstein, as well as Michael Carter, Peter Chelkowski, Ahmed Ferhadi, Mona Mikhail, and Frank Peters. The sincerest thanks and gratitude are owed to my primary Ph.D. adviser, Zachary Lockman, and the rest of my dissertation committee, Michael Gilsenan, Huri Islamoglu, Timothy Mitchell, and Salim Tamari. I am grateful also to the following scholars and colleagues far and wide who helped me with my research and commented on various drafts of the chapters in this book: Amin Abu-Bakr, Ibrahim Abu-Lughod, Boutros Abu-Mana, Iris Agmon, Samer Alatout, Ammiel Alcalay, Arjun Appadurai, Uzi Baram, Carol Bardenstein, Tom Bender, Homi Bhabha, Gid'on Biger, Breyten Breytenbach, Martin Bunton, Dipesh Chakrabarti, Beshara Doumani, Martin Peilstocker, Dov Gavish, Arnon Golan, Iris Graitzer, Jim Holston, Ruba Kana'an, Ruth Kark, Yossi Katz, Hassan Kayali, Sandy Kedar, Rashid Khalidi, David Kushner, Aharon Layish, Assaf Likhovksy, Haim Liski, Michael Lerner, Andre Mazawi, Tzvika Melnick, Gila Menahem, Benny Morris, Moshe at Vaikra Books, David Newman, Juval Portugali, Dan Rabinowitz, Hana Ram, Saskia Sassen, Edward Said, Armando Salvatore, Daniel Schroeter, Gershon Shafir, Hisham Shirabi, Amy Singer, Suleyman Skizittoprak, John Smith, Sasson Somekh, Ehud Toledano, Ilan Troen, Doron Tzafrir, Charles Wilkins, Gwendolyn Wright, Dan Yahav, Mahmud Yazbak, and Oren Yiftachel.

My research could not have been completed without the support and advice of my dear friend and colleague, Sandy Sufian, and my friends in and from Jaffa and Tel Aviv and in Turkey, including but not limited to Gabi 'Abed, Moussa Abou-Ramadan, Sami Abu-Shahedah, Yusuf Asfor, Nazih Ayubi, Filiz Baskan, Fatma Gelir, the Hamammi family, Alp Yucel Kaya, Thomas Kuhn, the Langotsky family, Erica Sigmon, 'Omar Siksik, 'Ali Yatim, 'Asma Agbarieh, and Abdul-Rahman al-Tayyara. I would also like to thank the staff of the following archives and libraries: Alliance Israelite Universelle, Paris; Central Zionist Archives, Jerusalem; Diplomatic Archives, Ministry of Foreign Affairs, France; Hagana Archive, Tel Aviv; Histadrut/Labor Archives (Elan Galper and Daphna Marcu); Israel State Archives, Jerusalem (Ronit Cohen); Middle East Center, Saint Antony's College, Oxford (Clare Brown); Museum of the History of Tel Aviv (Batya Carmiel); Palestine Exploration Fund, London; Public Records Office, Kew; Municipal Archives of Tel Aviv (Ziona Raz, Nelly Verzerevsky, Rivka Pershel-Gershon, Margalith Mugrabi, and Avraham Ben-Zvi); and the New York Public Library, New York City (Eleanor Yadin).

Sara Alexander, Jean Dupre, and Ghidian Qaymari gave me the pleasure of music, which kept me sane during my sojourns in Israel/Palestine and Europe. My brothers, Ronny and Larry LeVine, gave me invaluable support and life experience; my colleagues at *Tikkun* magazine and the Foundation for Ethics and Meaning reminded me that there is more to life than just academics; and faculty and colleagues at the 1998 Stuttgart Seminar in Cultural Studies and at the Mediterranean Programme of the European University Institute's Robert Schuman Centre for Advanced Studies provided intellectual and cultural inspiration.

The International Center for Advanced Studies Program on Cities and Urban Knowledges (in particular, Tom Bender and Barbara Abrash), the Kevorkian Center for Near Eastern Studies, the Graduate School of Arts and Sciences at New York University, the Middle East Research and Information Project, and the Society for the Humanities and the Mellon Postdoctoral Program at Cornell University (in particular, Dominick LaCapra) provided generous support while I wrote and revised my dissertation.

Finally, the nurturing and enthusiastic support of my outstanding colleagues in the Department of History at the University of California,

Irvine, and of Lynne Withey and the staff at the University of California Press (including the anonymous readers of earlier drafts of this book) provided the inspiration to complete the transformation of my dissertation into this book. I hope to be able to repay them all as our journeys continue.

Books

Introduction to Modernity (1995) by Henri Lefebure

Paradise Lost

Introduction

A geographical revolution [or overturning, lit. *mahapacha*] has
come to the world. Many once well-known and important places
have been long forgotten, yet Tel Aviv—this sandbank that rose on
the sands of Jaffa—has achieved a reputation in every corner of the
globe. I mean the world at large. In the domain of writers and
artists, in France, in Italy and Scandinavia, among men far from
our Yishuv. Experts in Tel Aviv know that this is one of the places
worth touring, and it has become part of the domain of their tours.

NAHUM SOKOLOV, "TEL AVIV," *Yediot Tel Aviv*, 1933

Modernity . . . is a word we are not even allowed to question.

HENRI LEFEBVRE, *Introduction to Modernity*, 1995

Orient = Arabs, Asians, Indians

Two years after the violence of 1929, Palestine had yet to heal. Faced with
the unenviable task of explaining the causes of the intensifying Jewish-
Palestinian conflict to the international foreign policy community, Supreme
Court Justice Felix Frankfurter said in part: "We who love the simple Oriental life in its beautiful setting may be pardoned if we regard with a sigh
its pulverization beneath the wheels of progress. Change is inevitable. It is
a mere accident that the Jews should happen to be its agents. . . . Palestine is
inexorably part of the modern world. No *cordon sanitaire* can protect her
against the penetration of the forces behind Western ideas and technology."[1]

Justice Frankfurter's paean to a Palestine Lost has few equals in its (no
doubt unwittingly) keen perception of the impact of Zionism and British
rule on the indigenous population. The pulverizing power of a penetrating
modernity to reshape the landscapes of Palestine, its ability to "overturn"
the existing modern(izing) geographies in favor of specifically Euro-
modern topographies of power and identity, and the inability of the indigenous inhabitants to protect themselves against modernity-as-disease—all
these point to the difficulty if not futility of resistance by a society whose
dialogues with modernity were often ignored by a desperately modernizing
Ottoman state and then actively suppressed by a mandatory colonial British
regime.

In the past two decades numerous authors have challenged the foundational myths and (mis)understandings that long dominated the historiog-

Frankfurter sees the violence as a necessary part of bringing

1

raphy of Palestine/Israel, a narrative that was inspired and sustained by the kind of modernist imagery saturating Frankfurter's remarks. This book follows in their footsteps but opens a new trajectory in the historiography of the country—and through it of the late Ottoman Levant—by using the various experiences of modernity in Palestine/Israel as lenses to explore the development of two of its most important cities: Jaffa, one of the oldest cities and ports in the world, and Tel Aviv, called "the first Hebrew city in the modern world," which was born alongside and ultimately overthrew Palestine's Bride of the Sea as the economic and cultural capital of the country.

But this book does not merely explore how Tel Aviv and its modernity "pulverized" Jaffa and the surrounding Palestinian Arab villages and communities, although that is what ultimately occurred. The six decades leading up to the catastrophe or miracle of 1948 witnessed a much more ambivalent if conflictual interaction among three interrelated matrices of modernity: Jaffa's cosmopolitan Mediterranean modernity, born out of the numerous and multiplying connections within and between Arab/Ottoman and European countries and empires;[2] an exclusivist-colonial modernity that arrived with Zionism and attained hegemony under British rule; and various "nonmodernities" within and surrounding the space of Euro-modernity in Tel Aviv—that is, Jaffa and its numerous villages "erased" by Tel Aviv's development and expanding imaginary and geographic domains. These evolved in response to what I describe as a mutually constitutive four-fold matrix of discourses—modernity, colonialism, capitalism, and nationalism—their attendant strategies of narration, and the innumerable binaries they create and sustain.[3]

An investigation of all three systems is crucial to composing a truly postcolonial historiography of Jaffa and Tel Aviv and of Israel/Palestine as a whole. Chapter 1 offers a critical discussion of varying approaches to the sociology and historiography of modernity, and chapters 2 and 3 offer a detailed account of the development of the Jaffa region and the birth of Tel Aviv during the last decades of Ottoman rule. Both methodologically and theoretically, the discussion seeks to broaden our understanding of the evolution of the discourse of modernities in Palestine/Israel. It does so by moving beyond the European, Zionist, and post hoc Arab sources (i.e., memoirs and other documents composed after the fact) that have long dominated the historiography of the country to an examination of Islamic court records, Ottoman documents, local press reports, early planning and architectural texts, cultural production (art, poetry, and literature), and oral histories. Together these sources give voice to important yet rarely encountered perspectives and data. They expose the dense web of relationships among various communities that participated in Jaffa's rise to wealth and prominence during the ninteenth and early twentieth century and allow me to explore the development and transformation of the Jaffa–Tel Aviv region during the late Ottoman period, the way in which the birth of Tel Aviv in 1909 permanently altered this trajectory, and the role of the conflicted modernization of the Ottoman state in Tel Aviv's rapid development and increasing power vis-à-vis Jaffa.

Such an investigation is crucial for understanding the shifting fortunes of the two cities and the national movements they represented under British and then Israeli rule, which are examined in chapters 4 through 8. In these chapters I challenge the notion that the transition marked a radical transformation from a backward, lawless Oriental system to a modern, progressive European regime by elucidating important similarities in the dynamics and ideologies underlying Ottoman and British rule in Palestine. I seek to advance our understanding of the autonomy and impact of modernization and centralization policies undertaken by the late Ottoman state, particularly in its Levantine provinces.

The East might have been "sick," as Frankfurter intimates, but the Ottoman state believed the cure for its ills was to be found not in cordoning itself off from Euro-modernity but rather in processes of institutional and economic centralization-cum-modernization that would have a profound effect on the development of Palestine during the last century of Ottoman rule by providing the fertilizer that enabled both Jaffa's increasing prosperity and Tel Aviv's and Zionism's blossoming on Jaffan soil.[4] Because of these policies during the course of the nineteenth and early twentieth century, modernity did not have to penetrate Jaffa (and to a significant though perhaps not equal degree, Palestine in general) through violence; as often as not it was welcomed by the local population through activities ranging from draining swamps to assimilating the latest European fashions, architecture, or agricultural technologies that arrived daily with the ever-increasing numbers of travelers at Jaffa's overburdened port.

Yet it is also true that in the final years of Ottoman rule, during the first decade of the twentieth century, new kinds of modernities emerged in Eurasia that increasingly would be imposed by Europe on non-European indigenous populations (and metropolitan European populations too, but that story cannot be recounted here). These penetrations caused symptoms of a disease that I demonstrate many Palestinians recognized and attempted with varying degrees of success to engage or (when necessary) resist.

Specifically, both Henri Lefebvre and Virginia Woolf inform us from seemingly different vantage points that around 1910 two powerful and contradictory discourses and landscapes of spatial production emerged that permanently changed "human character"—the first generated by colonial modernist ideologies of planning, the second by (post)modern Einsteinian physics—and through which the concretized, hierarchized modernist spaces could be shattered.[5] In 1910 the name of the Ahuzat Bayit neighborhood, now a metropolis, was officially changed to Tel Aviv. These two apparently contradictory experiences of space are central to understanding Tel Aviv's birth, history, conflictual, and ultimately fatal relationship with Jaffa.

That is, if we foreground the role of modern urban planning and architectural discourses in the imagination and building of Tel Aviv as a modern, exclusively Jewish city, we open new horizons for exploring both the power and the limits of modernity as a discursive and analytic project and for investigating the production of nationalist identities and subjectivities within it. At the same time, an analysis of the production of space in Palestine provides the means to shatter the existing modern(ist) visions of Tel Aviv and Jaffa—and through them, modernity at large—by offering a "strategy for leaving modernity" and the myriad lifeworlds it silences. Indeed, it helps us to rediscover the rich history of interaction and implication these discourses have obscured.[6]

Let us turn back the clock a bit farther, to a warm, late summer day in 1909, the day the founding members of the Ahuzat Bayit building society made a historic one-kilometer trek north of their homes in Jaffa to a plot of land known as Karm al-Jabali.[7] There they broke ground for what would soon become Tel Aviv, the capital of pre-1948 Jewish Palestine and today's "global" Israel; but the celebrations that day were frustrated by a group of local bedouins who went to court to stop construction, claiming that they had long used this sandy land to plant vegetables and graze their animals. The bedouins' victory was overturned by the local Ottoman authorities after European consuls intervened on behalf of Ahuzat Bayit; but they did not go away. During the next three decades, the bedouins "continually" passed through and used their former lands, making a general "nuisance" of themselves despite complaints by local residents and officials.[8]

I suggest that the contemporary historian would do well to take in the landscape of Palestine/Israel from a perspective similar to that of the bedouins and others living on the margins of the emerging political and social geography of Tel Aviv. Excluded from and thus unfettered by the numerous boundaries and divisions engendered by an emerging "sedentary and state space"—to whose striated landscapes they were unable or unwilling to conform—the bedouins continued to experience the space of Tel Aviv as open-ended and boundariless. For this reason they were viewed as a "plague."[9]

Yet the story of Jaffa and Tel Aviv can be understood as an operation of "trans-generational beduinity,"[10] one that rides astride the difference and ambivalence at the core of all unitary expressions of identity, traveling back and forth across Self and Other in order to flesh out selves and others whose voices have long been silenced, or at least muffled, by official "Zionist," "Israeli," "Palestinian," or "modern" personalities. This serpentine trajectory blurs the boundaries established by the modernity matrix and the numerous binaries and hierarchies it generates.

The various discourses embedded in the history and mythology of Tel Aviv and, through Tel Aviv, in the landscape of the Jaffa–Tel Aviv region need to be disaggregated before any reimagining of Jaffa or Tel Aviv can be attempted. This methodology allows me to explore the evolving relationship between Jaffa and Tel Aviv in a manner that opens up narratives heretofore largely silenced by the fourfold modernity matrix and to question the salience of "modernity" as a sociological and historiographical category, challenge the recent theoretical discussions about modernity's multiple pasts, presents, and futures, and perhaps move toward a critical leave-taking of the concept as a primary problématique, analytic, and project guiding the study and performance of identities and the discourses that have produced them in the post-Napoleonic Middle East.

BOUNDARIES OF THE MODERN

The discussion so far has perhaps not yet clarified why it is so important to investigate the history of the Jaffa–Tel Aviv region through a critical reading of the history of modernity as it unfolded in Palestine/Israel and the larger Levant. In fact, the region's history demands this line of inquiry, as the Jewish state was from the start conceived of by men such as Theodore Herzl as "a peculiarly modern structure," with Tel Aviv—literally, "Hill of Spring," a biblical name that was used as the Hebrew translation of Herzl's novel, *Old-New Land*—playing the role of the "thoroughly modern metropolis" at its heart.[11] Given the self-conception of Tel Aviv as the quintessentially modern city and the centrality of the discourses of modernity, modernism, and modernization in its development, any examination of the city's history needs to be contextualized in the larger project of European metropolitan and colonial modernities that inspired its founders and leaders and vis-à-vis the cosmopolitan Ottoman/Levantine modernities of late

Ottoman Jaffa with which it necessarily interacted and against which it defined and asserted itself.

Although Tel Aviv and Jaffa have since 1949 been considered administratively one city, Tel Aviv–Yafo, Tel Aviv was founded in 1909 to create a separate, specifically modern suburb that would provide its residents with a European style of living, in contrast to what was felt to be dirty, noisy, overcrowded, and essentially Arab Jaffa. Not surprisingly, for their part, Jaffa's residents and municipal leaders considered the region surrounding the city, including the Jewish suburb (at least until the late 1920s) and the surrounding Arab farms and bedouin communities administratively and culturally part of Jaffa.

Today the situation is reversed: officially Tel Aviv considers Jaffa an integral part of a united city, whereas the majority of Palestinian residents consider Jaffa historically and culturally distinct from Tel Aviv, even as they struggle to gain greater political and municipal representation. At the beginning of the twenty-first century, Tel Aviv–Jaffa remains as divided as it was after the British Mandatory Government granted the Jewish city "independence" from Jaffa.

We can learn much about the history of Tel Aviv, Jaffa, and the surrounding Palestinian Arab villages by following the movements and travails of the Palestinians and Jews living on the borders and margins of the city. Not just bedouins but also Yemenite and North African Jews, Houranis from Syria, Egyptians, Transjordanians, Circassians, Germans, Greek Orthodox, and Lebanese were part of the landscape of Jaffa before Tel Aviv's founding (soon to be joined by various unassimilable European Jewish immigrants). These communities were not part of the structured space of separation that would define Tel Aviv and thus were considered "bedouin" or "nomad."

Yet despite the modern, exclusively Jewish vision on which Tel Aviv was founded and built, these communities remained or became woven into the social, economic, and cultural fabric of the region.[12] Examining the boundary or frontier regions in which these populations lived—that is, examining Tel Aviv and Jaffa as frontiers of modernity (indeed, Jaffa was described in the Islamic court records in 1797 as a *thaghr*, or frontier location)[13]— reveals that Jaffa's relationship with Tel Aviv constitutes an especially profitable site for exploring the complex and problematic nature of modernity.[14] Put more strongly, it reveals the impossibility of separating the ideology and discourses of Zionism in general, and of Tel Aviv in particular, from the fourfold modernity matrix.[15] Yet, as I stated above, such an examination also raises the issue of whether modernity is the most useful prism through which to analyze and compare the development of Jaffa and

Tel Aviv, or for that matter, Jewish and Arab Palestines; as often as not, attempts by members of either community to demonstrate their modernity revealed the opposite lurking just underneath.[16]

Moreover, while most Zionists and British officials viewed Tel Aviv as a quintessentially "modern" city and Arab Jaffa (including the region's Arab Jewish population) and the surrounding villages as backward, the ability of many (often the least educated or sophisticated) Arabs to perceive and resist the consequences of the Zionist and British modern(ist) discourses suggests that there is a richer and more complex set of parameters than the European-inspired linear and teleological conceptualization of modernity through which to investigate the development of the two cities and two nationalisms. Indeed, using the fourfold matrix of modernity, colonialism, capitalism, and nationalism to analyze the space and communities of Jaffa–Tel Aviv helps us to recognize the local population as imaginers and producers (and not, at best, merely consumers) of their own modernity or perhaps better, nonmodernity, as the modernity that unfolded in Jaffa was free of, or at least not free to reveal, the colonial moment that I argue lies at the heart of the project (or attitude) of modernity.[17]

MODERNITY AT LARGE?

Any reconceptualization of the discourses of modernity (as problemátique or thematique) must engage the revolution in scholarship on the worldwide evolution of capitalist modernity that has challenged previously dominant conceptions of the centrality and uniqueness of Europe. This pride of place has, of course, helped to sustain Eurocentric, Orientalist modes of thinking that posited the long separation from and stagnation of the Ottoman and "Eastern" worlds vis-à-vis the rapidly modernizing West. In the words of Charles Issawi, "[T]he fact of Muslim decline itself stands plain."[18]

In reality, the story is not so neat or easy to follow. To begin with, the notion that European and Arab-Islamic cultures were so separate that they had to be bridged would have seemed strange to a twelfth-century Venetian or North African, let alone a sixteenth-century Ottoman or French diplomat (as they allied against the Hapsburgs).[19] More broadly, scholars such as Janet Abu-Lughod, Samir Amin, Peter Gran, Andre Gunder Frank, and Kenneth Pomeranz and Steven Topik have argued conclusively that the roots of capitalist modernity extend both temporally farther into the past and geographically wider across the globe than has been portrayed in earlier narratives.

Indeed, as Pomeranz argues, Europe was neither the center nor even the dominant power in the world economy until the nineteenth century (China held that distinction),[20] while closer to home, intra-Ottoman trade was more valuable than trade with Europe until the same period.[21] The teleological narrative of Europe as the prime mover of modernity and everyone else as responding to it must therefore be discarded in favor of constructing a narrative of a polycentric world with long-standing interconnections and no dominant center until the nineteenth century, when a combination of luck, geography (its location vis-à-vis the New World), and favorable resource stocks, especially coal, enabled the completion of a transformation from competitive to imperial capitalisms that Europe alone was fortuitously positioned to make.[22] This process necessitated a universalization of both the economic and the ideological aspects of modernity, and in so doing it constituted the "point of departure for the conquest of the world."[23]

Although considerations of space prohibit a detailed rehearsal of the debates over and most recent scholarship on the historiography of the late Ottoman Empire, an analysis of Palestine must be situated within larger discussions of the nature and scope of Ottoman state modernization and centralization policies—which took place "under conditions of inter-imperialist rivalry," particularly after the imposition of the Ottoman Public Debt Administration in 1882, yet maintained a fair degree of autonomy and agency[24]—and their impact on the country's economic, cultural, and political development. Only then can we understand how and why, with the imposition of British rule, a different kind of modernity emerged in Palestine, one that turned Jaffa into a space of nonmodernity vis-à-vis the increasingly Jewish landscape surrounding it.

If the Ottomans themselves understood their power to have begun to wane in the late seventeenth century,[25] the empire was considered one of Europe's "best colonies" by the late eighteenth century, an attitude that was naturally translated into European politics toward and scholarship on the empire even after its demise. Any attempt to refashion a less Eurocentric historiography of the late Ottoman Levant must therefore escape the well-laid trap of colonial rationality and instead decolonize Ottoman history by exploring the roots and dynamics of its many political economies vis-à-vis their own intentionalities and rationalities, which are much richer and more authentic than their depiction as pale copies of the European master narrative suggests.[26]

A more complex and accurate narrative would begin by understanding that far from being a period of decline, the sixteenth through eighteenth centuries were a time of the institutionalization and transformation of the empire, during which it was affected by many of the same processes that produced such dramatic changes in (at least northern) Europe.[27] Thus during the pivotal nineteenth century, although for very different and often contradictory reasons, both the European powers and the Ottoman elite sought to "modernize," "centralize," "individualize," and thus strengthen the Ottoman state,[28] which produced a set of institutions that made it more powerful, rationalized, positivistic, specialized, liberal, and capable of imposing its will on its subjects than ever before.[29]

Yet "rather than a wholesale importation of European modes of political and social organization, Ottoman modernity involved a process of mediation and translation to adapt new ideas from the West to radically different settings across the Empire."[30] One of the primary means to achieve this modernity was through the establishment of a "new" land regime (in 1858), and the tax revenues it would produce, whose goal was to establish title to every piece of productive land in the empire and in so doing establish a one-to-one correspondence between a piece of property and the person(s) paying taxes on it. If such a dynamic held in the more peripheral districts east of the Jordan, in the Jaffa region—one of the most productive in Palestine if not the empire—this Ottoman modernism would profoundly shape the region's subsequent history.[31]

In fact, the late Ottoman state consciously imagined and portrayed itself in quite modern terms. Yet "modern" did not have to mean "European" (it often meant just plain "new").[32] As Boutros (Butrus) Abu-Manneh argues, the well-known Hatt-ı Şerif of Gülhane, generally understood as inaugurating the Tanzimat period, can be interpreted as being grounded almost entirely in Ottoman-Islamic (and perhaps even Sufi) sources. Its resonance with "Western" or "European" modernizing discourses, at least until the second half of the century, was thus one of sympathy and correspondence rather than direct influence and imitation.[33]

In this sense, the "revival and regeneration of religion and state, land and community" could be interpreted as helping to usher in (or in some places, including perhaps Jaffa, solidify) a Levantine modernity—one in which "security of life, honor and property," public trials, and the extension of basic rights to all subjects could have created a noncolonial liberal capitalism if they had had the time to develop.[34] On the other hand, as the century wore on, the Sublime Porte increasingly considered itself a "modern member of the civilized community of nations" and the "committed advocate of reform in the Orient"; it even desired to emulate the other "civilized" nations by sending colonists to the "dark continent" to "bring the light of Islam into savage regions."[35]

In this vein, religious law, or *fiqh*, was updated to the "needs of modern times" and deployed to "civilize" the provinces, while in Palestine and other Arab provinces the state pursued an educational "mission civil-isatrice" in which the sons of prominent Jerusalem families (among others) were enrolled in new schools that used the "splendor of the spectacle" of Ottoman modernity to inculcate the "blessings of civilization to the Arabs . . . still in a state of nomadism and savagery."[36] Also of particular relevance to the Palestinian context—and indicative of the consequences of the modernity deployed by the state—is that while the Porte went to great lengths to prevent acquisition of land by "foreign" Muslims in key regions such as the Hejaz, it supported (or at least did little to prevent) such sales to Europeans, particularly Jews, in the Holy Land.[37]

In short, late-nineteenth-century Ottoman reforms often embodied an order that bore significant similarities to the colonial regimes that would replace the Ottoman state decades later.[38] But even as the Porte desired to join the European colonial club as a partner, by the Young Turk revolution in 1908—one year before the establishment of Tel Aviv—the imbalance of power between the empire and Europe was such that it could only be understood as taking place "in a colonial context," with the empire on the losing end of the equation.[39] Yet however negatively modern and deleteri-ous for its Palestinian subjects Ottoman political discourses became during the nineteenth century, in fin-de-siècle Jaffa at least a specifically noncolo-nial modernity seems to have developed that in turn created a specifically Levantine "third space" in which incommensurable subcultures were, for a time, spatially reconciled.[40] Put another way, a unique balance of political and economic power and culture existed in the region that produced a cos-mopolitan Levantine-Mediterranean culture that for several decades was free of the more pernicious effects of colonialism, nationalism, and even capitalism while retaining the hybridity and newness that have always defined modernity—and the modern city.[41]

The dynamics of this moment, and the forces that collapsed it, are dis-cussed in the chapters that follow. Here it should be noted that cosmopoli-tan modernities of this period were of a different order than the more unmediated colonial modernities arriving from Europe. However, in Pales-tine specifically, the more hybrid cosmopolitan identities produced by this matrix, which could situationally move back and forth between Muslim, Ottoman, Palestinian, clan and local and regional markers and loyalties, were no match for the militant identities of exclusivist-colonial national modernities of Europe—and thus of Zionism and soon enough of Palestin-ian Arab nationalism as well.

yeah, see how
did it *they did internalize*
it. did. internalize *it.*
internalize

Broadly speaking, then, in striving to "reach the level of European civilization," the modernity pursued by the Ottoman state was that imagined and unfolding in western Europe—that is, the dominant world imperial-colonial powers—and thus a modernity that was defined by ideologies shaped by colonialism and imperial capitalism, a fact that facilitated the Zionist development and modernization of the Jaffa–Tel Aviv region in the coming decades.[42] And with the increasing hegemony of a specifically ethnic Turkish nationalism within the Ottoman state, Palestinians were in a double bind, as the state was both inclined to support the privatization and marketization of land and disinclined to support anything that smelled of separatist Arab nationalism.[43]

Because of these dynamics, the formation of a powerful Palestinian Ottoman identity, one that could counter the specifically colonial Euro-modern identity of the Zionist movement, was frustrated; this situation led many Arab, especially Palestinian, deputies to determine that the Ottoman state was no longer able or willing to look out for their interests and that a specifically "Palestinian" nationalist identity needed to be forged.[44] But even as some sections of the Palestinian elite, particularly in Jerusalem and Gaza, were suspicious of the modernizing reforms of the late Ottoman state, especially the Committee of Union and Progress, others, including a good share of Jaffa's notable class, supported many of the "reforms" initiated by the center, most likely because the earlier generation of reforms had strengthened the urban notable class that dominated the city's politics and economy.[45] *So the politics was not black & white. Duh,*

Ultimately, the social pattern established by the Ottoman state's ambivalent modernization would contribute in the Mandate period to the inability of Palestinian Arabs to develop an urban proletariat, sustainable wage labor, and a political and economic force on a scale large enough to challenge the power of the landowning class in the countryside or Jewish industry and organized Jewish labor in the towns.[46] On the Zionist side, it encouraged (or at best, offered little resistance to) a Zionism in the soil of Palestine that could not but engender a "militant nationalism" against the indigenous non-Jewish population.[47] *fire with fire,*

But until Zionism ushered in the gradual hegemony of Euromodernity, a large share of the population of Palestine, particularly in the Jaffa region, was engaging processes of capitalization, marketization, monetization, and other aspects of "modernization" with ingenuity, rationality (in the European as well as local Arab-Muslim senses of the term), and success. Indeed, the work of Beshara Doumani, Ruba Kana'an, and Charles Wilkins pushes back the appearance of the benchmark economic barometers of modernity

Had it been left alone, it definitely had the possibility of developing successfully, even though it clearly would have similarities that I don't appreciate.

to the pre-Tanzimat era, at least to the turn of the nineteenth century in the immediate wake of Napoleon's invasion and perhaps many decades earlier, when Jaffa's citrus "gardens" were already the envy of Europe.[48]

As important as the dating of these processes is their complexity, which has been determined by the interplay of forces and interests of the Ottoman, Egyptian, and European states, local and regional Palestinian forces, and Mediterranean-wide processes of modernization at large. Such a complex set of actors, discourses, and interests suggests that we cannot engage what Doumani terms the "discourses of modernity"[49] in Jaffa and Tel Aviv without including two heretofore neglected discussions in the scholarship on Palestine/Israel: a detailed analysis of Janus-faced modernity and its many European, Ottoman, and Palestinian incarnations; and an investigation of the Ottoman perspective on the development of the Jaffa–Tel Aviv region and the emergence of the two nationalisms in this space.

No one would think of examining Mandate Palestine without making use of British records, yet few studies of late Ottoman Palestine, including the most important works of the past two decades, use Ottoman sources; this means that an important perspective is missing on the crucial years in which the two national movements emerged and developed alongside and often against each other. Given Jaffa's roles as a port city and the center of the Zionist *yishuv* (community), the local and central Ottoman perspectives on these issues would provide vital information and data on the development of the country in general, of the two (as yet) protean national communities, and of the role of the local Ottoman authorities and central government in these processes.

With such knowledge we can better compare the two triangular relationships—between Zionist Jews, Palestinians, and the Ottoman and then British (colonial) states—that defined the history of this period and helped to determine the contemporary dynamics and experience of neoliberal globalization in the region via Tel Aviv's role as Israel's "world city." Thus an important goal of the first three chapters of this book is to use Ottoman, local Palestinian (particularly Shari'a Court), and Jewish and Zionist planning sources to produce a broader and deeper knowledge of this period than has been possible using the traditional European and Zionist archival sources.

This approach has its limitations, particularly in that I do not have the space to engage fully the depth of information contained in the thousands of pages of Islamic court records or provide a detailed focus on one community or social group as Doumani, Agmon, Kana'an, and Wilkins have done in producing innovative and important contributions to the social history of

[margin, handwritten] Why would the West want to include Ottoman Sources??

Palestine; or that Kayalı, Deringil, and Makdisi, using Ottoman records, have demonstrated are crucial to obtaining a new and more nuanced understanding of the relationship between the Ottoman state and the Arab provinces. Yet by engaging the variety of sources I deploy, a broad perspective can be gained, one that I would argue is crucial to understanding the complex dynamics of Jewish-Palestinian interactions on the cusp of two great imperial regimes.

Moreover, most Zionist or Israeli and Palestinian studies of Jaffa or Tel Aviv have excluded the other city and community from their historical narratives when they explore their social and economic development and territorial expansion during the late Ottoman period (or at best have incorporated the other from an exclusivist-nationalist framework). This is true even of the most recent Israeli monographs exploring Tel Aviv's history, which contain little data or discussion of Jaffa and its Palestinian Arab population.[50] In contrast, the broad range of sources on which the narrative of the first three chapters draws allows me to situate the establishment and early growth of Tel Aviv within the larger narrative of Jaffa's rapid development during the period under review and to argue for their interaction, interdependence, and mutual influence.[51]

With chapter 4, the discussion moves into the Mandate period. Here I examine Jaffa and Tel Aviv from the point of view of the cities' economic development, labor and municipal relations, and spatial expansion during this period. Particular attention is paid to the interaction of the two communities and cities along the border regions that simultaneously divided and joined them. These regions were the fault lines out of and into which Zionist and Palestinian identities were imagined, negotiated, and, more often than not, contested.

In chapter 5 I momentarily step outside my historical narrative and examine the depictions of Jaffa and Tel Aviv in the literature, poetry, and press of each community. My examination provides further evidence of the influence of the exclusivist, modernist, and nationalist imaginings of Jaffa and Tel Aviv on the history and geography of the region. This lays the groundwork for the final three chapters of the book, which examine the architectural and town planning discourses that profoundly shaped the landscape of Jaffa and Tel Aviv during the late Ottoman and Mandate periods and which continue to exert a determinative influence on the reshaping (i.e., gentrification) of today's unified city of Tel Aviv–Jaffa.

Thus chapter 6 examines the discourses of architecture and town planning that were crucial to Tel Aviv's self-identity and at the same time its successful expansion of territory and power over Jaffa and surrounding

Palestinian villages. Yet while these discourses were deployed to separate Tel Aviv from Jaffa and ultimately to achieve the latter's discursive (and ultimately physical) "erasure," my analysis of architecture and planning in Jaffa reveals similarities to and even anticipation of developments in Tel Aviv that belie Tel Aviv's claim to be the sole representative of modernity among Palestine's cities if not the country as a whole.

However, as the title of chapter 7, "Planning to Conquer," suggests, I argue that the modernist architecture and town planning discourses deployed by Tel Aviv leaders during the 1930s and 1940s were instrumental to the city's expansion, and ultimately conquest and annexation, of Jaffa and the surrounding Arab villages. Chapter 8 examines how the contemporary spatial policies of the Tel Aviv municipality and the responses by the Palestinian population of Jaffa mark a continuation of patterns of struggle and contestation established almost a century ago. It concludes this work by returning to the theme of Tel Aviv's nonmodernity in order to ask whether the Jaffa–Tel Aviv region was ever "urban," or "public," or even a "city" according to the way in which these terms have been deployed by commentators as diverse as tenth-century Hanafi jurists and early-twentieth-century American urban reformers (including a certain future president whose views on the modernity of the nation would profoundly shape the post–World War I Middle East). Ultimately, by bringing into dialogue the voices of various sectors of the Palestinian and Jewish communities, Ottoman, British, and Israeli officials, and the odd American, Frenchman, or Baghdadi, the saga of Jaffa and Tel Aviv's troubled yet fascinating pas de deux can be explored with the richness and ambivalence it deserves.

History is anything but black and white, as is most of life and interpersonal relationships. But its easier to deal w/ black & white, as its easier to not face the realities of the world and the reality of our lives.

1 Modern Cities, Colonial Spaces, and the Struggle for Modernity in the Eastern Mediterranean

Why has modernity and its antinomies played such an important role in the history of the Jaffa–Tel Aviv region, and through it, in the larger historical and political history of Palestine/Israel? To answer this question we must first recall that the city has long been the most peculiarly modern of spaces, believed by many of the most enlightened reformers of the late nineteenth and early twentieth century to be the "hope of democracy" and thus of the nation.[1] In this context, Jaffa and Tel Aviv were each the "model" of urban modernity as it was imagined by the two national communities.[2] *No wonder these two cities are important to study.*

Yet the city was also the site where the ills of capitalism—both caused by, and necessitating, modernization—were glaringly on display, in particular, the extreme overcrowding, disorderliness, and disease associated with the rapidly expanding working-class quarters of European—and Palestinian Jewish and Arab—cities. It was out of the attempts to address myriad problems of life in the modern city that the discourses of planning and development, which are crucial to my story, arose. Perhaps the most well-known example was the destruction and planned rebuilding of much of Paris by Haussmann in the second third of the nineteenth century and the subsequent Haussmannization of other European capitals.[3]

As one French planner of this period, a Professor Barthelemy, described it, by "cleans[ing] the large cities . . . you cleanse the entire country."[4] Yet creating such a tabula rasa was a monumental undertaking in Europe; the task was much easier in the "backward" colonies, which were deemed ready for the radical (re)inscription of modern planning and development.[5] The colonial modernity that emerged in part out of this developmentalist impetus was doubly asymmetrical, designating both a break in the regular passage of time (i.e., modern versus traditional) and, as important, "a combat

cities were rebuilt to fit w/ the economic ideals and beliefs of the last 300 plus years.

15

in which there are victors and vanquished[, in which] [o]ther cultures 'bec[o]me premodern by contrast.'"[6]

Once the colonized space was vanquished and cleansed, the plan for and founding of a new colonial (and often capital) city would be "a civilizing event . . . giv[ing] form and identity to an uncivilized geography."[7] Central to this process was a logic of creative destruction whose power was especially strong in the space of the urban.[8] If, as the epigraph that opens this book suggests, the leaders of Tel Aviv believed that the birth of Tel Aviv was a revolution (or overturning, or even overthrowing, all connotations of the Hebrew word *mahapacha*) of geography—not just the geography of the Jaffa region but geography at large, in the "world at large" (*'olam hagadol*)—then it was through the process of creative destruction that this action was realized.[9] Indeed, this dynamic is a fundamental feature of the discourses of urban modernism and modernization, constituting an "aesthetic of erasure and reinscription" that is at the heart of modern ideologies of planning and development.[10]

In this manner, the founders of Tel Aviv, and those who recounted its history in words and images, were able to depict the land as "nothing but sand" and as empty and remote as "the Sahara desert," to lament the "primitive" practices of Arab sand carters when Jews were engaged in the same work, to depict the Palestinian inhabitants of Jaffa as "renters" and not owners of (i.e, not possessers of true rights to) the lands of Jaffa and Tel Aviv while Tel Aviv was considered a pure Jewish city. These themes made the depiction and perception of Tel Aviv as a modernist project and space sine qua non seem quite reasonable and even natural.

Tel Aviv, like other colonial cities sired and nourished by a "discourse of development,"[11] justified its various separations from its mother town by representing itself as a negation of existing conditions in Jaffa—a severing of ties that allowed for the discursive and ultimately physical erasure and cleansing of the territory, landscape, and history of Jaffa.[12]

Given these dynamics, I argue that if Zionist (and later, Israeli) identities and historiographies have sought to portray Zionism as both "modern" and something other than colonialism,[13] the epistemological and ontological premises of Zionism conclusively demonstrate just the opposite—that on the discursive and material levels, Zionism is a seminal example of the discourses of modernity and colonialism and their mutual embeddedness, demonstrating the impossibility of conceiving of one apart from the other. Thus the leaders of Tel Aviv were right to consider that city the highest manifestation of Zionist modernity, although not in the manner they presumed (i.e., as a symbol of progress and Enlightenment in a land otherwise devoid of both).

The link between modernism and colonialism may seem self-evident, yet in fact neither the pathbreaking analyses of Israel as a colonial or colonial-settler society by Rodinson, Kimmerling, and Shafir, nor the foundational writings on other colonial settings and colonialism at large by Fanon, Memmi, and Césaire, nor the most important recent philosophical and sociological critiques of modernity by Habermas, Giddens, and Harvey or postmodern contemporary critiques have accounted for the complexity and richness of the fourfold modernity matrix and the social and political-economic geographies it has produced.[14] It is crucial to address this lacuna if a more accurate and comprehensive historiography and sociology of Palestine/Israel, let alone of colonialism and modernity, is to emerge.

If we have isolated the city as an especially powerful site for the production of modernity, we have still to define the contours of modernity generated in the space of the urban. The project of modernity conjures numerous meanings, visions, and theories, many of which do not correspond to the experiences of Jaffa and Tel Aviv.[15] The most popular starting point is the Baudelairean description of modernity as the fleeting, the transitory, and the arbitrary; filled with both beauty and "the savagery that lurks in the midst of civilization."[16] This contradictory depiction of modernity stems from its experience as a new and accelerated mode of existence, one emerging from the dynamics of industrial production, circulation, and consumption that were generated by the rise and growing dominance of the capitalist market in various locations (and intensities) around the world.[17]

This mode of production was accompanied by a drive to be modern (at the most basic level, to be new and up-to-date) as well as a simultaneous development of universal, positivistic, and technocratic science, morality, and law.[18] The latter three discourses-cum-technologies were the only tools powerful enough for the burgeoning European and other bourgeoisies—and as important, workers, women, and other subaltern groups—to grasp and control a world in which change rather than tradition had become ubiquitous, in which the past had become a burden from which men needed to be freed.[19]

Contemporary critical thinking has transformed the contours of the modernity debates, most important, by discarding the traditional modernizational and teleological analyses based on the belief that there was only one route for a "culture" or "civilization" to achieve one possible "modernity." Instead, many (but by no means all) scholars accept that there is no one package or pattern of modernity.[20] In particular, Latin American scholars—perhaps because of the longer durée of Western imperialism-colonialism in the Americas vis-à-vis Africa or Eurasia—have developed concepts such as coloniality and transmodernity that help us to think modernity "out and through from the 'other end,' that is, from 'colonial modernities.' "[21]

Despite the numerous important advances in addressing the European bias of much of the scholarship on modernity,[22] however, many of the leading contemporary histories and sociologies of modernity either fail to capture the motivations or dynamics of Jaffa's and Tel Aviv's modernities (particularly the role played by colonial discourses and the creative destruction they unleashed)[23] or address the changes brought about by the contemporary, second wave of so-called globalization and thus events and ideologies that emerged decades after most of the events I am describing transpired.[24] One can include here such important discussions as those concerning secularization and religious transformation, the rise of second or risk-based modernities,[25] the modernity/Enlightenment dialectic,[26] and the role of the precise time-space zoning of social life as the source of modernity's "dynamic nature."[27]

Most recently, the "multiple modernities" approach has called for a far-reaching reappraisal of the classical visions of modernity and modernization, based on a realization that many seemingly traditional or otherwise nonmodern practices or beliefs (such as those associated with so-called Islamic fundamentalism) are in fact iterations of core elements of the modern condition-cum-project.[28] Its proponents thus call for developing new intellectual technologies to reenvision modernity as a transcultural space of interaction in which religion can play an important role, which encourages a reappraisal of modernity's European discourses and its non-Western expressions.[29]

Yet the multiple modernities perspective preserves a European-Western etiology and emphasis while focusing on issues such as individual autonomy and reason's supremacy, or on the possibility of interpreting contemporary "fundamentalist" movements as a form of "Jacobin modernity," that are less relevant to the situation in late Ottoman and mandate Jaffa–Tel Aviv (especially outside the bourgeois urban milieu) than they are to modernities' contemporary conditions.[30]

In fact, one could argue that "modernity," as it is understood and used in the social sciences, is both of quite recent vintage and located geographically and epistemologically in the United States—two reasons why we cannot easily transpose it to turn-of-the-twentieth-century Palestine.[31] For this reason it is not surprising that an accounting of the relationship between colonialism and modernity is absent in much contemporary scholarship outside of interdisciplinary analyses of "regions," such as the Middle East or the Indian subcontinent, where the importance of this relationship to the construction of accurate historiographies, geographies, political economies, or anthropologies is impossible to ignore.[32]

If we consider the other elements of the modernity matrix, it becomes clear that colonialism and imperialism were "the context that shaped nationalism."[33] I would argue that imperialism-colonialism and modernity are more than just the contexts of nationalism; together they constitute the "generative order" through which nationalism was manifested.[34] This genealogy was in fact recognized by Marx, who saw the birth of capitalism in the European overseas colonies and even before them, in the colonization of Ireland and Scotland; and recently it has led scholars to search for a heterogeneous account of the birth of colonial modernity.[35]

It is also clear that modernity's vision of itself is myopic—at once "purifying" and destructive (albeit creative), and constitutionally incapable of recognizing an Other whose otherness should be radically apparent by virtue of being fashioned out of something other than itself. Correcting for this myopia, we can view Jaffa as a space of "non-European alterity" that is simultaneously other than Tel Aviv and also constitutive of Tel Aviv, both materially through its land and economic wealth and ideologically and epistemologically in its role as Tel Aviv's Other.[36] The space of Jaffa (and all urban spaces for that matter) can thus be understood as a "prismatic structure of modernity" that continuously interacted with and helped to define and shape the spaces around it, especially Tel Aviv and nearby Palestinian cities.[37] Viewed this way, it becomes clear that at the moment Jaffa constituted Tel Aviv as a "modern Hebrew town" it revealed Tel Aviv *and* modernity to be powerfully "irrational myths,"[38] the kind that helped to transform Palestine into "a land without a people for a people without a land."[39]

All this suggests that we must (re)discover the "noncapitalist," "non-West," and "nonmodern" as more than just nondisposable specters or fictions of the colonial ideologies that helped to suppress Other, or indigenous, experiences and histories. Rather, we must see them as being at the core of the modern experience and condition,[40] a fact whose importance grows if we recognize that Nietzsche and his inheritors (among them Heidegger, Derrida, Bataille, Foucault, Deleuze) have all sought in one way or another to break out of "the prison of modernity."[41] To the argument that modernity is at once "the new, the historical and the ever-same" (another theme that returns to Nietzsche),[42] we can add that it is also at once the nonmodern, a condition possessing an epistemological and discursive coherence that demands acknowledgment and reflection.[43]

By acknowledging the dynamic interaction between modernity and nonmodernity, we can, for example, recognize the African "roots" of modernity without claiming that Africans were equally colonialist, nationalist, capitalist, and self-identified as modern as the Europeans who colonized them.[44] And if at a certain point colonized collectivities in Africa or South Asia began to articulate specifically modern(ist) discourses (usually through the nationalism axis of the modernity matrix), I would still argue that the possibility of fruitfully analyzing these modernities of the colonized should not suggest a similar profitability in analyzing the space of Jaffa and her inhabitants as one of a "modern collective subject" (as Chakrabarty and Chatterjee do for India), however heterogeneous and anormative a genealogy one grants a reimagined "modernity."[45]

Instead, an examination of Jaffa in the late Ottoman period, and even throughout much of the Mandate period, reveals significant differences from other sites of colonized modernity (e.g., the colonial "Bengali-modern"), both because until the 1930s Tel Aviv did not have the same power to shape Jaffan spaces and social discourses as British colonialism had in India and because a significant proportion of Arab inhabitants of the Jaffa–Tel Aviv region were not motivated by modernist ideologies or self-identities, as were Tel Aviv's.[46] Some, like the wealthy Palestinian Arab merchant mentioned earlier, could and did use modernity as a strategy or idiom for self-definition and even social advancement, but many others did not, since the rubric "modern" was claimed by Jaffa's hostile and expansionist neighbor (and thus represented a threat to Jaffa and Palestinians) or—more likely—since they had already been "modernizing" their landscape for several generations without having to define it as such (as was the case with local farmers who had drained swamps around the 'Auja/Yarkon River north of Tel Aviv, a quintessentially modernizing activity for Zionism).[47]

Making a nonmodern perspective more important is the impossibility of separating the ills of modernism and modernization from the positive goals and dreams of modernity as a project, as so many analyses of modernity attempt to do,[48] because the very philosophies and epistemologies underlying both—humanism, progress, enlightenment, freedom, and equality—are inextricably tied to colonialism-imperialism.[49] Indeed, the discourse of the Young Turks who assumed power in Istanbul in 1908 reacted specifically to this problem, displaying an ironic and often hostile view of "la vie moderne" symbolized by France and the other European powers.[50]

Following Bruno Latour, we could argue that even a "hybrid form of colonial modernity,"[51] let alone a pure distillation of the two discourses, was never a logical possibility, since modernity is (self-)defined by its refusal of hybridity.[52] And so, given the colonial basis of modernity, we could—and I would suggest, should—ask the following question, Can the colonized be modern? And would not the very act of shattering the exclusivist shell of "Euro-modernity" shatter its more liberatory ideologies and possibilities too? (This might explain why it has proven so hard for formerly colonized collectivities to grasp and use them, as they were purchased in Europe with their blood, sweat, and exploitation.)

My point is that only by taking full analytical and ethical cognizance of nonmodernity can we uncover the "mask" of modernity and challenge its existing spatializations (whose marginalization or elision of the non-West is even reproduced by a thinker as perceptive as Foucault).[53] New "narrative possibilities and story-telling options" are then open to us.[54] By acknowledging the presence of nonmodernities within and surrounding the space of Euro-modernity in Tel Aviv, we begin to understand the discourses of colonialism as the current that powers modernity and makes it, at best, a similacrum of what it imagines itself to be.[55]

Imagined thus, collectivities (or classes within collectivities) plugged in to colonial modernities' discourses in a grounded and well-shielded manner will draw limitless energy from this seemingly imperceptible voltage.[56] However, for those unshielded from its force, the voltage supplied by the colonial project and its power plants—from slave plantations to native armies—melts away modernity's "illusions," such as freedom or progress, or the promise of their future realization.[57]

This dynamism accounts for why it has always been those who were colonized by modernity who could see through the "ontology of sameness" that supports—or produces—modernity by simultaneously denying and creating the fundamental differences between modern and not-modern. This dualism is at the heart of the colonial project.[58] Thus it is because Tel Aviv's leaders knew—had to know—how similar the predicaments their city faced were to Jaffa's (which made Tel Aviv not modern, unless one redefines *modernity* to include the very properties it defines itself against) that the latter had to be erased to protect the modern self-image of Tel Aviv and Zionism.

It is for this reason, I suggest, that Palestinian Arab inhabitants of the Jaffa–Tel Aviv region could read modernity better than the Zionists or British. They understood that land was not "dead" just because the British changed a category of land tenure with the ostensible goal of helping to "develop" the land; they knew that in reality the planning schemes of

British- and Zionist-controlled town planning commissions were "not really a 'plan,' but rather a plan to take the land out of the hands of the owners," despite the "skillful justifications" of the former.[59] Even scions of Zionist technocracy such as Yitzhak Elazari-Volkani (founder of Zionist agronomy) were aware of the gap between the modernist claims and rhetoric of Zionist leaders (i.e., vis-à-vis the superiority of their "more rapid" methods versus supposedly "traditional" Palestinian practices) and the often "defective" reality of the Zionist agronomy on the ground.[60]

The contemporary perceptions by actors involved in the struggle over land and identity in the Jaffa–Tel Aviv region support the argument that the production of modernity "occurs *only* by performing the distinction between the modern and non-modern, west and non-west," an activity that always carries the danger of "contamination and disruption by the latter on the former."[61] Thus, by refusing to make these distinctions, by seeing through the modernist discourses, Jaffa–Tel Aviv's "bedouins" (or their contemporary counterparts) can be seen as not modern, even if many of their economic and cultural practices, such as the capitalization of land, had been modern for several generations. But it needs to be stressed that here I am not referring to the nonmodernity of modernity's imagination (i.e., as I argue below, the backward Other of its "spaces of representation")[62] but rather the productive nonmodernity of those who cannot stop translating modern ideologies into more hybrid realities.

REREADING MODERNITY

Thus far I have perhaps established how modernity's self-identity breaks down. Yet a positive point of reference must be established if I am to discuss modernity and its alter egos in Jaffa and Tel Aviv. A suitable framework for analysis can be found in Latour's argument that modernity has never been any more than a mode of classification or sorting, or better, an ideology and politics that accounted for how we classified and sorted. Modernity, in fact, hides its own nonmodernity, which can be retrieved by understanding its hybrid nature and following new rules based on the recognition that "we have never been modern."[63] This was obvious a century ago too, if we adopt the perspective of the bedouins, or even the cartoonists for Istanbul's "revolutionary" newspapers.[64]

For Latour, modernity can be understood as being based on two sets of practices, "translation" and "purification," which must remain distinct if they are to remain effective. Translation creates hybrids of nature and culture that link discourses from the realms of science, politics, industry, and art—and also "absorbs" the hierarchizing practices of what Mignolo terms "colonial difference" into the larger cultural imaginary of Western modernities.[65] At the same time, however, purifying practices create two entirely distinct ontological zones: that of human beings, on the one hand, that of nonhumans—that is, Nature—on the other.[66] So long as we consider these two practices of translation and purification separately, "we are truly modern." That is, though the experience of the modern condition is inescapably hybrid, it has to be portrayed as separate and purified in order for there to be a natural world that could be "rooted up"—as the French planner and architect Le Corbusier (who had great impact in Tel Aviv) described it—or "bulldozed"—to use Lefebvre's, and contemporary Palestinian Jaffan, imagery.[67]

What I am suggesting, then, is that in the sense outlined here the discourse-cum-project of modernity is in fact a *mis*reading of the modern condition because it assumes a purified, separated, striated, and hierarchized condition when the reality is much more messy, fluid, and "barbaric."[68] (And so instead of imagining a "radicalized modernity" as the appropriate denouement for what Habermas describes as an "unfinished project," we should perhaps consider modernity—which through colonialism has so often dehumanized the very "man" it created—as a project best left unfinished.)[69] What makes this misreading so powerful is that the ontological separation of Humanity from Nature is fundamental to the epistemology and discourses underlying colonialism—"an essentially *linguistic* discourse"—which require and (re)present a natural, nonhistorical conception of space, devoid (or better, made void—that is, purified) of all otherness.[70] In fact, modernity and colonialism share at their core a similar ambivalence that both must at all costs be sublimated through the production of difference, which, in the context of the modernity matrix, almost always involves various types of violence.[71] It is within this framework that we must understand the production-as-urbanization of space as an integral part of the making, maintaining, reproducing, and challenging of modern ethnonational relations.[72]

The "discursive condition of Zionist space" foregrounded the linguistic-discursive component of Zionism,[73] under which the production of space in Palestine was governed by a belief that the "new Israel" could only be erected on a *vacant* site. Thus Zionism was able to deploy itself only in a discursive space that was "natural, non-historical[,] . . . where all otherness [was] absent or neutralized."[74] As in all nationalisms, "the positivist Zionist discourse must 'clean' the site of the future society, must not see the Other."[75]

Just as the Parisian Barthelemy would have imagined, the Zionist discourses, especially their urbanist expressions, cleared the space of Palestine of all otherness before the act of colonization began.[76] Such a misreading, or "illusionary" vision, of Palestine was made possible by the modern/colonial imagining of space as both "transparent" and "realistic," that is, as fixed, natural (i.e., not social), easily intelligible, and able to be "objectively" studied (and ultimately reshaped) by the experts and planners who would fashion it to suit European tastes and colonial-imperial interests.[77] The relationship of this conception of space to the "systematic planning" that Herzl imagined would be central to the economical and efficient governance of his New Society and its capital city are evident on close examination of the urban history of the Jaffa–Tel Aviv region, as it is in other colonial urban settings.[78]

In this context, Zionist sentiments that the indigenous non-Jewish population of Palestine was "indolent and torpid," "living in the seventh century," and thus possessing "no right to rule the country to the extent that it has not been built up by them and is still awaiting its cultivators"[79] clarifies the chain of referents linking Tel Aviv to modernity, although not in the direct manner imagined by its leaders and chroniclers. Rather, it points again to the inherently colonial constitution of the project of modernity. In fact, I would claim that modernity and colonialism are not just embedded in one another but mutually generative and together generative of nationalism in the context of the worldwide development of capitalism.[80]

Thus Zionism, as a modern nationalist movement, is an inherently colonial discourse, and Tel Aviv, the "modern capital" of Zionist Palestine and now global Israel, cannot be understood or examined other than as a colonial city.[81] Once we begin to expose the cracks of this fourfold matrix of modernity, colonialism, capitalism, and nationalism the rich history of Jaffa and its struggle with modernity—long buried under the debris of Tel Aviv's perpetual "growth" and, today, gentrification—begins to emerge. However, the larger goal of shattering the existing historical narratives of Jaffa and Tel Aviv in favor of depicting a more fractured (yet at the same time, like light emerging from a prism, more interesting) landscape requires great effort.[82] It requires, as I suggested already, a critical leave-taking of modernity in its various guises and deployments.

I would therefore argue that the matrix of modernity must be recognized as unfolding (and, to borrow Juval Portugali's terminology, "enfolding") differently, not just in different bounded territories but within them. One could argue, with Gershon Shafir, that the material conditions generated by capitalism were the generative or dominant discourse in the development of agricultural-based Labor Zionism, while the discursive power of colonial modernity was dominant in the urban sector; or that in some cases colonial modernity can be joined by the modernity of the colonized (as in Chakrabarty's colonial Bengal), while in others nonmodernity is a better interpretive strategy for both modernity's victims and its analysts.[83]

Given these permutations, complex spaces of transcultural interaction, communication, and domination such as Jaffa–Tel Aviv need to be approached with the goal of freeing what Lefebvre terms the "representational spaces" of the clandestine, or underside, of life—that is, life as directly lived by the Jews and Arabs who daily challenged the official "spaces of representation" of the administrative-legal and ideological-nationalist boundaries that separated them.[84] Only then will it be possible to shatter the illusionary histories and landscapes that lie at the core of modernist, colonial, and nationalist discourse(s).[85] This "space of the inhabitants of the city" was characterized by Lefebvre as "imagined," and it is thus here that possibility of "reimagining" the spaces of Jaffa and Tel Aviv—and so of (non)modernity—can most felicitously be entertained.[86]

Accomplishing this reimagination requires an approach that understands both the "implicate" and "poetic" nature of the relationship between various places and communities within the space of Jaffa–Tel Aviv, and through them of the larger fourfold matrix of modernity as expressed there: implicate in that the communities and discourses "enfold" each other and cannot be investigated or understood separately;[87] poetic in that every process of social transmission—including scholarship[88]—implies a "poetic geography" in which events, distant in time and space, are the materials from which the two communities would build their future.[89]

Viewed implicately and poetically, Tel Aviv can be understood as an outstanding example of how Zionism is a Palestinian creation, both in the sense of being created on the ground-space of Palestine and, as important, in the sense of being the creation of Palestinians.[90] Thus any social geography of the Israeli-Palestinian conflict hoping to break free of the existing colonial-modernist paradigm must view these two societies as sociospatial wholes, or better, as a single sociospatial whole.[91]

If we examine Jaffa–Tel Aviv from the perspective outlined here, Tel Aviv—despite its self-perception—was and remains as much a space of nonmodernity as of modernity, as underneath its modernist veneer was an impure, nonmodern reality (Palestinians and other nomads, diseases and disorder), a fact supported by the ability of those most excluded from Tel Aviv's modern identity to see through the various discourses created to sustain it to the more muddied reality beneath. Indeed, Lefebvre's analysis helps us to see that in studying the spatial system composed of Jaffa and Tel Aviv, we are confronted "not by one social space but by many." "[T]he worldwide does not abolish the local,"[92] however much it might have wanted to. And modernity does not abolish the nonmodern—in fact, it helps to engender it.

CONCLUSION: NEW GEOGRAPHIES FOR PALESTINE AND ISRAEL?

"Writing has nothing to do with signifying. It has to do with surveying, mapping, even realms that are yet to come."[93] So argue Gilles Deleuze and Felix Guattari. If writing is an act of mapping and language a map, then the constitutive power of the Zionist discourses of Tel Aviv, as a grammar governing what could (and can still) be written about Tel Aviv and Jaffa, becomes apparent. So does the necessity of overturning it in favor of new, nonmodernist poetics of Jaffa–Tel Aviv before the goal of composing a more critical, yet holistic, geohistoriography of the region can be achieved.[94]

From this perspective, Jaffa's history—no less than any other—remains fully modern if we understand modernity to be "the name of all the discrepant histories" of our age.[95] Indeed, it is inarguable both that modernity is multiple and that every tradition is unique.[96] Not just my own work but that of scholars such as Khalidi, Doumani, Tamari, and Lockman demonstrate Jaffa's and Palestine's "modernity" in the sense of its experience of the processes and discourses and social changes that were played out there during the past century and a half or more, including the increasing desire by segments of Jaffa's Arab communities to engage in such a project of self-identification.

However, when we consider modernity as an ideological-discursive concept—and thus as a complex of modernity, colonialism, capitalism, and nationalism—Jaffan peasants in 1940, Ottoman and Chinese diplomats forty years before, or Islamist movements forty years later can perhaps be better understood as not-nonmodern, precisely because of their ability to see the link between modernity and the "new methods of destroying countries" unleashed by it (as a Chinese diplomat remarked to his Ottoman colleague over a century ago).[97] At the very least we should recognize that we live in "incomplete and mixed times of premodernity, modernity and postmodernity,"[98] just as we should recognize the right of the non-West to produce its own forms of cultural periodization, its own "transmodernization" based on strategies of endogenous creativity and local rationalizations.[99]

In this sense, expanding the definition of *modernity* to fit either late Ottoman Jaffa or late-twentieth-century Islamism both dilutes its power as a colonial discourse and refuses to allow that critical discourses, whether millenarian Islamism or peasant resistance to modernist townplanning, can indeed be "nonmodern" as projects, even if their goals and ideologies exhibit paradigmatic modern features.[100] Perhaps we can better locate modernity by viewing Jaffa–Tel Aviv as the "liminal" space of a modernity—not in the sense of moving toward some "post" modern state, but rather a more lateral transition to an Other, nonmodern condition.[101]

If this is the case, perhaps the critical leave-taking of modernity I call for can help to shift the balance of power between utopia and dystopia, which, especially in (post)colonial settings such as Palestine/Israel, seems more inclined toward the latter than the former.[102] In such a scenario, the descent—genealogically, not morally—into the nonmodern would no longer retain its negative or pejorative value, an artifice of the very modernizational literature most contemporary critical studies of modernity aim to challenge. In fact, we should talk about the multiple nonmodernities and do a nonmodern aesthetics of the history and/or geography of Jaffa–Tel Aviv.[103]

It is by moving out of the defeatism of believing there is "no other path" but modernity to confront its dystopic legacy that the truly liberatory promise of the modern project can see the light of day.[104] The chapters that follow explore how the discourses of colonial modernity have transformed the landscapes and peoples of the Jaffa–Tel Aviv region and what alternative readings of the region's history have always been, and remain, open to those who approach the topography–historiography from a less linear and more genealogical framework.[105]

2　From Cedars to Oranges

A History of the Jaffa–Tel Aviv Region from Antiquity to the Late Ottoman Period

A BRIEF HISTORY OF JAFFA

An examination of the conflicted histories of and relationship between Jaffa and Tel Aviv must be situated in the almost ten-thousand-year history of continuous human settlement in the Jaffa–Tel Aviv region. Jaffa is one of the oldest cities in the world and second perhaps only to Jericho as the oldest inhabited settlement in Israel/Palestine. The city has changed hands and has been partially or wholly destroyed more than thirty times in its fascinating and storied history. I begin with the last time it met destruction at foreign hands—the Napoleonic invasion of 1799, which is generally considered to mark the beginning of Jaffa's "modern" history.[1]

The majority of European and Zionist or Israeli studies of Jaffa have focused on the biblical through Crusader periods, ignoring the Ottoman period because of the assumption that Palestine experienced stagnation and even decline during this time; this ellipsis is also reflected in the archaeology of the city.[2] Such selective historiography has meant that the majority of the city's inhabitants throughout the modern period—non-Jewish Arabs—have not received due scholarly attention.[3] Instead, with the exception of the work of Alexander Scholch and Amnon Cohen,[4] Jaffa, like Palestine as a whole, has been described as a "forsaken district," which primarily through increased European influence was transformed from a conquered and destroyed town into "a new city, very different in size, character and layout from the traditional Middle Eastern town of the early nineteenth century."[5]

Here I attempt to correct this lacuna by exploring the role of both the pre-Zionist populations and the central and local Ottoman authorities in the city's rapid development in the late Ottoman period, specifically, the second half of the nineteenth century and the early twentieth century. This was a time of transition from one empire to another, from Ottoman political rule and relative economic autonomy to political and economic rule by Great Britain under a League of Nations mandate.

Jaffa's Premodern History

If there was one feature from earliest antiquity that put Jaffa on the map, it was the city's port. It was perhaps because of its port that Jaffa was conquered by the Egyptians as early as 1469 B.C.E. The city remained under Egyptian control until at least the second half of the thirteenth century B.C.E., when the "biblical," or "ancient" Israelite, communities first appeared in the city.

Jaffa Port was perhaps the only well-known harbor possessed or used by the Israelites during the biblical period. It was not just the port of Jerusalem, from which the cedars of Lebanon were unloaded for building Solomon's temple,[6] it was also the site from which Jonah attempted to flee from his prophetic calling (only to be swallowed by the famously mis-named "whale")[7] and where the apostle Peter received the call to convert pagans, as well as Jews, to Christianity.[8]

During the late Roman and Byzantine periods, Jaffa remained an important commercial center and port of exit for travelers from the central highlands of the country.[9] The city was conquered by Muslims in 639 and remained in Muslim hands until 1099, when it fell to the Crusaders. In 1196 the brother of Salāḥ Ad-dīn reconquered and destroyed the city, and its importance as a port diminished until it was rebuilt at the beginning of the Mamluk period (1268–1517).

By the fourteenth century Jaffa was once again a port city of some importance; in 1517 it fell under Ottoman rule. Though it went through many ups and downs in subsequent centuries—a 1726 description says that it has no walls, is "more like a farm than a city"—it redeveloped quickly.[10] Thus one source reports that by the mid-1760s,

> there were between four and five hundred houses, and several mosques. A marsh lying in the neighborhood had been drained and converted into gardens, making the atmosphere more healthful than it had been before. . . . The figs and oranges of Jaffa are noted for their size and flavor. The water-melons, which thrive on the sandy soil around, are in great repute, and are carried in great numbers to Alexandria and Cairo. Throughout all Syria, too, they have a reputation. The vegetables of Jaffa, too, are abundant and cheap: The soil yields as freely as it did centuries ago. The horticulturist Bove, who visited the place in 1832, was surprised at its great fertility. . . . The silks of Jaffa have for a long time had a good reputation in the East.[11]

This quotation contradicts the accepted historiography of Jaffa by demonstrating that it was a vibrant and growing town during the eighteenth and nineteenth centuries, a well-known player in the regional and even international system of trade in both agriculture and textiles, and that its sandy earth was remarkably fertile. But it supports Cohen's argument, based on a detailed examination of Ottoman and European sources, that the Ottoman state was engaged in a hard-fought—if not always successful—struggle to centralize control and revenue during the eighteenth century whose goal was the restoration of "a disciplined and orderly province,"[12] progress toward which was "greatly boosted by the country's involvement in international trade" and the tremendous profits and economic development it produced.[13]

By the mid-eighteenth century a "mukata'a of Jaffa Port" (i.e., a new revenue-administrative unit) was in place that was governed by a Mutaşarrıf (governor of the provincial subdivision) based at Jaffa Port, which by this time was profitable enough to have been strongly tied to the Vali of Damascus and to have been the object of significant struggles between various local and Ottoman authorities. These struggles in fact weakened the town toward the end of the eighteenth century after four decades of continual economic and demographic expansion, although the general picture in the region was still one of development and progress.[14]

Clearly, then, the Jaffa region was undergoing dynamic growth during the eighteenth century that set the stage for even faster and deeper growth in the next century. Yet the depictions of European travelers and accounts of local and Ottoman sources would be contested by the Zionist historiography of the city that began at the end of the nineteenth century.

Jaffa after the Napoleonic Invasion

In the decades preceding Napoleon's 1799 invasion—in fact, for much of the eighteenth century—Jaffa, like much of the coast of Palestine (from Acre to Gaza), found itself in the middle of numerous struggles between various local rulers and bedouin tribes, and pirates coming from across the Mediterranean periodically maurauded the town from the sea. This instability led the Ottoman government to strengthen its presence over the town by building a new watchtower with cannons and stationing more soldiers there.[15] Beyond these struggles and Napoleon's short but violent sojourn, Jaffa suffered two more sieges, one later in 1799 and another in 1803–5, and an outbreak of the plague as the nineteenth century began.

Despite the rough start of the nineteenth century, local evidence suggests that the fifty-year period that saw Napoleon's invasion at its center was one of economic, demographic, and physical and urban growth and was thus a crucial time for the development of Jaffa as a modern town.[16] It is not surprising that soon after the Ottomans recaptured Jaffa it began a dynamic period of growth that lasted until the end of the Ottoman period and profoundly reshaped its social geography. This development was not just limited to the immediate environs of the Old City but also included the small villages and farms in its immediate vicinity, which had already been settled for centuries.[17]

The person most responsible for Jaffa's renewed growth was the local governor, Muhammad Abu Nabut, who ruled the city from 1807 to 1818, and was described as "le père de la cité nouvelle."[18] A British traveler, Henry Light, wrote of his arrival in 1814, during Abu Nabut's time: "The shore appeared interspersed with sand and trees; on drawing nearer, cliff was seen, and Jaffa as a projecting rock of some extent, with bold precipices. Its features soon were distinguished. The walls batteries, towers, and houses, rising one above the other, presented a singular view, which even attracted the admiration of my fellow-passengers."[19] It is also worth noting, given the largely negative portrayal of the conditions at Jaffa Port in subsequent decades, Light's recounting of his landing: "[N]ot a moment was lost in unloading. . . . I never saw any disembarkation more expeditiously performed."[20]

The imposing walls were rebuilt by Abu Nabut, who also constructed a new mosque and fountain, which still stands, several markets—including one for women on land previously known as "the sandy land," an act of reclamation that predates a similar act by the founders of Tel Aviv by a century—and other religious and commercial buildings to serve the town's growing population. Together, these buildings demonstrated the growing importance of Jaffa as a "public" city, as well as Abu Nabut's desire to achieve greater power and status that reflected the larger growth in power of the a'yan, or notables, of Palestine.[21] As a result of his initiative, Jaffa quickly became the most important port in Palestine; the increasing activity helped to attract Sephardic (North African) Jews back to the city on a permanent basis beginning around 1820 and Askhenazi (European) Jews beginning two decades later, in 1839.[22]

The conquest of Jaffa by Ibrahim Pasha, stepson of Muhammad Ali, in 1831 had important administrative, economic, and demographic consequences. Within a year, new administrative procedures were in force, with a local council receiving reports on local affairs, tax collections, and public opinion.[23] Moreover, many Egyptian soldiers who came with Ibrahim Pasha settled north of the Old City in what eventually became the Manshiyyeh quarter.

Indeed, throughout the nineteenth century Jaffa was a center for migration of Arabs from other parts of Palestine and neighboring countries such as Egypt,[24] Syria, and Lebanon, as well as from North Africa and Afghanistan. Thus the Shari'a Court records document a large increase in the number of people—including foreigners—who wanted to confirm the sale of land outside the walls.[25] Even the Shari'a Court of Jerusalem contains records from the 1830s of transactions in Jaffa involving orchards that already had changed hands at least once.[26] Farther out, many of the surrounding villages had semisedentary bedouin populations, whose settlement was the result of the growing economic importance of and increased security around Jaffa.[27]

By the early to mid-1840s Europeans were being hired to survey and draft detailed maps and plans of the city, which was experiencing a "dynamic architectural change."[28] Ottoman sources reveal increasing attention to and improvements of the Jaffa-Jerusalem road (and later railway), as well as a demographic and religious transformation that resulted in the conversion of at least one church to a mosque.[29] However, the interaction between local and European cultures did not challenge the general European perception of Jaffa as being "old" and "backward," as becomes clear below.

The next major turning point for the development of Jaffa was the conclusion of the Crimean War, which initiated a remarkable upswing in Palestine.[30] Nowhere was this more evident than in Jaffa, which "literally burst its seams" during the next two decades, becoming the center of Palestine's economic life in general and of the "New Yishuv," the Zionist-inspired immigration to the country that began during the century's final decades.[31]

According to Lortet's *Syrie d'Aujourd'hui*, one of the most comprehensive guides to Greater Syria of the period, "The town of Jaffa, which possesses neither ancient ruins nor remarkable monuments, is nevertheless one of the most interesting of the towns that rise above the Oriental shores of the Mediterranean. . . . [It] is full of prosperity: It would be very important for France to establish there a financial institution, serious and honest, like Credit Lyonnais and the Banque Ottomane have established in a number of cities in the Orient."[32] The author describes Jaffa as exporting significant amounts of wheat, sesame, cotton, cured beef, and even vegetables (primarily to Alexandria) as well as its trademark orange. Its primary imports were English and American cotton fabrics, French goods (including perfumes), rice from lower Egypt, and American petroleum. The latter, vital product was described as crucial for Jaffa to "s'éclairer"—a word that means both to light streets and to be enlightened.[33] Lortet thus establishes a link connecting Jaffa, modernity, and the United States that is reminiscent of Tel Aviv's attempts to compare itself to California and New York City as symbols of modernity a generation later.

According to Lortet, the wealth of Jaffa was reflected in the shops in its market, which "ha[d] an originality that is impossible to describe" and were stocked with goods of every description, not to mention the vibrant and motley assortment of people, particularly women, from the Mediterranean and the Levant who lived and worked in and around the city.[34] Among these people were many Egyptians who took residence in the north and south of the city and engaged in cultivation and neighborhood building wherever they settled, including 'Ajami and Manshiyyeh, two neighborhoods that would become increasingly important to Jaffa after Tel Aviv was established.

ECONOMIC DEVELOPMENT DURING THE LATE OTTOMAN PERIOD

To analyze the economic development of the Jaffa–Tel Aviv region during the late Ottoman period, we must account for the relative lack of sources for urban production in Palestine in comparison with the data available for the agricultural sector and even the data available for the eighteenth century.[35] Nevertheless, it is clear that a combination of factors, particularly changes in land tenure symbolized (but not prompted) by the 1858 Land Code[36] and increased regional and European trade, created a new economic dynamic that significantly increased exports through the port and the com/ modification of land—and with them, the wealth of the city.[37]

Scholch's pioneering examination of the economy of late Ottoman Palestine summarizes the major European data on the Jaffa region and reveals the great expansion in exports and in land under cultivation in the wake of the Crimean War.[38] As important is the large increase in imports, especially of luxury foods and goods from Europe during this period, which helped to mark Jaffa's location as a modern, cosmopolitan Mediterranean city.[39] An 1872 account described Jaffa this way:

> The . . . town is picturesquely situated on a headland, the houses rising in terraces from the water's edge; it is entirely surrounded by a wall and ditch, to which the term fortifications is given, but, such as they are, they are falling rapidly to decay. Surrounding Jaffa are the orange gardens for which it is justly extolled, and which are a considerable source of wealth to the owners. The annual value of fruits grown in Jaffa is said to be 10,000 pounds. I have been greatly struck at times

when riding along this coast to see vines and fig-trees growing apparently in barren sand which abounds here; either there is a supply of
water beneath the surface sufficient to nourish the roots, or, what I
think is more probable, the sand is not more than a foot or two in depth
and the roots have been laid in good soil beneath.[40]

Led by the burgeoning orange trade, there was increased European economic penetration of Palestine in the years after the Crimean War, and,
concomitantly, increased European interest and involvement in the development of Jaffa. The most important reason for this intensified interest was
economic: oranges replaced cotton as the most important export crop to
Europe and especially to Great Britain, which led to the expansion of groves
in the area surrounding the town. An extensive 1902 study of the Jaffa
orange trade by two Zionist officials pays tribute to the growth of the
industry, the various Arab owners, and the wide reach of its markets (with
England, followed by Turkey and Egypt grouped as one unit, and, well
below them, Austria-Hungary as the primary markets).

Even as the study complains about the "primitive" state of Palestinian
Arab cultivation (Arabische Kulturmethode), the discussion of the costs
involved for Arab versus European proprietors bears out the praise of Arab
cultivation methods as much more cost-efficient than the supposedly more
modern Zionist-European ones made two decades later by the founder of
Zionist agronomy, Yitzhak Elezari-Valkani.[41] A similar rise in demand for
grain and sesame led to their increased cultivation in Jaffa's hinterland,
which had already seen "considerable economic activity," as reflected in the
drainage of swamps and the handing out of a concession for a water mill on
the 'Auja/Yarkon River, in the immediate wake of Napoleon's invasion.[42]

In addition, as the port of Jerusalem, Jaffa had become the most important foreign trade and debarkation point for tourists visiting the country,
with approximately 80,000 people disembarking annually.[43] Yet the city
lacked a proper harbor to handle the increased traffic in cargo and people,
as the port was one of the smallest in the Mediterranean, described in one
account as "little more than an open roadstead."[44] When combined with
the "constricting effects" of the city's wall and gates and the lack of a safe
and satisfactory connection with Jerusalem, the situation consistently frustrated European travelers.[45]

Despite these difficulties, the French vice consul in Jaffa, at least, believed
that its commercial importance and position as the port of Jerusalem in a
time of increasing tourism by Americans, British, and French justified the
continued use of Jaffa Port.[46] Not surprisingly, at least seven European and
Turkish proposals to develop the port were put forth during this period,

although none were implemented.[47] Yet the amount of trade moving through the port doubled just between 1893 and 1913, which puts it not far behind the tripling in the movement of goods through the eastern Mediterranean's major ports, Istanbul, Beirut, and Alexandria.[48]

Ottoman, Zionist, local Shari'a Court, and European consular records from the last half century of Ottoman rule testify to Jaffa's place in the larger Palestinian, regional, and world economies. An 1876 report from the French vice consul reveals that Jaffa was exporting fruits and vegetables from up and down the coast to numerous European countries.[49] Imports were deemed "relatively unimportant" and consisted mostly of European manufactures, although imports of petroleum and so-called luxury goods were on the rise, destined for Palestine's wealthy European and local residents.[50]

Although scholars such as Kark, Aviztur, and Scholch have focused on the dominance of European trade in Jaffa Port,[51] intraregional trade (i.e., within the Ottoman Empire and Egypt) also remained significant and even increased, as better terms of credit could be obtained from houses in Beirut and Alexandria than from European concerns.[52] Local industry included not just the well-known soap and oranges but also cosmetics, printing, textiles and clothing, bricks for building, smelting plants, perfumes, agricultural supplies, and condensed fruit juices.[53] By the 1870s there were 420 orange groves in the Jaffa vicinity; thanks to their "good quality,"[54] they yielded over thirty-three million oranges per year, one-sixth of which were consumed in Palestine and the rest exported to Egypt and Asia Minor on Greek ships and increasingly after 1875 to Europe.[55]

In fact, almost every category of exports increased significantly during this period.[56] By 1880 Europe had already taken over from Egypt and Turkey as the leading destination for most of Jaffa's exports, although the latter continued to lead in certain categories of imports, such as petroleum, "fancy goods," and cloths.[57] Even when agricultural exports suffered because of bad weather, the burgeoning tourist trade, now "central for the economy[,] . . . made up for the losses."[58]

The Shari'a Court records of Jaffa *(sijjil)* from this period also demonstrate the intimate connection between Jaffa and Jerusalem, its important role as the port of southern Palestine (and Jaffa's larger role as a "connecting link" between the Levant and Egypt and Europe), and the rapid economic, commercial, urban, cultural, and educational development of the city and its environs.[59] Although European trade became increasingly important, we should not assume a concomitant rise in European political influence. Instead, the merchants of Jaffa, like those of Haifa and Beirut, succeeded in establishing themselves as indispensable go-betweens for the import-export trade with Europe, in this way shielding the city from more direct political influence.[60]

Thus the French vice consul wrote in 1887 of his feeling of "profound lassitude" caused by the unceasing and even increasing difficulties he faced dealing with the local authorities, whom he felt (perhaps on secret instructions from Istanbul) hindered the fulfillment of the provisions of the capitulations for foreigners.[61] In fact, it was very hard for European agricultural or industrial private enterprises to establish themselves, despite their presence and influence extending well into the eighteenth century.[62] Many attributed this to the "constant mischief" to which they were subject, not just by the local population, but especially by what was described as a "highly corrupt" judiciary, which used "chicanery" to take advantage of the "subtlety of the law of registration" in the Ottoman Empire to disrupt real estate transactions involving Europeans.[63] (An alternative view is provided by a French chronicler in 1835, who wrote of the jealousies and the "guerre de prétention" among the European representatives in Jaffa, which were clearly generated by the city's growing economic importance.)[64]

Two decades later the Qa'imaqam, or governor, of the Jaffa District (*qada'*) would similarly write of the "importance of taking seriously the administration of the [Jaffa] Municipality and the functions of all the offices, from the lowest to the highest."[65] Yet there is an alternative understanding of the behavior attributed to local officials beyond greed and corruption, namely, that they were concerned about the ramifications of increased foreign land purchases on the economic and social health of the region and its poorer inhabitants. This could be one reason for the dispatches and reminders sent to Jaffa from Istanbul regarding the impermissibility of both European Jewish immigration and land purchases by Jews (in fact, the sultan, Abdulhamid, was aware that one of the "goals" of Jews in the country was to purchase land in Jaffa).[66] Even more, it perhaps reflected a general feeling of fear that "Ottoman culture ha[d] weakened . . . and foreign culture ha[d] become dominant" with the increased activities of European states and especially the British in Palestine.[67]

This drama would be replayed during the Mandate period (see chap. 7), with much the same differences of opinion between Europeans (i.e., British and Zionists) and local officials and residents (especially residents of the villages that were being threatened with displacement by the expansion of Tel Aviv). Yet despite the different perspectives of Europeans regarding Jaffa's development, reports from the British vice consul in Jaffa during the years 1880–1900 describe the "fairly flourishing condition" of the economy.[68] By the turn of the twentieth century it was obvious to all interested parties that "in the last twenty years Jaffa ha[d] progressed, expanded, and grown greatly."[69] The increasing economic activity, including a construction boom, prompted the French vice consul to advocate the construction of a square at the railroad station as a way to ameliorate the congestion in the area: "While it is true that doing this will lose picturesquensss of the place . . . the tourists, amateurs to the local flavor, will little regret it."[70] Business was so brisk, especially from increased trade with Nablus, that a special trade court had to be set up to accommodate it.[71]

This trend would continue into the first decade of the twentieth century, with the export of oranges increasing from 165,000 cases in 1885 to 1,608,470 in 1913 (the value of which increased from 26,500 pounds sterling to 297,700) and the number of ships visiting Jaffa increasing from 855 in 1900 to 1,341 in 1913.[72] (See table 1 for a yearly breakdown of the ratio of imports to exports.) It would appear that the economic position of ordinary Jaffans was significantly better than that of other inhabitants of the Middle East, such as Turks or Egyptians, whose purchasing power at the turn of the twentieth century was at best 16 percent of that of the British.[73]

Jaffa's Jewish community played an important role in the development of the city during this period, although its contribution should not be overemphasized.[74] But neither should we assume, as most Arab writers have done, that it played little role in Jaffa's economic life. In fact, the Jewish community was already important to the economy of Jaffa and the surrounding villages in the years leading up to the Crimean War, as Jewish petty traders and shop owners traveled back and forth between city and village.[75]

Jews also had a presence in the import trades, specifically, luxury and basic infrastructural goods, as the twentieth century began.[76] Yet they barely participated in the booming export market; even as late as 1907 David Smilansky, a founder of Tel Aviv, reported that the majority of the trades and commerce remained in Muslim and Christian control.[77] On the other hand, in 1913—the same year that Tel Aviv's leaders declared their desire to conquer Jaffa economically (see chap. 5)—the Damascus-based *al-Muqtabas* was reporting that in "Jaffa, the most important commercial city in Palestine[,] . . . most of the commerce is in Jewish hands, as if entering a Jewish city."[78]

SOCIAL RELATIONS

Jaffa's economic growth, not to mention the increased presence of European and American tourists and residents, hint at the societal dynamism that characterized the region in the decades after the Napoleonic invasion.[79] Social, economic, and spatial factors were mutually influential in the

TABLE 1. Imports and Exports through
Jaffa Port, 1893–1913 *(£ sterling)*

Year	Imports	Exports
1893	345,540	332,628
1894	273,233	285,604
1895	275,990	282,906
1896	256,090	373,447
1897	306,630	309,389
1898	322,430	306,780
1899	390,260	316,158
1900	382,405	264,950
1901	426,310	277,635
1902	405,550	203,390
1903	439,775	322,335
1904	473,320	295,300
1905	464,000	367,820
1906	660,000	500,000
1907	809,052	484,340
1908	803,400	556,370
1909	973,143	560,935
1910	1,002,450	636,145
1911	1,169,910	710,660
1912	1,090,019	774,162
1913	1,312,659	745,413

SOURCE: Avitzur, 1972, appendix, table 14.

dynamic changes that occurred during the century,[80] helping Jaffa become a center for immigrants from neighboring Arab countries and beyond. The many Egyptians who came to Jaffa with Ibrahim Pasha in the 1830s founded neighborhoods, such as Manshiyyeh, Abu Kabir (where the Biluim, the first Zionist pioneers, briefly set up a "commune" in the midst of the orange and lemon groves),[81] and Rashid, that clearly referred to their hometowns in the Nile delta.[82] There was also migration from Lebanon, influenced by the strong ties between the Christian communities of Jaffa and Beirut and the concomitant fact that many Lebanese owned land in Jaffa by the late nine-

TABLE 2. Jaffa's Population during the Late Ottoman Period

Year	Total Population	Muslims	Christians	Jews
1866	5,000	3,850	1,00	150
1875	8,000	4,300	1,745	400–600
1887	14,000	10,000	2,270	2,500
1891	16,570	10,500	2,875	2,700
1897	33,465	20,000	3,465	10,000
1904	30,000	18,000	9,000	3,000
1909	47,000	24,000	9,000	7,000
1913	50,000	30,700	9,3000	10,000

SOURCE: Kark, 1990, pp. 148–49. Other articles give slightly varying figures but do not conflict seriously with Kark's sources (cf. TAMA, 4/46, Arieh Yodfat, undated, "Va'ad Ha'ir Hachlelei Leyehudei Yafo ve-Pe'ulotav Beshanim 1912–1915").

teenth century.[83] The growing economy of the post–Crimean War period also led to migration from Jordan, Syria, Libya, North Africa, and even Afghanistan.[84] We can surmise that for the surrounding Arab world, Jaffa was, even before the Crimean War, as much a magnet for immigrants from the surrounding Arab lands as it and Tel Aviv would later be for Jewish immigrants from Europe (and North Africa). (See table 2.)

The social and economic development of Jaffa was such that in 1871 the Ottoman government established a bona fide municipal council in Jaffa with the support of town notables and consular representatives.[85] Along with increased trade and tourism, the rising European interest and economic and cultural influence in Jaffa was symbolized by the founding of educational institutions by various British, Scottish, French, Greek Orthodox, and Maronite churches in the last decades of the nineteenth century. These schools were considered by both the Ottoman government and the Europeans themselves spearheads of European colonialism and imperial rivalry.[86]

Specifically, by 1900 Jaffa had become a center of competition between British and French imperial interests; thus the French consul worriedly wrote to the Foreign Ministry to inform them that the British had created the position of vice consul, other commercial residences, and a new mission school in Jaffa, all of which were increasing their political influence.[87] In a later letter, the consul wrote: "The religious competition was always quite lively in this country . . . and now the dominance of Anglo-American tourists to the country [is] only going to increase it."[88] Yet the French established perhaps the best known, and still surviving, religious school in Jaffa, Saint Joseph College. This Catholic gymnasium, established in 1882, represented a coalition of interests: the French government, the Catholic church, and the Catholic community of Jaffa.

The rush of activity in Jaffa Port and the city's bazaars also indicated the mélange of peoples and goods making their way to and from Jaffa. Almost two decades before Lortet's description, in the decade after the Crimean War, Jaffa's bazaars were a "pele-mele" of foreigners and locals, of East and West,[89] and they would soon be called "among the best in Palestine."[90] An 1895 travelogue and an 1896 film showing scenes in Jaffa Port confirm the great mixture of peoples and styles of dress, as does a 1904 article in the Hebrew-language journal *Kedima*, which describes Jaffa, now "the spiritual center for the new [Jewish] *yishuv*," as containing "many different peoples, exchanging opinions, educations, and faiths, [and] . . . tourists from all countries and languages." Because of this flow of people in and out of the city, the social lives of residents "d[id] not exhibit a traditional character, determined specifically to themselves."[91]

The role of women in the social and economic development of Jaffa during the late Ottoman period should not be ignored, despite the fact that they rarely appear in contemporary and later scholarly accounts of the city. However, the *sijjil* contains much evidence of women (mostly from the Old City, but also immigrants from the outlying farms or even from Egypt)[92] participating in financial and real estate transactions such as land sales and purchases, granting and receiving loans, and taking on mortgages and leases.[93] For example, in a case from 1318/1900, a Muslim woman from Jaffa went to court to assess officially the value of her late father's house (located near the Abu Kabir neighborhood), of which she was an heir, so that she could then sell her share (of the house but not the land) to pay off a debt.[94]

The Islamic court records are also full of divorce cases, some from as far away as the Nablus district, many of them initiated by women. In one case, a woman sued her former husband for alimony of 20 French lira, arguing, "[F]our months ago [my husband] divorced me by saying 'my wife is divorced *(zawjati talaqa)*, my wife is divorced, my wife is divorced.' I ask for judgment for this divorce in the amount of twenty lira." The husband rejected her claim on the grounds that they had continued to live together; she in turn claimed that the fact that she had three menstrual cycles since the divorce proved that it was a valid divorce. Both sides brought witnesses to support their contentions; the judge ruled in favor of the wife.[95]

As Iris Agmon demonstrates, the assertiveness of women in protecting and even advocating for their interests in business as well as personal affairs suggests the importance of adding their voices to the already complex set of narratives that constitute the history of late Ottoman Jaffa in order to understand more fully the range of life activities in the Muslim community, as well as relations between women across ethnic and religious lines. Indeed, the changing situation of women reflected an increasing structural complexity of late Ottoman Jaffan society stemming from the newfound ability of peasants and the "middle class" to purchase land and establish orchards, which in turn enabled mobility between classes and societal groupings. Given this dynamic, it is not surprising that the Jaffa *sijjil* contain more descriptions of the development of neighborhoods outside the city walls than do the court records of other cities, such as Haifa.[96]

The relationship between the European Jewish and Muslim and Christian Arab communities in Jaffa in the late Ottoman period was, not surprisingly, even more complex and conflictual than intracommunal relations, particularly after the onset of Zionist colonization. For its part, the Ottoman government in Istanbul was aware of the increasing influx of Jews into and through Jaffa in the early 1880s and as a matter of policy opposed Zionist-inspired Jewish settlement, although this opposition was tempered by the desire to raise revenues through Jewish land purchases and other financial support.[97] A decade later Zionist representatives started hearing from Arabs in Jaffa that Jews "were beginning to incur ill-will" because they were building houses and vineyards without government permission.[98] According to a representative of the Alliance Israelite Universelle, the local Arab population treated Jews "in the most humiliating fashion. A Jew doesn't count for anything here."[99]

By the turn of the century it was clear that while there were instances of close personal relations between Arab and Jewish elites,[100] the "question of nationality" had by then become "the most difficult" in the city, with Jewish sources reporting that the Arabs feared that "the Jews came to impose [lit., *lehagdil*] a foreign Government upon [them]."[101] Thus in 1907 the Qa'imaqam of Jaffa, Muhammad Aşaf, wrote to the Mutaşarrıf of Jerusalem warning him that "a foreign foundation is now conquering the Jaffa region, important and most harmful, that threatens the future of . . . the country. These are the foreign Jews."[102] This document presents a very important perspective, that of a local Ottoman official, on the growing Jewish presence in the region in the years leading up to the establishment of Tel Aviv. The main concerns expressed by the Qa'imaqam deal with Jewish immigration and land purchases and the increasing scale and illegality of both.[103]

After reviewing the history of Zionist settlement in the Jaffa region, the Qa'imaqam complained that in recent years, "Jews have bought thousands of dunams of land" and have "turned the lands of Jaffa and its surroundings, all of which were state *(miri)* land, to private property *(mulk)* or *waqf*" in a manner that contravened Ottoman land law.[104] Moreover, these lands were supposed to be "subject to Ottoman laws and urban planning," but when they fell into "foreign hands, the Government [could not] do anything."

"To this day," the Qa'imaqam went on, "Jews and other foreigners continue to build hundreds of buildings without permission, until they abut state land and the land of their neighbors." As important, once in Jewish hands, the government would lose direct control of the land and its revenues, as the new owners interacted only with the government through foreign consuls. The Qa'imaqam writes, "[T]here is a great need to stop this phenomenon," as consular officials were further aggravating the situation by transferring land, even state land, to Jews.[105]

Because of his concern about immigration, the Qa'imaqam also focused on Jaffa Port, which in his view had been taken over by officials from various Jewish agencies and foreign consulates who waited for immigrants to disembark from the ships and then sold them visas for 40 gerush. The combination of increased immigration and land purchases led the Qa'imaqam to conclude: "[T]he goals of the Jews are clear: to live under various nationalities, sometimes Ottoman nationality, [in order] to widen every day, and through [numerous] intrigues against the power of the Ottoman State, to create a nucleus of thieves and swindlers, and to found here in a short time, after enough have come, an autonomous government."[106]

The relevance of the Qa'imaqam's concern with the gradual transformation of land from state control *(miri)* to private control *(mulk* or *waqf)* becomes clear in my discussion of the conflicts surrounding the purchase of and construction on the first plot of land that would become Tel Aviv. Indeed, there is evidence of significant levels of conflict between the local population and the state over the categorization of land, particularly valuable orchards, that had little to do with national concerns and everything to do with taxes.

Taxes were also of more than just passing concern during this period. Right at the time Tel Aviv was established, between approximately 1909 and 1915 (A.H. 1326–33), the government investigated the status of orange orchards outside of the Old City of Jaffa based on disputes over whether the land should be properly registered as *mulk* or *miri*. The basis for this seemingly lengthy inquiry was requests by the "owners" of the land for the abolition of the tithes (*ʿoshr*) on the orchards in return for continued payment of the *arazi-i miriye* tax at the rate of ten per thousand. Yet after an investigation by a commission consisting of local judges, tax farmers, notables, and other officials that involved an examination of the title deeds the "financial accountant of Jerusalem," one Akif, explained that the *tapu* (landownership) registers showed that "in practice the private orchards have begun to be included in the public orchards" (likely for tax purposes) and that the situation required further investigation.[107]

Over the course of the investigation the users ("owners") of the land in question "pretended" to pay the tithe on orchards planted on previously idle lands and then subsequently argued that they never paid tithes but only the *arazi-i miriye*, while the government gradually recognized the conversion from *mulk* to *miri*.[108] It should be noted that though the ʿoshr was due only when there was actual output on the concerned land, this was rarely a problem around Jaffa, and thus ultimately the users knew they would have to pay this tax; and because no minimum exemption was allowed and there was no one-year grace period before the obligation became due, the government would ultimately be assured of a steady flow of revenue from the orchards.

As important, the change in tenure made it harder to sell the lands or convert them into urban or residential use, which was increasingly profitable in Jaffa but which could have resulted in lower taxes accruing to the government.[109] The context would seem to be that the people of Jaffa were registering their orchards in whatever manner guaranteed the lowest tax obligation and, perhaps, would make it harder to sell to Jews (more evidence is needed to determine if this was an important motivation).

These maneuvers must be put into the context of the shifting strategies on the part of the Ottoman state, landowners, and peasant and smallholders, either to extract more revenue from land (in the former case) or to pay as little taxes as possible (in the latter two cases). According to a 1912 French-language manual, *Manuel de droit public et administratif de l'Empire ottoman*, there are three types of taxes on land *(propriété non bâtie)*. In the first scenario, one would have to pay "four per thousand"—which here means that whatever the land is valued in (gerush, lira), a 0.4 percent tax is assessed—on lands subject to the tithe, which was fixed at 10 percent. Alternatively, one would pay four per thousand on lands on which buildings could be erected *(terrains destinés à être bâtis/arsa)*. Both of these types of land are within the category of *mulk*, or private land. But one would pay ten per thousand on lands that were not subject to the tithe— that is, *miri*, or state-owned, lands that were clearly outside the built area of a village or town or were put to agricultural use. Therefore, one would pay more on land judged to be *mulk* than that judged to be *miri*, because the assessment would include the 10 percent plus 0.4 percent, as opposed to only 0.4 percent in the case of *miri* land.

In this framework the conduct of the people brought to the attention of the Ottoman tax officials in this document makes good sense: by converting their (apparently agricultural) land to *miri*, or state, land, they would not have to pay the much higher tax. Moreover, *miri* lands, while remaining under state ownership, were subject to traditional usufruct rights that could be exercised by anyone wanting to work the land—whether peasants or wealthy landowners. Thus the land could be used essentially as if it were private property. It seems that it was in the short-term interests of the people concerned to keep the status of the land in the kind of limbo of *arazi-i miriye*, even if we can say that in the long term they might have had more security in tenure had they converted it to *mulk*, especially after the British took over and changed the way state land was considered vis-à-vis those working the land.[110]

Similar investigations at around the same time revealed that the government was concerned to regain tax revenue from orchards that for one reason or another were granted exemption from taxes yet had subsequently had new trees planted on them, which meant that the produce, land, and gardens were all taxable. We also find conflicts between the "multezim"— the person responsible for collecting taxes over the specific land, although the title seems anachronistic for this period[111]—and tradesmen over the purchase of their products; though the details are sketchy, they seem to point to a conflict between the larger landowners and the urban petite bourgeoisie that would also suggest a gradual transformation of landownership and wealth in the Jaffa region from the former to the latter.[112]

One thing we can perhaps learn from these complex cases is that as the built-up and industrial area of Jaffa expanded, agricultural land was increasingly seen—or at least defined for the purposes of taxation by their owners—as urban land, which often resulted in situations in which the land wound up remaining *miri* while all buildings, trees, and so on, were classified as *mulk*.[113] This situation demonstrates a level of fluidity, conflict over, and even confusion in the nature and use of land in the Jaffa–Tel Aviv region that (as I demonstrate in detail in the next chapter) renders it difficult to determine the borders between "urban," "rural," or "barren" land.

What is clear is that the Qa'imaqam's suggestion regarding the Jewish-owned land to "destroy the buildings built without permission and return the land to a *miri* state and earn income from it [up to 3,000 lira yearly]"[114] contradicted the desire of the Ottoman state to sell (generally marginal) state/*miri* lands in order to increase its revenues; one reason for their differences could have been that the taxes would have remained in the Qa'imaqam's control and would not have been passed on to Istanbul.[115] Here we see the conflicting interests and perceptions regarding the status of the land at different levels of the Ottoman state, which helps us to understand how Zionist leaders were able to manipulate the ambiguities and ambivalences in Ottoman legal discourses surrounding land tenure to their advantage.

If there was one event that epitomized the fracturing relationship between Jews and Muslim and Christian Arabs and foreshadowed the further deterioration that occurred after the foundation of Tel Aviv, it was the violence of March 1908. On March 16, 1908, one day before the beginning of the Jewish holiday of Purim, fighting broke out between Muslim and Jewish youths in which one Muslim and thirteen Jews were wounded. According to the British consul, one of the causes of the violence was the increasing bitterness in Jaffa against the burgeoning Jewish population.[116] This assessment contradicts that of many scholars that Arab anti-Zionism had not yet emerged at the eve of the Young Turk Revolution.[117]

It was generally believed that the fighting was incited by the Jaffa Qa'imaqam. If true, his actions are not surprising; Arab propaganda against Jewish and Zionist immigration was increasing not just in Palestine but in Istanbul as well, inspired to a greater or lesser degree by the "Constitutional Revolution" then under way in Turkey under the leadership of the Committee of Union and Progress (CUP), which was active in Jaffa and offered a sharp critique of European imperialism and its effects throughout the empire that would surely have been noted by Palestinians who traveled to Istanbul.[118] In fact, by the last days of 1908 the "situation with the Arabs" in Jaffa had "changed considerably" for the worse and was dangerous enough to jeopardize the purchase of the land on which Tel Aviv would be constructed the next year.[119]

The increased violence in Jaffa in the period leading up to the founding of Tel Aviv, particularly between Arab youth and Jewish immigrants, prompted the chief rabbi of Jaffa to write to the local branch of the CUP urging them to stand up against the attacks against Jews.[120] Jewish workers, specifically, the Po'alei Tzion party (the largest prewar socialist-Zionist party in Palestine, established there in 1906) took matters into their own hands and formed a self-defense committee, Hashomer, in Jaffa later that year.

A new Qa'imaqam was appointed in the aftermath of the violence, but Jewish leaders were aware that he would not succeed in quieting the increasing hostility toward Zionism unless Jews took steps to ameliorate the situation, especially in the context of a reiteration of Ottoman policy against "accepting foreign refugees into Palestine."[121] A number of measures were thus proposed, including the creation of economic enterprises with Muslims and Christians, establishing a "collaborative, independent, and moderate" newspaper with Muslims, and, most important, radically curtailing nationalist actions: "Ces compétitions stupides, ces petitiesses et ces intérêts personelles. . . . Notre salut est dans le maintien de bonnes relations avec tous nos concitoyens."[122]

Perhaps because of this realization, the events of 1908 did not signal a total breakdown of relations between Jews and Arabs in Jaffa, and the CUP was unable to galvanize enthusiasm in Jaffa when it organized demonstrations there.[123] In fact, when the local French vice consul was asked by the foreign minister to report on the activities of the Muslim notables of the town the following spring, he reported that compared to Jerusalem, "Jaffa is not a center of political or Muslim religious action [and] the level of fanaticism here is less than in the majority of other villages of Turkey in Asia."[124]

The accuracy of this assessment is questionable, since on the next page the vice consul lists half a dozen of the town's principal notables who were more or less "fanatical" or "nationalist" or playing both sides of the political fence at the same time (the CUP, the Muslim League, the mayor).[125] Nevertheless, given the lackadaisical response to the CUP, the report would seem to suggest that the causes of the increased hostility toward Jews had more to do with the specific perceived threat of Zionism than with a general political ferment stimulated by events in Istanbul. And, indeed, in about 1912 the Interior Ministry in Istanbul sent an encrypted telegraph to the Syrian provinces, including Jerusalem, about "Arab nationalists" who were "inciting Bedouins and city-dwellers into insurrection against the Turkish community and Ottoman Government . . . and distributing newspapers to the villages" in and around both Jaffa and Haifa.[126]

From the available sources it is not possible to say conclusively how strong nationalist sentiment was in Jaffa during this period; what we do know is, first, that there was a history of political consciousness and at least protonationalist feelings going back at least to the 1881 'Urabi Revolt in Egypt (which had sparked riots in Jaffa),[127] and, second, that whatever the growing hostility on the national level, local Palestinian Arab merchants continued to work with their Jewish colleagues. For example, in January 1909 a group of Arab and Jewish businessmen, including Jaffa Mayor Omar Beitar and Ahuzat Bayit leader Meir Dizengoff, met to consider forming a joint company for lighting the city of Jaffa.[128] The next year Jewish and Arab orange merchants came together to form an export society.[129]

Even during World War I significant cooperation continued between Tel Aviv's leadership and local Ottoman and Arab authorities in Jaffa (although ultimately most of the Jewish quarter's population was exiled to nearby Jewish settlements). For example, when Tel Aviv leaders Meir Dizengoff and Yosef Schlotz wrote to the Qa'imaqam, Hassan Bey, in 1915 to request a receipt for 4,947 francs for their participation in the construction of Jamal Pasha Boulevard (the Jaffan answer to Tel Aviv's European-inspired Roth-schild Boulevard), he certified the letter and thanked them for their contribution, which, he wrote, "allowed the street to be built much more quickly."[130]

Yet on the whole, after the establishment of Tel Aviv in 1909, reports in the local Hebrew and Arabic press about opposition to Zionism from different quarters in Jaffa increased.[131] The reasons given for this included the "grabbing up" of land by Jews; the rise in the cost of living; Jewish social, commercial, and educational exclusivism; and the belief that Zionism was a spearhead for German or Russian influence in the Ottoman Empire.[132]

The Arabic newspaper *Falastin* reported that Tel Aviv's leaders would not allow Arab wagons to travel through its territory, had established a "fortress" in the town, and was using the Herzliyya Gymnasium as a "jail for Arab felahin."[133] A telegram to the Pasha in Jerusalem similarly explained: "The Jews in Jaffa are founding *a state within a state* in the new settlement of Tel Aviv, within the Gymnasium they are holding Arab prisoners, and within their Municipal Building there are two rooms used as a jail for citizens of the country."[134] This led the Ottoman authorities in Jerusalem to ban temporarily land purchases by Jews and prompted several Sephardic Jews to form a committee to mediate the increasing conflict between Jews and Muslim and Christian Arabs.

What is important about the perspective of Jaffa's Arab Palestinian leaders is that their words mirrored exactly the belief by Zionist leaders such as Dizengoff that the Jews had "created a state within a state in Jaffa" even before the establishment of Tel Aviv.[135] This situation made it clear that public hostility was rising over the increasing number of Jewish immigrants in Jaffa, and these sentiments apparently spilled over against the city's Christians as well.[136] *Falastin* called for the foundation of a society to purchase large plots of lands around the towns before Zionists could purchase them, and at least one notable who had conflicts with Jews over land surrounding Tel Aviv wrote for the paper against land sales to Jews.[137]

While a significant percentage of Ottoman documents relating to Jaffa have yet to be cataloged, files from a recently cataloged section of the DH.İD series provide tantalizing clues about the political, economic, and cultural situation in the Jaffa region during the last decades of Ottoman rule, when Zionist colonization was beginning in earnest. One thing that is clear from the files I have been able to examine is the growth in the town in general and in its commerce in particular. In fact, plans for a water project in Jaffa appear as early as 1880, and local calls were being made to build a new harbor to accommodate the increased trade at least as early as 1911.[138] However, the Jewish participation in that growth troubled local officials. More specifically, both economically and culturally the increasing participation of Jews in the orange trade seems to have worried local Palestinian Arab merchants as well as Ottoman officials.

On the one hand, the purchase by Jews of lands and mills well outside the Old City of Jaffa, including around the villages of Jerisha and Jammasin, raised eyebrows and led to complaints by local residents that the "sale of the mills to non-Ottoman Jews [was] improper."[139] The subject of concern actually extended from land and businesses to the products produced on and from them. A 1914 memo from a certain M. Ziya reported that some of the oranges exported from Jaffa have "Hebrew scripts, and also have some disadvantages." Among these disadvantages, according to the writer, were the following: "There are a lot of anti-Semites in Europe and the USA . . . who could act against Turkish exports," and the use of Hebrew "in this way . . . can cause a problem of Muslim and Jewish struggles similar to Muslim-Christian struggles" plaguing the empire. Most important, he said, the use of Hebrew "encourages Zionists."[140]

The problems generated by increasing penetration of Jews (especially Zionists) in what was heretofore a rather uniformly Palestinian Arab economy were exacerbated by the construction of new buildings by Jews in the Jaffa region, which caused "public reaction," struggles, and even physical violence between Jews and Palestinian Arabs.[141] There were also political repercussions, even when just the Ottoman Jewish citizens are considered. That is, at the turn of the twentieth century a debate broke out when the Jewish population of Jaffa increased to the point where local Jewish leaders petitioned the authorities (and apparently the local governor agreed) for representation on the city council. The participation of Jews and Christians was mandated under the 1877 reforms known as the Regulations for the Administration of the Provinces (Idare-i vilayet nizamnamesi), under which one Jew (as well as one Armenian) had to be appointed to the six-member city council.

Not surprisingly, Orthodox and Catholic leaders were opposed to Jews and Armenians being represented on the council, which led to petitions to the Interior Ministry. Catholic leaders went so far as to threaten to complain to France about the choice of a Jewish representative, and local authorities wrote to Istanbul about the difficulty of choosing members of the council and the court in the Jaffa district because of the opposition, even though the Interior Ministry specifically declared that the Mutaşarrıf "should make his duty to choose one member each from among the Jews and Armenians in Jaffa."[142] There are two interesting things about this debate; first, it takes place in 1909–10, at the time Tel Aviv was established; second, the opposition of the Catholics to inviting Jews to join the council was based on pre-Tanzimat logic. They argued that since they had not put the new law into practice, it should not be enforced in Jaffa. And with this justification they rejected the Tanzimat's granting of political equality to Jews, even though it did the same for Catholics, perhaps because Jaffa's Catholic leadership felt they had more power under the old system or because they felt the potential damage of Zionism was greater than the benefits of official equality.

Yet as important as the conflict over the increasing Zionist Jewish presence in the Jaffa region may have been, it was far from the only issue occupying the minds of Jaffa's leaders or the local Ottoman administration. Another major issue involved the integrity of Jaffa's local leadership, especially as it related to using their position to gain control of land and sell it to Jews. In one case in particular, residents of Jaffa sent a petition to Interior Minister Talat Bey accusing Omar Beitar, the mayor of Jaffa, of taking bribes, "acting unjustly, making big money from bribes and buying many lands."[143] Moreover, given the number of new buildings constructed by Jews in Jaffa, the fees for the permits alone should be much higher than the total revenues Beitar declared as having been received by the Jaffa Municipality.[144] And in fact we know from British documents listing Palestinian notables who sold land to Jews that Mayor Beitar sold a significant amount of land to Jews,[145] so there was likely good reason for the petitions against him. The support he received from his peers is likewise not surprising, especially considering that many of them probably also sold land to Jews.

The rising Zionist immigration through and to Jaffa did not just lead to increasing tensions between Arabs and Jewish immigrants, but also between the latter and the existing Jewish community of Jaffa. In fact, until the turn of the century it was the traditional, religious community that had the most influence and power within Jaffa's Jewish population.[146] The "new Jews" seemed to Palestinian Arab Jaffans radically different from the existing community, who were considered "sons of th[is] place" who had "repudiated the new Jews."[147]

The conflict between old-timers and newcomers was caused not just by the secular-religious divide that usually symbolizes the clash between the "old" and the "new" *yishuv* during this period (which, however, did lead to a "war of opinion and principle" between the two communities over issues such as education, profaning the Sabbath, and the like); it was also caused by struggles over political power and religious authority within the Orthodox and specifically Hassidic communities. The prevailing balance of power was reflected in the composition and activities of the first nonsectarian Jewish public body in Jaffa, the Va'ad Ha'ir (lit., "City Council"), which was formed in 1863 and was the primary representative of the religious, social, political, and economic interests of Jaffa's Jewish community until the establishment of Tel Aviv.

In fact, the year Tel Aviv was born, the Jewish Zionist workers' paper, *Hapo'el Hatza'ir,* celebrated the recent elections to the Va'ad Ha'ir (which included many of the founders of Tel Aviv) by declaring, "Mazel Tov! Jewish Jaffa is organized! From Ashkenazi Pharisees to Hassidic Ashkenazis, from Western Sephardis to just plain Sephardis, from old and young tradesmen (missing only Yemenites, but it's possible to take comfort in the hope that next year this lack will be repaired)."[148] Moreover, the local Sephardi-Maghrebi Jewish community continued to take its "Ottoman" identity quite seriously, for example, celebrating the Young Turk Revolution and the reinstitution of the 1876 Constitution with great fanfare at an event that none of the leading Ashkenazi residents of the town attended.

I would argue that, coming only a year before the founding of Tel Aviv, the public commitment to a renewed "Ottoman" identity by the Sephardic Jewish communities, which can perhaps be characterized as "Ottoman Zionism"—that is, a national although not strictly territorialist identity that mirrored the evolving Palestinian Arab identity of the period before the conflict with the Zionists and the weak Ottoman response led to an increasingly territorialist-national identity—along with their extensive relations with their Muslim and Christian neighbors, reveals that at this crucial moment an alternative form of Palestinian Jewish identity was possible to imagine, one that was foreclosed (at least in the Jaffa region) by the establishment of Tel Aviv and the modernism it brought to the region.[149]

To return to the activities of the Va'ad Ha'ir, by this time it had become increasingly "secular," and its power (and that of the older, generally religious communities it represented) inevitably began to wane.[150] Despite their overlapping membership, conflicts arose between the Va'ad, ostensibly representing the interests of the entire Jaffa Jewish community, and the Va'ad Tel Aviv, composed only of residents of the new neighborhood, over the role Tel Aviv would play in representing and administering the affairs of the Jewish residents of Jaffa (indeed, a similar struggle over who should represent Jaffa's Jewish population would be occur in the Mandate period;

see chap. 7). Each council felt that it should represent the growing Jewish population in Jaffa proper. For its part, the Jaffa Vaʿad argued in a 1912 election brochure that there was still a need for the Vaʿad in the "New Yishuv."[151]

The burgeoning rivalry between the two councils grew more intense with the first attempts to unite them, which occurred before the outbreak of World War I. The failure resulted from the difficulty of finding a unifying framework without having one (most likely the Vaʿad Haʿir) become dependent on the other.[152] Indeed, there were "many opponents of the Vaʿad from every side"; even "friends" of the Vaʿad wanted "to nullify it."[153]

By 1914 there were great debates over the question of the Vaʿad Haʿir's function, even existence, as pressure mounted to move the center of the Jewish community from Jaffa to Tel Aviv.[154] All in all, the relationship between the two councils was quite complex, and the strains between them, or between the established pre-Zionist *yishuv* and the increasingly dominant Zionist immigrants, were also accompanied by class antagonisms in the years leading up to the war. For many members of Jaffa's growing working class, there was apparently increasing resentment about the fact that more and more immigrants were going to Tel Aviv—a place where "only the rich live," meaning the "intelligentsia: the teachers, writers, officials and the like." And, to the workers' chagrin, facilities for "the people" had yet to be built.[155]

THE SPATIAL EXPANSION OF JAFFA AND TEL AVIV DURING THE LATE OTTOMAN PERIOD

As we have seen, even before the turn of the nineteenth century the walled city of Jaffa was surrounded by "famous" gardens and orchards that yielded palm, oranges, lemons, pomegranates, figs, and bananas "in profusion."[156] Although *Baedeker* considered the "interior" of the town (i.e., the Old City) "uninteresting" well into the 1870s,[157] the same could not be said about the area outside the casbah, as increasing construction by various foreign churches, governments, and private interests, coupled with the planting of new orchards (many with large houses) and the establishment of new neighborhoods by Europeans and local residents alike, continually altered the landscape.[158]

Numerous workers' neighborhoods, or *saknat*, had sprung up in the wake of the Egyptian invasion outside the walls of the Old City to the north, south, and east. Among these were ʿAjami, Nuzha, Hursih, Irshid, Jebaliyyeh, and Manshiyyeh. The development of these neighborhoods, which paralleled the establishment of Muslim neighborhoods outside the Old City of Jerusalem, led to new streets being cut through the existing orange groves, creating new spatial patterns that facilitated the urbanization of the region, including its villages.[159]

On top of that, one American and two German missionary associations established colonies and a "model farm" (Sarona and Walhalla were the names of the more permanent German settlements) after receiving permission from Ibrahim Pasha as early as 1837.[160] In fact, twenty new neighborhoods were erected in Jaffa between 1830 and 1880, and another sixteen (eleven of them Jewish) between 1880 and 1909, the year Tel Aviv was established.[161]

Moreover, similar to Jabal Nablus and other urban regions in Palestine, the increasing development of the Jaffa area further blurred the division between urban and rural spheres in late Ottoman Jaffa.[162] Indeed, while one could speak of Jaffa's "Old City" as an urban core of the Jaffa–Tel Aviv region, beyond its walls (at least what remained of them by the 1880s) there existed a complex patchwork of interwoven and constantly evolving land uses—agricultural, industrial, and increasingly residential—that defy attempts to characterize them as uniformly "urban." This would hold true, as will become important as the story progresses, even after the boundaries of the Jaffa and Tel Aviv municipalities expanded to encompass them, connecting the various regions into one "wider system" that cut across the various increasingly nationalized spaces.[163]

In fact, the notion of a firm dividing line between urban and other types of land was not present in the late Ottoman Middle East, as existing Ottoman and Islamic legal codes did not recognize a clear territorial differentiation between town and country.[164] This perhaps accounts for some of the difficulties and ambiguities of classifying land as *miri* or *mulk*. If we examine the opinions of the Hanafi school, which was historically dominant in Palestine (and officially in the Ottoman Empire as a whole), what we find instead is a "multidimensional definition": conceptually the city was a "comprehensive social and political entity"; geographically the all-embracing town was a large locality "in which there are streets and markets, to which rural districts belong," and whose size and economic and military importance warrant the permanent stationing of a representative of the state in the form of a "governor."[165]

More specifically, the city was the "center of an agricultural hinterland." What distinguished rural from truly urban spaces was the very relationship of dependence of the latter on the former, and as important, the fact that cities played a crucial "public" function because they possessed a "Friday mosque" that was the center not just for public worship but also for the interaction of the public and the state. In this sense Jaffa was already a "city" decades before it was officially granted municipal status in 1871, even before the Ottoman governor built a new mosque complex to support the rebuilding of the town after Napoleon's brief but violent sojourn in 1799, whereas the regions lying between the more fully urbanized quarters and the surrounding villages—including what would become Tel Aviv—could be considered *fina' al-misr*, or land that "served the common interests of town dwellers, not, however, the interests of individual, private persons."[166]

Such an imagination and categorization of the crucial frontier lands between Jaffa and the villages would be especially important as the boundaries between "urban" and "rural" became simultaneously more ambiguous (which mirrored the narrowing of differences between *mulk* and *miri* land) and more crucial to define.[167] A commentary on the 1858 Land Law demonstrates the ambiguity of the conception of the hinterland, or the "limits of the village or town." It explains:

> [T]he term "all the lands of a village or of a town" does not apply to the lands granted to a village or a town [by the sultan] at the time of its formation for the purpose of habitation, or as supplementary habitation, nor does it apply to the lands left and assigned for all the inhabitants of a village or town such as pasture grounds and places for woodcutting, but it signifies the lands required by the inhabitants as places for cultivation or arable fields. . . . [Yet] it is nevertheless possible to assign to a village or a town or to several villages or towns together, a piece of land situated within the limits of a village or town. For example, when it is required to set aside for the inhabitants of a village or of a town a place from which they can derive benefits of grazing, watering or woodcutting.[168]

It is in this context that we must attempt to make sense of the development and growth of the villages of Salama, Shaykh Muwannis, and Jerisha, the sister villages known as Jamassin East and West, and Summel (see map 1), which surrounded Jaffa and together encircled (and in so doing delineated) a zone of pastureland and agricultural land, roads (later railroads), rivers, and marginal sandy land that lay seemingly within the "limits" of the villages and of Jaffa as a rapidly expanding town. These villages, with their mixed populations of immigrants from Egypt and Jordan and bedouins from southern Palestine, all grew in the wake of the Egyptian conquest (and more so after the Crimean War) as increased security made settlements in open (as opposed to walled) areas more tenable.[169] In fact, they were an integral part of the social and spatial economy of Jaffa, as residents, including

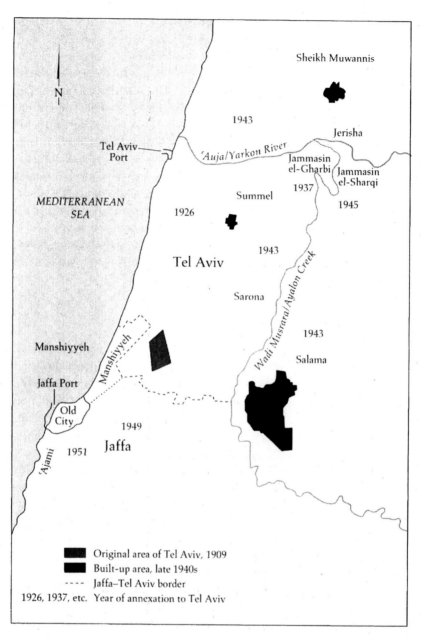

Map 1. Jaffa–Tel Aviv region with villages.

the seasonal bedouin populations, made frequent trips to Jaffa during this period to sell their produce and other goods or work in the town.[170] Many villagers used the proceeds to change building styles from adobe brick to stone and, later, cement. On the other hand, well into the Mandate period the villages were a favorite destination for Jaffans during summers and feast days, because of their "convenient location, near woods, and [Jaffa's] cafes, parks and gardens."[171] The villages gradually became integrated into the political economy of Tel Aviv as it expanded during the Mandate period.[172]

The most important spatial development in the post–Crimean War period was the increased capitalization of land in the vicinity of Jaffa. This process had actually begun by the mid-1830s, during the reign of Ibrahim Pasha; the capitalization of land was part of the larger process of monetarization of the local economy that would challenge and transform the system of land tenure well before the more well known 1858 Land Law was issued.[174]

In his examination of evidence of the social and economic development of Jaffa during the early Tanzimat period (1840–61) in the records of the local Shari'a Court, Wilkins points out that even if Palestine as a whole was marked by considerable political confusion, Jaffa still enjoyed significant economic expansion beginning with the Egyptian occupation (1831–39/40) and continuing through the next two decades. The principal features of this development, confirmed both by consular reports and local Shari'a Court records, were the physical growth of settled and cultivated areas around the old town and an increase in real estate investment by both Jaffans and residents of other Palestinian towns.[175]

By 1875 the main street of the Old City and the bazaar had begun to be paved, and the marketplace was extended through the area on which the former city gate and fortifications had stood, later continuing outside the town along the roads to Nablus and Jerusalem. In short, "viewed from the landward side, Jaffa had greatly changed its appearance within only a few years."[176] Two years later the walls of the city, already in decay, were being torn down and sold by the government to be used for new houses and stores, and the wealthy residents, including absentee owners from Beirut, were building large houses in their orange groves surrounding the Old City.

The scope of economic development and the accompanying spatial expansion and development is revealed by Theodore Sandel's map of Jaffa (c. 1878) and the surrounding area to the north, which clearly depicts numerous orchards, groves, farms, and villages that were connected by a network of roads to the old center, including the German and American colonies.[177] The capitalization of land in the Jaffa–Tel Aviv region was well enough established that Jaffa was known to be a town where "kulhum lamam," that is, "they're all riffraff," meaning that its money came from trade, citrus plantations, and other capitalized agricultural industries and thus had no "great families" (i.e., a patrician or landed class).[178]

As for Europeans (both government and church or other religion-based lay communities), they were attracted to Jaffa and its surroundings in the wake of the Crimean War not just for economic and touristic reasons but because of its strategic location, fertile soil, availability of land, and mild climate[179]—the same factors that no doubt prompted the influx of North African and, later, Ashkenazi Jews to the region.[180] In particular, the colony of Sarona, established in 1869 by members of the Temple Society (Templars) on the land of a recently defunct American colony, was one of two neighborhoods founded by Germans in the immediate vicinity of Jaffa's Old City during the second half of the nineteenth century. The second colony, Valhalla, was established in the years before World War I. Both made a great impression on Jaffa's European Jewish population.

Europeans and Sephardic (and later, Ashkenazi) Jews played an important role in the geographic expansion of Jaffa, though it was not as determinant as some scholars have claimed.[181] Several of the prominent Sephardic families realized even before the Crimean War that converting their liquid capital, earned from commerce and moneychanging, into real estate would prove in the future to have been a wise investment. By the 1870s, for example, the Shloosh family was "buying vineyard after vineyard" in the sands north of Jaffa, land that would form the nucleus of the pre–Tel Aviv Jewish neighborhoods of Jaffa, such as Neve Tzedek, Neve Shalom, Mahane-Yehuda, Mahane-Yosef, Shchunat-Aharon, and Kerem Hateimanim.[182]

Moreover, most of the walls of the Old City had been demolished by this time, which helped to fuel construction outside it, including government buildings and many large houses and new streets. The local government also "greatly improved" the road from Jaffa to Jerusalem through various public works projects between 1880 and 1888.[183] And the upsurge in tourism in Palestine, which by the beginning of the 1870s had become vital to the economic health of Jaffa, the country's primary port, was yet another important reason for Jaffa's literally bursting through its walls.[184] The increased economic and tourist activity led to the construction of the Jaffa-Jerusalem railway, which was opened in 1892. This in turn led to the construction of numerous public buildings by local and foreign governments and churches.[185]

By 1888, the year Jaffa's first Jewish suburb was established, the wall's dismemberment was complete—a major event in the cultural history of the city[186]—and streets, homes, and shops were being constructed on the now filled-in moat, many using stones that months before separated the old town from the surrounding neighborhoods. This rapid development led the government to commission a new map of Jaffa.[187] Two years later, "every meter of suitable land for planting [could] be sold for a high price [and] the farms ha[d] achieved a prestigious place in the commerce of Jaffa and apart from their enormous income, . . . employ[ed] many hands."[188] The 1892 *Murray's* guidebook described Jaffa thus:

> The first view of Jaffa, gained from the deck of the ship, is beautiful and entrancing. . . . [T]he sandy shore trends away in both directions in a monotonous line; but orange-groves, palms, and other Oriental trees combine to render the first view of the Holy Land for ever memorable to the European visitor. A disenchantment, however, follows from the very moment of landing. Jaffa is one of the dirtiest and most uncomfortable of all the towns of Palestine. The houses are crowded together[;] . . . the streets are narrow, crooked, and filthy [and] filled with groups of wild Arabs and eager traders. . . . Although Jaffa itself is dirty and uninteresting, its outskirts are delightful. New and well-built houses have sprung up amongst the splendid groves of oranges, and there are many signs of increasing wealth.[189]

This quotation is a good example of how Europeans, like Zionists in the decades that followed, could only conceive of Jaffa as an "old town"; that is, they seem to have been unable to let the "new and well-built houses" that sprung up outside the old walls challenge the biblical and Crusader imagining of the city. By definition, Jaffa's expansion outside the walls could not be recognized as an organic development and thus still "Jaffa." From an Ottoman-Islamic perspective, however, the region was part of the town.

At this point, European visions of the city did not have the power to shape reality, and government building activities in Jaffa expanded toward the turn of the century. In 1897 a new Saray, or Government House, was erected, and in 1900, perhaps the ultimate sign of Jaffa's—and Palestine's—full-scale entrance into the "modern" world, Sultan Abdul Hamid II had a clock tower built in a square opposite the new Saray (and in several other cities in Palestine) to celebrate his twenty-five years on the throne.[190]

By the first decade of the twentieth century even Arab peasants around Jaffa were purchasing land to build their own homes or rent to others; both merchants and peasants—many migrating from other parts of Palestine—understood that investing in Jaffa was good business.[191] The increasing influx of people and money led to a dramatic increase in land prices by the late 1900s.[192]

I have already mentioned the early involvement of Jews in land purchases outside the walls of the Old City. Although evidence from the *sijjil* indicates that Christians were much more likely than Jews to purchase land with Muslims,[193] Jews are also listed as copurchasers of land. For example, Yusef Moyal, partriarch of one of the most prominent Sephardic families of Jaffa, appears in a 1317/1898 case as a partner with Muslims and Christians in the purchase of land around the Old City, and he is described as owning "much land." This case is interesting because it served to confirm the sale after a third party had contested the seller's (one Shakr Bey) right to the land and because it contains a rich description of its topography, which included various kinds of fruit trees, a well with a spring and a pool for bathing, an irrigation wheel, and two houses, one of which was owned by a leading family of Jaffa, the Siksiks.[194]

The Moyal family registered Yusuf Moyal's will in the Islamic court, and Christians also registered land purchases in and brought disputes over ownership to the Islamic court;[195] both demonstrate the continued dominance of Muslim public and legal spheres through the end of the Ottoman period. Another case, from 1298/1880, documents the sale of an orchard and house that had been left to a Muslim woman named Fatima bint Muhammad al-Dawaʿ by her late husband.[196] The property was sold to a Christian native of Jaffa named Abdallah ibn Jirgis, perhaps a sailor (the last part of his name is "al-bahri"). What is interesting about this case is not just that a Muslim woman was selling land to a Christian but also the way the land is described. First, the neighborhood in which the woman lived, "Mahallah Sheikh Ibrahim al-Malahi," is labeled as "inside" Jaffa even though it is outside the Old City, while the orchard (located between another orchard and a vineyard to the south of the Old City, along what was called "al-tariq al-hilweh," most likely today's Yeffet Street) was considered "outside" Jaffa.[197] On the other hand, in a case involving the registration of the division of shares in a newly purchased vineyard, the scribe described the property as "kharij Yafa al-mahdud" (lit. "outside Jaffa the bordered"; i.e., what is definitely fixed or delimited as Jaffa proper)—an ungrammatical phrase that nevertheless demonstrates the ambiguity about what precisely was "Jaffa."[198]

Here it becomes clear that unlike Europeans, but in line with prevailing local Ottoman-Islamic geographic imaginaries, residents of the town took a larger view of what constituted Jaffa and thus would not have limited their evalutation of the city to conditions prevailing in the Old City.¹⁰⁰ The vineyard property was described as having trees, a spring, a well, an irrigation wheel, five mules, and a vaulted house with a European tiled roof and kitchen/bathroom facilities. This blending of local Arab vernacular and European architectural styles, which we can assume was under way (at least) in the decade before this sale (and perhaps as far back as 1845), demonstrates an economic and cultural intereaction between Arabs and Europeans that belies the traditional historiography of this period but whose erasure would be crucial to the imagination, expansion, and hegemony of Tel Aviv in the coming decades.

[handwritten note: Arabs bigger part of it than Zionism would admit]

3 Taming the Sahara

The Birth of Tel Aviv and the
Last Years of Ottoman Rule

THE FOUNDING OF THE AHUZAT BAYIT SOCIETY

It is in the context of the social, economic, political, and spatial changes in and around Jaffa that we must understand the course of events that led to the establishment of Tel Aviv. In the early 1880s Jews began to build on the lands they had purchased in the previous few decades, thereby joining the exodus of Christians and wealthier Muslims from the Old City to new and spacious suburbs. Agricultural land was purchased near the German colonies southeast of what would become Tel Aviv and orchards planted.[1] And in the sandy region north of the Old City, the first self-described Jewish neighborhood, Neve Tzedek, was established in 1887.[2]

Neve Tzedek was created specifically because the rapid expansion of the Jewish population in Jaffa and its environs made the region the center of the New Yishuv.[3] It and Neve Shalom, established in 1890, set the pattern for other Jewish neighborhoods—Mahane Yosef in 1904, Kerem Hateimanim in 1905, Ohel Moshe in 1906 among them—that grew up as these two became overcrowded.[4]

The founding and early history of Tel Aviv are not just contentious issues in the Israeli-Palestinian conflict. In fact, by the mid-1930s there was great debate within the city and its leadership over the details of its creation and early growth. Yet while the details of Tel Aviv's paternity remain at issue, the motivations underlying its conception and establishment are clear.

The course was set in 1906 when sixty prominent members of Jaffa's Jewish community, including both older Sephardic families and more recent European immigrants, decided to found a society for the purchase of land and the construction of homes in the Jaffa region. The name of the society was Ahuzat Bayit, literally, "Building Houses," and though the society's first meetings described its goal as the "founding of a new Hebrew *yishuv*,"[5] the word *modern* soon replaced *new;* that is, the goal quickly became defined as establishing a "modern Jewish urban neighborhood in a European style in the city of Jaffa."[6]

Most of Ahuzat Bayit's members were middle-class Jews living in Jaffa and engaged in trade, teaching, and Zionist public activity. The reasons for its formation were both practical and ideological: there was a need for healthy and sanitary housing, given the doubling of the population during the previous decade (from 3,000 to 6,000); and there were three specifically Zionist ideological motives. The first was the felt obligation to develop a nationalist-Zionist society in the city because it was the center of immigration to Palestine, which led to a desire to segregate the new immigrants geographically from Arabs in a place where they could nurture their national values by speaking Hebrew, developing Hebrew educational and cultural institutions, engaging in national activities, and the like.[7]

The second ideological motive was to stem the flow of Jewish capital into Arab hands through renting Arab houses, a major concern for Jewish leaders because it constituted the single largest drain of capital out of the Jewish sector. The third was to bolster Jewish national prestige as a prelude to raising the Jews' political status.[8] As one prospectus written by Ahuzat Bayit chairman Akiva Weiss explained, "We will preserve cleanliness and sanitation, and not follow the ways of the goyim [non-Jews], and like New York City[,] . . . our city in time will be the first gate to the [*sic*] 'Eretz Yisraelit.' . . . [It will be] an organized . . . modern city."[9]

Ahuzat Bayit was not the only group engaged in land purchases in the Jaffa region. Between 1908 and 1914 numerous land purchasing societies were established in cities around the world with the express purpose of providing land for settlement by Jews in the vicinity of Jaffa because of the general and specific advantages of the region.[10] The motivations and considerations underlying the foundation of Ahuzat Bayit are worthy of examination. As Yossi Katz has demonstrated, whereas the dominant view of Zionist ideology depicts it as focusing almost exclusively on agricultural settlement, the reality is that from the beginning the movement and its institutions attributed great importance to Zionist urban colonization.[11]

Against this background, we can understand the implications of a 1907 French publicity memorandum by Ahuzat Bayit:

> The Jewish emigration to Palestine begun some years ago has centered towards the cities exclusively. . . . Life in Jaffa has become so expensive and so difficult from an economic standpoint that it rivals the great

cities of Europe. . . . Thus we have set up here a *"COLONISATION JUIVE URBAINE,"* that is, the establishment of a Jewish element among the Arabs in the same city. . . . The result has been that we have quarters in which all the owners are Arabs and the renters Jews. . . . It is truly servitude. If we take into consideration the detestable sanitary state of the city of Jaffa, the lack of air in the Arab houses, and the frequency of eye diseases that have resulted, we will understand that for the Israelite population of Jaffa the question of housing has reached the crisis stage.[12]

The solution offered by Ahuzat Bayit was the construction of a new, Jewish neighborhood in a "healthy atmosphere and in hygienic conditions," each home "with a small garden and courtyard." "Who knows," the memorandum continued, "perhaps the model neighborhood in Jaffa [Tel Aviv] will soon be followed by similar neighborhoods in other towns." Other Zionist leaders concurred with this diagnosis of the problems in the existing urban *yishuv* and the potential of the Ahuzat Bayit "model" to rectify it. In fact, a 1909 lecture discloses wonderfully the mental gymnastics that on the one hand blamed Jaffa's squalor on her Jewish residents and on the other visualized the imagined "new" Jewish Jaffa as being free of such problems: "Arab Jaffa and its Jewish quarters with their filthy outskirts and lakes of . . . mud . . . made the arriving Jewish immigrants feel bad and caused them to dream of a new quarter, up-to date and spacious, pretty and clean." This new quarter would be "the new, the beautiful and clean—Jaffa of the Jews."[13] The implications of the town planning and architectural discourse surrounding the creation of Tel Aviv are discussed in chapter 6.

Given the ideological importance of Ahuzat Bayit to Zionist leaders, it is not surprising that once suitable guarantees were secured, the Jewish National Fund (JNF), backed by the Zionist Organization, agreed to guarantee a loan of several hundred thousand francs to be used to purchase land and build homes.[14] A fascinating Russian-language handbook on the JNF written in 1909 sheds light on the motivations underlying the Ahuzat Bayit project as well as its material, political, and national importance to the Zionist enterprise in Palestine. It explained: "[Ahuzat Bayit seeks] to constitute, in our own country, as soon as possible, not only an economic force but a political one. There is no doubt that we will not be able to own the country if we do not own the land. . . . The development of a Jewish urban community is without a doubt the most important stage in the bolstering of our position in the country."[15]

The importance of the idea that Zionists, then a minority among the Jewish minority in Palestine, already sought to "own the country" is discussed fully later. For now it is worth noting that this early chronology for the development of a "militant nationalism" demonstrates that Gershon Shafir's thesis that agricultural workers developed their exclusivist nationalism out of interaction and competition with the local Palestinian Arab workers reflected a similar process in the urban sector.[16]

At this point I will allow the handbook to continue to speak for itself, as it went on to explain that the JNF felt the urgent need to build an urban Jewish base not just for "material political, and national reasons" but also because "Zionism in Eretz Israel has found unhealthy lifestyles, similar to those in the ghettos of Europe. The Jews are now importing these [negative] qualities to Palestine. . . . In Jaffa one finds . . . a desire for congestedness, a disparagement of conditions which civilized people consider to be basic needs and which strongly affect man's physical and spiritual development. . . . If we do not intervene immediately, urban life in free Palestine will develop as in the ghetto.[17]

Given the belief that Jewish society, if left to its own devices, would not develop the healthy habits required by Zionism, it is no surprise that the director of the Palestine Office of the JNF, Arthur Ruppin, became personally involved with Ahuzat Bayit. In fact, he requested that a stipulation be added to the JNF loan to Ahuzat Bayit stating that the granting of the loan was conditional on approval of the building plans by a JNF expert so as not to "sacrifice hygiene and ignore the need to set aside areas for planting trees and parks and for public buildings."[18] Ruppin was also asked by Ahuzat Bayit to formulate the neighborhood regulations and ordered the latest writings on urban planning and building to help him develop the neighborhood's plan.[19]

THE ESTABLISHMENT OF TEL AVIV

The idea for the creation of Jewish neighborhoods outside the built-up region of Jaffa was not new to Tel Aviv. Neve Tzedek and Neve Shalom, established in 1887 and 1890 respectively, were only the first of almost a dozen Jewish neighborhoods of varying sizes to be established during the next two decades. As early as 1896, the Yafo Nof society had sought to establish a "modern" Jewish neighborhood modeled on the German colony of Sarona.[20]

These Jewish neighborhoods were part of the larger spatial expansion of Jaffa but with the beginnings of a nationalist rationale. As Hana Ram points out, their development was an integral part of the larger development outside the city's rapidly disappearing walls, and much of the land bought for the purpose by leading Jewish families such as Shloosh, Moyal, and Amza-leg was done with the understanding that with the coming of Zionism, Jews would no longer want to live among Arabs, even in "nice" neighborhoods.[21]

However, this was not ultimately manifest until Tel Aviv; before that Jews had built north of the Old City up to the sea around Manshiyyeh, but this was not "planned" and was not undertaken in order to surround Jaffa and cut off its development, as would be the case with Tel Aviv. Unlike Jerusalem, where the new Jewish neighborhoods were physically and socially separate from Arab Jerusalem, in Jaffa Jews continued to live and work with Arabs until the violence of 1921 set off mass (but by no means total) emigration to Tel Aviv.[22]

The plot of land chosen by Ahuzat Bayit, known as Karm al-Jabali (the vineyard owned by the al-Jabali family; in Hebrew, Kerem Jebali), was located slightly more than a kilometer from the Old City and was originally sold by members of the al-Jabali family in 1905 to a Jewish broker from Jerusalem. There is much to discuss in the name Karm al-Jabali, in terms of both how much of a "vineyard" it was and how many members of the al-Jabali family were listed as owning the land. Beginning with the latter, according to the recollection of Yosef Shloosh, Karm al-Jabali was owned by numerous heirs, some of whom had entered into contract with three Jewish brokers from Jerusalem to purchase the land.[23] How numerous were the heirs? Whereas A. Droyanov, in the official history of Tel Aviv, claims that there were nine,[24] a list of owners written in Hebrew, Arabic, and Ottoman at the Museum of the History of Tel Aviv lists an exponentially larger num-ber of heirs—as many as one thousand covering 106 pages.[25]

According to the contract of sale to Ahuzat Bayit, the borders of Karm al-Jabali were, on the east, the Nablus Road, on the west, Moyal's land (Nahlat Moyal) and Karm al-Baba (described as *mahlul*, or vacant, land),[26] on the south, the Ermani-Kapus land (Nahalat Haermani-Kapus), and on the north, the Shahin land—all for a price of 95 centimes per square meter.[27] These are not the same borders described in the original Arabic contract with the Jerusalem land brokers; there its boundaries are listed as the "private road" *(al-tariq al-khasusa)* to the south, the vinyeyard of Sheikh Hassan 'Ali and his partners to the east, Karm al-Mashrawi to the north, and Karm Salibi Shalyan wa-Shahin and the "general road to which all [the roads] lead" to the west (fig. 1).[28] Nor is it the same as those described in the original, official survey done by the Tabu office,[29] which lists both the north and south regions as being vineyards.[30]

One cannot fail to notice that the original contract, the survey (map 2), and the resale contract to Ahuzat Bayit do not describe the same borders or

Figure 1. Original contract of sale of Karm al-Jabali to Jewish land brokers, 1905/1323H. (Ram, 1996.)

even the same geographic landmarks. Nor is the area of the plot the same in each document.[31] In a very tangible sense, then, the three documents are not talking about the same plot of land. Beyond this (and there is certainly much more that can be said about these discrepancies, both theoretically and factually) the descriptions common to each demonstrated that the land of Karm al-Jabali was already in play for many years, had mixed Arab-Jewish ownership, mixed usage, and mixed tenure. It was certainly not just "barren sand dunes." What is more, when Karm al-Jabali makes an appearance in the *sijjil* in 1909 it is described as being "outside Jaffa to the north,"

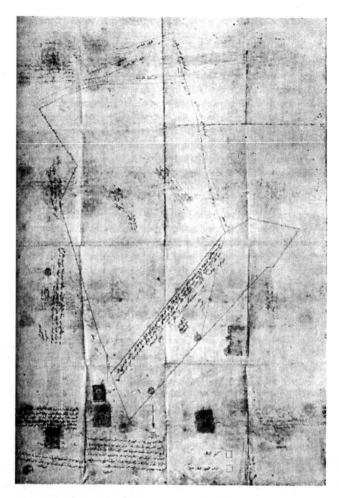

Map 2. Official survey of Karm al-Jabali at the time of sale, from Jaffa Municipality. (Droyanov, 1935.)

yet with different borders; also, the land is described as already having buildings on it and is owned by several people, including "al-khawaja,"[32] Mitrius (?) Cohen Ben Morris from Germany, and at least one other name, which is illegible.

The purpose of coming to the Shariʿa Court was clearly to register the lease and its terms, which state that the land is to be rented to a group of Jews—whose names match those of the members of Ahuzat Bayit—for 868 French francs per year for eighteen years; further, the lessees are allowed to make necessary "improvements and changes" as they see fit, and the rights to the land are transferable if the subsequent lessees abide by the terms.[33] Perhaps the "sale" of Karm al-Jabali to Ahuzat Bayit was recorded in the court records as a lease to avoid raising the eyebrows of the authorities; or it could indicate that another part of the Jabali land already had buildings on it, which is less likely. What is just as interesting is that the fact that Jewish sellers were non-Ottoman citizens did not cause a problem for the Shari'a Court judge or other officials, despite orders from Istanbul not to sell land to foreign Jews.

Although the original Arabic contract of sale stated that the then-sellers had "uncontested" ownership of the property, obtained both by inheritance and by purchase—and thus the subsequent purchase of Karm al-Jabali by Ahuzat Bayit should also have been uncontested—its sale was contested from numerous sides. One problem facing Ahuzat Bayit was that the land could not be openly purchased by either that organization or the Anglo-Palestine Bank but only by an Ottoman subject. This problem was overcome when two Ottoman Jews living in Jaffa agreed to register the land in their names in return for each of them receiving a plot of land in the neighborhood.[34] Complicating matters further was the fact that most of the land outside of the Old City, particularly in and around the villages, was *musha'a*, or at least not parceled out (i.e., *mafruz*), making purchases difficult; when it was *mafruz*, the shares were in the hands of each small shareholder, as was clearly the case with Karm al-Jabali.[35]

The context for this transaction was the tightening of restrictions on land sales by the Ottoman government in fall 1907 prohibiting the sale of *miri*, or state land, even to Ottoman Jews.[36] Given this policy, it is not surprising that the local Ottoman authorities—at least officially—opposed the foundation of Tel Aviv.[37] This had an impact on the purchase of the land when the Jaffa Municipality subsequently challenged the sale by claiming that part of the land of Karm al-Jabali was in fact *miri*. Another factor in the municipality's opposition was, according to Dizengoff, the belief that Tel Aviv would soon be a "complete" city.[38]

Specifically, correspondence between David Moyal, Ahuzat Bayit's attorney, and Meir Dizengoff—which was important enough that Hebrew translations (both handwritten and typed) were made of Moyal's French originals—reveals that Moyal was concerned about the sale for two reasons. First, he was having trouble determining from whom he could obtain final title on the land, that is, who the legal heirs of the property were. Indeed, as Shloosh describes it, "suddenly a new fungus [i.e., the bedouins] appeared—a real one—in that new owners announced their ownership of the place, after the sale of the land of Tel Aviv was completed, and inserted their tents and lived in them armed with swords and ready for war, claiming that the land was theirs, and only after compensation and much hesitation in time did we free the land."[39]

In addition, the Jaffa Municipality claimed at the time of the sale that one quarter of Karm al-Jabali was *miri*, and thus its purchase even by Ottoman Jews was prohibited—or in the best case scenario (assuming that the municipality disregarded the order from Istanbul, which was certainly not unthinkable), Ahuzat Bayit would have to purchase that portion of the land from the municipality, not the representatives of the Jabali family. Indeed, an official survey of the land states that the eastern borders were contested and that the land bordered vineyards on the north and south.[40]

Moyal advised Dizengoff that the claim for *miri* status by the municipality was "malfondée" because it was based on a well-known and faulty inscription on the cadastral surveys of the region; a tribunal would certainly recognize this if it came to that. The municipality also claimed that approximately fifty dunams (a dunam is about one quarter of an acre) of the northwest portion of the land was *mahlul*, or vacant (it should be pointed out that according to the sale contract, the lands to the west were *mahlul*, so it is understandable why such a claim would be made); however, in the end it would be found to be *mulk* also.[41] In the worst case, if the municipality won a verdict of *mahlul*, it would only affect the sale of forty dunams.

Thus, in the end Moyal believed that all of the land was *mulk* and belonged to the seller.[42] However, even if the municipality succeeded in its claim to ownership of this part of Karm al-Jabali, since Ahuzat Bayit had the land under contract it would have preference over any third party for purchasing the land unless the municipality decided to use the land for a "public utility" (which, if we recall the discussion in chapter 1 of this region as a *fina' al-misr*, would not have been surprising).[43] But barring this, the problem did not concern whether it would be allowed to purchase the land but from whom it was going to do so, and thus who was going to benefit from the sale, the al-Jabali heirs or the Jaffa Municipality.

Official opposition was not the only obstacle Ahuzat Bayit faced in its attempt to purchase Karm al-Jabali. Although a mythology of "Tel Aviv from the sands" quickly dominated the imagination and narration of the quarter (see chaps. 5, 6), the fact is that Karm al-Jabali was worked and occasionally lived on by the local Palestinian Arab population. Indeed, there were numerous conflicts awakened between the heirs and the Jerusalem Jews with whom they signed the contract, and many Arabs set up tents on the land with the claim that it belonged to them.

The government sent a detachment of gendarmes to what would become Herzl Street to block the construction (according to Ottoman law, it was forbidden to build close to army or police barracks), while Arabs from Jaffa arrived in a "festive procession." "Between the music of drums and trumpets they announced the riots *(paruot)* against the Jews."[44] The Arabs who occupied the land, perhaps from a small bedouin tribe, claimed that they harvested the supposedly "withered" vines and thus were the de facto occupants.[45]

However inevitable Moyal believed the approval of the sale was, Ahuzat Bayit was concerned enough to make sure a positive spin was put on the complications in reports by *Hapo'el Hatza'ir*,[46] and extra money was offered to the claimants in order to settle the conflict.[47] In the end, the leadership of Ahuzat Bayit, confident in their knowledge and ability to use Ottoman land laws, knew they would prevail, which they did when the local governor, under pressure from the Dutch consul, to whom the Jews brought their complaint, dispatched troops to evict the Arabs. The negative view of bedouins held by the Ottoman state, which had already attempted to register bedouin lands in several regions of Palestine, most likely facilitated the sale too.[48] Apparently, the bedouins were also paid a tidy sum to leave peacefully.[49]

(It is important to note that the Zionists were thoroughly familiar with Islamic land categories and knew how to manipulate them to their advantage. Thus we see that the Tel Aviv Council in 1917 specifically allocated money to plant trees on the surrounding *mahlul* land in order to claim it,[50] while Dizengoff understood the importance of *mahlul* land surrounding Tel Aviv for the city's development and wanted to use it to bring the city as close to the shore as possible so as to realize his dream of building a new port.)[51]

As I mentioned at the beginning of this story, though the founders of Tel Aviv succeeded in removing the bedouin "squatters" from their land, the latter did not simply give up and find greener pastures on which to graze their herds and grow their crops. Rather, they persisted in their resistance, and accounts from the early years of the new neighborhood describe it as being surrounded by robbers on all sides: "In this atmosphere of hatred and enmity, wishing for the worst and failure, Tel Aviv began its life. . . . It had to fight a continuous war, a daily war for its strength and growth."[52] This opposition by local Palestinian Arabs, the Jaffa Municipality, and the Turkish government was construed as being the result of "the Government's and the Arabs' hatred of the clean and modern city [which forced] Tel Aviv to become a city onto itself before the end of the Turkish period."[53]

Whether or not this was true, it is clear that the Palestinian Arabs took note of the distance of the new neighborhood from the center of town, as well as its separatist character: while the Shari'a Court records described older Jewish neighborhoods located near Manshiyyeh as "Manshiyyeh al-Yahud" (Jewish Manshiyyeh), Tel Aviv was referred to as "mahallah Tel Abib," or the Tel Aviv quarter.[54] Indeed, the unique position (geographically, politically, and culturally) of Tel Aviv vis-à-vis Jaffa was such that it was reported in the Arab press of Egypt, Syria, and Lebanon.[55]

Yet whatever the conflicts over Ahuzat Bayit, Arabs continued to sell land to and purchase land with Jews—although, as a rule, dealings were between Arabs. For example, in 1913 the court certified its permission to one Hassan al-Khatra to sell land to one Mr. Livnin for 10,000 Turkish lira.[56] In addition, at least five properties, totaling some 300,000 square meters, were purchased in 1912–13 from local Arab landowners for Tel Aviv.[57] In some cases Arab sellers agreed to parcel ("mafrouzer" is the French neologism used) land before sale, while one contract states that "the koushan is legal and the plan confirmed by the non-Jewish neighbors, by the municipal engineer, by the mukhtars of the quarter, and by the local imam."[58] There is also evidence of much other land around Karm al-Jabali owned by Arabs at the time of Tel Aviv's founding that was subsequently sold to Tel Aviv, such as the land of Sheikh Ali.[59]

Jews were not the only ones who built on the sands. The Shari'a Court records indicate that in 1911 the municipal engineer was authorized to create a(nother) new map of the town and "divide" the land for registration in the Tabu along modern lines, at least one of the reasons for which was to gain control of lands used by the bedouins of the region (here we see the link between Ottoman discourses of "civilizing" or "modernizing" the land and mapping and taking control of bedouin lands, as discussed in chapter 2).[60] Around the same time, building activity increased north of the Old City, along the shore in or near the Manshiyyeh neighborhood. This building was undertaken because the sands could support multistory houses and, perhaps more important, because the government wanted to strengthen control over both the main roads between the Old City and the villages to the north and the mouth of the 'Auja/Yarkon River, which it wanted to use for drinking water, electricity, and irrigation.[61] Jaffa's wealthier Christian families also expanded their agricultural holdings in the surrounding villages during this period.[62]

Given the complexity and contradictions surrounding the purchase of the land on which Tel Aviv began its development, it is not surprising that despite seemingly intense opposition from the local population, the Jaffa Municipality, and Ottoman authorities, in the end Ahuzat Bayit succeeded in completing its purchase of Karm al-Jabali. The foundation stone for Tel Aviv was laid on April 11, 1909.

The rules of the Ahuzat Bayit regarding planning and building in the new neighborhood are discussed in some detail in chapter 6. Here it is worth noting that it laid out specific and detailed requirements for what percentage of a plot could be built on, where outhouses could be located, and the design of buildings, and it reserved the right to approve all building plans and changes.[63] No stores or business or factories were allowed, and as late as 1912 *Hapo'el Hatza'ir* still reported that "in Tel Aviv they don't talk about business."[64]

Traditional Zionist historiography of the building of the early neighborhoods of Tel Aviv has, in the main, argued that "from the beginning Ahuzat Bayit and Tel Aviv needed very little from their Arab surroundings."[65] However, contemporary evidence suggests that the situation was such that by July 1909 Ahuzat Bayit's leadership felt compelled to "encourage members to use Jewish labor," although it cautioned that the bylaws did not allow it to force them to do so.[66] This led some property owners to hire Jews from Jaffa and the nearby colonies, but despite the workers' assurances of experience in building on and leveling the sand,[67] they demanded extra money and worked less,[68] and ultimately members of Ahuzat Bayit chose to employ Arab workers, who in fact built most of the first homes in Tel Aviv, accompanied from the start by Arab traders plying their wares to the new neighborhood.[69]

One solution was that Arabs would build stone houses and that Jews would build cement ones, or that Arab workers would be hired when there were not enough Jewish workers available.[70] Nonetheless, by 1910—at which point fifty houses, home to several hundred residents, had been completed—there were serious fights between Jews and Arabs working in the region of Tel Aviv in which six Jewish workers were seriously injured. This occurred at the same time that the neighborhood stopped using Palestinian Arabs as guards and replaced them with Jews.[71]

Thus it is clear that beyond the mere presence of Arabs, the fact is that Ahuzat Bayit likely could not have been built without them. By this I mean that although on the ideological level there was a general commitment to "Hebrew labor" as a defining principle for building the first modern "Hebrew" city, once it came down to choosing between highly skilled but cheap Arab construction workers and neophyte European Jews who demanded a "European" wage, many if not most owners naturally chose to employ Arabs (but only Jewish workers were allowed to build "public" buildings such as the Herzliya Gymnasium). Many also wanted to use "Arab stone" from Jaffa, but the leaders of Ahuzat Bayit forbade it.

In 1910, in the midst of these conflicts, the name of the neighborhood was changed from Ahuzat Bayit to Tel Aviv, in part because the new name reflected better the experience of establishing "magnificent buildings on the wilderness of sand."[72] The success of "Tel Aviv" led other Jaffan Jews to form similar associations to purchase land and build homes on adjoining land the same year. Thus the Nahalat Binyamin society bought what was actually a parcel from Karm al-Jabali that Ahuzat Bayit turned over to the Ge'ulah company in lieu of repaying a 40,000 franc loan.[73] The society began building in 1912 on a plot of land slightly more than twenty-five thousand square meters, and the same year the residents of Tel Aviv voted to merge with the new neighborhood, for which the latter paid Tel Aviv 10,000 francs.[74]

In 1913 Tel Aviv accepted Neve Tzedek's appeal to join with it on the condition that Neve Tzedek join its roads to Tel Aviv and adhere to the new quarter's strict sanitary regulations. When a field separating Neve Tzedek and Neve Shalom from Tel Aviv was purchased in 1912, the linking of the two original neighborhoods with Tel Aviv, Nahalat Binyamin, and another new neighborhood, Hevra Hadasha (established in 1913, also on land from the Ge'ulah society) was completed—together, they were a "New Jaffa."[75]

THE OUTBREAK OF WORLD WAR I

By the eve of World War I, Jaffa had grown from less than three thousand inhabitants at the turn of the nineteenth century to the second largest city in Palestine after Jerusalem.[76] According to *Hapo'el Hatza'ir*, one major problem facing the city in 1914 was the lack of definite boundaries or an existing "plan," the immediate creation of which would make possible the study of the conditions of the city and bring the hoped-for improvements.[77]

In the years between 1910 and the outbreak of the war, much of the land surrounding Tel Aviv, especially toward the sea, was purchased by Jews or if already in the hands of Jewish brokers, sold to one of the several land purchasing societies operating in the neighborhood. By 1913 it was clear that the majority if not all of the land between Tel Aviv and the sea was in the hands of Jewish proprietors, and the planning for newly purchased property was designed "so as to make it possible, ultimately, to amalgamate

[the] lots into one Jewish quarter."[78] In fact, enough land was purchased to cause significant debate during 1912–13 regarding the merits of continuing land purchases outside of Tel Aviv proper.[79]

All the activity in the Jaffa–Tel Aviv region led to rampant speculation in land, which by 1912 was seen by Tel Aviv's leaders as having left land prices "without any real foundation in the situation of the economic life of [the] city."[80] Speculation was also cited as a reason for the rapid development of Tel Aviv from a neighborhood to a city.[81] The Syndicate for Purchasing Land was thus established in 1914 to prevent speculation by buying land in the Tel Aviv vicinity whose disposition it could control.[82] *Hapo ʿel Hatzaʿir* explained, "[W]e need to say the truth: Tel Aviv has the power of attraction. . . . It is beautiful and also clean"—which is why reasonable people were paying unreasonable prices for land there.[83]

Another complaint regarding rising land and housing prices in the Tel Aviv vicinity was that they were accompanied by decreased security, as the neighborhood suffered a growing number of attacks and robberies.[84] It is not clear whether these attacks were nationalistically or criminally motivated, or some combination of both. Reports in the local Arab press—during this period, primarily *Falastin*—about increased crime among Arab regions of Jaffa and the surrounding orchards could have provided a clue, but a search of this period revealed no such reporting.

However, the recollection of one of the first Jewish guards in Tel Aviv, Saʿadia Shoshani, seems to suggest that the reasons for increasing "crime" were more nationalist in character. He remembered that in 1912 Arab bands from Jaffa were planning attacks on Tel Aviv during Purim (which would have been a repeat of the "attacks" of Purim 1908), which led workers to meet to arrange security for the neighborhood parade. As he explained, "The hatred against the development of Tel Aviv was so large that there was concern how to guard the neighborhood.[85]

HASSAN BEY AND THE END OF THE OTTOMAN PERIOD

One of the most interesting periods in Jaffa's late Ottoman development occurred at the outset of World War I. In 1914 a new governor, Hassan Bey (or Bek), was appointed to rule Jaffa, and he immediately began several projects to develop the city northward while also tearing down many buildings in the Old City in order to widen streets and improve roads to the port.[86] Whereas Jewish sources describe him as "unpopular,"[87] Arabic sources describe him in more mixed and ultimately positive terms, explaining that while local residents were upset at his tearing down of streets and houses, the city clearly profited from the improvements he made.[88]

There is good reason for Hassan Bey's unpopularity with the Zionist leadership in Jaffa and Tel Aviv.[89] First, like his predecessor, Mehmed Aşaf bin As'ad—who was also critical of the "mischievous Zionist" plans and "intrigues"[90]—he clearly understood that the Zionist leadership was interested in surrounding and then slowly "conquering" Jaffa. It was primarily for this reason that he founded a *waqf* on a large area well north of the existing built-up area of Manshiyyeh and built a mosque there. Although there was opposition by many Jaffans to the distance of the mosque from the center of Jaffa,[91] Hassan Bey felt that it was important to establish permanent control over this strategic area, fearing that the Jews would advance their building activities to the still-undeveloped shores north of the Old City and in so doing prevent Jaffa from expanding to the north.[92] In building his mosque, Hassan Bey actually shifted the center of growth in Jaffa away from the Old City and northeast toward Tel Aviv.[93]

Second, there was a clear concern on the part of the Ottoman government, which was surely reflected in Hassan Bey's policies, about the increasing Jewish settlement and even the expansion of Jewish institutions such as schools in the Jaffa region; this concern was heightened during the war, when the Public Security Office in Jerusalem sent telegrams to Jaffa announcing the need to "prevent Jews from acting against the country" and to forbid the return of expelled Jews, particularly Russian Jews.[94] There was also enough concern about the growing power of Jews and their educational institutions—epitomized by the Herzl Gymnasium—that the Public Security Office sent telegrams to the provinces informing them to "take precautions about the Jews who had graduated from the Jaffa Gymnasium [to] prevent them from causing harm."[95] These worries should be put in the context of the larger fear by the government that "the Ottoman culture ha[d] weakened in Jeruslaem and the foreign culture ha[d] become dominant."[96] The latter referred to the increasing activities of European states, especially Great Britain.

Thus the Hassan Bey mosque was built at a distance from the built-up area near the shore (where Jews had been building houses connected to Tel Aviv), to keep the land northwest of the Old City open for the northward spread of Jaffa and to block the seemingly inexorable advance of Jewish settlement surrounding Jaffa. Jaffa's last mayor, Yusuf Heykal, credited the the mosque and the surrounding *waqf* land with preventing the southward expansion of Tel Aviv.[97]

Another likely reason that Hassan Bey was resented by the region's Jewish population (although the Tel Aviv leadership worked with him on at least one occasion) was because his "plan" to develop Jaffa, in particular, the design of the region north of the Clock Tower and the boulevard layout of Jamal Pasha Street, was a direct Jaffan "answer" to the European planning of Tel Aviv, particularly of Rothschild Boulevard (see chap. 6).[98] Indeed, in 1914 the government restored "contracts and specifications" for the plans for an electric trolley and lighting and irrigation in Jaffa to the subprovincial *(liva)* level, which is a change from the desire for local partnerships between Jews and Arabs called for by leaders of Jaffa and Tel Aviv several years earlier, in 1909.[99]

In 1916 Hassan Bey was replaced by a new military governor, Shukri Bey, who was replaced by the end of that year by a new governor who ruled until Jaffa was conquered by the British on November 16, 1917. During this period, from March 28, 1916, until the British conquest,[100] all the residents of Tel Aviv, with the exception of a small "emergency committee" and a few guards, were expelled from the city; most wound up in the Jewish settlements of Mikve Israel and Petakh Tikva. Many Arabs also fled out of fear that the British would attack Jaffa from the sea.[101]

A "JEWISH" CITY, BUILT "FROM THE SANDS"?

Given the ideology of rebirth surrounding the establishment of Tel Aviv and its planning as a Garden Suburb—made possible, it should be noted, by the fact that Jaffa and its hinterland were a "Garden of Eden" in the late Ottoman period[102]—the quarter's development in subsequent decades actually transformed much of Jaffa's fertile areas into urban, densely built space.[103] Indeed, by the time Karm al-Jabali was purchased, future mayor Meir Dizengoff believed that "all the arable land in Palestine was cultivated by Arab tenants who were not the owners."[104] (See table 3.)

Although not a completely accurate statement, as there seem to have been some residents of the villages surrounding Jaffa and Tel Aviv who had de facto control over the land they farmed, his perception demonstrates why it was necessary for Karm al-Jabali to be conceived of as unarable and vacant land to justify Jews building on it. This cognitive reimagination of the region was made easier because "thieves and robbers hid" in the surrounding orchards and groves (these "thieves and robbers" would become the source of numerous attacks on Tel Aviv until 1948),[105] which provided another reason for wiping clean the slate to make way for Tel Aviv.

The importance of the imagination and description of the land on which Ahuzat Bayit would be built as vacant and dunes is clear from the 1935 official history of Tel Aviv, in which almost a dozen of the famous drawings of Tel Aviv by the artist Nachum Gutman, a native son, were included in the

TABLE 3. Land Purchases in Tel Aviv until World War I

Before the Foundation of Tel Aviv

Name	Year of Purchase	Area in Square Meters	Number of Houses	Nature of Land before Purchase
Neve Shalom	1884	58,639	177	Sand, a few vines
Neve Tzedek	1886	24,129	106	Same
Mahane-Yehuda	1886	7,094	40	Same
Shchunat-Brener and attached land	1891	60,000	100	Sand and vineyards
Ohel Moshe	1907	22,773	99	Sand and vineyards
Total in Jewish hands		172,635	522	

After the Foundation of Tel Aviv

Name	Year of Purchase	Area in Square Meters	Number of Houses	Nature of Land before Purchase
Central Tel Aviv	1908–14	338,059	538	Sand, a few vines
Ahuzat Bayit	1908			
Nahalat Binyamin	1910			
Hevra Hadasha	1911–14			
Mahane Yosef	1909	15,607	91	Sand, some vines
Kerem Hateimanim	1909	30,375	138	Vineyards and sand
Sha'ariat-Yisrael	1911	6,531	13	Vineyards and sand
Amin Nassif–Nahalat Yitzhak land	1912	123,424	132	A few vineyards
Zrifa Nestisin land	1912	12,577	15	Orchards
Ramadan land	1912	32,153	39	Vineyard
Kerem Mashrawi	1913	32,294	56	Vineyard and sand
Jazawi land	1913	30,705	35	Same
Merkaz Ba'alei Mal'akha	1913	66,380	130	Same
Kerem Khartum	1913	6,000	13	Same
Me'ah Sha'arim	1913	50,934	100	Sand
Shevat Ahim land	1913	15,505	33	Sand and vineyards
Matrikta'an land	1913	17,386	31	Same
Nahalat Yehoshua	1914	12,036	21	Same
Zrifa Tzava'ah land	1914	12,036	21	Same
Total 1908–14		890,274	1512	
Total 1884–1914		1,062,909	2034	

SOURCES: Various documents from CZA, TAMA, and MHA; Katz, 1994; Shchori, 1990.

chapters dealing with Tel Aviv's birth and early development. These drawings depicted the area as surrounded by a sea of sand extending to the Mediterranean, ignoring the existing Jewish, mixed, and Palestinian Arab neighborhoods of Manshiyyeh, Neve Tzedek, and Neve Shalom or the surrounding farms and orchards. These pictures were used to highlight the "jealousy" of Arab leaders in Jaffa, who, according to the official narrative under these drawings "could see that Tel Aviv would be a big city," even if it was then still "a reed inserted into a sea of sand."[106]

We can ask how this image corresponds to the description of Jaffa's hinterland almost a century earlier as a Garden of Eden with "vast quantities of oranges, lemons, citrons, pomegranates, apple and pear trees, with vines of black and white grapes[, as well as] . . . peach trees and melons: the latter form an article of exportation to the [Nile] Delta, and [are] esteemed the best in Syria."[107] Or how it corresponds to other nineteenth-century European descriptions of Jaffa as "a city full of life and prosperity surrounded on all sides by orange and lemon groves and trees."[108] There are also paintings, such as Thompson's 1864 scene (which seems to be a copy of an 1839 painting by Roberts) of a group of people—in fact, Jews of some wealth— picnicking north of Jaffa (probably on land adjacent to Manshiyyeh) in an area covered with a fair amount of vegetation.[109]

In fact, Lortet's 1884 volume, which describes the gardens surrounding the town as being "watered with abundance, luxuriant and containing magnificent trees," also mentions a "small village to the north of the town"— that is, Manshiyyeh—that was heavily cultivated by Egyptians using relatively large Egyptian cattle and, occasionally, European implements.[110] He includes an etching of the area that corresponds to the description in depicting the area north of the old town along the shore as extremely lush and, most important, with trees and vegetation growing out of the sands and right up to the sea (fig. 2). This depiction is validated by aerial photographs taken soon after World War I that show the area surrounding the built-up region of Jaffa and Tel Aviv as lush with vegetation.[111]

By now it should be clear that, in contrast to Jaffa's depiction in traditional Zionist-Israeli historiography and art, the "luxurious" fertility of the Jaffa region was long the focus of European descriptions of the area. M. V. Guerin's 1868 geography of Palestine notes that "all the world speaks about the superb 'vergers' of Jaffa[,] . . . the fabulous gardens[,] . . . the luxurious vegetation. . . . [It is] a veritable oasis."[112] Similarly, both the Palestine Exploration Survey and the 1876 edition of *Baedeker's* tour guide describe the region as very fertile. The latter reports, "About 1 1/2–2 feet beneath the sand there is excellent soil, and water is to be found everywhere at a

Figure 2. "Jaffa, North Coast," etching, 1884. (TAMA Library.)

moderate depth. Vines, though half buried in sand, thrive admirably."[113] Maps clearly demonstrate not only that the Old City of Jaffa was surrounded by orange gardens but also that they extended right up to Karm al-Jabali, where the sands began, and to the sea (map 3).[114]

If water was found beneath the sand, which overlies a rich soil, then the sands on which Tel Aviv was built were not "barren." Even if Karm al-Jabali was not under cultivation when it was purchased by Ahuzat Bayit, it—like all the orchards and vineyards of the Jaffa–Tel Aviv region, whether fallow or presently farmed—"ha[d] a history" of productive use.[115] Thus they could have been reclaimed with relatively little effort, giving support to the claims of the bedouins who protested the sale.[116] The numerous maps drawn of the Jaffa region reveal that there were vineyards extending north of the Old City to the sea—that is, on sand.[117] Sandel's 1878 map of Jaffa in particular clearly shows that there were vineyards very close to, if not on, the land of Karm al-Jabali (map 4).[118]

The clearest evidence we have of the state of the lands of the Jaffa–Tel Aviv region around the time of Tel Aviv's establishment comes from B. Z. Kedar's stunning book, *Looking Twice at the Land of Israel* (in Hebrew), which features aerial photographs and maps of Israel, including the Jaffa–Tel Aviv region, from the World War I period juxtaposed to photographs shot from the same angles and altitudes six decades later.[119] From the visual evidence of these documents, the following "facts" can be estab-

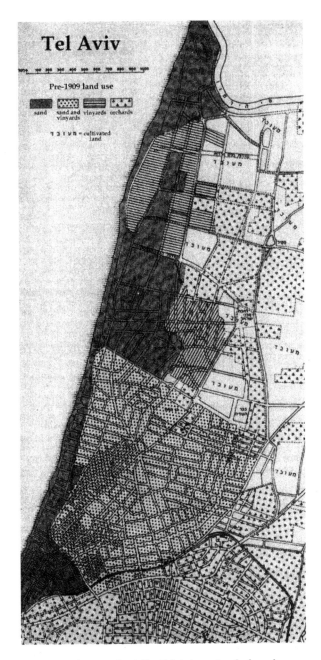

Map 3. Land use in the Jaffa–Tel Aviv region before the establishment of Tel Aviv. (Avitzur, 1997, from Droyanov, 1935.)

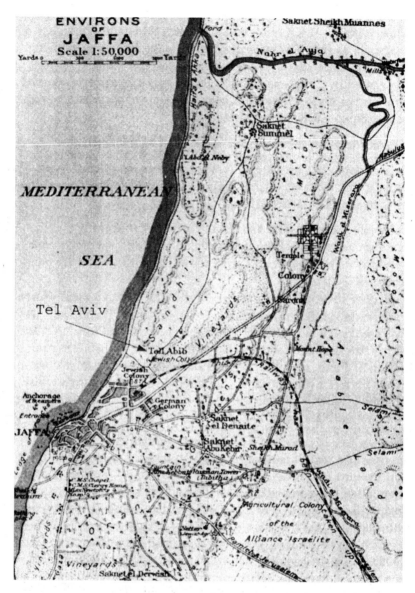

Map 4. "Environs of Jaffa," 1912. (Map by Theodor Sandel, TAMA Library.)

lished with a strong degree of certainty: unlike the Zionist descriptions and art surrounding Tel Aviv's birth (see chaps. 5, 6), the original neighborhood bordered densely planted agricultural land on its east and southeast (beginning directly opposite the railroad tracks), with the sandier land of the heart of the neighborhood (of varying depth, with vegetation scattered

Figure 3. Aerial photograph of Tel Aviv, Manshiyyeh, and surrounding farms, 1918. (Kedar, 1995, p. 90.)

throughout) giving way over the course of a few hundred meters to the north and northeast to increasingly densely planted land (approximately where Dizengoff Center stands today). As important, to its west was the already densely built-up neighborhood of Manshiyyeh, and to its southwest was, of course, Jaffa (fig. 3). Confirming the nature of the non-built-up land, a 1912 map puts Tel Aviv literally on top of "vineyards," surrounded by "arable land" and orchards on the east and south, while a wartime photograph of the German colony of Sarona taken from the southeast, and showing the region between it and Tel Aviv to the north, clearly shows dense, mixed planting (also indicated by a British map of this region from 1917) (fig. 4).[120]

Whatever its claims to creation ex nihilo, and thus to social and economic autonomy, Tel Aviv was born into and by the end of World War I had become part of a complex ecosystem of neighborhoods, "colonies," farms, "general" and "special" roads, vineyards, orchards, dunes, and sandy paths that defined the region north of Jaffa, tied it to the urban core, and wove it into the larger Jaffa region in innumerable ways.[121] It was hardly a "revolution" in the geography of the Jaffa region, although it would soon bring about an "overturning" of much of the region's landscape.

Figure 4. The German colony of Sarona facing northeast, c. 1917. (TAMA Library.)

CONCLUSION

All told, between the turn of the nineteenth century and the outbreak of World War I the population of Jaffa had increased more than fourfold and its built-up area had increased by a factor of fourteen, from approximately 100 to more than 1,400 dùnams (from 25 to 350 acres).[122] By the outbreak of World War I the Jaffa Municipality had greatly expanded its activities "to the benefit of both building infrastructure and inhabitants," and had even begun to impose an annual tax for "urban improvement."[123] There were reports before the war broke out that the Ottoman authorities had begun discussions to change the status of Tel Aviv to a city, the possibility of which was used by Tel Aviv to obtain a loan from the JNF for the amount of 500,000 francs.[124]

Tel Aviv itself grew from approximately 100 dunams in 1909 to 570 dunams at the beginning of World War I.[125] Its expansion was the combined result of haphazard and planned growth. In particular, one of the primary goals of Tel Aviv's development was to bypass north Jaffa/Manshiyyeh; by extending to the shore, the new neighborhood could block any possibility of Jaffa's northward expansion and spread without limits to the north and west.[126] As we have seen, this prompted Hassan Bey to build farther north than otherwise might have happened during the war; such cat-and-mouse expansion would characterize the growth of the two cities throughout the Mandate period.

However much Tel Aviv symbolized the hope for rebirth of the Jewish nation in its homeland as a modern community, Akiba Arieh Weiss, one its principal founders, explained, "[O]nly some years after the establishment of Tel Aviv, came the disappointment. All the good rules of Tel Aviv and all the modern improvements didn't lead to changes for the better of human nature and . . . to social justice. It appears that this desire for social justice of the author of this book [i.e., Weiss] was . . . hidden in the heart."[127]

As for Jaffa, its heretofore rapid development was stunted by the war, and the complex and contradictory relationship among the economic, social, and spatial aspects of its development also began to weigh on it. The conflict between the burgeoning sense of Palestinian national identity and the desire to partake in the equally burgeoning capitalization of land and culture would lead Jaffa notables to denounce Zionism one day and sell large plots of land to Tel Aviv the next.[128] Land transfers were officially prohibited, yet when made in the names of Ottoman Jews, they continued "quietly and without hindrance."[129]

Finally, the evidence presented here attests to the ambivalent nature of Ottoman rule in the last decades of its suzerainty over Palestine, reflecting conflicting needs of a modernizing and revenue-hungry state that still felt itself to some degree responsible for protecting the indigenous population against Zionist encroachment. Yet it should be noted that events in the Jaffa–Tel Aviv region that would have great consequence for the future of the two cities, and the two peoples, were viewed with little significance in Istanbul or by those writing for an Ottoman- or Turkish-language audience. There seems to be relatively little discussion of events in Jaffa and none on Tel Aviv in official Ottoman documents and little if any mention of either city in the Ottoman press. And of the three Ottoman Turkish books written on Palestine during the late Ottoman period, none included any significant discussion of Jaffa or any mention of Tel Aviv (even though they were published after the latter's establishment).[130]

All this would change with the arrival of the British army under the command of General Edmund Allenby on December 9, 1917, as it foreclosed permanently the possibility of Jaffa's autonomous development. In so doing, the onset of British rule in Palestine greatly influenced the relationship between the two emerging national movements and their two "capitals." The specifics of this process are the subject of the next three chapters.

4 Crossing the Border

Intercommunal Relations in the Jaffa–Tel Aviv Region during the Mandate Period

SOCIOECONOMIC INDICATORS OF DEVELOPMENT

When General Allenby rode into Jaffa in December 1917, the city and its environs—especially Tel Aviv—were reeling from several years of war. The situation had been made worse by the lengthy displacement of many of Jaffa's inhabitants, and most of Tel Aviv's, by the Ottoman military rulers when a British assault on the city seemed likely.[1] Luckily, the Jaffa–Tel Aviv region was not a target of the Allied forces, and it quickly began to recover after the end of the war and the return of the Jewish and Arab population.

Given the economic and political importance of Jaffa and Tel Aviv it is surprising that few records are available that break down the population of the two cities into Muslim, Jewish, and Christian communities. From the available data we know that between 1922 and 1944 the population of Jaffa grew from 32,524 to 94,310, of which the Muslim population increased from 20,621 to 50,880, the Christian population from 6,808 to 15,400 and the Jewish population from 5,087 to 28,000. As for Tel Aviv, its Jewish population increased from 15,065 to 166,300 during this period, while its tiny Christian and Muslim populations increased from 42 to 230 and 78 to 130 respectively.

The most important development that these data reveal is the growth of the Jewish population to more than 74.5 percent of the population of the Jaffa–Tel Aviv region by 1944, a figure that accounted for over one-third of Palestine's Jewish population.[2] Indeed, the Jaffa–Tel Aviv region as a whole had by far the greatest density of population in the country, but Tel Aviv's population grew much more rapidly than did Jaffa's by several orders of magnitude.[3]

What is most important for our purposes is that, nationalist rhetoric aside, the populations of the two cities were not homogeneous. Jaffa in par-

84

ticular had an increasingly large Jewish population, at least half of which lived in several "Jewish" neighborhoods that bordered Tel Aviv.[4] Much less is known about Tel Aviv's non-Jewish Arab population, although one source from 1933 explains that "the Arabs living in Tel Aviv are those who didn't sell their land and still live and work on it."[5]

The built-up and municipal areas of the two cities also increased significantly during the Mandate period. By 1938 the area of Tel Aviv was 6,600 dunams; Jaffa's area was 5,900 dunams.[6] By the end of this period, Jaffa's area expanded to 9,737 dunams—approximately the same size as the municipal area of Tel Aviv—and included seven major Arab quarters, six "saknat" (small neighborhoods) and seven markets.[7] (See maps 5, 6.)

Unfortunately, little comparative statistical data exist for comparing Tel Aviv's and Jaffa's economic development during the Mandate period. Whether in the 1930s or the 1980s, scholars investigating the economic development of Palestine of the period have been hampered both by a lack of data for the Arab sector and by the political passions surrounding the issue.[8] However, the difficulty of obtaining accurate data does not obscure the fact that Palestine's economy grew at a very high rate in the 1920–36 period, particularly during the world economic downturns that stimulated increased Jewish immigration to the country.[9] Thus, for example, the budgets of Jaffa and Tel Aviv increased from £P31,341 to £P203,335 and £P74,585 to £P1,512,203 respectively during the years 1928 to 1945.[10]

It is likely that Tel Aviv's budget surpassed Jaffa's sometime before 1926, when it was already greater than £E75,000.[11] By this time Tel Aviv had the largest municipal budget in the country. Jaffa's budget, in contrast, though it grew rapidly, was surpassed by Haifa by 1929 and by Jerusalem in 1935 and was severely hurt by the strike and revolt of 1936–39.[12] Nevertheless, taken together, the budgets of the Jaffa and Tel Aviv municipalities demonstrate that the region was at the center of Palestine's economic growth during the Mandate period. This growth was not limited to the two towns but also affected the surrounding villages.[13]

The statistics for imports and exports through the Jaffa and later the Tel Aviv port also demonstrate the growth during this period, particularly in the first half of the 1930s (see table 4).[14] Data on the development of specific local industries in Jaffa during the Mandate period either were never collected or have not survived. However, it is clear from the memoirs of former residents that local industries such as soap, textiles, cosmetics, and fishing also expanded, as did the local Arab press. Indeed, concomitant with Jaffa's economic development was its rise to the position of undisputed cultural

Map 5. British map of the Jaffa–Tel Aviv region, 1930s. (Hebrew University, Department of Geography, map room.)

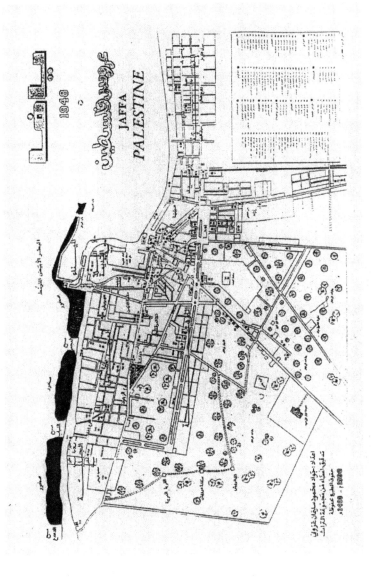

Map 6. Arabic-language map of Jaffa from a 1940s postcard.

TABLE 4. Comparison of Imports and Exports through Jaffa, Tel Aviv, and Haifa Ports, Selected Years until World War II *(in £ sterling)*

Year	Jaffa Imports	Jaffa Exports	Tel Aviv Imports	Tel Aviv Exports	Haifa Imports	Haifa Exports
1926	3,462,248	836,764	—	—	2,018,092	250,764
1931	3,055,626	853,117	—	—	2,410,470	480,763
1935	7,719,886	2,285,073	—	—	8,455,765	1,707,421
1936	3,182,817	1,513,507	601,581	55,948	8,627,065	1,690,025
1939	1,319,347	1,233,094	4,143,606	693,904	7,891,600	2,926,173

SOURCE: Avitzur, 1972, appendix, table 17.

center of Arab Palestine, home to innumerable clubs; youth, religious, and civic organizations; coffeehouses; theaters; and cinemas.[15]

The growth in the local economy was such that by the early 1930s *Falastin* was regularly publishing columns on commerce in the city, in particular, on the orange industry, which was considered by observers inside and outside of Palestine the most important economic activity in the country, accounting for some 60 percent of the customs revenues by the mid-1930s.[16]

The citrus industry was an example not just of the overall development of the region but also of the increasing dominance of Jews in the local economy: by the mid-1930s the Jewish share of the orange trade surpassed that of the Arab sector.[17] Another indicator of this trend is the fact that by 1935 construction in Tel Aviv surpassed that of Jaffa.[18] With the strike and revolt of the next year, Jaffa suffered permanent economic, social, and political damage, owing in great measure to the permanent diminution of its port as Tel Aviv built its own jetty and Haifa's harbor became the country's leading port. Compounding its woes, during the 1940s (perhaps earlier), the cost of living rose considerably faster in Jaffa than in Tel Aviv, as did the prices of basic commodities.[19]

An analysis of Tel Aviv's development, at least through the start of World War II, is a less difficult enterprise because a larger body of statistical data exists. At the broadest level, from its establishment in 1909 to 1925, during the first big wave of immigration in the Mandate period, the area of Tel Aviv expanded from 120 to 5,000 dunams, the number of houses grew from 60 to 3,000, and the budget increased from £E140 to £E75,000.[20]

If fluctuations in Jewish immigration influenced the general economic growth of Palestine, it played a determinative role in Tel Aviv's economic development: as it ebbed and flowed, so did the city's economy.[21] By 1930, 60 percent of all Jewish industry in Palestine (and 71 percent of its total production) was centered in Tel Aviv, as were 80 percent of the invested capital, 64 percent of the Jewish workforce, and 54 percent of the raw materials.[22]

The many achievements of Tel Aviv were often cited by Zionist officials as a positive exemplar of the Jewish-inspired development of Palestine. Yet Tel Aviv also experienced several downturns during the Mandate period. After an immigration-driven upswing in the early 1920s a depression in 1923 left the municipality incapable of coping with the "bitter reality" of continued immigration. The situation was bad enough to prompt both a questioning of the wisdom of continued immigration and calls to develop an "urban pioneering" ethos and movement in and around the city.[23] I return to the topic of urban planning at the end of this chapter and, in more detail, in chapter 6.

Although an economic upturn in 1924 and 1925 led the French consul in Jaffa to extol "the new Jaffa" (i.e., Tel Aviv) as the best symbol for Palestine's progress since the war,[24] the next two years brought depression and high unemployment and necessitated government intervention to help secure credit for the municipality's budget.[25] Various factors had created what even Zionist leaders felt was an "abnormal" situation in Tel Aviv when judged by "European standards"[26] but one they felt was understandable "in a country which is undergoing rapid process of transformation."[27] Indeed, as Ha'aretz reminded its readers, the "so-called economic crisis" afflicting the country was really centered "in one place—Tel Aviv."[28]

The 1930s got off to a much better start than had the previous decade, and by middecade, despite a worldwide depression, Tel Aviv's finances were "flourishing."[29] There were worries over the horizon for Tel Aviv's leaders, but interestingly, they did not involve Jaffa but rather Haifa.[30] In fact, the danger posed by Haifa's development was used by Dizengoff to justify building an "industrial city" next door to Tel Aviv that could compete with Haifa as a center of industry.

It is unfortunate that adequate statistics do not exist to determine the relationship of the economic upturns and downturns in Tel Aviv to the economic situation in Jaffa. If one accepts the traditional Zionist perspective of separate, dual Jewish and Arab economies, we might assume that Tel Aviv's problems remained within its "economic boundaries,"[31] with Jaffa remaining more or less unaffected by Tel Aviv's ups and downs. However, this was likely not the case.

Data on economic activity and growth in the Jaffa–Tel Aviv region during the 1940s are particularly scarce. From the available data we can conclude with some confidence that whatever losses were suffered during the war because of decreased commercial exports and imports (especially from a sharp decrease in citrus exports and influx of Jewish capital), they were likely compensated in great measure by wartime economic expenditures and related employment. Nor did the end of the war (1945–46) lead to an appreciable economic downturn in the region.[32]

JEWISH AND ARAB WORKERS IN THE JAFFA–TEL AVIV REGION

Arab Workers and the Histadrut in Jaffa and Tel Aviv

With this broad (if incomplete) understanding of the economic trends during the Mandate period, we can explore the situation faced by workers in the two communities—that is, the majority of the two populations—and cities during this time. If Tel Aviv was established by sixty bourgeois families from Jaffa, from the start working-class Jews and Palestinian Arabs as well were an important presence in the neighborhood-turned-city. It could not be otherwise, given the centrality of the region as a destination for the majority of Jewish immigrants and capital.

As the groundbreaking studies of Gershon Shafir and Zachary Lockman have demonstrated, from the beginning of Zionist colonization of Palestine Jewish workers and their leaders sought not just to "conquer" Arab jobs but at the same time to develop ties with Arab workers.[33] To help negotiate this contradiction, the Histadrut—a national Jewish trade union closely allied to the Zionist movement—published two Arabic-language papers, *Ittihad al-'Ummal*, which appeared in the mid-1920s, and *Haqiqat al-Amr*, which appeared in the late 1930s. Each was part of a broader effort to convince Arab workers that the Histadrut, and Jewish workers in general, were "comrades" rather than "enemies."[34]

The inaugural issue of *Ittihad al-'Ummal* featured a call by the Histadrut to Arab workers and *felahin* (peasants) to "awake from [their political and economic] slumber" that had overcome the country for hundreds of years.[35] As for the Jewish city of Tel Aviv, it was cited as a prime example of how "East meets West," of how "Zionism helps the East to reclaim its former glory," as evidenced by the wonders of the city and its government.[36]

Interestingly, whereas most of the activities of the Histadrut's Arab Department were centered in Jaffa, almost all of the examples of labor activity concerned Tel Aviv. Jaffa was hardly mentioned, except to assert that the Jaffa Workers' Council was the "only group" protecting the rights of workers in the city.[37]

Haqiqat al-Amr contained many more photographs than its predecessor, many of them featuring new buildings in Tel Aviv designed in the International Style that had come to stand for Tel Aviv's modernity (about which more is said in chapter 5). It is not surprising that no pictures of International Style buildings located in Jaffa appeared in the paper. The paper also provided a space for the Histadrut to present analyses of the causes of the inadequate working conditions in Jaffa Port, to counter accusations in the Jaffan Arab press about the alleged harm done by the Histadrut to Arab workers, and to justify actions of the Labor or municipal leadership that had antagonized the country's Arab population.[38] After episodes of violence *Haqiqat al-Amr* sought to remind readers that "their city [i.e., Jaffa] became . . . a nest for vicious messages,"[39] whose "immorality" was contrasted with the freedom and organization of Jewish Tel Aviv.[40]

Beyond propaganda, the local and national leadership devoted significant energy throughout the Mandate period to developing ties with Arab workers on the ground. The records of their successes and failures provide the best, often the only, documentation about labor conditions in "Arab" Jaffa. In 1921, for example, Jewish woodworkers sought, with varying degrees of success, to develop ties with Arab carpenters, bakers, government (railway, postal, and telegraph) workers, and camel drivers. In the latter case it was hoped to work together to get rid of the bedouin camel drivers, who were nicknamed the "fifth aliyah."[41] For their part, Arab port workers sought help from the Histadrut to alleviate their poor working conditions and combat the influx of cheap "foreign" workers from Egypt and Syria.[42]

As the 1920s wound down it appears that Arab workers began to heed warnings that the Histadrut was "helping" them only to further Jewish interests;[43] yet with the economic upturn of the early 1930s the Histadrut once again focused concerted energy on organizing Jaffa's Palestinian Arab workers,[44] who used this interest to press the leadership of its "Arab union," the Palestine Labor League (PLL; formed in 1932) to promise that the Histadrut would not seek to bring Jewish workers into Jaffa Port.[45] Despite concerns on both sides, however, the pace of Histadrut activity in Jaffa quickened during this period, as a new club sponsored by the PLL opened near the port and approximately one hundred stevedores belonged to an affiliated union.

By 1934 Arab port and factory workers in Jaffa were requesting advice, help, and even organization from the Histadrut and the PLL.[46] Their success in organizing Arab workers in Jaffa prompted *Falastin* to issue a "public call" for the creation of an Arab union in 1934, which led to the establishment of the Arab Workers Society (AWS) in Jaffa in October 1934.[47] As Reuven Zaslani, one of the point men for the Histadrut's Arab activities, put it, the success in Jaffa Port made it possible to see the day when "*we* will be the rulers in the port of Jaffa and will be able to do great things there, both politically and economically."[48]

From the vociferous resistance of Arab employers and religious and nationalist leaders to any attempt at cooperative work with the Histadrut, it is clear that Jaffa's Arab elite was—to say the least—suspicious of these activities (although it is also clear that not all leaders opposed the Histadrut for reasons of solidarity with workers).[49] The Histadrut, along with Tel Aviv Mayor Dizengoff, was thus portrayed as working against Arab workers and wanting to "cut their livelihoods,"[50] while Arab labor leaders protested to the government against the "judaization of the port" and other British policies in support of Zionism.[51]

Indeed, even the Histadrut's limited successes in organizing Arab workers led one Arab worker to ask, "Who is responsible for this comedy?"[52] The Arab press, specifically *Falastin, al-Difa'*, and *al-Jami'a al-Islamiyyah*, attempted to deflect attention from the lack of successful organization by Arab unions and to convince workers not to join the PLL by focusing on the Histadrut's Jewish-only labor policies and the desire of Jews to "rule Jaffa Port." Jewish-Arab cooperation of the type that occurred in Haifa Port, it was argued, would only lead to the "judaization of Arab Jaffa," a goal made more apparent by Jewish "attacks" on Arab land in the Jaffa Port area as well as in other areas of Jaffa.[53]

Nevertheless, Palestinian Arab workers continued to approach the Histadrut into the early part of 1936,[54] which led trade unionists to convene a national conference in Jaffa in February of that year. There it was resolved to beat the Histadrut at its own game by setting up pickets against Jewish workers in Jaffa that mirrored the Jewish union's actions against Arab workers in Tel Aviv. Soon the "first Arab Garrison in Jaffa" was formed, whose one hundred members tried to "prevent Jews from working in the middle of this Arab city," particularly on three new schools in Jaffa.[55]

The strategy clearly succeeded, for when the Arab Strike began on April 19, 1936, all the port workers in Jaffa quickly joined, and the very Arab lightermen and stevedores who worked with the PLL during the past two years were among its most vociferous supporters.[56] Yet if the outbreak of the strike and revolt in 1936 severed connections between the Histadrut and Arab workers, the latter once again contacted the Histadrut regarding even worse conditions at the port after it reopened in October of that year.[57] By the end of 1937 relations were much improved, and a "strong tendency" to organize Arab workers resumed in Jaffa and throughout the country as a whole.[58]

One reason for the success (albeit limited) of the PLL in Jaffa is that it filled a void by endeavoring to fight for the rights of Arab workers in situations in which no one on the Arab side would.[59] As one worker tearfully explained in an article in *al-Difa'*, seven hundred of his comrades who had joined the Histadrut did so because they were angry and exasperated. Unable to "escape the oppression of our bosses . . . and unable to feed our children," he wrote, the workers "entered the arms of the Histadrut because they despaired of ever getting justice from their bosses," who "summered" in the orchards around Jaffa or in Beirut.[60]

Under Histadrut auspices, "warm, friendly and cooperative" relations between Jewish and Palestinian Arab workers would continue on and off into the early 1940s.[61] Perhaps because of the PLL's continued success, in

1943 Palestinian Arab unions once again convened a conference in Jaffa, offering what were essentially the Histadrut's ideas and strategies as their alternative for organizing "their" workers.[62] Despite this new push by the Palestinian Arab labor movement, the PLL successfully organized the strike of Jaffa's municipal sanitation workers; even municipal workers aligned with the Palestinian Arab union supported cooperation with the PLL on the strike.[63]

In fact, during this period, the PLL also rented an apartment in a house owned by the deputy mayor of Jaffa and hired a young Palestinian Arab from a notable Jaffan family to run an office there. Spurred on by the success of the Sick Fund instituted for Arab members and hoped-for "practical economic work" to raise wages, there was a feeling that, despite great difficulties, workers were fully prepared to organize and the Jaffa branch could turn into an important, if not *the* important, center for Palestinian Arab workers in the country.[64]

With enough vigilance and effort, therefore, modest successes could still be achieved.[65] In January 1944 the PLL signed a labor agreement with the Jaffa Municipality to raise the basic wage and to provide clothing and shoes for workers. More interesting than the terms of the agreement were the comments of the deputy mayor of Jaffa to the PLL representatives, as reported by the latter. "Why do you bother us and meddle every day in the interests of the workers?" he asked, to which the PLL representative replied, "Times change, there is democracy, there is freedom to organize, justly and honestly." The deputy mayor did not appreciate this line of reasoning and answered, "What democracy? We don't have democracy, we scorn democracy. . . . We only understand one thing: the worker that puts forth demands to us is a worker that wants to be lord over us and this we will not suffer."[66] At this point another official entered the room and the conversation, declaring that the PLL only wanted to "upset our order" by getting involved with workers, which would hurt the unity of the Arabs and make it harder to have a united front against the Zionist movement as a whole.[67]

If accurate, this exchange reveals the contradictory position of the PLL-Histadrut in the larger arena of Palestinian Arab labor politics in Jaffa. Whatever its role in securing the overall "conquest of Hebrew labor" in Jaffa, its aims and activities were in many cases closer to the interests of Jaffa's Palestinian Arab workers than those of the latter's national leadership. However, as Palestinian Arab trade unions became better organized in the mid-1940s there was less reason for Arab workers to turn to the PLL, and its fortunes quickly began to wane. In Jaffa we can pinpoint this turn-around as May 1944, when protests by Palestinian Arab residents of Man-shiyyeh against residents who had joined the PLL, coupled with the "storming" of a PLL May Day celebration by Palestinian Arab workers, forced the union to move its office across the border to Tel Aviv.[68]

By year's end the vast majority of Palestinian Arab workers were reported to have lost faith in the intentions and abilities of the PLL, perhaps because of unheeded appeals to their "Jewish worker brothers" to hear their complaints against the Histadrut, and the PLL retained little if any presence in Jaffa.[69] Even the government no longer considered the PLL of great importance in the industrial life of the country.[70] In August 1945 a major Palestinian Arab labor conference was held in Jaffa that highlighted the "appreciable influence [of the movement] in the economic and social, if not political, life of the country," or at least in the towns.[71]

Arab Labor in Tel Aviv

As discussed in chapter 3, while Tel Aviv was conceived of and portrayed as a purely "Jewish" city, the reality was that Palestinian Arab workers had a small but significant and visible presence in the years following its estab-lishment. Palestinian Arabs continued to work in Tel Aviv after it was granted municipal autonomy in 1921, and as the Tel Avivan economy grew, so did the "problem" of "Arab labor" and even residency in the town.[72]

In fact, from the beginning of the Mandate period (and no doubt earlier) the Tel Aviv Municipality hired Palestinian Arabs to work at the post office and other public institutions in the city during the Sabbath,[73] and the town boasted its own club for Palestinian Arab railway workers (which had twenty-five members by 1931).[74] Even during the 1936–39 revolt, the PLL sought to bring Palestinian Arabs into Tel Aviv and tried to find three or four Arabic-speaking Jews to give three-month courses on such issues as "the Arab Community in Eretz Israel" and "the question of Jewish Arab cooperation and joint organization."[75]

But beyond the officially sanctioned presence of Arabs in the Jewish city, there was a much larger unofficial, and officially unwelcome, presence. Already in 1921 a Yemenite contractor wrote a letter to *Falastin* complain-ing about pressure from Russian Jewish workers to fire a Palestinian Arab under his employ.[76] The situation was so tense that the governor of the Jaffa district wrote to Dizengoff to ensure that the municipality would enforce a guarantee from the Histadrut not to interfere with Arab contrac-tors or workers.[77] In another instance, the United Rabbinical Council of Jaffa appealed to the Tel Aviv Municipality and the government to prevent

Figure 5. Permit issued by the Tel Aviv Municipality for two Arabs from Jaffa to sell wares in Tel Aviv, 1933. (TAMA, 4/345b.)

the "desecration" of the Sabbath in Tel Aviv by non-Jewish peddlers and traders;[78] Jewish shop owners similarly complained about "numerous Arabs without permission" daily setting up shop in front of their stores.[79]

By the mid-1920s Arabs in Tel Aviv were selling market wares at prices so low that Jewish merchants were forced drastically to reduce their prices to compete. Despite its best efforts, the municipality realized that it was "impossible to get rid of them," so it was decided to "force them to register" in order to "regulate them and charge taxes and control the situation."[80] That is, Palestinian Arabs could not be kept out of Tel Aviv but at best only regulated, like their Jewish counterparts (see fig. 5). Yet even this proved difficult, as in many cases Palestinian Arabs worked in unregistered or illegal or unofficial factories or restaurants located in Jewish residences in Tel Aviv.[81]

By the early 1930s the problem of Arab labor prompted renewed discussions between the local Histadrut affiliate, the Mifleget Po'elei Tel Aviv–Yafo (MPTAY), and the Tel Aviv Municipality to combat the problem.[82] Ultimately, the Histadrut was forced to admit that "Arab labor ha[d] encroached upon the first Jewish city." Whether in the commercial center, poorer Jewish neighborhoods, or the outskirts (where "supervision [wa]s difficult"), hundreds and ultimately thousands of Palestinian Arab workers were employed by Jews as construction workers and porters, with a significant increase in the years before the 1936 Revolt.[83]

In response to this situation the Histadrut Executive Committee, along with the MPTAY, decided in 1935 to take measures that included the commencement of a "public war" against contractors to use only Jewish labor in order to reduce the number of Palestinian Arab construction workers in Tel Aviv and renewed coordination with the Tel Aviv Municipality and other citizens' groups to "fight for Jewish labor."[84] Because of this increased pressure, Jewish businessmen seeking to continue to employ cheap Palestinian Arab labor began to "smuggle factories into the Palestinian Arab village (Summel), thus freeing themselves from the obligation to employ Jewish labor."[85] This is likely one reason why the municipality became so interested in annexing the land of Summel and other villages adjoining Tel Aviv in the ensuing years, and it demonstrates the increasing importance of administrative borders for policing the more porous national boundaries that were supposed to separate the Arab and Jewish communities and economies in the Jaffa–Tel Aviv region.

Relations between Jewish Workers, Labor Leaders, and the Tel Aviv Municipality

Though free of the national competition for labor that defined Jewish–Palestinian Arab relations, intra-Jewish labor relations were far from harmonious, a situation made worse by the fluctuating economy and generally high levels of immigration.[86] This was a major cause of the continual struggles between workers and their local and national representatives and the Tel Aviv Municipality.

In fact, by 1921 violent confrontations erupted between the Tel Aviv Municipality and workers, with the former accusing the latter of "conducting a war against workers" with the support of the government.[87] These conflicts led workers to attempt to win control of the municipality—which they did only once, in 1926–27—while the bourgeois town fathers enacted various election laws that excluded workers from the right to vote by limiting suffrage to "home owners." The combination of large-scale immigration, a tenuous job market (and larger economy), and competition with Palestinian Arabs also led to a "startling" increase in crime in Tel Aviv compared with Jaffa, in good measure as a result of a "large increase in the floating population of [the] area."[88]

Despite the innate and ongoing hostility between workers and municipal leaders, the Histadrut (especially its executive committee) was constantly involved in and had many links—personal, professional, political, and labor—with the municipality, to the point that the functions of the two bodies began to intermingle by the mid-1930s.[89] There were also conflicts within the workers' movement, most noticeably involving Yemenite and Mizrachi, religious, and women workers. Yemenites had long been considered by the labor leadership as a potential weapon in the war for Hebrew labor, as their presumed cultural affinity with Palestine's non-Jewish Arab population supposedly allowed them to work for the low wages and under the harsh conditions endured by the local population.

While the MPTAY broadened its activities into the Mizrahi and Yemenite communities in the 1930s,[90] the Yemenites' situation remained difficult; as late as 1936 (and probably later) there were hardly any permanent Yemenite workers in Tel Aviv, which forced the Histadrut to admit that it was not doing nearly enough to help Mizrachi workers.[91] Right up until the end of the Mandate period Yemenite workers complained to the Histadrut of the lack of "agreeable work" for them.[92]

Many religious workers refused to affiliate with the labor movement. Here the Histadrut's main antagonist was the Hapo'el Hamizrahi movement, which was established in Poland in 1918 and arrived in Palestine in 1920–21. Most of its members were unskilled or factory workers, and there were constant conflicts between Hapo'el Hamizrahi, the Histadrut, and the Tel Aviv Municipality over the division of labor between the two unions.[93] It was not until 1938 that the MPTAY and Hapo'el Hamizrahi agreed to a joint exchange to distribute jobs for both groups of workers, in which the latter's share was 11 percent.[94]

Given the scale and demography of immigration to Tel Aviv throughout the Mandate period, it is not surprising that women made up an important segment of the Jaffa–Tel Aviv labor force, or that they were disproportionately hit by unemployment.[95] In fact, the Zionist Organization's Women's Committee decided early on that urban as well as agricultural work was central to settling new immigrants. Thus factories were established in 1918 and 1919 to train young women in the trades and the "household economy," and two working women's groups received land from the Tel Aviv Municipality for housing and limited farming.[96] Women also worked in more physically demanding jobs, such as street paving and the construction industry, from the beginning of the Mandate period (fig. 6). Despite having to fight continually for "complete equality" with their male counterparts, they would enter the professions (e.g., teaching and nursing) in increasing numbers as time went on.[97]

Figure 6. Women construction workers in Tel Aviv, 1923. (Bernstein, 1987.)

While Jewish workers living in Jaffa faced the same challenges and were subject to similar dynamics experienced in Tel Aviv, their situation was not identical. In the downturn of the early to mid-1920s, for example, conditions were often worse and labor militancy greater in Jaffa than in Tel Aviv. This situation was exacerbated by the fact that the Jaffa Municipality did not employ Jews in its public works or health projects, although they constituted more than one quarter of the population by the early 1930s.[98]

However, relations between the Jaffa Municipality and Jewish workers were not unremittingly hostile. Well into the 1920s the MPY, with the help of the Jewish National Fund, purchased land for a workers' neighborhood in Jaffa after negotiations with the Jaffa Municipality.[99] Examples of such cooperation are not common, but they demonstrate that in the 1920s the competition for land had yet to become acute enough to prevent cooperation and also that the Jaffa Municipality, more than the Tel Aviv Municipality, was not uniformly opposed to helping members of the "other" national community who lived or worked within its borders.[100]

Jewish Labor in Jaffa, Jaffa Port, and Tel Aviv Port

As the space of the Jaffa–Tel Aviv region became increasingly nationalized during the Mandate period, Jaffa Port was defined by Arabs more and more as an exclusively "Arab" space.[101] Yet by the end of the Ottoman period, Jewish presence and influence in Jaffa Port was increasing. By 1920 Jews were working on Jewish boats such as the *Halutz* or *Pioneer*, and the Jewish press was writing of the importance of Jewish workers in Jaffa Port in light of increased immigration to the country.[102] On the administrative level, several Jews, including the mayor of Tel Aviv and several Jewish notables, had joined Jaffa's mayor and several Palestinian Arabs as members of the Jaffa Port committee.[103]

At the same time Tel Aviv's leadership sought to build a new port or harbor in which Jews would have greater presence, influence, and even control.[104] Thus in 1922 Dizengoff wrote to British officials advocating the construction of a new port closer to Tel Aviv. After asking rhetorically, "Have we in a single instance driven anybody out of the possession or the enjoyment of his property?" he argued, "[T]he lands which we have bought and which are now covered with this prosperous township, were nothing but sandy tracts, uninhabited, sterile, uncultivated, giving no income whatever to their owners or to the state. We bought them only from people who were, out of their own free will, content to part with that at a good price."[105]

This explanation is, of course, a wonderful summation of the entire Tel Avivan creation mythology. How did it affect Zionist national and municipal policy? Dizengoff continued: "If today it is possible to hope that in the very near future the town of Jaffa will witness the beginning of the construction of a modern harbour, this is due solely and exclusively to the initiative and energy of Jewish citizens of Tel Aviv."

Until such a port could be built, Jaffa Port was considered "a very important place for Jewish workers,"[106] since even in its "bad condition" it could provide Jews with forty to fifty jobs. One group, calling itself the Hebrew Coachman's Group, was established in 1922.[107] Working at the port was certainly not easy for the coachmen; in fact, they wrote, "[There is] no other group in all of Jaffa and Tel Aviv similar to us in the difficult conditions of work, and in the condition of continual war like us."[108] Yet they complained to Jewish officials that too few Jews were willing to work as porters or coachmen, even though these jobs could furnish a living to hundreds of families.[109]

By 1927 as many as forty Jewish carters, supporting up to 117 dependents, worked both in the port and on the 'Auja/Yarkon River. In a pamphlet published to celebrate the Hebrew Coachman's Group's five years of existence, the authors described the "vigorous hatred" (often expressed in violence) of the Palestinian Arab coachmen for the Jewish "pioneers"; however, the "young Jews" persevered. The pamplet went on: "[Eventually, we became] a natural part of all levels of work in the port. The penetration of Jews into the port was, like every important conquest, the fruit of the pressure of immigration and the necessity of absorbing immigrants. . . . The Arabs reconciled themselves to our presence in the port and got used to us; peace prevailed between them and us, and now there are friendships between us."[110]

A similar group was formed in 1933, as the Histadrut increasingly became interested in "expanding the conquest of Hebrew labor in Jaffa Port."[111] By the 1935–36 fiscal year, Jewish workers made up roughly 7 percent of the port's workforce.[112] If we consider that the majority of the port's workforce was composed not of residents of Jaffa or its vicinity—who numbered only four hundred or so—but rather of up to three thousand Hauranis and Egyptians,[113] it becomes clear that though Jews constituted only a small percentage of the overall workforce, their numbers were substantial vis-à-vis the local Arab population.

Yet whatever the limited success of Jews in gaining employment at Jaffa Port, the desire to move the port closer to the area of Tel Aviv, and the resistance of Palestinian Arabs to that demand, remained constant. Palestinian Arab leaders argued that "the Zionists want to move the port to Tel Aviv in order to kill Jaffa."[114] Conquest, as opposed to murder, would be a better description of the Zionist leadership's goal, but the perception that Jews wanted to build a new port rather than rebuild the old one was not inaccurate. Even when Dizengoff wrote to the government pressing for the establishment of a new port in Jaffa (to handle the increased traffic generated by the booming citrus trade) he presented many reasons why such an enterprise would be almost impossible at the port's present location and suggested the mouth of the 'Auja/Yarkon River—which he termed "the natural boundary of Tel Aviv and Jaffa"—as a good alternative location.[115]

Here we see how the geographic, cognitive, and administrative "borders" of Tel Aviv were elastic enough to conceive of the two cities as one unit when it served the interests of the leadership, even as they were reinforced in other ways. Yet however much the Tel Aviv Municipality desired to move the port closer to or within their jurisdiction, many of the Jewish merchants in Jaffa were against such a move, which Dizengoff derisively attributed to their desire to "remain in the *galut* [Diaspora] of Jaffa."[116]

Negotiations to introduce Jewish labor into Jaffa Port (in fact, to recognize officially their increased presence) ended with the government's negative reply on April 9, 1936, less than a week before the April 19 outbreak of the strike and closure of the port (although even after the outbreak of the revolt and the establishment of a "Jewish" port in north Tel Aviv, Yemenites continued to work at Jaffa Port as porters).[117] Again, labor leaders argued that the prohibition of Jewish workers was "tantamount to creating an economic pale for Jews in Palestine and placing Jaffa Port outside it."[118] It was perhaps prescient that only days before the outbreak of the revolt, the high commissioner asked the newly formed Jewish Lighterage Company to hold off for a year the introduction of Jewish workers on their lighters because of the fear that such an action would increase the risk of disturbance at the port.[119]

In the wake of the strike and revolt *al-Difaʿ* once again exclaimed that "Jews are attempting to 'kill' Jaffa Port" in revenge.[120] But even before the revolt the paper exclaimed: "This is a pure Arab port. . . . We here repeat and state over and over again, that this Port has been Arab since time immemorial and that it will remain Arab until the end of time, and if the Government continues to insist on letting the Zionist hands toy with this Port, then the Government alone will bear responsibility for the consequences of such action, consequences that the Government itself does not wish for."[121]

It took just over six months to the day after the port was closed for activity to resume; on October 19, 1936, two ships, loaded with hundreds of tons of grain, delivered their shipments.[122] Through much of World War II Jaffa Port did not operate at full capacity, It was only after the war that life finally returned to "normal" in the eyes of the city's Arab residents.[123] Normal, of course, meant that the life of the port was Arab and needed to remain Arab.

This sentiment was, of course, the mirror image of the Jewish vision for Tel Aviv and its hoped-for port, and it was precisely the strike and closure of Jaffa's port that allowed Tel Aviv's leadership to achieve this long-held goal, the creation of an independent, Jewish port within its borders. Indeed, with the eruption of the revolt the local and national Zionist leadership and their British supporters were unified in the belief that Jaffa and its port were no longer safe for Jews and that never again could Tel Aviv and its surrounding districts be placed "at the mercy of the Arab lightermen" of Jaffa.[124] Thus Jews had "no choice" but to build their own, independent port.[125] As I explain in chapter 7, in a manner similar to the discourses surrounding the annexation of land around Tel Aviv and other Jewish activities in and around Jaffa, the rhetoric of security was used to justify the establishment of a separate port in Tel Aviv.

Given this logic, within weeks of the port's closure Jews had constructed a jetty in northern Tel Aviv, which began unloading goods on the beach beginning on May 9, 1936. Formal permission to construct a port was given by the government on May 15, and construction of the new Tel Aviv Port was completed on Christmas Eve of that year. Not surprisingly, its creation was deemed the "most important event of the year" in the city's municipal gazette.[126]

Although the high commissioner initially approved the jetty as a temporary measure to deal with the closing of Jaffa Port, it quickly became clear that Jewish leaders and citizens were united in their desire to construct a permanent harbor in Tel Aviv so as to "avoid the necessity of Jews ever again being dependent on Jaffa Port." Despite government opposition, support for the port was so great and continued improvement in facilities sufficient enough so that permission was given for the landing of all categories of goods in August 1937 and of passengers in April 1938.[127]

Tel Aviv Port became a political symbol of Jewish sovereignty not just against the Palestinian Arabs but also against the British.[128] Yet while the port's share of traffic steadily increased, from the beginning its finances were deeply troubled.[129] Already by 1939, despite the coordinated efforts of the bourgeois municipality and the philanthropic Jewish leaders who administered the port, it was felt that there would be "no hope" for its survival unless the Histadrut assumed financial responsibility.[130]

Because Tel Aviv Port quickly and clearly became a major threat to the prosperity if not survival of Jaffa's port, the Zionist–Tel Aviv leadership several times attempted to explain their position to the Arabs. In the Histadrut-sponsored *Haqiqat al-Amr,* Moshe Shertok argued, "[T]he position of Jews in Jaffa Port was similar to that of a man renting a house from another and paying high rent and furnishing it and arranging it and making it center of his work . . . and suddenly the owner comes one cold night and throws him out and closes the door in his face and denies him any of his rights to [his home]. . . . This is exactly what the Arabs did to us with the strike in Jaffa Port [in] announcing that the port is an Arab port and only Arabs have the right to use it any time they want. . . . Now comes the ancient owner . . . returning anew to life in his country. So we want our own port where we can participate fully and [where] the rights of Jewish workers will be protected."[131]

Notice the ambivalence in Shertok's language: first Jews are "renters," then they are "ancient owners" returning to revive themselves and the ancient homeland. Yet in both depictions the Arabs have disappeared from the space of the port; they exist only as the much-despised landlord from whom Jews fled to Tel Aviv in the first place.

Another argument used to justify the existence of Tel Aviv Port was to claim that each port served the needs of "its" population.[132] According to this line of reasoning, Jaffa Port was conceived of as a purely *in*-port that served the needs of the city and its immediate surroundings (as if the city had no hinterland or relationship with other cities), whereas Tel Aviv's port handled both imports and industrial exports, connected the city to its "hinterland," and was deemed vital to the future "development" of Jerusalem.[133]

Perhaps the clearest description of the Zionist understanding of the role and function of Tel Aviv Port comes from an article from the Labor newspaper, *Hapo 'el Hatza 'ir*, in which the editors asserted, "[T]he conquest of the port in Tel Aviv is one of the biggest settlement activities of our movement. . . . We must see that this activity [the opening of the port] was much more than an answer to the disturbances of Jaffa. It is today one of the main links in the chain of our activities in opening up the country."[134] Tel Aviv is nowhere mentioned in this article, and it is clear that here the role of the port was understood more in terms of its national than its local significance.

The article concludes with the following argument: "The debate is not about sharing ports but [about] the vision of our port as a great settlement enterprise. The question is whether we proceed in the same way as agricultural colonization. . . . Only someone who doesn't see the port as a settlement enterprise would give up on its independence." In other words, the goal of "settlement" was to take spaces that were inhabited or used by both communities and transform them into exclusively Jewish territory. As Ben-Gurion wrote in a July 1936 diary entry, succinctly stating the Zionist view: 'I would welcome the destruction of Jaffa, Port and City. Let it come; it would be for the better. This city, which grew fat from Jewish immigration and settlement, deserves to be destroyed for having waved an axe at those who built her and made her prosper. If Jaffa went to hell, I would not count myself among the mourners."[135]

THE TEL AVIV AND JAFFA MUNICIPALITIES: CONFLICT AND COOPERATION

Municipal relations offers another arena in which to examine the clash between nationalist rhetoric and the needs and realities of everyday existence in a large urban center such as the Jaffa–Tel Aviv region.

The Tel Aviv Municipality: Internal Dynamics and Relations with the Jaffa Jewish Community

Given the ideological, economic, and demographic importance of Tel Aviv, it is not surprising that politics there was "dissimilar" to other Jewish and Palestinian Arab towns.[136] Its predominantly Jewish population (as opposed to mixed towns) and historically bourgeois leadership (as opposed to the power of the labor movement in the kibbutzim and other Jewish urban and rural settlements) made for municipal political conflict that was more intense than in the rest of the country. For their part, Palestinian Arab leaders viewed the electoral process in Tel Aviv as little more than a mechanism to increase Jewish control of the country.[137]

By the early 1920s the contests for power and resources between the different political factions, and the communities, constituencies, and visions of the city they represented, led to "internal wars [that] were bringing down the city," as more than a dozen parties—including various incarnations of the workers' parties, the Organization of Owners of Houses and Plots, the Orthodox, the Yemenites, the Haredim, the Revisionists, the Tenants, and the Non-Partisans—vied for control of the municipality. Each one felt, as the Yemenite List described it, that "only we can defend our rights."[138]

Adding to the turbulent political atmosphere was the continued complex, often conflictual relationship between the Tel Aviv Municipality and the Jaffa Jewish community during the Mandate period. For its part, the Jaffa Va'ad continued to press the case for representing the larger Jaffa–Tel Aviv Jewish community,[139] fearing that Jaffa's Jews were being "swallowed into" Tel Aviv.[140] Tel Aviv's leadership perceived its interests to lie in taking over the Va'ad's functions—thereby cementing its control over the entire Jewish population of the Jaffa–Tel Aviv region—and even engaged in secret negotiations with the government to that end.[141]

The Tel Aviv Municipality also had numerous conflicts with the religious community in the Jaffa–Tel Aviv region, particularly over such issues as women's suffrage and "guarding Shabat," which religious Jews saw as an essential task of the "first Hebrew Municipality in the world" but which went against the secular grain of the majority of the city's residents.[142] By the mid-1920s a state of "war" existed between the religious population of the Jaffa–Tel Aviv region and the Tel Aviv Municipality (also known as "the destroyers of Shabat"),[143] one that anticipated, and even set the stage for, the current hostility between secular and religious residents of the city and the country as a whole. But whatever the conflicts between the two va'ads and between the Tel Aviv Municipality and religious Jews, economic and political realities necessitated significant cooperation on the day-to-day level, particularly in the areas of social, health, educational, and religious affairs. Cooperation was naturally amplified in extraordinary times, such as the violence of 1921 or 1936, when they worked together to find housing and jobs for refugees from Jaffa.[144]

The Jaffa–Tel Aviv region was also a center of Yemenite life and activity in Palestine,[145] and the Yemenite and Sephardic communities there had their own problems with the Ashkanazi-dominated municipality that mirrored their conflicts with the Labor leadership.[146] This was compounded by the poverty and overcrowding from which the Yemenite community in particular suffered,[147] which in turn caused repeated friction with the authorities, who saw them as mendicant "hordes," and even a "plague," whose invasions of the city needed to be "stamped out."[148]

The description of the Yemenites as somehow not belonging in Tel Aviv, when in fact they lived in neighborhoods that predated the city by decades, is a good example of how the modernist conception of Tel Aviv turned people with deep roots in the region into "invading hordes" (a depiction that also applied to the local bedouins) or "floating populations" (as marginalized inhabitants of the region were described by a British judge). Yet despite the many hardships they had to endure, the Yemenites were among the most public-minded communities in Tel Aviv, coming out to vote in much greater numbers than their fellow citizens.[149] Clearly they felt they had a stake in Tel Aviv, however much of a problem they might have been considered by the British or their own municipal leaders.

The Jaffa Municipality

It is very difficult to write a history of the Jaffa Municipality because almost all of its records are lost, having been destroyed or taken into exile by municipal employees in 1948. The data that exist come mostly from reports in the local press and documents contained in Israeli and British archives and date from the 1930s and 1940s. I will thus focus on this period.

From reports in *Falastin* and other newspapers, it is evident that, like its counterpart in Tel Aviv, the Jaffa Municipality had continual difficulties coping with the economic ups and downs of the 1920s. Even during the boom of the mid-1930s, the municipality (again like Tel Aviv) had trouble meeting the social and educational needs of the population.[150] In fact, Jaffa's population envied both Tel Aviv's accomplishments and the fact that despite them the municipality was the subject of vociferous criticism by the Jewish press.[151]

Although it faced persistent financial problems, the Jaffa Municipality managed significantly to improve the city's infrastructure and services throughout the Mandate period. Much of its budget was spent on improving health services and paving or expanding streets in 'Ajami, Manshiyyeh, and other neighborhoods. It also engaged in more substantive public works projects with the support of government loans.[152]

Specifically, in 1931, 1933, early 1936, and 1943 the high commissioner and the municipality approved plans for improvements that cost upwards of £P1,000,000 and included establishing new building regulations, redesigning the "regional road system," and improving public buildings.[153] In fact, despite the problems associated with the revolt of 1936–39 several new construction projects had commenced by 1938.[154] A few were criticized in the local press.[155] The details of these critiques are discussed in chapter 6; here it should be noted that the municipality's seeming emphasis on achieving budget surpluses over making noticeable improvements in such areas as garbage collection and schooling was likely a contributing factor to the criticism.[156]

With the end of World War II the Jaffa Municipality looked forward (pending negotiations with the government) to building new hospitals, schools, and gardens in the city.[157] It brought over one of Egypt's leading town planners to design a new town plan for Jaffa, which cost £P3,000,000 and required three years to complete.[158] Mayor Yusuf Heykal expected "Jaffa [to] become the most beautiful of cities in Arab countries if Jaffa Municipality [could] implement the plan"; but to begin with the municipality could only hope to build five hundred of the planned three thousand apartments because the government was still settling several cases of disputed landownership within the plan's area.[159] However, although their construction began before 1948, within a few years of Jaffa's annexation to Tel Aviv in 1949 all signs of their presence and indeed of much of Jaffa's development had disappeared.

Relations between the Jaffa and Tel Aviv Municipalities

Along with the normal responsibilities of any municipal corporation, the Jaffa Municipality saw itself as responsible for the defense of the city's borders, economy, and culture from Tel Aviv. These policies became more militant in the 1940s under the influence of Arab nationalist politics.[160] Thus on more than one occasion the Jaffa Municipality wrote to the Tel Aviv Municipality complaining of border infringements; several times it asked the government for "British justice" or "strong measures" to protect its borders (especially in Manshiyyeh) against "criminal Zionist attacks on the city."[161]

The local press also placed this "defense" burden on the municipality. For example, right to the end of the Mandate period *Falastin* considered it fundamental for the city's leadership to "accept the responsibility demanded to protect Jaffa from conspiracies against her and [attempts to] plunder her Arabness, and lower her from her present rank to being [just] a suburb among the suburbs of Jewish Tel Aviv."[162]

The struggle against Tel Aviv clearly pitted the Jaffa Municipality against the city's Jewish residents, including the Jewish members of the council, who were reminded that Tel Aviv was "in reality a part of Jaffa" and accused of allegiance to the Jewish city's interests (they stopped attending council meetings in 1937).[163] Yet like its neighbor to the north, the Jaffa Municipality would ultimately demand the annexation of areas around Jaffa to expand its built-up area.[164]

While there were numerous confrontations between the two municipalities, there was also cooperation. Already in 1919 Jewish and Arab leaders in the two towns met to organize "an important project [not described] for our country and its people"; another proposed project involved the joint exploitation of the 'Auja/Yarkon River for irrigation and electric power.[165] In fact, only weeks after the May Day violence the mayor of Jaffa wrote to Dizengoff requesting a meeting to "coordinate" new town plans for Jaffa and Tel Aviv, and leaders sought to "reestablish friendly relations" in 1923.[166]

A particularly tangled relationship between the two municipalities—and thus much cooperation, confusion, and conflict—evolved with respect to the collection and division of taxes (particularly in Jaffa's "Jewish neighborhoods," to which Tel Aviv increasingly provided essential services in the 1930s and 1940s),[167] the paving and/or expansion of joint roads in border neighborhoods, the administration of common slaughterhouses, and the improvement of transportation from the Jaffa–Tel Aviv region to Haifa.[168] Often cooperation was the result of give-and-take; on one occasion the Jaffa Municipality agreed not to oppose the building of a bridge across the 'Auja/Yarkon River if the Tel Aviv Municipality agreed to support Jaffa's requests to the government on other issue.[169] The municipalities also cooperated in the construction of a new train station for the Jaffa–Tel Aviv region that would benefit both towns[170] and offered joint protests when too much port traffic was diverted to Haifa.[171] Finally, the two mayors often met under the auspices of the Jaffa district commissioner (sometimes with the mayors of the country's other major towns) to discuss issues as varied as fixing vegetable prices and enhancing municipal cooperation.[172]

Two statements by Tel Aviv Mayor Meir Dizengoff best capture the complex relationship between the two municipalities. At a 1922 dinner in honor of the high commissioner's visit to Jaffa and Tel Aviv, Dizengoff explained,

> It cannot be denied that a kind of a state of war exists between the Jews and our Arab neighbors ["fellow citizens" is handwritten above this], but it is, however, a peaceful war, a competition between different ideas and conceptions [and] between different kinds of energy and manners of life and work. Take for instance my friend Assem Bey Said, mayor of Jaffa Municipality and myself; he wants to improve and embellish Jaffa and erect customhouses and stores and I wish to embellish Tel Aviv, I am erecting bathing establishments, building roads and houses. The common result of all this will be that both Jaffa and Tel Aviv will soon be beautiful ["and modern" is handwritten above] European cities.[173]

Here we see a curious juxtaposition of the discursive borders that Tel Aviv's leadership used from the start to separate themselves from "galut" Jaffa, coupled with the recognition that whatever the different "ideas" and "energy" possessed by the two cities and their people, Jaffa's development could not be denied. It was clear to Tel Aviv's leaders from the beginning of the Mandate period that both cities, not just Tel Aviv, were in a period of rapid development.[174]

But beyond the "peaceful war" between the two municipalities, when the question of formally establishing Tel Aviv as an independent municipality arose in the mid-1920s, Dizengoff asked the government "not to completely separate us from Jaffa" because of joint revenues and Tel Aviv's "true business interests" in the city. In fact, the Jaffa Municipality was credited by Dizengoff for helping the Tel Aviv Municipality in many areas, from paving roads to turning over customs and Tabu revenues and providing land for and otherwise supporting Jewish factories in Jaffa.[175]

PAVING THE WAY FOR "CATASTROPHE"

*The Violence of 1921, 1929, and 1936
and the Partition of Palestine*

However rich and multilayered were the interactions between Jews and Arabs of all social strata in the Jaffa–Tel Aviv region, the defining events of the Mandate period for both Jaffa and Tel Aviv were the major clashes that took place on their mutual borders in 1921, 1929, and 1936.[176] Although relations would ultimately return to varying degrees of "normalcy" after these clashes, each permanently altered the social, economic, and geographic landscape of intercommunal relations in the two cities and ultimately led to plans to partition the country through the middle of the two towns. As one former member of the semiclandestine Zionist military organization, the Haganah, put it, "In Jaffa . . . at night our neighbors became killers."[177]

The May 1921 violence was not the first instance of intercommunal violence in Palestine. As we have seen, the clashes of 1908 gave credence to the desire of many of Jaffa's Jews to establish a separate quarter, removed from the center of Jaffa. Ten years later, only a short time after the British conquest, significant discontent on the part of the Palestinian Arab population of Jaffa vis-à-vis the Jews was noticeable, bordering on "popular hostility."[178] Thus when clashes broke out in Jerusalem in 1920 they quickly spread to Jaffa, prompting Tel Aviv's leaders to search for ways to improve relations with Arabs.[179] By 1921 Jaffa's rapid economic and demographic growth had made it the place "where you would get more information about political feeling than in any other part of Palestine."[180]

The "storm" of violence that broke out on May Day 1921 was more intense than that of the previous year, and spread rapidly to the rural areas surrounding Jaffa. The violence began at the close of labor demonstrations in Tel Aviv, during which a Jewish Marxist group clashed with the larger Ahdut Ha'avodah party.[181] Despite being guarded by a contingent of police, a group of fifty to seventy Marxists slipped away to the seashore and began to march toward Tel Aviv. The police attempted to disperse the Marxists into an open area on the border between Tel Aviv and Jaffa.

At the same time, Arabs had gathered on the Jaffa side, growing increasingly concerned that the Jewish groups were about to march into Jaffa and attack them. When the (British) police shot into the air to disperse the Jewish demonstrators, the Arabs thought that it was Jews shooting at them, and a mob spread through northern Jaffa (Manshiyyeh and Neve Shalom) and south through 'Ajami, smashing Jewish shops, attacking pedestrians, and breaking into the immigration house that sheltered newly arrived Jews.

The Arab policemen failed to stop the mob (and in some cases themselves attacked Jews),[182] and forty Jews were killed by the end of the second day, the extreme violence fed by rumors that Muslim women and children were being killed by Jews.[183] It is hard to know definitively who precipitated certain incidents within the larger violence, but the report of the Commission of Inquiry reveals that each side initiated some acts of violence, generating reprisals from the other side.[184]

For Jaffa's Arab population, the 1921 violence was, in the words of *Falastin*, a "revolt."[185] This contention was supported by both British and Zionist intelligence reports; one senior Zionist official cited the "unnatural" spread of the Jewish community and its "seiz[ing] and spreading" over the rest of the city into the surrounding orchards as a leading cause of the "*mountainous*" hatred between the two communities.[186]

The implications of this analysis are, I think, clear. To begin with, the spatial—and along with it, economic—impact of Jewish immigration on the surrounding (and at this point, still largely Palestinian Arab) agricultural lands, which were a primary source of the city's wealth, is evident. The increasing physical, cultural, economic, and political pressure of the growing European Jewish community on what was previously a predominantly Arab city could not but have set the stage for violence sparked by the spectacle of European Marxists parading through a mixed neighborhood preaching liberation for the Arabs as well as for the Jews. Tel Aviv's imminent separation from Jaffa and constitution as an autonomous local council (one stage below full municipal independence), which occurred on May 11, 1921, was certainly another compounding political factor. This was just one more indicator of the growing economic and political independence—and power—of the Jewish community in and around Jaffa.

The violence of May and June led thousands of Jaffan Jews to move to Tel Aviv. This influx caused great strains on the Tel Aviv Municipality; in one press release Dizengoff described the "great, unhealthy, and dangerous demoralization" that "paralyzed all the economic and social life and disturbed the functioning of the governmental mechanisms entirely."[187]

The 1929 violence, which began at the Wailing Wall in Jerusalem before spreading throughout the country, was again centered in the alleyways and the Hassan Bey mosque of Manshiyyeh once it reached Jaffa. Despite special precautions by the police to patrol the Jaffa–Tel Aviv border at Manshiyyeh (which were taken as soon as word came of the violence in Jerusalem), groups of Palestinian Arabs and Jews squared off and the Haganah patrolled the region surreptitiously.[188]

The British forced the Palestinian Arab funerals to be held in southern Jaffa ('Ajami), instead of Manshiyyeh, while the burial of slain Jews was allowed only in north Tel Aviv. As a result of the violence fifteen hundred refugees fled to Tel Aviv from Jaffa, particularly from mixed neighborhoods. This influx occurred just as the Tel Aviv Municipality was attempting to return its finances to a "healthy" state, and the resulting economic damage threatened to ruin the city and the municipality together.[189]

The lesson that Dizengoff drew from the violence, and the boycott that accompanied it, was that "Jews need to establish themselves in Palestine in the most isolated, rather than mixed, manner: the Jews who live in Hebron and Safed pell-mell with the Muslims have suffered from every point of view; while Tel Aviv and the colonies of Petach-Tikvah, Richon-le-Zion, etc., have not suffered at all."[190] If, then, the 1921 violence revealed the link between increased immigration and intercommunal tensions, Dizengoff's analysis of the lessons of 1929 demonstrates a new understanding of the role of Tel Aviv and other "Jewish" towns in combating Palestinian Arab hostility to the Zionist enterprise. Separation—physical, economic, political, and discursive—would define Zionist policy into the 1930s, just as the "land question" in the Jaffa–Tel Aviv region began to heat up.[191]

The next outbreak of violence, in October 1933 (subsequently referred to by Palestinians as the "Jaffa massacre"),[192] was not intercommunal but rather directed at the government in Jaffa.[193] Three years later, however, the longest and most serious violence of the Mandate period would rock the country—the "revolt," or *intifada*, of 1936–39. The causes and chronology of the revolt have been examined by many authors and need only be summarized here. Among the causes were the proposed National Assembly (which the Jews had rejected), rapidly increasing Jewish immigration, the discovery of a shipment of illegal arms destined for the Haganah at Jaffa Port, mounting unemployment and competition for jobs, the government's approval of the Huleh valley development concession to a Zionist company, and the crushing of al-Qassam's revolt in the north of the country.[194]

After al-Qassam's death his supporters, the Ikhwan al-Qassam, killed two Jews, leading to reprisal killings of Arabs and a mass funeral procession in Tel Aviv. This in turn led Arab politicians in Nablus and Jaffa to call for a general strike on April 19.[195] The strike was given additional impetus after Zionist Organization president Chaim Weizmann, speaking in Tel Aviv, enraged Arab leaders by claiming that the widening conflict represented the "forces of civilization" struggling against "the forces of barbarism and the desert"[196]—the boundaries between which, one can imagine, were nowhere more clear than the border zones between Tel Aviv and Jaffa.[197]

The most significant event of the revolt occurred on June 16, 1936, when the Royal Air Force destroyed large swaths of Jaffa's Old City as retribution for the continued support of the strike by Jaffa's residents. Although the stated goal of the action was to pave the way for an "urban improvement" project, the actual intentions—clear to everyone—were both to punish residents and to clear out wide new roads through the densely built Old City, which could then be more easily patrolled by British troops.[198] "The plan that terrified Jaffa" was how *al-Difa'* labeled the demolition that "redesigned" the Old City.[199] As the archdeacon of Jaffa reported to London, "large numbers of houses have and are being demolished as a punitive measure in Jaffa, even when no charges were brought against residents . . .

and even there was looting on the part of the British troops, even against the Archdeacon of Jaffa!"[200]

By July the strike had spread throughout Palestine and was being described as a "strike for life and honor," even the "eighth wonder of the world."[201] By the end of the year the revolt had waned significantly, although in many respects Jaffa remained a city under siege throughout the 1936–39 period.[202] In fact, Jaffa was so badly hurt by the strike in 1936 that few residents exhibited a desire to participate in the renewal of violence that began in late 1937.[203]

An appraisal of the various outbreaks of violence during the Mandate period in the Jaffa–Tel Aviv region demonstrates that each led to major "national victories" for Tel Aviv. The first, 1921, "turned Tel Aviv overnight into the center of the Jewish *yishuv*"[204] and was intimately connected to the announcement of Tel Aviv's new status as a "local council," or "township." As Ram argues regarding the timing of the announcement, "there appears to be no doubt regarding . . . the connection between the declaration and the riots in Jaffa."[205]

As for 1936, the strike and the closure of Jaffa Port paved the way for the realization of the long-held dream of building a "Jewish" port in Tel Aviv; as important but often overlooked was the annexation by the Tel Aviv Municipality of large swaths of land from the Palestinian Arab villages surrounding Tel Aviv, which began in 1937 and would not have received the level of government support it enjoyed had it not been for the ongoing violence.[206]

Another national victory, at least from the perspective of Tel Aviv's leaders, was the effect of the revolt on the ability of Palestinian Arabs and Jews to live in proximity to each other. For example, when the government proposed the construction of a new Palestinian Arab neighborhood (for refugees from the destruction of part of the Old City) near several of Jaffa's Jewish neighborhoods, Jewish representatives immediately sent memos to the high commissioner complaining that its proximity to a newly constructed (and in their minds, Jewish) road would defeat the road's function of connecting Jewish and avoiding Palestinian Arab neighborhoods and would even cut off the Jewish neighborhoods from each other. According to one memo, "[The settlement of Palestinian Arabs near these quarters is] plainly speaking, detrimental to our further developing this waste land and is also dangerous to our life and property [because it interrupts the] line of communication [and] afford[s] additional opportunity to the lawless and unruly elements of Jaffa to perpetrate crime upon us."[207]

As an alternative the group suggested that the new neighborhood be moved slightly in order to eliminate possible dangers to the Jewish neigh-borhoods. It was argued that such a move would benefit the Arabs because the original plan would have left the Palestinian Arab quarter surrounded on all sides by land belonging to Jews: "In our humble opinion it is to the advantage of the Arab refugees to be settled in appropriate Arab surround-ings." In fact, *Falastin* criticized the plan for similar reasons, contending that the original site was surrounded by Jewish land and would thus pre-sent a "danger of hunger and death" if disturbances again broke out in Jaffa.[208]

Perhaps the greatest victory for Tel Aviv resulting from the periodic vio-lence on its borders with Jaffa was the recognition by the government, and ultimately by the United Nations (in the 1947 Partition Plan), that Pales-tine as a whole and Jaffa–Tel Aviv in particular had to be partitioned. The idea of separation or partition was first proposed in the report of the Peel Commission in 1937, and the "alarming news" was immediately deemed a "catastrophe" in the Palestinian Arab press, because it would "divide this Arab nation" and separate Jaffa and its surrounding Arab villages from the rest of the country.[209]

The plan proposed to build a large fence (specifically, an "iron railing") to separate the two communities. Such a fence—that is, a national bound-ary—between Jaffa and Tel Aviv was proposed even though the govern-ment introduced the border by asserting that in reality Jaffa and Tel Aviv "form geographically a single town,"[210] a sentiment that mirrored those of the Scottish town planner Patrick Geddes, who designed a town plan for Tel Aviv in 1925 (see chap. 6).

Not surprisingly, in their proposals for redrawing the borders, Tel Aviv's leaders suggested annexing Jaffa's Jewish neighborhoods to Tel Aviv; moreover, they requested that almost the whole of Manshiyyeh, including Hassan Bey Mosque, as well as large parts of the Abu Kabir neighborhood, be transferred to the borders of the new Jewish city and state. For their part, Jaffa's leaders agreed to the transfer of only the northern part of one of the Jewish neighborhoods to Tel Aviv and requested the transfer from Tel Aviv to Jaffa of the entirely Jewish areas along the sea north of the existing boundary and part of the religious Jewish neighborhood of Neve Shalom.

The government opposed both of these proposals, suggesting instead an exchange of territory that would include transferring part of Neve Shalom to Jaffa and part of the Florentine and Shapiro quarters, which contained a mixed population, to Tel Aviv. The overriding concern of the government was both to design as straight a border as possible (to facilitate policing) and to "effect as large a reduction as possible in the Jewish population of Jaffa." This goal would be furthered, it was hoped, by the transfer of the remaining "other" populations in each town to its "national" home.[211]

Clearly, however much the government understood Jaffa and Tel Aviv as constituting one town, it was prepared to overturn that existing geographic reality in favor of one that supported the belief by most of Tel Aviv's leaders that Jaffa was irreparably "galut" and therefore not Jewish space, a theme that I discuss in greater depth in chapter 7. The Palestine Partition Commission hoped the proposed boundary modifications for Jaffa and Tel Aviv would reduce violence between the two communities by separating them and ensuring that no unauthorized crossings or contact occurred. Yet, as the discussion in this book demonstrates, far from separating people, boundaries—whether between opposing cities or between the national Self and Other—more often mask or even generate precisely the intermixing they seek to prevent. That is, boundaries and borderlands are "vague and undetermined" places created by the emotional residue of living with constricted identities; as such, they are the places from which the very "presencing" of the Other that is so threatening to the Self begins.[212]

The nationalist motivations underlying the multiple divisions of Jaffa and Tel Aviv, their two "economies," and their two communities are not difficult to discern.[213] However, the reality was that in all the various levels discussed in this chapter these very borders were "places of hybridity" that frustrated the political and ideological expectations of those charged with enforcing them, forming a truly "*inter*national space," whose ability to disturb the vision of Tel Aviv as the sign of the Jewish nation's modernity made its erasure and replacement with a more rigid and policeable space (however illusionary, as Lefebvre reminds us) a constant concern for Zionist and municipal leaders.[214]

The conclusions drawn by Tel Aviv's leaders from the episodes of violence that periodically rocked the region disclose a belief that Jews living in "mixed communities" suffered from a lack of economic and physical security and political power, whereas "purely Jewish" communities like Tel Aviv were immune from boycotts and thoroughly secure: "not even a single Arab band—however large it may be" was thought able to penetrate its borders.[215] In fact, Tel Aviv's borders did not provide the advertised economic or physical security. Economically, although Jewish leaders often played the boundary card, asking Jewish residents not to buy Palestinian Arab produce or frequent Palestinian Arab stores or restaurants in Jaffa, Tel Aviv, or the surrounding villages, the reality was that Jews continually engaged in these activities.

What is more, price fluctuations in "Arab" markets in Jaffa had immediate effects across the municipal line, a problem that angered Tel Aviv's leaders to no end and lead to fratricidal fantasies about Jews living in Jaffa.[216] As for security, it was precarious enough so that Jews living on the borders of the city conceived of themselves as "pioneers."[217]

Ultimately, despite the best efforts of Tel Aviv's leaders, municipal borders were never the ultimate arbiter of sovereignty or political, economic, or security control over land in Jaffa and Tel Aviv. A Haganah report explains:

> [In the 1920s] the Tel Aviv police could only guard *Jews* and could not guard outside the Jewish city, so they couldn't go to Sheikh Muwannis, but only up to the border. . . .[218] Concerning Jaffa and Tel Aviv there was [no] clear border—in Neve Shalom one street belonged to Jaffa here, and to Tel Aviv there, and these borders were not determined for defense. Defense and guarding during all these years was determined by whether a number of Jews lived there.[219]

Thus it is not surprising that during times of violence, especially in 1936, attacks on Jews were especially high in border areas and that surrounding orchards and Arab farms and villages were frequently the scene or launching points of attacks on Jews and Tel Aviv.[220]

CONCLUSION: THE BEDOUIN HORDES

Throughout the modern period, the Jaffa–Tel Aviv region has been a place of "attraction" to the Jewish and Arab population of Palestine and beyond. Like their fellow (im)migrants, bedouins too found the land on which Tel Aviv was built favorable for their travels and grazing activities, and the construction of a few hundred houses, or the erection of various administrative or discursive boundaries, did not change their perception of the landscape.

If some bedouins were wont to encamp "right opposite" Jewish houses in Tel Aviv;[221] other bedouins continued to use fields purchased by Jews or other European residents in the Jaffa–Tel Aviv region, sometimes coming from the village of Jamassin along the Wadi Masrawa/Ayalon brook to their traditional pastureland in southern Jaffa.[222] Moreover, "many destitute Arabs and gypsies were attracted to [public festivals] and took up their abode within the area. These nomads were, in the main, responsible for the many larcenies recorded."[223]

Perhaps even more important than the actual episodes with and complaints about the local bedouins[224] was the fear generated by the idea of bedouins and the periodic "aliyah" they represented. As an example of how the issue of bedouins could get blown out of proportion, the district commissioner of Jaffa once wrote to Dizengoff regarding several "rumours" circulating about an "alleged mounted party of 120 bedouins passing through Tel Aviv to the Manshiyyeh last night," which turned out to be nothing more than "a few youths returning from a picnic at El-Karem."[225]

As Homi Bhabha has argued, rumors can be symbols par excellence of the "ambivalence, fear and indeterminance of meaning" that lie beneath the surface in all exclusivist-nationalist assertions of identity. Thus from the perspective of Tel Aviv's leaders, the youths' unauthorized traversal of Tel Aviv seems to have created, however briefly, a space of "revolt and resistance" that produced an ambivalence within a Zionist identity founded on a purely Jewish Tel Aviv. This could not be tolerated by the city's leadership, most of its residents, or British officials, and thus a few youngsters returning from a picnic became a bedouin army headed for Manshiyyeh, ground zero of the battle for identity and supremacy in Jaffa and Tel Aviv.[226]

The anxiety or ambivalence produced by the real or imagined bedouin incursions in fact highlight the colonial nature of Tel Aviv as a city and a discourse, as it is in the colonial city, more than other "modernist" cities, that the inability to recognize and accept the past (in this case, the "bedouin" past of Tel Aviv) leads to the desire to erase the existing human geography of the place—the "most othering moment of colonialism."[227]

Yet not all relations with the bedouins were conflictual. As late as 1945 a representative of the "Watatwa bedouins," comprising some sixty families with 317 members who had lived for many years near Summel (they even had a post office box in Tel Aviv, #6002), wrote to the district officer in Tel Aviv asking if one of their elders could be appointed mukhtar of the tribe: "We beg to point out that all our business relations are with Tel Aviv citizens, Tel Aviv authorities and Tel Aviv police. It has become very important for us to have an officially recognized representative."[228]

As I demonstrate in Chapter Seven, while most residents of the surrounding villages protested against their gradual transformation into Tel Aviv's "hinterland,"[229] once incorporated into Tel Aviv town planning or the municipal area they chose committees to represent them to the municipality, used municipal services, and otherwise cooperated with the municipality—even involving it in internal disputes.[230] In the case of Summel, the Arab and Jewish residents together wrote to the Tel Aviv Municipality requesting that it resolve the following areas of concern: sanitation, garbage removal, medical services, electricity, telephones, and bus service from the farm to the city.[231]

The mixed neighborhood of Manshiyyeh was also a site of interaction between the two communities since the nineteenth century, as wealthy Jews began moving there as far back as the 1880s.[232] Along with the neighboring Jewish neighborhood of Mahana Yosef, it would later become home to many of the Jaffa–Tel Aviv region's poorest (mostly Middle Eastern) Jews, who generally maintained good relations with their non-Jewish neighbors.[233]

By the first years of the Mandate period Manshiyyeh had become a focal point of Arab-Jewish violence in times of strife and at the same time "the region which connected Jaffa with Tel Aviv,"[234] its "beautiful, big and clean beach" frequented by residents of both Tel Aviv and Jaffa.[235] A former Arab policeman who lived in both Manshiyyeh and Tel Aviv recalled working with Jewish policemen for the British to find arms being smuggled in to the quarter by Zionists, and oral histories of Jewish and Arab residents reveal cases of business partnerships and even intermarriage between Muslim and Jewish residents.[236]

The extreme ambivalence and multilayered texture of the space of Manshiyyeh is a microcosm of the forces that simultaneously pushed Jaffa's and Tel Aviv's Jewish and Arab communities together and pulled them apart during the last two decades of British rule (and which continue to do so in contemporary Jaffa). Ultimately, however, most Jews found it too difficult to live among Palestinian Arabs, and by 1946 nearly seven thousand Jewish residents of Manshiyyeh had moved to Tel Aviv because of the lack of security in the quarter. As one report asserted:

> The majority of landlords and landowners are Arabs. The population is mixed. The Arabs, landlords, live together with their Jewish neighbors and live off the rental income. . . . Who are the Jewish residents of Manshiyyeh? First of all, they're new immigrants from the Middle Eastern countries. They don't have any *economic or moral guides* in the country, and they naturally went to Arab surroundings. . . . The condition of life and the feel of the surroundings is closer to them than the Jewish *yishuv*, and influences them more. Many in Manshiyyeh were also born here, in Jerusalem, Tzefat [Safed], Tiberius. But they are our "Beduins," moving from place to place. And part of them live on the dole. . . . The family life is terrible. Women have no rights in the house and are treated with complete contempt by husbands. There are [also] women who show the free life of European women and continue to search for it, seeing it in licentiousness.[237]

The last area of complaint in this quotation reveals yet another site of Palestinian Arab-Jewish comingling—the body; that is, in sexual relations between Arab and Jewish men—and even senior British officials—and prostitutes from both communities.[238] This phenomenon certainly had a long history in a port town such as Jaffa. Yet it was not just Middle Eastern Jewish immigrants who were without economic or moral guidance; their European sisters also continued the long tradition. Thus in 1924 many of the new immigrant women were considered "not so decent." "Suddenly we began to see in the different streets of Tel Aviv cars of the wealthy Arabs and Christians from Jaffa arriv[ing] in Tel Aviv in the middle of the evenings and parked alongside the houses in which lived new female immigrants, [and] the wild debauchery continued until the wee hours of the night."[239]

In fact, Jews and Palestinian Arabs were in bed together in more ways than sex, as the ability of many of Jaffa's most prominent Arab leaders to simultaneously lead protests against and do business with—including selling land to—Jews and the large-scale Jewish employment of Arabs in what was officially an "exclusively Jewish" Tel Aviv, highlights the fluid lines of resistance and cooperation that simultaneously separated and connected the two communities.[240] And these lines were in many instances drawn symbolically around the "Arab" threat to Jewish sexual and social purity in border areas such as the beach north of Manshiyyeh. One worried Jewish resident of Jaffa wrote to Mayor Dizengoff on June 7, 1992:

> I would like to bring the following to your notice;–Arabs of a very inferior class are frequenting the Casino, and numbers are unfortunately increasing. It is hoped, however, that the entrance fee of P.T. 2 will keep them away. If not, I am very much afraid that the class of people that we are all desirous of seeing at the Casino will stay away.
>
> Mixed bathing is drawing the natives to the Bathing Resort, and to my knowledge, three Arabs have bathed there. They will spread the news that they are allowed to mix with the ladies, and there will surely be trouble.
>
> I very much regret worrying you, but I consider it my duty to inform you of what I see, think and hear.
>
> Believe me,
> Yours respectfully,
> L. M. Jeune
> POB 64 Jaffa[241]

It was not only concerned citizens or political leaders who saw the potential for interethnic mixing. Zionist planners also took an interest in this problem, whether mixing in the workplace or in social settings. For example, a 1940 study of the benefits of establishing an "urban kibbutz" in Tel Aviv argued that the various efforts to build the Jewish city were "a great source of 'infiltration' in the body of the urban worker," one that would no doubt reinvigorate a "pioneering spirit" whose diminishment over time had, according to the study's author, created a "crisis" of aims and direction in Tel Aviv.[242] The myriad forces that ultimately shifted the balance toward separation and conflict are examined in the remaining four chapters.

5 A Nation from the Sands?

*Images of Jaffa and Tel Aviv in
Palestinian Arab, Zionist, and
Israeli Literature, Poetry, and Prose*

A STRANGER LIVING IN MODERN TIMES

There is a long history of writing in various media about Jaffa and Tel Aviv.
The recurring themes and images in these two narratives deepen our
understanding of the motivations and strategies underlying the actions of
leaders and ordinary citizens in their decades-long struggle to develop their
cities and to gain control over the land, water, and resources of the region.

Two recent well-received books, one focusing on each city, provide a
good entry point for examining the historical and continuing themes
through which Jaffa and Tel Aviv have been represented to their peoples
and to the larger English-language public. The first, a 2000 novel by Linda
Grant titled *When I Lived in Modern Times*, describes the travels of a
young, adventurous woman from the safety and boredom of postwar
(1946) London to the adventure, danger, and intrigue of Palestine, Tel Aviv
in particular.[1] The book's title evokes the self-conception of Tel Aviv as a
peculiarly "modern city," or in the author's words, an "eccentric, disparate[,] . . . teaming metropolis."[2] But it was not just any kind of city: "We
drove through the orange groves till we reached the white city, and it *was*
white, then."[3] The whiteness of Tel Aviv, which reflects the dominance of
International Style architecture, is followed by her description of a photograph of "a small crowd of men and women . . . standing in the middle of a
dune."

> Emptiness stretched all around them—nothing, as far as the eye could
> see, unless you turned to the south and there was Jaffa, where Androm-
> eda was chained to the rock and Jonah set sail for Tarsus. . . . The
> ancient city was overcrowded and the group of pioneers standing opti-
> mistically in the sand in 1909 were holding a founding ceremony for

their new town, which they would call Tel Aviv. . . . I had seen nothing like this before—how could I have done, as a citizen of an old country? It was an entire town without a past. . . . I was in the newest town in the world.[4]

The imagery of the above quotation is pure Tel Aviv: the White City, built in the middle of the desert, modernity's home in the Middle East, with no past and a bright future. As for Jaffa, when it makes its entrance fifty pages later, at the halfway mark of the book, a friend of Grant's heroine exclaims, "We all expected it to be not a big city but at least a little Berlin. My God, it was more like a town in the Wild West that I had seen at the cinema. . . . The conditions were terrible in those days, *terrible*."[5] In contrast: "[Tel Aviv] was the absolute avant-garde of modernism. All our architects came from the Bauhaus, as you must know. We were building a European city and the Arabs were stuck in the Orient."[6]

Finally, the neighborhood of Manshiyyeh is brought in as a place of intrigue for the visitor now turned, literally, into a Zionist spy. A meeting was planned in the neighborhood because it "was a slum. . . . It's a no-go area for the British. It's out of bounds to their troops. . . . The ones you have to watch out for are the Arabs. . . .[7] What *was* that place? It was chaos. It was dirt and disorder, squalid and stinking. The white city didn't touch it."[8]

Manshiyyeh was in fact a mixed neighborhood, officially part of Jaffa, that "touched" Tel Aviv along their long mutual border. With this description of Manshiyyeh the description of the Jaffa–Tel Aviv region is largely complete: the gleaming modern White City, the ancient, terrible old town, and the dangerous, chaotic border region. These themes, which defined the portrayal of the region in the Zionist-Israeli literature during the past century, are reinvigorated for a new generation of readers.

The second book alluded to above is a memoir by the Palestinian lawyer and activist Raja Shehadeh, whose 2002 *Stranger in the House: Coming of Age in Occupied Palestine*, is in large part a memorium to "Jaffa, or more precisely, the memory of Jaffa."[9] This memoir is a reconstruction of and reconciliation with a lost world, "a better life":

[A]nd that life was left behind in Jaffa. Jaffa, I was told, was the Bride of the Sea. . . . Jaffa was a pearl, a diamond-studded lantern rising from the water[,] . . . affluence, a house with original oil paintings, and my grandfather's fully equipped Continental Hotel, which my grand-mother always boasted had a restaurant with enough china and silver cutlery for two hundred guests. Jaffa was where my father had developed a comprehensive law library in his office in Nuzha street, where there were courts, a busy nightlife, Dora, the Jewish seamstress from Tel Aviv who made my mother's clothes, tasty pastries from Kapulski's, and orange groves. And above all these, Jaffa was the sea. . . . How I yearned through my childhood for these imagined pleasures.[10]

In contrast, Ramallah, where Shehadeh's family fled during the 1948 war, was "backward," a place where he was always a stranger, and at best, "an observation point from which to view the Jaffa [he] had never known[,] . . . a glittering array of lights at night." Shehadeh continues: "Night after night [my father] stood motionless, hardly breathing, seemingly captured by this luminous world of Jaffa he had abandoned. To be a man was to be the way my father was in Jaffa. The good life was the nightlife of Tel Aviv."[11] Already we see Tel Aviv's place in the Palestinian imagination, as a center for the good life; and indeed, it was critiqued for these qualities by Palestinian nationalist writers on Jaffa because it would lure too many native sons to their financial and moral ruin.

Although there was always an appreciation of Tel Aviv (often masked as jealousy or fear), for Shehadeh and other Palestinian refugees, Jaffa, like Tel Aviv for the Jews, was still a shining city in its own right, representing "dynamism" and "the promise of youth." However, when Shehadeh's father finally returned to Jaffa after 1967 and saw what had become of Tel Aviv during the ensuing years, he

> realized that the glittering lights to which his eyes had been riveted for all these years were not the lights of Jaffa but those of Tel Aviv. For as the sun set, Jaffa lapsed into slumber and darkness. It was Tel Aviv that glowed with the glitter of the night lights. . . . [Traveling north into Tel Aviv] he now confronted the life that had been created by the new dwellers of this land. The Tel Aviv he had known was but a suburb of Jaffa; now the ghost town was the dead suburb of the living city.[12]

Indeed, his father then realized that he had missed the "vitality" of Tel Aviv all the years he lived in Jaffa, and now it was too late to understand what that vitality was trying to tell Palestinians before 1948—that there was a powerful national movement next door to them that they had better take seriously and prepare to confront; but alas life in Jaffa was too "frivolous" for that.[13]

Here we see most of the major themes in Palestinian representations of Jaffa and Tel Aviv: the lost wonder of Palestine's economic and cultural capital; the beauty of a sea that most Palestinians could never touch again; the frivolity of their lost life; and Jaffa's lapse into stagnation and decrepitude once the "new inhabitants of the land" replaced its rightful owners.

In the pages that follow I explore in greater detail the themes highlighted in the recent works of Grant and Shehadeh, each in its own way a work of fiction—or better, fantasy, as the (re)imaginings of the two cities that are central to their narrative often do not fit the reality of life for their residents during the twentieth century. Fantastical descriptions of the two cities have a long pedigree. In fall 1936, while Palestine was still reeling from the violence and strikes that had begun in April of that year, the official *Tel Aviv Gazette (Yediot Tel Aviv)* featured an article promoting tourism to the city. Ignoring the ongoing hostilities, the article explained, "Tel Aviv is not a city, but rather a house of cures, a house of health *(beit marfa', beit ha-vra'ah)*. If I was a doctor, I would send all the sick Jews . . . for three years in Tel Aviv, because this is a one hundred percent Jewish city, it is the best rest for all sicknesses. Tel Aviv isn't just Eretz Israel, Tel Aviv is life."[14]

Clearly one of the main justifications for the Zionist enterprise was the belief that Jewish life in the Diaspora had become inherently unhealthy, even sick, and that the establishment of a "National Home" (read: state) on the ancestral soil of Palestine was the cure. If Zionism was believed by its adherents to be the "cure" for what ailed European Jews of the late nineteenth and early twentieth century, Tel Aviv, as we see here, was both the pharmacy and the sanitarium where the cure could be administered in its purest and most potent form.

The problem with the cure was, of course, that another people inhabited the promised land. If the land was well populated and sustaining a growing and productive population, how could Zionist leaders justify Jewish resettlement after so many centuries of absence? Thus out of necessity as much as in imitation of other European colonial discourses the Zionist movement began to portray Palestine as largely vacant, its land as barren or sterile, and its Arab inhabitants as backward and unproductive—in this way creating the discursive and physical space for Jewish colonization and settlement. A verse from the Book of Amos, prominently displayed above the entrance to the home (now a museum) of Tel Aviv's first and longest-serving mayor, Meir Dizengoff, reads: "God will restore the fortunes of my people Israel, and they shall rebuild the ruined cities and inhabit them."[15]

The previous four chapters have set the stage for a more in-depth examination of how Zionist colonization, epitomized by the establishment and growth of Tel Aviv, led to the gradual erasure of Jaffa's borders, independence, and history. The mechanism of this effacement was, paradoxically, the erection of myriad new boundaries separating the two cities and communities; these in turn were supported by two powerful myths, whose centrality to the Zionist enterprise in Palestine and impact on the relationship between Jaffa and Tel Aviv have yet to be adequately explored. The first myth is that Jaffa, like the rest of Palestine, was mired in a period of stagnation and backwardness until the "arrival" of Europeans at the end of the nineteenth century. The second, related myth is that its daughter city, Tel Aviv, was born literally out of the sands, a parturition that denied Jaffa any role in the construction or rapid development of "the first modern Hebrew city in the world."

One of the central assumptions of the now-defunct Oslo peace process was the much-publicized Israeli belief that "separation equals peace," that is, that the physical and territorial separation of Israelis and Palestinians called for in the Accords (but, it needs to be noted, never realized) would bring a sufficient level of physical and psychological security to allow Israelis to take the "risk" of granting Palestinians some form of restricted sovereignty. Events during the past ten years, 1993–2002, have done much to discredit the logic of separation; yet while the al-Aksa Intifada that began in fall 2000 soured the hopes of whatever Palestinian constituency remained for the Oslo process, the Barak and then Sharon government and most mainstream Israelis have demonstrated continued fealty to the "logic of separation."[16]

The logic of separation in fact has a long pedigree in the Zionist movement and is intimately tied to the belief that Jews and Arabs were living in what was essentially two Palestines: one Jewish, modern, and progressive, the other Arab, traditional, and backward. Thus in 1941 L. V. Beltner explained that "the town of Jaffa, hard by Tel Aviv on the Mediterranean coast of Palestine, offers a case in point [of self-imposed Arab separatism]. Jaffa is an Arab town. The people are Arabs; they are Mohammedan by religion; they live and dress and work in the Arab way; and their customs fence them off from neighboring Tel Aviv, the town of the Jews."[17]

This understanding of the boundaries separating Tel Aviv from Jaffa, Jews from Arabs—not to mention the sublimation of the multisectarian Muslim and Christian Arab communities into the overly signified "Mohammedans"—needs to be put in the context of the Zionist justification of their enterprise and of Tel Aviv's role in its realization. Specifically, Zionist leaders explained that if one could "see through" the hostility to Jewish colonization, it would become clear how the "modernizing influence of Jewish immigration sets new standards of economic and social freedom and provides new means of liberation to the intellectual and materially enslaved Arab masses."[18]

Tel Aviv's role as both symbol and vehicle of this process of modernization was evident to leaders from all sides of the Jewish political spectrum. Thus Dizengoff wrote in a 1923 memorandum to the government, "Only thirteen years have passed since a small number of people went out from

Jaffa to establish a *modern* settlement. . . . As you surely will have seen already, the town of Jaffa has developed in the last years, *through* its borough Tel Aviv, especially in the direction to the north of the old town."[19]

Similar to Beltner's analysis, Vladimir Jabotinsky, founder of the Revisionist movement,[20] believed that "Tel Aviv is the most discussed city all the world over." Its development proved, first,

> that there is in Palestine both room and need for an *urban* colonization. . . . Second, that industry can find a footing in this ironless and coalless corner of Asia. . . . Third, Tel Aviv is an example and a lesson as to how two nationalities destined to live in one and the same country, can and should dwell side by side without stepping on each other's toes. This is, perhaps, the most "discussed" feature of Tel Aviv; to me, the most valuable. Two men of different habits may keep friendly for ever if each one has his own apartment, provided the walls be of sufficient thickness; but they are bound to lose their tempers if forced to room together.[21]

How did Jabotinsky come to believe (or believe he could seriously make the claim) that the "most 'discussed'" feature of Tel Aviv was its symbolic and exemplary function as a model for intercommunal relations? What kind of narrative would have to be constructed for Zionist leaders to imagine Tel Aviv in such a way? To answer these questions we need to return to the creation mythology that still defines the historiography of the city's establishment and development; that is, the idea that Tel Aviv was literally born out of the sands.

A City from the Sands? Part II

The story of Tel Aviv's miraculous birth from the sands is as central to comprehending the city's identity and self-perception within the larger Zionist mythology as the virgin birth is to understanding the story of Jesus. In *Tel Aviv: 'Ir Nifla'ot (Tel Aviv: City of Wonders)*, written on the occasion of the twentieth anniversary of the city's founding, Dizengoff explains that many people thought it was "crazy to build a city on the sand, without a hinterland." The story was framed by an iconic photograph of the sixty-odd families who founded the city standing on a sand dune, preparing to draw the lots that would divide up their newly purchased property (fig. 7). Tel Aviv, Dizengoff exclaims, proved its doubters wrong.[22]

But Tel Aviv's success was not preordained. As one account of the town's early days notes, the future seemed anything but assured. In describing the decision to build Ahuzat Bayit away from the center of Jaffa, the novelist Shai Agnon points out that there was much protest from those who wanted

Figure 7. Members of Ahuzat Bayit preparing to draw lots to divide their plot of land newly purchased from Karm al-Jabali, 1909. (TAMA Library.)

to remain close to Jaffa's public life and avoid the "danger" of building far from the foreign consulates, "on the sands."[23] Yet if the early years gave the impression that Tel Aviv was "a city standing on the sand . . . and likely to crumble with the slightest shake,"[24] after World War I confidence in her future grew. As Dizengoff wrote in the *Municipal Gazette,* twenty-five years after the foundation was laid in the "desert sands" north of Jaffa, Tel Aviv was on the way to becoming "another New York"; the "boldness and energy" of the population might even transform it into the industrial capital of the Near East:[25] "Today everyone knows that the city of the sands is perhaps the city with the most solid economic base in the country and perhaps even abroad."[26]

It is also clear that from the start Tel Aviv's leaders sought to make it not just a success in its own right but also the antithesis of all the feelings of disempowerment and weakness that plagued Jews in the Diaspora. As Agnon wrote, in Tel Aviv "we will do something, not like in our Jaffa. . . . Indeed, something great was brewing in the world. [One] could hear the tread of things to come."[27] But more than just geography had to be overturned to achieve this feat. As one of Tel Aviv's most famous writers, Haim Bialak, described it, the establishment of Tel Aviv was also "a decision against the creation of hundreds of years of the Diaspora *(galut)*."[28]

Only a powerful force and will could succeed in breaking the shackles of centuries of Diaspora life. Thus Tel Aviv became a "perpetuum mobile, dynamic, [full of] tempo and movement."[29] Most important, in contrast to Jaffa, there was "no voice of war and no smell of war, but rather a voice of building and a smell of settlement.... The workers sweating from the heaps of sand and joining in with the happiness of the owners of the house, and no one could know who was happier, the owners or those who built the houses."[30]

Despite their exclusion from Agnon's narrative, Palestinian Arabs played a role in the early building of Tel Aviv. But this exclusion made it possible to compare Tel Aviv's exuberant energy to Jaffa's supposed lack thereof. As an article in the *Palestine Post* put it, "It could not be otherwise considering, apart from the national factor, the enormous difference between the conditions in the two towns—the unprogressive Jaffa Municipality and the Jewish township seething with energy."[31] What was the source of this energy? Agnon explains that "in truth, all the people of Jaffa are people of peace," but as immigration increased with the onset of the second aliya, "war"—the "conquests of land and labor"—became the goal: "The goal was war . . . within and without. War was a mitzvah and war was momentum, war was war, and the whole country was full of war and victory."[32]

If this was war, the sands were the main battlefield. Numerous songs and poems refer to "the sands of Tel Aviv," their texts often juxtaposed to well-known photographs or drawings of the sands from which Tel Aviv was born.[33] In fact, as it developed and expanded into the 1920s, "Tel Aviv on the sands" remained an important theme in poetry and songs,[34] symbolizing a quiet, romantic space of diversion and amusement for the busy town. As a 1922 poem exclaimed:

> If you want, habib
> to waste an hour
> Run quickly to Tel Aviv.
> Go to the hills; there in the evening
> on the Sand, there you will see,
> You will find everything.[35]

For prose writers like Agnon and the first songwriters and poets of Tel Aviv, "the sands were the gardens of love of Tel Aviv, like the threshing floor in the moshav, and the vineyards of Ein Gedi."[36] That is, they were pregnant with life and waiting for their "cultivators," as Ben-Gurion described Jewish immigrants.[37] Songs depicted young couples enjoying a stroll on the sands and talking about their dreams; whoever did not enjoy strolling on the sands was "stupid."[38]

Thus the lyrics of one song: "Give me, give me the zif-zif sand [sand used for making cement]. Thus we build Tel Aviv."[39] Another focuses on the theme of fertility, or sex:

> And there on the sands, like lions,
> brooding pairs,
> In Tel Aviv there is no fear,
> For every question there is one answer . . .
> Come, let us strengthen them together in Tel Aviv.[40]

The sands were linked to the future: "Tel Aviv, Tel Aviv, City of the Future, filling [everything] with its brightness. On the sands of the sea, Noisy from all the people."[41]

The poems and songs about Tel Aviv also linked the Jewish quarter to Jaffa and the surrounding orchards. Thus one poet described his desire to "breathe in the atmosphere of Jaffa, one perfumed and revealing, spiced with all kinds of fragrances, the fragrance of 'Tel Aviv' and rebirth, the fragrance of citrus and writers. . . . I will go and sing joyfully on the way . . . to Yafo."[42]

However, poems about those areas where Arabs lived or worked either ignored[43] or appropriated that presence; that is, symbolically and discursively the immigrants became the original Arabs. For example, a poem about the Nordiah neighborhood (located on what is now the Dizengoff Center area) describes how "the *bedouins* that came from Poland" spread out over Balfour Street and lived in tents.[44]

In sum, then, Tel Aviv symbolized Israel, its labors, loves, and dreams, as described in this song from the late 1920s or early 1930s:

> Tel Aviv—the city that is Israel, all of it
> Jews are here—the wealthy and the workers
> It's good to live in Tel Aviv, in Eretz Israel
> Here to live and wait for the coming of the savior . . .
> After work, to the restaurant we go to eat
> And after that we go to walk on the beach, on the sand.
> There it's possible to love a girl like the moon, to tell her that she's
> beautiful like the moon.[45]

Moreover, if we consider the area of Jaffa and Tel Aviv as a "frontier,"[46] it is not surprising that Tel Aviv, in its function as a primary symbol of the rebirth of Jews in Eretz Israel, also took on the ethos of "pioneering" that would become more generally identified with the kibbutz, born the same year as the city. As the city was running out of open land on which to expand in the 1930s, the idea of the pioneer, a common theme in early songs, returned:

> Who will build, will build a house in Tel Aviv?
> Who will build, will build a house in Tel Aviv?
> We the pioneers will build Tel Aviv!
> Give us the clay and bricks—and we'll build Tel Aviv![47]

In examining the way Jaffa and Tel Aviv were depicted in the Hebrew-language fiction of the day, it is important to note that before the first houses of the neighborhood-turned-city were built many of the most important early-twentieth-century Hebrew writers, teachers, and intellectuals lived in Jaffa and its first Jewish neighborhood, Neve Tzedek.[48] No writer is more identified with the early years of Tel Aviv than Shai Agnon, who lived in Jaffa and then Neve Tzedek for five years. Many of his stories, including his *Tmol Shilshom*, describe the daily life of these neighborhoods in almost "documentary" detail.[49] Here is how Agnon first describes the land on which Tel Aviv would be built:

> Houses obscure in shape stood scattered in the sand. . . . There was no sign of life in them but puddles of sewage. . . . Yitzhak walked on the desert of Jaffa. . . . After a while he reached a settlement *(yishuv)*. Camels and donkeys and mules loaded with merchandise stood as if they bore no burden. Close to them sat several Arabs and long and assorted flutes in their mouths, and their eyes raised to the sky. Near them stood some Jews and they were arguing with the Arabs.[50]

In contrast, for Agnon, Jaffa was "white houses glistening in hills of sand, and its green orchards crowning it in good trees and a glorious radiance. . . . Spirits of the sea blowing between its dark cypress trees, and the azure of the sea playing with its sands, and the good fragrance wafting in from its vineyards.[51] But was it the fragrance of Jaffa or of Tel Aviv? For Agnon also writes that in Tel Aviv one could "take oneself out of the crowds of Jaffa and smell the fragrance of the land and see a good society."[52]

Toward the end of *Tmol Shilshom* Agnon returns to the landscape around Jaffa: "Out of one window one sees the green orchards without measure, and from another window one sees the valley that the train passes through, and from another the desert on which Tel Aviv would later be built, and from another . . . Neve Tzedek."[53] Though there was a sandy region north of Jaffa, it was surrounded by "orchards without measure" and was not the dominant feature of the landscape, as the prominence of the sands in Tel Avivan poetry and songs would lead one to believe.

Agnon repeats this window motif in one of his most famous short stories, "Hill of Sand":

> If you have never met Hemdat, you might as well meet his room. It stood in the dunes of Neve Tzedek and had many windows; one facing the sea, and one facing the sand that Tel Aviv is now built on, and one facing the railroad tracks in Emek Refaim, and two facing the street. And yet by drawing the green curtains, Hemdat could cut himself off from the world and bustle of Jaffa.[54]

Here the hustle and bustle of Jaffa reveal themselves, as does the mix of sand and life: "In the tender moonlight, the sand stretched for miles all around. The eucalyptus trees by the railroad tracks gave off a good smell, their branches whispering the heart's language in the wind. The surf sounded far away, and the bells of a departing caravan, chimed to the singing of the camel drivers."[55]

Whereas Agnon's stories paint a rich and ambiguous portrait of Jaffa and Tel Aviv and their inhabitants, others reflect a more stereotypical vision of the country and its Arab population. Thus a 1937 children's story about a boat trip on the Yarkon River proceeds:

> As [Mother] rowed, they felt that somehow they had left Tel Aviv far behind. Here before them was life as it had been hundreds of years ago. David was watching a few Arab women on the shore. They were shaking a basket up and down. "I can't imagine what those women are doing," he said finally. Mrs. Gordon smiled. "That is the primitive way of separating the wheat from the chaff," she said. As they passed these people, Mother said, "Do you see that the large straw hut over there? In its shade an Arab is seated, just as his father did, just as his grandfather did, and just as his ancestors did for hundreds of years before. . . . " "Listen to those Arabs singing," cried Tamar. "They are dressed differently from most Arabs." Tamar pointed to a group of well-dressed, dark-skinned people who were singing a sad, plaintive melody in a deep nasal tone. "These Arabs are not as poor as the others," said Imma. "They have learned about modern life, and they dress as we do. . . . " "Soon they heard the tinkling of a bell in the distance. When they look in the direction of the sound, they saw a caravan of camels led by one lone Arab . . . crossing the Yarkon." "That is the Arab's old-fashioned way of transporting goods from one place to another," said Imma. The children could not understand why these Arabs still followed their strange old customs when they lived so close to a modern city like Tel Aviv.[56]

One has to wonder how the scores of Jews who worked long hours for low wages as camel drivers and zif-zif traders along the Yarkon (bringing sand to building sites in Tel Aviv) would have felt about the mother's narrative. In any case, it is a prime example of the way in which conditions (such as the unsanitary state of both towns) and practices (such as habits or occupations) common to both communities and towns were singled out by Zionist leaders and writers as belonging exclusively (and negatively) to Jaffa and its non-Jewish population.

Tel Aviv and Jaffa in Post-1948 Israeli Literature and Film

Tel Aviv and Jaffa remained important settings in post-1948 Israeli literature. Ya'akov Shabtai's *Past Continuous,* which depicts the daily life of the 1960s and 1970s in Tel Aviv and Jaffa, is a more recent counterpoint to Agnon's turn-of-the-century portrait of the region.[57] In her insightful critique of the way Shabtai and other Jewish writers have depicted Arabs in stories about Tel Aviv and Jaffa, Tamar Berger writes that Shabtai "separates in his own way the Arabs from their Arabness. They become part of the landscape, a metonym of it[,] . . . not material. A symbol of something else, far, for the memory that was disappearing" (or alternatively: being erased).[58]

For the characters in *Past Continuous,* like for Agnon, Jaffa was an ambiguous space. On the one hand, as his main character walked along its familiar streets, he observed "the ugly stone houses[,] . . . grimy and dusty, full of high arched windows and little balconies with rusty iron railings . . . jumbled together and interspersed with junkyards and seedy garages."[59] Shabtai described "Yaffa," one of the female characters in the book, as growing "more and more enslaved to a past beyond redemption, which weighed on her like a gravestone, and on a couple of occasions she said to Zina that if only she could free herself from the past maybe she might still be able to get a little enjoyment out of the present."[60]

Yet Jaffa was still a place of beautiful color, particularly its port, which was (and still is) *the* place for good food and a nice view of the sea, "where the beachfront houses and pink church and the minarets of the mosques were already bathed in the strong light of the sun, white seagulls hovered, as always, above the water[,] . . . where a fleet of fishing boats bobbed on the waves with their lamps."[61]

Not surprisingly, Tel Aviv remained a buzz of activity, daily covering over more and more of the region's Jewish as well as Arab past. The following passage offers a paradigmatic description of the city during this period:

> Goldman . . . went on walking until he came to Dizengoff Street, on the other side of which a giant bulldozer was busy excavating. . . . From one

day to the next, over the space of a few years, the city was rapidly and relentlessly changing its face, and right in front of his eyes it was engulfing the sand lots and the virgin fields, the vineyards and the citrus groves and little woods and Arab villages . . . and also cypress trees and lemon and orange and mandarin trees, or buildings which attempted to imitate the architectural beauties and splendors of Europe, in the style of Paris or Vienna or Berlin, or even of castles and palaces, but all these buildings no longer had any future because they were old and ill adapted to modern tastes and lifestyles . . . and Goldman . . . knew that this process of destruction was inevitable, and perhaps even necessary, as inevitable as the change in the population of the town[,] . . . but . . . hatred and rage seethed in him more bitterly than ever and enflamed his longings for the streets and neighborhoods and landscapes which were being wiped out and vanishing without a trace, like the ugly neighborhood of the old shacks lying before him like an empty lot crossed by men and women who walked through it without pausing and cars which sped past without taking any notice.[62]

The dynamics of these rapid physical, architectural, and aesthetic changes are examined in detail in chapter 8. What is ironic in this description of Goldman's rage is how easily his vision and voice could be mistaken for a Palestinian's—perhaps one of the residents of the old Arab villages whose destruction he laments.

It is not just Israeli literature, poetry, and song that present these images of Jaffa and Tel Aviv. One of the most famous Israeli films of the past twenty years, *Late Summer Blues*, is set in Tel Aviv and features much of the same imagery.[63] The film, set during the War of Attrition along the Suez Canal in 1970, is about the experiences of a group of high school graduates during the summer before their induction into the army. One by one each character faces the reality that soon they will be leaving the comfort of Tel Aviv and quite likely going to the Canal, where soldiers (as would two of the group) were dying daily. Tel Aviv symbolizes for the friends everything that will soon be lost, "innocence, purity, stupidity." As each leaves for the army, the city becomes "a ghost town."

At the beginning of the film the narrator repeats "Time: June, 1970; Place: Tel Aviv," while the viewer observes the friends spending their last days together engaged in various prearmy rites of passage on the beach. Much of the film is shot on the beach (but what appears to be the beach of Jaffa, not Tel Aviv), and the sand and sea are its most prominent visual backdrop. In one scene at the beach the characters sing the following song, which also ends the film:

Oh Lord, Oh Lord, I pray these things never end
The sand and the sea
The rush of the water
The crash of the heavens
The prayer of man
The sand and the sea . . .

While the characters of the movie face their future on the shores of Jaffa, peppering their conversation with "Ahlans," "Yelas," and other collo- quial Arabic phrases (reminiscent of the "habib" of the 1922 poem quoted above), Palestinian Arabs themselves are nowhere in sight. In fact, this film, like Shabtai's novel, is an excellent example of what Amnon Raz- Krakotzin has described as "the constant distancing of the Arabs upon which even the 'liberal' Israeli approach to its minority population is founded.[64] Like Shabtai's *Past Continuous*, the Tel Aviv of *Late Summer Blues* is "an Arab-free zone, [it] remains the only city in the West without Arabs. It is a city that bars entry to residents of the territories. Even Israeli Arabs are not welcome there."[65]

"WE ARE IN A STATE OF WAR":
TEL AVIV AS PERCEIVED BY ITS OTHER

The city of Jaffa was both the economic and cultural center for Palestine's Arab community, its "gate of entrance and liberation."[66] Several of the most important literary clubs in Mandate Palestine were located there, and writ- ers such as Muhammed Izzat Darwazah and Muhammad Rafiq al-Tamimi, although not born in Jaffa, lived and did much of their writing there.[67] There were fourteen clubs, thirty-three educational organizations, and thirty-one printing houses by the Mandate period; the charitable organizations in par- ticular "participated in a remarkable way in the strengthening of the national, religious and cultural consciousness and political resistance to the British Occupation and the struggle of land sales."[68]

For Jaffans, the city's position as the cultural center of Palestine was inti- mately tied to the presence there of the country's press, which "was formed in Jaffa."[69] Beginning in 1911, three of Palestine's most important Arab newspapers were centered in Jaffa: *Falastin*, *al-Jami'a al-Islamiyya*, and *al-Difa'*.[70] There were eight newspapers founded in Jaffa in the late Ottoman period, and thirty-three during the middle of the Mandate period.[71] What is interesting for our purposes is that the Arab press, *Falastin* in particular, devoted considerable attention to events and developments in Tel Aviv, both positive and negative; for example, it reported on the municipality's budgets and Zionist conferences[72] and often translated articles from the Hebrew press. Thus, for example, *Falastin* often wrote about "the Future of Tel Aviv!"—the exclamation points serving as a warning or wake-up call to Jaffa to take notice of the rapidly advancing Jewish city.[73]

There was a clear conceptual and epistemological distinction between life in Jaffa before and after Tel Aviv was established, especially after World War I, when the Jewish town began to develop rapidly, threatening Jaffa's economy at the same time that it contributed to its growth.[74] On the one hand, the Arab press described Tel Aviv as "the modern Jewish city," or, as one Arab journal described it, "the most advanced city in Palestine."[75] On the other hand, Tel Aviv's rapid economic expansion and especially the "entrance of Jews into the commerce of Jaffa" led Jaffans to fear losing jobs to Jews,[76] and the frequent meetings between municipal officials and senior Zionist leaders led to charges that the Tel Aviv Municipality was involved in national Jewish politics.[77]

There was also the feeling that the government showed favoritism to Tel Aviv. An article in *Falastin*, "Tel Aviv Municipality: God's Contentment upon It," opined that Jaffa faced continuing hardship while the government lowered Tel Aviv's debt, using this as an example of the government's unequal treatment of the two cities.[78] Moreover, the Jaffa press portrayed the Tel Aviv Municipality as playing a major role in the taking of "Arab national land" (which was not far off the mark, as I explain in chapter 7).[79]

In light of this belief, and perhaps also in response to Tel Aviv's positive portrayal by Jews, Tel Aviv was described as "the most corrupt city in Palestine," or "the one pure Jewish city in Palestine but at the same time the city in which we see the most corruption."[80] Given the rampant corruption believed to be endemic to the Jewish city, the Tel Aviv Municipality was also described as "encouraging [the] transgression of public security in ways that are not found in other cities, linked to Jewish immigration."[81]

What is more, the historical connection between communist activity and violence in Jaffa and Tel Aviv (i.e., the violence of May Day 1921 that began on the border between the two towns after a demonstration by Jewish communists) meant that Tel Aviv was seen as a hotbed of "communism." An article in *Falastin* blamed Jews for "bringing Communism to this Holy Land": "Who harbors, maintains, and pays Communism and the Communists? Is it not Tel Aviv and the Jews? Does Mr. Dizengoff not know that a Communist and a Jew are synonyms in this country and throughout the Levant?"[82]

Indeed, for Jaffa's Arab press, Tel Aviv's corruption was contagious.[83] And so the entrance of Arabs, or Arab symbols, to this Jewish space was viewed negatively, unless such penetration was an act of defiance against the city and what it symbolized. In an article titled "The Fez in Tel Aviv," *al-Jam'iah al-Islamiyyah* explained, "[W]e are in a state of war . . . , and [cannot] deny ourselves any weapon or means to defend ourselves. And there is no [better] weapon than . . . holding on to our eastness. And I will confirm for you that the presence of the fez in Tel Aviv will be a great influence[,] . . . and I am the first to hold on to the fez."[84]

Perhaps no medium of communication more immediately reflected and shaped the attitudes of the Palestinin Arab public than the cartoons that appeared in the local press, particularly in *Falastin*. As Sandy Sufian demonstrates, political cartoonists were central players in the shaping of public opinion, especially during times of heightened tension such as the 1936–39 Revolt.[85] One reason for their power was their deployment of physiognomic ideas about the bodies and faces of Palestinian Arabs and Jews, which used the constructed hierarchy of race to represent and criticize the Other, to present recognizable yet stereotypical images of well-known personalities or groups. Fattened stomachs, long beaked noses, large hands, and exaggerated facial expressions were all used to convey "an overarching theme of deviancy" of both Zionist leaders and opposing Palestinians.

The cartoons in the Palestinian press thus helped to shape and reinforce visual markers of separation in the larger culture. Four illustrations from July 1936 issues of *Falastin* illustrate this point and are remarkable for what they say about how Arabs in general and Jaffans in particular conceived of Tel Aviv. The first cartoon, showing Tel Aviv Mayor Dizengoff presenting the high commissioner, Lord Wauchaupe, on July 24, 1936, with a "Magen David" and the commissioner's grateful acceptance demonstrates how Tel Aviv symbolized the evils of the Balfour Declaration and the continued cooperation between the municipality and the government, especially in the wake of the Arab strike that had begun earlier that year. Here it is important to note the physiognomic characteristics of the two men (especially Dizengoff), which clearly play on existing European stereotypes that have found their way into the Palestinian Arab press; thus Tel Aviv's mayor is slightly hunched over, with big hands signifying lack of intelligence and integrity.

The second cartoon, from July 14, 1936, depicts Dizengoff in a seemingly vaudevillian pose, saying "Shalom" to the mayor of Nablus, who will have none of it and replies, "No Shalom, No Salam, and no negotiation till Jewish immigration ends." Again, the physical characteristics are the same, and the Nablus mayor's rebuff of Dizengoff is clearly meant to pressure the actual mayors of Palestinian Arab towns to do likewise while both reflecting and mobilizing popular opinion against any cooperation with Jews. Again, Dizengoff is in a wide-open pose, his large hands and eyes open to the reader, while Nablus's mayor stands upright, with fine features and a reserved yet determined demeanor.

A third cartoon is illustrative of how Palestinian Arabs were supposed to imagine Tel Aviv and Jewish women in general (fig. 8). The scene would seem to be a court of law, specifically a divorce court, at which the archbishop is forced to choose between the two communities, represented by two very different women. On the left is a scantily dressed and provocatively posed Jewish woman, cigarette in hand, who clearly serves as the very antithesis of the Palestinian woman depicted in colorful yet modest traditional attire. The cartoon also appeals to the sentiments of Christians by having the archbishop tell the government, symbolized by John Bull, that he must divorce his second, Jewish, wife in order to make peace in his house.[86] Here we see the crucial role that Christians are described as playing (it should be remembered here that *Falastin* was a Christian-owned paper), as well as the clear sentiment in Palestinian culture—elite and popular alike—about the essential nature of the two societies as exemplified by the character of their women.

Indeed, John Bull is depicted with his usual corpulent body as he stands smoking his pipe and pointing to the Palestinian woman, who is pretty but shapeless in her traditional garb, with hands lowered in a completely non-threatening position. The Jewish woman is wearing mini-shorts and a rolled up blouse that reveal shapely legs and ample cleavage and is standing in an open pose on tiptoes, as if she is about to lunge at the reader (or the wronged Palestinian woman), with her hands in the air suggesting lack of control or modesty. The archbishop reflects the ambivalent position of the British, as he is staring down at the Jewish woman (perhaps right down her blouse) even as he admonishes Mr. Bull to divorce her.[87]

Finally, the fourth cartoon is a satirical commentary on the British desire for Jewish-Arab coexistence. Here the Jewish–Tel Avivan mouse and the Arab-Jaffan cat—the power imbalance between whom clearly implies Jaffa's victory over Tel Aviv in the ongoing strike—clearly reflects a logic of separation that mirrors the Zionist imagination of Arab self-imposed separatism explored at the start of this chapter.[88] This cartoon uses a standard technique of European physiognomy, theriomorphism, which compares and transforms humans into animals in order to attribute the qualities of the latter to the former.[89] Thus the mouse is wearing a Hassidic-looking hat, while the cat is, naturally, wearing a kaffiyyeh. All the animals are listening to radios that are broadcasting a speech by the colonial secretary (depicted with an

The man of the two wives

JOHN BULL :— My Lord , I married first an Arab woman and then a Jewess and for the last 16 years I have had no peace at home ..

THE ARCHBISHOP :— How did you manage to have two wives, are you not a Christian ?

JOHN BULL :— It was the pressure of the Great war, my Lord ...

THE ARCHBISHOP :— Well my son, if you are sincerely looking for peace you must divorce your second wife, because your marriage to her is illegal ...

الرجل ذو المرأتين

جون بول : اني يا سيدنا تزوجت امرأة عربية اولا ثم تزوجت عليها امرأة يهودية ومنذ ١٦ سنة حتى الانو الخصام قائم و مدفي بيتي...

رئيس الاساقفة : " وكيف تزوجت اثنتين ألست مسيحيا ؟؟

جون بول : لان ذلك تحت ضغط الحرب العظمى يا سيدنا...

رئيس الاساقفة : اذن عليك يا ولدي اذا كنت حقيقة ترغب في السلام ان تطلق الثانية لان زواجك بها غير شرعي ...

Figure 8. Cartoon from *Falastin* depicting prototypical Jewish and Arab women as symbolizing Zionist and Palestinian national characters, July 25, 1936.

oversized head and large nose), who stands astride the whole country while informing the world that "the whole object of His Britannic Majesty's Government is that Arabs and Jews should be able to live together in peace and amity."

Aside from these cartoons, the publication of innumerable violent images, of wounded and dead Palestinian Arab Jaffans during their various revolts, of the funeral of al-Qassam, of landless peasants, and so on, served both to "publicize" and "popularize" the struggle and sacrifices of individual citizens in the larger community.[90] There was also literal performance involved, as the young boys who sold the papers would shout aloud the headlines in the streets, even embellish the stories of the exploits of Palestinian Arab "heroes" in order both to sell more papers and to motivate people to themselves engage in violent resistance.[91] The 1936–39 Revolt was thus portrayed as a "war of the people," with the masses forging a rebellion through the efforts of the dispossessed, peasants, workers, students, women, and intellectuals—in short, the full spectrum of society.[92]

If Tel Aviv was portrayed in an almost uniformly negative light, descriptions of Jaffa in the Arab press served as a counterpoint to the perceived threat posed by its Jewish neighbor. Thus for *al-Difaʿ*, Jaffa, though "surrounded by Jews," or perhaps because of this fact, was the "city of the great revolution" during the 1936 Revolt, the "center of a new movement[,] . . . a movement of economic organization . . . bringing about the retreat of [our] opponent."[93]

When the Jaffa Port closed in 1936 and Jewish leaders called for a new port to be built in Tel Aviv, *Falastin* responded by exclaiming: "[I]f the Jews think they can do without Jaffa they are wrong, but Jaffa can do without Jews and their city. As for Tel Aviv, worthy of blame for everything, it is unable to make the adaptation, and if the Government helps to realize this idea . . . it will not enable it to do without Jaffa. . . . We are the ones who will proclaim the economic war on them, cutting them [off] forever."[94]

The confrontation between Jaffa and Tel Aviv was a key theme in Arab literature of the period.[95] Najati Sidqi wrote a collection of stories titled *al-Akhwat al-Hazinat (The Sad Sisters)* that discuss the social and political problems faced by the Arabs of Palestine and others through the prism of the experience of Jaffa. In the title story, he describes the transformation of Jaffa from a quiet, romantic Arab place into a busy city inhabited by aliens—Jews—who have introduced strange habits and ways of life.[96] In another story he examines the inability of a young man from a traditional family to adjust to the new conditions of life, including increasing emancipation for women.[97]

Even more important is the story *al-Malak was al-Simsar (The Angel and the Land Broker)*, by Muhammed Izzat Darwazah. Darwazah describes the methods used by Zionists to entice Arabs to sell their lands. It begins with a description of a typical Palestinian Arab family sometime in the late Ottoman period through the mid-1920s.[98] The head of the family, who is about forty, has spent all his life as an illiterate farmer and has never been exposed to the attractions of life in the cities. Under the influence of a Jewish land broker he makes his first visit to Tel Aviv. There he is introduced to a Jewish girl—no doubt resembling the one in the cartoon described earlier—who encourages him to spend himself into debt. The yield of the land he owns proves not enough to meet his obligations, and the land broker arranges for a mortgage. When the payment falls due, he cannot meet it. He has to sell the land to the broker for a price far below its value, and within a short time he spends the money and deserts his wife and children, becomes a beggar, and ends his life in a lunatic asylum. Darwazah's frankly political aim becomes clear toward the end of the story, when he describes in great detail the way in which other villages decide to create a fund to save land threatened by Zionist buyers.[99]

But the Jewish intimidation and manipulation were not confined to Tel Aviv, as we have seen. In one interesting scene, recounted in the memoir of former Jaffa mayor Yusef Heykal, the "nationalization" of the space of Jaffa into more and more of a Palestinian Arab space is evident: Heykal describes how a Jewish man and his son were walking through a street in Jaffa that was crowded solely with Arabs, unarmed yet in a "provocative manner." Though they were provoked by some Arabs, they blithely continued walking to their house and on entering, loudly shut the door.

The incident led Heykal to wonder why they would have put themselves in such danger (in fact, by now Arab teachers were instructing pupils that the Jews were their "mortal enemies"); his answer was that Zionists felt that they did not have to fear the Arab majority.[100] This incident demonstrates that by this time Arab residents of Jaffa felt that Jews, even residents of Jaffa, did not belong in their national space. Thus, far from just a purely territorial conflict between the two cities, the ideological and spatial boundaries between them have become completely intertwined in the memory of Jaffans past and present.

As Carol Bardenstein has argued, the Jaffa Orange was also mobilized extensively in Palestinian (and Zionist-Israeli) discourses as a "national symbol" of the ties between the people and soil of the country.[101] In the collective Palestinian imagination, the fragrance of orange blossoms in the dense orchards of the Jaffa region, the "shade" of individual trees in backyards, the lushness of the orchards and fertility of the soil—all elicit strong associations with the tragedy of 1948, intertwining the fate of Palestine's people and its oranges.[102]

For Diaspora Palestinians, especially women, conjuring the memory of their former homes has played an important role in "cohering the nationalist narrative of loss"; Palestine becomes "no more than a lemon tree in the backyard of the house she left in Jaffa. Not even a room, not even a facade of a house, but just a tree in the backyard, hidden away from the bustle of main street politics; the tree under whose shadow she always imagines herself sitting, dreaming away her days."[103]

"Memorial books" and other memoirs of Diaspora Palestinians constitute another important source of the way Palestinians imagined Jaffa before and after 1948. Memorial books were most often written about villages destroyed in 1948; they are like "village histories," belonging to a hybrid category of texts that in the past might have been conventionally assigned to the disciplines of anthropology or folklore, yet which today are being seen as important histories of the country.[104]

In her treatment of the role of collective memory in Palestinian identity, Susan Slyomovics focuses on a memorial book on the village of Salama, the largest of the villages neighboring Jaffa, as a premier example of the form and function of these books. In particular, she explains how the maps contained in this and other memorial books can be viewed as "folk maps" to accompany the "folk history" of the village as recounted by former inhabitants, not as a factual statement about "geographic reality." "Folk maps resemble notions, ideas, and opinions about the details of the past."[105]

I would say that they *are* statements about geographic reality, an alternative geography, if you will, of the region now controlled and inhabited almost exclusively by Jews.[106] Thus in the memoirs of Zaki al-Dajani, one of pre-1948 Jaffa's leading citizens, the author includes several crude, yet accurate, "memory" maps of various neighborhoods of the period (map 7). If we consider that very few maps have survived of pre-1948 Jaffa that highlight Arab points of interest (beyond religious or official buildings), Dajani's maps are important tools in helping to reconstruct an Arab landscape of the city, not just for historians, but also for its present Arab population.[107]

Another map included in the memorial book of Salama, this time of a bus route that ran from Jaffa through Salama to the surrounding villages, reveals the connections, or "integrated regionalism," that existed during the pre-1948 period between Salama and Jaffa to the west and the villages extending all the way to Birzeit on the east (map 8). Not only does the place-

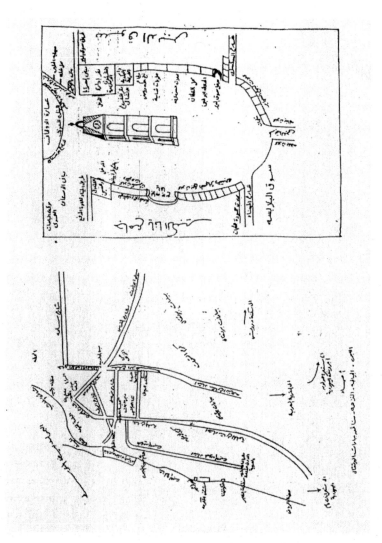

Map 7. Hand-drawn "Memory Maps" of the region outside Jaffa's Old City. (al-Dajani, n.d., pp. 41, 43.)

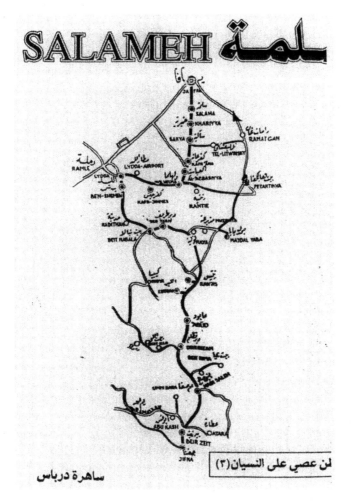

Map 8. Jaffa Bus Company bus route, 1940s. (Dirbas, 1993.)

ment of this map on the cover of the book elevate a once "mundane map . . . to iconic and mnemonic status,"[108] it also literally rewrites the modern geography or terrain of the region, reawakening connections between the coastal and central regions of the country that are otherwise difficult to imagine within its present geopolitical and demographic borders.

A closer examination of the Salama book reveals that it contains several reproductions of family lineages from an earlier memorial book on the village published by Birzeit University[109] and discussions of the families and clans of the village. Documenting the former presence is more important than the documentation itself; it is almost impossible to make out the names on what are clearly photocopies of the family trees from the Birzeit book. Copies of the schedule of the Salama Bus Company and letters from it to the government (complaining about what it felt was unjustified obstacles raised by the government to the route) are also provided, as are plans to annex the village to the Jaffa Municipality in last years of the Mandate period, a list of the "martyrs" from the village during the fighting of 1948, and, finally, photocopies of the surviving records of the village's Tabu (Land Registration) Office, which goes on for some sixty pages.[110]

All of this evidence is clearly amassed to demonstrate that the village of Salama, which Zionist-Israeli leaders wanted literally and figuratively to "erase" from the earth after the 1948 war,[111] was once a vibrant and living Palestinian space intimately connected to the surrounding landscape and participating in the struggle for Palestine.[112] To emphasize the contrast between then and now, the author includes a detailed discussion of current Israeli policies of expropriation of the land that was once the village, especially of an old cemetery on Muslim *waqf* land.

An examination of the memoirs of former (mostly bourgeois) citizens of the city also sheds light on how Jaffa was imagined by its citizens—as the "wide-open gate to Palestine," the country's "gleaming city," and the "center of Palestine's politics and national spirit."[113] In fact, Jaffa was considered both the "biggest economic center in Palestine" and "the greatest city in terms of culture and civilization"; its "excellent geographic position and advanced ways of life and fertility of its lands and abundance [lit. "gushing"] of its water" made it a "city of attraction, as is clear from its history."[114]

Two books written by an expatriate Christian Jaffan, Hana Malak, define the memoir genre. The first book, *Zukrayat al-Aʿilat al-Yafiyya: Bayna al-Madi wa-l-Hadar (Memoirs of Jaffan Families: Between the Past and the Present)*, is a collection of memoirs of his family in Jaffa; it contains the names and professions of numerous members of his and other leading families in Jaffa, descriptions of Jaffa's main neighborhoods, and its civil, cultural, and religious—particularly Orthodox—institutions. The second book, *al-Juzzur al-Yafiyyah (Jaffan Roots)*, further documents the histories of the city's leading families and provides more detailed descriptions of Jaffa's neighborhoods and cultural and commercial life, a lengthy description of the destruction of part of the Old City by the British in 1936, and Jaffa's conquest by Israeli forces in 1948.[115]

Malak himself demonstrates the continued connection felt by Jaffa's former residents to the city in the opening lines of the book, which features an ode to the "Children of Jaffa" in the Diaspora: "Our beloved Jaffa is [still] the bride of the sea in her sweet fragrance and perfume of blooming oranges and lemons, planted by out fathers' hands and renewed through the years on the sands . . . of its white sea."[116] Such exhortations demonstrate the pedagogical role intended by most authors for their books vis-à-vis the younger generation(s) of Palestinians, most of whom have never been to Jaffa and only know it through old photographs and the stories of their grandparents.[117] It can also serve as a problematic site for the (re)construction of the city's history by people still grappling with their seeming abandonment of it during its darkest hour.[118]

More recently, the local Arab Jaffan community organization, al-Rabita (Society for Jaffa's Arabs), published a children's book titled *Yafa: 'Urus al-Bahr (Jaffa: Bride of the Sea)*. The book gives us a broad picture of how the contemporary residents of the city view its history and future. Filled with poems, stories, and recollections by older people about Jaffa's beauty and past glory, its young narrators inform children that Jaffa was a "thriving, flourishing, and blossoming city that always loved the stranger."[119]

In fact, *Jaffa: Bride of the Sea* is clearly intended to prompt children to ask their parents questions about the city's history. As one young character asks his grandfather: "Tell us about every inch of Jaffa[,] . . . about the taste of its oranges, [its] fish[,] . . . about the orchards, the port."[120] Another young character exclaims, "How beautiful are the memories!"

The value of the memoirs and memorial books described here lies not in the historical information they provide, most of which can be found in Arabic encyclopedias such as *Biladuna Falastin* and *Mawsu'ah Falastin*. Rather, by focusing on the stories and memories of the families that lived there, they help us to understand how at least one segment of Jaffa's population saw the city in its prime and in doing so provide an important counterpoint to the dominant view of Jaffa as Tel Aviv's backwater, or more recently, tourist attraction and newest yuppie neighborhood.[121]

It is important to note that in almost all the books discussed here Jaffa's Jewish population is completely absent, despite its long tenure there and the important role it played in Jaffa's social and economic life (Jews constituted roughly one-third of the population by the 1940s). It is as if the effacement of Arab Jaffa from Israeli history, in particular, the Israeli narrative of Tel Aviv, has led to a corresponding elision of Jaffa's Jews by the city's former Arab residents. When Jews appear, it is almost always in the context of the fighting of 1921, 1936, and, especially, 1948, when they are depicted as conquerors of the Arab city.[122]

Thus in reading the recollections of Jaffa's city's last mayor, Yusef Heykal, one sees that Tel Aviv is described as late as 1918 as merely consisting of "several houses" near some vineyards north of Jaffa and dependently connected to it.[123] When Heykal describes his trips from Jaffa north to the ʿAuja/Yarkon River (which had to pass through Tel Aviv), there is no mention of Tel Aviv; it is as if the Jewish quarter was not considered worthy of mention by Jaffans, or as if looking back many years, Heykal did not see Tel Aviv even as he "passed through it."[124]

In fact, Tel Aviv as an everyday experience or space is rarely if ever mentioned in the memoirs of (former) Jaffans. Instead, it is usually described in conflictual terms, as having "impoverished and killed" what al-Ghouri describes as "the first port of Palestine,"[125] or as trying "to wipe the name of Jaffa from the map of the world and replace it with Tel Aviv."[126] Other memoirs and histories of Jaffa tend to follow a similar pattern of emphasizing the city's ancient history and then focusing on Jaffa's important role in the "national struggle against the British occupation and the Zionist invasion,"[127] framed by famous poems eulogizing the loss of the city to the Jews.

Usually when the expansion of Jaffa is discussed, there is no mention of the Jewish neighborhoods or of Tel Aviv, although the revolts and violence of the Mandate era are described at great length.[128] On the extreme end, one memoir recounts the danger posed by Tel Aviv to Jaffa by contextualizing it in terms of the larger "Zionist threat to the world," which is "demonstrated" by extensive quotations from *The Protocols of the Elders of Zion*, the authenticity of which, needless to say, is not questioned.[129]

In 1997, the Jerusalem-based Arabic newspaper *al-Quds* ran a nineteen-part series on Jaffa and its history by Abbas Nimr, director of Pious Endowments *(awqaf)* and Religious Affairs for the Palestinian National Authority. From the first installment, Nimr emphasizes Jaffa's past glory and beauty ("Jaffa is the city of beautiful poetry") and its potential for rebirth.[130] He then proceeds to a lengthy description of most of the important families of Jaffa—which, as we have seen, is a central component of almost all Palestinian histories of the city—and explains why Jaffa was the "bride of the sea": "Jaffa is a city of unanimous beauty, charming the peoples, and undergoing numerous changes from the dawn of history."[131] After recounting its history from earliest times to the late Ottoman period, he moves on to the twentieth century, never mentioning the creation or development of Tel Aviv.[132]

Instead, Nimr discusses the Jews in a separate section titled "The Jews of Jaffa," where he explains that they were not an organic part of the city's history. Finally, he compares the annexation of much of Jaffa's land during the Mandate period, and the encirclement of the city by Jewish towns, to the process of Jewish settlement building today, likening its present situation to that of Hong Kong before its return to China.[133] As I discuss in chapter 8, in the late 1990s the Arab community of Jaffa began to speak in similarly nationalistic terms about their neighborhood.[134]

ARAB POETRY ABOUT JAFFA AND TEL AVIV

In perhaps the most famous volume of memories of Jaffa by her former citizens, *Yafa: 'Utr Medina (Jaffa: Perfume of a City)*, nearly all the pieces mention two places, the sea and the vineyards and citrus groves.[135] The shore and orchards that surrounded the city were also well represented in poetry and songs about Jaffa.

If Jaffa was a city of "beautiful poetry," it is not surprising that poetry would reflect both the fond memories and the bitter longing of its former residents. Several poetry conferences in Jaffa during the Mandate period, sponsored by the city's cultural and religious organizations, featured some of the greatest Palestinian and Arab poets of the day.[136] When I asked the Palestinian poet Sa'ud Asadi about poetry on Jaffa, he opened a well-worn copy of one of his collections of poems and, explaining that the orange was the symbol of Jaffa for poets, wrote down one of his poems for me:

> From Jaffa, not from today
> My grieving for you has lasted for so long
> From the days when I was small and the world was secure
> And we ran after the [fruit] seller, And the world was wide,
> And we yelled: What are you carrying, ya Amm?! And from where
> have
> you come?!
> And he would say: From Jaffa, I'm carrying oranges.[137]

Indeed, poets wrote of the "tenderness and rearing" they felt in Jaffa, especially her "fertile land," which was compared to the love and rearing of a child by a parent.[138] Given such fond recollections, the desire to one day return to Jaffa is never absent from their minds. As one poet lamented, "Daily I come with the imaginary hope of return."[139]

Sorrow for the loss of Jaffa is palpable, the city symbolizing what the martyrs of 1948 fought and died for:[140]

> Jaffa, my poor city . . . Jaffa, my wounded city . . .
> Jaffa, my slaughtered country.
> Jaffa, to forget [you] my city, is to cut my throat.[141]

In between these cries are plaintive questions: "Where are the sons of the sea and their lofty pride? Where are the heroes of Tel ar-Rish? Where are the people of Manshiyyeh? Where are the sellers of the Askandar market?"[142]

The following poem combines most of the major themes in Arabic poetry about Jaffa: the fond memories of what was, the longing for return, the imagery of fertility, and life symbolized by the citrus orchards.

> Oh Jaffa, by God we will return to you, carrying the flag and crawling
> Watering your land with the blood of honor, and millions pushing
>   millions
> We will build and raise what was destroyed
> All your men, hand in hand
>
> Jaffa Oh Jaffa
> By God we will return to you
> Quenched by your sweet water for your gardens
> We will lay down under the lemon trees from which above sing the
>   birds.[143]

And again, a poem by al-Afghani, reads:

> Jaffa, upon you are greetings and peace; Jaffa, Bride of the East and of
>   Peace
> Jaffa, I remember you in the evenings, in the afternoons, in the
>   nights, when I wake up at night, and in my dreams
> Jaffa, I remember you when my tears wake me up, and I remember
>   your yesterdays, which stimulate my love
> Jaffa, it is hard for me that you suffer torture; Jaffa, your torture is
>   mine
> I am among the preservers of the promise, still Jaffa preserves my
>   sincerity. [144]

For poetry, as for the memoirs of former Jaffans, the sand and the sea were important themes:

> The sea of Jaffa is our sea
> How many times have we run on its dunes
> And frolicked and played on its beaches.[145]

The poet Kamal Nasr describes the beach with the longing of Diaspora memories:

> Oh the wounded shore in my chest, don't make me feel incapable
> I don't have the power to come here, are you to come to me
> Between us is a gap of suffering.[146]

Equally important, however, Jaffa is also depicted as a symbol of the Nakba, the disaster of 1948. The poet Mahmud Salim al-Hut writes:

> Jaffa, my tears have become dry and converted to blood instead.
>   When will I see you? Is life eternal?

In the evening and the morning my memory is renewed
It is carried in the folds of my soul forever.
How are my Palestinian sisters?
My desire for them is great, as if they are pieces of the Garden of
Eden.
How are you today, oh Jaffa?
Was Jaffa blessed by her conquerors after she was handed over?[147]

Yet the city is also a symbol of future redemption. If for many Diaspora Jaffans the last view of the city was leaving from its port, a well-known song from the Lebanese singer Fairuz, "Mina' Yafa" ("Jaffa Port"), offers hope of return. In it Fairuz—who met with members of the Jaffan community when a delegation from the local community organization, al-Rabita, visited Egypt—sings about fishermen setting out to sea from the port, getting lost, and being forced to battle a great storm at sea. Yet when the sun rose again the next morning the sailboat had miraculously made it back to shore:

But we returned, we returned with the morning.
We came with the wind, like a sea monster comes.
We filled the shore with shells; Oh, how good was our return to Jaffa.
When the wind was blowing like a storm, we said that we wouldn't
return to Jaffa.
When the wind was blowing like a storm, we said that we wouldn't
return to Jaffa.
And we will return, we return, Oh Jaffa; we will return, we return,
Oh Jaffa.[148]

Perhaps a poem introducing a 1997 brochure from al-Rabita most powerfully describes the feelings of the contemporary Arab Jaffan community about Jaffa and Tel Aviv:

Shall we begin in the destruction of Jaffa and its culture and Arab
civilization or in its judaization?
From where shall we begin, when Jaffa has been judaized for so many
years.
From where shall we begin when 90% of Jaffa's land and houses are
owned by
the Israel Lands Authority?
Shall we begin with the "late" agreements with Amidar and
Gadish?[149]
Or with Tel Aviv Municipality and its neglect concerning Jaffa and
her Arab residents?
Tel Aviv, this city that makes you really feel like you want to vomit
when you write "Tel Aviv–Yafo Municipality."
Where is Tel Aviv from Jaffa, here it embraces your history in
longing, for entering and enfolding your originality.

Here was created from the first moment relations between you and
between space and time.

In Tel Aviv strangers pass in front of you, they pass quickly, and
strange people and languages and dialects, foreign to you and far
from you.

Will it think that this "Tel Aviv" was created in the culture of the city
of Jaffa, and swallowed her blood and sweet nectar in this, what
symbolizes for us "Tel Aviv"?

Is it possible that this unplanned city to swallow the ancient
Cana'anite city, cleaving to its history and culture?

Did it come to pass for this rooted bride[150] to fear the culture of "Tel
Aviv"?

CONCLUSION

It is ironic that Tel Aviv, whose identity is intertwined with town planning
and architectural discourse, is derided as random or unplanned—an irony
most likely not lost on the local Palestinian Arab community, which is in
the midst of a fifty-year struggle with the Tel Aviv Municipality over control of planning and development in what today is Tel Aviv's "Arab quarter." What is most interesting is that while in many cases Jews are fighting
alongside the Palestinian Arab community against the municipality's policies and against Israel's invasion of Palestinian cities in spring 2002—even
jointly calling for making Jaffa an independent municipality—they seem
to be completely absent from the community's imagination of itself and
the space of Jaffa. Thus in summer 1997, on a chartered bus carrying a delegation from al-Rabita (I was among them) back from a Jaffa Festival sponsored by the Jaffan Diaspora community of Amman, the younger passengers spontaneously began to sing a medley (with the adults soon joining in)
that included a song about Jaffa and more nationalist lyrics:

On and on and on and on, Jaffa on my mind.
Jaffa is Arab; Muslims and Christians, on and on[!] Oh Jaffa.
This night, this night, this night for our sweet enjoyment.
This night, on and on, till the day . . .

We went to the street and raised the flag.
We sung for our country, the sweetest songs . . . songs of freedom,
and national unity, and popular war.
[It is our] way of winning; Rejoice, Oh my country . . .
In [our] hands, like a stone
We defeat [lit. "conquer"] the conqueror with stones.
Oh history, record each detail of what happened.

Here we see not only an obvious allusion to the first Intifada but also that neither Jews nor Tel Aviv are included in the Palestinian Arab imagination of Jaffa. In fact, as I listened to this song and watched the faces of its singers, I knew that it was only a matter of time before a new Intifada occurred in Jaffa, which it did in October 2000, when Jaffa and other Arab towns in Israel erupted in protest and violence in support of their Palestinian compatriots in Jerusalem, Nablus, and Gaza who were engaged in fierce battles with the Israeli Defense Forces after Ariel Sharon's visit to the Temple Mount/Haram al-Sharif in Jerusalem and in response to continuing and in some ways worsening political and economic discrimination against their own communities. The remaining three chapters shed light on how this came to be.

6 Ceci N'est Pas Jaffa
(This Is Not Jaffa)

Architecture, Planning, and the Evolution of National Identities in Jaffa and Tel Aviv, 1880–1948

> We shall not dwell in mud huts; we shall build new more beautiful and more modern houses. . . . Indeed, we shall build in a bolder and more stately style than was ever adopted before, for we now possess means which men never yet possessed.
>
> THEODORE HERZL, *The Jewish State*

> It seems to be no matter of mere chance but rather natural that it is the architect who should be among the first to realize the change in the structure of the world because he feels the structural elements to be his own personal prerogative.
>
> ERICH MENDELSOHN, *Palestine and the World of Tomorrow*

> Money we don't have[,] . . . a plan we do have.
>
> ONE OF THE FOUNDERS OF TEL AVIV

In its lead editorial celebrating Israel's fiftieth anniversary, the *New York Times* singled out the city of Tel Aviv for praise, noting that it has become "a hub of modern architecture and commerce" in an economy that "rivals Western Europe in per-capita wealth and technical sophistication."[1] Five years later, UNESCO announced that "the White City of Tel Aviv," that is, the central and northern neighborhoods that possess the greatest concentration of International Style architecture in the world, has been designated a World Heritage Site, specifically because they represent a "synthesis of outstanding significance of the various trends of the Modern Movement in architecture and town-planning . . . adapted to the requirements of a particular cultural and geographic context."[2]

This focus on Tel Aviv and its architecture as a symbol of Israel's modernity, prosperity, and Europeanness by the *New York Times*[3] and UNESCO is not a coincidence. It returns to the founding ideology of Zionism: in imagining the urban "old-new land" in which his utopian treatise, *The Jewish*

State, would unfold, Theodore Herzl populated his city with the most "beautiful and modern houses." He did this not just for the sake of the city's residents but also because he felt that the city's buildings—what he termed its "beautiful types"—would form "part of our propaganda."[4] More than a century later UNESCO confirmed his vision when it informed the world that Tel Aviv—as distinct from "ancient Jaffa"—represented "modern organic planning principles" and an "implementation of the modernist ideas into the local conditions" in a manner that today retains "universal value."[5]

Like his contemporaries throughout Europe and America, Herzl realized the important symbolic role of architecture in anchoring the quest for national identity in the built environment, that is, of endowing the "national home" with a suitable physical form.[6] Thus in 1911, two years after the founding of Tel Aviv, the professional journal the *Architectural Record* reported that "the problem of town-planning in its final form is essentially an architectural problem";[7] and the architect, now technocrat—as Derick Penslar has demonstrated, "technocracy" was as fundamental to Zionism as it was to French or German political and scientific discourses— "saw his superiority guaranteed in his power to outline plans, make projects."[8] Whether in Europe, the colonies, or Palestine, what made the plans and projects—and the men who conceived and implemented them—so powerful was the belief that the new "sciences" of urban planning and architecture were above politics and concerned only with the long-range public good.[9]

Yet as Gendolyn Wright has observed saliently, even the most aesthetic designs have political implications.[10] Perhaps the most important site for the contestation of politics and aesthetics or architecture during this period was in the debates over how much of a "clean slate" was required to create the "new" and what to "conserve" of the "old" in the (re)design of modern cities.[11] The conflicting motivations of planners and architects was well summarized in the London Town Planning Conference of 1910, at which one participant warned against the idea of "the iconoclastic city planner who yearned for a 'clean slate' that he might make designs untrammelled by the past."[12]

This admonition was particularly relevant to architects and planners working in the European colonies, where the physical and epistemological separation of "old" and "new" cities, cultures, and civilizations was a cornerstone of colonial discourse. Its relevance to Zionist architecture and planning in Palestine during the late Ottoman and Mandate periods will become clear in the course of this chapter, which reveals the history of architectural and town planning discourses in Tel Aviv and Jaffa to be a unique lens through which to investigate the unfolding relationship between the Zionist enterprise and the indigenous Arab population of Palestine.

The literature on the architectural history of Palestine/Israel is almost exclusively from a Zionist and Israeli perspective. These studies have tended to be descriptive and teleological more than analytic and critical. In view of this, I take up the call issued by the French architect and critic Georges Bataille to trace and expose the "cracks that frustrate plans and shatter [the] monuments" of modern, in this case Zionist, architecture, that is, to interrogate the epistemological and ideological underpinnings of Zionist planning and architecture during this period.[13]

A CITY FROM THE SANDS, PART III

In welcoming Lord Alfred Milner to Tel Aviv in 1922, Dizengoff described it thus: "This whole little town, as far as the eye can discern straight streets and modern buildings, is Tel Aviv. Thirteen years ago not a single house existed in these parts [note: this is not true], nothing but sand dunes covered the region."[14] What is particularly interesting about this assertion is the fact that the "modern" architecture of "Tel Aviv Haktana," or Little Tel Aviv, still used the local "Arab" idioms and construction techniques that were labeled "traditional" when used in the Arab (or pre-Zionist Jewish) parts of the city.

Dizengoff's narrative also reveals the first "crack" in the discourse of Zionist architecture, planning, and nationalism, a fissure that points to the importance of the International Style that came to dominate the city in the 1930s precisely because it was interpreted as a clear and radical visual break with existing Arab (and bourgeois European) architecture and thus culture. Particularly interesting in this regard is the work of the Tel Avivan artist Nahum Gutman, whose drawings illustrated the official history of the city as well as his own stories about life in the early years of Tel Aviv. For Gutman, Tel Aviv was literally situated in the middle of a sea of sand (fig. 9). There was no life around it; the Old City of Jaffa was a blur in the distance, while a guardian angel protected the new Jewish colony from above. And in fact Gutman's pictures were constantly used as illustrations of early Tel Aviv in books, articles, and the *Town Gazette*.[15]

In another well-known drawing of the first building of Ahuzat Bayit, Gutman depicts a completely barren landscape except for one tree, the train tracks, and three dung beetles. Underneath he writes: "[T]his is a view of the place on which was built the neighborhood 'Ahuzat Bayit.' . . . The beetles that are swarming in the sand—were the first citizens of this place."[16]

Figure 9. Drawing by Nachum Gutman depicting Tel Aviv before World War I. (Gutman, 1989.)

What makes Gutman's renderings so interesting, beyond the fact that they were inaccurate,[17] is that Gutman knew they were inaccurate and in fact discussed the interaction between Jews and Arabs, particularly the Arab laborers who built the suburb, in his stories and prose writings.[18] Although he could acknowledge the Arab presence in his writings, in his visual imagining the land had to be barren and empty, "a land without a people for a people without a land," as the well-known Zionist slogan put it.[19]

Indeed, if the area of Karm al-Jabali on which Ahuzat Bayit was built might have been primarily sand dunes, it comprised only about 6 percent of the land of Tel Aviv in 1922 and less than 1 percent by the mid-1940s. Perhaps a more appropriate moniker for Ahuzat Bayit would have been "the neighbourhood on the dunes."[20] Either way, it is clear that this notion of a city born out of the sands was a fundamental trope in the Tel Avivan self-imagination. Below I examine how the discourse of the sands was reflected in the city's architecture.

Ceci N'est Pas Jaffa

In writing "This is not a pipe" under his famous drawing of a pipe, the French artist René Magritte intended to call into question the validity of modern forms of representation and perception, as well as the power of writing to subvert what was before the eyes. Although such high philosophical and critical principles most likely did not motivate the founders of Tel Aviv, the numerous writings and visual depictions of Tel Aviv clearly display a similar intention to subvert the eyes of all who would view their new town after leaving Jaffa.

For Tel Aviv's founders, the attempt to separate physically as well as ideologically and espistemologically their new neighborhood from Jaffa and its existing Arab and Jewish quarters was a primary concern because they had more than just the presence of Jaffa to contend with: Tel Aviv was the eleventh Jewish neighborhood established in Jaffa since 1887, and at least twenty Muslim and Christian neighborhoods were established outside the Old City since the second half of the nineteenth century.[21] The creation of Tel Aviv was therefore part of a larger process of the city's physical and cultural expansion (in which Muslims and Christians also participated, even anticipated). Yet because it was not created ab nihilo, it was clear that Tel Aviv would have to be qualitatively different from Jaffa's Jewish neighborhoods that had been established beginning in the late 1880s.[22]

Neve Tzedek was envisioned by its founders as "a clean, well-planned neighborhood in the standards of those days. The homes were small and attractive, and although the streets and sidewalks were narrow, they were straight and clean. . . . The streets of Neve Tzedek were considered the broadest and the homes, the most beautiful in Jaffa."[23] This might sound like a good model on which to build the "first Jewish city" of Palestine, but the founders of Tel Aviv needed their quarter to be different. As one Zionist historian recounts it, for them, the founding of Tel Aviv had to be a revolutionary event. Here, for the first time, the urban Jewish *yishuv*—its national and cultural independence—would be revealed in the form of its houses and the character of its streets.[24]

Thus it was generally held that "as an Arabic city, or almost one, the Jewish neighborhoods . . . were built according to the 'taste' and 'order' of an Eastern city. . . . [T]here was no architectural plan, curved alleyways, heaps of apartments and filthy places—this is the accepted manner in all the neighborhoods of an eastern city and Jaffa among them . . . and in the Jewish neighborhoods in Jaffa."[25] Architecturally, as Ilan Shchori explains it, these early suburbs were of the "crowded East European style mixed with local Arab styles, like the first neighborhoods outside the old city of Jerusalem."[26] Homes had closed courtyards and high walls around them, with Arab-style flat roofs and arches; they were "not just Arab in ownership but also in plan, construction and form."[27]

This style was predominant, according to Smilansky, because "those who built in Neve Tzedek were Jerusalemites and . . . had no perception of more spacious neighborhoods and built densely in Jaffa as well. . . . This pitiful state of affairs was caused and continues to be caused even now by the fact that our brethren frequently inhabit the dwellings of Arabs, and when they began to build they imitated the style of Arab buildings. Another reason may have been that these homes were built by Arabs, using the methods and materials they knew best."[28]

Here two more cracks appear in the Tel Avivan discourse—first in the laying of blame for Neve Tzedek's "problems" on the fact that it had been built by Arabs when Tel Aviv, as we have seen, was also built by non-Jewish hands; second, between the "straight, clean and well-planned" streets envisioned by Neve Tzedek's founders and the "curved, unplanned and Eastern" Neve Tzedek perceived by the founders of the new suburb. Apparently, ideology has many powers, including the ability to warp space, in this case changing straight streets into curved alleys.

Nevertheless, it is clear that a central theme of the founders' debates was their desire to avoid building just another Jewish neighborhood of Jaffa. As I explained in chapter 3, their goal was to "establish a Hebrew urban center in a healthy environment, planned according to the rules of aesthetics and modern hygiene in the place of the unsanitary housing conditions in Jaffa."[29] As adjacent lands were purchased and other new neighborhoods planned, steps were taken to ensure that "attention will be paid to all the modern facilities of Europe."[30]

It was this "modern" rationality and consequent rejection of the older Jewish neighborhoods of Jaffa that has led scholars such as Yossi Katz to consider Tel Aviv "the first Zionist urban undertaking in Palestine,"[31] as a modern self-identity and rejection of the existing indigenous Palestinian Arab or Jewish culture were defining features of Zionist ideology. The most obvious way to achieve this was through physical and spatial separation from the existing Arab and, even more interesting, *galut* Jewish environment;[32] not surprisingly, the leadership of Ahuzat Bayit agreed that new land purchases had to be as far away from Arabs as possible.[33]

Yet the desire to separate physically from "Arab" Jaffa did not signal the abandonment of Jaffa; quite the opposite development was intended. After reviewing the situation in the Jewish neighborhoods of Jaffa, Arthur Ruppin, then head of the Jewish National Fund office in Jaffa, explained the function of Tel Aviv thus: "I do not think that I am exaggerating when I say that the creation of a well-built Jewish quarter will present the most important step toward the economic conquest of Jaffa by the Jews."[34] Similarly,

Dizengoff, who was proud of the fact that "the Jews created a state within a state" in Jaffa by the time Tel Aviv was established,[35] felt that the solution to the "Arab problem" in general and in Tel Aviv in particular would be to "channel resources as quickly as possible to build the economic infrastructure of a Jewish society, a rapidly developed, modern and efficient urban and industrial society."[36]

The implications of this "conquest" are clear. As an official from the Palestine Zionist Executive Committee wrote in a 1923 letter: "What [we] should like to do is to give the Arabs the same sort of interest in the Jewish national home as the *foreign* investor has in the stability of any country where his money has been put."[37] But while the official Zionist rhetoric saw the Jewish National Home and the Palestinian Arabs as inhabiting two separate and autonomous social, economic, *and* physical spaces, the Arabs living in and around Jaffa understood well the consequences of their estrangement from the social and economic space of the Jewish National Home.

Urban Planning and Architecture in Tel Aviv

The period in which Tel Aviv was born was a pivotal one in the development of the philosophy underlying both modern architecture and town planning in Europe. In 1909 the first proposal for the comprehensive town planning bill for London was put forth,[38] and only months before the groundbreaking of Ahuzat Bayit, the *Architectural Record* reported that "the best opportunities for effective work were in the undeveloped parts of cities, and here there should be a plan to which the city should gradually adapt itself."[39]

Moreover, because most of the Jewish architects in Palestine had come from or studied in Germany, the urban development and architecture of the region was deeply influenced by German planning's dual focus on the proper conceptualization of the nation-state–city relationship and the need to bring "order out of chaos";[40] the modern nation, Jewish or European, could not be born out of chaos. In the same vein, the building of Tel Aviv was seen as having a fundamental role in the realization of a Zionist homeland and the first step in the desire of Zionist planners to make Palestine a laboratory for urban design.[41] Whatever the competing socialist and capitalist visions for the city, each "envisioned Tel Aviv in terms of an integrated complex of values in which physical form not only reflected the city's social and political characteristics but contributed to shaping them."[42]

Similarly, in 1910 the *Architectural Record* opined:

> [T]he towns of today . . . are the embodiment of a wealth producing energy; and they have lost the joy of life. . . . They are pathetic fig-

ures—prematurely aged, unnaturally slow—lacking the efficiency that we must hope will come with years and with fuller development. Today the cities are illustrative of child-labor, straining against physical handicap, rather than rejoicing in their strength for labor. That is not right. We *city doctors* have no greater duty than to develop these half-grown child-cities into man-cities, fitting them or the men's work that they are so feverishly attempting to do.[43]

Recalling the discussion in chapter 1 of the cartographic-geographic nature of language, what David Prochoska has termed a "grammar of perception" had to develop, one that would help planners and architects to "read" the city and its new plans, which the great British town planner Patrick Geddes wrote were "no mere diagrams: they are a system of hieroglyphics in which man has written the history of civilization."[44] It was clear that only a scientist, a "doctor," could understand, manipulate, and implement the new system of town planning and the richly symbolic, uniquely powerful language that arose along with it.

From the Garden City design enshrined in Tel Aviv's charter to the International Style that dominated the city's architecture by the mid-thirties, architecture and town planning marked the locus of the material- and ideological-spatial discourses that emerged during this period. Significant work has been done on the architectural history of Tel Aviv.[45] Most of it, however, has compared the Tel Aviv "style" to European trends and either ignored the influence of local architecture or simply opposed the "modern" building styles and design of Tel Aviv to "traditional" Jaffa.

My research challenges the assumptions underlying these methodologies. There are many avenues through which to investigate the ideological implications of the changing architecture and urban design of Tel Aviv; my examination encompasses four: the Garden city design that marked the early development of the city, the eclectic architecture of the 1920s, the dominance of Bauhaus, or International Style, architecture in the 1930s, and the planning and architecture of the Ajami, the most "modern" part of Jaffa, which in many ways mirrored and even anticipated that of Tel Aviv. This discussion both opens the "official story" of Zionist architectural historiography and clarifies how each reflected the increased level of separation between the two communities.[46]

The Garden City model, developed by the English planner Ebenezer Howard at the turn of the twentieth century, was perceived by planners and the "more enlightened" public as the most progressive planning direction of the day.[47] As Zionism was seen by its leaders as a dynamic, progressive force, the founders of Ahuzat Bayit naturally chose a plan that would reflect their self-perception—the Garden City model.

According to Gilbert Herbert and Silvina Sosnovsky, the arrival of the Garden City idea was a "case of culture transfer" from Europe to the Middle East.[48] It arrived in Palestine via Germany, where it was first "allied with more progressive social and architectural trends" than were operating in England at the turn of the century. Once in Palestine, it underwent a process of adaptation to Zionist ideology, political realities, economic constraints, and what Lewis Mumford once called "the obdurate facts" of site.[49]

More specifically, the Garden Suburb design sought to provide a solution to the many problems endemic to European cities in the wake of the industrial revolution.[50] Jaffa, as Palestine's main port, center for immigration, and rising industrial city, suffered from the overcrowding and "disorder" common to most growing European cities. Thus "Tel Aviv was founded as a garden city for educated Zionists who still ha[dn't] completely forgotten the dream of moving to the country and engaging in self-labor."[51]

These symptoms of modern industrial urbanization were understood by the Zionist leadership rather to be symptoms of the city's backwardness. In contrast to this supposed state, the first clause of the bylaws of Ahuzat Bayit announced that "the aim of this group is the founding of a modern Jewish quarter in Jaffa."[52] To this day most Israeli historians and geographers see Tel Aviv as heralding an important turning point, not just for the Zionist enterprise in Palestine, but also "for the development of Jaffa[, which] rapidly became the nucleus of a city which was Jewish, modern, distinctive, and autonomous."[53]

In conceiving of Ahuzat Bayit as a Garden Suburb, the founders of Tel Aviv did not envision building a separate city; Jaffa would continue to serve as the urban center for the suburb's residents, providing services to its residents;[54] this is why Ruppin was so keen on "conquering it economically." Rather, the new suburb was to be built according to a master plan and be circumscribed by an agricultural belt.[55] Several architects—all from Germany or Austria—were asked to draw up plans for the new suburb, and after much discussion, the plan offered by the Viennese architect Wilhelm Stiasni was chosen because of its aesthetically pleasing design and central placement of the quarter's main street and public building, the Herzl Gymnasium, about which more below.[56]

In contrast to the earlier Jewish neighborhoods of Jaffa, Stiasni's plan and Ahuzat Bayit's bylaws limited the number of houses that could be built and provided for the allocation of ample open space and public and private gardens. Moreover, the bylaws "extended to *all aspects of public life.* Building laws were devised by experts, architects and physicians in such a way as to insure adequate space between houses, adequate room ventilation and clean courtyards"; "in general, attention w[as] paid to all the facilities of Europe."[57]

The members of Ahuzat Bayit hoped to create a "Jewish urban center in a healthy locality, laid out in a most comely manner and in observance of the laws of hygiene, so that instead of the filth and excrement in the present Jaffa houses we will find a resting place amidst gardens and fresh air."[58] In this they were following Howard's preoccupation with creating an environment to encompass proper "social processes," in contrast to the overriding importance of physical form in later Zionist architecture.[59]

The colonial twist to the Zionist implementation of the Garden City concept was the twin ideas that the new suburb should be spatially and ethnically segregated from the mother town. Thus it would have to be situated at a distance from the city in order to maximize its autonomy, and only Jews could live in the neighborhood (the bylaws prohibited the sale or renting of houses to Arabs).[60] Yet while the Garden City paradigm and the spatial expansion of Tel Aviv reveal the separatist ideology that was the raison d'être of the Jewish city's establishment, it was still too early to establish a Jewish national architecture, in contrast to the existing Arab or Arab-European hybrid architecture.[61] Thus the main arguments among members at the time concerned the desirability of using Arab building style and stone versus the lower costs and newer technology of cement block construction.[62]

The houses built during the first years of Tel Aviv were therefore of two types—the "Arabic-Yafo" style and "European." Both resulted in a practical and instrumental architecture, comprising local Arabic construction and adornments of the houses from different "European" and "Eastern" styles.[63] In contrast to the houses in Neve Tzedek and Neve Shalom, which were either walled or joined together, those in Ahuzat Bayit were separate, and all had gardens.

More important than the design, however, was that in adopting Howard's spatiality, Tel Aviv's founders territorialized his "hatred of the city" as an "outright evil and an affront to nature," a perspective that could not recognize any incarnation of the urban that "could not be abstracted to serve [Howard's] Utopia."[64] Of course, this sentiment could not, by definition, be directed toward *their* suburban-turned-urban utopia and so would increasingly be directed at Jaffa and the surrounding "Arab" geography.

A good example of this ideological understanding of architectural form and style is the debate surrounding the design of the Herzl Gymnasium, Tel Aviv's first and premier public institution, around which the neighborhood was built (it was said that "the Gymnasium built Tel Aviv" rather than the other way around). When the Herzl Gymnasium was designed the original plan met with a great deal of criticism because it was deemed too "Oriental," and critics were not satisfied until the size of the central dome was decreased and the "Oriental" ornaments were eliminated so that the building looked "less like a mosque" and the overall feeling was an "archaic Jewish style."[65] With these refinements, the Herzl Gymnasium would be the exemplar of a "practical architecture": local Arabic construction mixed with attempts to ornament using different styles but without the "ornate" and decorative ornamentation of "traditional" Arab architecture.[66]

Despite this attempt to achieve a new "archaic" Jewish style, most later commentators would see the Herzl Gymnasium as having been built using "specific Islamic styles";[67] and here another crack in the separatist Zionist architectural and town planning discourse appears, as the gymnasium was not just constructed of the traditional Arab stone building material but also reflected a desire to find a local style that would blend Occidental and European themes. Thus the windows and arches were inspired by traditional Muslim-Arab architecture, but the separation of the building into two wings with a main entrance and large steps in the middle reflected the art nouveau style then dominant in Europe.[68] This desire (however sublimated) to search for a "local" architecture that would combine Arab and European styles while remaining spatially exclusivist and separatist continued into the 1920s.

Architecture and Urban Design in Tel Aviv in the 1920s

Despite its ideological importance for the founders of Tel Aviv, the Garden City ideal could no longer offer a workable guide by the time the British arrived in 1917. The end of the war and the quickened pace of the city's growth—in particular, the need for industry after the influx of Jaffan Jews caused by intercommunal violence of May 1921—left this arrangement of space and form no longer practical.

It should come as no surprise that the leadership of Tel Aviv, especially in the wake of the Balfour Declaration, was overjoyed at the arrival of the British. For their part, British planners found "the transformation of the oldest country into the newest fascinating" and believed that "this paradox gives architects and engineers a golden opportunity,"[69] one that would be expressed in the eclectic style of architecture that had already become dominant in British and French colonies. As important, the British recognition of the importance of town planning allowed a renewed focus on the issue; the enactment of new town planning regulations allowed the Tel Aviv Council to hire at least seven builders and engineers (most of them from Europe), with "good results" achieved.[70]

I have elsewhere discussed the symbiotic relationship between the British and Zionist discourses of development in Palestine in the 1920s and 1930s, and the subject has also been well treated by Barbara Smith.[71] My research revealed that both had similar attitudes regarding the backwardness and stagnation afflicting Palestine and the ultimately beneficial impact of Zionist-inspired modernization. It is no surprise, therefore, that the arrival of the British by and large meant greater support for the growing dominance of Tel Aviv vis-à-vis Jaffa that the Hebrew city's founders had long hoped for.

The influx of people and money into Tel Aviv and the concomitant increase in construction[72] necessitated a new town planning scheme, drawn up by the eminent Scottish planner Patrick Geddes. It also called for a new style of architecture, one that would dominate the city in the 1920s and reflect the changing ideological self-conception of Jews in the city vis-à-vis their Arab neighbors. This style has been termed by most scholars the "eclectic" phase, or "Oriental Eclecticism," and its popularity reveals that architecture was still a meeting place, a liminal space between Palestinian and Jewish-Zionist cultures, during this period.

The term *eclecticism* originated in the nineteenth century, and its free and often inventive combination of European and "Oriental" motifs was a perfect reflection of the contradictions inherent in Zionism as both a "utopian" movement[73] that sought to be a beacon to the East (the emblem of Tel Aviv was the lighthouse, representing its role in bringing European modernity to the sleeping East) and as an exclusivist, settler-colonial movement.[74] It was not just a straight combination of Eastern and Western styles but is better understood as an "integral interpretation" of the two,[75] signifying an attempt to bring together forms from all periods to create a "complete style." One critic revealingly labeled it an "eastern-modern" style—a conjoining of two discourses rarely sanctioned in Zionist ideology, unless it is Zionists who are the agents of that conjoining.[76] The local architecture was thus believed to be, however "primitive," in "harmonious union with the landscape."[77] The buildings built during this period contained elements from styles as disparate as Moorish, neoclassical, neo-Gothic, and art nouveau.

Similar to the more accommodationist "cultural Zionism," and even binationalism, that reached its apex during this decade, many architects felt that only by coming to terms with and carrying on the local Arab tradition in architecture would the new Jewish national home become rooted, as opposed to remaining alien, to the country.[78] Yet it must also be noted that Zionist eclecticism emerged at the same time that the British were attempting to create a new "colonial" style in Palestine, at least in British government or church buildings.[79] And while the development of eclecticism in French colonies—to broaden the context—reflected an often sincere desire by administrators and planners such as Lyautey, Prost, and even Le Corbusier to achieve a harmonious mixing of East and West, such a balance did not disturb the basic hierarchy of culture and civilization on which colonial discourse was erected. We can therefore also understand the reasoning underlying this aesthetic as being rooted in a feeling that the local architecture was "exotic and romantic,"[80] a quaint sentiment that was part of the desire to built a "cocoon" that would be a simulacrum of the local environment while ultimately remaining separate and European.[81]

It is worth noting that the Revisionist movement (the non-"socialist," more openly nationalistic counterpoint to the Labor movement in the yishuv) was also interested in the fate of Tel Aviv. In fact, it believed that "cities [we]re key" to establishing the Jewish majority necessary for creating a state;[82] and even during the "eclectic" 1920s it felt that "the architect building in Eretz Israel must choose whether he is building in an Eastern style or the West."[83] For them, this was pivotal, because even if otherwise imbued with Jewish-Zionist culture, by living in an "Eastern" environment people would be "at war with [their] harmful surroundings."[84] By early in the next decade Tel Aviv's architecture would reflect the increasing militancy of the both the Labor and Revisionist ideologies.

International Style and the Increased Separation of the Two Communities and Cities

Developments in Zionist architecture and design in the 1920s were spawned both by the sincere desire to understand the indigenous society that was shared by many colonial administrators and planners and the continued attempts to arrive at a modus vivendi with the Palestinian population. The change in style with the onset of the 1930s—which mirrored a turn away from Oriental themes and toward modernism in Zionist-Jewish art—can be tied to the countrywide eruption of violence in 1929,[85] although even before this episode, by several accounts around 1927, Zionist architects had begun to "turn back to Europe."[86]

In response to this renewed threat to the emerging Jewish hegemony in Palestine,[87] and also to the economic upswing that was beginning after several very bad years of economic depression in the mid-1920s, a new form of architecture began to take hold that better reflected the increasing separation between the two communities and the ever-increasing need to justify the Zionist project as "an outpost of civilization" in the Middle East, as Zionist leaders from Herzl to Chaim Weizmann had long described it.

Looking back on the first buildings of Tel Aviv from the perspective of the 1930s, the Zionist architect Alexander Levi criticized the existing architecture for its bad form and lack of culture or planning.[88] For Levi, Tel Aviv "needed to be an Eretz Israeli city, not a new Pinsk";[89] more important, he and his fellow architects and planners felt they needed to "stop the creation of a second *galut* in Eretz Israel." They felt it was necessary to have a "Town Planning Commission to stop [their] building from resembling the Diaspora." "[T]he new building style [was] great propaganda," specifically because it aroused respect among people of culture and influence who came to tour the country.[90]

Such sentiments help to explain why the idea of Tel Aviv having been born "from the overturning of geography" was first expressed in 1933, at the height of the penetration of the International Style in the city. The negative focus on *galut* also reveals how the modernist architecture of the 1930s was imbued with the same spatial metaphors of home versus Diaspora that permeated the Zionist imagining of Tel Aviv versus Jaffa. The "turn back to Europe" was furthered by the closing of the Bauhaus school, where seven Jewish-Zionist architects had studied—with the onset of Nazism in Germany in 1933.[91] By the early 1930s, at the same time that many architects were returning from their studies in Europe, "a new architectural climate" developed in the Jewish population, one that opened new ways for building cities in Eretz Israel.[92]

The population of Tel Aviv tripled in the 1930s as thousands of German Jews fled Hitler. This led to increased pressure on the land and more frequent confrontation between Jews and Arabs, and the increase in the already dense population justified the expansion of the city's borders to include the lands of the surrounding villages.

It should come as no surprise that in the environment of the 1930s Zionist architectural discourse became ever more militantly "modernist," just as the larger Zionist argument that the Palestinians were incapable of developing the country, and thus undeserving of ruling or even remaining in it, became ever more vigorous. The International Style–Bauhaus vernacular accorded so well with the Zionist spirit of renewal that by the early 1930s modernism became the visual mold for the Zionist project.[93] Here we might recall the words of Justice Frankfurter that began this story: "Change is inevitable. . . . Palestine is inexorably part of the modern world. No *cordon sanitaire* can protect her against the penetration of the forces behind Western ideas and technology."[94]

The International Style, which also dominated the design of the agricultural kibbutzim in the 1930s,[95] was thus the perfect architectural reflection of the modernity of the West (and thus Zionism) and its ability to

עיר החולות
(ליובל העשרים וחמש לבנין תל־אביב)

Figure 10. Newspaper photograph of an International Style building in Tel Aviv with the words "City of the Sands" written above it. (*Do'ar Hayom*, 1932.)

"master" the "nature" of East. As the well-known German architect Erich Mendelsohn, who immigrated to Palestine in 1934, put it: "The Orient resists the order of civilisation, being itself bound to the order of nature."[96] Only Zionism and not the indigenous Arab population had the tools to master nature and build a modern, flourishing society out of the sand.

As David Ben-Gurion put it in a speech before the Twenty-second Zionist Congress, "development and progress" were the keys to rejuvenating Palestine—if the push toward International Style marked the conflation of economic, political, and ideological-aesthetic motives underlying "development and progress" in Zionist built space, there was no better measurement of their abundance in the Jewish sector than the block upon block of gleaming white International Style buildings being erected in Tel Aviv (fig. 10).[97]

Moreover, like Zionist ideology, International Style discourse refused any accommodation whatsoever to existing urban and social conditions: "The break with the past must be absolute."[98] Why? Because both European and Zionist adherents of International Style believed that if one changed the architecture, society would be forced to follow the program of social change that the architecture embodied.[99] Thus Zionist architects advocated a "triple negation: of Diaspora in favor of national home, bourgeoisie in favor of [socialist] working society, and Orientalism (in fact, of emerging Arab nationalism) in favor of a new collective image."[100] Not surprisingly, then, when the northern part of the city was built in the early 1930s it was composed almost entirely of International Style buildings, while the official history of Tel Aviv written in 1935 described the newer sections of the city as "the old nullified in the new."[101]

Much of the "cleansing" power of International Style discourse can be attributed to its intimate relation with the "functionalist" conception of urban space that dominated architecture and planning during the twentieth century, which was premised on the belief in the need to "to start from a clean slate[;] . . . in the triumph of Modernism, regionalism and environmental identity were ignored."[102] This was a power that Le Corbusier, for one, attempted to exercise on the widest scale possible. Le Corbusier (who was born in 1887, the same year the first Jewish neighborhood of Jaffa was established) had considerable experience in French colonial planning in North Africa, and his influence extended to Zionist architects; of the three principal founders of the Chug (the "circle" of Zionist architects in Palestine), Arie Sharon was a graduate of the Bauhaus and Ze'ev Rechter was greatly influenced by Le Corbusier.[103]

Le Corbusier's understanding of the force that impelled the modern town into existence is particularly relevant to our understanding of the ideology underlying Zionist modernist architecture because, according to him, it not only created order but also destroyed the "disorder" that came before it.[104] In *The City of Tomorrow and Its Planning*, Le Corbusier quotes a Turkish proverb: "Where one builds one plants trees. We uproot them [lit. "root them up"]."[105] This richly symbolic view demonstrates well the drive toward "creative destruction" that David Harvey, building on Schumpeter, has aptly described as characterizing the entire project of modernity[106] and thus Zionism as a quintessentially modern project.

It also helps us to understand how Zionist architecture and planning, especially in the 1930s and 1940s, signaled a "displacement" that both revoked the validity of the "Oriental" architecture and condemned it to an association with an ornamentalism that had no place in the functionalist aesthetic of Zionist modernism.[107] The Zionist architect Julius Posner pointed at the immanent connection between the "erasure of past memories" and the creation of a strictly new, 'modern, clean character of building.'" "We have come to the homeland to build and be rebuilt in it," he wrote. "[It is] the creation of the new Jew, but the creator of that Jew as well."[108]

Figure 11. Tel Aviv, "the White City," 1937. (TAMA Library.)

Even more important, as Lefebvre convincingly argued, International Style and the Bauhaus school represented a culmination of the emerging awareness of space and its production: Bauhaus "artists" had the power to "create" space through the uniting or art and technology under a "purified aesthetic" that was in fact motivated by a "strong political ideology."[109] This link between aesthetics, technocracy, and political-national ideology was particularly strong in Zionist architecture and planning. Viewed this way, it becomes clear that International Style was the first truly "social architecture" in Palestine,[110] where "social" is understood in the productively spatial sense. (See fig. 11.)

The popularity and power of International Style in Tel Aviv can also be linked to the discourse of the sands. Tel Aviv's leaders described Tel Aviv as being built "on the *still clean dunes* where they could live under European conditions not then obtainable in Jaffa."[111] Here we clearly see the functional and ideological connection between the discursive erasure implied by the Zionist–Tel Avivan discourse of birth from the sands and the subsequent dominance of the International Style in the city. As Alona Nitzan-Shiftan explains, the newly discovered absence of a shared visual heritage with the Arabs allowed the region to be constructed as a tabula rasa. Architects could build for the uprooted Jewish refugees "an apartment free from past memories"[112]—memories of the Diaspora and memories of the Arabs as well.

A final factor behind the rise of International Style as it evolved in Tel Aviv was its almost wholesale adoption by the Labor movement, specifically, in the construction of workers' housing at the same time that the movement was becoming both more powerful and more militant politically. During this period, the leading architects of the *yishuv* were integrated into its socialist leadership, which furthered the institutionalization of modern architecture in Tel Aviv and beyond. And to gain such a powerful position, they needed a clear message that reflected the greater public awareness of the social importance of architecture in Europe (particularly Germany) as well as Palestine but that would be perceived at the same time as "primarily a set of solutions to technical and sociological questions" and thus devoid of political implications.[113]

In this framework the deployment of International Style did not just signify a break with locally inspired idioms; as in Europe, it also signified a repudiation of (Zionist) bourgeois society and politics and the concomitant urge to make working-class neighborhoods stand out on the local municipal landscape[114]—a desire that was especially significant in Tel Aviv, since the Labor movement was consistently at war with the bourgeois leadership of the municipality.[115]

Yet although the International Style, with its functional contours, was initially a symbol of workers' cooperative housing in Tel Aviv—primarily because of the concentration of these structures in the large housing complexes—in the 1930s and 1940s it became "the accepted style in the city as a whole, including its private construction."[116] The symbolic force of the new architecture was put to much greater and better use in the larger nationalist discourse than it was in intracommunal Jewish class struggles. By the late 1930s Tel Aviv's leaders boasted of the "magnificent buildings" that "brought Tel Aviv fame as a modern and advanced [or "progressive"] city."[117]

As I have argued in the previous three chapters, Zionist urbanization, like European colonialism, could not provide for innovation or progress in Jaffa because Zionists had reserved this prospect for themselves.[118] Within this ideological framework, International Style architecture served as the ultimate expression of loyalty to the West and to "modernity" versus tradition. As the *Israel Yearbook* of 1995 explained in a special section on the International Style architecture of Tel Aviv, the "absence of any architectural tradition allowed for the fast growth of the modern style. . . . Although the architects wanted to achieve links to the East, their loyalty was to modernism and links to the West." Even more interesting, the Tel Aviv municipal architect Nitza Smok titled her monograph on International Style in Tel Aviv *Houses from the Sand*, which reveals both how by the 1930s all attempts at reaching an accommodation with the indigenous population were over—it was back to a creation ex nihilo scenario for the establishment of Tel Aviv—and how this paradigm still dominates current reflections on the influence of Bauhaus and on the larger historiography surrounding the creation of the city.

This ambivalence was reflected in the writings of architects such as Mendelsohn[119] and in the professional literature, specifically in the architectural journal of the Chug, *Habinyan Bamizrach Hakarov (Building in the Near East)*, that was started in 1934 by Jewish architects in Palestine "to guide the development of architecture in the country."[120] The journal contains numerous contradictions in its portrayals of Arab architecture. On the one hand, its editors believed that any comparisons of the modern parts of Jaffa and of Tel Aviv would "fall without any doubt to the better for Jaffa"[121] and reported that Arab architects were looking to Italy and France for inspiration. On the other hand, they criticized new Arab building in Jaffa (using the new water tower as an example, whose design they decried as resembling a minaret) by saying that it "lacks any expression of the life of the people, the connection with the society that created it."[122]

Moreover, in contemplating what elements of the local style to retain, the editors clearly constructed and referred to an "ideal" type of Arab house, one they claimed has not developed or changed over time, that could be juxtaposed to the progressive European type: "[T]he arrangement of the Arab apartment houses is unacceptable in building a Jewish apartment house, and that Arab apartment houses, as opposed to mosques, are not good, do not [achieve] the importance of the Arab art of building. So we cannot use Arab houses as models, specifically because the whole structure of Arab society and of gender divisions in the home means that Arab houses need to be divided in ways that Jewish ones do not."[123] What makes this analysis so interesting is that, as Nathan Harpaz points out, in the early years of Tel Aviv the "natural connection with Jaffa" was reflected in the style of the neighborhood's houses; thus even the design of the houses often was of the "Middle Eastern type," that is, one large central room surrounded by smaller rooms.[124]

THE VIEW FROM THE OTHER SIDE(S): PALESTINIAN ARCHITECTURE AND PLANNING IN JAFFA

While Europeans and Zionists might have the traditional Palestinian building styles inferior, no less an authority than Patrick Geddes, in his Town Plan for Tel Aviv of 1925, wrote that "it is important to realize that this [Arab] architecture and decorative art, at their best, are second to none in the world."[125] Geddes understood, as Shukri Arraf points out, that the existing Arab architecture served quite practical and "rational" ends. For example, the narrow, winding, covered streets of the Old City were not "unplanned" or irrational but rather were designed that way: The narrow and twisted roads were good for defense, as they would slow any army attempting to invade the city; the roofs shaded the markets and reduced humidity so that people could display their fruits and vegetables.[126]

The ambivalent relationship of Tel Aviv with Jaffa during the 1920s, represented ideologically in the eclectic style of architecture (and in Zionist art of the period),[127] was also reflected in Geddes's town plan. In fact, the Geddes Plan reflects the ambivalence of the British view of Tel Aviv and its development better than almost any other document of the period.

Of course, Geddes, an iconoclastic, non-Jewish Scotsman, was not going to view the Tel Aviv–Jaffa relationship with the same natural bias that Jewish, and even British, planners did. Although he felt uniquely at home in the Jewish city,[128] he began his Town Planning Report of Jaffa and Tel Aviv by writing, "[W]ith all respect to the ethnic distinctiveness and the civic individuality of Tel Aviv, as Township, its geographic, social and even fundamental economic situation is determined by its position as Northern Jaffa. . . . The old town, the modern Township, must increasingly work and grow together . . . for Greater Jaffa."[129] (For this reason alone, it is not surprising that he was ceremoniously thanked and saluted for his efforts by the city fathers, but the plan was never implemented.)

Geddes based his planning for Tel Aviv on his belief that "Tel Aviv of all places, from its very origin, [has been] a transition place and a link between the overcrowded cities of Europe and the renewal of Agricultural Palestine."[130] Because of this spatial and ideological position, he felt that the original Garden Village character of the city should be emphasized in, for example, new housing, particularly for workers in both cities. In this way it would avoid the problems of small, crowded streets that grew in the areas adjoining Manshiyyeh. He also stressed that the 'Auja River and adjacent streams needed to be "deindustrialized" if the natural character of the area was to be preserved and that new rail lines should be built to more efficiently connect Jaffa, Tel Aviv, and surrounding Arab villages, "in the course of which all separate townships will increasingly unite to cooperate as 'Greater Jaffa.' "[131]

Finally, Geddes noted, "[Tel Aviv] has many critics. At first it seems a mere medley, a struggle of individual fancies . . . [132] [While] it is only fair to recognize distinct tendencies towards improvement . . . still, the architectural style of most buildings is of distinctly North European character; whereas we are here in the Mediterranean." Therefore, he felt, an "Orientally" inspired architecture would make sense for geographic and climactic reasons. What is most interesting about Geddes's analysis of Tel Aviv's architecture is his belief that "the present magnificent recovery of classical Hebrew as the spoken language of the Jews of Palestine is of course a first step or re-Orientalisation; but others are needed. [But] it is encouraging to find the beginning of appropriate Oriental feeling in a good many buildings."[133]

Geddes's belief that the return to Hebrew was part of a "re-Orientalization" of the Jews betrayed a misunderstanding of the rationale for establishing the Jewish city, which was in fact to create a separate space, away from Arab and Oriental culture, where Hebrew could be spoken and the Jewish national renaissance could be achieved—without Arabs. It is clear that the Zionist leadership was thinking, not of building a "Greater Jaffa," but, as Dizengoff described it, a "Greater Tel Aviv," in which Tel Aviv would be the commercial, industrial, construction, cultural, educational, financial, and medical center of a region that would include all the surrounding Jewish farms and cities.[134]

Eclecticism and International Style were not confined to Tel Aviv but appeared contemporaneously in Jaffa. Eclecticism was particularly dominant not just in "Arab" Jaffa but in Palestine as a whole, incorporating several European elements imported by foreign architects and embraced by the local bourgeois population. According to Michael Levin, around the turn of the twentieth century "the Oriental elements had declined to a point where they could no longer be a source of influence or inspiration precisely at a time when the architects who came from Europe were eager to espouse them as models to be copied."[135] One can also see in the street layout of Manshiyyeh an attempt to create a European grid pattern as the neighborhood expanded.

An important if little-known study of 'Ajami by Daron Tzafrir, chief architect for Jaffa of the Tel Aviv Municipality (at the time of writing), demonstrates that the development of 'Ajami, in terms of both street design and architecture, mirrors closely the development of Tel Aviv. In fact, at the turn of the century, 'Ajami was thought of by Jews as the best and most modern place to live in Jaffa. Thus when one longtime Jewish resident of Jaffa was told about the coming establishment of Tel Aviv, he exclaimed, "Go live in 'Ajami and enjoy exemplary cleanliness. Move into an attractive, roomy house and stop wasting your time with foolishness."[136]

Just as Tel Aviv was started by a non-Muslim minority community, 'Ajami was started by Maronite Christians, who built a well-groomed neighborhood that would feature a mixture of five building styles, from the most traditional classic peasant house to the most modern International Style residences. Most of the traditional or classic houses were located at the older northern end of the neighborhood, which featured smaller and more winding streets. This style predominated in Palestine at the turn of the twentieth century, when residential quarters first began to be built outside the city walls in large numbers. With its red pyramid-shaped slate roofs, it was also the style of the Jewish neighborhoods created in the 1880s and 1890s as well as that of the Ahuzat Bayit houses that began Tel Aviv.

Slightly farther south one finds the "castle house" style favored by the wealthy of both cities into the 1920s (they are also found around Lilenblum and Nahalat Binyamin Streets in Tel Aviv), which were constructed of silicate instead of stone. For Tzafrir, this style reflected a changing urban view from the traditional to the modern, as it took on the air of a European-style villa though it retained many "Eastern" ornamentations.

Yet another housing style that became quite popular in the first two decades of the twentieth century was the "adorned" house, which represents the first attempt to build apartment houses in the city to ease overcrowding. It also combined local and European styles. Finally, moving farther south, the street becomes a bit straighter and International Style houses appear, which demonstrates that "as a port city Jaffa was always connected with Europe and was subject to its cultural influences. The modernist revolution did not pass over Jaffa."[137]

In Jaffa as in Tel Aviv, International Style signified "modern" building and was thus adopted as the style of choice in the 1930s and 1940s by many of the city's wealthier residents, as well as for public buildings. In fact, International Style was used as a propaganda tool by the Arab as well as Zionist movements in their respective presses and publications, which featured photographs and articles about the newest buildings in their respective cities.[138]

Yet we cannot deduce from the fact that there were International Style buildings that their inhabitants were the most "modern" or "Western" residents of the city. As one former resident noted when she visited Jaffa for the first time in many years: "We went past my great-uncle's house which is now the residence of the French Consul. It was and is a grand modernist Bauhaus mansion—all straight cream-colored streamlined lines. My aunt said that it had been his dream house and was one of the most modern houses in Palestine in the 1940s with all the modern amenities, including central heating. She also said he was from the most conservative end of the family—and his wife and girls rarely went out—so much for architectural determinism."[139] In other words, modernity, as Fredric Jameson has pointed out, had became a commodity or a status symbol, no longer (if ever) reflecting a larger cultural or epistemological weltanschauung.[140]

The owner of the home, according to his great-nephew, was a "home-grown entrepreneur, [a] self-made man," who did not come from a long line of rich people. Yet

> he became a citrus exporter, then a citrus grower, and was also an importer of machinery, mostly irrigation machinery, and the head of the Jaffa Chamber of Commerce and City Council member. . . . As for why he built a house in such an avant-garde style even though he was a conservative man; it would be important to understand the notion of conservatism of the time. Palestinian people were hungry for education and made sure that their children could go to schools of all kinds and levels. . . . Along with this hunger for education was a hunger for learning and acquiring technology of the time, including irrigation and pumping systems, flour mills, cement block making plants, and the basics of the age including foundries, etc. To the best of my knowledge, my uncle, who had visited Europe several times, had seen the modern style and wanted it for himself. People from the middle class of Jaffa thought nothing of acquiring the latest in needed practical technology, and therefore importers of machinery were important in supplying this need.[141]

Jaffa's development can be described from a planning as well as an architectural perspective. We can chart three distinct planning regimes from Napoleon's 1799 occupation through the late Ottoman period. The first was initiated during the tenure of Abut Nabut, the first Ottoman governor after the invasion, who sponsored the construction of several "beautiful markets" and stores as well as his more famous mosque and fountain. For subsequent Arab planners, this period was considered the beginning of Jaffa's "golden era," as the Egyptian town planner ʿAli Masʿud described it in his 1945 plan of Jaffa.[142]

As the century drew to a close, roads were constructed into newer neighborhoods or industrial-commercial areas outside the Old City, the most important of which was Boustros Street, which became the commercial center of the new part of town for both Arabs and Jews and featured buildings constructed in a range of styles.[143] By the beginning of the twentieth century Jaffa had undergone a transformation into the center of an urban region whose power and economy were expanding, which Arabs and Jews "saw [as] an urban center in which to expand their industrial, trading and cultural activities."[144] This is exactly why the fathers of Tel Aviv had the luxury of designing their city as a Garden Suburb, without an industrial or commercial district.

The next upsurge in "planned" development occurred during World War I under the rule of Hassan Bey, whom Masʿud called a "lover of development" because his projects "greatly improved and beautified the city."[145] As discussed in chapter 3, Hassan Bey strove to ensure that the land to the northwest of the Old City would remain open for development by Jaffa (not Tel Aviv), and thus he established a large *waqf* and built a mosque (which bore his name) as far north as possible, which quickly became a symbol of Jaffan, in fact Palestinian, resistance to Tel Aviv and Zionism until the end of the Mandate period.[146] As already mentioned, Jaffa's last mayor, Yusuf Heykal, credits the creation of the mosque and the surrounding *waqf* land with preventing the southward expansion of Tel Aviv.[147]

Hassan Bey also constructed or widened other streets, improved roads to the port, and tore down many buildings in the Old City to make way for new streets. The new region built north of the Clock Tower, particularly Jamal Pasha Street, which was cut through orange groves to the east of the Old City, was clearly a direct Jaffan "answer" to Tel Aviv's Rothschild Street, both of which had central promenades lined with trees.[148]

During the Mandate period, especially the 1930s and 1940s, there were numerous private and publicly sponsored development projects in Jaffa, which resulted from the "need to quickly implement plans to beautify the city and widen its streets" so that the "black stain" might be removed.[149] In 1931 (and again in 1933) new "plans to develop Jaffa," including new building regulations, were announced with great fanfare by the municipality. However, the press was skeptical whether the five-year, one-million-pound project, on the level of projects for Beirut and Damascus, would actually benefit residents.[150] The 1933 plan met with similar skepticism.[151]

The government approved plans, along with municipal initiatives, for enlargement of the area of Jaffa Port and the building of new hospitals and cinemas, construction of many new roads in the city's newer neighborhoods (in one case requiring the partial destruction of a mosque in the Irshid quarter) and widening or paving existing ones (such as Faisal, Jerusalem, and Irshid Streets, and others near the port), installing water and sewage pipes into homes throughout the city (and building a water tower in 'Ajami), and creating new gardens, particularly in the al-Basah land southeast of the Old City.[152]

The continued development of the city, coupled with the violence of 1936, led the government to reexamine its previous plans and possibly completely revise them.[153] The first plan considered in the wake of the revolt was to redevelop the area of the Old City, to "cover up" its partial destruction by the Royal Air Force in June 1936.[154] This plan, based more on military and public relations than on "planning" considerations, was never implemented. A second one was approved and initiated in 1937–38; it "molded the face of Jaffa as a 'Garden City' on the sea."[155]

The goal of the plan was to increase the built-up area of the city by constructing a garden suburb of 1,970 dunams in the south between the Jewish towns of Bat Yam and Mikveh Israel, on land that was partially orchards and partially sand. On the margins of the plan (and seemingly pushed as far away as possible from the center of town) was the rehousing scheme for residents of the Old City who became homeless as a result of the June 1936 demolition that was vociferously opposed by the adjacent Jewish neighborhoods.[156] When Mas'ud ultimately offered his 1945 plan, he ignored the "Jaffa Rehousing Scheme" proposed by the government; even more, he transformed the Garden Suburb into a new one that mixed straight grid patterns with winding streets, broad boulevards and circuses, squares and green spaces, all intended to give it the character of the best Mediterranean cities, making it—even more than Jerusalem—"the true capital of Arab Palestine."[157] (See map 9.)

In laying out the rationale for his plan, Mas'ud explained that were it not for Tel Aviv's surrounding the city on the north and east, Jaffa would have had much more room to expand and develop.[158] Because of this problem, he suggested expanding Jaffa's borders to include the surrounding small villages,[159] as occurred in other urban regions of the country. Given these factors, Mas'ud felt that two considerations were central to the implementation of his plan. The first was to strengthen the main arteries that connected central Jaffa to outlying neighborhoods on a "radial" grid, and from them, to Jerusalem, Gaza, and Haifa. This grid can perhaps be under-

Map 9. Town plan for Jaffa by ʿAli Masʿud, 1945. (TAMA Library.)

stood as recognizing the long-standing relationship between the city and surrounding peasant and bedouin communities. Indeed, this relationship was forged in large part through the annual Nebi Rubin Festival held near Jaffa, which for generations attracted pilgrims from throughout Palestine and was so important that according to tradition, "the Jaffa Mohammedan women [would] say to their husbands: 'Either you take me to Rubin or you divorce me . . . or I divorce you.'"[160]

The second consideration was to deploy a new grid system for new street construction and improve the existing street grid system to connect with it.[161] Masʿud also included a new train station in the eastern part of the city, new industrial and commercial regions, the renovation of markets, and expanding and improving the port region.

Map 10. Mas'ud town plan for Jaffa and map of Manshiyyeh with overlapping depiction of existing and future streets. (TAMA Library.)

Despite his concern about Tel Aviv's encirclement of Jaffa, it is clear that Mas'ud did not intend to isolate Jaffa from the Jewish town. In fact, he appears to have taken up Geddes's earlier call to unite the two towns into one region, as his redesign for Manshiyyeh, which necessitated the complete reconstruction of the quarter, replaced its old and narrow streets with wide avenues and promenades specifically designed to flow into the main arteries of both Tel Aviv and Jaffa (map 10).

CONCLUSION: TEL AVIV AND JAFFA AS "COLONIAL" AND "MODERN" CITIES

The town plans of Jaffa of 1937–38 and 1945 are distinguished by their shared vision of a Jaffa that was no longer confined to a narrow strip along the sea but rather was developed in a unique and well-planned manner to the south and east.[162] The numerous projects and instances of development described above demonstrate that Jaffa had been engaged in a decades-long process of economic and cultural "modernization" by the time Tel Aviv was founded that continued with varying degrees of autonomy until the end of the Mandate period.[163] On the other hand, to the extent that the city suffered from dirtiness, noise, and lack of planning, it must be remembered that such complaints were also made about the great metropolitan centers of Europe and the United States during this time.[164] Indeed, in 1926 the renowned Zionist planner Richard Kauffman would not include Tel Aviv in a comprehensive review of town planning in Palestine, because, having "grown into a town of more than 40,000 inhabitants, unfortunately it de[fied] all efforts to make it conform to a systematic scheme."[165]

The reality of Jaffa's "modernity" did not prevent her leaders from absorbing elements of the European and Zionist critiques of the city. Thus Aref al-Aref wrote in 1940: "Tel Aviv is a great city. There is no difference between it and the great cities of Europe. High buildings, spacious department stores, organized streets, and order that overwhelms your vision everywhere, one can almost think in walking in the streets of Tel Aviv that you're walking in the middle of a street in a European city. I saw this and became distressed, and said to myself, When will we, the Arabs, achieve this degree of wealth and riches? And how will it be possible for us to defeat this cultured, rich and advanced people?"[166]

In a similar vein, although not specifically referring to Tel Aviv, in 1945 Mayor Heykal expressed "the need to reorganize the city along modern lines and improve the culture within it," as he put it in the foreword to the Official Planning Scheme for the city.[167] Moreover, just as indigenous elites of colonized countries often internalized the belief in their "present back-wardness,"[168] Jaffan native Hisham Shirabi recalled his childhood in the city as "the golden age, the age of power and glory." "And in comparison to the past," he wrote, "the present was a painful process because it exposed the difference between them. It had guided and taught us to hate the West and to love it passionately at the same time."[169]

Mas'ud too believed that "modern progress necessitates this plan; the old city needs a plan for restoration, and the people of Jaffa want future generations to avoid the stumblings and mistakes of this generation."[170] Yet similar to the Zionist ability to forgive their city's failings, he stressed that "Jaffa's culture at the present time is traveling at a quick pace," despite the difficulties following in the wake of World War II.[171]

The evidence presented in this chapter demonstrates that in order to define "Jaffa" as backward and dirty, those doing so had to exclude from consideration all of the "modern" quarters of the city, particularly the upper-middle-class sections 'Ajami and al-Nuzhah, which is exactly what Europeans and Zionist leaders did from the beginning. In the next chapter I show that the Zionist leaders worked hard to ensure that this vision would not be realized.

An analysis of colonial cities has long been understood as crucial for obtaining a broader understanding of the larger discourse of colonialism, and even European urbanism,[172] precisely because of the intimate relationship between the aesthetic appeal of architecture and the "unrelenting quest for political control and economic modernisation" that lay beneath the surface of all colonial projects.[173] My analysis of the ideology underlying the development and deployment of Zionist architecture in Tel Aviv and Jaffa suggests that Tel Aviv possessed many of the characteristics of a colonial city; from the beginning the leaders of Tel Aviv, following colonial urban policy, had as their goal the physical separation of the newly arriving and indigenous populations.[174] As important, while the architecture of colonialism clearly sought to maintain the overriding theme of difference on which it was based, it nevertheless can be shown to reveal "levels of ambivalence and hybridity" that constitute the cracks and fissures that Bataille encouraged us to examine as an efficacious means of breaking down the master narratives of European (colonial) modernity.[175]

In fact, Anthony King's adaptation of Telkamp's schematization of colonial cities reveals that Tel Aviv possesses many of the characteristics of other colonial cities such as New Delhi, which also was built separate from but close to the existing indigenous settlement.[176] Yet he also points out that we must examine the new colonial city both in relation to the colonized society and territory and in relation to the metropolitan power. And it is here that Tel Aviv diverges from traditional colonial cities: it had no ties to a metropole the way major French or British colonial cities did, nor was it part of a larger empire.

Nevertheless, architecture in Tel Aviv clearly played a similarly important discursive and symbolic of keeping colonial and indigenous societies "in their places by constituting a visual marker of difference and separation from its Arab surroundings."[177] More concretely, as in Tel Aviv, the plans for the *villes nouvelles* had "in every case encircled the medinas with European development,[178] a development that in Tel Aviv, as elsewhere, "ensured the encirclement, indeed strangulation," of the native cities while guaranteeing that when growth did take place, it could not be "orderly."[179]

Whereas colonial administrators boasted of their desire to "preserve" the native city (and through it, native customs and culture), the leadership of Tel Aviv did not seek to leave the "older" city standing alone next door as a negative image of their own modernity but rather ultimately desired to take it over. Zionism, not having the burden of empire, never needed to "conquer the natives' hearts";[180] it needed to conquer the land and the economy, which is what ultimately transpired, not just in Jaffa, but throughout Palestine.

7   Planning to Conquer

The Role of Town Planning in the Expansion of Tel Aviv, 1921–1948

Since the British Occupation of Palestine the idea has gained currency that there is something mysterious about certain plain Turkish terms occurring in Ottoman land law. Often wrong meanings are ascribed to such terms to suit personal inclinations as to how the law should be read.

M. CALHOUN, LAND OFFICER,
"'Atif Bey—Commentary on the Land Laws—1939 Edition," 1944

The revisionist historiography of modern Palestine/Israel of the past fifteen years has only just begun to investigate the dynamics of urbanization during the pre-1948 period, especially in the Jaffa–Tel Aviv region.[1] Theodor Herzl's *Old-New Land* is still an accurate portrayal of the way the majority of Israelis (and Diaspora Jews) understand the unfolding of the Zionist-sponsored "development" of Palestine. In fact, while the setting for the conversation is Herzl's imagined Haifa of the future, the description was really of Jaffa, and thus his vision that of Tel Aviv, or the old-new land (Altneuland).[2] As he wrote:

"Pardon me sir!" cried Reschid Bey with a friendly smile. "But this sort of thing was here before you came—at least there were signs of it. My Father planted oranges extensively. . . ."

"I don't deny that you had orange groves before we came," thundered Steineck, "but you could never get full value out of them."

Reschid nodded. "That is correct. Everything here has increased in value since your immigration."

"One question, Reschid Bey," interrupted Kingscourt. "Were not the older inhabitants of Palestine ruined by the Jewish immigration? And didn't they have to leave the country? I mean, generally speaking. That individuals here and there were the gainers proves nothing."

"What a question! It was a great blessing for all of us," returned Reschid. "Naturally, the land-owners gained most because they were able to sell to the Jewish society at high prices. . . . I sold my land to our New Society because it was to my advantage to sell. . . ."

"But I wanted to ask you, my dear Bey, how the former inhabitants fared—those who had nothing, the numerous Moslem Arabs."

"Your question answers itself, Mr. Kingscourt," replied Reschid. "Those who had nothing stood to lose nothing, and could only gain. . . . Nothing could have been more wretched than an Arab village at the end of the nineteenth century. . . . They benefited from the progressive measures of the New Society whether they wanted to or not."

In this chapter I address this lacuna in the critical scholarship on urbanization in Jaffa–Tel Aviv, and through it, in Palestine as a whole. I examine the role played by the discourse of town planning and development in the attempts by Zionist–Tel Aviv leaders to expand the territorial limits of the city and gain control of its chief water resources, the 'Auja/Yarkon River and the Jaffa Port. This was a discourse that the Jewish leadership and the British Mandatory Government would continue to share despite increasing political differences and in which Jaffa and its Palestinian Arab population (and in some cases, its Jewish population as well) had little hope of participating, other than at best as the object of development.

My investigation proceeds in three parts: the changes wrought by the British on Ottoman land law in Palestine and its impact on the development of land and town planning legislation during the Mandate period; how the rapidly growing municipality of Tel Aviv used this legislation to annex lands from the surrounding Palestinian Arab villages; and the struggles over who would control and profit from the exploitation of the 'Auja/Yarkon River and the Jaffa and (later) Tel Aviv ports. Throughout the discussion, I analyze the resistance, and less often the cooperation, of different segments of the local Palestinian population in this process.

The evidence provided here demonstrates how the discursive erasure of the well-established Palestinian Arab presence in Jaffa and the half dozen villages to its east and north (including the 'Auja River) anticipated and, I argue, helped to bring about the very real disappearance of these spaces and the populations inhabiting them during the 1948 war.[3]

THE DISCOURSE OF TOWN PLANNING
AND DEVELOPMENT IN JAFFA—TEL AVIV
The Changing Categorizations of Land Tenure in Late Ottoman and Mandate Palestine

In a previous essay I analyzed the consequences of Zionist and British discourses of development in Mandate Palestine, particularly as they played out in the agricultural sector.[4] My examination revealed that the "modernist" worldview underlying both Zionist and British diagnoses of Palestine's (and its population's) problems, and their proposed solutions to develop and modernize the country, led inevitably to an understanding of development that—like all colonial-national projects—meant removing the local population from their land.[5]

The importance of this shared discourse of development is clearly evident in the ability of Tel Aviv's leadership to use British land and town planning legislation to gain control of large swaths of land from the neighboring Palestinian Arab villages. In chapters 2 and 3 I discussed some important aspects of land tenure and categorization in Islamic and Ottoman legal systems as they developed in Palestine. Here I focus on British land law in Palestine, which was based on the Ottoman Land Law of 1858 that enumerated six classes of land—*mulk, miri, waqf, mawat, mahlul,* and *matruka*[6]—that were also used by the British during their rule of the country.[7] As a senior British land officer reminds us, "[I]t is necessary to bear in mind one basic principle which dominates [Ottoman] law, namely, the absolute power and control of disposition of the Sovereign over all lands which have not been definitely and expressly alienated by him as . . . *mulk* property. . . . [Moreover, *miri*] grants are usually made with a view to providing the public Treasury with the funds necessary for the maintenance of the State."[8]

Of course, in practice the Ottoman state had much less power to enforce its will in Palestine during the last decades of its rule than the British state had during the Mandate period. In this context, the latter three categories are of particular importance because they were conceived of as being unused or empty and thus could be most easily converted into urban land, the precursor for development by Jews. *Mawat* lands were unoccupied, marginal agricultural lands that were not held by title deed and were situated far from inhabited areas.[9] As Stein points out, before the Mawat Land Ordinance of 1921, one could assume possession, cultivate, and gain title to *mawat* lands on payment of a tax on the unimproved value of the land. Many Palestinian Arab cultivators took advantage of this provision during the Ottoman period, and numerous towns and villages were extended and enlarged this way. However, the British wanted to retain full control of as much state land as possible, and the Mawat Land Ordinance made it an offense to cultivate *mawat* land.[10]

This marked an important change in the understanding of *mawat* land, because it shifted the meaning of the term from an emphasis on the land's unclaimed status and distance from built-up areas to an understanding of such land as being "waste" and "barren"—the perfect tabula rasa, for example, on which to build a "modern" European city such as envisioned by the founders of Tel Aviv. Thus the 1947 *Survey of Palestine* reports that "*mawat* land should have no significance and should be deemed undeveloped, vacant land proper which cannot be possessed except by allocation from the State."[11] Deemed "dead or undeveloped,"[12] *mawat* land was ripe for development and being state property, was more easily allocated to those thought capable of "developing" it, although "the nature of the reviver" would be considered in all reclamation cases.

Mahlul, or state land, was either land that reverted to government control if left uncultivated for three years or land that had been "rendered vacant" by the state for some reason and was "under option for re-grant."[13] Similar to *mawat* land, until 1921 the previous holder of usufruct rights could redeem the land by paying a tax, but here too the British reinterpreted the law so that the high commissioner could declare *mahlul* land "Public Land" and thus permanently at the disposal of the state to allocate as it deemed appropriate.[14] In 1917, during the transition from Turkish to British rule, the Tel Aviv Council attempted to claim surrounding *mahlul* (and also *miri*) lands by allocating money to plant trees,[15] yet also complained that the "book of 'Mahlul' registration [wa]s missing" at the Jaffa Survey Office, likely taken by persons "hostile to [the Council's] work and to the development of Jewish colonization in Palestine."[16] What should be noted here, however, is that from the perspective of Ottoman law there was a clear implication that "cultivation was a prerequisite for changing the character of the land in some way."[17] In other words, it would seem that "urbanizing" agricultural or outlying land was not considered the same as "reviving" it and would not have been considered a valid cause for changing its classification, unless the new town or village had specifically received a *firman* authorizing its establishment.[18] Yet even in the late 1930s *mahlul* lands (particularly in the north of the city) were considered for the city's development and thus claimed by Tel Aviv on the rationale of using them for the building the Tel Aviv port.[19]

Matruka lands were among the most complicated sites of tenure and usage in Palestine and were thus a prime location for the "heresies" in the interpretation of Ottoman land laws when viewed by officials reading backward to the 1858 reforms from the perspective of the Mandate period. Broadly speaking, they were public or communal lands, such as roads or pastures, and were especially important in the Jaffa–Tel Aviv region, where at least three villages had semisedentary bedouin populations. Such lands could either be "left" to the public's use (like outlying roads) through *ab antiquo* usage or "assigned [by the state] to the inhabitants of a village, or town, or group of villages or towns" for pasture, threshing floors, storage of timber, or similar uses.[20] It was prohibited for anyone other than the village to which the land belonged to encroach, cultivate, or plow *matruka* land, and ownership was not transferable during the Ottoman period.[21]

During the Mandate period, there were several struggles over whether the high commissioner had, or should have, the power to change the categorization of *matruka* land.[22] The Palestinian Arabs were particularly worried about the high commissioner assuming this power, because in most cases where it became possible to "reclaim" *matruka* land Palestinian Arab cultivators would not have the funds with which to develop such areas themselves, the assumption being that "the Jews would be allowed to buy up land which is impossible for them to obtain under the present law."[23] Indeed, a report on the various debates over *matruka* land prepared for the government in 1944 specifically argued for the right of the government to vacate current users because "since the British Occupation the position [of *matruka* land] changed radically[,] . . . creat[ing] vested interests in favor of the communities registering as profits à prendre beneficiaries [i.e., the residents of a village who used the *matruka* land] and of immobilizing vast stretches of vacant Public Lands to primitive users or usage detrimental to the preservation of the soil [and to] a progressive land policy. . . . It has also the effect of withdrawing the vacant lands from the reserves available for development."[24]

That is, keeping the land "immobile"—and thus impossible to "turn over" productively, an image that brings to mind tilling the soil to keep it fertile and prevent "erosion"—is clearly linked to "primitive" use that, by definition, prevents the land's natural "progress" and "development." This is a perfect summary of the way in which the discourse of development shared by the British and Zionists affected the land regime in practice. It is in this context that we must understand that under British rule the categories *mawat*, *mahlul*, and *matruka* were brought under tighter control than in the previous period, essentially becoming de facto, if not de jure, *miri* (i.e., state) land. (This process can also be seen as a natural continuation of late Ottoman attempts to gain more control of untaxed lands that had the potential to bring in revenue through use or sale.) Thus the semi-official 1935 *Land Law of Palestine* describes a case heard at the Jaffa Land Court in 1926 in which the presiding judge declared that "cultivation . . . must be effective and 'maintained.' Operations must be carried out which result in a *permanent* and definite change in the quality of the land. The wilderness must be made to blossom."[25] This new dynamic of "permanently" altering the "quality" of land and the concomitant change in its status is in marked contrast to the local experience of marginal or "unclaimed" land, in which it was brought into use when needed and left fallow during other times—a dynamic that is not recognized by this more rigid interpretation of land reclamation.

What makes this transformation so important is the fact that traditionally, and even more so during the Mandate period, "all land situated within the boundaries of towns and villages [was] treated as *mulk* . . . [regardless of] whether the land [was] cultivated or not."[26] While only the High Commissioner had the power[27] to convert urban *miri* into *mulk* land, the author of the *Land Law in Palestine* describes the process as usually being "automatic with the extension of urban boundaries."[28]

In fact, this rigidification of what had formerly been (and in the villages outside of Jaffa at least, continued to be) a more plastic negotiation of bundles of rights to and control over land was inevitable. This is because the 1858 Land Code itself sanctioned the process of transforming the meaning of control over land from the power to distribute "bundles of rights" to outright "ownership" by the state or "private" parties. In this sense the claims by the Ottoman drafters of the 1858 Land Code that they were "conserving" rather than transforming existing land laws is problematic, whereas the similar claim by the British some seventy-five years later can be said to possess some validity, since the transformations symbolized by the 1858 code can be understood as having reached their logical conclusion in the more rigid British reinterpretation.

Yet if the British sought to give Ottoman land law the appearance of being a body of immutable rules and procedures, land law during the Mandate period remained "a contested domain, continually being created and re-created pending the requirements and assertions of the participants in particular historical situations."[29] Confusing matters even more was the fact that British officials often had trouble finding copies of Ottoman laws, especially in English, and it was not until the late 1920s that anyone had the requisite knowledge and experience to compose an authoritative and reliable English digest of them. Thus the very foundation of Mandate land law was literally copies of copies, or translations of translations,[30] of Ottoman laws. No wonder that 'Atif Bey would write, "Many heresies are current in regard to Ottoman land law and tenure."[31]

Urbanization and the Development of Town Planning Legislation in Palestine

Along with the "recodification" of the country's land tenure system, the British enacted numerous pieces of town planning legislation during their almost three decades of rule. These had a significant impact on the development of the Jaffa–Tel Aviv region in general and in the history of Tel Aviv's expansion in particular. To begin with, the British prohibited all transfers of immovable property in Palestine during their first three years of rule. In 1920 the Land Transfer Ordinance was enacted, the objectives of which were (1) to stimulate the economic growth and capital investment that accompanied the development of land and (2) to regulate the purchase of land in order to prevent speculation and protect small landowners and tenants against eviction. Yet the restrictive elements of the 1920 ordinance were removed, one by one, over the course of the decade.[32]

In 1928 the Land Settlement Ordinance was enacted, followed the next year by the empire-wide Colonial Development Act of 1929. In 1930 existing town planning ordinances were consolidated so as to deal with the increasing importance of the land question in the wake of the 1929 violence.[33] Also resulting from the violence were four reports—the Shaw Commission, the Passfield White Paper of 1930, and the Hope-Simpson and French reports of 1931—that all prescribed severely limiting future Jewish immigration and land purchases.

The French report called for five steps to be taken to address the issue of Palestinian Arabs displaced by Jewish land purchases, the "prerequisites for which it determined where the acceleration of survey and settling of title to lands, the speedy partition of *musha'a* lands, and Government control of lands and water resources in areas slated for development."[34] While these measures were intended to ensure that the *fellahin* most threatened by displacement from Jewish land purchases remained on the land, the colonial pedigree of the ideology underlying "surveying, settling and partitioning" the land was such that, particularly in urban regions such as Jaffa–Tel Aviv, Zionist leaders and planners were able to use them to continue to gain control of Palestinian Arab land, even in the wake of the restrictions on land purchases ushered in by the 1939 White Paper.

As for the need for government control of "developable" land and water resources, this idea was understood to be so "distasteful to the Jewish Agency" as to preclude "successful cooperation with Jews in any scheme of development" under government control,[35] and prompted the Secretary of State for the Colonies to suggest not appointing anyone "too closely connected with actual development work" to committees dealing with land settlement.[36] Thus development and planning were to be guided largely by ideological and political considerations and not the goal of maintaining *fellahin* on their land. The subsequent development of Tel Aviv would epitomize this process.

From the perspective of Tel Aviv's leaders, there was a strong link between the need to reform the country's land laws and the need to increase the power of its Town Planning Committee and the size of its Town Planning Area. Thus, for example, Tel Aviv's municipal engineer said that the dearth of open spaces in Tel Aviv arose because of an "inadequate municipal town-planning area" and because of the "system of landownership."[37] Just as important, in describing the region surrounding Tel Aviv, he said that "unlike other cities which are surrounded by large unbuilt-on areas and have wide town development possibilities, Tel Aviv is bounded on the west by the sea, on the south by Jaffa, on the north by the river and to the east by Sarona."[38] Despite being written in 1942, at a moment when the Tel Aviv Municipality was engaging in a "war" over land with the surrounding villages, there is no mention here of the six villages that also surrounded Tel Aviv, several of which would soon see large parts of their lands annexed to the city. Such lacunae typified the process of the discursive, and then physical, erasure or disappearance of these villages.[39]

In the administrative structure that was consolidated during the 1930s the High Commissioner and Central Town Planning Commission on the national level and the district[40] and local town planning commissions (composed of British and local representatives) assumed the exclusive power to designate Town Planning Areas and regulate planning and development. Until this time municipal councils such as the Jaffa Municipality retained these powers; thus Jaffa had enacted its own town planning legislation as early as 1923.[41]

It is significant that representatives of Garden City associations or similar bodies concerned with the development of a town could also be invited to join the town planning commissions, since such development was almost purely a Jewish concern. Moreover, the powers included the rights to tear down and reconstruct overcrowded or congested areas, to control the design of buildings, and to expropriate lands within the Town Planning Area for the construction of new houses or new roads—a tactic that the Tel Aviv Municipality would use in Sheikh Muwannis, as we shall see.[42]

Finally, in the 1930s the importance of "land settlement" in the Palestinian context cannot be overstated, particularly because the cadastral survey and newly established land registry offices mandated by it facilitated the purchase of land at the same time that a recession was making it harder for the often debt-ridden Palestinian smallholders to resist the speculative prices offered for their lands.[43] The process of "settling" the land involved the use of the cadastral surveys called for in the 1928 ordinance to determine boundaries, categorization, and other "registerable rights" to plots of land,[44] which would then be recorded in land registers. Such settlement of title to land was considered by the British the fundamental ingredient in improvement and development.[45] As important, the *Survey of Palestine* points out that the idea of land settlement *"must not be confused with the settlement of people on the land."*[46]

There was good reason for this admonition. As Scott Atran argues, through the discourse of land settlement, British and Zionist interests could continue to coincide on policy even when their political interests differed.[47] Thus the director of lands explained to Jewish officials that the proper settlement of rights to land was "the only way to made lands available for the Jews without political complications."[48] Not surprisingly, "settling" the land inevitably "encouraged fragmentation and dispossession of landholdings as well as social dislocation and disaffection."[49] The villages surrounding Tel Aviv were particularly affected by this process.

The history of and strategies underlying the expansion of Tel Aviv during the Mandate period reflected the development of town planning legislation, especially during the 1930s and 1940s. Even before the establishment of Tel Aviv, Zionist Jews boasted of creating a "state within a state in Jaffa."[50] During its first twelve years Tel Aviv's leadership attempted to make the town "completely independent" from Jaffa despite the fact that the quarter, like other recently established neighborhoods, enjoyed no separate legal status or autonomy from Jaffa.[51] As we saw in the last chapter, the goal, as stated by Arthur Ruppin as early as 1913, was to "conquer Jaffa economically."[52]

Central to the achievement of both autonomy and conquest was the expansion of the town's territory, and thus "Tel Aviv had intentions of expanding from the very beginning."[53] During the last years of Turkish rule, it was hoped that additional land acquisitions would succeed in bypassing the Palestinian Arab Jaffan neighborhood of Manshiyyeh and create a link to the sea, an accomplishment the leaders of Tel Aviv believed was a precondition for the very survival and development of the suburb because it would block any possibility of Jaffa's northward expansion while allowing Tel Aviv to spread without limits to the north and west.[54] By 1914 Tel Aviv had encircled Manshiyyeh and permanently blocked Jaffa's expansion to the north, although thanks to Hassan Bey, perhaps farther north than its leaders would have liked.

In June 1921 Tel Aviv was granted municipal autonomy as a local council.[55] During the Mandate period, there were two main causes for Tel Aviv's expansion. On the political level there was the Zionist strategy of attempting to gain possession of as much of the coast of Palestine as possible, which was believed to hold the "key to the country's economic future while strategically dividing Arab-controlled regions."[56] Yet just as powerful were the more mundane reasons for its rapid growth, such as the rapid increase in population and the speculatory rise in land prices in both Tel Aviv and Jaffa that it fueled.[57]

Thus members of the town council described how the need to cope with the "difficult and troublesome question" of building houses for workers and immigrants (many of whom were living in cramped unsanitary tent and barrack compounds scattered throughout the city) caused a "hunger for land" in Tel Aviv that led the municipality to begin serious if "chaotic" efforts to purchase small parcels north of the city (up to the ʿAuja/Yarkon River) as well as east (to the village of Salama).[58] While the purchase and parcelization of land in the north of Tel Aviv was made easier by Geddes's town plan, the presence of Palestinian Arab orchards to the east created "legal-official difficulties" that hampered land purchases and subsequent planning in the neighboring villages during this period.[59]

In fact, during the 1920s, there were conflicts with the local Palestinian Arab sellers—but these were mostly over money, not the purchases themselves, as the landowners and Jewish brokers sometimes increased the sale price after contracts had been entered into. Even the mayor of Jaffa, perhaps not wanting to curtail his own power, wrote to the Central Town Planning Commission in support of the taking of land for public purposes by the Tel Aviv Municipality, which he stated was permissible under Ottoman law.[60]

In 1927 and again in 1934 ordinances were enacted that separated Tel Aviv from Jaffa and then constituted it as an "independent local authority no longer in any relation of subordination to the Municipality of Jaffa."[61] The latter ordinance came into force one year after a new municipal law was enacted that gave municipalities greater powers to expand their borders, a right that until then had been "totally lacking" and was "so important that it [wa]s almost a question of the life of Tel Aviv."[62] With its new freedom Tel Aviv attempted to gain control of much of the agricultural land directly east of the city, as well as parts of the Jewish and Palestinian Arab neighborhoods on its borders.[63]

It was during this period that Tel Aviv ran out of uncontested land onto which it could expand.[64] Even within the municipal area of the city, much of the sandy lands in the north were still in the hands of Palestinian Arab owners and were becoming more difficult to purchase because the rise in land prices led owners and land brokers to sell smaller parcels to increase their profits.[65] The subsequent "war" over the expansion of Tel Aviv's borders was so fundamental to the city's development that the mayor, Yitzhak Rokah, wrote that "the history of the borders of Tel Aviv is the history of the city and its birth pangs."[66]

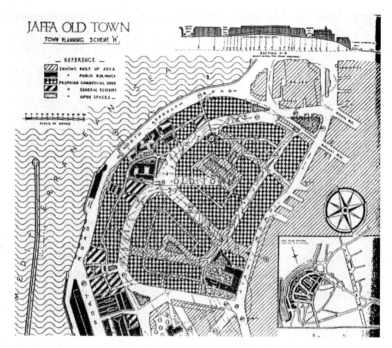

Map 11. British "improvement" scheme for Jaffa Old Town, 1936. (PRD, CO814/12.)

The Palestinian Arab revolt that began in Jaffa in 1936 led to closer cooperation between the British and the Zionists than had been seen since the 1929 uprising, and the shared focus on "security" issues—the citrus groves of the surrounding villages were frequently the staging ground of attacks on Jews—and town planning facilitated the annexation of village lands during the remainder of the Mandate period, especially after the 1939 White Paper limited the ability of Jews to purchase agricultural land. In fact, as discussed in chapter 3, the British provided an excellent example of the conflation of security and planning when they destroyed large swaths of the Old City of Jaffa in June 1936 in retaliation for the Palestinian Arab Revolt but justified their actions as an act of town planning, as "renewal" and "improvement" (map 11).[67]

"Settling" the Land: The Annexation of Village Lands by the Tel Aviv Municipality in the 1930s and 1940s

The practical experience of the discourse of "rights"—particularly of rights to land—in Mandate era Palestine, and its complex relations with municipal politics and administration, illustrates why it was so difficult for the British to fulfill their obligation (enshrined in both the Balfour Declaration and the Mandate) to "safeguard the civil and religious rights of the existing non-Jewish communities in Palestine." More specifically, the experience of the Palestinian Arab villages surrounding Tel Aviv during the 1930s and 1940s offers a good opportunity to examine how land settlement worked in practice during this period and why, despite the advice of the *Survey of Palestine*, it is hard not to confuse settling rights to land and settling people on land.

Table 5 contains data regarding the villages that were ultimately incorporated into Tel Aviv. I begin with the village of Summel because it was located closest to Tel Aviv, literally beginning where the streets of the city ended. Summel was perhaps the oldest village in the immediate vicinity of Jaffa, and its residents worked primarily in the citrus groves that surrounded village's built-up area. Despite the crucial role of citrus farming in the region's economy, in 1930 the central Land Settlement Office reported that the part of Summel situated in the Urban Property Tax Area of Jaffa–Tel Aviv was not being "settled" and the local Land Office was "accordingly authorized to effect dispositions respecting lands within that area without reference to [the Land Commissioner]."[68] The land was thus authorized to be allocated for the new housing and industrial enterprises generated (and necessitated) by the demographic and economic expansion of Tel Aviv.[69]

Again, in September 1933, the town planner of Tel Aviv presented a plan to the district commissioner of Jaffa to develop the lands east of Tel Aviv,[70] claiming that the "existing population north of Sarona [i.e., Summel] is very sparse and . . . presents the only possibility of expansion of these urban areas."[71] Summel in particular was to be reserved "for commercial development[,] . . . lending additional value to the property to attract investment in its *re*construction."[72]

Here we see how the terms "settled" and "unsettled" were understood simultaneously as involving the "rights" to and population density of a piece of land, thus creating previously nonexistent distinctions between and within the lands of a village that made possible its reclamation and urbanization by Jews. In fact, in a 1937 meeting of the Boundaries Commission, Tel Aviv Mayor Rokah pressed for the annexation of Summel and the adjoining part of Arab el-Jammasin el-Gharbi, then still part of the "Rural Area," into Tel Aviv's boundaries by claiming that "these lands are rural but have acquired an urban value."[73] A decade later one of the leaders of Sarona described this process when he advocated that any town

TABLE 5. The Arab Villages surrounding Tel Aviv

Village	Date Founded	Population, 1922	Population, 1931	Population, 1944	Land Ownership, 1944 (in dunams, [number of houses])	Comments
Jammasin Gharbi	Eighteenth century	200	566	1,080	1,365 total (529 Arab, 714 Jewish)	89% land cultivable; residents raised buffalo and marketed meat and milk in Jaffa, also citrus and bananas, cereals
Jammasin Sharqi	Seventeenth century	n.a.	395	730	358 total (286 Arab, 54 Jewish)	95% cultivable; same as Gharbi
Jerisha	Before 1596 Ottoman census	57	183	190	555 total (397 Arab, 93 Jewish)	87% cultivable; site of well-known mills and which Jaffans frequented for rest and recreation

Summel	Before 1596 Ottoman census; perhaps Crusader period	449	658	850	2,091 total (1,048 Jewish, 1,043 Arab; Jews owned 587 out of 762 dunams of orange groves in 1938)	127 houses, elementary schools, and mosques in 1931; close economic ties to both Jaffa and Tel Aviv; many Jews living there by end of Mandate
Salama	Before 1596 Ottoman census	1,187	3,691	6,730	6,782 total (5,633 Arab, 885 Jewish)	93% cultivable; wheat, barley, beehives; services; 2 primary schools, 1 high school
Sheikh Muwannis	Eighteenth century	664	1,154	1,930	15,972 total (11,456 Arab, 3,545 Jewish)	91% cultivable; 2 elementary schools, 1 high school; granted status of local town planning commission in late 1930s

SOURCES: *Survey of Palestine*; *Biladuna Filastin/Diar al-Yafiyya*: Vilneh, 1965.

planning scheme for the area respect the region's "rural character" even as part of it was zoned for heavy industry. As he explained, "Leav[e] all the rest open for future development, to a time when the land has gone or is to go out of the hands of the present agricultural population and thus has fallen ripe for urban settlement."[74]

It is here that the two meanings of the term "land settlement," which the authors of the *Survey of Palestine* admonished readers not to confuse, necessarily become conflated. For as Atran wrote, fixing, or settling, of the rights to the land was the necessary precondition to its physical settlement by Jews—in this case, making possible its use for the expansion of housing and industry necessary for the development of Tel Aviv.[75]

Thus during the 1940s, Summel, along with parts of the villages of Jammasin el-Gharbi and Jerisha, were again in the sights of British and local Zionist town planners. These lands were still considered "practically undeveloped," and it was considered vital to bring them under "complete municipal authority" because only the "legal and administrative machinery of a municipal corporation" would have the power to draw up a "creative or positive machinery of development" through which Tel Aviv could "redeem some of these defects which have deformed and stunted its past growth and to prepare for a better planned and more spacious urban future."[76]

The government was not of one mind as to the merits of annexing these lands. The attorney general and the solicitor general opposed it, but the district commissioner (the senior official of the regional town planning commissions) felt that "the concentration of industry in a suitable place . . . is of the greatest importance both to Tel Aviv and to Palestine as a whole." (Note the conflation of the two.)[77] The next year a similar divergence of views occurred when the Tel Aviv Municipality requested permission to annex land from Salama and Sarona for the erection of cheap dwellings to relieve the acute housing shortage in Tel Aviv.[78] The Colonial Office was more skeptical of Tel Aviv's intentions, while town planning and local officials believed that building them within the current borders of Tel Aviv would "completely spoil the whole layout of the area which is intended for residential houses of a more expensive type."[79] Another official said, "[T]here may well be some Palestinian Arab outcry and press comment, but on the whole I feel that the transaction is justified in the interests of the good administration of the country and that any such outcry will not be of true substance. . . . Meantime, no opportunity of promoting municipal enterprise that promises a betterment of the situation should be disregarded."

Because of its size and location on the banks of the 'Auja/Yarkon River directly north of Tel Aviv's built area, the village of Sheikh Muwannis was also a prime target for annexation by both the government and the Tel Aviv Municipality, particularly in the 1930s, when numerous "workers' neighborhoods" began to be built in the north.[80] In 1925 and again in 1929,[81] the government attempted to gain title to the sandy lands lying to the west of Sheikh Muwannis to the seashore, in the first case claiming that the land was *mahlul* and in the second *rimali* (sandy)—in both cases, "waste and uncultivated." The residents of the village promptly sued to prevent the expropriation; although it is impossible to determine which of the two sides' claims were true (i.e., whether or not the lands had been under cultivation by the villagers),[82] what is clear is that the government clearly reinterpreted (if not misinterpreted) the Ottoman law in claiming that "nobody has a right to waste uncultivated land."[83]

In fact, preference could have been given to the villagers to obtain rights to the land, as opposed to either leaving it uncultivated state land or transferring it to Tel Aviv for urban and industrial development, which the government considered doing. Instead, the director of lands noted that the land was "a very valuable site for urban development purposes,"[84] and it ultimately was incorporated into Tel Aviv.

Clearly, the government's concern was to fix permanently the status of the land based on its present condition in order to facilitate land purchases by Jews as well as urbanization. Yet permanently determining or "settling" the categorization of land is nearly impossible in the case of sandy land or coastal dunes, both because the borders continually changed and because such lands could, when needed, easily be used for planting vegetables or even citrus groves. This was, not coincidentally, the very claim made by the local bedouins regarding the "sands" on which Tel Aviv was to be built when they tried to block the suburb's construction in 1909.[85]

Thus the local population understood, as one Sheikh Ragheb pointed out before the Palestine Supreme Court, that "sand does not make [land] *mawat*," that is, "dead" land,[86] and it is clear from numerous cases in the Tabu and Land Office files that the British were aware of this.[87] Yet because such "reclaimed" land easily "vanish[ed] from the face of the earth" (as one British judge held), it was often impossible for the Palestinian Arab inhabitants to obtain "rights" to it from the government.[88]

Despite or because of the fluid condition of the land, its present state was used to justify Jewish development while specifically excluding the possibility that the local Palestinian Arab population could themselves reclaim it. In fact, the Jewish Agency touted the "transformation" of Sheikh Muwannis as a model for the benefits of Zionist-inspired development of the country, claiming that the sale of 1,500 of the village's 19,000 dunams of land to Jews between 1924 and 1932 fueled a "complete transformation" of the village, in which "all lands without exception [were] cultivated."[89]

Assuming that the figures and analysis are correct, they are quite telling: the claim that all the village's land was being cultivated underscores the stakes involved in the later attempts by the Tel Aviv Municipality to annex it, which would make villagers even more dependent on a town whose mayor, as we will see below, confessed to the district commissioner that he wished he could "blow up with bombs" a new Jewish market because it sold Palestinian Arab produce (some of which certainly would have come from the fully cultivated lands a mile or so north).[90] Moreover, in the context of the "massive planting" in the rapidly expanding citrus industry of the 1930s, the annexation of these lands by Tel Aviv foreclosed the possibility of many Palestinian Arabs engaging in this profitable business, which was increasingly dominated by Jews.[91]

The residents of the area had their own experience "reclaiming such lands for productive use." Nevertheless, by 1943, as a result of the "expenditure of great efforts" by Tel Aviv's mayor, Israel Rokah, the municipality succeeded in having large parts of Sheikh Muwannis incorporated into its town planning area, "a great victory for Tel Aviv," as it was described in the city's *Official Gazette*.[92]

Palestinian Arab Responses to the Discourses of Development and Town Planning in Jaffa and Tel Aviv

Clearly, while British and Zionist officials tended to see the lands of the villages surrounding Tel Aviv as being at best "agricultural" (and thus disconnected from the "urban" city of Jaffa) or even "waste" or "dead" land, the reality was that the social and economic geography of the villages around Jaffa was very complex during the late Ottoman and Mandate periods and intimately connected—socially as well as economically—to Jaffa. In particular, the status and uses of the land were very fluid, an understandable and normal state of affairs for a multiclass (and in some cases multiethnic) population struggling to adapt to the rapidly changing economic, social, and natural environment in a village located close to a port city.

Villagers were familiar with and used the Ottoman and British Land Codes to change or protect the status of their lands in their internal battles for control of territory.[93] And they had begun to improve their lands during the Ottoman period[94] and subsequently worked with the Mandatory Government to that end, especially to drain swamps.[95] In fact, from the very beginning of the Mandate period villagers petitioned the government to "reclaim and cultivate" *mawat* lands.[96]

By 1930, as Tel Aviv and the government began encroaching on their lands, the residents of the villages felt that their traditional grazing lands were in jeopardy and petitioned the government not to allow the land to be sold to anyone, realizing that such an eventuality inevitably would have led to their being alienated from it.[97] Indeed, realizing the importance of control over planning, the leaders of Sheikh Muwannis requested permission to form their own town planning council as early as 1935.[98]

Clearly, too, the British were not alone in their ambivalence toward Jewish land purchases of village lands. In fact, many leading Palestinians, several of them from Jaffa (including two mayors),[99] were involved in land sales at the same time that they publicly criticized British support of Jewish land purchases.[100] For example, while the mayor of Jaffa "emphatically rejected" a proposal by the Tel Aviv Municipality to annex part of the Jaffa border neighborhood of Manshiyyeh, when it came to the annexation of village lands, his first concern was that the "owners of the lands" were not being consulted.[101] The majority of the residents concerned would have had little say in how the land on which they lived and farmed was disposed.

In another case involving a new road scheme being debated by the Sheikh Muwannis Local Town Planning Council, government officials noted that though "the unofficial minority was strongly opposed to the whole scheme, the official majority supported it on the understanding that the financial aspect would be dealt with by the District Town Planning Commission to whom they referred it."[102] That is, the wealthier landowners did not mind having the land expropriated because they knew they would receive adequate compensation, while the poorer residents of the village were against any expropriations because they knew they would receive nothing.[103]

If some segments of Jaffa's Palestinian Arab elite were ambivalent about the impact of Tel Aviv's expansion onto the land of the surrounding villages, the rest of the population exhibited no hesitation in condemning the annexation of their land. Moreover, they understood that the British changes to the Ottoman land system aimed at securing and extending British control over the land and the country as a whole.[104] Thus British attempts to "codify" the land system in Palestine met with protests by Palestinian Arabs from the beginning of their rule, with the 1920 Land Transfer Ordinance being cited as one of the causes of the May 1921 revolt.[105]

A concise description of the methods employed by the Tel Aviv Municipality to gain control of land was offered by an attorney representing Palestinian Arab families in Salama who were threatened with expropriation of their lands: "[T]here are in the vicinity other plain and bare lands which do not yield any income but which are not being acquisitioned for the simple reason that they are Jewish lands, and that the whole object of this formality is to expropriate Palestinian Arab lands and convert them into Jewish property. [While] it may look as though it were an innocent expropriation for purposes of housing ex-servicemen, it is in fact not so because the endeavors exerted by the Jews to obtain this orange grove from my clients dates back to a number of years. Finding that they were unable to obtain the [land,] . . . they resorted to another measure; i.e., they filed an action in the Magistrates Court of Tel Aviv for sale of the property at auction on the ground that the property was not capable of partition [the Jewish and Palestinian Arab shares could not be divided into parcels]."[106] When this too failed the idea of expropriating the land under town planning ordinances was conceived of and executed.

In another case, when the Tel Aviv Municipality attempted to build a road on Palestinian Arab land the Jaffa-based religious daily *al-Jami'a al-Islamiyyah* complained:

> In reality the plan in the Town Planning Commission now including Sheikh Muwannis is not really a "plan" but rather a plan to take the land out of the hands of the owners. . . . We have farmed land north of the 'Auja for a long time and then Jews came and wanted to buy it because it is close to Tel Aviv, and we said no, and they tried to get it through various means, including using the Government to push a plan to open a road through our farmland . . . after it proved incapable of gaining ownership through [other] means. [We declare] that this project has no benefit returning to the village, either from a planning or moral perspective.[107]

Again, a 1939 debate in the Sheikh Muwannis Local Town Planning Commission over a new road scheme for the village reveals that while the wealthier landowning residents who were on the commission supported the plan, the majority of the residents were dead set against it. In objections filed with the commission they explained: "[O]ur village is principally an agricultural village and certainly does not need an extravagant scheme and roads. . . . Ours is not a *CITY* but just a *VILLAGE* in the true and real sense. To make it imperative that every building plot must have a minimum area of 1000 m² is, to say the least, an unwarranted extravagancy and waste of land."[108]

The villagers clearly had their own, quite practical and rational notions of what constituted "waste" land. More generally, they offered a sophisticated critique of planning practice as it affected them, declaring, "[T]he essential wisdom in constructing a road is to shorten distances, with the least possible inconvenience to property owners, thus helping to serve the inhabitants in the best and most economic manner. There is at present a road . . . which has and still continues to serve the inhabitants. . . . The old road passes by the village itself, thus serving the inhabitants to the best manner possible, while none of the projected roads pass by the village."[109] For the Tel Aviv Municipality to "seek and get those facilities under the guise of a Town Planning Scheme amounts to an unlawful and most uncommendable attempt that should never be allowed."[110]

The Jaffa Municipality did not always pay sufficient attention to protecting the interests of the residents of the surrounding villages; it was, however, concerned to protect the sand dunes south of the city (which ultimately became the Jewish towns of Bat Yam and Holon). For Jaffa's leaders, the dunes "were the only outlet left to it for expansion," and thus the attempts by non–Palestinian Arab companies to purchase land signified an attempt to "complete the encirclement of Jaffa and choke it out of existence."[111] As one Palestinian Arab newspaper editorialized, "Since the Jaffa Municipality has already asked for those lands and as they are Jaffa's only outlet, it would be unjust to dispossess it of them. We have no doubt that the authorities would soon hasten to annex them to Jaffa in the same way that they annexed Sheikh Muwannis village to Tel Aviv—although there is a difference between the two cases."[112]

The contest for the lands of the villages surrounding Jaffa and Tel Aviv continued until the end of the Mandate period. In 1947 the Supreme Muslim Council and the Department of Awqaf in Jaffa wrote to the government asking it to disallow the inclusion of certain *waqf* lands in Tel Aviv's town planning scheme, explaining that despite government assurances to the contrary, "the annexation of the *waqf* land . . . involves the Government's support of the realization of the ambitions of those who wish to acquire the land to serve their interests by means for which they have become very skillful in creating justifications."[113]

Most important, they understood the relationship of Zionist and British town planning discourses, the granting of monopolistic concessions to Jewish interests, and the specific battles to control the land and resources around Jaffa. Thus they wrote: "Since *waqf* land could not be sold, the Jewish Concessionaire, Pinhas Rutenberg, gained control of the land in 1921 by obtaining a concession from the Government for generating electricity from the 'Auja River." They concluded: "[T]he Jews intend to use the 'Auja concession for swallowing up the *waqf* and the Arab-owned lands. Since the *waqf* land was invulnerable, they resorted to annexing parts of it to the Town Planning Area. . . . Naturally, it will continue to annex the whole *waqf* land bit by bit first to the Town Planning Area, then to the Town

Planning Scheme. Later, it was be added to the Municipal Area of Tel Aviv, Ramat Gan, Petakh Tikva, and other Jewish settlements. In this way, the Jews will have succeeded in obtaining what they could not obtain from the 'Auja Concession."[114]

AUTONOMY, SEPARATION, OR ANNEXATION?
THE STRUGGLES OVER JAFFA'S JEWISH NEIGHBORHOODS

From its establishment, Tel Aviv's leadership strove to ensure that neighboring Jewish quarters adopted what they considered the most modern town planning, architectural and hygiene standards. Thus town planning and hygiene considerations were written into the agreements uniting Tel Aviv and the Hevra Hadasha neighborhood and for new quarters constructed outside the boundaries of Karm al-Jabali, on which these two neighborhoods were built.[115]

In September 1920 several smaller Jewish neighborhoods agreed to join Tel Aviv. In July 1922 Tel Aviv and Neve Tzedek, the first Jewish neighborhood built outside the Old City of Jaffa, completed negotiations for their unification.[116] As Tel Aviv expanded the Jewish National Fund continued to pursue Jewish settlement in Jaffa proper, which was still considered a goal of "great national importance."[117]

Not all of Jaffa's Jewish neighborhoods were able or wanted to unite with Tel Aviv; in fact, throughout the Mandate period there were numerous discussions and debates between the Tel Aviv and Jaffa Municipalities over which should have jurisdiction over Jaffa's rapidly expanding "Jewish neighborhoods."[118] By far the most contentious battle involved the neighborhoods of Shapira, Givat Herzl, and Florentin and, to the south, Beit-Vegan, Agrobank Shikun, and other adjacent lands (with a population of more than twenty thousand Jews and constituting 10 percent of the city's area).

In the wake of the outbreak of the 1936 revolt, the residents of these neighborhoods called for their immediate annexation to Tel Aviv, claiming that they were "like a foreign body in the Jaffa Municipality." From a town planning perspective as well as "geographically, ethnically, and organically," they were part of, or at least "a natural continuation" of, Tel Aviv.[119]

In supporting the demands of the neighborhoods, the Jewish Agency argued, "The aspiration of these Jewish quarters to be attached to Tel Aviv is based both on geographic and ethnic considerations. . . . It is surely not unnatural for the inhabitants of these quarters . . . to feel anxious to be taken under the wings of the neighboring Jewish city from which they are divided by a mere artificial boundary."[120] Another memo, from 1938, argued:

> Historically, all these quarters are the outgrowth of Tel Aviv. Geograph-ically, they form one compact unit with it. Their streets are direct con-tinuations of the streets of Tel Aviv. If you enter Tel Aviv from the southern end of Herzl Street the only way by which you can find the dividing line between the areas of Jaffa and Tel Aviv is by watching the street lamps. . . . [121] The character of the areas as a whole [is] one com-plete zone of Jewish urban development. . . . It is, furthermore, true that all the four sections enumerated contain patches of Arab land and some Arab houses, but their complete contiguity with Tel Aviv is not affected thereby. . . . On geographical grounds, therefore, there appears to be no reason either for the retention of these quarters within the boundaries of Jaffa Municipality.[122]

The richly descriptive language of the arguments—the "artificial boundary" keeping the neighborhoods ("one complete zone of Jewish urban development") under the rule of their evil "stepmother" and away from their "natural" mother, Tel Aviv—illustrates the powerful cognitive, ideological, administrative, and even emotional borders deployed by Zion-ist leaders to separate Jews and Arabs who in fact lived in the same city, even in the same neighborhood.[123] Nonetheless, neither the Jaffa Munici-pality nor the government accepted the above portrayal of the situation, arguing that the Jaffa Municipality had tried to provide services but was "obstructed" by residents, who only availed themselves of its services when it benefited them.[124]

In this decade-long struggle one document, from May 1940, sheds par-ticular light on the internal Zionist debates over the future of Jaffa's Jewish neighborhoods and whether it was more beneficial from a "national" stand-point for them to remain part of Jaffa or be annexed to Tel Aviv. This is the protocol of a very lengthy meeting of the representatives of the directorate of the Jewish Agency, the Tel Aviv Municipality, the Va'ad Le'umi (National Council), and the Jewish neighborhoods of Jaffa.[125] Because of the rich and descriptive language of the conversations, I present below lengthy excerpts from the text, with commentary as the discussion progresses.

Three opposing perspectives were represented at the meeting: remain-ing part of Jaffa, becoming an autonomous local council, or being annexed to Tel Aviv. Those advocating the first option included the Jaffa Municipal-ity member Ben-Ami (no first name provided) and the Jewish Agency's Moshe Shertok. Shertok presented the most strategic reasoning for remaining part of Jaffa (even after describing the establishment of a local council as the most "practical option"): "If we leave these neighborhoods in

Jaffa and don't demand their separation, we can concentrate a population around Jaffa and bring to pass that the city of Jaffa itself will have a Jewish majority."[126]

Ben-Ami's argument for remaining part of Jaffa came in response to the assertion by a militant rabbi from the neighborhoods, Rabbi Ostrovski, that they were in a state of "war" with Jaffa and thus "the most dangerous places" in Jaffa–Tel Aviv. Ostrovski argued:

> It's impossible to say that the national organization has to lead the war. The war has to be led by the residents of the neighborhoods them-selves. If the [national] organizations encourage them to fight, it will not succeed. It is up to the people of the neighborhoods to be ready for anything. . . . Who among us now is ready to make peace with the Arabs, who is interested in peace with the Government? We have no need now to search for peace. But sometimes you have to pay a price for no peace, then you need to consider the gain against the loss. What will giving up give us? I think that this will be a big mistake if we make peace. We need to continue the war until finally the neighborhoods will be joined to Tel Aviv.[127]

In reply, Ben-Ami asserted that up to 90 percent of the residents of the neighborhoods did not want annexation but instead would opt for a local council because they could not afford to pay Tel Aviv's high taxes.[128] More-over, he argued, "I do not believe that our relations with the Arabs will be in the coming generations one of hatred. I know the Arabs better than Rabbi Ostrovski, I know that it is possible to get along better."[129] He went on:

> I don't see any decisive and obvious reason to break from Jaffa. . . . I'll go so far as to say that indeed there were victims in Jaffa and part of the victims were residents of the [Jewish] neighborhoods, but there were also many victims from Tel Aviv itself. If someone happened to be in Jaffa—that day they fell victim.
>
>   I don't know if we are discussing now from the point of view of principles. From this point of view there are many reasons to remain in Jaffa. These neighborhoods are not entirely separated and do not con-stitute a geographic unit. If I come through Salama to Jaffa, these neighborhoods are the natural continuation of Jaffa; if you're going on Herzl Street, they are the direct continuation of Tel Aviv. If we consider from this point of view that we want to augment the Jewish *yishuv* in Jaffa—then it's clear that we should [not] leave the neighborhoods in Jaffa.[130]

Tel Aviv Mayor Rokah was not at all happy with Ben-Ami's remarks:

> I feel myself in a strange position here. If I knew that I would hear the people of the neighborhoods talking like this I wouldn't have come.

Don't think that I will demand annexation with the mood like this.
Now I understand why we sit on different sides of the table, I on one
side and him [Ben-Ami] on the other. What I heard today puts us in a
position such that I need to say that we're [not] interested in kidnap-
ping you to Tel Aviv. . . . I speak from the national point of view.[131]

For Rokah, the divide between Jaffa and Tel Aviv was such that any Jew—
like Ben-Ami—who chose in some way to identify with Jaffa was considered "on different sides of the table" from him, that is, somehow existing
in a *galut* space that was the very antithesis of Tel Aviv. He continued in an
obviously exasperated state, and the confusion and contradictions in his
remarks are revealing:

These neighborhoods are part of Tel Aviv in their constitution, and
their reality in Jaffa is a terrible blow, an economic, political and
national blow . . . If this region returns to Jaffa the blow will be
stronger . . .[132] In Tel Aviv there is a Shabat Law. How well we keep it is
another thing, but there is something. [In Jaffa] there is nothing, nothing. I ask you not to give a hand to this. This debate about whether or
not we will conquer Jaffa is already obsolete. If Haifa was already going
the way of Tel Aviv, we might have another port. We saw that Jews
couldn't approach the Haifa port. Were it not for Tel Aviv we couldn't
approach Jaffa Port, even if there was a Jewish majority. . . . Tel Aviv
has so many big assets, even if we have many faults, but Tel Aviv has
its own schools [and] port, and no one can be ashamed of it, and what
do we want to do? To conquer Jaffa? With these neighborhoods, with
the mood that you heard today, you will conquer Jaffa? On the contrary you will weaken your Tel Aviv, and of course economically you
will weaken the Hebrew economy.

I will tell you what it was. This morning the new District Commissioner told me, "We received confirmation for a new open market in
Kerem Hateimanim, the plan will be executed by Jews from Kerem
Hateimanim who want to establish a modern market in their neighborhood." I said: "If I could I would blow it up with bombs." The District
Commissioner told me that the plan to establish the market was
approved, but he is a *goy* [gentile], so he doesn't understand anything
. . . [and] said, "This market is designed for the people of Tel Aviv."
[But] it's clear that it will be a cancer for Tel Aviv. . . . The clear intention is to ruin our economy. . . . Already today this part is a cancer on
the Hebrew economy, and what will happen if they built a big modern
market? And this in the borders of the Jaffa Municipality. You see that I
can't stand there with a guard making sure no one goes to this new
market. This is also the situation in the south [of Tel Aviv].[133]

Rokah's argument is very interesting, as it demonstrates the shift in
perception by Zionist and Tel Avivan leaders since the late Ottoman period,

when conquest was of great national importance. Clearly, the development of Jaffa was such that in the minds of the present leadership of Tel Aviv economic conquest was no longer possible through increased settlement in Jaffa proper. Perhaps it also is a reason why Tel Aviv was then in the midst of attempting to annex and "settle" large swaths of land from the surrounding villages, to "strangle" Jaffa, as the Arab press described it.

In critiquing Rokah's willingness to abandon Jaffa, Menachem Ussushkin, of the Jewish National Fund, explained the historic shift in Zionist strategy represented in Rokah's position. Noting that there were "a lot of good things in Jaffa," he asserted that there were historically two tendencies underlying Zionist colonization. The older strategy, dating back to the beginnings of Zionist colonization in the late nineteenth century, was to "enter into the Arab body and conquer it, to penetrate into all parts of the country from Dan to Be'er Sheva, on both sides of the Jordan, in every place with the goal of turning the Arabs into a minority, not expel them. This is the tendency that says we need to conquer every place possible and not leave it to others."[134] More recently, he clearly lamented, the leadership chose an "easy, good, and nice" strategy, one based on a desire to

> leave the difficult places and concentrate in nicer and easier places, to leave the geographical and historical positions and limit ourselves to new and nicer places and adapt ourselves to them. This tendency fights for the division of Jerusalem into an old and new city, this tendency leaves Hebron. . . . [It] has many merits, it's more secure and easier, we see the advantages already before our eyes today. If you walk through Tel Aviv, you see a world alive, you're in a Jewish place, you don't see any *goys*.[135]

This was perhaps also a generational conflict, as Ruppin, Ussushkin, and the older leadership who had fond memories of Jaffa as the cradle of the Zionist yishuv were loath to abandon it. On the other side, Rokah and the younger generation of Tel Aviv's leaders thought primarily of the city's interests (even against the larger national interest when necessary), basing their actions on the realization that no amount of Jewish settlement in Jaffa would further the aims of the conquest of labor or land, since Jaffa was irredeemably *galut* as long as it was under Palestinian Arab control.

Thus Rokah emphasized securing Tel Aviv's borders from infiltration from Jaffa, and while many residents desperately sought annexation to Tel Aviv, Rokah chided those who would remain:

> If you want to remain in Jaffa—you have my blessing, stay in Jaffa. We of course will do something, will restrict our services within the municipal borders of Tel Aviv. . . . There is no value to the theory that we

need to conquer Jaffa, that we need to leave a huge Jewish community there when Tel Aviv is next door. Jaffa is not Jerusalem. Maybe in Jerusalem I would be of a different opinion . . . that there is value to live within an Arab community, since you can't rip Jerusalem out of Jews' hearts. In Jaffa there isn't a Western wall, a holy place and ruin.[136] From the other side this is a very difficult blow not only for Tel Aviv but for the Jewish agricultural *yishuv,* by the lack of clarification that there is in these borders—residents of the neighborhoods in Jaffa under Arab and half-Jewish control, etc.[137]

Ussushkin responded by admitting that were he not afraid of Rokah's reaction, he would suggest annexing two neighborhoods from Tel Aviv to Jaffa, so that the Jews would be even closer to forming a majority there: "You talk about erasing Jewish Jaffa from the map of Eretz Israel. If you talk about crimes—this is a crime. This is a great historical name, the first port of Jerusalem.[138] In Jaffa Port we have a part. Didn't you, Shertok, see the ugly map that the Government gave us in the Land Law [of 1939, which forbade Jews to purchase land in what were defined as "Arab" areas], the prime area in Jaffa that we're forbidden to buy land [Area A], this is only because it's an Arab city and all its neighborhoods are Arab."[139]

Ben-Ami also challenged Rokah's interpretation of events:

You [lit. "they"] tried to scare us in various ways. Thus the way of Rokah to throw a bomb here and a bomb there. I say that you can't build a fort on the border of Tel Aviv [to keep out] Arab products. These products flood all of Tel Aviv. This is something that we apparently can't stop. Here there is an economic war of cheap versus expensive, and in the natural way when there isn't interference it's difficult to fight against it. It's clear that there is the possibility and right to influence Jews not to buy these products but to fight the products and not absorb them into our market—this is impossible.[140]

Here we see the ambivalence caused by living in the border between the two cities, the two nations, under half-Jewish and half-Palestinian Arab control, and why it would cause consternation to Rokah, who could not understand how any Jews would want to live in Jaffa with a Jewish community "at whose head is [Jaffa mayors] Omar Beitar or Assam Bey [Bek]."[141]

Ussushkin suggested further to Rokah:

You grow and glorify in the north and the east and leave the south for Jaffa. . . . Are [we] to leave a city in which Jews live, in which the Jewish *yishuv* began, and that is very connected to our memories[?] Thank God it's impossible to move the Western Wall to Tel Aviv. If it were possible to do such a thing I'm sure that they would have decided by majority opinion to move it. In the synagogue a few years ago on Yom

Kippur they joked: "Next year in Tel Aviv." And . . . you will lend a
hand to the erasing of the name of Jaffa and making it *judenrein*
[cleared of Jews]. Think about that. . . . Why do I talk like this with
such emotion? It's obvious they will remain in Jaffa.[142]

Finally, Ussushkin exhorted residents of the neighborhoods:

> [B]lessings will come to you if you fight with all your power against
> taking the Jews from Jaffa. . . . [I]f you can [take] this sacrifice, to suffer
> in Jaffa and guard that Jaffa will be a Jewish city with a big majority[,]
> . . . then all the *tzuris* [aggravation] that we would have from the Arab
> world wouldn't be as much as if Jaffa was free of Jews and they could
> create an Arab state there. . . . All this geography about how the neigh-
> borhoods stand, I'm not interested in it. I didn't look at the map,
> because this for me is a principal political question of the first degree.[143]

Most of the neighborhood representatives no doubt agreed with
Ussushkin's characterization of the importance of the issue, but for some
the action it demanded was the opposite of that which he advocated; while
they too felt that "the matter of the neighborhoods is a very big settlement
issue," the primary concern was never again to have to "go and bow my
head again in Jaffa," as one resident exclaimed.[144] Thus the solution for
them was annexation to Tel Aviv. In either case, Ussushkin's argument is
fascinating in its striking similarity to contemporary debates within Israel
over whether it is worth the *tzuris* to continue the Occupation and support
(and even expand) the Jewish settlements that it protects—that is, whether
the "Arab state" that would emerge if the territory were vacated would
ultimately be more problematic than the "sacrifice" necessary to maintain
the status quo.

Other residents spoke for and against the three options of remaining in
Jaffa, establishing a local council, or being annexed to Tel Aviv.[145] The
strongest sentiment was expressed by one resident who exclaimed: "To
return to Jaffa means to return to the *galut*, and we will not return to it in
any way. . . . All of us are sons of Tel Aviv. I think that the expansion of Tel
Aviv will go towards the south and not towards the north. If the border will
become Salama, I am sure that in a couple of years we'll need to encroach
[on] the border [i.e., expand Tel Aviv's borders to encompass Salama],
because there aren't any people in the neighborhoods who will agree to live
under the patronage of Jaffa."[146]

At this point David Remez of the Histadrut joined the conversation. Perhaps influenced by his experience both fighting against and organizing
Arab labor, he also believed that the neighborhoods were joined to Jaffa
artificially. "Haifa, Jerusalem, Nablus, and Be'er Sheva," he said, "are separate issues."

It's impossible to generalize and say, "Go assimilate them!" [At which point Ussushkin interrupts: "Not assimilate but conquer!"]. . . . These neighborhoods are next to Tel Aviv. You [Ussushkin] folded the map, and good for you, but you can't ignore the *fact* that these neighborhoods are *within Tel Aviv.* Geography isn't something you can cancel by folding a map. I take one step from Tel Aviv and already I'm in the neighborhoods. There's nothing in common between them and Jaffa. . . . [T]hey're *in* Tel Aviv [and] this is one *yishuv.* What do you want me to do, *cut off a limb* from life without mercy and *feed* Jaffa. I say, maybe we need to make a *sacrifice* such as this for the good of the front, but I'm not yet ready for this. . . . As a Tel Aviv Jew I see a great danger for Tel Aviv in giving up on the claims of the neighborhoods and leaving them in this way as part of Jaffa. . . . A *breach* such as this next to Tel Aviv is a dangerous explosion for the entire Tel Aviv economy. It's not correct that in the matter of products it's so simple. If this were in the area of Tel Aviv it would be a *fortress,* the way Allenby [Street] can be a fortress. Also Allenby is a relative fortress. But to be part of [lit. "a citizen of"] Jaffa—this is another matter entirely.[147]

After Remez finished speaking and the meeting began to wind to a close, Shertok again spoke:

I too have "lived among them [Arabs]." When my family came to Jaffa 34 years ago we lived in 'Ajami, this was *penetrating* Jaffa. The first immigrants' house was in Jaffa, this was penetrating Jaffa. We saw the results of this penetration. You didn't suggest to persist in this tendency of penetrating Jaffa. Now it's happened that Tel Aviv is the city that's expanding and it's expanding on the land of Jaffa. You want this [expansion] to remain in the municipal framework of Jaffa? I say, you will attempt to force reality. In *fact* this is Tel Aviv, in *law* this is Jaffa. There is here an *anomaly* that can be eliminated only by returning it to a *normal* condition, adjusting the legal situation to the municipal situation, *don't force reality to fit the legal framework.* . . . The argument of Ben-Ami that the neighborhoods are in the region of Jaffa isn't an argument at all, because the whole city of Tel Aviv was built on Arab land and because in the beginning it was part of Jaffa Municipality. But the aim was to free [ourselves] and be independent and the goal went stage by stage. And this liberation isn't complete. In the meantime reality has conquered parts of Jaffa for Jews, but the *municipal liberation* lagged behind and needs to overtake this thing. Now we're in a transitional stage and it's slow, and the question is how we can survive in this restricted stage by remaining in a situation of anarchy or [creating a more] known transitional form. But in my opinion we can't be debating the main *goal of development.*[148]

Once again the rich, ambivalent, and often contradictory language of the last two quotations (some of which I have italicized so as to facilitate their juxtaposition) tells us much about the myriad considerations and emotions involved in this seemingly political debate. Thus we see, pace Rokah's earlier description of the "reality of the neighborhoods in Jaffa," that for Remez, while in *law* they might be in Jaffa they were *in fact within Tel Aviv*; only a lag in *municipal freedom* keeps them from reaching the natural *goal of development* in the annexation to Tel Aviv—anything less not only mutilated the Jewish body and landscape but also provided nourishment to the enemy.[149]

Whatever their views on how to resolve the question of the neighborhoods, it was clear to all that Jaffa should (and for most, would ultimately) be "Jewish." The Jewish connection with the city of more than two thousand years was emphasized, while the Palestinian Arab history and presence in the city was ignored if not erased. Jaffa was *galut* as long as it was under Palestinian Arab control, but that was an *artificial* situation, as the region was *geographically* and *naturally* part of Tel Aviv; the legal *anomaly* could be made to conform to that *fact* by adjusting the municipal boundaries. Once again, we see the overturning (literally and figuratively) of geography that defined the Zionist approach to Jaffa, as the neighborhoods were considered "geographically" part of Tel Aviv even though they were still administratively and juridically part of Jaffa.

The meeting ended with an apparent consensus to push for the establishment of a local council, but there was no way that Jaffa's leaders would agree to such a move, fearing that it would "crumble the Municipality" by triggering other Jaffan neighborhoods, especially the majority Christian neighborhood of Ajami, to follow suit.[150] In December 1940 a compromise between representatives of Jaffa's Jewish neighborhoods and the Jaffa Municipality was reached in which the Jewish quarters dropped their claim to establish a local council for the time being in exchange for the Jaffa Municipality's writing off their arrears.[151]

By 1945 there were an estimated thirty thousand residents in Jaffa's Jewish neighborhoods; the Tel Aviv Municipality continued to press for the transferral of "all the Jewish area and not just the built-up area of the neighborhoods."[152] Yet at the same time, perhaps not coincidentally, the neighborhoods' representatives were complaining that in their still ongoing negotiations with the Jaffa Municipality to achieve some kind of autonomous status, "The Jaffa Municipality [wouldn't] agree to any solution." "They don't want us," they said, "not just in Jaffa, but in Eretz Israel."[153]

These two quotations clearly reflect the paradoxes that lay at the core of the Zionist settlement enterprise both in the Jaffa–Tel Aviv region and in Palestine as a whole; the continual "conquest" of territory went hand in hand with intense feelings of persecution from their Arab neighbors who were being conquered (or at best, "assimilated"), which then presented another justification for settlement, development, and security. Indeed, not just the land but also the sea became embroiled in the conflict as the two communities struggled over control of the Jaffa and then the Tel Aviv port.

But these struggles over and nationalization of the territory and water of the region did not go unchallenged, particularly by the Palestinian Arab population. In fact, while the European Jewish financier Pinhas Rutenberg acquired a concession for irrigation and electricity using the waters of the 'Auja/Yarkon River, which effectively linked the mouth of the river to the nearby Tel Aviv Port (angering Jaffa's leaders and population to no end),[154] both communities continued to use the river for fishing and other activities.

Thus when workers at the Tel Aviv Port evicted licensed Palestinian Arab fishermen attempting to moor their boats between the mouth of the 'Auja/Yarkon River and the port in fall 1936, *al-Jami'a al-Islamiyyah* indignantly asked, "Has the 'Auja River become Jewish and consequently Arabs are not allowed to fish there?"[155] The Jewish port workers complained that "the foreshore was a Jewish foreshore and was not to be trodden by Arab feet" and that they "could not work any longer seeing the Arabs gradually come nearer and nearer." But more interesting is the reply of the leader of the fishermen, who answered that "the strike was off, and that half of the Moslems were in Tel Aviv and half the Jews in Jaffa, and therefore he too came, to fish."[156] That is, as I have attempted to demonstrate throughout this and previous chapters, spaces that were nationalized within exclusivist and bounded notions of identity during times of trouble (when boundaries are always most clearly drawn) were experienced by many Arab residents of the Jaffa–Tel Aviv region as having reverted to the more open (yet vis-à-vis the hegemonic nationalist discourses, more "clandestine") reading of space "as lived by its inhabitants," as Lefebvre described it.

However, for the Zionist leadership and Jews committed to maintaining a rigid separation from the *galut* environment, once the space was nationalized there was no turning back. Thus as a result of this incident an official prohibition against Arabs fishing in that area was enacted,[157] and a river that had served all the residents of the Jaffa–Tel Aviv region for generations took one step closer to becoming an exclusively Jewish space.

CONCLUSION: THE BORDERS OF THE ABSURD

In a 1940 discussion between a Zionist official and the chief secretary, the latter suggested, taking an "absurd case," "might it not happen that the

Jews would acquire and occupy so much land of Jaffa that the rest of the municipal area would not be able to run its municipal affairs on its reduced income if the whole of the Jewish area were to go over to Tel Aviv?" The Zionist official replied that "from the practical point of view there was no such likelihood. Jaffa was a town of some 40,000 Arab inhabitants and there was no question of Jews acquiring such vast areas in Jaffa as to leave that town without the means of running a municipality on its own."[158]

While the chief secretary's scenario did not play out, we have seen that it was far from absurd. As I have demonstrated, the local and national Zionist leadership had as their goal the control of Jaffa, its waters (sweat and salt) and its agricultural hinterland—whether through "conquest," "assimilation," or encirclement. Indeed, even after the conquest of Jaffa the Zionist-Israeli leadership at the highest levels remained concerned about the neighborhoods on the borders between Jaffa and Tel Aviv.

Thus in a meeting of the Provisional Government a month after the conquest of Jaffa, Ben-Gurion stressed the importance of "preventing the return" of Jaffa's Arab population, using as an example the border neighborhood of Abu Kebir: "If we can prevent from here taxis in the streets at night—this would be a real relief. If there will be [an] Abu Kebir again—this would be impossible. The world needs to understand that we are 700,000 against 27 million, one against forty. . . . It won't be acceptable to us for Abu Kebir to be Arab again."[159] The symbolism here—Abu Kebir as a synechdote for the Palestinian presence in Jaffa, the iconic imagery of siege (the proverbial few against the many) when the reality in the Jaffa–Tel Aviv region at least was the reverse; that is, Tel Aviv and its Jewish satellite neighborhoods and towns had surrounded Palestinian Arab Jaffa—reveals the interpenetration of local and national spatial imaginaries in the Zionist-Israeli political discourse.[160]

As I have also demonstrated, the discourse of town planning, development, and modernization was a vital tool in the arsenals of the Tel Aviv and national leaderships in their "wars" over the land, port, and river of Jaffa. As the French theorist Manuel Castells argues, the very terms *urbanization*, *development*, and *Westernization* are not "innocent" but in fact, qua theoretical ideologies, are central to the creation and support of the "myth of modernity."[161] It is this myth of modernity, so central to the self-definition of the Zionist enterprise as a whole and Tel Aviv in particular, that necessitated the discursive exclusion of the land, waters, and population of Jaffa and the surrounding villages from territory or resources needed for Zionist urbanization or development, until (to repeat the words of the gentleman from Sarona) such time as they would "go out of the hands of the local population and be ripe for urban settlement."

What is most interesting about this discourse is how often the British bought into it and how easily many segments of the Palestinian Arab population saw through it. This should could as no surprise, for as I have elsewhere demonstrated, one of the foundational themes of the relationship between the Zionist leadership and the British was the language of development they shared and from which the Arab population was by definition excluded.[162] Indeed, this chapter bears out the belief expressed by the preeminent Jewish town planner, Richard Kauffmann, that the town planning of Jewish settlements in Palestine could not be understood apart from the character and objects of the Zionist movement and its goals of settling and renewing the Jewish people—although most likely not in the manner in which he was conceiving it.[163]

Yet if the exclusivist goals of the Zionist–Tel Avivan enterprise are apparent in the evidence I have presented, the microlevel analysis of the day-to-day interactions of the Jews, Arabs, and British reveals a much more nuanced, complex, and even ambiguous reality. Moreover, the evidence demonstrates that even if "the Arab population did not deeply suffer economically from the gestures accorded to Zionist interests" vis-à-vis enterprises such as the Rutenberg Concession, it was still meaningful on much more than a "symbolic" level.[164] Rather, the material-economic and symbolic levels were bound together very successfully by the Zionist leadership through the town planning and development discourses.[165] Moreover, the response of many *fellaheen* to Tel Aviv's town planning strategies demonstrates that they were *not* "terrified of Land Registry offices and the courts"; nor can we assume that they "were not cognizant of their legal rights and status before the law" or that "the Arabs' primary experience was of survival against nature, and they had little experience in confronting the bureaucratic and legislative machinery introduced by the Ottomans and British."[166]

To argue thus is to assume both that the Ottoman state was not actively involved in transforming the nature of land tenure and use for its own benefit and that the peasants had no stake in or ability to adapt to and even challenge their evolving political-economic environment. Instead, it is clear that at least those living in or near the city of Jaffa were as cognizant of the effects of the Zionist-inspired urbanization of the region as they were of the changing legal field in the late Ottoman period and that they both understood their rights vis-à-vis the new land laws and knew how to work the system to attempt to foil the Zionists' goals.[167] It was a combination of British "incognizance" and the fact that wealthier landowners benefited from Zionist "development" that did them in.[168]

My discussion expands the framework for applying the insights of scholars such as Gershon Shafir and Derick Penslar to the analysis of Zionist urbanization. That is, the integrated idea of collective agricultural settlement as an answer to the twin problems of land and labor that Shafir presented in *Land, Labor and the Origins of the Israeli-Palestinian Conflict* had an equally important counterpart in Zionist urbanization, as did the Zionist "technocracy" described by Penslar in *Zionism and Technocracy.*

Most important, as the meeting of Jaffa residents and officials from Tel Aviv and the national Zionist leadership makes clear, in the trenches of the "war" between Jaffa and Tel Aviv for control of the land, water, and resources of the region, local, municipal, and national interests often clashed in ways that both challenge(d) and put into conflict the official ideology and historiography of Tel Aviv as, on the one hand, an autonomous, independent, and exclusively "Jewish" city and, on the other, as a "beacon of light" for its neighbors to the north, east, and south.

8 The New-Old Jaffa

Locating the Urban, the Public, and the Modern in Tel Aviv's Arab Neighborhood

JAFFA AND TEL AVIV AFTER THE 1948 WAR

In 1947 United Nations General Assembly Resolution 171 partitioned Palestine into Jewish and Arab states. Despite being surrounded by Tel Aviv and other Jewish towns within the territory of the proposed Jewish state, the city of Jaffa, because of its majority Palestinian Arab population and status as the cultural and economic capital of Arab Palestine—its "Bride of the Sea"—was included in the territory of the Arab state. Fighting in Jaffa began in December 1947 and continued until the city's surrender on May 13, 1948, which followed the flight of all but 3,500 of the city's prewar Palestinian Arab population of 70,000.[1]

At the end of the war all of the twenty-six Palestinian Arab villages in the Jaffa subdistrict were emptied or destroyed; Jaffa itself had "totally collapsed."[2] Prime Minister Ben Gurion envisioned that Jaffa was to be resettled entirely by Jews: "Jaffa will be a Jewish city. . . . War is war."[3] On April 24, 1950, Jaffa was officially united with Tel Aviv.

According to one soldier-turned-architect who participated in the capture of the neighboring village of Salama, "From the beginning the Municipality decided to *erase* historic Salameh and build in its place something completely new."[4] In previous chapters I discussed how the discourse of "erasure and reinscription," as James Holston has termed the guiding force behind modernist planning, was a major theme in the planning and architecture of Tel Aviv.[5] As such, it was given biblical justification: recall the passage from Amos greeting visitors to the Tel Aviv Museum, "I will restore the fortunes of my people Israel, and they shall rebuild the ruined cities and inhabit them."[6] Thus the municipality changed almost all the

Arabic street names in Jaffa to numbers, until such time as they could be renamed in Hebrew, the etiology of which were discussed at length in the short-lived Hebrew Jaffa paper, *Yediot Yafo (News from Jaffa)*.[7]

While the municipality was reluctant to annex Jaffa because of the cost of postwar rehabilitation, ultimately the two cities were united into one municipality because the government saw it as vital to achieving the goal of "the disintegration of Jaffa and the demarcation of the boundaries of a united city of Tel Aviv and Jaffa."[8] Their unification was announced on April 24, 1950, with "Yafo" attached to "Tel Aviv" to preserve the historical name,[9] while "Tel Aviv" symbolized the Jewish settlement renewing itself in Israel.[10]

In the course of this book I have attempted to demonstrate that architecture and planning were essential to the visual and discursive separation of "modern, Jewish" Tel Aviv from "ancient," "Arab" Jaffa, marking the city as a premier symbol of Jewish-Zionist rebirth in and of Palestine. As the *New York Times* pointed out in its lead editorial celebrating Israel's fiftieth anniversary, Tel Aviv's International Style architecture continues to symbolize the city's, and the country's, modernity. Yet the overriding focus on Tel Aviv and its architectural heritage has obscured Jaffa's impressive architectural heritage, both its early influence on the design of homes in Tel Aviv and the frequent deployment of International Style by the city's bourgeoisie before 1948 to declare their, and Jaffa's, modernity.[11]

In light of the discussion of the previous two chapters, this chapter has two goals. In the first part I examine the battles for control of and identity in what remains of Palestinian Arab Jaffa during the late 1980s and 1990s, a period in which it has become an object of "development" as both a site for tourism and as a new and chic neighborhood for the burgeoning Jewish elite of "global Tel Aviv." More specifically, I examine how, in the face of creeping dislocation, accompanied (and supported) by daily media and television portrayals of Jaffa as poor and crime-ridden *and* chic, exotic, and romantic (and thus the ideal tourist site), Palestinian residents have attempted reimagine their "city" and open up new spaces for agency and empowerment through which they can articulate a more autochthonous synthesis of the city's history and its architectural traditions—one that will allow them to remain on the land and develop Jaffa for the benefit of the local, as well as international, community.

The second part of this chapter serves as a conclusion to the book as a whole. Here I return to the argument with which I began—that the Jaffa–Tel Aviv region, and even Tel Aviv itself, is in many ways a "non-modern" space—and draw out two corollary postulates, that the Jaffa–Tel

Aviv region has over the course of the past century of conflict become neither "urban" nor "public" and thus perhaps no longer a "city"—regardless of its status as one of the "cities of the world."

A centerpiece of my analysis is one of the newest sites of controversy in Jaffa, on which the Peres Center for Peace was supposed to begin construction until the al-Aksa Intifada put the project on hold indefinitely. The center was to be the physical embodiment of former Prime Minister Shimon Peres's vision for a "New Middle East," with Israel as its economic and cultural engine; its mandate is to "build an infrastructure for peace" by sponsoring joint projects between Israelis, Palestinians, Jordanians, and other regional actors. I argue that the relationship between the architecture of the proposed center (which sought to create "a local architecture without local features" that would "contribute to the reawakening" of Jaffa) and the ambivalent dynamic of its worldview and programs symbolize the Oslo-era politics of space and identity in Jaffa and Tel Aviv and in Palestine and Israel.

BACKGROUND OF THE PRESENT
SOCIOECONOMIC SITUATION

The post-1948 remnants of the Palestinian Arab community of Jaffa were the poorer Arabs from the surrounding villages and a few Jaffans who remained. Jewish immigrants, mainly from the Balkans, were settled in empty Palestinian properties in the early 1950s. Later, when many of them moved to newer neighborhoods in the Tel Aviv region, Palestinians resumed renting and buying properties and moved back to live in Jaffa.

After a precipitous drop in the Tel Aviv metropolitan region's population during the 1972–83 period, the 1980s began a period of transformation of Tel Aviv into a "postindustrial era" that saw the relocation of most of the major financial and industrial corporations of Israel to the city, and with it, numerous "yuppie/dinkie" couples.[12] This immigration was augmented by the wave of Soviet Jewish immigration that began in 1989. The Palestinian population of Jaffa almost trebled since 1972; in contrast, the Jewish population of the two predominantly Palestinian Arab neighborhoods of Jaffa—'Ajami and Lev Yafo—fell dramatically, down to less than 3 percent in the case of 'Ajami.[13] Table 6 shows how the population of Jaffa and Tel Aviv changed during this period.

Discrimination has continually played a central role in the social life of Jaffa's Palestinian residents. It is a major factor in wage differentials, access to jobs, and educational level between Palestinians and Jews,[14] all of which has been exacerbated by the large increase in its Palestinian population and

TABLE 6. Population of Jaffa and Tel Aviv, 1961–2002

Year	Palestinian Arab Population of Jaffa (% of total population)	Total Population of Tel Aviv–Yafo
1961	5,782 (1.5)	386,070
1972	6,351 (2)	363,750
1983	9,455 (3)	327,265
1992	15,005 (4.2)	356,911
1997	15,800 (4.5)	Approx. 355,200
2002	360,400	

SOURCES: Government of Israel, Bureau of Statistics; Tel Aviv Municipality, 1997, *Statistical Yearbook*.

the influx of Russian immigrants who took jobs and housing from the local population after 1989.

Thus, despite claims by the municipality that conditions in Jaffa had actually improved in the past decade, in fact they "meaningfully deteriorated" in recent years, to the point that Palestinian Arab Jaffa has become the most depressed and disadvantaged community in the entire country[15]—an important cause of the renewed "intifada" in Jaffa in fall 2000.

THE CONTEMPORARY SYMBOLIC FUNCTIONS OF TEL AVIV AND JAFFA

In previous chapters I have argued that the symbolic and discursive functions of Tel Aviv and Jaffa within the Zionist enterprise have always been as important as their economic and political functions.[16] Consequently, they have exercised a determinative influence on the current political-economic situation in Jaffa. If the "first modern Hebrew city in the world" was from the start broadly contrasted with Jerusalem (the religious and cultural capital of pre-Zionist Jewish Palestine), "modern," "clean," and "well-planned" Tel Aviv was even more categorically distinguished from "backward," "dirty," and "unplanned" Jaffa—a mythology with such staying power that even UNESCO (not usually an organization sympathetic to Zionist narratives) ignored the significant presence of International Style architecture and other evidence of modernization in Jaffa, as well as its "organic" if conflicted linkage with Tel Aviv, to justify the designation of central and northern Tel Aviv as a World Heritage Site (an honor certainly well deserved even when based on a more accurate representation of its history and geography) without ever mentioning the words *Arab* or *Palestinian*.[17]

In the post-1948 period this dichotomy has continued to be a major theme in the Israeli and Western imagination of both cities, in no small part due to the trend in the past two decades (the era of postmodernist planning and architecture) for cities to seek to distinguish or differentiate themselves through their architecture, particularly through selling their image.[18] Thus the *New York Times* recently reported that "to many Israelis, the battle of the left-wing and secular Tel Aviv against the nationalist and religious Jerusalem is a struggle for the soul and destiny of Israel."[19]

Other American and European publications have also contrasted "secular," "normal," "cosmopolitan," "unabashedly sybaritic," and, most important, "modern" Tel Aviv with "holy," abnormal Jerusalem:[20] "a visitor wanting to see what the 50-year-old Jewish state is really all about would do well to plunge into the casual, self-consciously secular and thoroughly modern metropolis on the sea back where the dunes used to be"—as if Jerusalem and the seemingly interminable conflict it symbolizes are in fact a mirage on the "Sahara Desert" on which Tel Aviv was imagined, then built.

The "discourse of the sands" is intimately connected to an aesthetic of erasure and reinscription, which itself lies at the heart of most modernist planning ideologies, particularly Zionist-Israeli planning. Not surprisingly, the discursive erasure epitomized by the symbolism of sands and the changing of street names continues today. As the *Economist* explained in comparing Tel Aviv and Jerusalem, "Unlike Jerusalem, Tel Aviv contains hardly any Arabs. It has swallowed the old Arab port of Jaffa, but in the main it was built by Jews, for Jews, on top of sand dunes, not on top of anybody else's home."[21]

The purported absence of "Arabs" from the land on which Tel Aviv was built is an important reason why Tel Aviv is not considered a "national" space in the way that the *New York Times* conceives of Jerusalem, an ironic development considering that Tel Aviv was created as the living embodiment of a Zionist—that is, Jewish national—utopia.[22] It was also created as the living embodiment of the *modern* project, in which dreams of utopia all too often turn dystopic, particularly for those considered Other than the group for whom the utopia is being created.[23]

THE CONTEMPORARY TEL AVIVAN IMAGINATION OF JAFFA

The precise renditions of Tel Aviv's creation mythology by the Western media have had a profound impact on the way Jaffa has been imagined by

Israelis and foreign writers during the past fifty years, because the land-scape of Jaffa has remained central to the Tel Avivan self—and thus Other—definition. If Palestinian Arabs were discursively (and ultimately physically) erased from Tel Aviv, the process was even more determined in Jaffa. Two contemporary depictions of Jaffa, one negative and one quaint and "aggressively restored,"[24] have framed its envisioning.

On the one hand, Jaffa has been and continues to be visualized as poor and crime-infested. The neighborhood is the site of many crime and war movies and television shows since the 1960s[25] because "it resembles Beirut after the bombardments—dilapidated streets, fallen houses, dirty and neg-lected streets, smashed cars."[26] This image is reinforced by the media and government depictions, and to a lesser extent, the reality, of the neighbor-hood as a major center for drug dealing in the Tel Aviv metropolitan area.

On the other hand, specifically designed for tourist consumption, Jaffa is depicted as "ancient," "romantic," "exotic," and "quaint." "Old Jaffa . . . is the jewel of Tel Aviv," is how an official brochure described it.[27] These depic-tions of Jaffa are linked to its reimagining as a historically Jewish space, one that was "liberated from Arab hands," as the museums and tourist bro-chures inform visitors.[28] These visions of Jaffa are connected to Jaffa's place as a historic, archaeological, and thus tourist site in Tel Aviv: "A port city for over 4,000 years and one of the world's most ancient towns, Jaffa is a major tourist attraction, with an exciting combination of old and new, art galleries and great shopping. . . . Great care has been given to developing Old Jaffa as a cultural and historical center."[29]

In fact, the "city of the sands," imagined without a past or history, has always required Jaffa to complete its identity: "Once Tel Aviv became Tel Aviv–Yafo the young city all at once acquired itself a past—the 3000 years of ancient Yafo. . . . [And it] was ready for the great leap forward which transformed it into a metropolis. Yafo[,] . . . one of the oldest cities in the world, acquired a future and renewed youth, with widespread progress streaming its way from its youthful neighbor."[30]

Not surprisingly, contemporary Jaffans protest the way in which their city has become little more than "a margin on the name of Tel Aviv" since 1948.[31] One reason is that pre-1948 Jaffa was considered the "jewel" of Arab Palestine and was continually depicted in the Palestinian press as the country's most beautiful and important Arab city. As *Falastin* described it, "No one doubts that Jaffa is the greatest Arab city in Palestine, and it is inevitable that visitors to Palestine will stop by to see the model of Pales-tine's cities."[32] That is, Jaffa was the symbol and epitome of Palestine's modern urban landscape.

Yet many Diaspora Jaffas have come to accept the erasure of Jaffa, particularly those returning to visit the city in recent years, who have come to regard present-day Jaffa as a "figment of the imagination," or at best an object of critical nostalgia that borders on cynicism.[33] In many ways Tel Aviv has displaced Jaffa in the Palestinian imagination. When the facilitator of a peace mission in Palestinian-controlled Nablus asked people what their vision of peace was, a Palestinian artist replied, "Visiting Tel Aviv and watching the sun set,"[34] a sentiment whose echoes return to the pre-1948 period, as we saw in the discussion of Shehadeh's *Stranger in the House*.

On the other hand, the attachment of the remaining Palestinian population to Jaffa has grown significantly in the past two decades, in part in line with the larger trend toward increasing "Palestinianization" of "Israeli Arabs" in the wake of the reuniting of all of Mandatory Palestine after the Six Day War and then the outbreak of the Intifada in 1987.[35] Yet this nationalistic reimagining of Palestinian-Israeli identity also added greater relevance to the question of territoriality.[36] There have been several violent protests in Jaffa during the 1990s—most recently during the al-Aksa Intifada that began (and within Israel, ended) in October 2000—and leaders of the Palestinian community have called for Jaffa's municipal independence.[37]

Indeed, more than four years before the latest intifada, in response to continued attempts by the Tel Aviv Municipality to evict longtime Palestinian residents of Jaffa, the community's leadership threatened a "housing Intifada in the streets." They said they would declare "with a loud voice," "[W]e are planted here and . . . they will not be able to uproot us from our homes the way they uproot the orange and olive trees."[38] Both intifadas shared a focus on rootedness that is deeply embedded in the Jaffan, and the Palestinian, psyche, as evidenced by figure 12, a painting done by a young Jaffan artist, Suheir Riffi, that depicts a mother nursing her child, rooted in the earth and connected through it to her dilapidated home.[39]

GLOBALIZATION, ARCHITECTURE, AND PLANNING IN TEL AVIV–YAFO

The specificities of contemporary Jewish and Palestinian imaginings of Jaffa have influenced the way the Jaffa–Tel Aviv region has experienced the impact of globalization and the attempts by Israel's leadership, Tel Aviv's in particular, to make Tel Aviv into a "global" or "world" city. The drive to globalize Tel Aviv is understood as being part of the city's leaders' desire to shape and deploy a unique identity, separate from the rest of the country, especially from Jerusalem. Such an identity leaves planners, architects, and

Figure 12. Painting of woman and child next to dilapidated home by the Jaffan artist Suheir Riffi.

commentators to wonder "what to do with a world city that is so different from the rest of the country in which it is located."[40]

Naturally, Israeli social scientists have begun to analyze Tel Aviv as a global city, focusing on its entrance into the international market,[41] the increasing disparities between rich and poor, the "marketization" of social services such as the educational system,[42] and the influx of increasingly illegal migrant guest workers (tens of thousands of whom live in the Tel Aviv metropolitan area).[43]

Most architects working in Tel Aviv have refused to criticize the municipality's planning policies for "Global Tel Aviv," which call for building numerous high-rise projects throughout the city to maximize the market value of the land. One fantastical project, called Tel Aviv on the Sea, which would build several islands off the coast connected by bridges that would each contain several "millennium towers" of up to 170 floors, has been developed by researchers from the Technion in Haifa. At least one architect, Massimiliano Fuksas, the designer of the new Peres Center for Peace, sees such towering buildings as creating order out of urban "chaos."[44]

However, the eminent Dutch architect Peter Kook, who has worked in Tel Aviv, has described the present Tel Aviv "style" as "paranoia on the one hand, and the world wide trend of the worship of money on the other. The paranoia is reflected in the fact Israeli architects are closed to any outside styles, they only see what the Housing Ministry does, and not what's going on in the wider world. The power of money rules here in a dominant way on both aesthetics and on urban planning. . . . Also, there is a psychological factor. Israeli architects take the fortress as their model.[45] They are afraid to do more elegant architecture here, with more feeling, because maybe something will [destroy] the building."[46]

What is interesting is that in striving for "elegance" and "order," which Fuksas has achieved in his design for the Peres Center, both the design and the center it will house play into a century-long Zionist imagination of Jaffa as the antithesis of both.

ARCHITECTURE AND PLANNING IN TEL AVIV AND JAFFA DURING THE 1980S AND 1990S

The political, economic, and discursive roles architecture has played in Jaffa and Tel Aviv in the twentieth century bear out Michel Foucault's belief that "architecture and its concomitant theory never constitute an isolated field to be analyzed in minute detail; they are only of interest when one looks to see how they mesh with economics, politics, or institutions."[47] Certainly, both cities, particularly Tel Aviv, used town planning as a tool of the "war over land" in the Jaffa–Tel Aviv region during the Mandate period.

Yet, not surprisingly, much of Israeli planning literature has avoided any discussions of the Palestinian minority that would disturb the apolitical suppositions on which it is based, focusing instead on planning as "change-oriented activity" to "shift attention away from the document—the plan—to the political process whereby intentions are translated into action."[48] Thus, for example, in a 1997 edited volume on planning in Tel Aviv, a chapter titled "Conflict Management in Urban Planning in Tel Aviv–Yafo" consisted of a case study on underground parking in stores in central Tel Aviv;[49] the powerful realities of the state's dual "passive-regulatory/active-developmental system" have rarely been discussed, especially in Tel Aviv.[50]

Another example of this tendency comes from another chapter in a recent volume in the Social Processes and Public Policy in Tel Aviv–Yafo series, this one by Baruch Yoscovitz (at the time Tel Aviv's chief municipal engineer). According to Yoscovitz, there has been very little true planning in the Jaffa–Tel Aviv region since the town plan drawn up by Geddes in the mid-1920s: "Instead of comprehensive planning, these days we have 'pragmatic planning.'"[51]

What Yoscovitz fails to mention in his lengthy analysis of the Geddes Plan—to recall the discussion in chapter 6—is that Geddes clearly expressed his belief that whatever the "ethnic distinctiveness and the civic individuality" of Tel Aviv, it was geographically, socially, and economically part of Jaffa and should therefore "work and grow together" with the Jaffa Municipality "for Greater Jaffa."[52] Moreover, however "pragmatic" the dynamic of planning in Tel Aviv, the chief municipal engineer himself has been an important actor in the ongoing battles between the municipality and the Palestinian residents of Jaffa over the development of 'Ajami and Jaffa Port. It is worth noting in this context that the UNESCO report, which highlights the Geddes Plan in justifying Tel Aviv's designation as a World Heritage Site, also ignores Geddes's linkage of Tel Aviv with Jaffa.[53]

What my discussion makes clear, then, is that it is precisely the documents, or texts, that are pivotal to understanding the larger discourse of planning, particularly when planning takes place in "frontier" regions such as Jaffa's Palestinian neighborhoods.[54] This dynamic is especially relevant in the postindependence period of settler colonization movements such as Israel's; when we consider Jaffa as a frontier of this type, the link between discursive-cognitive landscapes and legal-administrative boundaries becomes apparent.

In frontier regions spatial policies can be used as a powerful tool to exert territorial control over minorities; on an urban scale, majority-controlled authorities can exercise subtler forms of spatial control through land use and housing policies, and in so doing create segregation between social groups.[55] This is particularly true when the government takes almost all the power out of the hands of local Palestinian communities to plan their own development.[56]

The discussion thus far suggests that the object of analyses of planning in Tel Aviv and Jaffa should be to clarify the complex web of relations among governmental, semigovernmental, and pseudogovernmental organizations and institutions that control the planning system in Israel. The number of institutions involved and the complexity of their relations[57] indicate that despite claims to the contrary, planning is highly politicized and ideological.

What is new in this equation is the increasingly prominent role of private interests in planning and development in Israel, in Jaffa in particular, and how this development is shifting the internal boundaries in the land and planning system while maintaining the traditional focus on permanent Jewish ownership of as much land as possible. Thus, for example, the pseudo-governmental Jewish National Fund (JNF)[58] announced in November 1998 that it was severing ties with the Israel Land Authority, the semigovernmental agency that administers both state and JNF-owned lands (and which heretofore has been composed of both government and JNF representatives), precisely because by going "private" it could buck the legal trend toward equality between Jews and Palestinians in the government sector and ensure that its huge reserves of land remained "in the hands of the Jewish people."[59] As I explain below, one can understand the transfer of the land on which the Peres Center for Peace is to be built as serving a similar goal.

Fueled by the larger discursive, even epistemological shift toward privatization in Israeli society, the strategic shift toward privatization in city planning has led to a situation in which planners chart a course of development focused on middle- and upper-class Israelis and implemented through private developers that pits Jews against their Palestinian fellow citizens. Thus Palestinian land is expropriated, the construction of new, privately developed Jewish housing on that land is subsequently approved, and the new Jewish "owners"—often self-described liberals and supporters of Palestinian rights—naturally take the lead in fighting against the claims the previous (or now, "illegal") Palestinian inhabitants, since by then they have invested time and money in their new homes. This is how the government, working through private developers, brings the economic interests of liberal Israelis in line with its perceived "national" interests vis-à-vis increasing Jewish ownership, control, and presence on the land.[60]

The evidence presented in chapter 5 suggests that a stroll through Jaffa, or a glance at a map, would reveal that from both an architectural and a planning perspective, Jaffa's pre-1948 development, ʿAjami's in particular, closely mirrored that of Tel Aviv.[61] However, in the postwar and unification planning of the early 1950s, Jaffa and the surrounding villages were considered "slums" and scheduled for rehabilitation, the goal of which was, "Today slums, tomorrow seashore parks."[62]

By the early 1980s a new generation of "renewal" efforts began in the older neighborhoods of Neve Tzedek and Lev Tel Aviv, a process that was closely linked to the larger ideologies and historical dynamics surrounding Israeli architecture and planning throughout the country, as well as in the Occupied Territories.[63] The renewed activity was prompted by the structural reorganization of the city's economy that began in the previous decade and sought to "reviv[e] the region as a space for living in the center of the city by drawing a mainly young population to it."[64] Both neighborhoods featured architecture that made them attractive for gentrification. Lev Tel Aviv, having already undergone extensive reconstruction in the 1930s, featured the International Style buildings that put Tel Aviv on the architectural map. Neve Tzedek featured much older buildings and attracted a bohemian crowd trying to escape both the austere, International Style architecture that dominated the city from the 1930s through 1970s and the more recent postmodern fetishization of consumption that took the ironic form of an easily identifiable uniform "postmodern style."[65]

In fact, there has been something of a rebellion by many residents, and even some architects, to the consumer-driven architecture of the 1970s, symbolized by the numerous residential and office towers in or near Neve Tzedek.[66] This is a major change from the early 1970s, when the municipality bragged that the "leap up into the skies . . . improved the appearance of the city, adding an extra beauty to its landscape."[67]

The renewed appreciation of the city's older architecture can be interpreted as part of the general trend in "postmodern architecture," reacting against modernism's clean break with the past, to employ a type of "historicism; historical quotation; an architecture of memory and monuments[;] . . . a search for 'character,' unique features, visual references."[68] Yet as important, it can be explained as part of the process in which architecture, and art in general, has become a commodity catering to consumer tastes—an ironic development in light of the desire to move away from a visually consumerist lived environment. Seen in this way the "renewal" of neighborhoods like Neve Tzedek can be understood not as "preserving" the past but rather as "rewriting or inventing" it, since buildings and districts are renovated, restored, or rehabilitated to correspond to ideal visions of the past and satisfy contemporary needs and tastes by incorporating new technologies and designs.[69]

If the gentrification of Tel Aviv's older neighborhoods generates and reflects contradictory impulses and desires, the process is much more complicated in Jaffa, which is officially part of Tel Aviv, yet is heavily invested with symbolism that portrays it as Tel Aviv's alter ego. How is this separation mediated? The answer becomes clear when we understand that through the various Zionist-Israeli visions of "ancient" Jaffa the neighborhood becomes "a discursive object created by Israelis as part of turning Israel . . . into particular socio-political spaces."[70] If we view Jaffa as a frontier region—indeed, as a frontier region of a frontier region; that is, as Tel

Aviv first saw itself—it further becomes clear how the spatial policies of the municipality are used as a powerful tool (much like the power of Orientalist discourse as described by Said) to exert territorial control over and physically shape this discursive yet material space.[71]

In the resulting process of cognitive and physical boundary between Tel Aviv and Jaffa, the Jewish yuppies moving to Jaffa "see residential exclusivity and the redeeming modernizing impact of Zionism as simply engendering a demarcation between two types of territory."[72] In this vision Jaffa is the ontohistorical Other of Tel Aviv, against which Tel Aviv defines itself. At the same time, having been "liberated" from its Arab identity and "united" with its daughter city, Jaffa is continuously undergoing a process of "renewed youth and progress," the lifeblood of which are the architectural and planning policies of the municipality. Yet the neighborhood's renewal is dependent on its permanent fixture in time and space as "ancient" or "quaint"—the ideal site for tourist and elite development.

In fact, if architecturally Tel Aviv has become a "tragedy"[73] because architects are afraid to build imaginatively there, Jaffa has become the space where the imagination, although remaining under government supervision, has had freer rein. That is, as "picturesque" has become the architectural fashion, the government realized that "old, dilapidated Arab neighborhoods have an 'oriental' potential."[74] Thus the function of the numerous rehabilitation projects of the past two decades has been to expand commerce, tourism, and hotels in line with the "specific character" of the area.[75] "Today the slogan is, 'Gentrify!' As land becomes available, it is sold on stringent conditions that only the wealthy can meet."[76] Thus the current style among the Jewish architects practicing in Jaffa is to build with arches, "thousands of arches, wholesale," as one architectural critic put it.[77]

The end result of this process has been expressed in "the systematic erasure of the identity of the city of Jaffa as a Palestinian Arab city."[78] This may seem ironic given the "Oriental" feel of current building styles, but in fact Jaffa has had to be emptied of its Arab past and Arab inhabitants in order for architects to be able to reenvision the region as a "typical Middle Eastern city" and construct new buildings based on this imagined space, unaware that such a city only ever existed in the worldview of the architects.[79]

It is within this framework that Kook has explained why recent attempts to "preserve" Jaffa cannot be taken at face value: "This is not 'preservation,' this is Disneyland. The old city and the new projects that attempt to preserve the Arab architecture are cheap imitations, more decorative, intended for tourists. . . . It's for entertainment or amusement, so why not?"[80]

TOURISM AND THE NEW MARKET DISCIPLINE

As the world economy and the peace process have faltered, Israel's economic leaders believe that the key to continued economic growth is the real estate market, of which the Tel Aviv metropolitan area is the center. This view has clear implications for the current "renewal" efforts in Jaffa, as the municipality has even less freedom or incentive to commit scarce resources to rehabilitating a poor minority community that is sitting on valuable land whose marketization is seen as essential for the country's economic health.[81]

The influence of the market discourse is readily apparent in current planning in Jaffa and should be used to contextualize statements such as Mayor Ron Holdai's campaign promise that "the time has come to lower the walls between Jaffa and Tel Aviv."[82] Thus while current policy guidelines declare that the new regional plan for Tel Aviv must involve residents in planning and increase housing for young couples,[83] when Palestinian community leaders have complained that most young Palestinian couples cannot afford to live in Jaffa officials have responded by explaining that "the market is the market"[84] and that "selling some apartments more cheaply would hurt profits."[85]

The most important impact of the marketization of planning in Jaffa has been the partial or total privatization of several of the bodies directly responsible for the rehabilitation of the quarter since the mid-1990s. Until then, as much as 90 percent of the housing units in Jaffa were partly owned by the government,[86] and a large part of the real estate in Jaffa was in the hands of quasi-governmental companies such as Amidar and Halmish. The transfer of the development projects to private developers was described by Jaffa's Palestinian councilman (in the same language, it is worth noting, used by the Jaffa newspaper al-Jam'iah al-Islamiyyah in 1932 to describe the burgeoning land conflicts in Jaffa–Tel Aviv and Palestine as a whole) as a major turning point for the quarter.[87]

One of the projects partially transferred to private developers involves the redevelopment of Jaffa's port, home to a fishing industry that supports two hundred fifty families. The stated aim of the project is to "resurrect and develop old Jaffa's harbor as an area of tourism, recreation and sea sport"[88] by linking it directly to the lived area of the Old City through the construction of up to four thousand elite residence and hotel units.[89] Yet the symbolism surrounding the port gives a clue to how the project will be realized: thus the official *Tel Aviv–Jaffa* guide of the Ministry of Tourism says, "[T]he old city today is alive, her buildings and alleys restored amidst cobbled streets and green parks as a thriving artist's colony. . . . [G]reat care has been given to developing Old Jaffa as a cultural and historical center while preserving its Mediterranean flavor. . . . Jaffa Marina [part of the development project] has been established in the heart of the ancient port . . . and offers all a sailor could desire. . . . Visit Old Jaffa anytime. By sunlight and starlight, it is the 'jewel' of Tel Aviv."[90]

"Project Shikum [Rehabilitation]" is also ostensibly designed to "develop and rehabilitate Jaffa." It was turned over by the municipality to a private developer, Yoram Gadish, in 1996, and when mismanagement and concerted local opposition led the government and the municipality to terminate Gadish's contract, a new private company headed by former Tel Aviv Mayor Shlomo Lahat was awarded the contract to continue the neighborhood's gentrification.[91] The relationship among the Tel Aviv Municipality, a historic and tourist landmark inhabited by Palestinians, and a private development company headed by a former mayor is identical to the situation in East Jerusalem vis-à-vis the "City of David" project, headed by former Mayor Teddy Kolek, although the specific legal and planning mechanisms by which control over land is secured differ in the two cities.[92]

An interview with representatives from the Gadish company while it administered Project Shikum reveals the thinking underlying both the Jaffa and Jerusalem projects—and thus the discourse governing Israeli planning on both sides of the Green Line. According to Gadish, the goal of the project was

> to develop Jaffa because Jaffa is not developed[;] . . . that is, develop infrastructure, sewers, streets, schools, etc., and . . . the empty lands in Jaffa. We want to revolutionize Jaffa *[lhafokh et Yafo]*, to change Jaffa from a neighborhood with so many problems to a tourist city—there's lots of potential for development into a tourist city. . . . But you need to have a *plan*, and like New York or anywhere, sometimes you have to destroy a building as part of development for public needs, and we're working with a committee of architects and the Municipality. . . . However, there residents want to keep the status quo because development increases prices, and their children won't be able to live and buy apartments there; also Arabs won't go to other cities like Bat Yam, Herzliyya[,] because there are no services for them. They *can* go to Lod and Ramle, but they're not *ready* to go and don't want to develop[,] . . . but with Jews [Jaffa] becomes more beautiful and develops.[93]

In the late 1990s a more official quasi-governmental body, Mishlama leyafo, has assumed responsibility for administering Jaffa, from providing municipal services to residents to supervising the quarter's gentrification. Its goal, in the words of Tel Aviv's mayor, is nothing less than to "to build

Jaffa, to revolutionize [*lhafokh;* lit. "overturn"] Jaffa into a dream space."[94] Another initiative, cosponsored by Tel Aviv University and two private philanthropic organizations called the Price Brodie Initiative in Jaffa, also believes that "Jaffa can be developed in the spheres of education and community," to which the project hopes to contribute by assessing the "needs of the community as presented by representatives of the Tel Aviv Municipality and the community. . . . In close cooperation with the governance of Jaffa [we] can give Jaffa a momentum for change which it has needed for many years."[95]

Several aspects of the statements by Gadish, Mishlama, and Price-Brodie representatives deserve comment. First, the root of the verb "to revolutionize," *lhafokh*, is the same as the verb for "overturning" in the phrase, "A geographical revolution has come to the world," as Yitzhak Rokah described it, with clear implications about Jaffa's existing geography in 1909. Indeed, this perspective was quite similar, one could argue, to the implications of the Gadish representative's statement. Second, the importance of having a "plan" was also fundamental to the genesis of Tel Aviv; as one of its founders wrote before the first house was built, "Money we don't have, a plan we do have."[96] Today the plan is for Jaffa, not Tel Aviv, but the implication that Jaffa requires transformation under Zionist-Israeli supervision is a long-standing discourse in Zionist and Israeli writing about and policies toward the city. The issue is whether the Jaffa-as-"dream space" can answer the dreams of the local Palestinian (and working-class Jewish) population, or the wealthy Jewish and foreign populations bent on remaking Jaffa in their more "Disney-fied" image.[97]

The Andromeda Hill Project

Perhaps the paradigmatic example of the intersection of the new global, market-based, postmodern architectural discourse in Jaffa and the almost century-long Zionist-Israeli imagination of the city is the Andromeda Hill project, where units start at well over U.S.$300,000. Constructed on property at the top of the ʿAjami Hill, with a commanding view of the port and ocean below, Andromeda Hill bills itself as "the incomparable Jaffa . . . the New-Old Jaffa" (fig. 13).

To orient prospective customers on its Web site, the Andromeda Hill virtual brochure explains that "historic Jaffa" lies to the north of the development, the "picturesque fishermen's wharf of Jaffa" to the west, and the "renewed ʿAjami district, where the rich and famous come to live," to the south. The Hebrew version stresses the architecture of the place even more, in line with the greater importance of architectural discourse in Israeli cul-

THE SEA, THE AMAZING VIEW, THE INCOMPARABLE JAFFA

The first original has been sold. The second original has been sold. The third original has been sold. And now there's Building No. 4 - 3 rooms apartments for sale - $390,000. Andromeda Hill by the sea - to live in the original.

ANDROMEDA HILL, an exclusive residential project is being created in Tel Aviv, offers a unique complex designed to harmonise with old Jaffa's charm and character along with magnificent views of the port and sea. Secure and beautifully landscaped grounds with paved walkways and quiet gardens will provide unmatched tranquility. Entrance to the complex is through a guarded lobby, for pedestrians only, while internal motor traffic will utilize a network of underground roads and tunnels. At ANDROMEDA HILL you will enjoy all the facilities of modern living, including private health club with swimming pool and gymnasium ... Yet you will be just moments away from the cafes, restaurants and shops which create Jaffa's special ambience. You can select your luxury apartment from a choice of two to six rooms or a magnificent penthouse, each elegantly and luxuriously finished to the highest standard.

ANDROMEDA HILL - THE NEW-OLD JAFFA

Please visit our site office/show flat at 38 Yaffet st.
Tel: 972-3-6838448. Fax: 972-3-6837499 Jaffa, Tel Aviv, Israel.
representative in the U.K: Loretta Cash at Russel Cash Overseas, Tel: 0181-420 6422, Fax: 420 6450
representative in the U.S.A: Tel: 202-4628990, Fax: 202-4628995
ANDROMEDA HILL on the Internet: http://www.andromeda.co.il
Developers; Mordot Hayam Ltd.
Developer & Building Contractor: [logo] Ilan Gat Engineers Ltd.

Figure 13. Advertisement for Andromeda Hill development.

ture.[98] Moreover, the section of the Web site titled "The Legendary Jaffa" recounts the Greek legend of Andromeda, which was set on a large rock facing the city outside of Jaffa's port and explains that "Andromeda became a symbol of awakening and renewal, and it is not by chance that the project was named 'Andromeda Hill,' expressing the rebirth of old Jaffa."

When asked why and how the architectural design and advertising campaign was chosen for Andromeda Hill, one former employee replied:

> The Municipality decided on the style—the windows, the columns, the materials—after going around Jaffa and looking at the buildings. . . . The style was very eclectic—Arabic from the beginning of the century influenced by European [specifically Italian] architecture. . . . Arches were a main symbol in a project of this size. . . . We didn't use real stone [except in a few places] but rather a man-made material called GRC, which is fake stone.[99] In terms of the ads, you have to think about who's going to buy there. . . . [T]hey expected people from abroad to buy it. Jaffa today is not a nice place, you have to think about the future, what will be attractive. People aren't living there because of the sea, because there's sea all over Israel, they're living there because of the nostalgia, the atmosphere.

The Andromeda Hill discourse, like that of Gadish, exemplifies the conflation of architecture and planning, market forces and government control, that comprises the forces at play in the continuing "war over land" in ʿAjami.[100] When I visited the complex in 1988 I was shown a short video before the tour whose narration concluded with the point that "Andromeda Hill is, in essence, a city within a city." This is almost identical to the language used by the founders of Tel Aviv to describe the Jewish position in Jaffa almost one hundred years ago, when they celebrated having created "a state within a state in Jaffa." The social, political, and spatial implications of such a discourse are also identical; that is, in each case, Jaffa is the object of "economic conquest"—as Ruppin described it ninety years ago—by Jewish residents from Tel Aviv.[101]

If we recall Kook's equation of Jaffa with Disneyland, this imagery takes on added significance in light of the belief by proponents of Global America that "the wretched of the earth just want to go to Disneyland if given the chance."[102] Like Disneyland for most of the world's poor, the virtual reality[103] that increasingly cohabits the space of contemporary Jaffa can only be viewed from beyond a "secured gate" by most residents of ʿAjami.[104] In Isra-Disney, Jaffa, as symbolized by Andromeda Hill, becomes an "urban masterpiece," a site of "artistic renaissance," and "a museum of magnificent architecturally designed buildings"[105]—a carnival of sites, sights, and sounds that excludes those who cannot afford the steep entrance fee.

The Peres Center for Peace

The most recent—and in many ways most timely—example of the interrelationship of architecture, planning, and discourses of identity and control in Jaffa involves the planned construction of the Peres Center for Peace in 'Ajami. I examine both the symbolism of the architecture of the center's new building and how it relates to the ideology underlying the programs that will be housed there.

The Peres Center for Peace was founded by Shimon Peres in 1997 and is "dedicated to the promotion of peace in the Middle East . . . in the context of globalization and international stability."[106] The center sponsors dozens of projects that bring together Israeli, Palestinian, and Arab (mostly Egyptian and Jordanian) scholars, policy makers, and businesspeople on issues such as technology, agriculture, municipal peace links, tourism, energy, health care, culture and media, education, and how the Israeli-Palestinian peace process can serve as an example for other war-torn regions.[107]

The structure was designed by the well-known Italian architect Massimiliano Fuksas and will be located on a 1¼-acre lot on the seashore in 'Ajami, on which the (Palestinian Arab) Donolo Hospital once stood. According to a review of the design by the Israeli architecture critic Esther Zandberg, the overall effect of the "compact and urban" structure will be one of "simple sophistication," that is, a local architecture without "local features."[108] The building will be a return, for the first time in decades, to a "straightforward Israeli architecture . . . without borrowed elements, an architecture that attempts . . . to be here without blending in."[109]

Zandberg continues (it is worth quoting her at length):

> The location of the structure . . . in Jaffa's 'Ajami neighborhood makes the achievement even more significant since Jaffa, with the encouragement of mandatory municipal directives, has long since become a Disneyland of Orientalized building styles.[110] This time the municipality backed off from its demand for the use of these gestures, such as arches or a tiled roof. . . . It is one of the most desirable and challenging plots of land in all of Tel Aviv-Jaffa. . . . The hope is that the center will contribute to the reawakening of Jaffa and perhaps even repeat some of the unprecedented and longed-for success of the Guggenheim Museum in Bilbao, Spain.

Because requests to the Peres Center for Peace and the architects for a rendering or picture of the design were refused, below I present Zandberg's description of the structure in detail:

> The structure is a narrow, long rectangle, an almost-schematic box in the positive sense of the word, and is attractive without being pompous. Three of the sides will be faced with strips of concrete and windows of varying sizes. The walls, whose thickness varies from half a meter to one meter, will involve a new and as yet untried method that will

enable people outside to look in and vice versa. At night, as Fuksas explains in the film he produced about the building, the structure will shine like a lighthouse. The fourth side, facing the sea, is of transparent glass—a great temptation and a difficult challenge becaue of the climate. The solution to this, and other complex technical difficulties, will be discussed in the detailed plans. . . . The building planned for Jaffa is very similar to another building designed by Fuksas for the Peres Center for Peace and the Palestinian Authority in Tul Karm, part of Area A (which is under complete Palestinian control). . . . The similarity between the two designs, in such different geographical areas, could be embarassing, but it could also open up the trite debate over "building in context" to a cultural and not only geographic perspective.

The nods to Jaffa's geography that are obvious in the Peres Center plans are the adaptation to the slanted lot and the glass wall overlooking the sea. The cultural gesture common to it and the plans for the center in Tul Karm is the attempt, under cultural conditions that are not completely different, to create a local architectire with "local" ingredients. By landing on the Jaffa shore, the building somehow developed symbolic gestures that were not obvious in Tul Karm. From the total, perfect box, two sculptural, flying canopies extend toward the sea—berets, waves, cloudiness or "wings of peace"—an image that Fuksas develops in his film to the point of poetic meditation, of the sort that lofty aims such as peace often coax from the mouths of architects.

Peres Center officials promise "that the center will also be available to Jaffa residents and will not close itself off." According to them, "the plan to erect the center was worked out together with Jaffa community leaders and senior Palestinian Authority officials."[111] Yet no community "leader" with whom I spoke as late as 2003 had been contacted by the Peres Center for Peace in any capacity, and none—from establishment school principals to young activists—believed that in the end the community would have any real access to the site apart from visiting it like any other tourist or that the projects the Center hopes to develop will involve or have an impact on them in any significant manner.[112]

Their view of the prospects for any real relationship between the center and the local community are in fact seconded by my interviews with the center's staff. When I called to arrange an interview to discuss its relationship with the local community a staff member with whom I spoke immediately became agitated and said, "What do you want to talk about that for, we have nothing to do with Jaffa or Tel Aviv," a point she went on to stress again later in our conversation. Similarly, the International Operations officer of the center admonished me not to focus on the potential projects or relationships with the locals, explaining that at least until the center is built in 'Ajami, such coordination and cooperation is not on the agenda.[113]

Yet Fuksas has said, "[T]his is the first time I feel that I am doing something that is not just beautiful but that will serve an important purpose as well. This will be the site of communication and Internet and a meeting place for peoples. That is the nature of peace. . . . We must forget the past and go forward."[114] Such a modernist vision fits perfectly with the ideology governing each of the various stages of Tel Aviv's architectural history, from Garden City to eclectic to International Style. Indeed, Fuksas "likes materials that are time transforming," a power that Tel Aviv has long been depicted as possessing over the peoples and nature it envelops.[115]

Fuksas says:

> [The Peres Center for Peace was designed] to shed some light on the main principle of architecture, that is Ethics—and to caution that it is going to be trapped in the bounds of aesthetics. In the dawning of the new millennium, where the world stands before harsh problems of over-population, architecture cannot stand solely on aesthetics, but must develop a sense of responsibility, and distinguish between good and bad. . . . I believe that we architects can change the world with our knowledge. . . . This building is optimistic. . . . The building is constructed on levels—like the history of this place. And once in a while, light beams out of these levels, like a big communication center. The building is not light from outside, but rather it will shine from within—this is the first symbol.[116]

This lighthouse image is central to Tel Aviv's history, as it long was (and to my knowledge, still is) an official symbol of the city. Moreover, although Fuksas focuses on levels of history, not once in the lengthy interview are the local Palestinian residents mentioned, their history seemingly forgotten. Fuksas did state, however, in response to a question regarding the urgency of this building in light of the major infrastructural, educational, and housing problems in the quarter, that "the peace center will be a home for all. . . . It will develop the Jaffa economy." He continued: "I totally agree with the Peres ideology that economic prosperity reinforces Democracy. . . . Israel is the most culturally diverse and authentic place I know, and it works here better than most places in Europe, believe me."[117]

The Peres "ideology," as I explore in a moment, is one firmly grounded in the market, tourism, and other discourses that few of Jaffa's nonelite residents have found to be living up to their promise. But here let me complete the analysis of the style of the building, which Fuksas explains was allowed to come to fruition after he persuaded the Tel Aviv Municipality to agree to a "totally unethnic building with no arches, stone face bricks, but with bare concrete," in Jaffa based on a "willingness to regulate Israel's architectural past, of which concrete plays an essential role."[118]

What is most surprising about this comment is that one of the most outstanding examples of Bauhaus architecture in the whole country is a former—and self-consciously modern—Arab house (now the French embassy), located only a few hundred meters from the site of the new Peres Center and which was designed by an Italian architect. Not to mention the many other International Style buildings—concrete, of course—located in the immediate vicinity.[119] Indeed, the reason for these elisions is clear by the manner in which the interview progresses. About midway through Fuksas stops talking about Jaffa and begins referring to "Tel Aviv," as in "Tel Aviv interests me so much more than Jerusalem. . . . You can only ruin Jerusalem. . . . Your opportunity is here, in Tel Aviv. So many meeting places and young people, and a vitality you don't find in most European cities. Not it is time to do good things in Tel Aviv. I dream of planning a skyscraper in Tel Aviv. It is so beautiful, the buildings, the towers in Tel Aviv."[120] Here again he repeats the traditional view of Tel Aviv as a "young vibrant" city where one can do "good things." That is perhaps why the Tul Karm–Palestinian version of the center is viewed as out of "context"—perhaps a bit too "Disney," without the modern surroundings of Tel Aviv.

Turning from the center's architecture to its activities, its projects in the areas of tourism and culture are most relevant for this discussion. In terms of the former, a major goal is the Palestinian-Israeli Tourism Cooperation project, although interestingly, Jaffa and Tel Aviv do not seem to figure into the "regional tourism packages" they are developing.[121] In the areas of culture and media most of the energy is devoted to coproduced theatrical productions and films (mostly documentaries), while municipal cooperation pairs Jewish Israeli municipalities with Palestinian towns across the Green Line.

The ideology underlying the center's activities and architecture is apparent from Peres's best-selling book, *The New Middle East*: "To save the future of the Middle East it is not enough to settle differences bilaterally or even multilaterally. We must build a new Middle East. Within this framework, peace is the means for security."[122] Peres's vision of the now-defunct Oslo process was that it would help to bring the Palestinians, "a group who had never been a people," into the status of peoplehood at the dawn of the era of globalization (thus the "new" in the new Middle East), when "the scale has tipped in the direction of economics rather than military might."[123] Yet this claim is belied by the senior staff of the center, among them Uri

Savir, former director general of Israel's Ministry of Foreign Affairs and chief negotiator of the Oslo Accords, and Carmi Gillon, former head of the General Security Services who is director general of the center.[124]

Indeed, this elision of the continuing military and political Occupation in the West Bank and Gaza in favor of an economistic-as-optimistic vision of the future can be juxtaposed to the headline and picture from Jaffa, published by the Arabic weekly *al-Sabar* during the Intifada inside Israel, which depicted fully armed Israeli soldiers patrolling the darkened main street of Jaffa and asked, "Yefet Street in Jaffa or al-Shahda Street in Khalil (Hebron)?"[125] Such erasures are not surprising given the neoliberal framework that sustains Peres's vision (in which the violence of the market either does not exist or is explained in nonpolitical terms).[126]

Yet the reality of the violence of the dominant and supposedly market-driven vision for Jaffa is such that the deputy mayor of Tel Aviv–Yafo, Michael Ro'eh, a member of the "progressive" Meretz party, predicted several years ago (in the context of the rapidly expanding gentrification of 'Ajami and seemingly without much disappointment) that "in ten years 75% of Jaffa's Arabs will be gone from the city."[127] Nevertheless, in describing the value of the proposed center in 'Ajami, he explained that it "would service all the residents of Jaffa. There will be seminars and meetings there between Jews and Arabs. This will be the development of the "New Middle East" [in] 'Ajami. This can be an anchor for change."[128]

The reality of Peres's New Middle East is evident—ironically—in the presence of (usually) "illegal" Palestinians from Gaza early each morning on Jaffa's Gaza Street hoping to get a day's work from local contractors. Despite complaints of local residents about their ubiquitous presence, "the connection between Jaffa and Gaza is by no means easy to cut. Just as Jaffa has its Gaza Street, so Gaza has its refugee camps named after Jaffan neighborhoods."[129] These workers are among the tens of thousands of foreign workers—many of their main competitors are similarly illegal Arab migrants from Egypt and Jordan (a resumption of at least a century-long pattern of "foreign" Arab migration to the Jaffa–Tel Aviv region)—who are following employment trajectories similar to their counterparts living in the vicinity of most of the "world cities."[130]

What is most interesting for our purposes—and for the Peres Center—are the words of one Gazan–Jaffan worker spoken prophetically only weeks before the violence erupted in October 2000: "We're at a stage where we don't ask what can be done. [Arafat] has enough prisons to last us a hundred years. Israel too we endured to the point where we blew up. The same will happen with the PA [Palestinian Authority], apparently. The rage will grow until we explode."[131] Importantly, the economic conditions driving the Gazan workers to Jaffa were a main cause of the al-Aksa Intifada; and many of the main protagonists of the protests in Jaffa were these workers from the Occupied Territories.

Moreover, although Peres believes the future is economic, his vision of the region is one dominated by the "spector of Islamic fundamentalism," which he believes is "inherent[ly] resistan[t] to modernism per se."[132] From this perspective, how will the Peres Center for Peace fit in 'Ajami, which even to its Muslim inhabitants has "grown each year more and more to resemble Tehran," with its black-chadored women and bearded men?[133] Can the Peres Center for Peace "introduce a new framework" for the Middle East, one that "will provide the potential for economic and social growth, extinguishing the fire of religious extremism and cooling the hot winds of revolution," if it is unwilling or unable to do so in Jaffa?[134]

There is much work to be done if the Peres Center for Peace, on the sands of Ajami, is to be a lighthouse of modernity and peace for Israel, Palestine, and the Middle East as a whole and not just another entertainment or amusement center. Not least is overturning the modernist vision on which it and Tel Aviv have been constructed.[135]

CONCLUSION: SPATIALIZING PALESTINIAN JAFFA
Locating the Modern, the Urban, and the Public in a Postcolonial Landscape

More than a century ago Theodor Herzl explained what was necessary to create a Jewish state in Palestine: "If I wish to substitute a new building for an old one, I must demolish before I construct."[136] Five decades later, at the height of the era of modernist planning, Le Corbusier—several of whose disciples became prominent Zionist planners and architects—quoted a famous Turkish proverb to epitomize the modernist ethic: "Where one builds one plants trees. We root them up."[137] Lefebvre explains the process more critically when he informs us that "the 'plan' does not remain innocently on paper. On the ground, the bulldozer realizes 'plans.'"[138]

The evidence presented in this chapter, like that presented in earlier chapters for the pre-1948 period, has demonstrated that Jaffa can be understood as a space of both negation and identification for Tel Aviv. This ambivalence to Jaffa mirrors the larger relationship of the Israeli state to the Palestinian communities living within its pre-1967 borders. The entry of the Palestinian into the Israeli "national self," or the self-definition of the Israeli state, is both ambivalent and paradoxical. It is ambivalent in that postmodernist architectural sensitivity to Jaffa's Palestinian Arab heritage has remained "superficial" and economic in orientation. The place-oriented postmodern architecture is used to catch a "global"—and implicitly, non-Arab—elite, and disallow potentially political identification from Jaffa's Palestinian community. The double economy of fixing Jaffa for an Orientalist gaze, on the one hand, and developing it along the line of a changing market economy, on the other, represents both the economization and depoliticization of the Palestinian community.

The contested space of Jaffa and Tel Aviv further epitomizes the complex manner in which architectural and planning movements are inscribed in the politics of national identity in Israel: erasing "tradition" (through International Style architecture) and reclaiming or reinscribing it (through discourses of heritage promoted by postmodernist architecture). As such, both are expressed in the economic as well as political idioms that in turn are central to the process of ethnopolitical identity formation in Israel as a modern nation-state. This is the dynamic governing the politics of urban design in contemporary Jaffa.

However, the linkage of the metaphors of erasure and rebuilding, and their function as ideological underpinnings of the "Jewish state," has long been recognized by Jaffa's (and no doubt the country's) Palestinian population.[139] Thus community leaders objected to a 1985 development project by explaining that the development policies of the Tel Aviv Municipality and national government agencies had generally involved using "legal" and "planning" mechanisms to destroy homes and expropriate Palestinians' land.[140]

Indeed, the concerted efforts to preserve/erase Jaffa's Palestinian Arab character and heritage have had a profound effect on the way residents experience the city: artists paint Jaffa as empty and vacant (fig. 14), while residents attempt to reclaim the city by referring to streets by their original Arabic names rather than the Hebrew names given them by the municipality after the postwar annexation of Jaffa. On the other hand, many residents, including the former chair of al-Rabita, the local Jaffan community organization,[141] have expressed their belief that the policies of the Tel Aviv Municipality have only strengthened the ties of most of the Palestinian community to Jaffa and its Arab identity.[142]

Prevented from expressing its identity through the design and planning of its lived environment, Jaffa's Palestinian population has articulated its identity through "spatializing social activity"[143]—through art festivals, original theater, organized protests (which became violent in 1994 and 1996), fighting to return streets to their original Arabic names, or barring

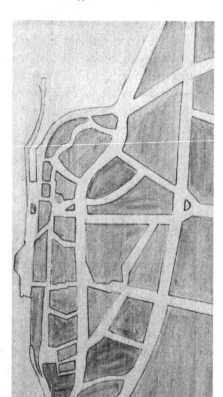

Figure 14. Painting of vacant Jaffa by the
Jaffan artist Suheir Riffi.

that, appropriating the language of ʿAjami's luxury developments and
deploying it to document its consequences.[144] Thus a 1997 festival jointly
sponsored by local Jewish and Palestinian grassroots organizations in support of a large group of families threatened with eviction from their land
was called the Sumud Festival—*sumud* being the well-known Palestinian
slogan for remaining rooted on the land against repeated attempts to evict
them—and featured a poster of a bulldozer with a fist, rooted in the earth,
blocking its way and a caption reading, "Here we remain. . . . We are not
alone" (fig. 15).[145]

These activities should be seen as a form of architecture; indeed, the only
form of architecture available to them since Palestinian residents are prohibited from planning or building their own lived environment.[146] By con-

Figure 15. Poster for "To Live within a Picture" exhibition, held in Jaffa in 1997.

structing an alternative landscape, or "poetic geography," to that of Zionist-Israeli Tel Aviv, the Palestinian community has "cognitively redefined the borders of Jaffa," which today have expanded to include parts of Tel Aviv, such as Neve Tzedek, that historically lay outside Jaffa's borders.[147] This has provided the impetus to calls for "autonomy" from Tel Aviv.[148]

I would contend that the network of practices represented by Andromeda Hill and the Peres Center is inseparable from the notable rise in religious (Muslim) and nationalist (Palestinian) self-identification by Jaffa's Palestinian community. In fact, while many scholars explain the recent upswing in Islamic-Palestinian or Jewish-Zionist sentiment in terms of the enduring national conflict between Palestinians and Jews, my research[149] reveals the extent to which the increase in religious-cum-national self-identification in Palestinian Jaffa can be understood as a "cultural architecture of resistance" against the globalization of Israel initiated by the country's secular Jewish elite, the strategic (and largely illusionary) "fading away" of the state that has accompanied it, and the material and cultural manifestations of these processes in the various fabrics of the city.

Locating the City

Throughout this book, I have argued that Tel Aviv—and through it modernity—has never been quite what it has been claimed to be. We are reminded that cities too are as much Other than as they are what they claim to be: Tel Aviv no less than Brasilia or New York is a modern city in the fullest sense of the word, as UNESCO has confirmed; yet it is also a colonial city, a capitalist city, and a nationalist city. And it is not modern in the way its protagonists imagined and idealized it, at least not most of the time. It is now clear that Tel Aviv and the city more generally contain Other spaces—perhaps surviving only as in a palimpsest: hidden beneath the continual creative destruction of the dominant landscape and visions that produce it but there nonetheless if one knows where and how to look—that are excluded from its master geography and narrative but whose silenced voices can tell us much about the nature and boundaries of the urban.

How and where can we locate the hidden (in Lefebvre's terminology, "clandestine") cities beneath Tel Aviv the myth and contemporary reality? In the case of Jaffa–Tel Aviv we have seen that the Palestinian-Arab and other overturned and marginalized—but once well-traveled—spaces were shaped by a decades-long process of centralization-cum-modernization by the Ottoman state that profoundly transformed the political economy of Palestine, providing the fertilizer that enabled both Jaffa's increasing prosperity and Tel Aviv and Zionism's blossoming on Jaffan soil. This process opened the possibility—however brief—of a "cosmopolitan Levantine modernity," that is, a specifically Levantine "third space" in which incommensurable subcultures were, for a time, spatially reconciled.[150] The lessons of this period have much to teach those who would build a shared future a century later.

Yet if Jaffa was considered not just the "jewel" of Arab Palestine but also the "mother of strangers" *(um al-gharib)*,[151] was it still a "model" and "maternal" city in the wake of Tel Aviv's creation and rapid development? Could Tel Aviv as a colonial city and Jaffa as an increasingly colonized city be considered "cities"? And where in fact were "Jaffa" and "Tel Aviv"? Can we really define their borders? And can a city exist without borders?

A return to pre-British and Zionist legal and geographic norms hints at the answer. If we take Jaffa, though one could speak of Jaffa's "Old City" as an urban core of the Jaffa–Tel Aviv region, beyond (what by the 1880s remained of) its walls we have seen that there existed a complex patchwork of interwoven and constantly evolving land use—agricultural, industrial, and increasingly residential—that defies attempts to characterize these uses as uniformly "urban," even after the boundaries of the two municipalities expanded to encompass them. Moreover, the Jaffa–Tel Aviv region contained numerous and "difficult" border/frontier regions that had to be continually traversed by inhabitants of both cities/nations, joining the urban and agrarian spaces of the region into one "wider system."[152]

To contextualize this landscape we must recall that the notion of a firm dividing line between urban or city and other types of land was not present in the late Ottoman Middle East, as existing Ottoman and Islamic legal codes did not recognize a clear territorial differentiation between town and country (one that became increasingly important as Tel Aviv developed and expanded during the Mandate period). The Hanafi understanding of the city defined it as a "comprehensive social and political entity"; the Ottoman law focused on "civilization" as a defining element of the city and its hinterland. Together they helped to define the city as an urban-rural system in such a way that it raises the question of whether a Palestinian city could be said to continue to exist if its hinterland—the "bridge" between civilization and the countryside—were removed from the control of the town.

Indeed, the various Islamic and Ottoman definitions of the boundaries of cities placed them between three and ten miles outside the urban core, which in our case would clearly include not just Tel Aviv but also the surrounding Arab villages. This means that the land on which Tel Aviv would be built was clearly part of Jaffa's hinterland and could be considered *fina' al-misr*, or land that "served the common interests of town dwellers, not, however, the interests of individual, private persons."[153] If we understand the *fina' al-misr* as "the spatial embodiment of the town dwellers as a collective unity," as a bridge between the built-up areas of the town, its agricultural surroundings, and the open countryside, the ramifications of the birth of Tel Aviv for the future of Jaffa as a city in its own right become clear.[154]

Given the ambiguity of Jaffa's borders, it seems appropriate, even necessary, to ask, Where in fact was Jaffa? Was Jaffa a city? A "district" (as it was in the late Ottoman period)? A "region" that included the old town, newer neighborhoods, and surrounding villages? A cosmopolitan personality that was only vaguely related to an identifiable space with clearly defined borders? These are crucial yet difficult questions to answer, and they are tied to the specific fear by local Ottoman authorities that Jews were trying to take over the region and create a "state within a state" and the more general fear that Ottoman culture was becoming fatally weakened with the increasing power of European-Zionist technologies of penetration and control.

And indeed, with the passing of the land of Jaffa and its environs into Zionist hands, the very nature of the space of the region was transformed. The patchwork of residential, market, industrial, and agricultural lands that constituted "Jaffa" was falling under the control of "Jews and other foreigners" who "live under various nationalities" yet pursue their own nationalist goals by "continu[ing] to build hundreds of buildings without permission, until they abut state land and the land of their neighbors."[155] At the very least, we can say that "Jaffa," what and wherever it was, was quickly becoming something other than what it had been and was on a trajectory to become before the arrival of Zionism.

Here it is worth noting Raymond Williams's interrogation of the city/country dialectic, in which he argues that the development of the modern European city (especially in his native England) could not have occurred were it not for the transformation of the traditional relationship between city and country wrought by colonialism and imperialism, a process that occurred on "an international scale." "Distant lands became the rural areas of industrial Britain,"[156] while the country's own rural areas increasingly became a "site of play, of capital, not of land," and extreme poverty grew on the city's margins. The widening economic gap was in fact crucial "to the construction of the space of London as a city."[157] In a similar manner, today's "quaint, old" Jaffa, like yesteryear's quaint English vicarage, has been transformed by the forces of globalization into a site of "amusement" for the nation's nouveau riche.

This process is epitomized in the contemporary luxury projects in Jaffa such as Andromeda Hill and the Disneyland atmosphere they generate with their "fake" style and materials intimately tied to how the imagination of these spaces of Israeli and international capital as a "city within a city" within what remains of Palestinian Arab Jaffa, in language that is almost identical to that used by Ottoman authorities and Tel Aviv's founders to describe the Zionist-Jewish position in Jaffa right before Tel Aviv's establishment. And here we see how the city and the state—more specifically, the "nation-state"—are inextricably tied together through "urban masterpieces"[158] such as Andromeda Hill. But to understand fully how the city, or at least Tel Aviv, functions as a synechdote and spearhead of the state we need to explore the nature of the public spheres and cultures that evolved in Jaffa and Tel Aviv during the twentieth century.

Is the City Public?

Is Disneyland, or World, a "public" space? The literature on mall culture, and on Disney as well, would seem to suggest that this most commodified of places can spawn momentary publics, although they possess neither the self-consciousness nor the "insurgent" potential to constitute a lasting public sphere.[159] But in our case the question is much larger, territorially and morally: Can a "world" city that is a vortex for processes of neoliberal globalization-as-privatization yet retains many characteristics of a colonial city sustain truly public spaces or cultures, let alone provide the spaces and materials out of which "insurgent citizenships" can be constructed (that is, identities that nourish and transform the larger city, public, and nation even if they never achieve hegemony)?[160]

We can define the public spheres and cultures of the city as involving ongoing contests over terrain—not just physical territory but also public spaces such as newspapers, schools, and places of leisure. The struggles to shape complex historical and global processes within the public sphere generate "prismatic structures of modernity" that are simultaneously local and interactive with other cities, with cultures, and with modernity at large.[161]

In this context the struggle between Tel Aviv and Jaffa over whose city, public, nation, and modernity would emerge victorious ended more than half a century ago, Tel Aviv having decisively won that battle in 1948. Yet we should remember that the pre-1948 city of Jaffa was home to a vibrant and powerful public sphere. Indeed, I would argue that a mortal weakening of Jaffa's public sphere with the flight of the city's bourgeois elite in late 1947 and early 1948 made inevitable its conquest and takeover by Tel Aviv and the continuing inability of the Palestinian Arab community to engage in successful collective action.

Moreover, with respect to Tel Aviv the city-state dynamic alluded to above raises the question of what kind of public sphere can exist in a city that is also a "state," specifically, a colonial state whose leaders are intent on using legal, administrative, economic, ethnic, and religious technologies and ideologies to prevent those who do not belong from having access to formerly well-traveled landscapes? And what impact do such restrictions have on the experience of Jaffa and Tel Aviv as "cities" by those thus excluded? There is no definitive answer, but it is clear that both communities increasingly saw the other city as simultaneously enemy territory and a space that needed to be redeemed for the good of the(ir) city and nation,[162] that the more people from the two communities mixed together, the more important it was for the public spheres and popular cultures they attempted to direct to (re)enforce the boundaries between them, and that these sentiments inevitably lead to the "deadening" of the urban experience if not the death of the city itself.[163]

At the very least, the desire by Palestinian Arab residents—or at least their leaders—to "hold on to [their] eastness"[164] in the face of the Euromodernity of Tel Aviv reveals a crucial dynamic: At the same time the "elite" of the two cities-as-nations saw the other city as both irredeemably Other and as a space whose redemption was crucial for the survival of the nation as a whole. Yet this dynamic made it impossible for there to arise a common public among the various communities inhabiting the Jaffa–Tel Aviv region, and the conflict between the ultimately divided publics surely made the core experiences of the urban—let alone of the modern—difficult to sustain.

And it is not just Palestinian citizens who have been affected by these discourses, as the majority of Mizrahi (or "Oriental") Jewish residents of Jaffa are incorporated into the larger Israeli polity specifically through the deployment of a powerful combination of religious and "ethno-class" discourses by a state whose goal is specifically to prevent conviviality between Jewish and Palestinian "Arabs," and thus any shared notion of publicness between them.[165] If we understand "public" to mean an arena, or zone, where "different interests, commitments, and values collide and resolve themselves into a reciprocal, multi-voiced, perhaps even carnivalesque civic sense that is shared as a relation, not as sameness or consensus,"[166] can a colonial city ever have a truly "public" culture, or even a "public" at all? At the very least, the exclusion (or inclusion via strategies of ethnic and cultural difference and exclusion) of significant portions of the population from the public sphere of an urban space challenges the Habermasian depiction of the public sphere as an idealized and inclusive space[167] and raises the question of whether a publicless urban space can be said to constitute a city.

This situation raises a question that is central to understanding the relationship between the city and the nation: If one of the main characteristics of the modern city is that it continuously and matter-of-factly generates a public "culture" or "life" composed from "life in the streets and other public places,"[168] can Tel Aviv (or any municipality) be considered a true "city" if it denies "public" participation to entire communities, no longer just "Arabs," but today also tens of thousands of "illegal" Nigerian, Thai, Romanian, and other workers who live in the city's poorer neighborhoods? Indeed, if at the heart of the metropolitan experience is supposed to be a mechanism that connects various urban collectivities whose "coming together in fact constitutes the public culture of the city," can we characterize the space of Jaffa–Tel Aviv as truly public or metropolitan beyond the narrowest and most denotative sense of these terms?[169]

On the Borders/Frontiers of the City as Nation

The founders of Tel Aviv were quite interested in the latest trends in planning and design in Europe and the United States. It is thus worthwhile to compare the planning discourses at play in the creation of Tel Aviv with those in, for example, New York, where progressive urban thinkers saw the city as providing a "vital platform for men and women to think themselves into politics, to make themselves into citizens."[170] Indeed, the "modern city" was considered by many "the hope of democracy."

In this context we should recall that from the start Tel Aviv compared itself to "New York City" as an "organized . . . modern city."[171] Yet a perusal of the list of books used by Tel Aviv's founders to educate themselves on the most modern trends in city planning finds no reference in them to writings such as Howe's *The City: The Hope of Democracy*, which was published in 1905, the year the original land of Tel Aviv was purchased,[172] or Wilcox's *The American City: A Problem in Democracy*, which was published a year later, when Ahuzat Bayit was founded.

Wilcox specifically argued that the "city is the center of the complex web of national life" and as such had the power even to "save the nation."[173] Woodrow Wilson (better known as the great advocate of the rights of nations) similarly saw the city as the *locus primus* for grasping the relations between societies and their politics, and so believed that "participatory urban democracy" was the best means to achieve a democratic society. Yet he also warned that a city—and thus a nation—can be "whole and vital only when conscious of its wholeness and identity."[174]

Tel Aviv's leaders clearly believed that their city had the power to save the Jewish nation; but as Jane Jacobs argues, cities whose publics do not recognize the fundamental connections between the various diverse spaces, communities, and cultures out of which they are composed become "dull and inert," containing "the seeds of their own destruction and little else."[175] This may be true in the long run, but as I have argued throughout this book, the discourses of colonial urban modernity that power a city like Tel Aviv are designed precisely to misread, erase, and otherwise overpower such hybridity in favor of supposedly pure selves whose Others are no longer in sight.

How, then, can we determine whether a city is "successful," particularly if, returning to Raymond Williams, the city is always somehow "false— every street a blow, every corner a stab"?[176] Perhaps by defining them vis-à-vis their potential to be "fantastically dynamic places," an experience made possible by their simultaneous location as the nation's most "strategic" places and their function as the entrepôt of the "nonlocal, the strange, the mixed and the public"—and therefore, if we recall Latour, of the non-modern.[177] In this context, what Jacobs terms "unsuccessful cities" can be understood as lacking the networks of "intricate mutual support" that make the nation's Others—consciously or not from the state's perspective—central to its strategy of self-realization. The goal of holistic and transformative (in Jacob's words, "real") city planning and design would then be to catalyze and nourish diversity and the "right to the city" by all its inhabitants.

Such a sentiment was also evidenced by the Hanafi jurists who defined the city (in contrast to a village or countryside) as a "comprehensive social and political entity embracing various groups, rallying different factions into one community and uniting them under one leadership" in a manner that transcends ethnicity or tribal loyalties.[178] Yet by this criteria neither Jaffa nor (especially) Tel Aviv could be considered a healthy city if a city at all.[179] At the very least, we can imagine that neither Jaffa nor Tel Aviv, nor their respective nations, was or is a successful enterprise, because only by fostering the broadest right to the city can nations "sustaine their own civilization."[180]

Indeed, the material fact of the city's existence does not guarantee the development of a city life.[181] That is why its relationship to the nation is so important. Planners, designers, and scholars of cities and the nations they help to define need to recognize the full extent of the permutations, complex spaces of transcultural interaction, of communication and domination that have constituted places like Jaffa and Tel Aviv; they need to approach them with the goal of freeing what Lefebvre terms the "representational spaces" of the clandestine, or underside of life—that is, life as directly lived by the Jews and Arabs who daily challenged the official "spaces of representation" of the administrative-legal and ideological-nationalist boundaries that separated them.[182] Only then will it be possible to shatter the illusionary histories and landscapes that lie at the core of modernist colonial urban and nationalist discourse(s).[183]

Such a "space of the inhabitants of the city" was characterized by Lefebvre as "imagined," and it is thus here that possibility of "reimagining" the spaces of Jaffa and Tel Aviv, of Israel and Palestine, can most felicitously be entertained.[184] To reiterate my argument at the beginning of this story, Lefebvre's analysis helps us to see that in studying the history of Jaffa–Tel Aviv, we are confronted "not by one social space but by many." For "the worldwide does not abolish the local,"[185] however much it might have wanted to.[186]

Notes

Dates in the notes are given in day/month/year (2/12/69) order.

ABBREVIATIONS

BAIU	Alliance Israelite Universelle Archive and Library, Paris.
BOA	Başbakanlık Arşivleri, Istanbul.
CZA	Central Zionist Archives, Jerusalem.
DAMFAF	Diplomatic Archives, Ministry of Foreign Affairs, France, Paris.
HA	Haganah Archive, Tel Aviv.
ISA	Israel State Archives, Jerusalem.
JA	Jabotinsky Archive, Tel Aviv.
JICR	Jaffa Shari'a Court Records, Haifa University Library.
KKL	Keren Kayamet LeYisrael Archives, Jerusalem.
LA	Labor Archives, Tel Aviv.
MHTA	Museum of the History of Tel Aviv, Tel Aviv.
PEF	Palestine Exploration Fund Archive, London.
PMAJ	Protocols of the Muslim Association of Jaffa, Jaffa.
PPCMECSAC	Private Papers Collection, Middle East Center, Saint Antony's College, Oxford.
PRO	Public Records Office, Kew.
RA	al-Rabita Archive, Jaffa.
TAMA	Municipal Archives of Tel Aviv, Tel Aviv.

INTRODUCTION

1. Frankfurter, 1931, p. 18.
2. Indeed, Jaffa was pre–Mandate Palestine's most important port and the

center of its famed citriculture; as such, it was bestowed with those two veritable markers of modernity, a railroad station and a clock tower.

3. Such a matrix allows for a much broader and deeper interrogation of modernity than, for example, Jameson's argument that "the only satisfactory semantic meaning of modernity lies in its association with capitalism" (Jameson, 2002, p. 13; p. 40 for modernity as a "narrative category"), precisely because it recognizes that capitalism was generated with, by, and through colonialism, nationalism, and modern ideologies and technologies of autonomy, mastery, self-reflexivity, and power. The fourfold modernity matrix is dense enough to ground the kind of "power-knowledge" matrix whose exploration was a central concern of Foucault, particularly in *Discipline and Punish* and the three-volume *History of Sexuality*.

4. Indeed, by the early nineteenth century a process of centralization was well under way and had returned the balance of power between the state and the provinces in the former's favor; it was helped by an expansion of foreign trade in which Jaffa, as Palestine's primary port, participated fully (Pamuk, 1987, pp. 9, 11).

5. On the one hand, Lefebvre argues, a transformation in contemporary society took place in which the notion of space first came to the fore socially: "Planning as ideology formulate[d] all the problems of society into questions and space and transpose[d] all that comes from history and consciousness into spatial terms. It is an ideology which immediately divides up" (Lefebvre, 1996, p. 99). On the other hand, Lefebvre informs us, "around 1910 a certain space was shattered. It was the space of common sense, of knowledge *(savoir)*, of social practice, of political power, a space thitherto enshrined in every discourse, just as in abstract thought, as the environment of and channel for communications." Here he was referring to the impact of an "epoch-making event," Einstein's theory of relativity, and the shattering of the concretized, hardened understanding and experience of space it heralded (Lefebvre, 1992, p. 25). The term *shatter* is borrowed from the architect and theorist Georges Bataille (see Hollier, 1993, p. 3; LeVine, 1998). Cf. García Canclini, 1995; Foucault, 1999; Argyrou, 2002). Woolf wrote that "on or about December, 1910, human character changed" (from "Character in Fiction," cited by Jameson, 2002, p. 104).

6. García Canclini, 1995.

7. The approximately 100-duman plot of land purchased three years earlier from several Jewish land brokers.

8. The bedouins were in fact a long-term "nuisance" in the Jaffa region, going back at least to the eighteenth century, when there were often battles between the tribes for control of the surrounding hinterland (see A. Cohen, 1973, pp. 110, 149, 152). Almost twenty years after the founding of Tel Aviv the residents of the neighboring German colony of Sarona wrote to the mayor of Tel Aviv complaining about the "damage done" by the presence of a bedouin camp on land belonging to Tel Aviv on their mutual border, especially by "the bedouin wives." Two years later the mayor of Tel Aviv wrote to the president

of Sarona, similarly complaining, "[B]edouins have encamped right opposite their houses, causing a great nuisance to the residents of the latter. We shall therefore be greatly indebted to you if you could please arrange for the bedouin camp in question to be transferred to some distance from the boundary of Tel Aviv so as to avoid the continuation of this nuisance" (Tel Aviv Municipal Archive [hereafter TAMA], 4/334b, 31/10/28 letter from Sarona Council to Tel Aviv Mayor; 17/7/28 letter).

9. Jaffa's Jewish leaders believed they had created a "state within a state" in Jaffa well before the creation of Tel Aviv, as Tel Aviv's first mayor, Meir Dizengoff, described it (Dizengoff, 1931, pp. 6–7; for a similar view by Palestinian Arabs in Jaffa, see Ram, 1996, pp. 260–61), from memoirs of Ben-Hanania. For the open-ended, nomadic, boundariless versus state-centered and sedentary conceptions of space, see Deleuze and Guattari, [1980] 1987, pp. xiii, 281.

10. Deleuze and Guattari, [1980] 1987, pp. xii–xiii, 53. "Trans-generational beduinity" is how one Jaffan native evocatively described his intellectual and genealogical travels in, from, and through Jaffa and Tel Aviv (Andre Mazawi, "Trans-Generational Beduinity," in Jaffa Diaries, at www.jaffacity.com).

11. This is how the *New York Times* described it, unwittingly paraphrasing Herzl's description of his still-imaginary Tel Aviv as "thoroughly European" (Herzl, [1896] 1988, pp. 61, 137; Serge Schmemann, "What's Doing in Tel Aviv," *New York Times*, December 21, 1997). In fact, Herzl envisioned Haifa as the capital of the New Society Jews would build in Palestine, as Tel Aviv had yet to be built when he wrote *Altneuland* in 1902.

12. It is a commonplace that a central component of the creation of communal—and especially modern national—identities is the setting off of the Other as its antithesis of the Self; in this case, positioning Arabs as the antithesis of "modern" European Jews. This led Europeans and Zionists to portray Jaffa as being the antithesis of "modern" Tel Aviv, an Otherness that was essential to create the bifurcation between Jewish and Palestinian societies necessary to establish a space of modernity within the boundaries of the Jewish city (cf. Mitchell, 1999a).

Indeed, throughout the late Ottoman and Mandate periods Jews and Palestinians of all varieties worked and did business together in vineyards, family factories and restaurants, brothels, carting sand for cement, in the port, and selling land. Examining the boundary, or frontier, regions in which these populations lived—that is, examining Tel Aviv and Jaffa as frontiers of modernity—reveals that Jaffa's relationship with Tel Aviv constitutes an especially profitable site for exploring the complex and problematic nature of modernity, which was how it was envisioned by those who dreamed of and founded it. Thus Theodor Herzl depicted the Jewish presence in Palestine as the "forces of civilization" struggling against "the forces of barbarism and the desert" (Herzl, from *The Jewish State*, quoted in Lesch, 1979, pp. 120–24; and Rodinson, 1973, p. 43). Zygmunt Bauman argues that "modernity is an inherently transgressive mode of being-in-the-world . . . roll[ing] into one the act of drawing a frontier and the resolve to transcend it. . . . Were the modernizing thrust ever to grind to a halt, this would not augur the completion of modernity, but its demise" (Bauman, [1989] 2000, p. 38).

13. We can understand frontiers as "denot[ing] the (material or metaphoric) 'twilight zones' at the edge of a collective's control. They delineate directions for expansion and growth, and provide basic symbols, legends challenges and myths used for the construction of national identity" (Yiftachel, 1996, p. 3). This understanding of boundaries is important because it links the process of boundary creation and the act of "pioneering" with the essentially "poetic" act of creation— whether of a new collectivity or of new spaces (cf. Bernstein, 2000, p. 85). For Jaffa's description as a *thaghr*, or frontier location or citadel, see JICR, Book 7, pp. 12–13, 1211h/1797 (also cited in Kana'an, 1998, p. 33)

14. Mignolo uses a similar strategy with his "border thinking" as a way of upsetting the dominant epistemology of "colonial difference" in analyzing colonial modernity in the Americas (Mignolo, 2000).

15. There are other fourfold matrices of modernity that can be compared with mine. The most well known is Giddens's matrix of capitalism, surveillance, military power, and industrialism as the "organizational clusters," or "dimensions," of modernity (Giddens, 1990, chap. 11). I believe that this matrix, while recognizing key processes and technologies, misses both the discursive force of modernity and the temporal and geographic axes that arise when recognizing colonialism as a core dimension. Shmuel Eisenstadt offers another matrix with the following dimensions: (1) structural-organizational, (2) institutional, (3) capitalist-political economies, and (4) distinct cultural programs (Eisenstadt, 2000, p. 176). Again, the absence of colonialism diminishes the efficacy of this matrix for examining modernity in Jaffa–Tel Aviv. Finally, the modernity matrix helps us to understand Partha Chatterjee's discussion of the power of the "bourgeois-rationalist conception of knowledge" to perpetuate colonialism (Chatterjee, 1986, p. 11).

16. Thus filth, poverty, and disease continually plagued Tel Aviv despite its being the "most modern city" in the Middle East, while one of Jaffa's richest merchants built the most modern International Style home in either city, yet rarely allowed his wife and daughters outside its walls.

17. Cf. Chatterjee, 1993, pp. 5, 13; Latour, 1993; Foucault, 1984, pp. 38–39, on modernity as an "attitude." See Jameson, 2002, p. 38, for a description of modernity as an "effect." As Ranajit Guha writes of the relative autonomy of Indian peasants from both colonial and indigenous elite ideologies: "There were vast areas in the life of the people which were never integrated into their hegemony" (Guha, 1982, pp. 5–6). Ashis Nandy also uses the term "nonmodernity," but in his usage it represents the "innocence" of the "nonmodern cultures and traditions" that confronted Western colonialism—that is, it retains the temporal and technological notions of the modern; yet he also explains how outside the small sectors of the Indian population exposed to the full thrust of colonialism "the ordinary Indian ha[d] no reason to see himself as a counterplayer or antithesis to the Western man" (Nandy, 1988, pp. 2, 72).

18. Cf. Issawi, 1995; and the works of von Grunebaum, Lewis, Vatikiotis, Gibb and Bowen, Watt, and Davison.

19. Alcalay, 1993, p. 7.

20. Frank, 1998, p. 30.

21. Quataert, 1994, p. 770. However, for goods produced or at least exported specifically from the Jaffa region, it seems that Europe was already a significant and perhaps majority recipient by the mid-nineteenth century, although Egypt, Lebanon, and the western coast of Asia Minor were also major export destinations (Scholch, 1993, pp. 80, 106, using British consular reports from Jaffa, 1857–75). Quataert demonstrates that the value of intra-Ottoman trade, for example, was greater than trade with Europe. Moreover, as Gran points out, the data show how trade during that period was vigorous, whereas Europe itself accounted for only perhaps 15 percent of Egypt's world trade, while demonstrating how the Ottoman elite benefited from the increasing capitalization of the economy (Gran, 1998; Abou-El-Haj, 1991).

22. Pomeranz, 2000; Mandel, 1997. By this, he means that no matter how efficient European capitalism became, it still could not compete with the local primitive accumulation because the latter could always squeeze wages lower to keep prices competitive. Thus the only way for European capitalism to conquer the foreign markets was to weaken or even cripple the indigenous capitalist sector, which it did through a process of capitulations, commercial treaties, debt, and finally military conquest and occupation. (In this respect Gran shows the importance of minority merchants in squeezing out the indigenous merchant class [Gran, 1998].)

23. By this, Amin means that the "acute awareness of European superiority" preceded the crystallization of economic dominance while leading to a conquest of minds and values as the latter set in. Moreover, as Shohat explains, as the European economic system was imposed to cement their superiority, a concomitant appropriation of "cultural and material" production occurred while the Europeans would at the same time lay the blame for the failure of the Middle East to adopt the European capitalist system on internal failure rather than the result of a process in which their underdevelopment was intertwined with Europe's "progress" (Amin, 1989; Shohat, 1994; Pomeranz and Topik, 1999; Pomeranz, 2000).

24. For a discussion of the Public Debt Administration as a "tool of European imperialism," see Blaisdell, 1966; Pamuk, 1987, p. 72. Indeed, the balance of power between the state and local elements was strongly enough in favor of the former that the European powers were forced to work through the state more than they would have liked, which further solidified the power of the centralizing state (cf. Pamuk, 1987, p. 133).

25. Thus the 1839 Hat-ı Şerif of Gülhane, which launched the Tanzimat, exclaimed that the period of decline and loss for the empire began "in the last one hundred and fifty years" (excerpted in Hurewitz, 1975, pp. 269–71).

26. Laroui, 1982; Islamoglu-Inan, 1988; Asad, 1993; Gran, 1996. Thus, for example, if we examine the series of reforms and treaties signed by the

Ottoman and various European states during the nineteenth century the com-bination of autonomous self-interest and foreign intervention becomes clear. The 1820 and 1838 treaties and the 1867 *firman* lowered tariffs, opened up the Ottoman economy, and hurt the ability of local merchants to compete with the Europeans. Yet as Abou-El-Haj argues, the 1839 and 1858 Tanzimat and land reforms must be understood as the result of two hundred years of local ad hoc solutions to the changing economy and called for policies such as security and freedom of persons, religious freedom, and rationalization of legal codes, which would lead to increased supervision of peasants, decreasing freedom, and increasing private property, all of which are central components of the moder-nity matrix. Kayalı argues that the Tanzimat reforms were focused on assert-ing greater control over Arab commercial centers and port cities—such as Jaffa—that were given more importance than European or Anatolian provinces of the empire (Kayalı, 1997, p. 32).

27. Gerber, 1987; Abou-El-Haj, 1991. Cf. Doumani, 1995, Introduction, for how these changes were experienced in the Palestinian hinterland.

28. That is, European governments encouraged centralization because it would make it easier and more profitable to dominate the empire's market through a single centralized administration rather than through multiple provincial leaders. Of course, the Ottoman state also wanted to centralize to gain greater control of its populations and sources of revenue, both to "mod-ernize" and to pay off the European debt.

29. Quataert, 1994, pp. 762–63; Deringil, 1999, p. 136. Cf. Kayalı, 1997, p. 78, for the Ottoman fear of lawlessness in the absence of centralization. In Palestine, the centralizing political and educational policies of the government helped to tip the balance of power vis-à-vis the local elites in the former's favor, the stage for which was shaped decades earlier when the Jerusalem region was separated from any other Ottoman province and put under the direct author-ity of Istanbul (Khalidi, 1997, pp. 36, 42, 151). See Rogan, 1999, pp. 12–15, for a discussion of how the Tanzimat state sought to individualize responsibility to the state through private ownership, taxes, censuses, and the like.

30. Rogan, 1999, p. 12.

31. Ibid., p. 83.

32. Brummett, 2000, p. 289.

33. Abu-Manneh, 1994.

34. Thus the focus on justice, equity, security, stability, and fighting cor-ruption and abuses of power had clear Islamic-Qur'anic precedents (Abu-Manneh, 1994, esp. pp. 191–94).

35. Deringil, 1999, pp. 136–37, 148, 154, quoting Ottoman official corre-spondence.

36. Ibid., pp. 93–94, 101–2.

37. Ibid., p. 56. The primary reasons for its support was a combination of the need for the tax revenue resulting from sales of land and modern perspec-tives as to the best manner to productivize land through capitalization and pri-vatization. Another possible reason why officials in Istanbul did not actively

oppose the Zionist enterprise is that many Zionist leaders, including David Ben-Gurion, lived and studied in Istanbul, in part to build ties with the burgeoning Young Turk movement (cf. Farhi, 1975, pp. 197–98).

38. Deringil, 1999, pp. 50–52. Deringil concludes that the Ottoman concept of "civilizing nomads" was based on the same premises as European colonialism (Deringil, 1999, pp. 136–37, 148, 154).

39. Brummett, 2000, p. 10.

40. That is, where hybridity was a fundamental condition of interaction among parties with varying positions of power who nevertheless had to live in the same space. For a discussion of the notion of the "third space" and a useful critique of Bhabha's use of the term, see AlSayyad, 2001, p. 8.

41. Perhaps one factor that encouraged this freedom was that the so-called Young Turk movement was actually more "Ottoman" than the earlier "Young Ottoman" movement. The Young Turks realized that ethnoterritorial nationalism was not a realistic political option in the context of the empire; thus membership was broad-based geographically and ethnically and diverse religiously and supported (at least for a short time) a multiethnic and multireligious empire (Kayalı, 1997, pp. 4–15).

42. Deringil, 1999, pp. 158–71. Here it should be pointed out that imports and exports in the empire as a whole only constituted between 6 and 7 percent of total production through the 1870s and that the trade crisis of the last quarter of the nineteenth century that affected Europe and the empire together did not seem to affect Jaffa significantly, based on shipping statistics through its port (see chap. 2, table 1; Pamuk, 1987, p. 13).

43. Quataert, 1994, p. 766; Khalidi, 1997. This antipathy toward Arab nationalism existed even as Turkish national sentiments grew stronger. Cohen describes a process of de facto privatization of land—or at least the state's giving up permanent control to *mukata'a* holders (who were called *sahib*, or owners of the rights) as long as they remitted sufficient taxes and were capable of "governing the *mukata'a* in an orderly and disciplined fashion" that would result in the "development of the country" (A. Cohen, 1973, pp. 181–22, citing Firman dated 22 Muharram 1120/12.4.1708 [Maliye, 9497, p. 5; and Maliye 9546, p. 6]).

44. Kayalı, 1997, p. 22; Khalidi, 1997. A policy that symbolized the fracturing of loyalties between the Turkish and Arab political elites was the CUP state's enforcement of Ottoman Turkish as the official language of the empire—a move that clearly pointed toward modern ethnonationalism as the primary basis of identification with the Ottoman state (Kayalı, 1997, pp. 61, 79).

45. PRO: FO 424/238 Consul McGregor to Sir G. Lowther, 12/4/13, report on nationalist sentiments among Arabs in Palestine. Cf. Smith, 1984, pp. 20–25.

46. Thus the only form of resistance left to the Arab rural population was military opposition to colonial power—but this lacked corresponding political and economic progress with any kind of class basis and led to the failure of the Great Revolt (Graham-Brown, 1982, p. 155; cf. Tamari, 1982, pp. 182–84).

47. Cf. Shafir, 1989, p. 16.

48. Doumani, 1995; Kana'an, 1998; Wilkins, n.d.

49. Doumani, 1995.

50. See Shavit and Biger, 2001, which covers the birth of Tel Aviv through 1936, uses few if any Palestinian/Arabic–language sources, and does not discuss in any detail Jaffa or the surrounding Palestinian Arab villages or the relations between the two communities.

51. By "exclusivist framework," I mean that the typical nationalist historiographies of the two cities treat the "other" community as somehow alien to "their" city and thus as having little influence (except for the worse) on its perceived autonomous history and development.

CHAPTER 1

1. Bender, 1999, p. 21.

2. As David Harvey points out, the city has always been viewed as the high point of human achievement, objectifying the most sophisticated knowledge in a physical landscape of extraordinary complexity, power, and splendor (Harvey, 1989b, p. 23). The modern élan particularly evokes the fast-paced experience of large cities, awhirl with recent fashions and exciting activities, constant changes in the environment, and a great diversity of people who come into some kind of contact with one another (Wright, 1991, p. 9; cf. Sassen, 1998, p. xxx). From an economic perspective, the city played a crucial role in the appropriation, mobilization, and geographic concentration of the surpluses of capital and labor power in commodity form that were central to the rise of industrial (and late imperial) capitalism. Modernism, then, as an ideology, was a system of values that could be realized most effectively in the city (Castells, 1983, p. 9).

3. Holston, 1989, p. 48.

4. Quoted in Wright, 1991, p. 16; cf. p. 319 n. 8.

5. Holston, 1989, p. 83. The planners possessed a teleological view of history in which capitalist modernity signified an advance in human civilization that began in Europe and would spread to the "backward" regions.

6. Latour, 1993, p. 39. He continued, "Native Americans were not mistaken when they accused the Whites of having forked tongues. By separating the relations of political power from the relations of scientific reasoning while continuing to shore up power with reason and reason with power, the moderns have always had two irons in the fire. They have become invincible" (p. 38).

7. Holston, 1989, p. 68. The modern nation-state process, Nico Poulantzas (2001) has observed, has always involved the eradication of the traditions, histories, and memories of the nations dominated as part of its self-creation and expression. This process is even more pronounced when the state in the making is a colonial-settler state (cf. Swedenburg, 1995, pp. 3, 8).

8. Harvey, 1989, 16. Cf. Schumpeter, 1976. Mitchell explains why the city magnifies the power of the creative destruction at the heart of the project of modernity: "The identity of the modern city is in fact created by what it keeps out. Its modernity is something contingent upon the exclusion of its own oppo-

site. In order to determine itself as the place of order, reason, propriety, cleanliness, civilization and power, it must represent outside itself what is irrational, disordered, dirty, libidinous, barbarian and cowed" (Mitchell, 1988, p. 165). Thus for most people(s), especially outside of the metropolitan countries, the creative destruction engendered by the growth of capitalist modernity meant imperial (if not colonial) domination of Europe, accompanied by the destruction of existing indigenous dialogues with modernity.

9. This creative destruction was helped by the emerging disciplines of geography, sociology, and political "science," which were in the process of overturning existing ways of seeing, mapping, governing, and living in the world. Thus Said argues that "imperialism after all is an act of geographical violence through which . . . space . . . is explored, charted, and finally brought under control" (Said, 1982, p. 10).

10. Cf. Holston, 1989, p. 5. Jameson similarly describes the "trope of 'modernity' [as] always in one way or another a rewriting, a powerful displacement of previous narrative paradigms" (Jameson, 2002, p. 35).

11. LeVine, 1995.

12. Cf. LeVine, 1998a, 1999b, 1999b. In fact, as Scholch points out, the "need" for colonization in order to "improve the country" became a fundamental element in the European understanding of Palestine by the 1860s (Scholch, 1993, p. 70).

13. As Shamir explains, Jews constructed and imagined their experience in Palestine as neither colonizers nor colonized, positing a distance from both Arabs and British and insisting on the uniqueness of Jewish nationalism (Shamir, 1999).

14. As I explain below (see n. 81), one cannot find the word *modernity* in the classic texts of Rodinson or Césaire, aside from one brief mention in the latter by way of a quote of the Frenchman Carl Siger in support of French colonialism (see Césaire, 1995, p. 40). Indeed, Césaire talks of Hitler being at "the end of capitalism," but he does not complete the circle to its beginnings or extensions in colonial modernity (1995, p. 37), as would a scholar like Bauman.

15. We must be careful not to confuse various connotations of modernity as a period of time, a condition, an epistemology or ontology, a project, an analytic or problématique, a set of institutions, etc.—all of which are expressed in different permutations in different sociotemporal-spatial axes.

16. It was Baudelaire who gave the concept of *modernité* its "modern" meaning in his essay, "The Painter of Modern Life." As Habermas explains, Baudelaire "puts the word 'modernity' in quotation marks" (Habermas, 1985, p. 9). But it was Hegel who perhaps initiated modernity as a philosophical discourse, developing the "critical concept" of modernity through a dialectic residing in the principle of the Enlightenment in order to ground the modern project (Habermas, 1985, p. 21). Cf. Frisby, 1985, p. 19, citing Baudelaire's *Les Fleurs du mal*. Similarly, Nietzsche focused on the "decadence of modernity and its lack of genuine passions, its false truths, its empty historicism, its eternal recurrence of the ever-same" (Frisby, 1985, p. 29).

17. Giddens, 1990, p. 6. It is for this reason that the period between 1750 and 1850 is seen as representing a threshold in which the actual breakthrough of modernity occurred in European social and cultural history, as it produced the specifically modern conceptuality that captures the increasingly accelerating transformation of experience (Lichtblau, 1995, p. 29).

18. Harvey, 1989a, p. 35.

19. Giddens, 1971, p. xi. Indeed, the second half of the nineteenth century saw a new project of sociopolitical modernization: the demand for social justice evolving out of the revolutions of 1848 and the labor movements and women's movement, claiming for universal suffrage and civil rights for women and workers and fair redistribution of resources of state and society (Dann, 1999, p. 27).

20. Höfert and Salvatore, 2000, p. 28. Thus we must be wary of even the recent work of leading scholars such as Anthony Giddens who describe modernity as emerging in Europe in the seventeenth century, which recent scholarship (Pomeranz, Abu-Lughod, Mintz, Frank, Gilroy) has demonstrated is a simplistic and geographically narrow location for its emergence. Cf. Arnason, 2000, p. 73.

21. Dussel, 1995a, 1995b, 1996; Quijano, 1992, 1995, 1998; cf. Mignolo, 2000, p. 52. In fact, we can say that the "counterdiscourse" against modernity has been going on for at least five hundred years, since the first Spanish ships landed in the "new world," as opposed to the much more recent, Euro-centered counterdiscourse described by Habermas (Dussel, 1996, p. 135).

22. Dussel, 1996, p. 131.

23. Thus, for example, Habermas's examination of the "philosophical discourse of modernity" is a misreading of modernity because it leaves out colonialism and imperialism (cf. Friese and Wagner, 2000, p. 27).

24. Not to mention that recent trends in academia have led to a "systematic recontainment of [modernity's] theoretical energy as such" (Jameson, 2002, p. 3).

25. Reflexive modernization is defined as the possibility of a creative (self-) deconstruction and reembedding of the entire modern-industrial epoch through another modernity (cf. Beck, Giddens, and Lash, 1994; Beck, 1992; Lash, 1999, p. 267). But in the context of late Ottoman and Mandate Jaffa–Tel Aviv, the issue is not the obsolescence of industrial society and the emergence of a "risk society" in which the social, political, economic, and individual risks increasingly tend to escape the institutions for monitoring and protection of an industrial society (cf. Beck, Giddens, and Lash, 1994, p. 5). What is more, the call for a new "reflexive" modernity is never squared by Giddens, Beck, and Lash with Habermas's claim that reflexivity was always inherent in modernity (cf. Luhmann and Habermas, 1971).

26. That is, the debate over whether modernity and Enlightenment should be severed to preserve the liberatory potential and meaning of the latter is not relevant to the period covered here (cf. Wokler, 2000; Habermas, 1985).

27. Giddens, 1990. To the question, "What are the sources of the dynamic

nature of modernity?" Giddens answers, the "separation of time and space and their recombination in forms which permit the precise time-space 'zoning' of social life, the disembedding of social systems (lifting out of social relations from local contexts of interaction and their restructuring across indefinite spans of time-space), and the reflexive ordering and reordering of social relations" (Giddens, 1990, pp. 16–17).

28. Based on the recognition that the expansion of modernity has to be viewed as the crystallization of a new type of civilization, not unlike the expansion of great religions or imperial powers in past times (cf. Eisenstadt, 2000). But modernity does not unfold the same way and at the same time for different (even if neighboring) communities. For the winners, it can seemingly fulfill its utopian promise, whereas for the vanquished it seems "essentially" dystopian (Kay and Strath, 2000, p. 11).

29. Salvatore and Höfert, 2000, pp. 14–17; Hefner, 1998a. Hefner criticizes most models of modernity for "overlook[ing] the far-reaching influence of religious ideals and networks on non-Western nationalisms . . . [and] fail[ing] to acknowledge the complexity of religious change" (1998b, pp. 87–88). Jameson's most recent work critiques these "alternative modernities" for merely effacing unpalatable elements of modernity through the reassuring cultural notion that all are now free to fashion their own modernity as they please—a valid point but one that fails to note that the multiple modernities perspective (which he does not directly address) in fact analyzes multiple historical and sociological trajectories to the present, not the Habermasian perspective of modernity as a project for the future (cf. Jameson, 2002, p. 12).

30. Cf. Eisenstadt, 2000, p. 179. Wagner considers modernity a situation in which the reference to autonomy and mastery provides for a double imaginary signification of social life, that is, one in which "man was to be fully autonomous and in complete control over . . . an increasingly rationalized world " (Wagner, 2001, p. 8; cf. Jameson, 2002, p. 145). The expression of individual autonomy can be extended to forms of collective autonomy and freedom, including colonial oppression (Wagner, pers. com., June 2001); yet can we still say that "the basic trajectories of political modernity have been, and probably still are, the emancipation of the individual and the rationalization of social relationships"? (Müller and Strath, 1999, pp. 7, 17). At least some participants in the multiple modernities discussions seem still to envision an "original," Western modernity that achieves its "purest" state in mid-twentieth-century America (cf. Eisenstadt, 2000, p. 176; cf. Wagner, 1999, p. 41, citing Alexandre Kojéve). Most Jaffans, however, were not the Romantics, nationalist intellectuals, or Jacobin revolutionaries who are the subjects of multiple modernities studies.

31. As Wagner points out, America has been *the* space of modernity in Euro-American theorizing over the past two centuries (Wagner, 1999; 2000, p. 3). Thus Woodiwiss critiques even leading cultural theorists such as Stuart Hall for misdefining modernity by not recognizing the term's American pedigree (from a sociological standpoint) and by abstracting the term to the point of denuding it of analytic content (Woodiwiss, 1997, p. 10). It is only in Simmel

(not in Marx, Weber, or Durkheim) that *modernity* is used to refer to a social *condition*, as opposed to an aesthetic context, with its current sociological usage evolving out of terms such as *capitalism-modernity, modern society,* or *modernization* (whose meanings are by no means identical to *modernity*) in response to the collapse of Parsonian modernization theory (Woodiwiss, 1997, p. 4; Wagner, 2001, p. 2).

32. Thus for Wagner "modern society denotes a social order that gains its modernity from a particular structural and institutional arrangement" (Wagner, 2001, p. 12). Although such a definition can include colonialism and imperialism in its arrangement, Wagner's analysis is limited to Europe and thus does not.

33. Mitchell, 1998, p. 417.

34. This was accomplished through the specificities of colonial and nationalist discourses of domination and hegemony. The idea of "generative order" is taken from Portugali (1993, p. 44), who adopted it from the physicist David Bohm. Harvey also makes use of Bohm's theory of generative orders in his most recent monograph (Harvey, 1996). That is, modernity—both as deployed by the colonizer and "desired" by the colonized—is "inextricably bound with domination" (Abdallah Laroui, quoted in Pandolfo, 1999, p. 122).

35. Marx, 1967, vol. 1, pp. 681, 703; cf. Mitchell, 1999b; Mitchell, 1999a, p. xvi; Chakrabarty, 1999.

36. See Dussel, 1995a, p. 65.

37. Appadurai and Breckenridge, 1995, p. 15.

38. See Dussel, 1995a, p. 66. For Dussel, the myth of modernity is based on the understanding of modern European civilization as the most developed and superior in the world, which then obliges it to "develop" the more primitive, barbarous civilizations along the same lines as its own.

39. With this insight, Habermas unwittingly affirms the power of colonialism and the larger fourfold modernity matrix in shaping "modernity," which would seem to "threaten or destroy" his hopes for reviving it as a liberatory philosophical discourse (cf. Habermas, 1985, p. 41). Rodinson similarly describes the power of colonialism and imperialism in the context of Zionism and Israel to "threaten or destroy" indigenous societies (Rodinson, 1973, p. 81).

40. Cf. Mitchell, 1999b, p. 12.

41. Cf. Habermas's exploration of these thinkers (1985).

42. Cf. Frisby, 1985, p. 14.

43. The concept of nonmodernity can be linked to Daniel Monk's recent interrogation of monumental-religious architecture in Mandate Jerusalem and the way it was used to forge Palestinian Arab and Zionist Jewish identities. Monk writes that he "persistently privileged the nonidentity that pervades each claim for the identity of history and its designated instantiations. . . . Jerusalem's monuments . . . actually rehearse the struggle's long-standing inability to account for itself" (Monk, 2002, p. 131).

44. Cf. Piot, 1999, p. 21. Indeed, when modernist or modernizing resistance to colonial modernity was offered by Others, it usually served to reproduce the

conditions of their own domination rather than bring them freedom and equality with the metropole (Chatterjee, 1986, p. 10; Argyrou, 2002). That is why, though I understand the desire by scholars such as Dussel and Mignolo to problematize the epistemologies of colonialism and modernity through empowering formerly "subalternized knowledges," I do not necessarily agree that the best way to do this is to demonstrate the modernity of the subaltern (cf. Mignolo, 2000, p. 59; Dussel, 1995a, p. 68). Indeed, it is for this reason that many contemporary Muslims "dismiss the European project of modernity and . . . its principle of subjectivity" (Tibi, 1995, p. 5; cf. LeVine, 2002).

45. Cf. Chatterjee, 1999; Chakrabarty, 1999. For example, Chatterjee's description of European colonial pedagogical missions as a "driving force of colonial modernity" does not hold for Jaffa (Chatterjee, 1999, p. 38).

46. Thus while for Laroui Arabs only crossed the threshold of modern times "in the pain of defeat, occupation, and servitude," this was not the experience of modernity in Jaffa, at least until the 1930s when the planning discourses of Tel Aviv grew powerful enough to facilitate the annexation of swaths of the surrounding Arab-owned territory (Laroui, [1967] 1982).

47. Cf. LeVine, 1998, sec. 2.

48. See the discussion below.

49. Said, 1978; Bracken, 1973.

50. Brummett, 2000, p. 84.

51. As Mitchell argues (1999b, p. 24).

52. As García Canclini argues for Latin America, being a land of "pastiche and bricolage" with many concurrent temporalities and aesthetics has made it a land of postmodernity for centuries (García Canclini, 1995, p. 6).

53. See Bhabha's critique of Foucault, as described by Mitchell, 1999b, p. 16; García Canclini, 1995, p. 7.

54. Jameson, 2002, p. 32.

55. García Canclini, 1995, p. 7. Jameson describes the act of affirming modernity as generating a kind of "electric charge" (Jameson, 2002, p. 35).

56. As Said demonstrates in his critique of the colonial foundation of European literature (Said, 1993).

57. From such an analysis we can conclude that Parsons's belief in a "sociologized Enlightenment," for example, in which human affairs would be self-regulating once freedom and reason were permitted to have their way, is unrealizable by the very conditions of modernity as a colonial discourse (cf. Wagner, 2001, p. 3). The "illusionary" nature of the hegemonic discourses of modernity are discussed in detail later in this chapter and in note 82.

58. Cf. Argyrou, 1999, pp. 35–37.

59. For a detailed analysis of Palestinian responses to British and Zionist architectural and town planning discourses, see LeVine, 1998, 1999a; and chaps. 6–8 below.

60. Thus (as I have elsewhere demonstrated in detail) the prominent agronomist Yitzhak Elazari-Volkani ridiculed the Zionist-inspired "transformation from primitive to modern agriculture in Palestine," demonstrating that in

many cases Zionist and not Palestinian agricultural practices were "defective" and castigating the "rapidity" of European-Zionist production techniques as "having no economic value" compared to the Palestinian peasants' more "traditional" methods (Elazari-Volkani, 1925). For a detailed analysis of Volkani's argument, see LeVine, 1995). Two decades earlier, Young Turk satirists lampooned the supposed speed of modern transport and the utility of other modern conveniences such as trams that "put horses out of work" (cf. Brummett, 2000, pp. 294–300).

61. Mitchell, 1999b, p. 26; his emphasis. That is, there are two registers of difference, one providing the modern with its characteristic indeterminacy and ambivalence, the other with its enormous power of replication.

62. Cf. Mitchell, 1999b, p. 27, clearly using Lefebvre's categorization.

63. Latour, 1993. Mitchell (1999b) argues that because these modern modes of classification are about political representation, they are—in contrast to the modernist explanation—in fact inseparable from the epistemological representations underlying colonial modernity. The unprecedented power of the "Anglo-American" free-market version of modernity at the turn of the millennium led a senior German official to exclaim that "if we want to be modern we have to get rid of" all sorts of social protections that characterized the post–World War II European welfare state, since "modernity has simply become a word for the conformity to such economic constraints" (Oskar Lafontaine, quoted in Jameson, 2002, p. 9). This is a crucial insight, because in fact the Oslo peace process was based on just this kind of modernizational neoliberal economic vision, which had disastrous effects on the Palestinian population and on lower- and working-class Israelis as well (see Peled, 2002; Yiftachel, 2002). This situation made it impossible for Palestinians to achieve the kind of modernity advertised to them as Oslo's reward.

64. Interestingly, the young Jewish guards who protected Tel Aviv (and who replaced what were originally local Palestinian Arab guards) often dressed as "bedouin calvarymen" to impress the local population (cf. Yehoshua, 1969, p. 220). For a discussion of how satirists and cartoonists during the Young Turk Revolution depicted the "ludicrous, hilarious or bewildering" attempts to Europeanize Istanbul, see Brummett, 2000, chap. 7.

65. Mignolo, 2000, p. 3. Latour uses the example of an article in his daily newspaper about the depletion of the ozone layer in which he sees all these various social spaces seemlessly woven together, "mix[ing] together chemical reactions and political reactions. A single thread links the most esoteric sciences and the most sordid politics. . . . The horizons, the stakes, the time frames, the actors—none of these is commensurable, yet there they are, caught up in the same story" (Latour, 1993, p. 1).

Latour's point is that the constitutional dualism of modernity in fact, as opposed to law, permits and encourages the invention and innovation of a host of hybrids that violate modernity's categories and guarantees (i.e., of Tel Aviv's Jewish purity, modernity, etc.). For Latour, the central dualism of modernity is that nature is transcendent (i.e., universal in time and space and thus scientifically and objectively "true") while society and the subject are immanent (i.e., changeable). But as he points out, the sociology of science has demonstrated the mythic character of this dichotomy and the hybrid nature of reality it obscures.

66. These practices "establish a partition between a natural world that has always been there, a society with predictable and stable interests and stakes, and a discourse that is independent of both reference and society" (Latour, 1993, p. 11). Evoking Latour's focus on purity, Wagner argues that modernist approaches come from "*decontaminating* understanding" by thinkers of all but the few "indubitable assumptions from which theorizing can safely proceed" (cf. Wagner, 1999, p. 43; emphasis added). Similarly, Quijano argues that the epistemological principle of modernity is the splitting of the knowing subject from the known object and the relationship of this action to processes of colonial domination (Quijano, 1992).

67. Le Corbusier, 1947, p. 82; Lefebvre, 1991, p. 191; cf. García Canclini on the failure of Latin American attempts to be both "modern and culturally pure" (1995, xiii). Urban "pioneers" would sing of the motherland, "We shall cover thee with a gown of concrete and cement" (Bernstein, 2000, p. 83); even earlier, as Shafir has shown in his study of early Jewish-Arab relations in the rural sector of Palestine, the indigenous population became "invisible" to the Zionist settlers; but while for him the roots of this action lay in the competition between Arab and Jewish workers, in the case of the city, the rendering invisible was done beforehand, discursively, creating a "space of representation" (to use Lefebvre's terminology) that helped to shape the reality on which it was imposed. Indeed, Bauman demonstrates that the processes of abstraction and classification essential to modernity "effaced the face" when the owner of a category was transformed from being an individual to a specimen: "Claims for ethical purification are easily transformed into claims for ethnic purification," thus linking colonial modernity to the Holocaust and thus certainly to nationalism (Bauman, [1989] 2000). Finally, it should be noted that for Nietzsche, "the illusory nature of the world in which we believe to live is the most certain and secure thing which our eyes can still catch hold of," even as it is symptomatic of a "total extermination and uprooting of culture" (Nietzsche, *Untimely Meditations*, p. 229, and *Sämliche Werke*, vol. 7, p. 817, cited in Frisby, 1985, p. 30; cf. Le Corbusier, 1947).

68. As Walter Benjamin describes it, although his tone is perhaps strangely positive, until we realize that barbarism was, in the wake of World War I, a positive and advantageous concept because it lacked evil and therefore makes a tabula rasa, a new start, possible. Such a power is directly related to the colonial basis of modernity (although Benjamin did not complete this lineage); and thus the "barbarism" of the post–World War I avant-garde could never realize the positive dreams of their anticivilizational discourse (Benjamin [1933] 1977, p. 215). Interestingly, the origin of the Latin term *modernus* as first used by Pope Galasius in the fifth century A.D. was related to the break between "classical" and (then) "contemporary" culture brought on by the rise of the Gothic—that is, barbarian—empire (cf. Jameson, 2002, p. 17).

69. See Césaire, 1995, p. 4, where he writes, "Colonization, I repeat, dehumanizes even the most civilized man." Cf. Jameson, 2002, p. 11; Bauman, [1989] 2000, pp. 228–30, 240. Bauman rightly points out that the phrase "unfinished project" is a tautology because modernity, by definition, can never be completed. At the same time he describes its most prominent feature as the need simultaneously to fix and transcend boundaries, an activity whose relevance for this discussion has already been well established.

70. Eisenzweig, 1981, pp. 267, 271, 278; emphasis added. Similarly, Juval Portugali asks whether in existing social science, "there [can] be a non-stratigraphic, spatial, and thus non-totalitarian theory, that is, a theorization of a system of differences and plurality?" His answer is no: "Such a theory never originated in social theory because . . . social theory never seriously challenged the mechanistic world view" (Portugali, 1993, p. 55). In Latour's terminology, it never challenged the separation of the spheres of "purification and translation"; that is, it has not ceased to be modern. Thus Portugali, like Deleuze and Guattari, looks outside of the traditional social science canon to find conceptual tools for developing such a theory. Portugali attributes this naturalization of space to the "aspatiality of geography, planning, and social theory as a whole" and believes it is at the root of their difficulties in adequately describing the dynamics of modern cities (Portugali, 1994, p. 217).

71. Chow, 1997, pp. 132–33; cf. Bhabha, 1997; Bauman, 1993.

72. Yiftachel and Meir, 1998, p. 7.

73. Eisenzweig, 1981, p. 262.

74. Ibid., pp. 265, 267. As Robert Sack points out, "[A] modern use of territory is based most of all upon a sufficient political authority or power to match the dynamics of capitalism: to help repeatedly move, mold, and control human spatial organization at vast scales. This modern use of territory is first a matter of degree and intensity. But at some point it begins to lead to a qualitatively different sense of territory and space. Territory becomes conceptually and even actually emptiable and this presents space as both a real and emptiable surface or stage on which events occur" (Sack, 1986, p. 87).

75. Eisenzweig, 1981, p. 280. Cf. Shafir, 1989.

76. As Eisenzweig explains, "The nuance is important, even crucial, to comprehending the Israeli imagination." Why? Because "the respective functions of the positivist discourse and that of the more traditional Russian Jewish pioneers are complementary but not identical. The positivist discourse clears the way by forming the dreamed-of and natural space, that is by emptying the territory of all troublesome presence. . . . It is precisely in order not to see the Palestinian that they are obliged to form a vision that conceals him" (Eisenzweig, 1981, p. 280).

77. Here I am referring to Lefebvre's and Soja's analytics of space, a fuller discussion of which appears in note 85 below.

78. Herzl, [1902] 1941, p. 78, cf. p. 93. See LeVine, 1995, 1999a, 1999b; and chapters 3, 4, 6, 7, 8 for empirical analyses of planning in Palestine/Israel. The discipline of geography, which has always been *the* theory and methodology of

urban and regional planning, emerged as the academic discipline most strongly oriented toward the colonies, where cities as well as the rural countryside still seemed fixed, harmonious settings (Wright, 1991, p. 71). Thus it was among the most prominent sites in which social scientists "attempted to apply rational thinking, science and technology to the sociopolitical domain in a practical way" (Portugali, 1994, p. 307).

79. Ben-Gurion, quoted in Flapan, 1979, p. 132; Cohen, 1912, p. 26; Ben-Gurion, quoted in Gorny, 1987, p. 140. Also see Gordon, 1916, p. 244, where he writes that the country's supposed decrepid state is a "sign that the country is waiting for us, reassurance of our *right* on the land" (my emphasis).

80. My understanding of modernity and colonialism as being mutually generative, and together generative of nationalism, is informed by the work of scholars such as Amin, Wallerstein, Abu-Lughod, Mintz, Prakash, Stoler, and Mitchell, all of whom have demonstrated how the discourse of the nation can be understood as a product and effect of colonialism (cf. Mitchell, 1999a).

81. Here I return to a point made at the beginning of this chapter—that my argument significantly expands on existing analyses of Israel as a "colonial" or "colonial-settler" society. To take perhaps the most well known critique of Zionism as a colonial discourse, Rodinson's *Israel: A Colonial-Settler State*, a reading of this text reveals that while Rodinson fits Zionism squarely into the historical typology of European colonialism-imperialism, demonstrating its ideological and political shaping of Israel as a colonial "fact," he focuses on the political aspect of colonialism as "occupation with domination," and nowhere in his study can one find the word or concept "modernity" (Rodinson, 1973, p. 92). This is also true in Césaire's *Discourse on Colonialism* (1995). Rodinson concludes that "the advancement and then success of the Zionist movement occurred "within the framework of European expansion into countries belonging to what later came to be called the Third World. . . . Once the premises were laid down the inexorable logic of history determined the consequences," which would be the "destruction" of the existing Arab society (Rodinson, 1973, pp. 77, 81). Such an analysis, however powerful and salient, misses the larger framework provided by the fourfold matrix I use and thus cannot account for the history and sociology of the two societies in all their complexity.

82. Precisely because of the discursive power of the historiography and sociology generated out of Zionism as a modern, colonial discourse. Influenced by the larger Zionist view of Palestine's Arab population, "for a long time Israeli sociology simply evaded the specific geopolitical context which encases Israeli society . . . [particularly] regarding Israeli Palestinian relations" (Ram, 1993, p. 332). At best, Palestinians were treated as an "object of history," in a social science that was "based on the articulation of a historical narrative through the Modernization perspective, which locates societies on the spectrum of traditionalism-modernity" (Sa'di, 1996, p. 395). Lash paraphrases Latour to argue that it is only when we are no longer modern that rights and representation, that rights to speak and be represented, will have been granted to and claimed by "the object"—in our case, Palestinians (Lash, 1999, p. 269).

83. Shafir, 1989; Chakrabarty, 1999.

84. Lefebvre, 1991, p. 33. Lefebvre explains how these varying discourses produce two experiences of space that both conflict and interact: "representations of space" and "representational spaces." The first is the space-cum-"spatial discourses" of those who make maps—scientists, planners, technocrats, and engineers—"the dominant space in any society (or mode of production)" (ibid., p. 39; 1991, p. 220). This corresponds to the space of the Zionist and British planners and leaders who designed and administered the city, as well as the European (i.e., more recently immigrated) Jewish Jaffan elite who first moved there. Significantly, this space can actually be "engendered by and within" the theoretical understandings that attempt to describe and maintain it, a mutual effectivity that is especially relevant in the case of Zionist urbanization as it played out in Tel Aviv and Jaffa.

Lefebvre's second category, representational spaces, embodies complex symbolisms, sometimes coded, sometimes not, that are linked to the clandestine or underground side of social life (Lefebvre, 1991, p. 33). This is the space "as directly lived through its associated images and symbols," and hence the space of "inhabitants" (p. 39). Lefebvre characterizes this dimension of space as "imagined," and it is thus here that possibility of "reimagining" the spaces of Jaffa and Tel Aviv can most successfully be entertained (cf. Harvey 1989a, p. 219).

85. As Soja points out, this "illusion of transparency" prevents us from seeing the social construction of the concretization of social relations embedded in spatiality (Soja, 1989, p. 7). The first illusion is that space is transparent—that is, easily intelligible and free of "traps or secret places" (Lefebvre, 1991, pp. 27–28). It is also tied to the idea that what is spoken or written about a particular space—especially by experts—is taken for actual social practice. Thus the Zionist-European discourse of development was accepted by most Jews, the British Mandatory Government, and some Arabs as the valid description of the lived experience of both the Jewish and Arab communities and so accorded a validity that sublimated the actual and often discordant Palestinian reality. Moreover, Lefebvre explains that in the "transparent" understanding of space "communication [i.e., Zionist discourse] brings the non-communicated [i.e., Palestinians] into the realm of the communicated"—that is, speaks for the mute Palestinian who "has no existence beyond an ever-pursued residue" (Lefebvre 1991, p. 28).

The second illusion is that space is "realistic" or "opaque," and in this illusion the rational understanding and explanation of space is "naturalized," becoming like hard clay that requires the hands of an experienced sculptor—or architect-planner—to be molded into a work of art (cf. Lefebvre, 1991, p. 30). As Soja elaborates, in this understanding space is conceived of and experienced as fixed, inert, and undialectical, which allows those who study and govern it to do so empirically and "objectively," to focus only on surface experiences and see space as a collection of "things" that can be appropriated and manipulated (Soja, 1989, pp. 6, 122–23; cf. Harvey's [1996, chap. 2] discussion of his "dialectical" methodology, which aims precisely to avoid this perception). In the process of reducing spatiality to pure physicality, "naturalizing [it] back to a first nature," which is then susceptible to "scientific" manipulation, any existing human geographies or landscapes are erased and replaced by new landscapes, perhaps those of the architect (cf. Soja, 1989, pp. 122–23).

86. Harvey describes the process as "mental inventions" or spatial discourses that imagine new meanings or possibilities for spatial practices (Harvey, 1989a, p. 219).

87. The word *implicate* comes from the Latin root meaning "to enfold inward," and for Portugali it indicates the enfoldment of societies and the territories they inhabit (Portugali, 1993, pp. xiii, 63).

88. Argyrou points out that anthropologists exclude from their accounts all those things that undermine the credibility of their story, yet include "poetic, literary forms that transform 'dry' data into a vivid, lively and entertaining story," even as they accuse "natives" of being able to operate intellectually only at the level of the poetic (Argyrou, 1999, p. 30).

89. Portugali, 1993, p. 140. Portugali argues that poetic geography "is the very principle of nationalism: it uses past, distant events as materials with which to construct the modern society and its nation-state" (p. 52). Thus poetic or richly symbolic descriptions of space summon certain emotions, memories, visions, imaginations, and cultural meanings that have the power to spur people participating in the discourse to take action toward realizing the larger project in which it is subsumed. In the case of Palestine/Israel, a poetics of the territory of Palestine that imagined or portrayed it as vacant, sterile, or "unhealthy" was instrumental in preparing the ground, and its arriving "cultivators," for their mutual rebirth through the redeeming activity of Zionism.

Similarly, Vico's geography—from which Portugali's is derived—implies that every new geographic present is to be seen not as a new, disconnected stratum but as an enfoldment and extension of past and distant geographies; a "poetic wisdom" that is the basis for the construction of the present and future. Poetry was important for Vico because for him the "creators" of humanity—the Greeks—were poets and sages (Vico, [1774] 1968, p. 117). Bachelard also developed his "poetics of space" based on the "speaking being's creativeness" and imagination, which constituted "a major power of human nature" (Bachelard, 1964, pp. xxiv, xxxiv; cf. Lash's [1999, p. 217] use of the notion of "poesis" as the productive counterpoint to instrumental rationality).

The historian Peter Gran convincingly argues that Israel/Palestine long served as the original locus of European and Western civilizational identity, as which biblical Israel (as a people and a territory) provided the matrix for the Western nationalist imagination. In this sense, the poetics of European imperialism in the Middle East were nourished by the same images as the Zionist imagination they shaped (Gran, 1998).

90. Portugali, 1993, p. 21. He uses Tel Aviv as a specific example of the utility of this approach, explaining that "Tel Aviv can be seen as a relatively independent city; at a deeper level Tel Aviv enfolds all the other cities in its metro-

politan space by being the destination of metropolitan commuters; at a yet sub-tler level, Tel Aviv enfolds also the Occupied Territories, etc. From this perspec-tive the rigid administrative boundaries of Tel Aviv are a thought abstraction in the explicate domain" (p. 130).

91. Ibid., p. xii.

92. Lefebvre, 1991, p. 86.

93. Deleuze and Guattari, [1980] 1987, p. 5.

94. The resulting maps would be multidimensional, the product of a "trans-disciplinary" endeavor that uses novels, poetry, film, and other nontraditional source materials—"the 'real' and the fictive more and more woven together in intertextual discourses" (Westwood and Williams, 1997, pp. 12–13)—to consti-tute a new narrative space that can provide us with a much deeper commentary on the people, institutions, and cities of Jaffa and Tel Aviv in both the pre-1948 period and today.

95. Mitchell, 1999b, p. 24.

96. Cf. Hefner, 1998a.

97. Rebecca Karl's recent work on Chinese-Ottoman relations at the turn of the twentieth century has revealed that Chinese diplomat-scholars with experience or interest in the Middle East well understood (in a manner similar to Muslim thinkers such as Jamal al-Din al-Afghani) the inherent connection between imperialism and ethnonationalism—"Europe has two new nouns" is how one Chinese scholar introduced these two terms—and modernity, which was described as a "new world . . . with new ideas, new learning, new political forms, new laws, new people[,] . . . and also new rules for destroying countries" (quoted in Karl, 1999, pp. 9, 14).

Even if we agree with scholars such as Wagner or Beck that "organized modernity" has met its demise in favor of a possible "extended liberal" or "experimental" modernity that is more fully inclusive, such a development is too late for Jaffa and Tel Aviv of the late Ottoman and Mandate periods, as their residents did not have recourse to such reimagined modernities (cf. Wagner, 2001, p. 7; Beck, Giddens, and Lash, 1994, p. 59).

98. Calderón, 1995, p. 55.

99. Cf. Beverley, Aronna, and Oviedo, 1995, p. 2, quoting Octavio Paz on the right to indigenous cultural periodization; Brunner, 1995, p. 43. For Dussel, "another way of thinking and feeling" is at the heart of the project of trans—rather than post—modernity (1995a, p. 9; 1996)

100. Cf. Eisenstadt's discussion of the Jacobin modernity of contemporary religious fundamentalist movements (Eisenstadt, 1999).

101. Thus, following Szakolczai, by "liminality," I intend more than its nar-row meaning as the "middle phase in rites of passage" in which the social order is temporarily suspended, only to be returned as the ceremony is brought to a close. Instead, Szakolczai sees modernity as a case in which temporary liminal conditions become permanent, and thus he expands its meaning to encompass world-scale transition in which the taken-for-granted order of things has actu-ally collapsed and cannot be restored, leading often to "an escalating spiral of

violence" (Szakolczai, 2000, p. 219). I would argue that modernity's liminality is not permanent but in fact can be transcended via a move toward nonmodernity.

102. Following Kaye and Strath's argument that utopia and dystopia are the two poles of modernity (Kaye and Strath, 2000). This dystopia is what Césaire describes as the "sickness" of capitalism, although he does not make the link explicit between capitalism, modernity and colonialism (Césaire, 1995, p. 39). In this manner I would strongly disagree with Tibi's argument that "cultural modernity cannot be equated with colonial rule on any terms" and that Muslim critics of modernity "confuse" what in his mind—erroneously, I believe—are the separate spheres of a "institutional dimension" and a "cultural project" of modernity (see Tibi, 1995, pp. 8–9). For me, the institutional and cultural dimensions of modernity arose out of the same matrix and are thus inseparable.

103. Thus we cannot follow Lash's recent call to find the "ground" of and for "another modernity" and a "different rationality"; his "aesthetic" focus on this other modernity is in sympathy with the need to engage in a "poetic geography" of Jaffa–Tel Aviv and of modernity. For Lash, this second, reflexive modernity is "largely aesthetic" and is one in which individuals find rules to use to encounter specific situations—that is, analogical rationality—rather than a determinate judgment based on a preexisting set of universal possibilities, as defined the first modernity (Lash, 1999, p. 13).

104. This belief was put forth by Abdallah Laroui in his pathbreaking study on contemporary Arab ideologies in the context of colonialism and modernity (Laroui, [1967] 1982).

105. That is, the kind of complex, alinear, and nonteleological reading strategy that Deleuze and Guattari describe as "rhizomatic" produces a complex multitude of entrance and exit points that can pierce through the protective shell of the fourfold modernity matrix (Deleuze and Guattari, [1972] 1983).

CHAPTER 2

1. Thus historians such as Ruth Kark and, more recently, Ruba Kana'an, who differ in their portrayal of Jaffa's post-1799 history, nevertheless begin their studies that year (see Kark, 1990a; Kana'an, 1998).

2. Interview with senior archaeologist for Jaffa at the Israeli Antiquities Authority, June 1997. For an in-depth examination of the consequences of this policy, see Baram, 1996, p. 17.

3. Indeed, the variety of sources used in this chapter confirm Roger Owen's call to move beyond the employment of oversimplistic or reductionist modes of explanation when dealing with the socioeconomic transformation of Palestine during the late Ottoman period. For their part, Palestinian histories have tended to downplay the Jewish presence in Jaffa over the centuries. Most Zionists, like their European counterparts, visualized Jaffa as "little more than an overgrown village until the late 1840s," believing that only at the end of the

nineteenth century, "with the coming of the German settlers, and after them the Jewish immigrants, did Jaffa develop" (Owen, 1982, p. 7).

In *Jaffa: A City in Evolution*, Kark asserts that "until the last quarter of the nineteenth century, the population of Jaffa remained traditional in character" (Kark, 1990a, p. 157). This supposedly stunted development and the over-crowding and lack of sanitation that accompanied it were attributed to the "nature" of Muslim cities (cf. Shavitz, 1947, pp. 145–47) and led teleologically to Jaffa's modern "Jewish twin Tel Aviv, founded by Zionists on the sand dunes north of Jaffa in 1909" (Kimmerling and Migdal, 1994, p. 38; and see p. 47).

4. Cf. Scholch, 1993; A. Cohen, 1973.

5. Kark, 1990a, pp. 15, 43, 53. Kark suggests that "a more balanced portrayal can be obtained" by citing such Zionist leaders as Arthur Ruppin. Ruppin's work is invaluable, yet he also sought the economic conquest of Jaffa (see chap. 7). Moreover, this view of the (lack of a) role of the city's Palestinian Arab population leads directly to the teleological assertion, common to most mainstream Israeli historiography, that it was Jews and Europeans who were responsible for the undeniable development of the city. From this perspective, the "uninterrupted course of growth and development" during the late nineteenth century led to the birth of Tel Aviv—which "rapidly [became] the nucleus of a city which was Jewish, modern, distinctive, and autonomous" (Kark, 1990a, p. 108).

6. II Chron. 2:10.

7. Jonah 1:3.

8. After leaving Lydda Jesus stayed in the home of one Simon the Tanner in Jaffa (Acts 9:36–42; 10:9).

9. Shachar, 1971, p. 1251.

10. Tolkovsky, 1963, pp. 327–28.

11. Ritter, 1866, pp. 253–59. It is worth noting that the port of Acre is not mentioned in this description. Moreover, this depiction contradicts Ram's assertion, drawn from the account of one European visitor, that "Jaffa remained in the main a 'measly farm' ('ir 'aluv) to the point that travelers could not believe that there was ever a city there" (Ram, 1996, p. 13).

12. What is interesting is that the desire and language of "order and discipline," which was used by the Porte vis-à-vis Palestine as early as a 1708 *firman* (Maliye, 9497, 22 Muharram 1120–13/4/1708, p. 5) reflects a potentially modern(izing) set of technologies and discourses of government, which raises numerous issues regarding the etiology and development of modernization in the empire that requires greater attention by scholars (cf. A. Cohen, 1973, p. 182).

13. A. Cohen, 1973, p. 19. We should be aware, as Cohen rightly points out, that the development of the "economy" should not lead to the assumption that the majority of the inhabitants of Palestine saw greater prosperity (p. 88). Yet his focus on official Ottoman edicts (i.e., a "top-down" view from the Porte) and European commercial records cannot elucidate the relationship between Jaffa and its hinterland, or other more local dynamics (Kana'an, 1998, p. 6).

14. A. Cohen, 1973, pp. 145–50, 154–56. Cohen's review of the Mukata'a records leads him to conclude that the upward trend in taxation can be understood only as an outcome of growing prosperity in the area (p. 156).

15. Abu-Bakr, 1996, pp. 109, 133; Kark, 1990a, pp. 8–9. Abu-Bakr describes the city as a "vortex" of these struggles.

16. Kana'an, 1998, pp. 17–18; Jameson, 2002, p. 31, for a discussion of the development of modernity in Europe during the seventeenth and eighteenth centuries via Descartes, Kant, and Hegel. A British chronicler in 1871 wrote, "The modern town is believed not to be more than one hundred years old" (Stewart, quoted in Kana'an, 1998, p. 21).

17. Cf. map by M. Jacotin, 1810, in Kark, 1990, p. 17.

18. The Belgian traveler Michaud, 1830–31, cited in Kana'an, 2001b, p. 134.

19. Light, 1818, p. 138.

20. Ibid., p. 139.

21. Kana'an, 2001b, pp. 134–35; Malak, 1993, pp. 49–50. For a more detailed discussion of the decades leading up to and after the Napoleonic invasion, see, respectively, al-'Awra, [1936] 1989, pp. 88–94, 299–311, 381–88; Kana'an, 1998.

22. Light describes Jews arriving at Jaffa Port with him in 1814 and others traveling to Jerusalem and at least sojourning if not living in the Old City (Light, 1818, pp. 138–44).

23. Kark, 1990a, p. 24.

24. There is evidence of the increased Egyptian immigration in the Shari'a Court records. See JICR, book 17 (1845/1261–1848/1265), p. 213; book 48 (1888/1306–1890/1308), p. 88.

25. Abu-Bakr, 1996, p. 370.

26. Thus an 1837 document in the Jerusalem *sijjil* refers to the "plantation outside the port of Jaffa" that bordered "the plantation of the sons of al-Hurani, known previously as the plantation of Yusuf al-Mahuri." Muhammed Ghosheh, quoted by Robert Schick, Islamic Studies Fellow, W. F. Albright Institute of Archeological Research, Jerusalem, e-mail comm., Sept. 1999).

27. See Biger, 1987a, pp. 53–56.

28. As Kark describes Tobler's 1845 account (Kark, 1990a, p. 67).

29. BOA, MV 180/12/1331, Irade-i nafia 1701, Irade-i nafia 1302/1884.

30. Graham-Brown, 1982, p. 55. For example, the value of Jaffa's exports doubled between 1856 and 1882, and the area of land under cultivation in the Jaffa district quadrupled in just one year, from 1862 to 1863, as extensive new olive and orange plantations were planted (Scholch, 1993, pp. 89–91).

31. Scholch, 1993, p. 142; cf. Kark, 1990a, p. 189.

32. Lortet, 1884, pp. 363–64.

33. Ibid., p. 365.

34. Ibid. Lortet described French and, more recently, English and Italian firms as the principal intermediaries in the town's foreign trade.

35. Scholch, 1993, p. 118; cf. the detailed information provided by A. Cohen's (1973) use of the Miliye records for Jaffa during this period, which I was unable to locate for the late Ottoman period.

36. The notion of a self-contained Palestinian economy lying fallow and waiting for European revivification has been shown to be far off the mark. The so-called self-contained and autonomous nature and behavior of peasant farmers in Palestine, so important for the traditional Zionist conceptualization of the Arab economy, did not exist even in the nineteenth century (Graham-Brown, 1982, p. 135). By that time the shifting power relations in the Ottoman Empire resulting from the land and tax reforms led to a restructuring of agriculture. A whole new relationship between the owner of the productive resources—land or capital or both—and the peasant tenant–operator, called *sharika*, or partnership, developed in which many owners "farmed out contracts" in such a way that it gave the peasant new entrepreneurial opportunities (Firestone, 1975b, 189; cf. Scholch, 1993, pp. 110–17).

37. Scholch provides an excellent summary of the dynamics underlying Palestine's (in particular, Jaffa's) development during this period (Scholch, 1993, p. 285).

38. See Scholch, 1993, pt. 2.

39. Ibid., pp. 108–9, table 33.

40. *PEF Quarterly*, 1872, Captain Stewart's Letters, 15/12/1871, p. 35. This is the same time Conder noted that the coastal plain near Jaffa was being bought up by Jewish, Greek, and Maronite "capitalists" (cited in Scholch, 1993, pp. 112–13).

41. Aaronsohn and Soskin, 1902, pp. 342–59; cf. Elezari-Volkáni, 1925.

42. A. Cohen, 1973, p. 157, for the swamp drainage and water mill concession. Scholch describes the "multidimensional character of European aspirations for Palestine and emphasizes that "the Zionist movement represented only *one* of many European movements during the nineteenth century that were dedicated to the 'reclamation' and colonization of Palestine" (Scholch, 1993, pp. 47–48; emphasis in original). Cotton had previously been a primary crop in the Jaffa region (although its cultivation was on a comparatively small scale, so that Muhammad 'Ali instructed his son Ibrahim not to install a monopoly on its trade). It was overtaken by other commodities during this period because the integration of Palestine and the commercialization of its agriculture made other crops, especially the Jaffa orange, much more profitable for export to Europe (Doumani, 1995, pp. 103–5). I believe this change was pivotal for Jaffa's relative autonomy during this period because Europeans had less control over the orange trade than they did over cotton. Scholch similarly argues that French demands for sesame, the increase in grain prices during the Crimean War, and the increasing organization of orange exports "brought cotton cultivation to a complete standstill" (Scholch, 1993, pp. 86–87).

43. Scholch, 1993, p. 134.

44. Jaffa Port in fact bore "the unenviable distinction of being classed at Lloyd's as one of the worst harbours in the world" (*MacMillan's Guide to Palestine and Syria* [London, 1910], p. 9).

45. Scholch, 1982, p. 33.

46. Diplomatic Archives, Ministry of Foreign Affairs, France [hereafter

DAMFAF], Jaffa CCC, 20/4/1879 letter to Foreign Ministry from Jaffa Vice Consul.

47. Ibid. For example, the French vice consul deemed it important to build a new port and railway because of the importance of the town and its function vis-à-vis Jerusalem. For a list of the plans to develop the port, see Avitzur, 1972c, pp. 92–112. For example, in August 1878 a French company obtained a concession to construct a harbor at Jaffa, although nothing came of it (for a project to develop the port in the period immediately before the war, see CZA L51/30, "Projet d'un quai a Jaffa"). There was also talk of using the waters of the 'Auja River for irrigation and other purposes, but while the British consul reported that the Porte had granted a concession for irrigating Jaffa gardens with water from the 'Auja River, no company was formed to carry out the scheme. After World War I the developer Pinhas Rutenberg received a concession from the British to build an electrical power plant near the mouth of the river (Smilansky 1981, pp. 72, 97–98, discusses this plan).

48. See table 1; Harlaftis and Kardasis, 2000, pp. 241–42.

49. The countries included France, Austria, Italy, Russia, and England, with most of their ships providing postal service (DAMFAF, Jaffa CCC, 20/4/79 letter to Foreign Ministry from Jaffa Vice Consul). In total 408 ships landed in 1878.

50. Scholch, 1982, p. 21. These included watches, clocks, porcelain, perfume, jewelry, and other "fancy goods" (DAMFAF, Jaffa CCC, 28/9/97 report to Foreign Ministry from Jaffa Vice Consul).

51. See Scholch, 1982; Kark, 1990a, chap. 5.

52. DAMFAF, Jaffa CCC, 28/9/97 report to Foreign Ministry from Jaffa Vice Consul. Five hundred to six hundred tons of cotton were imported from Damascus, Homs, and Hama. Cotton was also important from Egypt and Turkey and wools from Turkey and England; oranges from Jaffa went to eight European and Asian countries, in addition to the majority destined for Great Britain. Exports and imports increased every year in the last half of the decade according to French statistics and included cereals, grains, vegetables, olive oil, soap, wools, skins and hides, livestock, matting, oranges and other citrus fruits, holy objects, honey, and fresh and dried fruits.

53. Scholch, 1993, p. 142; Malak, 1993, pp. 55–56. The produce of southern Palestine was exported mainly through Jaffa, with its main export commodities in the 1856–82 period being wheat, barley and dura, sesame, olive oil and soap, oranges and other fruits, and vegetables, the exports of all of which doubled during the period (cf. Scholch, 1982, pp. 13, 18). In fact, oranges are listed as the second most important export from Jaffa Port as early as 1857 (Scholch, 1993, pp. 84–85).

54. "Namely their early ripeness, transportability, aroma, and almost complete lack of seeds" (Aaronsohn and Soskin, 1902, p. 342). Orange exports in fact jumped from 667,800 francs in 1885 to 2,480,000 in 1894, an almost fourfold increase in less than ten years (3.71 to be exact). For more on the growth of the orange trade, see Scholch, 1993, pp. 90–92.

55. Scholch, 1982, p. 17. The orange trade was important enough in the 1890s to warrant a special report from the French vice consul in Jaffa to Paris The report on commerce from the next year also listed wine, flour, leather and hides, and soaps among the major local products (DAMFAF, Jaffa CCC, 1/5/94 and 5/6/95 reports to Foreign Ministry from Jaffa Vice Consul).

56. Wool increased elevenfold and oranges 3.25 times, while exports in general rose from 15.6 million Turkish pounds in 1857 to 37.8 million in 1882 (Scholch, 1982, p. 62, tables 1.9, 1.10). The exports of soap, most of it manufactured in either Jaffa or Nablus, also jumped dramatically during the 1885–1913 period, from 13,722 to 200,000 pounds sterling annually (431 tons to 1,635 tons) (Avitzur, 1972c, p. 48).

57. PRO, Parliamentary Papers, 1881, "Report by Consular Agend Amzalak on the Trade and Commerce of Jaffa for the year 1880," p. 1098. Cf. Parliamentary Papers 1880–1900.

58. Hoteliers, merchants and sellers of pious objects, boatmen, porters, and railway workers all benefited from the increase in tourism (DAMFAF, Jaffa CCC, 30/6/96 report to Foreign Ministry from Jaffa Vice Consul).

59. Cf. al-Tarawnah, 1997; Wilkins, n.d.

60. Doumani, 1995, p. 74.

61. DAMFAF, Jaffa CCC, 2/7/1887 letter to Foreign Ministry from Jaffa Vice Consul.

62. Cf. the sources used by A. Cohen (1973) for this period, especially those of the French (vice) consul.

63. In fact, it was above all in the affairs of real estate that the "chicanery works its greatest and most striking success," because of the venality of the magistrates. After a sale is completed a new person enters the scene with a fraudulent, supposedly older title and makes a claim that winds up in the judicial process, resulting in an "open auction between the plaintiff and defendent to the profit of the judges" (DAMFAF, Jaffa CCC, 2/7/87 letter to Foreign Ministry from Jaffa Vice Consul).

64. M. Michaud, quoted in Kana'an, 1998, p. 56.

65. Jaffa Qa'imaqam Ahmed Bek to Jerusalem Mayor Fizi Effendi, then traveling in Jaffa, August 1, 1908, in Kushner, 1995, pp. 176–77.

66. The Porte had prohibited land purchases and immigration as early as 1882 and attempted to be kept informed about Russian Jewish settlement in Jaffa (BOA, DH.ŞFR, 38/110, S/24/1333H, Encrypted telegraph to Post and Jurisdiction of Jerusalem; see also BOA, DH.ŞFR, 72/129, R/7/1335H telegraph from Head of Public Security office to the 4th Army Commander Jemal Pasha concerning making regulations to prevent Zionist from "acting against the country" and how to handle prosecutions involving Jews during wartime). Cf. the quote by Sultan Abdulhamid after his meeting with Herzl, cited in Farhi, 1975, p. 194.

67. BOA, DH.İD 34/18, 1329/1910.

68. PRO, Parliamentary Papers, 1892, C.6550, #1023, Trade of Palestine for 1890–91, p. 2.

69. *Luach Eretz Yisrael*, 1899, #4, p. 8.

70. DAMFAF, Jaffa CCC, 30/6/96 Report to Foreign Ministry from Jaffa Vice Consul.

71. Gharbiyyah, 1975(?), p. 68; cf. Doumani, 1995.

72. The value of imports and exports during the 1893–1914 period jumped from 345,540 to 1,312,659 LP and 332,628 to 745,413 LP, respectively (Avitzur, 1972c, appendix, tables 1, 11, 12, 14).

73. Williamson, 2000, p. 49. He points out that perhaps the eastern end of the Mediterranean "did not share in the retardation" that appears to have affected many other Mediterranean countries.

74. Thus we should not see the Jews of Jaffa as *the* "economic artery" of Jaffa who brought "renewed life" to the orange trade once they began to purchase groves around the city (Droyanov, 1935, p. 45), although they were certainly an important force.

75. Droyanov, 1935, p. 22.

76. DAMFAF, NS Turquie, 1897–1917, Palestine, Cons. de Jaffa, #430, 15/3/10 and 2/9/10 reports. For example, the confectionary trade was in Jewish hands (TAMA, 1/20. Article in *Kedima*, 1904, p. 438).

77. Smilansky, 1981, p. 39.

78. CZA, Z3/115, German translation of 8/4/13 article in *al-Muktabas*. The article claimed further that most of the hotels were Jewish owned and that Jews owned bigger orange orchards, averaging 100 dunams versus an average of 50 dunams for Arab-owned orchards.

79. In fact, it would seem to refute the standard historiography of Jaffa, which posits that "generally speaking there was little cultural-social activity in Jaffa among the Muslims" before World War I (cf. Kark, 1990a, p. 163).

80. Already in the period following the Crimean War, for example, the increasing practice of constructing new floors on top of existing buildings for use as apartments or stores allowed people to see down into what until then were private areas for women in the compounds of Jewish and Muslim families. This led to several lawsuits to restrict such construction and is clear evidence of the "changing physical environment of the town and the challenges it presented to prevailing social mores" (cf. Wilkins, n.d., p. 7).

81. Yahav, 1990a.

82. Wilkins, n.d., p. 7. Mention of the Jebaliyyah neighborhood, located south of Jaffa, is found in the court records as far back as the beginning of the nineteenth century. An impressive listing of agricultural properties owned by the village shaykh at the time of his death is provided in JICR, book 5, case #104 (c. 1241/1825 or 1826).

83. Malak, 1993, p. 12. Malak describes the lineages of almost every major family in the city, showing their ties to other Arab countries and the extensive network of relationships, business and family, between the city and other Arab metropolises (Malak, 1996).

84. Malak, 1993, p. 43; Kark, 1990a, p. 159. The portrait of the Bouri family of Jaffa, presented in Malak (1996), illustrates the connection between town

and village quite well. Malak informs us that the Bouris owned a large mercantile concern in Jaffa, which imported and assembled bicycles, lamps, and other products. They were also involved in the film industry in the 1920s and owned quite a few citrus groves in the outlying areas that were worked by the villagers (Malak, 1996, pp. 130–32). In fact, many of the orchards that surrounded the city were owned by city dwellers, some of whom built summer villas in them.

85. This was in accordance with Jaffa's role as a *qada'*, or central town of the Jerusalem Mutaşarrıf as designated in the 1864 Vilayet Law (cf. Yazbak, 1998, chap. 2, for an excellent summary of the law and its implications). The goal of the municipality was to improve the city by enhancing its cleanliness and installing street lighting (Kark, 1990a, p. 33).

86. Mostly because they spread the culture and language of their respective countries (Ichilov and Mazawi, 1996, p. 7).

87. DAMFAF, NS Turquie, vol. 131, letter from French Consul to Foreign Ministry, 13/11/03. The consul was especially worried that the British school would increase the knowledge of English among the city's youth, leading to an increase in British influence such as occurred in Egypt. By 1905 the consul felt more assured that the local French school was succeeding in increasing French influence to the point that "everyone speaks French, giving the illusion of a French city," although the prospective opening of a new Greek Orthodox school was similarly worrying (ibid., 20/7/05).

88. DAMFAF, NS Turquie, vol. 131, letter from French Consul to Foreign Ministry, 20/7/05.

89. Guerin, 1868, pp. 2–11.

90. Palestine Exploration Fund, 1882, vol. 2, pp. 254–55; Heykal, 1988, p. 177.

91. TAMA, 1/20. Article in *Kedima*, 1904, p. 438. Film discovered by Tel Aviv University Professor Andre Mazawi and exhibited at the Mahrajan Yafiyya in Amman, July 1997. Cf. Kean, 1895, pp. 3–6, for a good description of the market and the "marvelous" and "faultless" products made by Jaffa's artisans.

92. Cf. Agmon, 1994, p. 55.

93. The work of Aharon Layish and, more recently, of Iris Agmon, has uncovered numerous examples of women buying and selling property to resolve or collect debts or purchasing wheat in order to retail it (cf. Layish, 1975, p. 529; Agmon, 1994).

94. JICR, book 80 (1318/1900), case #9, pp. 7–8. Beyond their involvement in commerce and real estate transactions, the Shari'a Court records clearly indicate that women were as quick as men to seek divorce as a remedy for unfulfilled marriage vows (particularly regarding economic security, which would be demanded through matrimony). A good example of the large number of matrimonial cases is JICR, book 83 (1900/1318–1905/1323), which contains at least a dozen cases.

95. JICR, book 160 (1914/1333–1916/1334), case #446, pp. 1–2. Cf. JICR, book 160, p. 27, for a case from Sheikh Muwannis, and p. 32, for a case from

Nablus. This volume contains mostly divorce cases, contested wills associated with divorce, and child custody cases. Agmon (1994) and Yazbak (1998) each present detailed discussions of the role of women in late Ottoman Palestinian society based on a close reading of the *sijjil* of Jaffa and Haifa, respectively.

96. Cf. Agmon, 1994, p. 19 (of English summary), pp. 41–42 (of Hebrew text).

97. See Mandel, 1976, pp. 168–72, for a good discussion of the tensions from the perspective of the Porte vis-à-vis increased immigration and land purchases by Jews.

98. As recounted in Mandel, 1976, p. 39.

99. Bibliothèque Alliance Israelite Universelle [BAIU], Israel IC/4761/1, letter to the President of the AIU from M. Angel, dated 15/9/1896; Israel XXXIV.E 101/6/1894, "Rapport Moral, Mai et Juin, 1894."

100. For example, the Qa'imaqam of Jaffa (the district governor, who also controlled the surrounding villages) was very close to some of the leading Sephardic families of Jaffa, particularly the Shloosh family (Shloosh, 1931, pp. 33, 39).

101. TAMA, 1/20. Article in *Kedima*, 1904, p. 435. The author continues that the Arabs called Jews "children of death" but more recently came to respect them because Jews were showing signs of "life." It is worth noting that "nationalist" sentiments were also evident two decades earlier in the support Jaffans demonstrated for the 'Urabi Revolt in Egypt (Scholch, 1993, pp. 278–81).

102. Jaffa Qa'imaqam Muhammad Aşaf to Mutaşarrıf of Jerusalem, July 9, 1907, document contained in Kushner, 1995, pp. 62–68.

103. An attachment to the letter contains a list of major Zionist land purchases in the Jaffa region; it describes large purchases in the villages around Jaffa extending all the way to Petach Tikva but does not include any of the Jewish land purchases in the immediate vicinity of Jaffa, such as the eleven Jewish neighborhoods that surrounded the town by 1907 (see Document 9 in Kushner, 1995, pp. 82–83).

104. Kushner, 1995, p. 63.

105. Ibid., pp. 64–65.

106. Ibid., p. 65. The Qa'imaqam was particularly concerned about "subversive groups" of "young Jews" and "anarchists" who were having "secret meetings" (p. 66 and Document 6, Jaffa Police Commander to Jaffa Qa'imaqam, December 6, 1907, p. 68).

107. BOA, DH.İD 122–22, 1333H, pp. 1, 11, 13, 19–22. The tax was on the value of the land, and in cities, on the houses and cultivated plots, whether used by the owner or rented out to others.

108. Ibid.

109. For a detailed discussion of these issues, see Heidborn, 1912, vol. 2.

110. For a detailed discussion of various Islamic taxes on land and agricultural production, see Cummings, Askari, and Mustafa, 1980; esp. p. 29 for a dis-

cussion of the '*oshr* tax, which explains that typically the amount due depended on the quality of the land (e.g., 5 percent on irrigated land, 10 percent on rain-fed land). It was applied to gross output, before the deduction of most production-related costs; however, it was obviously denominated in terms that recognized some production costs.

111. Cf. A. Cohen, 1973, for a discussion of the changing systems used by the Porte to collect taxes in Palestine.

112. BOA, DH.İD 122–22, 1330/1910, p. 24, DH.İD, 181–12, 1329/1909, DH.İD 122–2, 1333/1914, pp. 19–20, all documents concerning conflicts over the payments of taxes on orange or other citrus orchards. The taxes would seem again to have been the '*oshr*, at ten per thousand, the *virgu-u senevi* (annual tax) on the plot of land and the garden. Perhaps in some cases a "life-lease contract" was given on *miri* land that would have had the effect of making it practically *mulk*, or at least *malikane*. Indeed, Ehud Toledano explains that, in the words of "an old village mukhtar from the Galilee, who had been a large landowner during the Mandate[,] . . . while there were different laws for each type of land, in practice '*mulk*, *miri*, it didn't matter—all the lands of the village were private'" (e-mail comm., May 2002).

113. Indeed, a similar process happened when *miri* land was included in *waqf* property, producing the well-known "waqf ghair sahih," or incomplete or faulty *waqf*, because of the ambiguous status of the whole space. I would like to thank May and Michael Davie for informing me of a similar situation in Beirut during the same period (e-mail comm., May 2002).

114. BOA, DH.İD 122–22.

115. A precedent for this existed in the eighteenth century when the Vali of Damascus diverted taxes due to Istanbul to him (cf. A. Cohen, 1973).

116. PRO, FO 195/2287, 25/3/1908 letter from Blech to Barclay; cf. Mandel, 1976, p. 27. Similarly, one Zionist official in Jaffa reported that "the hatred towards the Jewish Community is increasing daily under the quidance of the *mutaşarrıf* of Jerusalem and the *qa'imaqam* of Jaffa" (quoted in Farhi, 1975, p. 195).

117. Mandel, 1976, p. 55. Both Khalidi's and Kayalı's discussion of the complaints of Palestinian representatives to the Ottoman Parliament also demonstrate a well-developed sense of the dangers of and hostility to Zionism by the time the revolution had occurred (cf. Khalidi, 1997; Kayalı, 1997).

118. This led to his rebuke from the governor of Jerusalem (cf. CZA, L2/26I, 4/vi /o9 letter to Ruppin from the Central Zionist Bureau, Köln). CZA, L2/321, "Exposé de l'incident du 16 Mars 1908." Cf. Eliav, 1973, pp. 152–97. The Qa'imaqan apparently accused the Jews of using the occasion of the Purim celebration to organize a plot against the government (BAIU, Israel, 1C/2936/3, 27/3/08 letter to the AIU President from Astrue). For a discussion of the CUP-inspired critique of European imperialism, see Brummett, 2000.

119. Dizengoff feared that unless the sale of the land to Ahuzat Bayit from Etinger was completed quickly, it might not go through; meanwhile, another

member of the Vaʿad Ahuzat Bayit was giving an unspecified sum of money to the Arabs to quiet protests (TAMA, 1/279, protocol of Vaʿad Ahuzat Bayit, 30/12/08).

120. The violence continued into 1909 and was particularly incited by Christian Arab Jaffans, who perhaps were most threatened by the Jews as competitors (cf. Ram, 1996, pp. 259–61).

121. BOA, DH.İD 45/8, 1392/1910, reply to complaint of German Embassy.

122. CZA, J85/618, 1/2/09 letter to Bril and Dizengoff from JCA in Jerusalem, illegible signature.

123. According to the French consul, the crowd "remained indifferent" (ibid.).

124. DAMFAF, NS Turquie, Vol. 132, letter from Jaffa Vice Consul to French Foreign Ministry, 26/5/09.

125. CZA, J85/618, 1/2/09 letter to Bril and Dizengoff from JCA in Jerusalem, illegible signature.

126. BOA, DH.ŞFR 39/19, vol. 1, no. 6561, R.21.1332/1913. Telegram from Private Office to Syria and Beirut Provinces and Post and Jurisdiction of Jerusalem.

127. PRO, CO 226/204, no. 37, cited in Kayalı, 1978, p. 15. In 1905 notables from several cities, including Jaffa, were imprisoned by the Ottoman authorities for smuggling Najib Azoury's *Le Réveil de la nation arabe* into the country, while at least two Jaffan literary clubs were involved in nationalist activities (Kayalı, 1978, pp. 18, 30).

128. TAMA, 2/14b, protocol of 17/1/09 meeting between Jewish and Arab notables of Jaffa.

129. Including the Pardess Society (started at the turn of the century), the Berouti Brothers, Georges Aramane, and Boulos Habib (DAMFAF, NS Turquie, 1897–1917, Palestine, Cons. de Jaffa, #430, 15/3/10 report).

130. Private collection of Hana Ram.

131. Cf. *Falastin*, 16/9/1911; Mandel, 1976, pp. 121–22.

132. *Falastin*, 29/5/1912, p. 1; 5/6/1912, pp. 1–2. Cf. Mandel, 1976, p. 129.

133. Recounted in Ram, 1996, p. 260. She cites *Falastin*, 2/11/12, as her source for this report, but I was unable to find this information in that issue. The same report is also cited in Yehoshua, 1969, p. 220.

134. Recounted in Ram, 1996, pp. 260–61, from the memoirs of Ben-Hanania; my emphasis. Yehoshua also reports that the Arab press described Tel Aviv and its goals in similar terms (Yehoshua, 1969).

135. Dizengoff, 1931, pp. 6–7. For the significance of Dizengoff's remark, see chap. 7 below.

136. CZA, L2/615, letter from Albert Antebe to Meirovitch, 22/9/12. Cf. *Falastin*, 17/8/13, p. 1, for an article discussing the "oppression" of Christians.

137. *Falastin*, 12/7/1913, p. 1; 30/8/1913, pp. 1–2.

138. BOA, Y.A. Res., 6/70, *Yafa'ya su celbi içün icrâ-yı keıfiyyât hakkında*

ruhsatnâmedir, 6 ıaban sene 297 ve fî 2 Temmuz sene 296 (14 July 1880); DH.İD 74/19, 28/5/1911 letter to Interior Ministry from the Department of the Navy.

139. BOA, DH.İD, 160-1/23, İç: 3/1, memo to the Finance Ministry, 19/12/1912.

140. BOA, DH.İD, 108-2/14-2, letter from M. Ziya (1/30/1914).

141. See, for example, the case involving a German Jew in Ramla named Colet who built a structure in the town that led to a fight in which someone's tooth was broken and that even led the German Consulate to ask for permission to build a police station to prevent future outbreaks of violence. BOA, DH.İD, 67-1/22-2, 19 Eylul 1326–2/10/1910 telegraph to the Interior Ministry by Mutaşarrıf Azmi.

142. For files related to this conflict, see BOA, DH.İD, file nos. 140-2/1-9, 140-2/1-18, 140-2/1-22a, 140-2/1-22b, 140-2/1-48, 140-2/1-52a, 140-2/1-73, 140-2/1-75, 140-2/1-81, all dated between 1909 and 1919.

143. Beitar's name is misspelled in this document as "Battal."

144. See BOA, DH.İD 215/10-7, 11 Kânûn-ı evvel sene 330 (24 December 1914, Petition to the Interior Ministry by Deputies from Jerusalem defending Omar Battal, describing him as a "good and honest man" and denying the validity of the charges, DH.İD 215/10-9, 7 Receb sene 1330 (22 June 1912), for the opposite view, with Jaffa residents accusing him of bribery, and DH.İD 215/10-36, 23 Mayıs sene 330 (5 June 1914) and DH.İD, 215/10-47/1 11 Kânûn-ı evvel sene 330 (24 December 1914), elaborating on the accusations.

145. Stein, 1984, p. 229, Appendix 3.

146. Ram, 1996, p. 161.

147. Cf. Yehoshua, 1969, p. 218.

148. *Hapo'el Hatza'ir*, 16/9/10, p. 3. The Va'ad consisted of sixty members and a seven-member executive committee (*Hapo'el Hatza'ir*, 1909, #15, "Organization of the Jewish Community in Jaffa"). Meir Dizengoff, Yosef Shloosh, David Moyal, Yosef Thon, and Betzalel Yaffe were on both councils.

149. For an innovative and important analysis of the evolving Ottoman Jewish Palestinian identity, see Campos, 2001. Campos is also examining this in her dissertation project at Stanford University.

150. Cf. Smeliansky, 1907, p. 28. A report by the Va'ad Ha'ir from 1908 includes a census of professions of immigrants arriving during the years 1905–7, which informs us that 658 professionals landed in Jaffa, constituting more than 10 percent of the population (AA, IV/104/118, report on the situation of the New Yishuv). The categories include doctors, lawyers, agronomists, traders, and the like.

151. LA, IV/104/118, report by Menachem Sheinken titled "Towards the General Elections of the Va'ad Ha'ir in Jaffa," 1912. Beyond providing for the general needs of the Jewish community through its expenditures, "there [were] many other things, arrangements, and repairs" it engaged in, including a restaurant in the port; a supervisory committee on health and sanitation in the city and slaughterhouses; a charity fund for workers; registering of births, mar-

riages, and deaths; merging the Ashkenazi and Sephardic slaughterhouses, and reducing food prices (e.g., the budget of the Va'adad Ha'ir in 1913 was 25,263 francs, with the administration of slaughterhouses taking the most expense [*Hapo'el Hatza'ir*, 19/12/13, p. 11]).

152. Cf. Ram, 1996, pp. 247–53.

153. TAMA, Protocol of the Va'ad Ha'ir, #67, 5/12/13. The words are those of Menachem Shenkin, a leader of the Jaffa Va'ad and a founder of Tel Aviv.

154. *Hapo'el Hatza'ir*, for example, called for "revisiting anew the basis for the existence of the Va'ad Ha'ir in order to be able to fulfill its function as the representative to the outside and director of the internal interests of the city." It stated that a modus operandi for cooperation between the Va'ad Ha'ir and the Va'ad Tel Aviv was the best way to accomplish this (*Hapo'el Hatza'ir*, 26/12/14, p. 17).

155. *Hapo'el Hatza'ir*, 18/9/12, p. 20. The conflict between workers and the bourgeois residents of Tel Aviv was exacerbated by the continuing influx of Yemenite Jews, whose immigration was encouraged because it was believed they would be willing to work for wages comparable to those paid local Arabs. The Yemenite community became more organized after the establishment of Tel Aviv but remained among the poorest residents of the Jaffa–Tel Aviv region throughout the Mandate period (cf. *Hapo'el Hatza'ir*, 16/3/11, p. 16). Shafir (1989) provides an important discussion of how Zionist leaders sought to use Yemenite Jews in the agricultural sector as inexpensive workers who could live on "Arab wages" and thus help them to realize the conquest of labor.

156. Schiller, 1981b, p. 42; Palestine Exploration Fund, 1882, vol. 22, pp. 254–55; Heykal, 1988, p. 177.

157. *Baedeker's*, 1876 English ed., p. 131. In concluding his description of the development of Jaffa during this period, Scholch contradicts this assessment, writing that "at least on the land side the appearance of Jaffa had indeed changed rapidly within a few years" (Scholch, 1993, p. 143).

158. Kark, 1988, p. 47; Wilkins, n.d. p. 8.

159. For example, by 1904 land was also being put up for sale in the village of Salama (CZA, J85/602, protocol of 19/5/04 meeting of unnamed group, including Levontin, Yafo, and three other men).

160. Eisler, 1997, p. 36. "Reconnaissance" trips to Jaffa to ascertain the situation there began as early as 1848 (p. 47), and a reasonably priced plot of land was found by 1850 in the gardens northeast of the Old City. These trips also played an important role in pushing for the development of a better road connecting Jaffa to Jerusalem.

161. Cf. Kark, 1990a, pp. 10–11.

162. Cf. Doumani, 1995, p. 55.

163. Williams, 1973, pp. 7, 264.

164. Our knowledge of how they differentiated between them, and in fact the primary sources themselves, are vague and have yet to be properly elucidated. Fortunately, there has been some work done on Hanafi writings on this topic, which are relevant to this case study because the Hanafi legal school was

(and remains) the dominant Muslim legal school in Palestine/Israel. The most important writing on this subject has been done by Baber Johansen (1981, 1999).

165. Johansen, 1981, pp. 141–43, citing Abu Hanifa. That is, economically it was defined as the center of commodity production that supported all types of specialized craftsmen; militarily its inhabitants should have been able to defend themselves against outside attacks.

166. Johansen, 1981, p. 147. In that sense, the sandier lands that included the nucleus of Tel Aviv that were not privately owned could be categorized as *matruka*, or common land that was "near to civilization [and] left to the public for grazing grounds, threshing floors and for cutting wood," as the 1858 Land Code describes it (Art. 1271, quoted in Eisenman, 1978, p. 57). For a detailed discussion of *matruka* and other categories of land tenure, see chap. 7.

167. That is, agricultural lands, which were normally *miri*, increasingly became de facto if not de jure *mulk* as the built-up regions of the city expanded, and as the government needed to assure returns on long-term investment in nominally "state-owned" land.

168. ISA, M/46/236/D/119, "ʿAtif Bey—Commentary on the Land Laws—1939 Edition," pp. 1–2.

169. However, the settled part of the villages, where the houses were, were still on the highest and most easily defended ground.

170. Shloosh, 1931, p. 15. Even in the late 1990s older Jaffans related to me their fond memories of the village of Jamassin (located 6.5 km north of the Old City), which was where their milk came from (the village was named for the cows and buffalo that were raised there).

171. Khalidi, 1992, p. 246.

172. Droyanov et al., 1935, p. 22.

173. As Firestone points out vis-à-vis land tenure and agricultural practice in Palestine, they were far from stagnant; in fact, the changing patterns of landownership in the late nineteenth century present "the clearest example of how Islamic patterns are intimately woven into the fabric of communal society. . . . [They] smoothed its adjustment to final absorption into the world market centered on Western capitalism, [and were] an adaptation to deal with poor public security, benefits of scale operation, [and] equalize economic opportunities[,] . . . [all of which is] only natural in economies like the Middle East, where production is subject to such uncertainties" (Firestone, 1975b, pp. 186–88).

Even more important was the expansion of a dominant commodity market fueled by Jewish immigration, in which land more than anything else was most rapidly and decisively converted into a commodity at the very time the peasants were increasingly losing control over it (Graham-Brown, 1982, pp. 105, 113). Moreover, the intensive cash crop system that was offered by the British and Zionists as a solution to the *fellahs'* woes in fact strengthened the hand of large landowners and therefore contributed further to their extraterritorialization. It should thus come as no surprise that the Arabs were frightened of and opposed changes in both landownership and agriculture because they were convinced that the changes and "improvements" in fact threatened their entire way of life, or that they fought such changes from the initial, predominantly European Christian land purchases of the mid-1800s.

174. Wilkins, n.d., p. 507. Although the ground was perhaps prepared by the gradual "privatization" of land through the conversion from *iltizam* to *malikane* tax farming in Palestine during the eighteenth century, which meant that the state would receive higher immediate revenues from the person granted a *malikane mukata'a* (tax concession) but would give up future taxes and control over the land (cf. A. Cohen, 1973, pp. 186–90).

175. Wilkins, n.d., pp. 1, 3. The Shari'a Court records document four major trends: the surge in rental of unoccupied *miri* lands for agricultural purposes, the extension of moneylending networks, the "vertical" expansion of the old town with the addition of new floors on existing buildings, and the formation of new settlements near Jaffa. Wilkins's examination of the Shari'a Court registers revealed numerous petitions by people from all over the country to lease *miri* lands for agricultural purposes.

176. Scholch, 1982, p. 39.

177. A copy of the map is available in Kark, 1990a, p. 68. The 1875 British-sponsored *Survey of Western Palestine* also made note of the five villages in the area immediately surrounding Jaffa. All told, the Jaffa district had twenty-three villages within approximately 16 kilometers of the city (Khalidi, 1992).

178. This analysis is drawn from the oral histories of Jaffa collected by Salim Tamari, particularly his interview with Wadie an-Nazer, a member of an established "aristocratic" Hebronite family. When asked about the great families of Jaffa, an-Nazer replied, "Great? There is nothing great about Jaffa's families, kulhum lamam! [they're all riffraff!]" (Salim Tamari, "Akka Is Not Jaffa: A City of Riffraff," Jaffa Email Group, 5/12/96).

179. Cf. Kark, 1990a, pp. 94–95.

180. In fact, the early Sephardic "aliyot" are of equal importance to the later, specifically Zionist "aliyot" for understanding the history and development of the city's Jewish and other communities. There was also an increasing influx of Yemenite Jews to Jaffa during the last two decades of the century, around the same time as the first European aliyah (Ram, 1996, pp. 30–51).

181. For example, Kark concludes that it was cultural "penetration" from outside that was the impetus for development. This is certainly true, but the evidence equally suggests that Europeans were drawn to Jaffa precisely *because of* its development. As she writes, "in concert, the Ottoman Empire, Western powers, churches, Jewish institutions, philanthropic organizations and new immigrants set Jaffa on the road to population growth and economic prosperity and transformed it into Palestine's leading city" (Kark, 1990a, p. 302).

182. Shloosh, 1931, p. 20. What is important about this description of the land is that it clearly demonstrates that what would become the Tel Aviv region was both sand and vineyards at the same time (in spite of his later description that there were some "withered vines planted here and there, abandoned and

left"), a point of fact whose importance for understanding the history of Tel Aviv is discussed below (Shloosh, 1931, p. 143).

183. PRO, Parliamentary Papers, C.5618, #529, Report on Trade of Turkey/Jaffa for 1888, p. 3.

184. Cf. *PEF Quarterly*, 7/1872, p. 77.

185. For example, by 1894 the Greek Convent had constructed a series of one hundred shops and stores just outside the old gate of the town, with new houses on top of them (PRO, Parliamentary Papers, C.7293, #1350, Consular Report for Turkey/Jerusalem, 1893, p. 6).

186. Heykal, 1988, p. 214. However, Heykal is mistaken in claiming that it "signaled the extension of the 'umran, or built-up area of Jaffa, for the first time, outside the gates to the north and south and east." This process began decades earlier.

187. BOA, Y.EE 132/29, Letter of Abdurrahman Zekai, Inspector of Land Registry Office, to Shakir Pasha. Another document reveals that the English were authorized to conduct a topographical survey of Palestine north of Gaza for a new map, although it is not clear whether this was ever undertaken (BOA, DH.KMS 6/25, 1332H).

188. Smilansky, 1890, quoted in Schiller, 1981b, p. 47.

189. *Murray's Handbook for Travellers in Syria and Palestine* (London, 1892), p. 2. Contrary to this view of Jaffa being filthy, which was prominent in Zionist accounts of the city, the French vice consul wrote to his superiors that public health was excellent in Jaffa in 1891, although there was concern over the adequacy of the quarantine of Jaffa Port (DAMFAF, Jaffa CCC, 19/10/1891 report to Foreign Ministry from Jaffa Vice Consul).

190. As Kark explains, these clock towers were built throughout Palestine and other Ottoman domains, usually near new government buildings, to express the sovereignty of the Ottoman Government and the modernization of the region (Kark, 1997, p. 2).

191. David Smilansky (from 1907), quoted in Kark, 1990a, pp. 125, 142. Cf. JICR, book 80 (1899/1317–1901/1318), case #9, which discusses the sale of an orchard.

192. This was worsened by brokers whose lust for profits hurt the tenants and peasants together (Smilansky, 1981, p. 40; cf. Granovsky, 1940, p. 43)

193. For example, JICR, book 129 (1911/1329), pp. 66–84, which contains a case involving several Muslim families and the Roks, a leading Christian family in Jaffa.

194. Ibid. Also see JICR, book 87 (1900/1318–1905/1323), case #1029, for another instance of Moyal purchasing property, this time from the Chialdi family of Jerusalem.

195. JICR, book 160 (1914/1333–1916/1334), case #14, p. 2. The registration noted that he bequeathed 5,000 lira for the poor and commissioned the construction of a synagogue in his name. For an example of several Orthodox Christian partners to a land deal bringing a dispute over how to divide rental

income from a *waqf,* see JICR, book 160 (1914/1333–1916/1334), case #137, p. 98.

196. JICR, book 83 (1298/1880), case #1014, pp. 3–4.

197. The assumption that this neighborhood lay outside the Old City is given further credence by Ruba Kanaʾan's exhaustive study of the Old City during the time of Abu Nabut. Kanaʿan confirms that she never came across "Mahallah Sheikh Ibrahim al-Malahi" in the *sijjil* or other documents (e-mail comm., Mar. 1999).

198. JICR, book 104 (1907/1325–1909/1327), p. 100.

199. A more thorough review of the *sijjil* during this period would no doubt find numerous instances of placing certain neighborhoods inside or outside of "Jaffa," the mapping (in both place and time) of which would yield much insight into the changing nature of the Jaffan conceptualization of the "borders" of their town as urban and agricultural development increased.

CHAPTER 3

1. Shloosh, 1931, p. 29.

2. Ibid., pp. 20, 76–77. For a summary of Neve Tzedek's history, see Archive of the Museum of the History of Tel Aviv [MHTA], A/6–8, *Neve Tzedek, Reaching 55 Years since Its Establishment* (Hebrew), 1945–46, p. 4. Neve Tzedek was envisioned by its founders as "a clean, well-planned neighborhood in the standards of those days. The homes were small and attractive, and although the streets and sidewalks were narrow, they were straight and clean. . . . The streets of Neve Zedek were considered the broadest and the homes, the most beautiful in Jaffa" (Tel Aviv Municipality, 1967, pp. 5–7; Kark, 1990a, p. 114).

3. MHTA, A/6–8, *Rules of Moshav Neve Tzedek* (Hebrew), p. 1.

4. Interestingly, the experience of straightening the sands, so prominent in the creation mythology of Tel Aviv, was not unique to Tel Aviv. The poorer residents of Neve Tzedek had to straighten the sands as partial payment for their land. In fact, flattening the sands in preparation for construction was a source of work for many immigrants in Jaffa who otherwise would have been unemployed in the years before World War I (*Hapoʿel Hatzaʿir,* 28/2/13, p. 19; 14/2/13, p. 16, where it is reported that dozens of unemployed were in Jaffa).

5. TAMA, 1/279, protocol of meeting of Ahuzat Bayit, 14/6/06.

6. Quoted in Katz, 1984, p. 161.

7. The geographic isolation, whereby immigrants could develop national values, would suggest the "demographic importance of [the] Jewish population as a basis for achieving political goals in Palestine" (Katz, 1992, pp. 2, 4).

8. Katz, 1992, pp. 2, 4; 1994, pp. 163–65, 280.

9. Copy of brochure in Shchori, 1990, p. 23.

10. Katz, 1983, p. 140.

11. Katz, 1992, p. 1; cf. Katz, 1994, chap. 1. To begin with, the city's founding must be put in the context of the larger Zionist discourse and the supposed

emphasis on agricultural rather than urban colonization. As Penslar points out, the European Great Powers provided the Zionist leadership with (colonial) models for settlement, and they studied domestic and colonial policies in order to learn how to erect a new Jewish society in Palestine (Penslar, 1991, p. 42).

12. CZA, J15/4352, 19/2/08 memo, "Construction des maisons à Jaffa." The similarities between this description of Jaffa and that of Herzl in his *Old-New Land* are likely not coincidental (cf. Herzl, [1902] 1941, p. 42).

13. TAMA, 1/20, newspaper clipping titled "Ahuzat Bayit" from a 1921 issue of *Hatzvi*.

14. In fact, when Ahuzat Bayit first applied to the Anglo-Palestine Bank for a loan of several hundred thousand francs, it was turned down because of insufficient guarantees.

15. Chelnov, quoted in Katz, 1992, p. 11. It continues, "[T]he process of agricultural colonization is slow and requires large investments and funds, whereas the expansion of a Jewish urban population is quicker and easier."

16. Cf. Shafir, 1989, p. 16.

17. Chelnov, quoted in Katz, 1992, p. 12.

18. Ruppin, quoted in Katz, 1992, p. 18. In fact, one version of the contract of sale of Karm al-Jabali to Ahuzat Bayit from the Jewish brokers stipulated specifically that houses must be built with "good materials and regulations, stones, trees, roofs, windows," and the like (CZA, L51/52).

19. These included Ebenezer Howard's *Garden Cities of Tomorrow* and the German architect J. Stubben's *Handbuch der band Staatebau.*

20. Cf. CZA, A/109/108, undated memo on Yafo Nof. The German Templar colonies also engaged in "modern" construction and industry beginning with the last decade of the nineteenth century (cf. Eisler, 1997, pp. 107, 122).

21. Ram, 1996, p. 129.

22. Ibid., p. 141.

23. Shloosh, 1931, p. 131.

24. Droyanov et al., 1935, p. 85.

25. MHTA, uncataloged notebook listing the names of the heirs of Karm al-Jabali in Arabic and Ottoman and English, with dates of birth and death and position in the family. The document was most likely created in fulfillment of article 5 of the contract of sale from the Jerusalem brokers to Ahuzat Bayit, which required that such a list be supplied in case someone challenged the sale.

26. A detailed description of the various categories of land under late Ottoman-Islamic law is provided in chapter 6.

27. MHTA, Ahuzat Bayit Box/Neighborhoods, A/I Ahuzat Bayit; undated contract of sale in Hebrew. The original survey map for the sale to the Jewish brokers lists both the north and south regions as being "kerem," or vineyards (map in Droyanov et al., 1935, p. 90).

28. As certified in the Tabu in 1877/1294. A copy of this contract is found in Ram, 1996, appendix, p. 47.

29. Or some other official public institution, as there are Ottoman tax stamps affixed to the map.

30. The survey map is in Droyanov et al., 1935, p. 90.

31. Thus in the Arabic contract it is listed as 21 1/2 qirat, which is not a unit of measure in itself but refers to a percentage of a larger plot of land to which the one being sold belongs, sold for 2,580 French francs, as compared to the 109 dunams described in the Ahuzat Bayit contract.

32. "Khawaja" was a term of respect for well-to-do foreigners.

33. JICR, 111, pp. 268–70, 29 Ramadan, 1327h (pagination from copy of Jaffa *sijjil* at the Center for Documentation and Research, Jordanian University, where this document was photocopied from microfilm, which differs from the original pagination done in Israel).

34. The two were Rabbi David Yellin and Dr. Aharon Mezi (Droyanov et al., 1935, p. 87).

35. Cf. Katz, 1983, pp. 139–48.

36. Mandel, 1976, p. 26, citing a 11/9/09 telegram from Antébi to Fernandez under Alliance Israelite Universelle letterhead.

37. Shloosh, 1931, p. 143.

38. Dizengoff, 1925, pp. 148–49.

39. Shloosh, 1931, p. 144. A memo dated 17/6/09 to the Anglo Palestine Company (probably from Ruppin) stressed the importance of ending the dispute with their "neighbors" and parcelizing the land as soon as possible (CZA, L2/71).

40. A photo of the survey map appears in Droyanov et al., 1935, p. 90.

41. He writes, in somewhat confusing French, that just that day the local authorities "said the actual owners of the said vineyard are liable because there was a statute of limitations that had long since passed, and so it is no longer in their authority" (n'a point inquieté les propriétaires actuels de la dite vigne dans leur jouissance de sorte que la prescription a couverte depuis fort longtemps tout droit aléatoire de l'Autorité) (MHTA, Dizengoff Archive, MhhD/II1, 12/3/1908, "Consultation donnée à Monsieur Dizengoff en ce qui concerne l'achat de la vigne Djebale sis à Jaffa").

42. MHTA, Dizengoff Archive, MhhD/II1, Hebrew minutes of 12/3/1908, "Consultation donnée à Monsieur Dizengoff en ce qui concerne l'achat de la vigne Djebale sis à Jaffa."

43. Lit., "construire un établissement d'utilité publique" (MHTA, Dizengoff Archive, MhhD/II1, 15/9/1908 letter from Moyal to Dizengoff, in French).

44. Shure, 1987, p. 68.

45. Ibid., p. 67, citing CZA J85/27.

46. MHTA, Dizengoff Archive, MhhD/II1, 3/1/1909 letter to *Hapo'el Hatza'ir* from members of Va'ad Ahuzat Bayit. See also MHTA, Ahuzat Bayit Box/Neighborhoods, A/I AB.

47. Shloosh, 1931, p. 131. In the end the purchase was completed with the payment on the name of our three [brokers] and the price was determined for each member, at 85 centim per meter. But after they divided the land into sixty parcels the members still had a large plot of land for new members.

48. BOA, DH.MUY, 12–1/26, 1327H, registration of bedouin lands in Birusseb, Jerusalem, Hebron, and Jaffa.

49. The complex, often contradictory motivations and reactions of people to

the Jewish presence in Karm al-Jabali/Tel Aviv was a repetition of events some thirty-five plus years earlier in the villages nearby Jaffa. Thus in 1887 the Palestine Exploration Fund reported that "the men of Yazur were particularly enraged [at the sale of some of their village lands to the Mikveh Israel school], as it had for a long time been their custom to plant gardens on the extreme edge of the land they cultivated, and then sell them to the people of Jaffa, in this way disposing of crown land for their own benefit. Thus cut off, by the interpolation of the Jewish colony, from a source of large revenue, they naturally became bitter opponents of the Agricultural School, which at this moment, however, employs from 80 to 100 fellaheen . . . from Yazur. The men of Yazur vow that they are completely ruined, but they were still able, some three months ago, to offer . . . 4,000 dillem of land which the Government wished to dispose of to the south of their village" (*PEF Quarterly*, 7/1887, p. 78).

50. Protocols of TAC, Meeting #118, 14 Tishri, 1917, TAMA: 1/282a. For an even earlier Zionist analysis of land tenure in Palestine, see CZA, L1/57, "Der Landeinkauf," undated but probably around 1905.

51. *Yediot Tel Aviv*, 1936, #5–6, p. 43. While the conflict surrounding Karm al-Jabali worried many members of the mother society of Ahuzat Bayit in Russia, it is clear, as Yossi Katz points out, that Dizengoff and Ahuzat Bayit's other leaders in Jaffa knew well the effects of this and other land purchases on the Arabs living on the land. Thus in a letter to the Geula Land Redemption Company in Odessa, which sponsored much of the early land purchases around Jaffa, Dizengoff explained that all the arable land in Palestine was cultivated by Arab tenants, not the owners, and thus by buying good agricultural land the company would by definition be in the position of having to evict them: "Without disputes one cannot purchase land in Palestine. It is more difficult now to buy land in Palestine than to part the Red Sea" (quoted in Katz, 1994, p. 99).

52. Droyanov et al., 1935, pp. 124, 127, 147.

53. Shloosh, 1931, pp. 146–47. Moreover, at least one "effendi" bought land adjacent to Tel Aviv, which the Va'ad at first thought was done with the intention of selling them the land at a profit but which they quickly realized was rather "out of hatred for the Jews," that is, out of a desire to prevent Tel Aviv from expanding. On another side, Tel Aviv bordered an old neighborhood (not named) that had very narrow alleyways that Ottoman law forbade building next to (Shloosh, 1931, p. 149). In a search of relevant catalogs at the BOA I was unable to find any files dealing with or even mentioning Tel Aviv.

54. JICR, book 148 (1912/1331–1913/1332), p. 344; book 166 (1914/1333), p. 170; book 196 (1920/1339–1921/1340), p. 383. Cf. Abu-Bakr, 1996, pp. 600–601.

55. As documented by Yehoshua, 1969, p. 220.

56. Private collection of Hana Ram. There are also documents suggesting that at times there were attempts to sell land without permission from the owners, or land that was sold was later found to belong to a third party and not the seller, or a third party claimed ownership. Private collection of Hana Ram. Letter from members of Dbagh family informing attorneys that they cannot

sell a parcel of land because they did not give permission; letter explaining that a plot of land near Tel Aviv off Nablus Road was being disputed by a neighbor who claimed the parcel belonged to him.

57. To be exact, 358,118 square yards (CZA, L18/68/2, German list of five properties: Kassar, Bamia, Bedrani-Kassar, Bedrani-Moyal, and Emin Nassif, purchased for Tel Aviv). There were also attempts to purchase more than 8,000 dunams belonging to the village of Sheikh Muwannis, which was considered a "good find" because of the fertility of the land and proximity to Jaffa, but these failed owing to the complicated title of the lands and to the residents having no reason to sell and move to less favorable surroundings (cf. Katz, 1983, p. 147). A February 1914 memo on potential land purchases in Jaffa informs us that there were two vineyards for sale, one of them quite close to Tel Aviv (CZA, L18/68/2, 22/2/14 memo on land purchases in Jaffa by Barski).

58. CZA, L18/68/2, contract between Thon and Cassar, dated 13/2/13.

59. TAMA, 1/120, undated memo from the Va'ad of the Society for Supporting the Children of Israel, Odessa. Cf. 1/114.

60. According to Abu-Bakr, the goal of these land reforms was to gain authority over the lands of nearby bedouin tribes, but it was ultimately Tel Aviv and not Jaffa that would take advantage of the reforms (Abu-Bakr, 1996, p. 513; cf. BOA, DH.MUY, 12–1/26, 1327H, registration of bedouin lands in Birusseb, Jerusalem, Hebron, and Jaffa; and BOA, Y.EE 132/29, ll Kanun-i Evel 1312H/6/5/1895, letter of Abdurrahman Zekai, Inspector of Land Registry Office, to Shakir Pasha).

61. Abu-Bakr, 1996, p. 600; JICR, book 98 (1906/1324–1911/1329), pp. 1–162.

62. JICR, book, 128 (1911/1329–1912/1330), pp. 1–2; book 129 (1910/ 1328–1912/1329), p. 344; book 166 (1914/1333), p. 275. The purchases by Christians (particularly the Rok family), which included lands of the Jerisha and Summel villages, began about 1904 (cf. JICR, book 85 (1901/1319–1902/1320), pp. 36, 71, 166; book 86 (1901/1319–1902/1320), pp. 126, 130, 292; book 91 (1904/1322–1906/1324), p. 90; book 139 (1911/1329), p. 258; book 148 (1912/1331–1913/1332), pp. 68, 220–326; book 156 (1914/1333), p. 153).

63. TAMA, 1/4, typed copy of rules of Ahuzat Bayit. Cf. TAMA, 1/43, letter to members of Va'ad Tel Aviv, 29/6/11, regarding placement of outhouses.

64. TAMA, 1/280, protocol of 17/11/09 meeting of Va'ad Ahuzat Bayit. *Hapo'el Hatza'ir*, 18/9/12, p. 19.

65. Shchori, 1990, p. 71.

66. CZA, L2/71, 18/7/09 resolution by Va'ad Tel Aviv. Ruppin also became involved in attempts to make sure Jewish workers were hired to build the first homes in Tel Aviv (CZA, KKL2/63, 5/7/09 letter from Ruppin to JNF).

67. MHTA, Ahuzat Bayit Box/Neighborhoods, A/I AB, 6/9/1909 letter to Va'ad Ahuzat Bayit, signature illegible. One letter from Jewish workers to the Va'ad Ahuzat Bayit reported that they already had experience straightening the sands, would not ask for higher wages, expected "no unpleasantness," and thus hoped that the Va'ad would not transfer the work to Arabs (TAMA, 1/40, 9/10/09 letter from workers to Va'ad). See also Carmiel, 1987, p. 91.

68. MHTA, Ahuzat Bayit Box/Neighborhoods, A/I AB, 6/9/09 letter to Va'ad Ahuzat Bayit, signature illegible; cf. MHTA, 1/2, unsigned letter to Ahuzat Bayit dated 6/9/09; TAMA, 1/280, protocol of 3/10/09 meeting of Va'ad Ahuzat Bayit.

69. Ram, 1996, p. 248. It is interesting to note that the year before Tel Aviv was established Dizengoff, in his capacity as adviser to Jewish plantation owners in Palestine, strongly advocated the employment of Arabs against the demands of Jewish workers, basing his position on the following: "We cannot but settle in our land fairly and justly, to live and let live" (quoted in Shafir, 1989, p. 79).

70. Cf. CZA, L2/171, 23/7/09 letter from Ruppin to the Committee for the Interests of Workers and Builders in Ahuzat Bayit.

71. MHTA, 4/2, redaction of article in *Davar* on the history of Tel Aviv, 4/6/26. The Arabs were originally hired to protect the neighborhood because they could be paid less than Jewish guards.

72. Shloosh, 1931, p. 141.

73. Cf. CZA, J56/3–4, undated letter from Nahalat Binyamin Society to Va'ad Ahuzat Bayit; Katz, 1994, p. 109.

74. *Hapo'el Hatza'ir,* 18/9/12, p. 22.

75. Katz, 1994, pp. 110–11. CZA, L18/1682, Rule of Hevra Hadasha, 1913. Cf. TAMA, 1/113, 31/12/12 letter to Va'ad Hevra Hadasha from Va'ad Tel Aviv. TAMA, 1/280, protocol of 9/10/13 meeting of Va'ad Tel Aviv, discussing union with Hevra Hadashah.

76. *Hapo'el Hatza'ir,* 11/23/14, p. 14. The 1914 budget of Jaffa Municipality totaled 554,700 kirsh for income and 532,000 for expenditures. The city engineer's salary, street cleaning, and lighting were the leading expenditures.

77. *Hapo'el Hatza'ir,* 11/23/14, p. 14.

78. CZA, L18/68/2, publicity announcement for sale of Mattari lands, including bill of sale from Mattari to Immobilien-Gesellschaft Palästina.

79. Some leaders felt that there was already more land than could be built on in the immediate future; others felt that the prices were very good and likely to rise, which justified more purchases (CZA, L18/68/2, 17/6/13 memo to Dr. Ruppin from Dizengoff and twenty-three other men, most likely Va'ad Tel Aviv). One memo listed 1.2 million square meters of land in Jewish hands, enough for one hundred houses and for building for twelve years. All of the Palestinian Arab land listed in a subsequent chart of "the land around Tel Aviv" was already bought by Tel Aviv by this time, although some land in Jewish hands had not yet been purchased (ibid.; also see L2/615, 22/7/13 memo to Antabi and L18/68/62, regarding the new "Syndicate to purchase land in Jaffa," which states that though prices were rising from week to week, there was enough land for 1,200 houses, which would last for ten years). Tel Aviv also bought land owned by David Moyal that was located between the Sarona orchards and Summel road in 1913 (CZA, L18/70/1, letter to Eretz Israel Office received 17/11/13).

80. TAMA, 1/281, protocol of Va'ad Ahuzat Bayit, 29/4/12. It is clear, in fact, that Tel Aviv not only did not solve the housing problem of Jews in Jaffa,

since it was specificaly created by and for the wealthier section of the population, but worsened it because of speculation. Local newspapers were full of complaints against the Tel Aviv Va'ad's "incompetence" regarding keeping housing prices low and other problems associated with the birth of Tel Aviv (cf. Katz, 1992, p. 20).

81. *Hapo'el Hatza'ir*, 17/10/14, p. 8. Cf. *Hapo'el Hatza'ir*, 11/28/13, p. 14, which reports that housing prices were rising "all over" in Tel Aviv, Neve Tzedek, and Neve Shalom.

82. TAMA, 1/281a, protocol of Va'ad Ahuzat Bayit 29/4/14. TAMA, 1/281, 3/5/14 protocol of Va'ad Ahuzat Bayit concerning the creation of a syndicate to purchase land.

83. *Hapo'el Hatza'ir*, 5/22/14, p. 14.

84. Cf. *Hapo'el Hatza'ir*, 1/11/12, p. 21.

85. Hagana Archive [HA], 87.20, Oral History of Sa'adia Shoshani, 5/6/52.

86. Kark, 1990a, p. 49. Cf. Schiller, 1981a, p. 37. For the document appointing Hassan Bey military commander of Jaffa (I was unable to find a document appointing or mentioning him as Qa'imaqam), see BOA, DH.ŞFR, 57/258, 1333.Z (Safr).24, Reply telegram from Officials Office to 4th Army Commander Cemal Pasha.

87. This feeling was perhaps because of his earlier participation, when stationed in the Galilee region, in government roundups of suspected Jewish spies for the British during the war (cf. Samuel, 1932, pp. 100–104).

88. Mas'ud, 1945, p. 10. Jamal Pasha Street replaced several narrower streets as well as several markets, which were on *waqf* land and had to be destroyed quickly to avoid protests by the *waqf* authorities (Heykal, 1988, p. 75).

89. Hassan Bey is usually described in Jewish sources as bordering on evil, with a "stormy and violent personality" (Nidbah, 1978, p. 175). Also see Droyanov et al., 1935, p. 214.

90. BOA, Yıldız, Perakende Evrakı, 289/1. Mehmed Aşaf bin As'ad qa'immaqam of Jaffa, to Adulbhamid II, 3 Nissan 1324/16 April 1908; also cited by Farhi, 1975, p. 206.

91. Heykal, 1988, p. 76.

92. In fact, Ruppin's diaries reveal just this intent (Ruppin, 1971, p. 123).

93. Kana'an, 1998, p. 22.

94. BOA, DH.ŞFR, 48/33, 1333.M.29, telegraph to the Public Security Office about the Jewish Layonat School in Jaffa; DH.ŞFR, 48/110, 1333.S.24, telegram to Post and Jurisdiction of Jerusalem about movements of Russian Jews settled in Jaffa; DH.ŞFR, 64/294, 1334.Ş.11, telegram from Public Security Office to Port and Jurisdiction of Jerusalem regarding the possibility of a decision to forbid expelled Jews to return; BOA, DH.ŞFR, 72/129, 1335.R.7, reply telegram from Public Security Head Office to Jamal Pasha; BOA, DH.ŞFR, 75/59, 1335.C.12, telegram from Public Security Head Office to Halep Province about treating Romanian and Italian Jews expelled from Jaffa and Gaza to Halep as enemy subjects; BOA, DH.KMS, 18/41, 1332H, telegram from Interior Ministry about the increased settlement of Russian Jews.

95. BOA, DH.ŞFR, 83/99, 1336.R.2.

96. BOA, DH.İ;D, 34/18, 1329H. There was also a suggestion to open a university in Palestine at which Ottoman Turkish would be taught.

97. Heykal, 1988, pp. 77, 80.

98. Tzafrir, 1994, p. 9. The word *answer"* should not imply that such planning would not have been undertaken without the the influence of Tel Aviv, although certainly the presence of Tel Aviv influenced the urban development of Jaffa.

99. BOA, DH.UMVM, 74/10, 1334H telegram.

100. Already by December 1914 it was clear to the British that "the recent trend of events in Turkey render an eventual landing at Jaffa almost unavoidable. If through certain political and strategical considerations, without which the lay mind may not be initiated, a regular occupation of Palestine be at present impraticable or unadvisable, then a mere occupation of the port of Jaffa, which alone may serve the present purpose, might still, with advantage be advocated, in as much as it may involve a comparatively unimportant diversion of the forces which the political and strategical exigencies in Egypt might require." It was felt that the local authorities might welcome a British takeover because of the potential economic disaster that would befall the city if the port were closed by the war (PRO, FO 368/1437, letter from Storrs, 5/12/14).

101. Cf. CZA, A153/144/1, Protocol of meeting of the Emergency Committee, in Jaffa, 30/9/14. The situation was dire enough that Dizengoff worked tirelessly to raise $50,000 for the community from donors in the United States for war relief. As Israel Gengold describes it, the U.S. government set up a "sea train" to Jaffa to ensure that the aid arrived (*Et-mol*, 8/85, p. 3). Fear of Arab attacks on Tel Aviv during their absence was one catalyst for the Haganah's formation.

102. As one European described Jaffa in 1854 (quoted in Schiller, 1981b, p. 45).

103. Schiller, 1981b, pp. 42–47.

104. December 1909 letter from Dizengoff to Odessa, quoted in Katz, 1994, p. 98.

105. Droyanov et al., 1935, p. 124.

106. Ibid., p. 149. Droyanov continues that "Arab officials from Jaffa realized immediately that Tel Aviv was from the beginning a 'complete city,'" and because a *firman* from the sultan was needed to build a new city, the municipality attempted to stop work on the neighborhood.

107. As Light described it in 1814 (Light, 1818, p. 144). For a description of Jaffa as a Garden of Eden, see quote in Schiller, 1981b, p. 45.

108. Schiller, 1981a, p. 34.

109. Ibid., p. 33; Saba', 1977, p. 16. For the postwar photograph, see Vilai, 1965, p. 64. Also see Saba', 1977, p. 47, for a painting that depicts 'Ajari during the 1830s Egyptian occupation.

110. Lortet, 1884, pp. 376–80.

111. Kedar, 1995, chap. on Tel Aviv and Jaffa.

112. Guerin, 1868, pp. 2–11.

113. *Baedeker's*, 1876 English ed., p. 131.

114. *Baedeker's*, 1880, maps on pp. 3, 5.

115. Yithak Rokah wrote of the orchards that were once the lands of Tel Aviv "cut off by time" from their previous agricultural identity. While he probably was not thinking of Karm al-Jabali, his comment is valid in this instance too (Rokah, 1965, p. 31). He goes on to describe the village of Summel, which by the late 1930s was surrounded by Tel Aviv, as an "oasis in a sea of sands"; the municipality building and the opera house were built on orchards that belonged to long-standing Jaffa families as well as the vice consul of Holland (pp. 33–34).

116. Thus while Biger (1984b, p. 53) points out that Karm al-Jabali was the one piece of land in the area of the villages northeast of Jaffa that was not really cultivated, it could easily have been (and was) resown when the need arose. There was precedent for such activity; as far back as the 1870s, when the sultan granted the local Mikveh Israel agricultural school permission to build a farm on land near Jaffa (sponsored by the French Jewish Alliance Israelite Universelle), the land was cultivated by the villagers of Yazur, south of Jaffa. As one member of the PEF's 1875 expedition wrote, "Though the land belongs to Government, the Fellahin, from long usage, have got to look upon it as virtually their own, and resent its occupation by any other person. In this case the men of Yazur . . . were particularly enraged, as it had for a long time been their custom to plant gardens on the extreme edge of the land they cultivated, and then sell them to the people of Jaffa, in this way disposing of crown land for their own benefit" (Palestine Exploration Fund, 1875).

117. Sandel and Baedeker map, in Kark, 1988, p. 47.

118. Kark, 1990a, p. 68.

119. Kedar, [1991] 1995, opening two-page photograph of the Jaffa–Tel Aviv region in 1917, photographs of Tel Aviv and the larger Tel Aviv–Manshiyyeh region from 1917 and 1918 on pp. 13 and 15, and the collection of maps and photographs on pp. 86–103.

120. See Kedar, [1991] 1995, maps and photographs on pp. 86–87, 89, 93.

121. *Palestine News*, *A Tour-Guide of Southern Palestine*, map on p. 29, probably the 1918 British Survey of Palestine and Egypt map of the environs of Jaffa. The sandy paths were used by camel drivers—Jewish and Arab—to bring the zif-zif sand necessary for Tel Aviv's growth from the other side of the Yarkon/ʿAuja river.

122. Gilbar's figures are 98 dunams in 1841 and 1,280 in 1917 (Gilbar, 1990). Scholch cites Ben-Arieh: 2,750 inhabitants for 1800, 10,000 for 1880, and (no doubt including Tel Aviv) 47,700 for 1922 (Scholch, 1993, p. 38).

123. Kark (1990a, p. 46), cites *Falastin*, 8/17/12, for this information, but when I checked the microfilm there was no issue from that date and those before and after it were consecutively numbered.

124. Ram, 1996, p. 254.

125. Katz, 1994, p. 287. I use this approximate figure because the various legal documents concerning its purchase have different numbers; moreover, whereas Katz gives a figure of 85.5 dunams, the official records and histories of the city list the original area as 109 dunams.

126. Katz, 1994, p. 287.

127. Weiss, 1967, p. 9.

128. For example, notables such as Alexander Rok and Antun Qassar (see Mandel, 1976, p. 55).

129. Mandel, 1976, p. 172.

130. I am referring to *Filistin Meselesi—Sionizm Davasi*, which is apparently a Zionist propaganda pamphlet, *Filistin Ric'ati*, and *Filistin Risalesi*. The last includes a basic description of the Jaffa region (pp. 3–11), but there is no discussion of the contemporary socioeconomic or political situation in the region. For a list of catalogs in the BOA consulted for this book, see bibliography.

As this book was going to press, a two-volume study of Jaffa's modern history based on an exhaustive review of the Islamic Court records was published (Ali Hasan al-Bawab, *Mawsu'ah yafa al-jamilah*, Beirut: al-Muassasah al-Arabiyah lil Dirasat wa-al-Nashr, 2003). Al-Bawab documents that the Ottoman government used increased customs revenues to make improvements to Jaffa—sometimes referred to as "yafa al-bahiyyah," or "Jaffa the Magnificent"—during the latter half of the nineteenth century. He concludes that most land outside the casbah was made up of gardens, orchards, or vineyards. As for Tel Aviv, Shari'a Court records describe the land on which it was built (i.e., Karm al-Jabali) as sandy "with vineyards spread over it owned by the people of Manshiyyeh" (p. 574).

CHAPTER 4

An earlier version of this chapter was presented at Borders and Beyond: The Annual Conference of the Israel Anthropological Association—Nazareth 1999.

1. As the Jaffa Va'ad described in its annual report for that year, "the residents of Tel Aviv were expelled, but Tel Aviv had to and needed to live." A small group of young guards thus remained to watch the neighborhood (TAMA, 1/90, report of the Va'ad Ha'ir Leyehudei Yafo, 1917–18, p. 29).

2. *Hapo'el Hatza'ir*, 27/11/46, p. 6, table; *Hapo'el Hatza'ir*, 6/1/40, p. 15. One reason for this increase is that over 90 percent of the Jews who arrived in the country by the 1930s remained in the Tel Aviv region. For example, of the 27,862 immigrants in 1933, 25,086 stayed (*Yediot Tel Aviv*, 1934, #5, p. 189).

3. Jaffa's population grew 59.5 percent between 1922 and 1931 and 81.8 percent between 1931 and 1944. Tel Aviv's population grew much more rapidly: it increased 203.6 percent between 1922 and 1931 and 361.5 percent between 1931 and 1944. The population density of the Jaffa–Tel Aviv region was almost five times higher than the next most densely populated subdistrict, Haifa.

4. "Jaffa's Jewish neighborhoods" would be the subject of much controversy and enmity between the two municipalities as well as within the Jewish community of Jaffa–Tel Aviv (see chap. 6). Their population was a combination of spillover from the official borders of Tel Aviv as the city expanded and of Jaffan Jews who no longer wanted to live in "Arab" neighborhoods because of increased intercommunal hostility.

5. *Yediot Tel Aviv*, 1933, #10, p. 341.

6. LA, IV/219b/37, "A guide for unity toward determining the borders between Tel Aviv and Jaffa."

7. Malak, 1993, p. 50.

8. Himadeh, 1938, p. 240; Abed, 1988, p. 16. The following is an example of the political bias underlying many analyses: "Palestine was before the war a backward country principally devoted to agriculture, with a few insignificant industries. . . . [Today] Palestine industry is practically all Jewish" (Ziman, 1946, pp. 100, 143).

9. Abed, 1988, p. 25.

10. PRO, CO/821/13, 1938 and 1945 *Blue Book of Palestine Government Statistics;* 1938: pp. 320–21, 1945: p. 320. The unit of measure is the Egyptian pound, and after 1931, the Palestine pound.

11. *Yediot Tel Aviv,* 1/2/26, p. 9. Note that the Egyptian pound was the official currency in Palestine until March 31, 1928, when the Palestine pound came into circulation, at a conversion rate of £P1.00 equals £E0.975.

12. PRO, CO/821/13, 1945 *Blue Book of Palestine Government Statistics,* Finances of Municipalities Total Revenue and Expenditure, p. 320. One reason for the disparity between Jaffa and Tel Aviv was the level of taxation and the debt incurred by each municipality, which were both much higher in Tel Aviv (cf. PRO, CO/821/13, 1938 *Blue Book of Palestine Government Statistics,* pp. 320–32; cf. PRO, CO742/19, *Palestine Gazette,* 8/i/42, p. 33; 18/6/42, p. 731).

13. Sheikh Muwannis's budget rose considerably during the 1940s, when figures were available, from 3,000 pounds in 1941 to 6,268 in 1942, 9,668 in 1943, and 18,312 in 1944 (Government of Palestine, 1944–45 Statistical Abstract, p. 85).

14. Already by 1926 the two ports had roughly equal amounts of cargo discharged and loaded; Haifa moved ahead in discharging by the next year, although loading remained fairly equal until 1937 (Himadeh, 1938, p. 337). Significantly, the number of ships moving through Jaffa Port decreased from 1,376 in 1921 to 1,198 in 1935 because of increased activity in Haifa and then fell to 510 in 1936 because of the strike (Avitzur, 1972c, appendix, tables 1, 5).

15. Malak, 1993, pp. 54–56.

16. Quoted in *Falastin,* 4/7/36, p. 7; *Falastin,* 21/2/34, p. 1. *Falastin* ran numerous articles on the orange trade in Jaffa that discussed not just the status of exports around the world but also technological and historical analyses of the orange and the industry and celebrations of Jaffa Orange Shows, which prompted a "special illustrated" issue (*Falastin,* 17/2/27, p. 1; cf. 1/1/32).

17. The Jewish share of exports surpassed that of Arabs by the mid-1930s to reach 6,900,000 boxes, as compared to 4,244,000 boxes for the Arab sector, in 1937–38 (Himadeh, 1938, p. 139). While the ratio of Arab to Jewish landownership in Palestine as of 1943 was decidedly in the former's favor (approximately 24.5 million to 1.5 million dunams), the Jews owned almost the same amount of citrus and urban land as Arabs (*Survey of Palestine,* vol. 2, p. 566).

18. Government of Palestine, 1944–45 Statistical Abstract, p. 201; *Biladuna Filastin,* p. 248. The number of permits issued in Jaffa peaked in 1932 at 748 and

varied wildly in the next decade, whereas the number issued by the Tel Aviv Municipality was sometimes as much as tenfold that of Jaffa (TAMA, *Yediot Tel Aviv*, 1936 Yearbook, pp. 55–59; Government of Palestine, 1944–45 Statistical Abstract, p. 201).

19. The cost of living index rose from 100 in January 1942 to 152 at the end of 1944, compared to 138 for Tel Aviv at the end of the same period, while prices in Arab markets in Jaffa also rose faster than in Jewish ones in Tel Aviv.

20. LA, IV/321/9, 12/9/25 letter from Dizengoff to High Commissioner.

21. TAMA, 3/146, "Note sur la crise économique à Tel Aviv," by Dizengoff.

22. "Urban Development in Palestine," *Palestine & Near East* 21–22 (1930): 434.

23. *Hapo'el Hatza'ir*, 20/7/23, p. 17.

24. DAMFAF, Consular Reports, Jaffa, 19/6/25 report "La Palestine: Rapport de l'Attach Commercial." All three cities were mentioned, but only Tel Aviv was typed in capital letters and underlined.

25. CZA, S25/713/94, Notes on an Interview at Government House, 28/10/26, with High Commissioner and senior Palestine Government personnel and Col. Kisch of the Zionist Executive. Cf. TAMA, 7(6) /27, Plan of Action to Organize and Develop Urban Settlement; TAMA 3/97, 14/2/21 letter from Mo'etzet Po'alei Yafo to Tel Aviv Municipality; CZA, S25/713/94, 22/12/26 meeting of the Crisis Alleviation Commission of the Jaffa and Tel Aviv Communal Council.

26. These included the increased speculation in land and the concomitant reliance of a large proportion of the population on the building and allied trades.

27. CZA, S25/734/201, Memo on the Economic Position of the Urban Jewish Population in Palestine, 29/1/26.

28. The reason given for this was the reliance of the economy on construction and related industries, which meant that when the "building fever" passed the construction industry and thus the whole local economy went into a tailspin (*Ha'aretz*, 7/4/26; translation of article in CZA, S25/713/94). Another cause was the economic crisis in Poland (the source of most of the Jewish immigration to Palestine during this period) ("Urban Development in Palestine," *Palestine & Near East* 21–22 (1930): 436;. cf. *Ha'aretz*, 7/4/26; CZA, S25/518II).

29. TAMA Library, Report of the Annual Meeting of the Tel Aviv Chamber of Commerce, 1935, p. 12. As Dizengoff explained it, "The last few years have witnessed the wonderful growth of Tel Aviv. Its development has been extremely successful, and it succeeded in equipping itself with all the paraphernalia of a modern great town in an incredibly short time" ("The Development of Tel Aviv," MHTAY, MHHDI/II8, Dizengoff Archive, undated but probably 1933 or 1934, pp. 1–2). He continues: "We believe that we are not going beyond the truth by asserting that it is unlikely that any other city has shown such great growth during the same period. . . . With the vast hinterland of agricultural settlements and orange groves we are becoming a great agglomeration." It is important to understand the spatial implications of such arguments.

When Zionist economists celebrate the transfer of "industrial enterprise to areas outside the cities"—in this case, using Ramat Gan, an industrial satellite of Tel Aviv, as a prime example of this phenomenon (Ze'eman, 1946, pp. 100, 143)—it must be kept in mind that Arab towns such as Jaffa did not have the luxury of developing industrial hinterlands to encourage and cope with increased development, as they were increasingly surrounded, or "strangulated," by Tel Aviv.

30. Or more specifically, the looming creation of Haifa Port, an event that induced panicked discussion of "Haifa versus Tel Aviv," or of how Haifa "threatened" Tel Aviv's "very existence." The concern was that unless Tel Aviv put in place "the necessary safeguards," it might find itself "entirely eclipsed by the development of Haifa" ("The Development of Tel Aviv," MHTA, MHHDI/II8, Dizengoff Archive, undated but probably 1933 or 1934, p. 20).

31. To use a phrase from Metzer's recent economic history of the Palestine during the Mandate period (Metzer, 1998, p. 7).

32. According to figures provided in the supplement to the 1947 *Survey of Palestine*.

33. In the Jewish sector, no less than forty localities responded to the Histadrut's appeal for Arabic classes for Jews, and almost six hundred people signed up.

34. Cf. Lockman, 1996.

35. *Ittihad al-'Ummal*, 4/1925, inaugural issue, pp. 1–2.

36. *Haqiqat al-Amr*, 19/5/37, p. 1.

37. Cf. *Ittihad al-'Ummal*, 4/25, inaugural issue, 10/6/25, 10/11/25, 1/2/26.

38. Particularly the attempts by Tel Aviv to annex Jaffa's Jewish neighborhoods (cf. *Haqiqat al-Amr*, 31/3/37, p. 3; 14/4/37, p. 4; 26/2/47, p. 3). Thus when Tel Aviv Port opened, *Haqiqat al-Amr* explained that Tel Aviv was forced to build its own port after being "slapped in the face" by Arabs with the strike at Jaffa Port—this after all the work and money Jews had poured into the port over the years (*Haqiqat al-Amr*, 14/7/37, p. 3). Readers were thus counseled that Tel Aviv Port should not be considered an issue of "national concern for Palestinians"—the exact words *Falastin* used to describe its creation—and that attacking the new port would neither benefit trade and commerce in Jaffa nor relieve the "chronic sickness" of Jaffa Port (*Haqiqat al-Amr*, 7/4/37, p. 3).

39. *Haqiqat al-Amr*, 31/8/38, p. 1.

40. "Tel Aviv shows the ability of Jews to direct their own social affairs and to live free as a people, and [we] hope the visit of the [Anglo-American] Committee will show that Jews and Arabs can live together" (*Haqiqat al-Amr*, 2/7/47, p. 1). One story described the "strange sight" during the revolt of a group of Arab families fleeing from Jaffa to seek refuge in Tel Aviv. They requested asylum and houses from the Tel Aviv Municipality from the "evil of the terrorists that still rule Jaffa." The story continued: "The parents and children stared, their eyes full of wonderment and amazement at the great movement in the streets of Tel Aviv, and they were met by smiles at times and [also

by] bewilderment and confusion, exclaiming, 'Truly this is a place of completely free movement between Jews'" (*Haqiqat al-Amr*, 4/12/38, p. 3). The refugees were North Africans who had lived in Jaffa for the past thirty to forty years and were led by one Sheikh Haram Sar.

41. Lockman, 1996, pp. 74, 129, 155. These attempts were spurred on by the low wages paid to Arab workers, which made them natural competitors against their Jewish counterparts.

42. The willingness of these workers to work for very low wages naturally pushed down the already low wages of local Palestinian Arab workers (LA, IV/208/1/4487b, 14/6/34 letter; LA, IV/208/1/4495, several letters in Arabic in this file; cf. Lockman, 1996, p. 217; cf. LA, IV/208/1/4487b, 19/10/34 letter from Zaslani to Crosby).

43. Cf. Lockman, 1996, p. 95, citing *Falastin*, 19/8/27. Hapo'el Hatza'ir felt negotiations held during this period were entered into hastily and recklessly, to protect the status quo and prevent the Arab camel drivers from establishing a foothold in Jaffa (*Hapo'el Hatza'ir*, 13/11/25, p. 15). While "Arab effendis" were blamed for "stabbing" Jewish camel drivers "with knives" by running zif-zif sand into Tel Aviv, the reality was that the Jewish drivers could not supply all of Tel Aviv's needs (LA, IV/208/1/642, 10/3/33 report on Jewish transport work in Tel Aviv).

44. The PLL shifted its focus from Haifa to Jaffa because of the importance of the citrus industry and the port, where workers were increasingly discontented and ripe for organization because of the long hours and low wages paid by Arab contractors, as well as by foreign competition (Lockman, 1996, p. 217).

In determining a strategy for how to proceed with joint organization, it was felt that "to interest the Arab worker in trade union action and induce him to make joint cause with the Jews, a certain period of preparation is necessary during which the Arab worker should undergo an apprenticeship in matters of discipline and social organization" (CZA, S25/2961, Report on Activities of the Arab Secretariat, January–June 1931). In Jaffa and Tel Aviv one of the first groups to be approached was the mostly Greek Orthodox and Armenian drivers, who had organized independently of existing Arab unions (Lockman, 1996, p. 207).

45. The Palestinian Arab dock workers and lightermen were the main force behind this drive (Lockman, 1996, p. 226). Needless to say, this was a promise they certainly could not make since the raison d'être of the Histadrut activities in Jaffa, and the PLL in particular, was specifically to facilitate the conquest of Hebrew labor there and elsewhere in Jaffa

46. The workers approached the MPTAY in February 1933 with a request on behalf of workers on fifty boats to join the Histadrut to establish a cooperative or union (LA, IV/208/1/4487a, 28/2/33 letter). In general, there was the feeling that their activities in Jaffa had been very successful and that they had improved working conditions (CZA, S25/2961, Report of Agassi and Zaslani, 20/11/34). The year 1934 was significant for the Histadrut's efforts to organize workers through the PLL. The accusations that Jews were taking Palestinian

Arab jobs were "rebutted" by promising that no Jewish workers would be brought into Jaffa Port to take Arab jobs (CZA, S25/2961, Report of Agassi and Zaslani, 20/11/34).

47. The AWS was established in July 1934 in Jerusalem by a member of the Nashashibi family and was thus supported by *Falastin,* which also had ties to the Nashashibi camp. The call by *Falastin* led to a public meeting that was attended by more than four hundred workers from different industries (*Falastin,* 19/9/34, p. 2; 21/9/34, p. 3; 23/9/34, p. 7).

48. CZA, S/25/2961, letter from Zaslani to Hoz, 14/10/34 (emphasis in original), quoted in Lockman, 1996, p. 219. In fact, although there were several subsequent "great defeats" and continual "weakness," the PLL's organizing activities had not failed, since the ultimate goal (at least in Jaffa) was not to help Arab workers—however sincerely they worked for that end—but rather "to succeed in inserting Jewish workers into the Port" (LA, IV/104/49/1/76, 28/2/36 meeting of the Arab Committee of the Histadrut).

49. Thus the secretary of the Arab Labor Federation of Jaffa asserted resentfully in 1937: "The Histadrut's fundamental aim is 'the conquest of labour.' . . . No matter how many Arab workers are unemployed, they have no right to take any job which a possible immigrant might occupy. No Arab has the right to work in Jewish undertakings. If Arabs can be displaced in other work, too, that is good. If a port can be established in Tel Aviv and Jaffa Port ruined, that is better" (from George Mansur, *The Arab Worker under the Palestine Mandate,* quoted in Lesch, 1979, pp. 45–46).

50. *Falastin,* 9/8/33, p. 7.

51. A good example of the reasoning behind Palestinian Arab opposition to the activities of the Histadrut in the Arab sector comes from a 1935 article in *al-Jami'a al-Islamiyyah* that accused the Histadrut of "playing with fire" by trying to involve itself in "the Arabic Jaffa Port," explaining that "the Zionists (and we can't forget that the men of the Histadrut have taken [control] over Zionism today) did not fail to find a group of people from among the workers themselves . . . to make it easier for them to take possession of the port and to be the agent of strife *(fitna)* and lighting the fire of disaster and injustice *(sharr)* there." The newspaper proceeded to publish the names of those Arabs at the port who were helping the Histadrut (*al-Jami'a al-Islamiyyah,* 22/5/35, p. 4).

52. LA, IV/208/1/3348a, "A General Proclamation." The writer, a "mechanical worker" named Salih al-Tiar, named those responsible as being "first, our pseudo-national organization, second, our enlightened workers, and third, the fellahin who roam about [because they] sold their land to Zionist agents and treacherous brokers."

Specifically, these workers wanted help with forming a trade union that would get them better wages and fight the influx of foreign Arab workers. As Agassi recalled it more than forty years later, in 1934 Arab workers from the village of Yazur who worked at the Masrawi factory in Jaffa approached the executive committee of the MPTAY to organize them, and Dov Hoz was called to Tel Aviv to help (CZA, S25/4618, undated memorandum on cooperation between

Jewish and Arab workers through the Histadrut; LA, IV/208/1/3348a, Meeting of the Arab Committee, 29/4/35; cf. CZA, S25/4618, undated memorandum on cooperation between Jewish and Arab workers through the Histadrut).

53. LA, IV/104/143/30, Agassi file; clippings from *al-Difa'*, 22/1/35 and 28/1/35; *al-Jami'a al-Islamiyyah*, 23/1/35; *Falastin*, 23/1/35.

54. For example, assistance with securing promised (but undelivered) wage increases was sought from a member of one of the most prominent nationalist families in the city, Azmi Bey Nashashibi (LA, IV/208/1/4495, Arabic list of workers with Hebrew notes).

55. The construction of which was originally contracted by the government to a Jewish company that did not employ Arabs (*Falastin*, 21/2/36, p. 5; Lockman, 1996, p. 236). Two schools were located in the Nuzha quarter and one in 'Ajami. As many as one hundred Arab workers went to one of the building sites in Nuzha and demanded that the Jewish workers stop working, after which the group left guards to make sure Jews did not continue working there and then went to the site in 'Ajami, at which point the police were called to break up the demonstration. A similar incident, this time leading to the arrest of one worker, occurred several days later.

56. This is in contrast to Haifa (where a more pro-Zionist municipal and port leadership made it much harder for Arabs to support the strike) (Lockman, 1996, pp. 241–42).

57. LA, Oral Memoir of Eliyahu Agassi, 22/2/72.

58. CZA, S25/2961, PLL, Report of Activities, June–December 1937. The report explained that it was the workers' "shaky faith" in their power to organize themselves more than any hostility to the PLL and the Histadrut that was a hindrance. One group that approached the PLL was already represented by two lawyers, one a Jew from Tel Aviv and the other an Arab from Jaffa. About sixty Arab workers showed up for a meeting with the PLL; by July 1937 the Jaffa branch had between sixty and seventy members, mostly tradesmen, with the main concern of the group finding work for its members (CZA, S25/2961, PLL, Report of Activities in Jaffa–Tel Aviv, June–December 1937). While the "spirit living in the group" was described as "positive and not deterred by anything," for the most part the Arab workers in Jaffa "stood as spectators from afar—interested and impressed indeed, but not yet decided in [their] souls to join the group" (CZA, S25/2961, PLL, Report of Activities in Jaffa–Tel Aviv, June–December 1937).

59. In one instance, the PLL succeeded in getting the government to investigate labor conditions at Jaffa Port, but the British port manager prevented any action from being taken as a result of the investigation. Another reason for its success likely was, as Lockman points out, that the Arab workers were not the unaware, docile, or easily manipulated labor force that Labor Zionist and Arab nationalist leaders believed them to be but rather understood that "several rival labor organizations were seeking to win their support and sought to turn that rivalry to their advantage" (Lockman, 1996, p. 227).

60. LA, IV/104/143/30, Agassi file; clipping from *al-Difa'*, 18/1/35.

61. HA, 105/199, "Baʿayot Hayom," 19/1/41. For example, in 1940 Arab workers once again approached the Histadrut to ask for help organizing a cooperative work–contracting society to fight the hiring of casual laborers and work lockouts (LA, IV/08/1/2046, 16/2/40 letter to Chief Secretary from Hoz). Apparently, according to a meeting of the Arab Secretariat held the day before this letter was sent, in the current climate the Arabs were more inclined to "warm to the light of the Histadrut" than to set up a separate organization. But it was decided to act cautiously and not proceed too quickly lest both sides wind up disappointed, and thus the best way to act, according to Dov Hoz, was to create a "durable nucleus that would benefit both them and [the Histadrut]" (LA, IV/08/1/2046, 15/2/40 meeting of the Arab Secretariat of the Histadrut).

62. Thus they urged the establishment of a newspaper for workers and promised to work to increase wages, widen "reforms," establish a "sick fund," and open new workers' clubs in the cities and villages (*Falastin*, 23/1/43, p. 3).

63. LA, IV/219/233, protocol of Arab Secretariat, 4/10/43. The workers complained to the PLL that they feared the municipality was "ready to swallow them" and demanded their help, which they did, focusing their efforts on those in Manshiyyeh, which met with "some success" (LA, IV/219/239, 5/9/44 and 22/10/44 meetings and diaries of PLL). After this success the power of the PLL grew and "120 workers saw the bureau of the PLL as their home," while attempts by the Arab union to separate the workers did not bear fruit (CZA, S25, 3107, Report of the activities of the PLL, 1936). The victory with the Jaffa Municipality "not only tightened the connections of the sanitation workers to [the PLL] but led other municipal workers to be interested in working with the PLL, and both Jaffa Municipality and the government continued to negotiate with the PLL for all municipal workers. What is interesting about these developments is that Manshiyyeh was both the place where the Histadrut achieved its greatest success organizing Arab workers and also the place where some of the biggest conflicts occurred between the two communities.

64. LA, IV/219/233, 23/4/43, and 29/6/43 meetings of the Arab Secretariat.

65. The PLL also organized workers at the Wagner factory in Jaffa, but ultimately the leaders of the Arab Section were forced to admit: "In this city we have today only around one hundred men and . . . it is clear to us that it is forbidden to be satisfied with this situation. In Jaffa, one of the most Arab cities in the country, there will always be attackers lurking around us from among the nationalistic groups. And because of this situation we cannot give up on it after we've gone and opened . . . in most factories" (CZA, S25, 3107, Report of the activities of the PLL, 1936).

66. LA, IV/219/239, 23/5/44 protocol of Arab Secretariat.

67. Ibid. Harsh treatment and illegal wages led a group of his 160-odd workers to contact the PLL for assistance. Arab workers in the Wagner factory chose to join the PLL rather than the Arab Workers Group because they believed that the Histadrut was better able to defend their interests. Immediately after they joined the PLL they approached the Wagner factory and demanded better working conditions and higher wages, but the owner con-

tacted the Arab union to fight the PLL and divide those who joined it, which he succeeded in doing (HA, *Yediot me Yafo*, 28/11/43).

68. HA, 105/205, intelligence report, 1944.

69. Cf. Lockman, 1996, p. 312. For a detailed description of the appeal by Arab workers to their Jewish comrades, see LA, IV/490/2, "From Arab Workers to Jewish Workers," 1944.

70. On the other hand, the Arab trade union movement was judged by the British to have recently become an important force that exerted considerable influence on the economic and social, if not political, life of the country, especially in the towns (LA, IV/219/233, Department of Labour, Report on Arab and Jewish trade union activities, December 1945). The Palestine Arab Workers Society (PAWS), which had been in existence since 1925, was felt to be finally coming into its own and was "destined to play a part in the Arab community similar to that played by the [Histadrut] amongst Jews"—a situation that led to "considerable friction" with the PLL. Also see LA, IV/219/233, Department of Labour, Progress of Arab Trade Unions in the year ending 1944; LA, IV/208/1/4217, 8/5/47 meeting of the Arab Secretariat; CZA, S25/3107, PLL, Report of Arab Section, 2/I/45, for information on the Arab unions and the Histadrut.

71. *Survey of Palestine*, vol. 2, pp. 763–65.

72. Thus in the aftermath of the May Day 1921 violence, the Va'ad Tel Aviv discussed expelling Arabs working in the Tel Aviv market, but it was decided that those Arabs who had helped Jews during the violence would be given special permission to continue working in the Jewish town (cf. TAMA, 2/38b, 1/2/22 letter; Shchori, 1990, p. 324). In Jaffa too Arab labor was enough of a problem in the "Jewish" economy to prompt the Jaffa Va'ad to study ways of "combating" the employment of Arabs by Jews (cf. TAMA, 8/57, Report of the Va'ad Ha'ir Leyehudei Yafo, 1925).

73. A fact that was used to placate an angry chief rabbi of Jaffa and Tel Aviv who believed the municipality was employing Jews on Shabat (TAMA, 2/68a, 9/11/23 letter from Dizengoff to the Chief Rabbi of Jaffa–Tel Aviv). *Davar* reported in February 1935 that several Arabs were hired as message boys and cleaners at the Tel Aviv Post Office to replace Jewish clerks (CZA, S25.4618, quoted from 12/2/35 issue).

74. LA, IV/208/32a, 3/31 report by the Arab Secretariat of the Histadrut.

75. LA, IV/208/1/1287, 11/11/36 meeting of Arab Secretariat of Histadrut.

76. When he turned to the Va'ad Tel Aviv they advised him that he needed to annul his contract with the Arabs and then things would quiet down. This letter aroused "great concern in the Muslim Association. . . . in the context of continuing unemployment in Jaffa, [which] also was causing the governor much concern" (LA, S/EC/H, 8/12/21 meeting).

77. TAMA, 2/38b, 7/12/21 letter; emphasis in original.

78. Ibid., 22/1/22 letter to Governor of Jaffa District.

79. TAMA, 4/334a, 14/7/27 (14 Tamuz, Tarpaz) letter to Tel Aviv Munici-

pality from Betzalel Apel. Like the United Rabbinical Council, he too asked the municipality to order the Tel Aviv police to expel the Arabs.

80. TAMA, Protocol of Town Council, 11/8/24. The Tel Aviv Council voted to revoke all permits to traders and issue only temporary ones.

81. There were also problems with Arab zifzif traders, who were bringing zif-zif to the streets of Tel Aviv where Jewish carters were purchasing it and selling it again to building sites in the city (LA, IV/250/72/1/2594, Report of the Secretariat of the MPY, 1923–24). The MPY asked the Jewish carters to make arrangements with the Jewish Cameldrivers Committee, and they agreed as long as the MPY would stop the Arab zif-zif trade in the streets of Tel Aviv.

82. Including the increase in the number of guards against Palestinian Arabs working at Jewish businesses and building sites (LA, IV/208/1/642, protocol of 18/6/34 meeting of Va'ad Hapo'el of MPTAY).

83. These included many "unlicensed" bedouins, Houranis from Syria, and Egyptians, who together "reigned almost supreme" in the porterage, construction, and zif-zif trades (CZA, S25/4618, clipping from *Ha'aretz*, 19/9/34). Jewish Labor officials felt that "if not dealt with by appropriate means, the percentage w[ill] only continue to grow, [but] all activities to stop it so far have not been successful" (LA, IV/208/1/642, 14/5/34 meeting of MPTAY with EC/H).

84. LA, IV/208/1/642, 14/5/34 meeting of MPTAY with Executive Committee of Histadrut (EC/H).

85. CZA, S25/4618, clipping from *Davar*, 26/3/35.

86. Jobs and housing were the two main concerns facing most Jewish workers, with unemployment, "tent and barracks" life, and, at times, "absolute undernourishment" their main scourge. For discussions of unemployment in the Jaffa–Tel Aviv region, see, in chronological order: LA, AC/H, 14/12/21 meeting; LA, S/EC/H, 20/2/22 meeting; CZA, S25/566, 31/10/23 letter from Dizengoff to Col. Kisch; LA, EC/H. 4/10/23 meeting; LA, EC/H, 8/11/23 meeting; LA, IV/208/1/11, Protocol of November–December (Kislev) 1923 meeting of MPY; *Kuntres*, 9/1924, p. 16; LA, EC/H, 26/2/25 meeting; LA, S/EC/H, 1/7/26 meeting; TAMA, 7(4)/1g, 21/2/27 letter to District Commissioner, Jaffa, from Tel Aviv Mayor Bloch; *Hapo'el Hatza'ir*, 25/1/29, p. 13; ISA, M/612, "Labor Conditions in Palestine," 9/9/33 report by Hathorn Hall; *Falastin*, 2/3/37, p. 3; LA, EC/H, 28/6/37 meeting; LA, EC/H, 6/1/38 meeting.

87. More specifically, "the democratic foundations of the yishuv and the Zionist movement," which was built by workers (TAMA, 1/256, 22/7/21 meeting between Tel Aviv Council and MPY; LA, IV/235/917, flyer dated 14/11/28); *Hapo'el Hatza'ir*, 22/11/35, p. 7; 29/11/35, p. 2). The 1921 violence was over working conditions and wages for public works jobs such as street paving. Thus there were continued conflicts between workers and managers and bourgeois town leaders in general, which made it harder to organize in Tel Aviv than in other Jewish or mixed towns (LA, IV/250/72/5/93, MPTAY, *Numbers, 1939*, p. 4).

88. Jaffa District Judge, quoted in *Palestine Post*, 2/5/35, p.2

89. Especially in the wake of the municipal elections of late 1935, which for the Histadrut were "a great success, answering all [their] hopes" (Labor won more than 40 percent of the vote), and the 1936 revolt (cf. LA, EC/H, 1936, #28, 9/1/36, and #30, 1/11/36 meeting, *Hapo'el Hatza'ir*, 20/12/35, p. 1). Cooperation was particularly strong in developing public works projects to ease unemployment and in establishing workers' housing and neighborhoods in Tel Aviv (CZA, S1/532, 4/2/26 letter to Col. Kisch from ZE). For details on these projects see CZA, S25/4618, "Notes on the Histadrut, 1936."

90. They describe their increased activity among Bukhari, Damascene, Yemenite, Salonokim, and Iraqi workers in the Jaffa–Tel Aviv region, especially among the youth of these communities (LA, IV/208/1/642, 7/34 report on activities of the MPTAY).

91. LA, IV/250/72/1/1184, 22/1/36 letters to the Executive Council of MPTAY; LA, IV/250/72/1/1246, Plan of Action for Yemenite Workers in the Country, 1937 or 1938. Two Yemenite clubs were established in Tel Aviv (LA, IV/250/72/1/1648). Yet members still complained about the unfair division of labor that they claimed the MPY (Jaffa Worker's Council, which expanded later into the MPTAY) had done nothing to relieve, even after the Yemenites agreed to join the union. Moreover, they felt that there was a complete "lack of justice and lack of equality in the division of work" between them and their Ashkenazi counterparts (LA, IV/250/72/1/1184, 22/1/36 letters to the Executive Council of MPTAY) and that there were getting little help from the MPTAY (LA, IV/250/72/1/1246, 16/3/37 letter to MPTAY from the Yemenite Workers Club).

92. LA, IV/250/72/1/585, 10/II/47 letter to MPTA by Yiha'el Adaki; LA, IV/208/1/642, 9/4/33 report to S/EC/H.

93. Fishman, 1979, pp. 55, 133; TAMA, 6/5, 1923 public proclamation by Tel Aviv Municipality on the issue. Thus, for example, in early 1923 Hapo'el Hamizrahi put up flyers all over Jaffa and Tel Aviv accusing the Histadrut of "spilling blood" and of "scandal" in the conflict over access to jobs (*Hapo'el Hatza'ir*, 20/7/23, p. 20).

94. LA, IV/208/1/4755, 27/2/38 contract/agreement.

95. Particularly since more than 20 percent of female immigrants were young and unmarried (this percentage would drop in the 1930s) and rents for single-room flats were exorbitant in Tel Aviv (Bernstein, 1987, pp. 31, 38, 45). It should also be noted that there were major class differences between working- and middle-class women.

96. LA, IV/230/49; TAMA, 1/234, letter dated 26/2/29 or 28/3/29 (the Hebrew date is written as Adar 16, but because there were two months of Adar in 1928–29, Adar Aleph and Bet, it is impossible to know to which of the two Gregorian dates it corresponds. The former date is for Adar Aleph and the latter for Adar Bet); *Hapo'el Hatza'ir*, 27/7/19, p. 18; LA, IV/230/49, 10/3/27 letter from General Council of Women Workers.

97. TAMA, 1/165, letter dated 13/3 (29 Adar)/18; LA, IV/208/1/642, letter dated 30/7/34; cf. Bronstein, 1987, pp. 31, 117. Bronstein explains that women wanted to be involved in physical labor so they could participate in the build-

ing of the country. The General Council of Labor Women wrote to the Tel Aviv Municipality: "The difficult situation of women workers in Tel Aviv is known to you of course. We, the Council of Labor Women, are doing everything we can to find work for women laborers. . . . [T]he municipality is going to donate land for the first women's economy in Tel Aviv (in Kerem Shaban), fourteen women presently work there and dozens more will." They then asked for 12 to 15 dunams more for flower growing, raising chickens, and other semiagrarian occupations (TAMA, 3/97, 27/5 [14 Sivan]/26 letter). Yet the MPTAY was also the first local worker's council in the yishuv to address issues related to working women and ultimately set up a women's council to create a "bridge between the working women and the working mother," an event that "was important in the life of working women in Tel Aviv" (LA, IV/230/1/315, Annual Report of Women's Division of the MPTAY, 1937–38).

The plight of female workers was aggravated by the revolt and the fact that workers' housing was spread around the city, making coordination more difficult (LA, IV/230/72, Annual Report of Mothers' Organization, 1/10/36–1/10/37). At the end of the Mandate period living conditions were difficult enough to push larger numbers of women away from the workers' movement (even working mothers' groups), in favor of remaining at home and caring for children (*Hapo'el Hatza'ir*, 23/9/47, p. 20).

98. It reached the point that the executive committee of the Histadrut decided "it [was] necessary to remove a number of workers from Jaffa." The committee reported: "Those that were removed from Jaffa last year have not returned." (LA, EC/H, 5/10/23 meeting; cf. CZA, S25/4618, memo on Work in Ports, Railway, etc., Public works, 1929).

99. LA, IV/250/72/1/2594, undated report of the MPY, 1920s.

100. In fact, during this period, the MPY looked into purchasing lands in the neighboring villages of Sheikh Muwannis, Salama, and Beit Dajan for workers' housing, but speculation made the land too expensive, and the *kushans*, or deeds, were not in order (CZA, S1/532, 25/6/25 letter to the Shchunat 'Ovdim Committee).

101. *al-Difa'*, 13/1/36, p. 4; *Falastin*, 8/10/45, p. 3. Jaffa was an "Arab" port since at least its reconquest by Salaḥu Ad-din's brother (who was in fact a Kurd) at the end of the twelfth century.

102. HA, 40.00023, Oral History of Elchas Steinberg; *Hapo'el Hatza'ir*, 13/2/20.

103. TAMA, 1/231. Specifically, the Jewish members were Dizengoff, David Ismojik, and David(?) Alonzo; the Palestinian Arab members were Jaffa Mayor Assem Bey Said, Nejib Beirouti, and Abdullah Dajani.

104. Not surprisingly, this was also the time that *Falastin* began warning its readers about the Jewish desire to move the port near or to Tel Aviv (TAMA, 20/20, clipping of *Ha'aretz*, 6/10/20; *Falastin*, 14/9/21, p. 1).

105. TAMA, 2/81a, 1922 letter to Lord Alfred Milner.

106. LA, IV/250/721/1831, 15/7/28 letter to Jaffa Labor Council, signature illegible.

107. Ibid.

108. LA, IV/250/72/1/1831, letter to the Va'adat Hagiyus (Mobilization Committee) from the port workers' committee, 28/8/27; cf. 9/3/28 letter to District Commissioner from, initials, Z.P.; LA, IV/250/72/1/1831).

109. LA, IV/250/72/1/1831, 7/6/25 letter, no signature.

110. LA, IV/250/72/1/2468, "Hebrew Coachmen's Group in Jaffa Port," Passover Eve, 1927. Most of the Jewish businesses importing through the port, and even some non-Jewish ones, used their group.

111. LA, IV/208/1/642, 8/7/34 memo, "A Suggestion for the Establishment of a Partnership for Work in Jaffa Port"; LA, IV/208/1/642, 2/4/34 meeting of MPTAY. More specifically, Jewish coachmen formed another cooperative in 1933, with thirty members, although their situation was harmed by government opposition and low-wage Palestinian Arab workers. There were also three other groups of Jewish workers in Jaffa Port with about twenty members, but they vigorously resisted attempts by the Histadrut to organize them. At the same time the local press protested strongly against the "provocation" (Shaghab) of the Histadrut in Jaffa Port in the beginning of 1935 and warned workers against working with an organization whose goal was the judaization of the port (*Falastin*, 17/1/35, p. 5, cf. 6/3/35, p. 2, 26/5/34, p. 6; cf. LA, IV/208/1/635, 1934 contract between the Histadrut, MPTAY branch, and two Jewish, Tel Aviv–based contractors for an example of the Histadrut's attempts to obtain Jewish-only contracts with Jewish firms working at the port.

112. CZA, S25/4618, Employment of Casual Labor. There numbers were 17,388 man-days of casual labor by Jews versus 244,634 by non-Jews.

113. CZA, S25/4618, memo, Non-Jewish Immigration from Neighbouring Countries. There were 100 Syrian workers employed in Jaffa Port in June 1935, mainly in unloading goods, and when the government refused to allow them to continue to work the main lightermen's cooperative society intervened and asked the port administration to give the Syrians permission. All told, there are about 3,000 foreign workers at the port, mostly for the winter season, and 400 local Jaffan workers (CZA, S25/4618, memorandum, "Non-Jewish Immigration from Neighbouring Countries . . ."; clipping from *Davar*, 22/1/35).

114. *Falastin*, 20/6/24, p. 1.

115. TAMA, 3/102, Memorandum to Mr. Palmer. Dizengoff explained that Patrick Geddes, who would soon design a new town plan for Tel Aviv, had suggested this location as the best for a new port. In August the local press reported that the Jews had asked the government to build a port on the 'Auja/Yarkon River (*Falastin*, 16/viii/33, p. 3; cf. LA, IV/250/72/1/3208, 8/7/34 memorandum titled "Suggestions on Establishing a Partnership for Work in Jaffa Port"). The Palestinian Arab press also monitored the Jewish press for discussions about the creation of either a separate port for Tel Aviv or a joint port for both cities (*Falastin*, 1/4/37, p. 1). Thus it would report on Jewish members of the port committee who attempted to move the port to lands closer to Tel Aviv, according to *Falastin* (*Falastin*, 14/9/21, p. 1).

116. TAMA, 6/40, 6/10/25 meeting of the "Executive Committee." The

conception of Jaffa as a Diaspora, that is, an inherently foreign and alien space that was the antithesis of Tel Aviv, would pose numerous problems for Zionist leaders. On the one hand, this depiction is central for the Tel Aviv imagination as the space of the unfolding of Zionism; on the other hand, Tel Aviv's leaders could never decide whether Jaffa, as *galut* space, should be slowly "assimilated" into Tel Aviv or abandoned until such time as it could be "conquered."

117. Despite the national conflict surrounding Jewish workers at Jaffa Port, they had more mundane concerns: "We do not demand special rights, we only want to work like the rest of the port workers," was the way one worker expressed the issue, and their main concern was how to face the day-to-day difficulties of working in a port (LA, IV/250/72/1/1834, Minutes Book of Yemenite Workers Club, 1936–37, 3/2/37 meeting).

118. CZA, S25/4618, "Evidence on the Jewish Share in Public Works, 1936," p. 6.

119. CZA, S25/4618, 9/iv/36 letter from Chief Secretary to Jewish Agency.

120. *al-Difa'*, 23/10/36, p. 2. Not surprisingly, Jews felt similarly threatened. In the wake of the strike, the Jewish Port Committee reported: "[T]he hands of the Arabs are upon us to the point that it is impossible to bring Jewish workers to Jaffa Port and even to enter the port area without danger" (CZA Library, *Namal Tel Aviv* [Tel Aviv Port], p. 46, quote from 26/4/36 meeting of Port Committee).

121. *al-Difa'*, 2/2/36. The government was annoyed at the constant attempts by the Palestinian Arab press to give nationalist interpretations of "petty incidents" that were part of the "normal . . . daily quarrels" between lightermen and porters (ISA, untagged file, report dated 10/2/36). Cf. ISA, untagged file, leaflet dated 29/11/36, for the Palestine Communist Party's opposition to the construction of a port in Tel Aviv.

122. *Falastin*, 20/10/36, p. 5.

123. *Falastin*, 8/10/45, p. 3.

124. In PRO, CO733/362/10. In the margins of the Marine Trust Ltd. Statement on the Jaffa Port (by S. Hoofien), one Colonial Office official wrote, "What about Haifa?" which raises interesting questions:Why did these problems not occur in that city, and why did the Jews not push for a similar "separation"? For an in-depth examination of these questions, see Lockman, 1996, esp. chap. 6.

125. Again, a Colonial Office official noted in the margins, "Yes, but in their *own* interest and therefore at their own risk" (PRO, CO733/362/10, ibid., emphasis in original; cf. PRO, CO733/298/8, 17/7/36 telegram from High Commissioner to Secretary of State for the Colonies). In another dispatch to the secretary of state for the colonies the high commissioner wrote, "[I]f this were an ordinary commercial undertaking this condition might perhaps constitute an insuperable objection to its profitable operation. Economic considerations, however, are not conclusive in the present case for it is a matter of fact that many Jewish enterprises of a 'national' character, which may be intrinsically uneconomic and unprofitable, are successfully maintained by the financial

support of Zionist sympathizers" (PRO, CO733/398/8, 22/8/36 telegram from High Commissioner to Secretary of State for the Colonies).

126. *Yediot Tel Aviv,* Yearbook, 1936–37, p. 79. As *Hapoʿel Hatzaʿir* wrote, "What had only been a dream eight months ago, already appears before us as a block of living reality" (*Hapoʿel Hatzaʿir,* 21/1/37, p. 23). In the words of the Marine Trust, the strike "starved out" Tel Aviv, and this led to the creation of the Harbour and Communications Council of Tel Aviv consisting of representatives of all classes of the community, business, government (local and the Jewish Agency) and the Tel Aviv Municipality, which then laid the groundwork for the creation of the jetty-turned-port in May 1936 (LA, IV/208/1/1253b, memorandum on Tel Aviv Harbour).

127. ISA, M/(14)/LD, 12/3508; 30/9/41 letter to Marine Trust from Chief Secretary, with enclosures.

128. And thus *Falastin* followed the developments of Tel Aviv Port very closely (see *Falastin,* 26/1/37, p. 6). In a fascinating 1940 letter to the financier Pinhas Rutenberg from the Marine Trust, which administered the port, the "political importance" of extending the port was stressed to demonstrate: "At this historic moment, [we must] ostentatiously undertake this act of independence on the part of the Jewish people in the sphere of national expansion. . . . [Moreover,] after the issue of the White Paper we must come out with an act of non-cooperation by starting the construction of the Western breakwater of the extension scheme. . . . [T]he building of the western breakwater is the act of occupation, the actual fixing of a new boundary. We cannot do less, we need not do more" (LA, IV/208/1/1736a, 16/5/39 letter).

129. Tel Aviv Port was moving more than 12 percent of the country's citrus exports by 1940 versus 35 percent for Jaffa Port (CZA, L9/422, Tel Aviv Harbour, 1936–46, Official Handbook of the Maritime Trust, Tel Aviv, 1946, p. 14; LA, IV/208/1/1736a, Memo to the Board of the Marine Trust from the General Manager, 1939; cf. *Hapoʿel Hatzaʿir,* 28/10/38, p. 4, for an account of the "bitter debate" over the port's future; and LA, EC/H, 21/3/40 meeting, p. 14, for a discussion of Histadrut intervention to prevent its closing).

130. LA, EC/H, meeting, 11/12/39, p. 12. "The port can't breathe anymore" was how one EC member described the situation (LA, EC/H, 6/11/39 meeting, p. 2).

131. *Haqiqat al-Amr,* 14/7/37, p. 3.

132. "Jaffa, with its 77,000 inhabitants, provides for the requirements of the Arab population, its orange exports and its imported general goods. Tel Aviv serves the needs of the Jewish community, supplies the necessities of a population of 250,000, raw materials for the industries around Tel Aviv, and caters for industrial and orange exports. In addition, it has to serve the closely populated centres of the colonies in the plains north and south of Tel Aviv. The development of Jerusalem, in particular, will greatly depend on the facilities provided by the port of Tel Aviv" (PRO, CO733/418/22, "Jaffa Port and Tel Aviv Harbour, 1940," Introductory Memo: Tel Aviv Port, 24/5/40, by Dr. Joseph Sagall, p. 5).

133. In a 30/9/41 letter from J. S. Macpherson, Chief Secretary, to Hoofien, Chairman of Marine Trust, Macpherson rebuts Hoffien's desire for the administrative separation of Tel Aviv Port from Jaffa Port, saying that the claim that the good management of Tel Aviv Port calls for its administrative separation from Jaffa Port is not true, and in any case, "the Government has no intention to allow Tel Aviv Port to be separated from the Jaffa Port area" (PRO, CO733/435/20, Jaffa Port and Tel Aviv Harbour, 1942).

Whatever the national implications of this enterprise, we should not forget the local concerns and aims of the people running the new port. Most important, as the 1946 Report of the Marine Trust put it, "[Tel Aviv's] own district and Southern Palestine generally are its legitimate hinterland, and the fact is too patent to require any proof." That is, all of southern Palestine (with its largely Palestinian Arab population) was now to be served by Tel Aviv Port, while Jaffa Port was to be restricted to servicing only the Palestinian Arab economy of Jaffa and its immediate surroundings. This argument is a good example of how the economic and communal boundaries that already had been deployed by Zionist researchers to "describe" separate and autonomously developing Jewish and Palestinian Arab Palestines were also used to justify policies derived from these "scientific" analyses.

134. *Hapo'el Hatza'ir,* 5/7/37, p. 9.

135. Ben-Gurion, Diary entry, 11/7/136, quoted in Teveth, 1985, p. 175.

136. *Hapo'el Hatza'ir,* 22/11/35, p. 6. The leadership made continued attempts to restrict the right to vote so as to weaken the political power of the Labor movement in Tel Aviv (TAMA, *Yediot Tel Aviv,* 15/6/26, pp. 14–15).

137. While promoting factionalism in the mixed towns (cf. *Falastin,* 10/2/34, p. 2; cf. 16/2/34, pp. 3, 5; 20/2/34, p. 7).

138. JA, 2/B 10G, Election Committee to the Fourth Council of Tel Aviv, 31/12/28; TAMA, 4/4024, 31/8/26 letter to District Officer, Jaffa; *Hapo'el Hatza'ir,* 17/5/35, p. 1. At this time only 27,000 of the 120,000 residents had the right to vote. Interestingly, in 1935 the Homeowners' List imitated the Labor list, beginning its electoral pamphlet with the slogan "Homeowners of the all parties, Unite!"—clearly copying (disparagingly, no doubt) the socialist rallying cry (CZA, A174/16, Pamphlet of the General Union of Homeowners). The Labor faction was still fighting for the right to vote for all citizens as late as 1946 (*Hapo'el Hatza'ir,* 9/1/46, p. 3).

The Labor faction finally won the municipality for a brief period in 1926–27 when Dizengoff resigned, after being overruled in a decision regarding the abolition of school fees (cf. *Kuntres,* 21/1/26, p. 24). Another story has it that Dizengoff retired in a fit of anger over a dispute with the Labor Party over representation on the main committees of the Tel Aviv Municipality, which the council approved despite Dizengoff's objection. This also occurred at a time when the housing situation in Tel Aviv was worsening (*Hapo'el Hatza'ir,* 12/6/25, p. 1). As the crisis in the now labor-dominated Tel Aviv Municipality worsened, *Hapo'el Hatza'ir* blamed a relentless and unfair attack on the city's new leadership by not just Dizengoff but also the Ba'alei Habatim faction in whose hands he was nothing more than a "game ball" and who wanted from the beginning to "free themselves from the prison of the Left" (*Hapoʿel Hatzaʿir*, 7/1/26).

Relations between the municipality and the Revisionists became more strained in the late 1920s because the latter felt the municipality did not appoint enough of their members, and their national leadership wanted to boycott municipality elections unless the matter was resolved. Moreover, Jabotinsky was totally against running on the same ticket as the United Center (UC) party of Dizengoff, although he was not against a separate list allied with the UC. However, the Tel Aviv branch was forbidden to do it under one list because Jabotinsky opposed the "general worldview"; thus working under one list "would only upset [their] work now and in the future" (JA, 2/2 G10, Protocols of the Zionist Revisionist Organization, Tel Aviv branch, 2–12/1928).

139. While Tel Aviv would constitute only an "internal neighborhood committee" (TAMA, 1/90, report of the Vaʿad Haʿir Leyehudei Yafo, 1917–18, p. 32). "There is enough work for both of us," it said, especially since it focused on religious issues of the larger community (and thus had the support of the Haredim, who in any case despised the Tel Aviv Council because of the Shabat law controversies) and many people did not vote in the Tel Aviv elections (TAMA, 2/42a, Protocol of meeting of the Vaʿad , 26/4/27; cf. TAMA, 8/327, 3/9/21 letter to Tel Aviv Council from Vaʿad).

140. In fact, only days after Tel Aviv was granted municipal autonomy and the Tel Aviv Council was established, the Jaffa Vaʿad wrote to the latter asking to meet to discuss uniting the two councils (TAMA, 1/259a, 27/5/21). However, in the Vaʿad's opinion, "The Tel Aviv Town Council stepped over the line . . . [a]nd became a representative committee of the Jewish community in Tel Aviv; to the outside there is not much difference between the representation of the community of Tel Aviv itself and of Jaffa itself, and thus it appears as if Tel Aviv fulfills the same function as the 'general' Vaʿad" (TAMA, 1/200a, 21/5/21 [14 Ayar, Tarpa], letter to Tel Aviv Town Council from the Jaffa Vaʿad).

141. TAMA, 2/68a, 22/12/22 letter from the Vaʿad to Tel Aviv Town Council; cf. TAMA, 8/301b, Report of the Vaʿad Haʿir Leyehudei Yafo, 1923, p. 3. Nevertheless, by 1922 it was determined that the jurisdiction of the Vaʿad included "all the Jews living permanently within the borders of Jaffa and its neighborhoods," and its functions included rabbinical affairs, education, charity, buying land for public purposes (synagogues and cemeteries), representing the affairs of Jews before the government, finding public works for the unemployed, immigration, taxation of Jews, Jewish civil court, and the "rest of the economic and civil interests of the Jewish citizens of Jaffa" (TAMA, 1–1922–1, Rules of the Vaʿad Haʿir Leyehudei Yafo)

142. As early as 1910 the chief rabbi of Jaffa provoked a bitter debate in the Tel Aviv Council with his opposition to diligence service from Tel Aviv to Jaffa and other public desecrations of the Sabbath (Shchori, 1991, p. 14; TAMA, 2/14B, 24/5/23 letter to Dizengoff). Not surprisingly, women were a main

symbol in the battle over Tel Aviv's identity, and it took a great deal of effort on the part of women's organizations such as the Union of Hebrew Women for Equal Rights to ensure, for example, that they retained the right to vote in elections for the Va'ad (for flyers supporting each view, see MHTAY, A (Municipal Services), A/1–3).

143. Over the issues of allowing cars to be driven or stores and restaurants to remain open on Sabbath (CZA, A174/31, 24/5/34; cf. *Hatzofeh*, 4/i/39, p.1, 20/2/39, p. 1). Thus the labor newspaper *Hapo'el Hatza'ir* complained, "[Y]esterday it was 'women,' today it is 'Shabat'—this time the question is more serious." The newspaper is referring to the fact that the issue of women had helped them to bring down the council and the Va'ad Ha'ir, but the issue of Shabat—that is, the passage of a new law requiring all stores to be closed on Shabat, among other restrictions—which was cited by the new neighborhoods as a precondition for their participation in the next elections, could be used as a way to extend their political reach into everyone's private lives (*Hapo'el Hatza'ir*, 4/5/23, p. 1).

144. TAMA, 8/353, 13/3/27 letter to the Va'ad Hale'umi Leyehudei Eretz Israel from the Jaffa Va'ad; cf. TAMA, 8/60, Protocol of meeting of the leadership of the Va'ad, 9/7/36. As early as 1914 the Tel Aviv Council agreed to contribute to the cost of putting up lanterns in Jaffa's Jewish neighborhoods (TAMA, 8/715, Dizengoff letter to Chief Rabbi of Jaffa, 1/7/14), while Dizengoff was an active member of the Jaffa Va'ad in 1912 and long after that (TAMA, 8/715). The Jaffa Va'ad and the Tel Aviv Municipality worked together to lower the prices of meat and fish (TAMA 2/68b, letter from Va'ad Ha'ir to Tel Aviv Municipality 14/4/36), and even to coordinate elections (TAMA, 2/1, letter to Va'ad Ha'ir from Dizengoff, 4/10/22).

145. LA, IV/250/72/1/1184, "Maskirat Merkaz Ha'ovdim Hateimanim," undated, pp. 92–94.

146. In fact, the Committee of the Jewish Sephardim Community in Jaffa had many of the same functions as the Jaffa Va'ad, including its own rabbinical establishment and other communal institutions (cf. TAMA, 2/1, 17/12/22 protocol of the Committee of the Jewish Sephardim Community, Jaffa.

147. By 1922 the Yemenite neighborhoods were so overcrowded that the Yemenite Committee, meeting in Jaffa, felt the need to buy more land around the neighborhoods so that could be used for the local economy and house poor families (*Hapo'el Hatza'ir*, 28/2/22, p. 28). Despite their supposed ability to compete with Palestinian Arabs for low-paying jobs, the reality was that the employment situation of the Yemenite population was "horrible" (LA, IV/104/1252/11, 12/32 memo by Israel Yeshiyahu).

148. TAMA, 4/334G, letter from the Deputy District Superindendent of Police of Jaffa to the Divisional Inspector of Police in Tel Aviv dated 20/7/30.

149. *Kuntres*, issue resh/aleph, 1925, p. 32.

150. Thus *Falastin*'s complaint in late February 1936 that kids were in the streets and that despite some private donations to construct new buildings, the government was not doing enough (*Falastin*, 25/2/36, p. 3).

151. Thus *Falastin* marveled, somewhat jealously, at both the fact that 24,000 students were enrolled in schools in Tel Aviv, 20,000 of them in municipal schools ("!") and the fact that despite these numbers, the Jewish press continually criticized the city's educational policies. Moreover, it lamented that in comparison to Tel Aviv the Palestinian Arab municipalities, including Jaffa, fared badly despite the tens of thousands of pounds paid to the Jaffa Municipality by parents to educate their children (*Falastin*, 8/7/41, p. 2).

152. These included a housing project, a water tower, a park, and a sports stadium (*Falastin*, 23/10/32, p. 4; 1/9/34, p. 1; 6/9/34, p. 4; 24/10/34, p. 3; 6/8/35, p. 5; 1/4/37, p. 1; 3/6/38, p. 5; 5/6/38, p. 5; 1/3/40, p. 4). The development would consist of twenty-seven houses, each on approximately six-tenths of a dunam of land, which would be paid for by the new residents over a three-year period. The location was considered especially good because it was elevated, the air was not too humid, there was good bus transportation, and a new road was being built (*Falastin*, 25/8/35, p. 10).

153. *Falastin*, 15/7/31, p. 4; 28/11/33, p. 6; 4/1/36, p. 2.

154. *Falastin*, 3/6/38, p. 5; 5/6/38, p. 5.

155. *Falastin*, 22/7/31, p. 1, 23/7/31, p. 1.

156. Thus the municipality achieved a 40,000-pound surplus in its budget by cutting expenses in health and other areas, but *Falastin* was critical because there was "garbage in the streets" and "devastating" health problems. Moreover, although there appeared to be a surplus, in fact the money was taken from schools and hundreds of children were on the streets (*Falastin*, 23/11/43, p. 3). Again, when the Jaffa Municipality enacted an education tax *Falastin* complained that tens of thousands of pounds remained in banks and had not been allocated to the schools (*Falastin*, 4/6/44, p. 2).

157. HA, 105/204, Arabic and Hebrew newspaper clippings, 1944.

158. HA, 105/50, Arabic and Hebrew newspaper clippings, 1946.

159. Ibid.

160. According to a Haganah intelligence report, Jaffa Mayor Beytar became more militant after his return from a trip to Syria in 1941 because he thought he could become the leader of the Palestinian Arabs in the absence of the Mufti, whom he did not believe would return to Palestine in the near future (HA, 105/200, 10/10/41 report).

161. TAMA 4/334a, 21/4/29 letter. Also see articles in Falastin, 14/5/38, p. 5, 22/7/39, p. 5, 26/11/43, p. 4; HA, 105/50, newspaper clippings, 1946. Cf. TAMA, 4/3349, 22/7/29 or 22/1/29 (date illegible); HA, 105/206, "Yediot me-Yafo," 16/87/44.

162. *Falastin*, 2/5/47, p. 1.

163. Thus when there was discussion over whether the train station should move from Lod to either Jaffa or Tel Aviv, the secretary of the municipality castigated the two Jewish members of the municipality for their concern only about Tel Aviv's interests, and he reminded them of their obligation to "remember the name of Jaffa" in their deliberations, in part because "Tel Aviv was in reality a part of Jaffa" (*Falastin*, 23/10/32, p. 4; cf. CZA, A173/15).

164. *Falastin,* 14/5/38, p. 5; 22/7/39, p. 5; HA, 105/50, Arabic and Hebrew newspaper clippings, 1946. In one case it complained that Tel Aviv police were entering the Carmel market on the border between the two towns and harassing the Palestinian Arab merchants there (TAMA, 4/334a, 21/4/29 letter). In another it sued Tel Aviv Municipality over allegedly stealing water from its pipes for the Florentine and Shapiro quarters (*Falastin,* 25/12/31, p. 8), and the two municipalities fought over the distribution of rationed items such as eggs, with Jaffa Municipality complaining, for example, that some of its eggs went to Tel Aviv (*Falastin,* 26/11/43, p. 4). Also see TAMA, 4/334g, 22/7/29 or 22/1/29 (date not clear) letter; HA, 105/206, "Yediot me-Yafo," 16/8/44, for information about intermunicipal relations.

165. Private collection of Hana Ram, 14/5/19 letter from Anton Jelal, Nahle Beiruti, Musa Yusef Rus, and two other Palestinian Arabs to Shloosh and Barsky; cf. CZA, A174/28, 18/5/19 letter.

166. TAMA, 1/258, letter dated 21/5/21; cf. TAMA 2/48a. The mayor also requested a copy of the "new plan of Tel Aviv," so that it could be included in the "general plan of Jaffa." It is not unlikely this request was motivated by the fear that Tel Aviv's new town plan would damage Jaffa's interests. On at least one occasion, Dizengoff wrote to the mayor of Jaffa to request that special consideration be given to a Palestinian Arab resident who had written to him complaining that he was fined and jailed for not being able to pay a fine for building without a permit (private collection of Hana Ram, 1928 letter).

One of the most prominent Palestinian Arabs involved in "reestablishing friendly relations" was none other than Abdullah Dajani, ostensibly one of Jaffa's leading nationalist figures, who only days later wrote to Dizengoff (?) warning him that the government had given Issa el-Issa permission to start *Falastin* again, which Dajani felt would lead to a return of "anti-Jewish agitation and would spoil all [their] joint efforts to establish harmony between Jews and Arabs" (CZA, S25/517, 24/1/23 letter to High Commissioner from Dizengoff (?)).

167. For example, in the 1944–45 Jaffa municipal budget, 20,000 pounds were transferred to Tel Aviv for education, social services, and hospitalization services extended by Tel Aviv Municipality to Jewish taxpayers of Jaffa (HA 105/206, clippings from Hebrew, Arabic and English press, 7–10/1944). The municipality also contributed to a Jewish workers' hospital in Jaffa in 1920 (TAMA, 1/166, 20/7/20 letter to Tel Aviv Town Council from Kupat Holim, Jaffa).

168. TAMA, 2/47b, 21/3/22 letter from Tel Aviv Municipality to Jaffa Municipality; TAMA, 2/66b, 19/11/23 letter from Jaffa Municipality to Tel Aviv Municipality; 2/33a, 15/1/24 letter from Dizengoff to Assem Bey El-Said; TAMA, 2/66b, 11/x/25 letter from Tel Aviv Municipality to Jaffa Municipality; TAMA, 2/33b, letter from Jaffa Municipality to Tel Aviv Municipality, dated 8/9/23; Protocol of 5/9/23 meeting of the Tel Aviv Council; *Falastin,* 16/8/34, p. 2; *Palestine Post,* 16/8/34, p. 5.

169. TAMA, protocol of 38th meeting of the Tel Aviv Council, 8/3/25.

170. *Yediot Tel Aviv*, 1/11/28, p. 42. Although the services along joint streets were not always equal. Thus only in the parts of Kerem Hateimanim within Tel Aviv's borders was there electricity into the mid-1930s, and the parts under the jurisdiction of Jaffa Municipality "exist[ed] under the government of heavy dimness," lit only by moonlight (*Ha'aretz*, 25/6/34, "Kerem Hateimanim . . . Orchard? Of Course Not").

171. TAMA, 2/47b, 21/3/22 letter from Tel Aviv Municipality to Jaffa Municipality; TAMA, 2/66b, 19/11/23 letter from Jaffa Municipality to Tel Aviv Municipality; 2/33a, 15/1/24 letter from Dizengoff to Assem Bey-Said; TAMA, 2/66b, 11/10/25 letter from Tel Aviv Municipality to Jaffa Municipality; TAMA, 2/33b, letter from Jaffa Municipality to Tel Aviv Municipality, dated 8/9/23; Protocol of 5/9/23 meeting of Council; *Falastin*, 16/8/34, p. 2; *Palestine Post*, 16/8/34, p. 5.

172. *Falastin*, 12/3/43, p. 3; 16/12/42, p. 3. There were times when the Tel Aviv Municipality did not mind that its products were taxed in Jaffa, such as when the Jaffa Municipality began taxing meat slaughtered in Tel Aviv that was being sold in Jaffa. At a meeting of the executive committee of the Tel Aviv Municipality, Bograshov pointed out, "[I]t is good that Jaffa Municipality will raise the tax on meat sold in Jaffa because it will allow us to raise the tax on meat slaughtered in Jaffa and sold in Tel Aviv" (TAMA, 6/40, 22/9/25 meeting).

173. TAMA, 2/81b, 3/3/22 speech.

174. TAMA, 1/283, Protocol of Council Meeting #21, 2/4/21; TAMA, 1/283, Protocol of Council Meeting #21, 2/4/21.

175. TAMA, 16/2/24 meeting of the General Committee of the Tel Aviv Town Council.

176. HA, 22.00003, Oral History of Herzl Habas, 1950.

177. The violence of 1921 and 1936 actually began in Jaffa, whereas the 1929 violence began in Jerusalem and then spread to other cities, including Jaffa and Tel Aviv.

178. CZA, L4/829, 21/5/21, Testimony of Captain Chisholm Dunbar Brunton before Committee of Inquiry into 1921 riots.

179. For example, they ordered their propagandists to "turn down the heat[,] . . . to tell [their] newspapers to soften their stories, not so openly broadcast Zionist goals." There was a large demonstration in Jaffa on February 27, 1920, sponsored by the Muslim-Christian Association, including a general strike and the closing of stores. The demonstration was against Zionism generally and against, as the sign on one store read, "the idea that Palestine will be a National Home for Jews" (CZA, L18/119/3, 1/3/21 letter to Ussushkin from Shertok, with accompanying summary of speeches at demonstration). Among the suggestions for improving relations were Jewish participation with them in business, making loans available to the working class, opening an Arab newspaper to separate "Arabs [i.e., Muslims] and Christians," and hiring Palestinian Arabs as Arabic teachers (CZA L18/119/3, 5/iv/20 protocol of meeting from Va'ad Hatzirim le'eretz Israel to Ussushkin). The official, Deputy Mayor Rokah, continued, "We can engage in our politics, do practical activities, but

without declaring and publishing them in newspapers that will only enrage our neighbors."

180. CZA, L4/829, 21/5/21, Testimony of Captain Chisholm Dunbar Brunton before Committee of Inquiry into 1921 riots. This was specifically because there was "more trade[,] . . . more population, and more of the proletariat[,] . . . [q]uarters like Manshiyyeh and Tin Town where you find poorer people living together." Not only did many "Bolshevik" (i.e., Eastern European) Jews live in Manshiyyeh; the community was also home to some Yemenites, who could more easily spread the Marxist propaganda (including "well-written" Arabic-language pamphlets) that the local Palestinian Arab religious and political leadership found so threatening.

181. As the High Commissioner, Herbert Samuel, described Manshiyyeh, it was 'the mixed Moslem Jewish Quarter of the town" (ISA, M/144/4, 3/5/21 cable to the Colonial Office by High Commissioner Samuel).

182. ISA, M/144/4, 3/5/21 cable to the Colonial Office by High Commissioner Samuel; CZA, L4/861, copy of 8/5/21 letter to Zionist Executive in London, no signature. The Tel Aviv police were actually sent to guard the Mopsim who were marching to Manshiyyeh. One of the policemen recalled how the Palestinian Arabs began attacking them and even pursuing them to the borders of Tel Aviv, and many Palestinian Arabs gathered around the border of Manshiyyeh and Tel Aviv. The Palestinian Arab policemen, according to the recollection of one Tel Aviv police officer, "not only did not do anything" to prevent the violence "but themselves participated in the acts." At the same time violence exploded in Manshiyyeh it also began in ʿAjami, where the Immigrants' House and Vaʿad Hatzirim were (HA, 180.29, "The Municipal Police in Tel Aviv").

183. Lesch, 1979, pp. 204–5.

184. *Falastin* tried to show evidence that Jews from Tel Aviv fired first and attacked Palestinian Arab houses in Manshiyyeh (*Falastin*, 14/5/21, p. 3). Jews continued to be attacked through June in the Manshiyyeh and ʿAjami quarters, and *Falastin* continued to describe the situation in Jaffa as "very tragic and grave—as if in a time of war" (*Falastin*, 29/6/21, p. 3; PRO, Parliamentary Papers, C.1540, 1921, "Report by Commission of Enquiry into Jaffa Riots, 1921," pp. 26–37).

185. *Falastin*, 14/5/21, p. 3.

186. Private Papers Collection, Middle East Center, St. Antony's College [PPCMECSAC], Brunton papers, 13/5/21 report by Brunton to General Headquarters; cf. PRO, Parliamentary Papers, C.1540, 1921, "Report by Commission of Enquiry into Jaffa Riots, 1921," p. 24; CZA, KKL3/35, letter from the Director of the Herzliyyah Gymnasium to Menahem Ussushkin, 7/v/21; emphasis in original.

187. TAMA, 2/81a, "Notes sur la situation générale à Jaffa." He also noted that though Bolsheviks and recent immigrants were blamed for the fighting, in fact "most Jews arrested and accused of diverse crimes are Sephardim—longtime inhabitants of the city." Refugees were housed in some 182 tents in Tel

Aviv after the violence, leading Dizengoff to write urgently to the district governor asking for 2,000 pounds to build housing, or at least barracks, to ease overcrowding and unsanitary conditions (TAMA, 2/38b, 21/10/21 letter in French).

188. *Hapo'el Hatza'ir*, 30/8/29, p. 11; HA, 18.00009, Oral History of Niota Halperin; CZA, S25, 4606, file on 1929 riots. In fact, "while the speeches at the Great Mosque in Jaffa were more 'pacific,' more militant people went to the [Hassan Bey] mosque in Manshiyyeh, and after speeches came out to inaugurate attacks on Tel Aviv—a huge crowd tried to attack Tel Aviv from several directions, but were repelled by the British . . . while attacks continued in Abu Kebir and Neve Sha'anan."

According to one Haganah report, Palestinian Arabs ran toward Tel Aviv shouting, "To Manshiyyeh, to Tel Aviv, ya Shebab, to Tel Aviv, from the Sea, from below" (CZA, S25, 4606, file on 1929 riots, 20/10/29 summary of evidence). Jews living in the north of Tel Aviv, near the village of Sheikh Muwannis, also feared attack (HA, 40.00023, Oral History of Elchas Steinberg).

189. In the wake of the fighting, Dizengoff wrote to a friend, "[T]he Arab attacks . . . have been transformed in front of our eyes into economic attacks: All the Christian and Muslim Arabs have declared a fierce boycott against Jewish products and against Jewish commerce" (CZA, S25, 4606, file on 1929 riots). In Dizengoff's words, the violence threatened to bring "a great calamity[,] . . . to ruin economically the city and the Municipality together" (TAMA, 8/301A), Meir Dizengoff, "Tel Aviv: Its Needs and Future," 1932; TAMA, 7(6)/2a, 28/10/29 letter to Monsieur Grunblatt; cf. CZA, L4/829, 21/5/21 testimony of C. D. Brunton before Commission of Inquiry into 1921 riots, p. 8 for a comparison with the 1921 boycott).

190. TAMA, 7(6)/2a, 28/10/29 letter to Monsieur Grunblatt.

191. Thus the violence of 1929 also led to the "revival . . . of [the] old project of creating a jetty in Tel Aviv," which until then had been politically as well as economically unfeasible but whose prospects were "radically changed" by the violence: "Everyone, merchants, industrialists of Tel Aviv and the Jewish colonies, orange exporters and growers, all recognize the necessity . . . of now having our jetty here on the sea independent of Jaffa and the Arabs and their *marins*" (TAMA, 7(6)/2a, 28/10/29 letter to Monsieur Grunblatt). Yet just as interesting, Dizengoff said, "[N]ow would not be a good time to throw into the debate and into the 'melee' a new cause of separation or discord, but because of the pressure of the population, including the members of the Municipality, I see an obligation to take up again the question and study it at first in the new circumstances that we have entered and to see perhaps if it is justifiably necessary to strike the iron while it is hot" (ibid.).

Further: "[T]he futility of the boycott movement is perhaps best illustrated in the case of Tel Aviv. In theory, the boycott movement should have reduced Tel Aviv, the center of Jewish industries, to the position of a beleaguered fortress economically isolated and cut off from its sources of existence. In fact, however, Tel Aviv seems far from being prejudicially affected. . . . The Jewish economic structure in Palestine is a largely independent unit which does not look for its income and profit to the local Palestinian Arab population, mainly formed of a backward rural element with a few primitive needs. The reverse is rather the case, and it is because of this that the anti-Jewish boycott is a weapon which the Arabs will discover to be double-edged" (M. Lehman, "Palestine in 1929: An Economic Analysis," in *Palestine & Near East*, 31/1/30, p. 7).

192. Kayyali, 1978, p. 173.

193. The demonstrators numbered about 3,000 Palestinian Arabs (including women), many of them armed with sticks, knives, and other weapons, and began at the office of the Muslim-Christian Association. It became violent as it moved up ʿAjami hill to the Suk el Salahi (PPCMECSAC, Faraday, 1/3(1), 25/10/33 Police Depositions for 27/10/33). The skirmishes injured numerous people; fifteen Palestinian Arabs were sentenced to prison for leading the demonstrations (for pictures of the protest and resulting violence, see *Falastin*, 12/11/33; for discussions and copies of the official investigations into the demonstrations, see *Falastin*, November and December 1933 and March 1934).

A reorganized Haganah, having learned from the 1921 and 1929 violence, set up five or six concentration points around the Hassan Bey mosque, which perhaps contributed to the lack of intercommunal violence in Manshiyyeh (HA, 122/26, Oral History of Yosef Carmin, 1960).

194. There were several articles in *Falastin* regarding the proposed National Assembly (cf. *Falastin*, 8/4/36, p. 1). The awarding of the concession raised fears of large-scale displacement of villagers.

195. At the mass funeral in Tel Aviv demonstrators tried to march on Jaffa, and in return, Palestinian Arabs tried to march on Tel Aviv after the district commissioner refused to grant them a permit to march in Jaffa. Fearing violence, middle-class Palestinian Arabs hastily formed local committees that they hoped could organize a nonviolent strike to channel the Palestinian Arabs' explosive anger. But the strike spread rapidly through the Palestinian towns, and a week later the heads of the political parties gave it their support, forming the Arab Higher Committee (Lesch, 1979, p. 217).

196. Lesch, 1979, pp. 120–24.

197. Many of the Jews attacked in the early days of the revolt in Jaffa were in or leaving government offices, working in Palestinian Arab establishments or for Palestinian Arab contractors, or even on the street in central Jaffa or the surrounding neighborhoods. Others were shot from orange groves (CZA, S25/4244, Chart 7).

198. *Falastin* and *al-Difaʿ* for June and July 1936 contain detailed descriptions of the demolitions and reactions from residents.

199. *al-Difaʿ*, 19/6/36, p. 4.

200. PPCMECSAC, J&EM, 66/2, letter to Archbishop of Canterbury from Archdeacon of Jaffa, 23/11/38.

201. *Falastin*, 27/7/36, p. 7.

202. As described in a 1939 letter from a British resident of Jaffa to the archdeacon there (PPCMECSAC, J&EM, LXVI/2, 16/11/39 letter).

203. One memorandum on Jaffa during this period explained, "It is correct to say that it was the best-behaved town in Palestine until trouble started in the Manshiyyeh quarter in June [1937] (on the provocation of Revisionist Jews). Things then settled down again until August, when reports were current of the presence of rebels who were levying taxes on the tradespeople. It was not until after the bomb of August 26 that the rebels really took charge" (PPCMECSAC, J&EM, LXVI/2, "Memorandum on the State of Jaffa").

In fact, Jaffa suffered so much from the strike of 1936 that "its main preoccupation since then has been to keep the work of the Port going so that it may get something to live on; its unwillingness to take part in the troubles which have been afflicting Palestine for the past year was shown by such good behavior up to the middle of June that the Jaffa–Tel Aviv police force was used as a reservoir from which to reinforce the police in other parts of the country, leaving insufficient here to deal with the trouble when it began" (PPCMECSAC, J&EM LXVI/2, 23/11/38 letter to Brigadier-General H. Wetherall from the British chaplain in Jaffa).

Yet at certain points during the revolt the city "was in the hands of the rebels," as rebels attacked the port, murdered officials, raided the municipality and shot patients in the Government Hospital—all the time the government could give the majority of the population no protection against the rebels (PRO, CO/733/372/18, District Commissioner's report to Chief Secretary, 8/10/38). The rebels went so far as to attempt to assassinate future Mayor Omar el-Beitar, as well as Deputy Mayor 'Ali el-Mustaqim, and two attempts were made to burn the house of Mayor Assam Bey El-Said and set up alternative "rebel courts" to which people were forcibly summoned while being warned not to go to the government courts. In addition, Jaffa's financial situation was so bad that the Municipal Council was formally warned to put its affairs in order or face "drastic steps" by the government, despite the latter's understanding of the difficulty the Jaffa Municipality faced collecting revenue during this period. As one report summarized it: "The Arabs will give no information as to who the rebels are or where they are to be found because they know that such action is tantamount to suicide as the Government can give them no protection. The Government can give them no protection until the Arabs give them the information which will enable them to lay hands on the rebels. As the Government can take no action to produce information as drastic as the rebels are taking to prevent it being given, it follows that the Government is playing a losing game and must adopt some other policy which will restore some confidence in their power to protect" (PPCMECSAC, J&EM, LXVI/2, "Memorandum on the State of Jaffa").

204. Ram, 1996, p. 338.

205. Ibid., p. 337.

206. There were conflicting accounts as to the role of the neighboring Palestinian Arab villages in the revolt. As one Haganah member recounted, "In the days of the 1936–39 disturbances, Tel Aviv was surrounded by an Arab environment, Jaffa and its orchards around it. And the Arab farms were hostile. On the border of Jaffa–Tel Aviv there was firing and arson fires, killings, sabo-

tage, etc., and I was sent to the Jaffa–Tel Aviv border and the end of Shabazi road that bordered with Arab Manshiyyeh with the Haganah, with legal and illegal weapons, and we, the Jewish guards, were responsible to these Haganah people. There were fires set in Manshiyyeh that did not spread to Tel Aviv, and shooting from Manshiyyeh into Tel Aviv" (HA, 180/21, Oral Interview with Moshe Nahmayas, 1960?). On the other hand, according to a Haganah report from 1941, Palestinian Arabs from Jamassin were "almost not at all active [in the revolt], apart from isolated firing on the street and on Ramat Gan," while Sheikh Muwannis was "almost not at all active," and Jerisha also "was not active." However, Summel and Jamassin el-Gharbi were somewhat active, firing in the night across to Tel Aviv. But Salama, Yazur and Beit Dajan, were used by the "bands" as crossing points because the "street passed between Jewish settlements and was a connection between the bands in the mountains and Jaffa" (HA, 105/200, Activities in Arab farms in 1936–39 revolt).

207. LA, IV/333/2/180, 28/12/36 letter to High Commissioner from representatives of Kiriyat 'Avoda, Agrobank, Green, and Beit Vegan quarters.

208. *Falastin*, 29/12, p. 5, "memo" titled "Government Land for Housing Arab Refugees of Jaffa!;" 13/1/37, p. 7. It also reported that the Jaffa Municipality decided to annex a huge tract of land from Salama and Yazur and thus the sands around Beit Vegan to Jaffa Municipality (*Falastin*, 1/11/36).

209. *Falastin*, 10/7/37, p. 1; 11/7/37, p. 2; 21/7/37, p. 2; 22/7/37, p. 2.

210. PRO, C.5854, "Palestine Partition Commission Report," 10/38, chap. 5, p. 40.

211. Ibid., p. 43.

212. Bhabha, 1994, p. 5. Also see Anzaldúa, 1999.

213. In a year end review of economic developments of 1929, *Palestine & Near East* magazine, a Zionist publication, celebrated "the character and nature of the economic processes taking place and of the results achieved in the restoration of a backward and primitive country to a new economic life. . . . [T]wo specific factors influence the trend of economic fluctuations in Palestine: the coexistence of an advanced and a primitive economic system and a continued immigration movement. In Palestine, side by side with a modern economic structure, there exists an economic system which is still largely based on primitive semifeudal conditions of a past age [and] still largely follows laws of development of its own. But the determining factor in the country's economic destinies is Jewish immigration" (*Palestine & Near East*, 31/1/30, p. 3).

214. Bhabha, 1994, pp. 25, 38; emphasis in original. Bhabha further writes that "so long as a firm boundary is maintained between the territories . . . aggressivity will be projected onto the Other or the Outside" (pp. 145, 149). Bhabha's analysis underscores the importance of border or frontier regions in destabilizing the very (national) identities they are meant to protect, and can fruitfully be combined with Lefebvre's analysis of "representations of space" versus "representational spaces"(see chap. 1) to begin the process of establishing an analytics of the simultaneous (de)construction of modern ethnonational identities.

215. CZA, A174/20, "The Possession of Land [is] the foundation of Pales-

tine politics," memorandum of the Nachlat Avoth of Palestine, Ltd., written in 1938.

216. LA, IV/250/72/1/3084b; TAMA, 3/101, 7/12/24 letter to Tel Aviv Municipality.

217. Thus the residents of the Brener neighborhood, while boasting that their "settlement of this area got rid of Arabs in favor of Tel Aviv," nevertheless spoke of the continual danger they faced living on the Jaffa–Tel Aviv border; as a consequence, they saw themselves "fulfill[ing] the function of 'pioneers' of Tel Aviv in this region" (TAMA, 4/2974, 4/7/33 letter to the Committee for Arranging the Interests of the Brener Neighborhood, signed by fifteen residents of the neighborhood). A similar sense of danger was felt by Jews living in other border regions of Tel Aviv and Jaffa or the surrounding villages (cf. TAMA, 4/1255, 4/1/34 letter from the Shchunat Histadrut Hashchanim to the Tel Aviv Town Council).

218. The report continued: "It must be remembered that in those days Sheikh Muwannis was 'very far.' The second border was in Neve Shalom, next to Jaffa. . . . We knew that any new disturbances would begin in Neve Shalom as it had in 1921 . . . [so we gathered] there whenever an outbreak of violence seemed likely, and members of the Haganah would gather around the borders to guard."

219. HA, 180.29, file on Haganah activities in Tel Aviv. The text continues: "If they did [live there] we attempted to guard it, or if [Jewish] children came out onto the streets to play we were obligated to guard it even though officially it was forbidden for us to enter the place. . . . We had many functions in this period. If there was a murder in Jaffa and it involved Jews from Tel Aviv, members of the Haganah would go arrest him, because for an Arab to come to Tel Aviv and arrest a Jew wouldn't be so simple and easy a thing." The Haganah became well organized in the mid-1920s as members stole guns from British officers and watched both Palestinian Arabs and the communists, "who were totally anti-Zionist." In fact, one of their functions was to make sure there was no Jewish-Jewish violence in Tel Aviv.

220. See note 206 above. In fact, a 1941 Haganah intelligence report lists 109 suspected members of Arab "gangs" in the Tel Aviv region: eight from Summel, ten from Sheikh Muwannis, five from Salama, and three from Jamassin (not specified whether East or West) (HA, 105/200, 26/6/41 list).

221. TAMA, 4/334b, 17/7/28 letter.

222. ISA, M/34/1 GP/3501.

223. PPCMECSAC, Faraday, 1/4, Report on criminal activities, 1932, p. 30.

224. TAMA, 3/79, letter from Dizengoff to Asst. District Commissioner, 27/7/25.

225. TAMA, 2/48a, 15/7/22 letter. I have not been able to determine the location of el-Karem. It was not a village in the Jaffa district and was likely just a vineyard on the northeastern outskirts of Jaffa–Tel Aviv, perhaps near the Wadi Masrawa/Ayalon, which was frequented by local Palestinian Arabs for recreational activities.

226. Bhabha, 1994, pp. 200–203. The mixed neighborhood of Manshiyyeh, in particular, Hassan Bey Mosque, was a central site of contention between the two communities and municipalities throughout the Mandate period, the starting point of larger incidences of violence as well as intense intermingling between the two communities. Thus when police in the Jaffa–Tel Aviv region heard about the outbreak of fighting in Jerusalem in 1929 they immediately took special precautions at the Jaffa–Tel Aviv boundary in Manshiyyeh (CZA, S25, 4606, file on 1929 riots).

It should be noted that the headquarters of the Marxists, or "mopsim," was located in Manshiyyeh, which for some time had been a mixed quarter both ethnically and economically; many of Jaffa's poorest residents lived there, but so too did the mayor and some of its wealthiest Palestinian Arab and Jewish citizens. The Hassan Bey Mosque was a central starting point for the violence, as was Neve Shalom (HA, 35.00001, Oral History of Uri Nadav; HA, 40.00023, Oral History of Elchas Steinberg). During the 1936–39 revolt in particular, groups of Palestinian Arab youths traveled through Manshiyyeh trying to prompt people to volunteer for local "guarding" duty, mirrored by clandestine Haganah patrols that focused on the quarter's winding streets and central mosque (cf. *Falastin,* 27/5/36, p. 5; 9/9/39, p. 3; 9/1/37, p. 6). In one incident, bombs exploded in a Jewish house in Manshiyyeh (*al-Dif 'a,* 1/7/36, p. 6).

227. In a comment on an early draft of the introduction and chapter 1, Dipesh Chakrabarty described this desire to erase and reinscribe the existing landscape as a "death wish" for the national Other that is the hallmark of the colonial moment (comment made as panel discussant at the conference "Uncertain State of Palestine: Futures of Research," University of Chicago, February 1999).

228. TAMA, 4/2237, letter dated 1/5/45 from Suliman Ibrahim Abu Eid Qatatwa. In another letter sent to the mayor of Tel Aviv, they wrote that "to have a mukhtar is so important for us that we hereby declare our readiness to refund to Government or any other authority any salary that will have to be paid to the new mukhtar by them" (ibid.).

229. It is important to understand how Tel Aviv saw itself vis-à-vis the surrounding region, especially near the end of the Mandate period. As a 1946 report of the Tel Aviv Harbour Commission explained, Tel Aviv "will soon have a quarter of a million inhabitants, [is] surrounded by a large and populous semi-urban district, situated on the seaboard, a town to which a very large part of the country's entire import trade is diverted, and a district from which the largest part of its export trade derives. . . . Its own district and Southern Palestine generally are its legitimate hinterland, and the fact is too patent to require any proof" (CZA Library, *Tel Aviv Harbour,* 1946, p. 16).

230. TAMA, 4/2237, 24/2/44 letter in Arabic to Tel Aviv Municipality from elders of Mas'udiyyeh village. For example, villagers slaughtered their sheep in Tel Aviv's slaughterhouse under municipal supervision (TAMA, 4.2237, 28/2/44 letter to Tel Aviv Mayor from District Food Controller). In one case, a petition from thirty notables of the village to the Tel Aviv Municipality asked

that the mukhtar of Summel be removed for not performing his job well (TAMA, 4/2237, 14/2/45 letter to the "qa'immaqam" of Tel Aviv from thirty Summel notables).

231. TAMA, 4/2237, letter dated 19/12/43 to Tel Aviv Municipality from Summel residents, in Hebrew, but with Arabic signature at bottom.

232. Glass and Kark, 1991, p. 117.

233. Biger, 1987b, p. 51.

234. Hamuda, 1985, p. 13.

235. Heykal, 1988, 112. Although, as Leila Nusseibah recalls, people from the different groups did not partake in the same activities: "The English swam, the Christians walked on the beach, and the Muslim women sat on the beach happily observing the activities" (Diyab, 1991, p. 163).

236. Diyab, 1991, p. 203; the cases of intermarriage were recounted to me by Tzvika Melnick, archivist of the Geography Department of Tel Aviv University, who conducted fieldwork in Manshiyyeh in the 1980s.

237. MHTA, Manshiyyeh File, 1946 clipping from *Davar Po'elet*, titled "Manshiyyeh's Refugees"; emphasis added.

238. If we are to believe this story: a Diaspora Palestinian Jaffan who was active in the underground during the 1930s and 1940s recounted in a memoir that after hiding in several Arab countries to avoid arrest for killing a British policeman in the 1940s he was able to have his record "cleaned" by paying off the British military governor of Jaffa with an expensive meal and two of the best prostitutes from the Akarakhaneh brothel on Dizengoff Street, with whose madam, Zohra, he was apparently on good terms (Husni Abu Eid, "Memoirs of a Rebel Arab Vagabond in Jaffa," in Anwar Abu Eishe's *Mémoires Palestiniennes: La terre dans la tête*, excerpt translated by Fawziyyeh Hammami and sent to author as part of Jaffa Email Group, 25/8/98).

239. HA, 180.29, "The Municipal Police in Tel Aviv." Apparently, taxi owners also worked with the women in these activities. *Falastin* reported on a "school of pickpockets in Tel Aviv—Arabs and Jews among its youthful students" (*Falastin*, 17/6/34, p. 8).

240. For example, Alfred Rock, who was a frequent business partner of Jews in Jaffa and Tel Aviv and sold a great deal of land to them, also played a part in the disturbances of 1933 and was active among Palestinian Arab youth in Jaffa; and Ibrahim el-Shanti, publisher of *al-Difa'*, is described by the government as "writ[ing] with a vitriolic pen and is constantly opposed to the Government," yet Zionist sources also describe him as being on their payroll (PPCMECSAC, Tegart file, 1/3b, Description of Arab and Jewish political parties). The Citrus Board also had its headquarters at Jaffa and had both Arab and Jewish representatives (cf. *Survey of Palestine*, vol. 1, pp. 336–42).

241. TAMA, 164/1, letter from L. M. Jeune to Dizengoff, 7/vi/22.

242. Shai Gelbatz, Kibbutz 'Ironi (Urban Kibbutz), pamphlet published in 1940 by the Kibbutz Ha'ironi Publishing House; document at the LA library. See esp. pp. 6–7, 13–14.

CHAPTER 5

1. Grant's book was awarded the 2000 Orange Prize for fiction.

2. Grant, 2000, inside dust cover flap.

3. Ibid., p. 70; original emphasis.

4. Ibid., pp. 70–72.

5. Ibid., p. 118; original emphasis. "Those days" were 1933.

6. Ibid.

7. This is one of the few descriptions of "Arabs" in the book.

8. Grant, 2000, p. 208; original emphasis.

9. Shehadeh, 2002, p. 3.

10. Ibid.

11. Ibid.

12. Ibid., p. 63.

13. Ibid., pp. 28, 64.

14. Shalom Esh, "Tel Aviv," *Yediot Tel Aviv* 3–4 (1936): 116.

15. Amos 9:14. Isaiah 58:12.7 reads: "And your ancient ruins shall be rebuilt; you shall raise up the foundations of many generations; you shall be called the repairer of the breach, the restorer of streets to dwell in." See also Ezekiel 36:10, 33.

16. Numerous critiques of the ideology and political and military calculations underlying Prime Minister Barak's attempts to force a "unilateral" separation with Palestinians can be found in *Ha'aretz*, September–December 2000.

17. TAMA, 4/3565, "City of the Jews," by L. V. Beltner, August 1941.

18. "The Real Issue," *Palestine & Near East*, 15/2/30, p. 1.

19. TAMA, 3/102, 4/ii/23 memorandum, "On the Importance of a Habour at Jaffa," presented to Mr. Palmer of the Palestine Government. Emphasis added.

20. The Revisionist movement was created in 1931 by Jabotinsky and others who had more militant views regarding the means if not ends of achieving Jewish sovereignty in Palestine than the more "pragmatic" Labor movement, with whose "socialism" they also disagreed because most adherents were bourgeois. The Likud and other right-wing Jewish Israeli parties are the ideological and political descendants of the party.

21. "The Meaning of Tel Aviv," *Palestine & Near East*, 1929, p. 110a.

22. Vardi, 1929, p. 6.

23. Agnon, 1957, p. 438. As one early resident described it, "I remember . . . the first impression I had of the houses of Tel Aviv . . . some scattered buildings in the sandy desert. Like packed suitcases stood the squares of houses, like baggage unloaded in a transit station, they were ready to be removed" (Abraham Sholonski, quoted in Yafeh, 1980, p. 40).

24. Meir Dizengoff, "Toward the Anniversary Exhibition of Tel Aviv," *Yediot Tel Aviv*, 1933, #10, p. 235. Even election-year poetry made sand a central image, as evidenced by the following "Song for the Elections in Tel Aviv":

"A strong city do we have—this is Tel Aviv. . . . In great sadness and in bitterness for us, within swaying and unsure steps, on plains of sand, in the desert of generations it arose and revived."

25. Tel Aviv is described as "how modern, how American!" in a 1949 book on the "future" of the Middle East (Hindus, 1949, p. 17). (In *Tel Aviv: City of Wonders*, Milton Gall also compares Tel Aviv to New York [document in TAMA library, p. 46].)

26. Meir Dizengoff, "Toward the Anniversary Exhibition of Tel Aviv," *Yediot Tel Aviv*, 1933, #10, p. 235.

27. Agnon, 1957, pp. 172, 121. The history and miracle of Tel Aviv "risen from the sands" was a prominent theme at the Palestine exhibition at the 1939–40 New York World's Fair. (Cf. Gelvin, n.d.)

28. Quoted in Yafeh, 1980, p. 44.

29. *Hapo'el Hatza'ir*, 3/11/33, p. 3. "It [wa]s difficult to understand how in such a little town, with so few people in it, there was so much sound" (Hacohen, 1985, p. 18).

30. Agnon, 1957, p. 448.

31. *Palestine Post*, 27/6/38, p. 6.

32. Agnon, 1957, p. 132.

33. Cf. Hacohen, 1985, pp. 22–23.

34. Rafael Klatzkin, "Tel Aviv on the Sands," in Hacohen, 1985, p. 31.

35. TAMA, 20/18, newspaper clippings file, "Tel Aviv," *Ha'aretz*, Purim, 1922.

36. Hacohen, 1985, p. 22. For an in-depth discussion of the image of sand in early Zionist literature, see Yekuti'eli-Cohen, 1990.

37. Quoted in Gorny, 1987, p. 140.

38. Uri Kisrei, " On the Sands of Tel Aviv," in Hacohen, 1985, p. 23; Uri Kisrei, "There on the Sands," in Hacohen, 1985, p. 22. "Before that, they came to a dune called the Hill of Love. . . . The dune was a lovely place on which to sit at night. The sand was dry and fragrant" (Agnon, 1995, p. 112). "Lie down slowly on the sands, lie down slowly on the soft bed" (lit. "platform") was how the poet David Shuonovitz described it in 1918 (Shmuonovitz, "On Jaffa's Beach," in Haretz and Rabin, 1980, pp. 7–11). See also the next poem, "With Jaffa's Sea," by Saul Tchernohovsky (pp. 12–13).

39. Levin Kipnis, "Song of the Camel," in Hacohen, 1985, p. 50.

40. Zalman Sheir, "In Tel Aviv," in Hacohen, 1985, p. 41.

41. Amnoel Harusi, "Himnon Tel Aviv," in Hacohen, 1985, p. 60.

42. Shmuonovitz, "On Jaffa's Beach." Another poem exclaims: "In Tel Aviv, This cute, loveable hill, with the fragrances of oranges and blossoms, We will realize a dream, Tel Aviv of peace, Here we'll build a wondrous nesting place" (Yosef Oksenberg, "Between Fruits of the Garden," in Hacohen, 1985, p. 39).

43. Cf. Shlomo Tanai, "On Dizengoff Street," or Asher Dayakh, "Agav Tiyul Le-yad Hayarkon," in Haretz and Rabin, 1982, pp. 45, 63.

44. Avot Yisharon, "Eresh Poem for Shchunat Nordiah," quoted in Berger, 1998, p. 143; emphasis added.

45. Avidgdor Hameiri, "Praise and Thanks to Tel Aviv," in Hacohen, 1985, p. 45.

46. As I briefly explain in chapter 2 and discuss in more detail in chapter 8.

47. Levin Kipnis, "Who Will Build?" in Hacohen, 1985, p. 65.

48. Including Haim Bialak, Shai Agnon, Ben-Tzion, and Abraham Sholonski.

49. Yafeh, 1980, pp. 22–23.

50. Agnon, 1957, pp. 42–43.

51. Ibid., p. 98.

52. Ibid., p. 180.

53. Ibid., pp. 411–12.

54. Agnon, 1995, p. 89.

55. Ibid., p. 94. Elsewhere, he describes "busy Jaffa" (p. 106). Again, "At night, when the town had gone to sleep, even sandy Jaffa . . . and its little houses stood soundlessly half-sunken in sand" (p. 106). As another character described Neve Tzedek: "Oh, look, the sun is going down. I've never seen anything so gorgeous. I wouldn't leave this place for the world. Happiness for me is going out to my backyard and seeing all the fig trees and dates. It's beyond me how Mrs. Ilonit goes around complaining all the time. Why, it's paradise here!" (p. 99).

56. Braveman, 1937, pp. 68–69. The book was written in English and thus was clearly intended to influence young Jews in the Diaspora about both Tel Aviv and the surrounding Palestinian Arab population.

57. Cf. Berger, 1998.

58. In Hebrew, *holekh venimhak* (Berger, 1998, p. 86). Thus when Barbara Mann explains that early Zionist-Jewish art in Palestine strove for "the creation of a new, 'native' Hebrew culture in Palestine," we must understand the creation of this "new native" as being dependent on the disappearance of the existing native population (Mann, 1999, p. 234).

59. Shabtai, 1985, p. 375.

60. Ibid., p. 358.

61. Ibid., pp. 243, 245. For Haim Gouri, Jaffa was also a symbol of plenty: "I go to Jaffa, to the melodies without end, and the great patience, to the vanilla ice cream and other delicacies" (Haim Gouri, *Hasefer Hamshuga' [The Crazy Book]*, quoted in Berger, 1998, p. 85).

62. Shabtai, 1985, pp. 268–69.

63. Directed by Renen Schorr, 1987, Blues Productions.

64. Amnon Raz-Krakotzin, "Cover to Cover: Tracing the Trail of History through Dizengoff Center," *Ha'aretz*, 2/9/98.

65. Ibid.

66. Cf. al-Dumaniki, 1928, p. 729. He further describes Jaffa as "beautiful" in myriad ways, "important" strategically, and very "fertile" (p. 833).

67. Al-Tamimi in particular played a leading part in opening a literary club in Jaffa, the Cultural Athletic Club, and publishing numerous articles and pamphlets throughout the period (Abu-Ghazaleh, 1973, p. 24).

68. Nimr, series on Jaffa's history in *al-Quds*, 12/8/97, 16/8/97, and 25/8/97, p. 23.

69. Cf. recollection of Dr. Akram al-Dajani, in Diyab, 1991, p. 152. And in fact there was an important link between cultural, sport, and military-nationalist activities, both actually and discursively (Diyab, 1991, Recollection of Abd ar-Rahman al-Habbab, p. 200). *Falastin*, 29/8/40, p. 1.

70. For an in-depth review of the politics of these newspapers (although curiously, *ad-Difa'* is missing from his analysis), see Khalidi, 1997, chap. 6.

71. Nimr, *al-Quds*, 12/8/97, 16/8/97, and 25/8/97, p. 23.

72. Cf. *Falastin*, 12/1/40, p. 3; 22/7/40, p. 2.

73. One article discussed at length an article by then former Mayor Dizengoff on the present state of Tel Aviv and his views on what needed to be done to develop Tel Aviv for the future, complete with statistics on the Jewish town's economy *(Falastin*, 7/8/26, p. 1). The relationship between Jews and the Haifa Municipality was also detailed (*Falastin*, 16/7/33, p. 3). Other articles reported on the movements of Jewish cooperative companies in the country, the majority of which were located in Jaffa and Tel Aviv (*Falastin*, 18/5/29, p. 1), and a special "Notes on Jaffa and Tel Aviv" section featured statistics comparing the port and railways of the two cities (cf. *Falastin*, 26/7/28, p. 1). They were quite worried about the decision to move the railway from Lydda to Tel Aviv (*Falastin*, 18/1/28, p. 1).

74. Cf. *al-Jam'iah al-Islamiyyah*, 25/12/32, p. 8.

75. *Falastin*, 13/3/29, p. 1; TAMA, 3/145, *al-'Umran*, undated, p. 605.

76. "The presence of ten thousand Jews in Jaffa is cutting Jaffa Municipality off from us and from our workers" (*Falastin*, 26/10/32, p. 9). Cf. *Falastin*, 7/7/31, p. 7. Also, cf. 31/5/34. p. 3.

77. *Falastin*, 5/9/29, p. 4.

78. *Falastin*, 20/7/30, p. 1. In particular, the Levant Fairs, international trade expositions sponsored by the British government and the Tel Aviv Municipality, were clearly understood by the Arab press as symbols of Tel Aviv's growing dominance and thus important vehicles of propaganda for the city and the Zionist movement as a whole. Thus the fairs received a great deal of coverage in the Arab press, which saw these exhibitions as directly linked to attempts by Jews to take over the country's economy (and Tel Aviv over Jaffa in particular). Thus papers such as *Falastin* and *ad-Difa'* urged people not to attend the fairs and criticized Arab countries such as Egypt for participating in them (cf. *Falastin*, 31/3/32, p. 7). In "Observation on the Tel Aviv Fair," from 1932, *Falastin* reported that the area of the fair was incredibly dirty, a situation made worse by the way the pavilions were constructed and its promenades built on sand, which made it very difficult to walk.

79. *Falastin*, 24/9/32, p. 6.

80. Ibid.

81. *Falastin*, 8/12/33, p. 7. To emphasize the point, demonstrations in Tel Aviv, especially violent ones, were often reported on (see, in particular, *Falastin* in late 1933 and early 1934, which featured numerous articles on the violent protests by Jews in Tel Aviv in December 1933).

82. "Mr. Dizengoff Goes on Doting," *Falastin,* 12/8/36, p. 3. This equation of Tel Aviv and communism, so inaccurate since Tel Aviv was in fact a bourgeois creation, returns to the late Ottoman period (see chap. 3).

83. Thus when the Arab National Conference was held in Tel Aviv in 1933 (for reasons not explained in the article), *al-Jam'iah al-Islamiyyah* labeled it "reckless," "scornful," and "contemptible" and saw it, in conjunction with the incidences of Arabs going to cafés or engaging in other activities in Tel Aviv, as "signing a contract of slavery and servitude to the Jews."

84. *al-Jami'a al-Islamiyyah,* 6/9/32, p. 2.

85. See Sufian, forthcoming.

86. This portrayal of Jewish women is quite significant in relation to Tel Aviv and to Dizengoff in particular; in fact, it is not far from the way Jewish Tel Avivan men imagined the prototypical Tel Aviv girl. One middle-aged native of Tel Aviv told me that the colloquial Hebrew verb *lehizdagef* was coined to describe the way girls would promenade up and down Dizengoff Street in front of young men.

87. The woman clearly represents the type of prostitutes that were, according to Salim Tamari, frequented by Palestinian Arab men coming from Jaffa.

88. See TAMA 4/3565, L. V. Beltner, "City of the Jews," August 1941.

89. Sufian, forthcoming, p. 2.

90. See, e.g., *Falastin,* 24/4/36, for a special photographic issue devoted to the rebellion (cf. Najjar, 1975, p. 138).

91. Cf. Najjar, 1975, p. 141.

92. Ibid., p. 163. Four out of the five newspapers that appeared during the revolt were in Jaffa (table, p. 211).

93. *al-Difa',* 18/10/36, p. 4.

94. *al-Difa',* 9/5/36, p. 1, "Jaffa and Tel Aviv."

95. Palestinian Arab writers treated Arab national issues somewhat different from other Arab writers because they saw it from the perspective of the threat posed by Zionism, and the flood of polemical tracts, booklets, articles, and essays published by Palestinian writers during the Mandate period provided ideological support to the armed resistance of other segments of the population (Abu-Ghazaleh, 1973, p. 39).

96. Sidqi, n.d.

97. As recounted in Abu-Ghazaleh, 1973, p. 62.

98. The story appears to be set in the 1920s, but the grandson of the author has informed me that it was written in the late Ottoman period, around 1913 (Dr. Izzat Darwazeh, e-mail comm., March 2000, citing information provided by his father, the author's son). There are no surviving copies that I was able to locate; my discussion is based on the detailed description in Abu-Ghazaleh, 1973.

99. Recounted in Abu-Ghazaleh, 1973, p. 63.

100. Heykal, 1988, p. 115.

101. Bardenstein, 1997.

102. Ibid., p. 7. See Ghassn Kanafani's *Ard al-Burtaqal al-Hazin (Land of Sand Oranges)* or Yusri al-Ayyubis's *Bustan al-Burtuqal (The Orange Orchard).*

103. Quoted in Slyomovics, 1998, p. xx.

104. Slyomovics, 1998, p. 1. One must exercise caution, however, not to use these self-consciously nationalist (and almost exclusively bourgeois) narratives—which often border on hagiography—uncritically in one's attempt to "rediscover" Palestinian historiography; the difficulty of this task is increased by the relative dearth of detailed Palestinian historical writing on Jaffa or other cities and villages.

105. Ibid., p. 7.

106. That is, a geography, or territory, of "representational spaces"—to return to Lefebvre's terminology.

107. This point was stressed to me by Dr. Andre Mazawi when we found the book at a Jaffa Festival in Amman, Jordan. Moreover, younger Palestinians in Jaffa also relate to the maps in this way and expressed great interest in having me send them copies of all the memoirs of former residents I have collected during my research, believing they are "very important to preserving the identity of the younger generation today" (interview with a young Arab Jaffan, November 1998).

108. Slyomovics, 1998, p. 9.

109. Kanaana and 'Abd al-Hadi, 1986.

110. Dirbas, 1993.

111. See chapter 8 below for the significance of this explicitly stated desire to "erase" Salama.

112. Thus the diary of one of the village leaders from 1947 tells of his being prevented from commencing a trip because of an important call from the Mufti of Jerusalem (Dirbas, 1998, photostat of Diaries of Sheikh of Sheikh Muwannis).

113. Heykal, 1993, pp. 82–85; Diyab, 1991, p. 14. For Hisham Shirabi, the city was a "new world" when he visited it as a child, standing for everything prohibited him in the "daily grind of school life," its "wonderful" food, sea, streets, and cinemas providing his first taste of freedom and adventure. Another former resident described her father's feelings about the city thus: "My father talked a lot about Jaffa. To him it was the most beautiful place on earth. He talked about its warm, clean shores where he swam every day with his friends. In Jaffa, he would say, 'There were plenty of fruits. We used to buy a full camel load of oranges and watermelons for only one shilling.' He liked being a student and a boy scout" (Tamari, Jaffa Email Group, 1996).

114. Malak, 1993, p. 43; Culture Committee of the Fund for a Free Jaffa, 1990, p. 15; al-Dajani, n.d., pp. 84–85. Hisham Shirabi, who wrote two memoirs of his youthful experiences in Jaffa, similarly explains that "there is not doubt that the social and cultural life [Jaffa] was more advanced that the other cities of Palestine" (see Diyab, 1991, esp. p. 16).

Emile al-Ghouri, a native of Jaffa, described his feelings on his return home from years of study abroad: "I was really delighted to return to Jaffa, and when I saw it from the sea, I found that it had grown and developed, and had grown much larger from the city I had left. . . . But I felt at that time that this defiant national citadel would not hesitate to meet the evil at the hand of the British and Jews" (al-Ghouri, 1972, p. 151). As interesting are his feelings on seeing the Old City, which for Europeans was the symbol of backwardness and decay: "And the Old City of Jaffa, on the sea, came into view, and it looked just like a high mountain, its houses and inhabitants lost in it and in the sea and its power. . . . As we approached the port . . . my eyes filled with tears of joy because [it] was still alive" (ibid.).

115. The books were self-published in Jerusalem in 1993 and 1996. In other books Jaffa is described as being the target historically of numerous invasions because of its important strategic location, which led to its large press and political consciousness (cf. Culture Committee of the Fund for a Free Jaffa, 1990, p. 21). It is also described as the center of many of the major revolts during the Mandate period, with special emphasis on the violence in and around the Old City in 1933 and 1936, as well as the battle for Manshiyyeh in 1948, where the role of the "terrorist" Irgun is highlighted (p. 25; al-Dajani, n.d., pp. 172–73).

116. Malak, 1996, p. 9.

117. The following excerpt from a dialogue between a father and son (the former raised in Jaffa, the latter living his whole life in Gaza, to where the father fled in 1948), contained in a documentary on the conquest of Jaffa by Jews in 1948, highlights the difficulty of maintaining the attachment to one's native soil through even one generation:

Son: "Yafa, Yafa, Yafa. . . . Do you remember what my grandmother, your mother, gave to me? The key to our house. You know what I did after the peace agreement? I threw the key away."

Father: "However many years pass, our life will always be bound up with our country, Palestine."

Son: "I kept the key for 35 to 40 years, but I don't have it anymore because the house doesn't exist. It's like hanging on to something that doesn't exist. It's gone; finished."

Father: "But the key is like part of your own body. It will always be that way so that one day you can go back."

Son: "If they rebuild Jaffa for you here in Gaza, if they reconstructed the mosques, buildings, streets and houses, How would you feel then?"

Father: "Listen, what is the point of drawing a map of Palestine so that I can hang it on my wall here when my whole life and every breath I take is bound up with Jaffa? I don't even want to go back and reclaim my house. Let me go to where my houses once was, that place so dear to my heart . . ."

Son: "What you are telling me gives me no hope for the future; either to stay and prosper here or to go back to Jaffa . . ."

Father: "On Judgment Day, if I am brought before God and given the choice of either going to Heaven or returning to my home town, I'd choose to go and live in Jaffa. I shall leave God's Heaven and say, 'Please let me go live in Jaffa because it's my home town.' Life isn't about eating and drinking, it's about one's peace of mind." (*Going Home*, directed by Omar al-Qattan, Med-Media Programs of the E.C. et al., 1995).

We can see how the father and son, the two generations, are talking past each other, in fact are talking about two different times and spaces even as they both talk about Jaffa.

118. In 1997 there was an interesting, sometimes angry and hostile exchange of e-mails on the Jaffa Email Group in which the issue of why so many of the city's bourgeoisie left Jaffa when their lives were not in imminent danger was hotly debated.

119. Badarna, 1997, p. 56.

120. Ibid., p. 13.

121. As one Palestinian described his return to Jaffa, his desire to chart the landmarks of his childhood was frustrated after running into a tourist guide narrating an alien history of the city to a group of tourists. He saw through the listeners eyes the "cute reconstructions" of Old Jaffa that erased any trace of its formerly vibrant Arab character and "plastered" over this site of his romantic longings into art galleries, discos, expensive restaurants, and the like. "No tourist or Israeli my age could ever guess that thirty-five years ago this was the vibrant, flourishing Arab center of Palestine. No trace of it is left" (Shehadeh, 1982, pp. 20–23; cf. Swedenburg, 1995, p. 71).

122. Cf. Culture Committee of the Fund for a Free Jaffa, 1990, p. 14.

123. Heykal, 1988, p. 69.

124. Ibid., p. 181.

125. al-Ghouri, 1972, p. 151.

126. Heykal, 1988, p. 216.

127. Cf. al-Dajani, n.d.

128. Cf. Gharbiyah, 1975(?), pp. 65–79.

129. See Y. al-Dajani, 1991.

130. Abbas Nimr, "Jaffa . . . The Eternal Longing," *al-Quds*, 17/5/97, no page number on offprint.

131. Nimr, *al-Quds*, 22/5/97, no page number on offprint.

132. Nimr, *al-Quds*, 12/7/97, no page number on offprint.

133. Nimr, *al-Quds*, 7/7/97, p. 16. He explains that Hong Kong was returned to China because China would have otherwise taken it over by force. Regarding its encirclement by Jewish towns, Nimr says that Jaffa was not given the name "Jaffa the Great" (Yaffa al-kabira), as were cities like Cairo or Amman, because although it was "the most beautiful city on the shore of Palestine," its biggest commercial city, and an important port and transit point to other cities, they were able to "stunt its area," even as they were unable to succeed in thwarting its economic and cultural development (Nimr, *al-Quds*, 27/9/97, p. 21).

134. Thus when one enters the office of one of the local community organizations one is greeted by a Palestinian flag and framed letter of thanks from Yasser Arafat on the wall, along with paintings of scenes of Palestinian defiance

against Israel. The 1997 Jaffa Festival cosponsored one of the local organizations and the Diaspora Jaffan community of Amman was imbued with Palestinian national symbolism, as it opened with the singing of the national anthem and included many nationalist songs (e.g. "Muntasib al-Qama Amshi" and "'Inni Akhtaratik Ya Watan") and descriptions of Jaffa as being eternally part of Palestine. This was followed by the showing of a recently discovered film of the earliest footage of the city, featuring scenes from Jaffa Port in about 1896, with narration explaining that the variety of peoples, dress, and activity demonstrated Jaffa's modernity and progress at that time. Afterward, old pictures of the destroyed Manshiyyeh quarter were shown, a play was performed about contemporary life in Jaffa by Jaffan playwright Gabi 'Abed, and several nationalist songs were sung at the close of the festival. See chapter 8 for a more detailed discussion of these issues.

135. Cf. Diyab, 1991, pp. 147, 155. According to Nizzam Sharabi, "Most of the residents of the Palestinian cities came to Jaffa to swim [in the sea], to sit in the cafes close to the sea" (p. 219).

136. *Falastin*, 8/xii/46, p. 3; HA, 105/311, Arabic newspaper clippings file on Jaffa, 1945, "The Great Poetry Festival in Jaffa."

137. Cf. al-Ayubi, 1990.

138. "Son of Palestine," in al-Dajani, n.d., p. 213.

139. Ibid.

140. Cf. Walid al-Hilias, "Yafa of the Martyrs," in al-Dajani, n.d., p. 214.

141. Ishkantana, 1964, pp. 3–4.

142. More recently, the poem "The Psalm of Isaiah's Grandchildren," asks: Arise today/Go up and cry in the streets of Tel Aviv/A Thousand woes to him/Who does not seek the Lord/A thousand sorrows to him/Who goes into Egypt/Bringing the cross to the East (Arurui and Ghareeb, 1970, p. 22; author's name not given).

143. No author given, in Fund for a Free Jaffa in Kuwait, 1990, p. 27. The poem continues: "Jaffa Oh Jaffa/By god we will return to you with our weapons/Free in death or living free/Our power is our faith in our return, mighty with a burning like fire/Pushing the torch on our way, tomorrow millions of free men are coming/Jaffa Oh Jaffa." Also see Kamel Nassir, in al-Dajani, n.d., p. 216. Mahmud Darwish similarly summarized the feeling of longing: I make pilgrimage to you oh Jaffa/you are to me a wedding of an orchard *(ma 'i 'aras bayyarah)*/Calling it from the port. . . . From the port Calling her/Pulling me and pulling her/to the strings of a guitar/Commemorating the gathering of the neighborhood/and the longing of the heart for the Henna (of marriage) (Fund for a Free Jaffa in Kuwait, 1990, p. 28; also featured in Gharbiyyah, 1975(?), p. 10).

144. Ibid.

145. Khoury, 1997, p. 29.

146. Quoted in al-Dajani, n.d., p. 216.

147. From a poem by Mahmud Salim al-Hawt, title not given, in al-Dajani, n.d., pp. 212–13.

148. From the album *Nejma al-'Arab al-Awali*. Lyrics in Badarna, 1997, pp. 11–12.

149. Two Jewish companies, one government and one private, that were contracted to "develop" the Arab neighborhoods of Jaffa.

150. See chap. 8, fig. 13.

CHAPTER 6

1. *New York Times*, 26/4/98, Week in Review, p. 14.

2. UNESCO, 2003, p. 61.

3. As opposed to the "romantic but fading memory" of the kibbutzim, as the editorial described a few paragraphs later.

4. Herzl, [1896] 1988, p. 108.

5. UNESCO, 2003, pp. 57–58.

6. Nitzan-Shiftan, 1996, p. 154. According to the *Architectural Record* soon after Tel Aviv was founded, "The character of the city is most evident when seen through the medium of its color, but it is also seen through its texture and its form. The buildings and the outline of the streets, to be a fit complement to modern city life, should be regarded in the first place as a background and a foil. In their form and outline they should be simple and strongly composed. Their surface should be hard and their enrichments delicate to a degree. . . . The characteristics of a city expressed in its color, its texture, and its form, reflect on the citizen himself" (*Architectural Record*, August 1910, p. 142.)

7. *Architectural Record*, November 1911, p. 506.

8. Georges Bataille, "Architecture," in Hollier, 1993, p. 45.

9. Rabinow, 1989, p. 289. Thus the Jewish Organization of Engineers, Architects and Surveyors in Palestine would say, "Until today we have not worked in politics" (Labor Archives, IV-421–67. Press Release dated 10/41).

10. Wright, 1991, p. 8.

11. In fact, Hegel attributed the beginning of art, which is the object of aesthetics, to architecture (Hollier, 1993, p. 4).

12. *Architectural Record*, excerpts from London Town Planning Conference, December 1910, pp. 456–57. The speaker continued: "Cities are not only made but grow. . . . The growth is conditioned not only by physical but by human environment, and is closely dependent on history. To wipe out that history's evidence may be to take away more than the town planner can give."

13. Hollier, 1993, p. 3.

14. TAMA, 2/81a.

15. A typical example of the use of Gutman's drawing is in the town gazette in 1944 in which the caption "Tel Aviv in its first years" was written over the now-famous drawing of the guardian angel presiding over a sea of sand (*Yediot Tel Aviv*, August 1944, #3–4, p. 40). More than half a century later, the great Zionist Bauhaus architect Arieh Sharon would use this very picture to illustrate the chapter on Tel Aviv in his *Kibbutz + Bauhaus* (Sharon, 1976, p. 50). He began the chapter with the words "the planning and architectural panorama of Tel Aviv, the town built on sand dunes" (p. 45).

16. Gutman, 1989. A similarly sandy landscape is offered in Reuven Rubin's famous 1922 painting, *Tel Aviv*.

17. A more accurate portrait of the Tel Avivan landscape can be seen in the work of Tel Aviv–Jaffa artist Tsionna Tagger's 1924 *The Railway Crossing on Herzl Street*, which is perhaps due to the fact that she grew up on Rothschild Street, in a house that was bordered on one side by vineyards and on the other by dunes (cf. Mann, 1999, pp. 235–37).

18. Cf. Carmiel, 1987.

19. Not surprisingly, then, the official history of Tel Aviv describes its creation as "just a 'reed' stuck into a sea of sand," or more elaborately, "from the south of Jaffa we see the wide region of sand, from the north, Tel Aviv, and after . . . again sand" (Droyanov et al., 1935, pp. 149, 270). That there was a huge village, Shaykh Muwannis, and bedouin lands, both directly north of the 'Auja river, is ignored. Interestingly, this metaphor was not always understood positively. Thus Revusky writes that "the criticism was often heard that Tel Aviv was 'built on sand,' that it had no solid economic foundations, that its occupational structure was top-heavy and white-collar men would prove very dangerous in case of economic adversity" (Revusky, 1945, p. 113).

20. Meroz, 1978, p. 38.

21. Kark, 1990a, pp. 110–11.

22. Thus while Neve Tzedek possessed some of the broadest streets and most beautiful homes in Jaffa (Kark, 1990a, p. 114), it could not serve as a model for Tel Aviv because the founding of Tel Aviv had to be a "revolutionary event," in which would be revealed the urban Jewish *yishuv* for the first time. Its national and cultural independence would be demonstrated in the form of its houses and the character of its streets. In fact, the Arab landlords built special houses for Jews with the specific goal of maximizing profit, not a healthy deployment or distribution of space and form. But these were not the houses in which the middle and upper classes of Jaffa lived. However, the chroniclers of the new Jewish town did not draw this distinction between the way Arab landlords built housing for Jews and the way many Arabs lived in the relatively wealthy town of Jaffa (it is similar to assuming that turn-of-the-century New York or London slumlords lived like their immigrant tenants).

23. Tel Aviv Municipality, 1967, pp. 5–7; Kark, 1990a, p. 114.

24. Arlik, 1980, p. 214.

25. Droyanov et al., 1935, p. 63.

26. "The Influence of European Architectural Styles on the Vision of Construction in the Founding of Tel Aviv at the Turn of the Century," located at the TAMA Library, 14–138, p. 20.

27. Arlik, 1980, p. 218. He continues, "The houses were built with too limited means, cheap materials, without plan. The builders were masons—Arab contractors—while at least some Arab houses paid tribute to Islamic architectural tradition, there was nothing in the Jewish houses . . . the old Jewish yishuv, like the Arab population, lived in the remnants of the old. The new was inferior in quantity and quality."

28. Smilansky, quoted in Kark, 1990a, p. 116. In a sense, Jerusalem was the

galut for the predominantly "modern" secular culture forming in Tel Aviv, a situation reversed today in that the dominant religious-nationalist Zionism of the post-1967 era looks at "left-wing and secular" Tel Aviv as the antithesis of "religious and nationalist" Jerusalem (*New York Times,* 30/4/98, p. A19).

29. Quoted in Meroz, 1978, p. 35. When writing to the Head Office in 1907 to request money to build Ahuzat Bayit, Arthur Ruppin, head of the Jewish National Fund office in Jaffa, similarly considered it "extremely important that there be a Jewish quarter both in Jaffa and Jerusalem which will stand in comparison with the quarters of other nations and, in regard to hygiene, will not suffer from the short-comings of the present Jewish quarters in these towns (Ruppin, 1971, p. 121; cf. Donovitz, 1959, pp. 10, 13). Moreover, as Ahuzat Bayit member Akkiba Weiss described it, replying to Meir Dizengoff's claim that the neighborhood could still be constructed with less money than originally planned, "We don't want to build a new Neve Shalom [Another Jaffan Jewish neighborhood, founded in 1890] with all the sickness and filth" (TAMA: Protocols of Ahuzat Bayit, 1908, p. 42).

30. CZA, L51/71, Bylaws of the Nahalat Binyamin society; quoted in Kark, 1990a, p. 121.

31. Katz, 1986, p. 405.

32. Thus the leaders of Tel Aviv would often speak of even the Jewish neighborhoods of Jaffa as being *galut* (cf. CZA S25/5936, meeting 16/5/40; although the title of the protocol says ". . . Jewish neighborhoods within the borders of *Tel Aviv,*" that is clearly a mistake).

33. TAMA, Protocols of Ahuzat Bayit, 1908, p. 21.

34. Quoted in Droyanov et al., 1935, p. 77. Elsewhere the verb used by Ruppin is given as *to rule over* Jaffa's economy ("The Foundation of Tel Aviv," in Aricha, 1969, p. 38).

35. Dizengoff, 1931, pp. 6–7.

36. Dizengoff, quoted in Troen, 1991, p. 23.

37. CZA, S25/665, 6/12/23; emphasis added.

38. The passage of which gave French planners the sense that their country "was falling dangerously behind" even England's late start (Rabinow, 1989, p. 267). There were also several major conferences on town planning and architecture that year in the United States and Europe, including one held at Columbia University in New York. The "Notes and Comments" section of each issue of *Architectural Record* lists these publications and conferences.

39. *Architectural Record,* June 1909, Notes and Comments, on lecture by N. P. Lewis on city planning, p. 449. Just as interesting, if we examine the discussions and debates in the *Architectural Record* during the period 1909–11, it is clear that however much planning was on the agenda in Europe the reality was that the "laissez faire method of town building had proved in the last half century both its hideousness and its wastefulness," which necessitated "greater organized control in architecture as well as street planning" (*Architectural Record,* December 1910, excerpts from London Town Planning Conference, pp. 456–57). Even in England there "was not a single really decent example of how a town should be planned" (*Architectural Record,* September 1909, pp. 77–78).

German planning, which exerted great influence on urban development and architecture in Tel Aviv and Palestine as a whole, was similarly based on the belief that "the sense of a new cultural standard could not be developed in the old city because the cultural social system, with its traditional values, precluded the opportunity to attempt change in a comprehensive framework" (Mullin, 1982a, pp. 117, 125).

40. Mullin 1982a, p. 118.

41. Troen, 1991, p. 10.

42. Ibid., pp. 10–11.

43. *Architectural Record*, December 1910, p. 458; emphasis added.

44. *Architectural Record*, November 1911, p. 509; Prochaska, 1990, pp. 207–9. His vantage point, that of a late-twentieth-century urban historian, is of course quite distinct from that of the planners his study of Bone interrogated, and his "reading" of the city includes its physical scale and social distance as countervailing factors (i.e., residential and social segregation, the way Europeans speak to Arabs with *tu* instead of *vouz* or call them all "Ahmed"). Yet the need to "read" the city has not changed.

45. See, e.g., Levin, 1984; Smok, 1994.

46. That is, while both Zionist architecture and the larger discourse of Zionism were ultimately reduced to an official, teleological, and modernist understanding of modern architecture, the reality was that well into the 1930s Zionism and Zionist architecture remained "plural movements still debating their eventual forms" (Nitzan-Shiftan, 1996, p. 147). My methodology avoids falling into the paradigm, still accepted by many Israeli writers on this topic, that in attempting to create a new autochthonous "Hebrew" style the early Zionist architects "created something from nothing" (Harlap, 1982, p. 42). Harlap describes the process this way because "it must be remembered that unlike other colonists, who drew upon the architectural heritage of the mother country, the Jewish settlers in Palestine had no real architectural tradition that they could call their own," or that the hybrid "eclectic style" that dominated architecture in the 1920s was, because of its hybridity, an "artificial style that imposed old forms on new ways of life" and thus "was inevitably doomed to die out and give way to the emerging modern style" (p. 46).

47. Howard is considered one of the "titular figures" of modern urbanism. His most important work was *Garden Cities of Tomorrow*, published in 1902, which is often referred to as founding modern city planning (Rabinow, 1989, p. 257).

48. Herbert and Sosnovsky, 1993, p. 60.

49. Ibid., p. 63. For an in-depth discussion of the Garden City idea in Germany, see Hall, 1988, chap. 4. One of which certainly was the local Arab population, which by definition was not included in the "new spatial and social arrangements" (Rabinow, 1989, p. 212) heralded by the Garden City movement as the best method to solve urban problems.

50. For a good description of the problems facing European cities during this period, see Hall, 1988, chap. 2.

51. Droyanov et al., 1935, p. 301.

52. Ibid., p. 156. According to Katz, the Zionist leadership felt that the creation of airy and clean Jewish suburbs next to the cities was the best way to settle new immigrants (Katz 1984, p. 109). Ahuzat Bayit and Tel Aviv became the model for the desire to create numerous such suburbs or towns in the first decade and a half of the twentieth century, including in Haifa, Safed, Jerusalem, Petakh Tikvah, Rishon Letzion, and even near Gaza.

53. Kark, 1990a, pp. 107–8.

54. Katz, 1994, pp. 281, 289. As Biger points out, the Garden City paradigm combined the idea of having "gardens" in each plot of land with two other characteristics of any residential suburb—a measure of separation from the city center and a degree of dependence on it (Biger, 1986, p. 4).

55. As Katz points out, contemporary sources did not fail to remark the great success of the Garden Suburb as against the Garden City (Katz, 1986, p. 407). While Howard saw his garden city as being small-scale manufacturing centers, the members of Ahuzat Bayit decreed in their original bylaws that no stores could be built in the neighborhood so as to maintain its pristine quality (TAMA, 1/4). For an in-depth rehearsal of the debates over allowing stores in the neighborhood, see Shchori, 1990, p. 50. All the land would either be publicly owned or under the control of the building society that initiated the project.

Howard, like all radicals, believed that the "land question"—the concentration of the ownership of land in Great Britain in the hands of a few—was the "root of all our problems." Thus he wanted to extend powers to the Garden City Company as the sole landlord, thereby affording greater public ownership and control of land (Fishman, 1994, pp. 40, 47, 49). Between 1889 and 1892 Howard created the basis for his ideal community: "a garden city as a tightly organized urban center for 30,000 people surrounded by perpetual 'green belt' of farms and parks. . . . [T]hey weren't supposed to be satellite towns for a great metropolis but rather he foresaw the great cities of his time shrinking to insignificance" (p. 40).

56. For an in-depth discussion of the debate surrounding the planning of the neighborhood, including pictures of several of the plans, see Droyanov et al., 1935, pp. 102–8.

57. TAMA, Protocols of Tel Aviv Town Council, 1920, p. 4, emphasis added; bylaws of Nahalat Binyamin Society, CZA, L51/71. From this description it is clear how one can consider the development of Tel Aviv and its effects on Jaffa from a Foucauldian understanding of the sociopolitical and spatial effects, that is, power, of the modernist discourses surrounding Tel Aviv.

58. TAMA, Protocols of Ahuzat Bayit, April 6, 1907.

59. Cf. Hall, 1988, p. 93.

60. CZA, L18/105/4, L51/52, L2/578; TAMA, Protocols of Ahuzat Bayit, June 6 and July 31, 1907. Apparently, as Katz points out (1993, p. 284), in purchasing the land at Karm al-Jabali the members of Ahuzat Bayit felt that they were "beyond the city limits of Jaffa." The Jaffan authorities, not surprisingly, considered the area within their jurisdiction.

61. A discussion of the houses built during the first years of Tel Aviv, and the two types of architecture—"Arabic-Yafo" style and "European"—can be found in Arlik, 1987b, p. 9. The houses in Ahuzat Bayit were distinguished from those in Neve Tzedek and Neve Shalom not only by having gardens and by being separated from one another but also by the regulation that only a specific percentage of the land could be built on.

62. It is interesting to note the envy also felt by Jews for the "castles and palaces" built by Jaffa's wealthier Arab residents on the city's "more attractive streets" (1906 description in Kark, 1990a, p. 128); Ruppin, looking back fifty years, lamented the "monstrous" houses that were built due to lack of funds, which led to the use of cement and a lack of detailed architectural plans for many of the original houses (Ruppin, "The Foundation of Tel Aviv," in Aricha, 1969, p. 40.)

63. Arlik, 1987, p. 9.

64. Cf. Jacobs, [1961] 1993, pp. 23–26.

65. Quoted in Meroz, 1978, p. 48.

66. Arlik, 1980, p. 219.

67. Ibid.

68. A similar design can be seen in the Technion Building in Haifa, also built around 1910.

69. Abercrombie, quoted in Herbert and Sosnovsky, 1993, p. 189.

70. TAMA, 1/283, Protocol of Tel Aviv Council, 2/4/21.

71. LeVine, 1995, 1998; Smith, 1993.

72. The rapid growth of the town had led to annulling the ban on stores and business by World War I.

73. Cf. Gorny, 1984. Gorny describes three types of utopianism at work in Palestine in this period: comprehensive national utopianism, socialistic, class-oriented utopianism, and kibbutz utopianism (p. 23).

74. As Prochaska explains, settler colonialism is a discrete form of colonialism that is distinguished from other varieties. Whereas in the majority of colonial situations there are two primary groups involved—temporary migrants from the colonizing country, administrators, military, merchants, traders, missionaries—and the indigenous people, in settler colonies the settlers constitute a third group. It is not simply the existence of settlers that makes a difference but rather the implications and consequences of their presence that is significant. It follows from the very manner in which a settler society is formed that stratification is based more on race and ethnicity than on socioeconomic class (Prochaska, 1990, pp. 9–10; cf. Shafir, 1989).

75. Arlik, 1987, 115.

76. Nathan Harpaz, 'Ir 'Ivrit—Adricalut 'Ivrit," article found at TAMA, pp. 279, 281.

77. Levin, 1982, p. 233.

78. Epitomized by personalities such as Martin Buber and groups such as Brit Shalom (Covenant of Peace).

79. TAMA library, article by Harlap, title page missing, p. 45. During this period, Zionist architects such as Alexander Baerwald attempted to use classical and Islamic architecture as a "legitimate" combination and adaptable for the countries that would be new and up to date from the technical aspect of construction while remaining close to the Islamic styles of the country. Baerwald also studied the inner workings of Arab and Mediterranean architecture in order fully to understand the forces affecting its shapes and forms.

As Michael Levin points out, there were two "eclectic" styles operating in Palestine in the 1920s—one motivated by a sincere desire "to create architecture based on a profound understanding of the Eastern world view, its system of proportions and formal vocabulary with an almost archaeological fidelity to the sources"; and another, freer use of indigenous forms as "ornamentations" on top of fundamentally European designs, "with positive and negative results" (Aba Elhanani, "The Founding Architects," in *Et-Mol*, June 1994, p. 6).

80. Arlik, 1987, 116.

81. Cf. Troen, 1991, p. 18. This simulation of the indigenous architecture would seem to involve an epistemological operation similar to that described by Timothy Mitchell when Europeans constructed the Middle Eastern exhibitions at the great world exhibitions of the late nineteenth century; that is, the construction of a "peculiar distinction between the simulated and the real" (Mitchell, 1988, p. 7). In fact, the eclectic architecture of the 1920s in Palestine was similar to the colonial architecture of Morocco, a style termed "Arabisances," which mixed functional and romantic motifs that followed "modern" guidelines for sanitation and new construction without foreclosing any of the regional adaptations to climate, such as terraces and courtyards. In this way, European architects "freely adapted" local designs (cf. Wright, 1991, p. 108). Moreover, French architects attempted to define a "Mediterranean" architecture that focused on the shared aspects of the "Oriental" and the "Occidental" (cf. Celik, 1997, pp. 102, 115).

82. Jabotinsky Archives [JA], G10/B17, 1/30 Bulletin of the Tel Aviv Chapter of the Revisionist Movement.

83. *Hatzafon*, 23/4/26, p. 3.

84. *Hatzafon*, 14/5/26, p. 3. This war extended, it should be noted, to the surrounding Arab farms, whose dominance of the agricultural sector around Tel Aviv also presented a dire threat to the *yishuv* (ibid). Because of this feeling, in their electoral platforms the Revisionists (and it should be noted that Mayor Dizengoff, though not himself a Revisionist, often ran on the Revisionist-aligned ticket) demanded that the government both give the city all the government land within its border and institute a Jewish-only labor policy in "the city and its surroundings"—that is, the surrounding Arab farms and ultimately even Jaffa (Jabotinsky Archives, Collection of campaign propaganda for Municipal Elections, 12/3/26). The link between Jewish-only labor practices and the desire for spatial segregation, and thus between spatial and ideological boundaries, is clear.

85. The fighting broke out in response to an argument over the Jews instituting new religious practices at the Western Wall in Jerusalem that disturbed

the agreed on religious status quo there. In fact, it was a spatial argument, that is, over their erecting a spatial separation between men and women praying there. For similar discussions, see the accounts of French colonialism in North Africa by Wright, 1991; Abu-Lughod, 1980; Rabinow, 1989.

86. Arlik, 1987, p. 11; Zalmona, 1998, p. xii.

87. By this I mean that the 1929 violence and the many official investigations it prompted (such as the Shaw Commission and the Passfield White Paper of 1930 and the Hope-Simpson and French reports of 1931) constituted the first real threat to British support for Zionist policies in the country (cf. LeVine, 1995).

88. *Mishar ve-Te'asia*, #3–4, TAMA, 4/3563, n.d., p. 100. Similarly, Arieh Sharon says of his return to Tel Aviv after studying at the Bauhaus, "I was very depressed by the architecture" (Sharon, 1976, p. 46); and Dizengoff lamented the "unsuitability of earlier buildings to the conditions of the place and the goals for which they were built" ("The Question of Housing in Tel Aviv," *Yediot Tel Aviv*, 1937, #6, p. 178).

89. TAMA, 4/3563, article in *Mishar ve-Te'asia*, #3–4, year not specified, p. 99; see also TAMA 3/146. In an article in the *South African Jewish Chronicle* dated June 30, 1933, Marcia Gitlin describes the same feeling.

90. TAMA, 4/3563, article in *Mishar ve-Te'asia*, #3–4, year not specified, p. 103.

91. There was intense opposition to the Bauhaus and much of the rest of International Style architecture in Germany, which had become so prominent in the 1920s, by conservative thinkers and architects, in particular the Nazis, who accused it of being culturally "decadent," "materialistic," "nomadic," "Jewish," and "Bolshevik" in its aims—"the cathedral of Marxism . . . a cathedral, however, which damned well looked like a Synagogue" (quoted in Lane, 1968, p. 162; also see pp. 139, 147–49, 164–67).

92. Sharon, 1976, pp. 47–48; cf. Graicer, 1982, 1990.

93. Nitzan-Shiftan, 1996, p. 151; cf. Monk, 1997, p. 96.

94. Quoted in LeVine, 1995, p. 105.

95. Levin, 1984, p. 31. In fact, there was an "urban kibbutz" movement that ultimately saw the creation of a kibbutz in the northeast frontier area of Tel Aviv, where it was surrounded by "hostile Arab villages" (presumably Jerisha, Jammasin, Summel) and citrus groves on land of what is today Ramat Gan (cf. Yahav, 1994). However, this kibbutz did not have the funds to deploy a sophisticated International Style architecture when it was founded in 1947, and it was dissolved by 1951.

96. Quoted in Levin, 1984, p. 36. He continued, "This is why I am so strongly attached to it, trying to achieve a union between Prussianism and the life cycle of the Muezzin. Between anti-nature and harmony with nature." This "attachment" to the "East" distinguished Mendelsohn from most of his Jewish colleagues, yet the perceived dichotomization and hierarchization between the two cultures remained central to both variations of Zionist International Style architecture.

97. There was such a "fear of growing old" that the city went through sev-

eral cycles of destruction of monumental buildings that were themselves symbols of its "modernity" when they were built only years before (Gered and Zilberman, 1989). These include the original municipal building, the municipal
museum, the National Theatre, the opera house, and ultimately, in the post-
1948 period, the destruction of the first architectural metonym of Tel Aviv, the
Gymnasium Herzliyya, to make way for the monstrosity called the Shalom
Tower.

98. Holston, 1989, p. 53.

99. Ibid., p. 57.

100. Nitzan-Shiftan, 1996, p. 153.

101. Droyanov et al., 1935, p. 313.

102. Trancik, 1986, p. 21. Thus International Style and the Bauhaus school
were "the most influential force in defining functionalism" (Trancik, 1986, p.
23). It is also worth noting that one of the most important architects, Julius Ratner, was also prominent in the Haganah, and as Daniel Monk points out, "one
is compelled to speculate whether Ratner's aesthetic confrontation with the
Oriental did not assume another form in 1947 when, as one of Ben-Gurion's
military advisers, he argued for an 'aggressive defence' against Arab attacks by
responding with a 'decisive blow, destruction of the place or chasing out the
inhabitants, and taking their place' " (from Morris, 1987, p. 32, quoted in Monk,
1997, pp. 98–99).

103. If this were an architectural survey, I would explain the influence of Le
Corbusier's design innovations on architecture in Tel Aviv. In the context of
this analysis, it suffices to point out that the leading Tel Avivan architects
believed that the introduction of "Corbu's" pilotis (pillars) into—or rather
under—Tel Aviv's "dull townscape" was their main achievement, because raising the buildings about one story off the ground meant the lowest floors were
no longer parallel to the dusty, noisy, and dirty streets, while an effect of a continuous garden area connected with similar areas in the adjacent houses and
with the streets was also achieved (Sharon, 1976, p. 48).

104. Trancik describes three important principles underlying Le Corbusier's influence on modern urban space: the linear and nodal building as a
large-scale urban element, the vertical separation of movement systems, and
the opening up of urban space to allow for free-flowing landscape, sun, light,
and air (Trancik, 1986, p. 27). Only the third element was realized in Tel Aviv
because the small size of the city precluded grand development schemes.

105. Le Corbusier, 1947, p. 82. It should be pointed out that Le Corbusier
(along with the CIAM) was in fact the first person to use the word *modernisme*,
for which he "diligently" worked at constructing its ideology (Jameson, 2002,
p. 167).

106. Harvey, 1989a, p. 16. This need to destroy the existing cultural and
political landscape in the process of creating a new, and by definition modern,
social landscape is common to most national movements—especially of the settler colonial type, where conflict with the indigenous population plays a central
role in the fashioning of national consciousness (cf. Shafir, 1989).

107. Monk, 1997, p. 95. Thus the emergence of a modernist vernacular was intimately connected to a progressive erasure, or stripping, of connotative Orientalist inflections from the body of Zionist building, in effect, out of the austere silence of the Neue Sachlichkeit that arrived in Palestine with German Jews. By invoking the *sachlich*, or objective nature of modernist architecture, Zionist architects defined Bauhaus against not just existing European architecture (and culture) but also the "vulgar orientalism" of Arab architects (p. 97).

108. Nitzan-Shiftan, 1996, p. 155.

109. Trancik, 1986, pp. 23–24. By this Lefebvre meant that space was a "social product" whose production is, especially in the late modern period, in the hands of supposedly apolitical "experts" such as planners and architects, who have the unique power to manipulate the concretized, hardened, and objectified space, in fact, to "engender" space "by and within" their theoretical discourses (Lefebvre, 1990, esp. pp. 27–40, 123). In analyzing the production of colonial space in Morocco, Rabinow similarly describes how *la cité* began in the 1920s to imply "a more abstract space—a socio-technical environment—upon which specialists would regulate operational transformations" (Rabinow, 1989, p. 320).

110. Graicer, 1990, p. 288.

111. TAMA, 4/3563. 9/12/33 letter to Editor of *Crown Colonist*. Emphasis added.

112. Posner, "One Family House in Palestine," *Habinyan* 2 (1937): 1; cf. Nitzan-Shiftan, 1996, p. 158.

113. Miller, 1980, pp. 44, 132.

114. Graicer, 1990, p. 300.

115. Ibid., pp. 290–94. More specifically, the municipality consistently (and with the support of the British) attempted to prevent the working classes from voting and refrained from establishing neighborhoods for workers (as municipalities in Europe did), so as to prevent the growth of "labor" voters.

116. Graicer, 1990, p. 300.

117. Museum of the History of Tel Aviv-Yafo, Sea-shore file, Memo on the Creation of a Modern Promenade/Plaza in Tel Aviv, March 1938.

118. Cf. Wright, 1991, p. 159.

119. Thus Mendelsohn chastises the belief that the reentrance of the Jews into the Arab world means only "'civilization fighting the desert as originating from the political mentality of the rational Western world.'" He felt that the fertile soil of the "organic culture of the East rooted in the unity of Man and Nature needs only to be dug with the mature technique of the western hemisphere in order to secure the common future of the Semitic world" (Mendelsohn, [1940] 1986, p. 12). Clearly the return of the Jews represented that mature technique and "new life" to a "dormant" country (p. 14; cf. p. 9). For Mendelsohn, "the Moslem is entirely the child of the desert—he values the power of nature higher than human energy. Hence his fatalism resulting from the endless glare of the sun. He values the riches of fantasy higher than technical inventions. That is why his architectural creations are not constructive

but abound in richly colored materials like the desert spring flowers suddenly rising after the first winter rain" (p. 8).

120. It described three functions for itself: to find the construction and materials best suited for the needs of building in Eretz Israel; to make architectural form of building and conditions of the country agree for the needs of the population and its desires; and to help solve the problem of apartments for the masses, which more than the other two it felt had yet to be addressed (December 1934, p. 16).

121. February 1935, p. 76.

122. Ibid., pp. 75–76. While Monk points out that Jewish architects constantly referred to the illustrations in *The Palestinian Arab House: Its Architecture and Folklore,* by the Palestinian architect Canaan Tawfik (quoted in Ingersoll, 1994, p. 152 n. 5), an examination of the work reveals that Tawfik's analysis mirrored the European and Zionist understandings of Arab architecture. Thus he writes, "It may be assumed that, in general, the present people of Palestine are housed in a manner not greatly different from the manner usual in ancient times." And "the old city houses represent *true* Palestinian architecture. . . . It is wrong to suppose that old town dwellings embody modern European features and technique" (*Journal of the Palestine Oriental Society* 12 (1932): 225, 231; emphasis added).

123. February 1935, p. 54.

124. Nathan Harpaz, "'Ir 'Ivrit—Adricalut 'Ivrit," found at TAMA, pp. 279, 281.

125. Ibid., p. 40. Though he still began his praise with the caveat, "Without recommending any more adoption of Arab Architecture . . ."

126. Arraf, 1994, p. 135. Another explanation is, as Wright argued in her study of the colonial Maghreb, that much of the chaos in the design of the older cities resulted not from any inherent structure of the Islamic city but rather from land speculation and illegal building in response to increased European penetration (Wright, 1991, p. 100). The local Palestinian population designed their houses in accordance with the nearby environment and indigenous traditions while interacting with European styles, which is why throughout the country one can find houses with red roof tiles, an adaptation of European and Ottoman building styles (Arrag, 1994, p. 147). The city's last Arab mayor, Yusef Heykal, explains the centrality of the courtyard of his family's house in a manner that reveals its aesthetic function to be quite similar to public gardens of Tel Aviv (Heykal, 1988, p. 70).

127. For an in-depth discussion of the similar ambivalence in Israeli art during the 1920s, see Zalmona, 1982.

128. "I was the only Gentile, but I found cordial acceptance of a plan the most ambitious I have ever made, enlarging a city of 30,000 to 100,000 or more, with a new port and with every city block arranged within as something of a garden village" (Geddes, 1972, p. 94).

129. Geddes, 1925, p. 1.

130. Ibid., p. 16.

131. Ibid., pp. 7, 9. Interestingly, in view of Jaffa's position as the major port of Palestine and the unfeasibility (and undesirability) of building a second port, "it is impossible to make Tel Aviv a second Jaffa. . . . This existing residential seaside town, and this too costly and artificial Jetty Port, could not [but] spoil each other, with resulting deterioration—indeed practical failure to both" (p. 9).

132. That is, as a result of the eclecticism then dominating the building in the city. There would seem to have been considerable British ambivalence about Tel Aviv, visually, culturally, and politically. Some "expressed distaste on aesthetic or political grounds for the Jewish National Home, its bustling enthusiastic Zionist settlers, and its proudest achievement, the burgeoning city of Tel Aviv, always contrasted with the picturesque and suitably 'oriental' ambience of Jaffa. 'It's all very efficient,' pronounced one young English visitor about Tel Aviv, 'but gruesomely go-ahead—everything bubbling over with expansion— these trodden people from the ghettos have a right to be proud, but it's rather nauseous in a way, this bristling prosperity, and absolutely unscrupulous. An English journalist found Tel Aviv, 'perfect freak in Palestine,' 'without any flavor of the east'" (Sherman, 1997, p. 87).

Yet a British soldier expressed admiration in a 1943 letter to his sister back home: "Tel Aviv is considered the most modern city in the ME [Middle East]. Ten years ago, there was barely a building there. Most of the population originally came from Russia, and they are quite a nice set of people to mix with. We went practically all around the town, and saw the wonderful buildings they have recently built there" (Sherman, 1997, p. 170).

133. Geddes, 1925, pp. 39–40.

134. Dizengoff, 1925, p. 70.

135. Levin, 1982, pp. 228–29.

136. Quoted in Kark, 1990a, p. 116.

137. Tzafrir, 1995, p. 19.

138. For the Zionists and the Labor movement in particular, the goal of such photos was to "assist the Arab in broadening his outlook and educational background," as the Zionist labor organization, the Histadrut, described it (LA, IV/208/1/4217b, Survey of Histadrut Activities, submitted to UNSCOP, July 1947, p. 72). For examples of the Zionist labor use of photographs and articles on International Style, see the Arabic-language newspaper of the Histadrut, *Haqiqat al-Amr*, 19/5/37, 22/12/37, 12/i/38, 27/1/39. From the Arab side, *Falastin* ran a front-page photo of the newly opened al-Dajani Hospital, a wonderful example of International Style, in 1933 (*Falastin*, 17/7/33, p. 1; 10/12/33, p. 1).

139. Salim Tamari, *Compilation of Reminiscences collected by Tamari of various former residents of Jaffa*, e-mailed to author, August 1996.

140. Jameson, 1994.

141. E-mail comm. from Hassan Hammami, 3/3/98.

142. Mas'ud, 1945, p. 3.

143. Cf. JICR, book 83 (1889/1317–1902/1319), #1045. Agmon also cites this case and provides descriptions of several houses recounted in the *sijjil* during this period (Agmon, 1994, pp. 224–26).

144. It is clear that by the late Ottoman period, Jaffa was not just a "bustling port city" but had undergone "noteworthy development in a number of areas" in industry as well as culture and that beyond the physical development of Jaffa, the town was also the center of the burgeoning Palestinian nationalist movement (al-A'udat, 1990, pp. 807, 810). As one resident of the city whose families roots go back generations put it, "We can say that Jaffa was considered the biggest economic center in Palestine, and also the greatest city in terms of culture and civilization" (Malak, 1992, p. 43). Hisham Shirabi similarly writes that "there is no doubt that the social and cultural life [of Jaffa] was more advanced than in the other cities of Palestine" (Tzafrir, 1994, p. 8).

145. Mas'ud, 1945, p. 3.

146. Heykal, 1988, p. 77. During times of violence, snipers often used the mosque's minaret to shoot at Jews in Tel Aviv and Manshiyyeh. Interestingly, while Kark describes Hassan Bey as "unpopular," the Arabic sources, such as the memoirs of Jaffa Mayor Yusef Heykal and City Engineer 'Ali Mas'ud, describe him in more mixed and ultimately positive terms, noting the concern of local residents at his tearing down of streets and houses but also noting that the city profited from the improvements he undertook (Mas'ud, 1945, p. 10).

147. Heykal, 1988, p. 80.

148. Tzafrir, 1994, p. 9.

149. *Falastin*, 4/1/36, p. 3. The "stain" was from the lack of services and modern plumbing and the like that too many residents still suffered with.

150. *Falastin* complained that the whole process—plans, maps, discussion—took too long, while previous promises to improve the 'Ajami and Manshiyyeh neighborhoods by the mayor were still unfulfilled, and questioned whether homes would have been destroyed (some of them very old) to widen roads if their owners were Jewish (*Falastin*, 22/7/31, p. 1; 23/7/31, p. 1).

151. For the text of each plan, see *Palestine Gazette*, 16/6/31 (#285); 5/1/33 (#337).

152. *Palestine Post*, 9/8/34, p. 2; *Falastin*, 18/6/32, p. 3; 22/7/32, p. 1; 23/7/32, p. 1; 4/1/36, p. 2; 19/1/40, p. 3; 27/1/40, p. 3; 1/8/41, p. 3; 12/1/45, p. 3.

153. Gavish, 1993, p. 143.

154. For a discussion of the destruction of the Old City, see chap. 7.

155. Gavish, 1993, p. 143.

156. Ibid., p. 148.

157. Ibid., p. 150, where Mas'ud is quoted.

158. Mas'ud, 1945, p. 11.

159. Ibid., p. 13.

160. Canaan, 1927, p. 216.

161. Ibid., pp. 3–4.

162. Gavish, 1993, p. 154.

163. Wright describes the process of modernization as involving a shift

from local markets to international capitalism, from production based on self-sufficiency and exchange to a system that responds only to distant consumer markets, as well as the built infrastructure of highways and railroads, factories and plantations, banking and insurance firms—all of which, to lesser or greater degrees, were occurring in Jaffa, which, as I've described above, had the very "fast-paced experience of large cities, awhirl with recent fashions and exciting activities and constituent changes in the environment and a great diversity of people" (Wright, 1991, p. 15).

164. Such as Paris at the turn of the century, where there was, in fact, a "sheer intransigence to change" (Wright, 1991, pp. 16–18).

165. Kauffmann, 1926, p. 97.

166. Aref al-Aref, *Gaza Diary* (Arabic), January 1926, 1940, copy from St. Antony's College, Oxford, given to me by Assaf Likhovksi.

167. Mas'ud, 1945, p. 1.

168. As the editor of an Egyptian journal described it at the end of the last century (Mitchell, 1988, p. 169).

169. Shirabi, 1977, p. 19. Yet we should note, as Wright points out, that the policies for colonial cities in the 1910s and 1920s sought to address many problems that plagued France: overcrowding, poor sanitation, economic stagnation, class and ethnic antagonisms, fears about immorality, and aesthetic squalor (Wright, 1991, p. 54).

170. Mas'ud, 1945, p. 1.

171. Ibid., p. 10.

172. In fact, Europeans looked to the projects in colonial cities for examples for how to better plan their own cities (Wright, 1991, p. 107; cf. Rabinow, 1989).

173. Celik, 1997, p. 5; Wright, 1991, p. 83. The French believed that the three perceptual and social values of any piece of architecture were social responsibility, expressed in the facade; a program, affirmed in the interior plan; and urban design, which translates the relations of the building itself into the larger fabric of the city (Leandre Vaillat, quoted in Wright, 1991, p. 107). This is quite similar to the way architecture was conceived of in Tel Aviv in the 1930s, in the "urban communes" in particular.

174. Abu-Lughod, 1980, pp. 144–45. A clear separation of the two cities (old/new) would have three main advantages: political, that is, keeping natives and Europeans from mixing and thus coming into conflict; hygienic, that is, avoiding direct contact with the dirty and diseased indigenous population; and aesthetic, that is, design and construction in the most modern, efficient, and elegant way possible.

175. Celik, 1997, pp. 1, 6. Here she defines ambivalence as being connected to "hybridity," in which the Other's original is rewritten but also transformed through misreadings and incongruities, resulting in something different. Similar to Geddes's understanding of the power of architecture, just as colonialism and colonization "imposed on the country not only its authority, but a whole set of descriptive symbols [that] replaced and repressed" the existing sociosemiotic system (Wright, 1991, p. 89). Architecture has a "legibility" that plays a social

role that embodies elements that lead to the emergence of collective memories and symbols (Celik, 1997, p. 2). This was particularly true of International Style.

176. Cf. King, 1991, pp. 18–19. It has also been suggested to me that Shanghai underwent a similar development.

177. Abu Lughod, 1980, p. 187.

178. Wright, 1991, p. 153.

179. Abu-Lughod, 1980, p. 160. As Fanon explained, "The European city is not the prolongation of the native city. The colonizers have not settled in the midst of the natives. They have surrounded the native city; they have laid siege to it. Every exit from the Kasbah . . . opens on enemy territory" (quoted in Abu-Lughod, 1980, p. 131).

180. Wright, 1991, p. 1.

CHAPTER 7

1. These include Ruth Kark's *Jaffa: A City in Evolution* and related articles, Yossi Katz's *The Business of Settlement, Private Entrepreneurship in the Jewish Settlement of Palestine, 1900–1914*, and related articles, and articles and dissertations by Ilan Troen, Gidon Biger, Iris Graicer, Iris Agmon, and Andre Mazawi. Though there have been a fair number of studies of architecture in Tel Aviv, most have not looked at its relationship to the larger discourse of town planning or Zionist identity in a critical way, and only two (Tzafrir and Mazawi) have looked at architecture in Jaffa. Tamari's recent edited volume on the modern history of Jerusalem as well as Ruba Kana'an's dissertation and related research are beginning to fill this gap.

2. Theodor Herzl, *Old-New Land*, trans. Lotta Levensohn (New York: Bloch, [1902], 1941), pp. 121–24.

3. This included the flight of at least 90 percent of Jaffa's non-Jewish population, numbering perhaps seventy thousand people, including the entire populations of the surrounding villages.

4. LeVine, 1995.

5. Just as important, it also showed how Palestinian agriculture, and in fact the entire Palestinian understanding of the goals of economic life, had a different logic from the Zionist and British notions of modernization, planning, development, and progress, one that was misunderstood because each of the latter two groups' agendas did not permit them to understand the economic situation from the Arabs' perspective.

6. In fact, as Huri Islamoglu points out (interview with author, March 1999), the Land Code dealt only with "state" lands, *mawat, mahlul,* and *matruka,* and the categories of *mulk* and *waqf* were not included. It is important to note that while *mulk* is generally understood as being "private" property, this is not an accurate reading of the pre-1858 reality, in which it was specifically a claim to revenue over land, which was balanced against parallel and sometimes competing claims to usufruct and title *(rakaba).* That is, it was one of a bundle of often competing rights under constant negotiation by the

state and other social classes. However, with the enaction of the Land Code the state became the outright "owner" of new state lands, instead of the possessor of the power to "distribute" various rights to different competing groups in society. Most important, as the "owner" of land, in a sense no different from the "private" owner of the now redefined *mulk* property, the state could then sell lands to raise money, as opposed to the previous practice of distributing rights to revenue (primarily through tax-farming).

It is in this context that we must understand the post-1858 categories of land tenure that the British would ultimately inherit and rigidify. Specifically, *mulk* land was privately owned land, located primarily in urban areas, which could be disposed of as the "owner" saw fit. *Miri*, or "private usufruct" land—considered as a specific category of tenure and not as the general understanding of state ownership over *mawat*, *mahlul*, and *matruka* lands (according to an official commentary, *matruka* was a subspecies of *miri* land and thus was ultimately at the disposal of the state to allocate, unless it was specifically *ab antiquo* common land) (cf. ISA, M/46/236/D/119, "'Atif Bey—Commentary on the Land Laws—1939 Edition")—was land in which the *rakaba*, or title, rested with the state (and thus was owned by the state outright). Occupiers had permanent usufruct rights as long as they cultivated it and paid the tithe, and could dispose of them subject to the state's consent via the local Cadastral Office. Until 1913 *miri* owners had to get special permission from the state to use this land for industrial purposes, or even for vineyards or orchards or dwellings, as the state believed (mistakenly) that these restrictions would keep the largest amount of land available for agriculture (Stein, 1984, p. 11). *Waqf* lands were dedicated to religious or charitable purposes and were divided into two types: those dedicated from *mulk* lands *(waqf sahih)* and those dedicated from *miri* lands *(waqf ghar sahih)*.

In addition to the official six categories of land, another important classification in use in Palestine was the *musha'a* system, which essentially meant collective village ownership or tenure of a plot of land, with the land being redistributed on a periodic basis so that all members of the community had equal access to the best land. *Musha'a* came under more criticism than perhaps any other form of tenure in Palestine, as it was believed by the British and Zionists that collective ownership prevented the capitalization of land that was the prerequisite for privatization and modernization of the agricultural sector.

7. Eisenman points out that the 1858 Land Code was "an original Ottoman creation . . . neither European nor completely Islamic" (Eisenman, 1978, p. 53), by which he means that existing and evolving conditions in the empire going well back into its history affected the conceptual tone and substance of the legal regime it instituted. This view accords with Abu-Maneh's regarding the larger Tanzimat-era legislation, of which this was an important milestone (Abu-Manneh, 1994).

8. ISA, M/46/236/D/119, Report on "'Atif Bey—Commentary on the Land Laws—1939 Edition" by M. Calhoun, long version dated 4/44, p. 47. Eisenman similar argues that the main goal of the 1858 Land Code was to reg-

ularize the situation concerning *miri* land (Eisenman, 1978, p. 56). Yet he also points out that because partition was provided according to the procedures of the Shari'a the Land Code marks a further indication of the assimilation of *miri* into *mulk* (p. 57), which would account for the confusion regarding the registration of orange orchards outside Jaffa (see chap. 2).

9. Generally having the character of hilly, scrub, or woodlands, or grazing grounds

10. Stein, 1984, p. 13.

11. *Survey of Palestine*, vol. 1, p. 233.

12. Ibid., p. 226.

13. The change in classification usually occurred because of negligence by its owners or because the owner died and left no heirs. The term literally means "the untying of the bond" (Cohen, 1973, p. 298; 'Atif Bey—Commentary on the Land Laws).

14. This was subject to the "right of *Tabu* by any claimants to the land," but in order for someone to have such a "right" the land had to be surveyed and registered, which was impossible for many residents of the villages.

15. TAMA: 1/282a, Protocols of Tel Aviv Council, Meeting #118, 30/9/17 (14 Tishri).

16. CZA, L4/176, 1/5/18 letter to Major Ormsby-Gore from the Tel Aviv Committee.

17. Eisenman, 1978, p. 59.

18. Ibid.; ISA, M/46/236/D/119, 21/5/35, " 'Atif Bey—Commentary on the Land Laws."

19. Dizengoff, quoted in *Yediot Tel Aviv*, 1936, #5–6, p. 43.

20. ISA, M/46/236/D/119, 21/5/35 file containing numerous government documents and analyses related to the definition and uses of *matruka* land in the Ottoman and Mandate periods. The file cites instances of the Porte granting this status to the "Rishon Sand Dunes" (p. 4).

21. In Ottoman times land was designated as *matruka* by an imperial rescript, or *firman*. While Stein believes that "possibly the matruka category did not exist in Palestine" (Stein, 1984, p. 14), in fact, it played a prominent role in several disputes among Jews, Arabs, and the British government during the Mandate period.

22. A particularly relevant example of this was a discussion in 1935 to change this law, which was considered to "cause great inconvenience and . . . an obstruction to the proper development of the country."

23. The High Commission's Executive Council noted in September 1935 that "the proposal to grant a general power to change the category of Matruka land would give rise to popular suspicion as to the use to be made of that power. It was likely to excite fear among Arabs that the power would be employed for the purpose of bringing Arab common land into Jewish hands" (M34/34/L280/299, memo to Chief Secretary, 16/9/35, and ISA, M56/236/D/119). Despite this realization, there was general support for giving the High Com-

missioner the power to convert certain specified areas of *matruka* land into *mulk* or *miri* for a definite purpose only, although this power was supposedly limited in such a way that Arabs would understand that it could not be used arbitrarily to alienate them from their communal lands.

24. ISA, M/46/236/D/119, Report on "'Atif Bey—Commentary on the Land Laws—1939 Edition" by Land Officer M Calhoun (?), dated 15/10/44, p. 7.

25. Goadby and Doukhan, 1935, pp. 48–49; emphasis added.

26. Ibid., pp. 38–39.

27. By the Palestine (Amendment) Order in Council 1933, article 16A.

28. Himadeh, 1939, p. 79.

29. Bunton, 1997, pp. 26, 75. In fact, in 1930 a British colonial legal expert derisively described the land laws of Palestine as "an unintelligible compost of the original Ottoman laws, provisional laws, judgments of various tribunals, sultanic firmans, administrative orders. . . . Public Orders, Orders-in Council, judgments of various civil and religious courts" (quoted in Bunton, 1997, p. 63). Palestinians did not accept the notion that the British administration left the "indigenous" laws unchanged (p. 32).

30. Often from Ottoman to French to English, with the added problem that "the Old Turkish language is very difficult to translate into English as sentences run into each other without punctuation and as the order of the sentences is reversed. Since it is not always easy to ascertain where one sentence ends and another begins, phrases which happen to be between two sentences can easily be attributed to either of them" (ISA, M/46/236/D/119, Report on "'Atif Bey—Commentary on the Land Laws—1939 Edition" by M. Calhoun, long version dated March 1944, p. 36).

31. ISA, M/46/236/D/119, "'Atif Bey—Commentary on the Land Laws—1939 Edition," p. 2.

32. This began as early as the next year with the Amended Land Transfer Ordinance in 1921 (Smith, 1993, p. 92).

33. As Stein points out, the land question in Palestine reemerged after a decade in which several economic crises, a shortage of funds for land purchases, and the focus on immigration had overshadowed the question of land purchases (Stein, 1984, pp. 218–19). For the Colonial Development Act, see Morgan, 1980; and the official publication: *The Colonial Development Act, 1929,* and *Colonial Development and Welfare Acts, 1929–70: A Brief Overview,* June 1971.

34. PRO, CO733/214/87402; minutes to Secretary of State for the Colonies by the High Commissioner Wauchope, 2/1/32.

35. PRO, CO733/214/97049; "Development Scheme and Report of Mr. French," by O.G.R. Williams, 14/1/32.

36. PRO, CO733/214; letter to High Commissioner Wauchope from the Secretary of State for the Colonies, 29/1/32. Just as significant, in minutes to senior officials dated 15/1/32, the High Commissioner explains that while the French report offers "long range and large-scale" suggestions, what was needed

immediately were concrete proposals for the resettlement of displaced Arabs and development with a view to Jewish colonization on the smallest scale politically and financially feasible. The possibility of Arab development is completely absent from his thinking.

37. Y. Shiffman, "Tel Aviv: Today and Tomorrow," in *Palestine & Near East*, September 1942, p. 167.

38. Ibid.

39. In his analysis of the role of modernist town planning discourses in the creation of Brasilia, James Holston describes a fundamental feature of the discourses of urban modernism and modernization as being an "aesthetic of erasure and reinscription" that is closely linked to an ideology of development (Holston, 1989, p. 5).

40. Which coincided with six administrative districts created in 1936 to implement the policy of decentralizing the Town Planning Commissions.

41. *Town-Planning Handbook of Palestine, 1930*, New York Public Library, SERA, p. 5. See *Falastin*, 27/2/23, p. 3, for article on the new landownership law enacted by Jaffa Municipality.

42. As significant, the High Commissioner could grant both public bodies, such as municipal corporations, or private individuals or bodies, such as Zionist land-purchasing organizations or concessionary bodies, the power to expropriate land, as long as it was designated for "public use."

43. Owen, 1991, p. 7.

44. The High Commissioner would publish an order in the *Palestine Gazette* constituting a "settlement Area," then the settlement officer would publish two notices and proceed with the actual work of settlement of a given village, with claims recorded, posted, and adjudicated.

45. Bunton, 1997, p. 9.

46. *Survey of Palestine*, vol. 1, p. 234; emphasis in original.

47. "Although the British Administration might roundly condemn Zionist 'arrogance,' and profess to champion the *fellah*'s 'needs,' no official British policy statement or plan ever questioned the necessity for land settlement" (Atran, 1989, p. 724).

48. Quoted in Atran, 1989, p. 725.

49. Atran, 1989, p. 737.

50. As Tel Aviv's first and most famous mayor, Meir Dizengoff, described it (Dizengoff, 1931, pp. 6–7).

51. TAMA, 4/2667b, undated memo in Hebrew on the history of Tel Aviv's borders and development. One way of both achieving and demonstrating this "independence" was through enacting specific town planning regulations intended to differentiate Tel Aviv from the Arab quarters of the town. These regulations were put into place between 1909 and 1921 when several nearby Jewish neighborhoods joined the new quarter and demonstrate that town planning was already an important component of the Tel Avivan self-identity. The new neighborhoods thus had to agree to follow Tel Aviv's bylaws in terms of town planning, architecture, and hygiene and its prohibition against selling land to Arabs.

52. Ruppin, 1971, p. 121.

53. Kark, 1990a, p. 124.

54. Katz, 1994, p. 287. In fact, according to Ruppin, it was the successful purchase of the land north of Manshiyyeh that constituted the decisive step in the transformation of Tel Aviv from a suburb to a city (CZA, A7/9, L2/615; cf. Katz, 1994, p. 288).

55. The newly constituted Local Council of Tel Aviv was established by the High Commissioner under his authority to constitute a council in a quarter of a town that was "distinguished by its needs and character from the rest of the municipal area." The council would have the right to impose taxes, raise loans, enter into other contracts, or pass bylaws to secure order.

56. Along with the territorial continuum in former *musha'a* lands in the plains (Atran, 1989, p. 736). It should be noted that the French Report of 1931 implicitly endorsed this strategy by calling for "the improvement and intensive development of land in the *hills* in order to ensure the fellah a better standard of living" (PRO, CO733/214, 23/12/31, p. 3; emphasis added).

57. Particularly in 1925–26 and 1933. Abraham Granovsky points out that "the wave of speculation of 1925 began with trade in urban land and had its inception in Tel Aviv" (Granovsky, 1940, pp. 43, 50). In fact, the population of Tel Aviv more than doubled, from 16,000 to 38,000 in the years between 1923 and 1926, while land prices increased 250 times from the beginning of the city to the mid-1920s. During the period 1923–39, the area of the city increased ninefold, with land purchases concentrated in the north and east of the city and south of Jaffa (p. 79).

58. *Yediot Tel Aviv*, 1928, # 6–7, pp. 9–11, 39. Approximately 62,000 lira were spent by Tel Aviv Municipality between 1924 and 1928 to purchase upwards of 1,000 dunams of land, which ultimately housed 1,500 families.

59. Ibid., p. 49.

60. Ibid., pp. 21, 24, where one council member complained, with regard to the Jewish intermediaries who brokered some of the sales, that "in dealing with land purchases you're not dealing with the 'cleanest' people."

61. PRO, CO733/158/7, Despatch from H. C. Luke, Acting Officer Administering the Government, dated 9/8/28, to the Secretary of State for the Colonies.

62. *Yediot Tel Aviv*, #6–7, 1934, p. 252.

63. Including the neighborhood of Manshiyyeh, which had a large Arab majority (TAMA, 4/2667b, Memo on proposed changes of boundaries between Jaffa and Tel Aviv, undated but probably 1934).

64. As Granovsky described it, "one of the greatest obstacles to the normal development of Tel Aviv was the absence of the land necessary for its expansion" (Granovsky, 1940, p. 177).

65. Cf. Graicer, 1982, p. 138.

66. *Yediot Tel Aviv*, #12, 1934, p. 154. The word *milhama* (Hebrew for "war") was used to describe the struggle to expand the city's borders, and given that the Arab Revolt of 1936–39 began in Jaffa the martial imagery is not surprising (cf. CZA, S25/5936). An examination of the surviving records of the

Criminal Investigative Division of the Mandatory Government, other police and intelligence files, and newspaper reports reveal that the border areas of Jaffa–Tel Aviv and surrounding Arab villages and orange groves were also the site of constant tension and often violence between the two communities. What is interesting is how both Jews and Arabs saw the surrounding "other" presence as a clear threat to its security (cf. ISA, M46/236/D/119).

67. For an excellent and extensive review of the events surrounding the destruction of the Old City, see Gavish, 1994.

68. TAMA, 4/2667a, Letter to Registrar of Lands, Jaffa, 24/12/30.

69. Granovsky, in his 1940 *Land Policy in Palestine,* helps to contextualize the "settling" of Summel's land when he explains that "the evolution of prices in Sarona [the German colony located next to Summel] is an instructive example of the effect of the advancing values of urban lots upon the prices of agricultural land. Drawn into the vicinity of the city by the expansion of Tel Aviv, Sarona land could be sold as urban land" (p. 41). This is a clear example of how "settling" the rights to agricultural land adjacent to a Jewish urban area ultimately meant its urbanization and incorporation into the city's municipal or town planning boundaries.

70. Including parts of the German colony of Sarona and the lands of the villages Montifiore, Summel, and Jammasin.

71. TAMA, 4/2662b. Explanatory notes in connection with the proposed skeleton town planning scheme for the land east of Tel Aviv.

72. Ibid., p. 3; emphasis added. It would appear that in the mind of the writer, the region had once been "constructed" but because of Arab backwardness, fell into disuse or dilapidation.

73. TAMA, 4/2667b, Minutes of Meeting dated 13/7/37. He continued, "I received one claim from owners of a piece of land situated at the 'Auja River for the extension of boundaries so as to include the land." He further explained that Tel Aviv would offer municipal privileges to all owners and that some owners already asked for pipelines. It is not specified whether it was municipal or town planning boundaries.

74. Ibid., "Comments to the skeleton town planning scheme for the area east of Tel Aviv," by Gotth. Wagner. Toward the end of the Mandate period, another district commissioner admitted that if town planning and zoning regulations would not suffice to create the industrial zone because of "politics and prices," he was "in favor of the much more heavy-handed method of compulsory acquisition as it is difficult to obtain benefits for the public in any other way in so far as the urban areas of this District are concerned." The solicitor general and attorney general were more skeptical: the former said that he saw the "very greatest objection to taking land compulsorily from one man in order to give it to another for the purpose of making a profit, which is what this scheme ultimately amounts to" (ISA, M/46/L176316, note by Solicitor General dated 4/3/47).

75. In fact, to buttress their claims to the land, Tel Aviv's leaders began advocating the formation of "some kind of county authority" during this

period that would coordinate planning and development for the larger region of Tel Aviv, the surrounding villages, and neighboring Jewish satellite towns such as Ramat Gan, which was located next to Summel (Y. Shiffman, "Tel Aviv: Today and Tomorrow," *Palestine & Near East,* September 1942, p. 178).

76. Interview with Y. Shiffman, in *Palestine & Near East,* January 1943, p. 12.

77. ISA, M/46/L176316, note dated 6/6/47.

78. Thus one Colonial Office official who reviewed the file wondered why the schemes contemplated could not be carried out by using undeveloped land lying within the existing municipal boundary (particularly the larger area lying in the north of Tel Aviv).

79. ISA, M/44/89/L/308; unsigned note dated 21/6/45. The ambivalence of the government to the repercussion of Zionist town planning in Tel Aviv is clearly evident in this case. Thus a Colonial Office official declared that whatever the merits of the housing scheme, it was not "one of those schemes which fall with[in] the scope of the functions of a municipal corporation." Yet he also noted, "Unfortunately, usually the case when local authorities expropriate lands adjacent to their built-up areas is that the agricultural uses to which these lands had previously been put must thereupon be curtailed. Such lands however, have invariably derived a great increase in value from their proximity to developed areas. Thus in this case a grove must be sacrificed and a tenant family dispossessed, whilst high compensation will doubtless be paid to the Samara family" (ibid., Memo Chief Secretary dated 17/10/45). The High Commissioner certified the acquisition of the lands in June 1945.

80. Cf. Graicer, 1982.

81. Cf. ISA, M/18/LD8/3411, letters from 1929.

82. Ibid. The villagers' counsel "[did] not deny that the area is bounded by Sand Dunes." "But," he continued, "they do not cover all the land we claim. It has not been planted with trees but vegetables and there are two wells now covered by sand."

83. As the government claimed in its defense against the villagers' suit. Barbara Smith writes, "Not only did British officials misread the previous land laws, but they failed fully to understand local agricultural practices and appreciate the unusual post-war conditions" (Smith, 1993, p. 99). Evidencing the government's reinterpretation of Ottoman practice and policies is that in the Jaffa region the Ottoman state worked to impose taxes on orchards that were planted on previously unused lands, not to claim the lands themselves (cf. BOA, DH.İD, 122–22, documents from 1329 and 1330 on conflicts over the imposition and assessment of taxes in orange orchards). Moreover, one could interpret the prevailing understanding of *miri* land in Ottoman Palestine as having been de facto private land because in practice if not in law, by signing a long-term *miri* lease (usually either forty-nine or ninety-nine years), the government undertook not to seize the property as long as the appropriate taxes were paid (Ehud Toledano, e-mail comm., May 2002, citing interview with village Mukhtar from Galilee on this issue).

84. ISA, M/18/LD8/3411, letter to Department of Agriculture dated 7/2/28.

85. The *Survey of Western Palestine* of 1878 noted that fertile soil lay only a few feet under the sands, and Kallner and Rosenau noted in their 1939 discussion, "The Geographical Regions of Palestine," that "almost everywhere the coastal plain has sufficient underground water at moderate depths" (*Geographical Review* 29 [1939]: 63).

86. ISA, M/48/G184/3529, Land Appeal No. 171/26, 16/5/27.

87. Thus in one case, the director of lands wrote to the registrar of lands in Jaffa that a particular Arab, "Aly El Moustakeem" (a prominent Jaffan who served as deputy mayor), was buying land in Sheikh Muwannis in 1927 that he planned to convert into an orange orchard and that he "suspected" sand dunes to be included in a part of the *musha'a* plot he was buying. Because sandy land was by definition *mawat* it belonged to the government and thus could not be cultivated or sold without its permission (ISA, M/18/LD8/3411, letter from Registrar of Lands, Jaffa, to Director of Lands, Jerusalem, 19/5/29). This and similar cases also reveal that while the concept of *musha'a* land was being singled out by both the Zionists and the British as perhaps the greatest obstacle to bettering the position of the smallholder, the fact was that while land often might have been registered as *musha'a*, "[it] is actually partitioned amongst the share holders and each is in possession of a separate portion " and thus privately owned in all but name.

88. This was the language Goadby and Doukhan report a British judge used in dismissing a claim to *mawat* land (1935, p. 49).

89. PRO, CO733/230, "Jewish Agency Observations on the French Report." The income, according to the Jewish Agency's statistics, was invested in improving housing conditions, planting small orange groves, modernizing the village's irrigation and plowing systems, and increasing vegetable cultivation and marketing to Tel Aviv and other Jewish towns—all of which led to the absence of unemployment, as "those without land were steadily employed as laborers, and even bedouins and villagers from the neighborhood were attracted to Sheikh Muwannis for work."

90. CZA, S25/5936; meeting of representatives of Tel Aviv Municipality, Va'ad Le'umi, Jewish Agency and residents of Jaffa's Jewish neighborhoods, dated 16/5/40.

91. Cf. Metzer, 2000, p. 380.

92. *Yediot Tel Aviv*, #12, 1943, p. 148. Yet even after increasing the town planning area of Tel Aviv by more than 50 percent (from about 9,000 to 14,000 dunums), the municipality was not satisfied and demanded an extension. Several months later the city was awarded another 9,000 dunums, bringing the new total to approximately 22,000 dunums (*Yediot Tel Aviv*, #12, 1943, p. 151).

93. ISA, M/R.21129/3704. Thus one resident explained, "Jammasin did not cultivate any part of the [lands]. It had been a part of our grazing lands. Jammasin improved the rest of the old swamp, we did not do so by lease from Sheikh Muwannis people. . . . I claim defined lands in the disputed area. I do

not give up my claim in favor of any grazing claim. I first claimed land at Land Settlement some five to six year ago before that Government went out to land. I do not know that certain of our people then claimed it as grazing land, but I have heard that a matruka claim was made."

94. ISA, M/R.21129/3704. A resident said, "Drainage of the swamp took place fifteen to twenty years ago and work lasted for two to three years. I have cultivated in the lands for some sixteen to seventeen years in my patches, but even before the British came I improved some places." This activity in the region can be traced back at least to the first decade of the eighteenth century (cf. Cohen, 1973, p. 157, where he discusses how considerable economic activity in the closing years of the eighteenth century was reflected by the draining of swamps).

95. ISA, M/R.21129/3704. Yet at least on one occasion, a respondent complained, "When land was improved we had insufficient grazing land." This is not surprising, considering the importance of watering places for the residents of the villages who still depended on grazing buffalo for their livelihood; but it demonstrates that from their own experience "improving" the land, villagers had learned that reclaiming land for intensive cultivation was in some cases ill advised, particularly when the land had been used for grazing their cattle.

The testimony of one "W. of Jammasin Arabs" on May 19, 1941, states, "We used to live on produce of buffaloes and cattle. . . . Now we have improved lands and we improved them after the British Occupation. Before recent years no one opposed us in our work of improvement. The buffaloes used to wallow in pools. The Bassa was also for grazing and it was a forest. We cultivated vegetables and wheat on the land. Public Health dug ditches and waters receded. This was [in 1920]. We helped at the work. P.H.D [Public Health Department] had it cleaned by us. That is at our expense. We also worked at wages at cleaning. We improved lands in Bassa with picks and some with ordinary ploughs. We have no internal disputes among ourselves. We cultivated on high places in scattered patches. Where we also had our tents. We used to live in tents and arbours. We did this in western parts of sands, too much water was in eastern part for tents or cultivation in olden days."

96. And thus, considering the short distance to the village, was more appropriately categorized as *matruka* since it was used for pasturage (ISA, M/R.21129/3704, 15/7/21 report [#10] on lands lying in vicinity of Sheikh Muwannis and Petakh Tikva/Mulebbes).

97. ISA, M/R.21129/3704. After declaring the boundaries of their grazing lands, which lay in the Jammasin (al-Sharqi) village between Jerisheh and Petakh Tikva), they exclaimed, "Whereas [our] cattle have, since time immemorial, been grazing in the said lands and whereas they have no other grazing land for [our] cattle and whereas almost all the inhabitants of the said village live on the milk and butter they raise from their cattle which graze in the above mentioned lands, therefore the grazing lands are indispensable and necessary for them" (petition dated 13/4/30, on letterhead of the Jaffa Waqf Administration).

98. Cf. *Falastin*, 21/11/36, p. 4. The paper was annoyed that the two bodies considering this issue were Tel Aviv Municipality and the Office of the District Commissioner.

99. Stein, 1984, p. 178. The list included Mayors El-Said, Alfred Rok, and 'Omar al-Baytar, the latter's brother, 'Abdul Ra'ouf, Abu-Khadra, Yaqub Dallal, and others (See Stein, 1984, appendix 3), although, according to Stein, there were no lands in possession of absentee landlords in the Jaffa subdistrict in the early 1930s, and the lands sold, except for one parcel by El-Said, were not in the Jaffa area. All these men were prominent members of the nationalist parties.

100. Gabriel Baer has also noted that it was the economically stronger groups in villages that were more interested in the permanent partition of common lands as a way to both minimize uncertainty and strengthen their economic and political position (quoted in Kamen, 1991, p. 138).

101. Although he well understood that "in the case of inclusion within the Municipal area of Tel Aviv, the burden of taxation on Arab owners of lands will be so high that they will be forced to sell. The Government will then levy urban property tax and the Municipality of Tel Aviv, a general rate, so that owners will have to pay tax and rate, sometimes more than the actual income received."

102. ISA, Z/183/37, Letter dated 6/12/30.

103. In another land expropriation case in the village of Salama, an official noted that while there would probably be some Arab criticism of the expropriation of the plot, "the actual owners were anxious for such expropriations as providing a means of enabling them to dispose of their land to Jews without incurring odium!" (ISA, M/44/89/L/308, note initialed M. F. to the A/Chief Secretary dated 13/6/45. The exclamation mark was handwritten).

104. Bunton, 1997, p. 33. He continues, "It is evident that a great deal of discretion was given to the courts to ensure that rules relating to property rights always converged with the administrative necessities of the colonial state" (p. 62).

105. Thus the Muslim-Christian Association of Jaffa criticized the unlimited authority given to the High Commissioner in the 1920 Land Transfer Ordinance. Interestingly, Stein suggests that it was the small notable landowning and land-benefiting class whose livelihoods were threatened by the British management of the land market who were most vocal during the 1921 revolt (Stein, 1984, p. 49).

106. ISA, M/44/89/L/308.

107. *al-Jami'a al-Islamiyyah*, 21/12/37, p. 3. The consolidated town planning regulations of 1930 gave a local town planning commission the right to build roads as a first step toward executing a town plan.

108. ISA, Z/183/37, petition signed by "villagers of Sheikh Muwannis" to Lydda Town Planning Commission, 10/11/39. They continued: "If the intention underlying the projected roads is to serve the inhabitants, we will now readily declare that we are amply served by our existing roads and are happy with them. If, however, the intention underlying the projected roads is to serve our neighbors, then we will readily declare that charity begins at home and

such neighbors should serve themselves out of their own and not at the expense of others." Another complaint, described by the district commissioner as an "average individual complaint," objected that although the 1936 Town Planning Ordinance gave residents the right to claim compensation, in reality, "[Local Commission] does not constitute a juristic person and is not financially responsible," and thus there was really no one from whom compensation could be claimed (ibid., letter to District Commissioner from Said and Yusef Beidas, dated 13/11/39). Notice what the villagers considered a "waste" of land.

109. That is, a bypass road, and in fact it is clear from the description of the eleven new roads that would be built that they literally carve up Sheikh Muwannis for the benefit of Tel Aviv residents while also creating an industrial zone in what was, as the residents described it, an agricultural village.

110. ISA Z/183/37, petition signed by "villagers of Sheikh Muwannis" to the Lydda Town Planning Commission, dated 10/11/39.

111. Ibid. The area of Jaffa is 6,100 dunums, but the town planning area of the city is 14,500 dunums. In a 1944 editorial, *al-Difaʿ* found it "interesting" that the expansion of Jaffa only went toward the east despite the fact that there was so much land to the south and suggested that the way to deal with the problem of expanding the borders of Jaffa would be for the local town planning councils of these areas to be canceled and for the Jaffa Municipality to annex these regions. What is interesting is that the land to the east came from the villages of Salama and Yazur, but no one from those villages complained the way they did when Tel Aviv attempted to annex village lands.

112. ISA, M/12/1/46 DEM/122, Review of Palestine Press, 4/8/44. A petition signed by dozens of residents of Jaffa to the High Commissioner further explained that "those dunes were known as the Jaffa Sand Dunes so the people of Jaffa have priority over [them]." And because extension to the north had been "blocked by Tel Aviv . . . should this land be given to the Jews the future growth and extension of Jaffa would be undermined. The only remaining alternative for the growth of Jaffa is the east. This is made up of orange groves, and in ordinary circumstances is an important source of income and livelihood for many of the population. The grant of this land to the Jews would inevitably result in tightening the grip made by the Jews around Jaffa, with the purpose of crippling the growth of major Arab towns" (ISA, ibid., telegram to High Commissioner from 26 Jaffan notables, undated).

Similarly, a petition from twenty-six "Jaffan notables" declared, "The Government [has] agreed to the annexation of pure Arab villages (Summel, Sheikh Muwannis, Jerisheh, Jammasin) to the Tel Aviv town planning area in spite of the fact that the land of these villages is purely agricultural and is the main source of sustenance to the people of these villages. The strong fair protest of the villages to this annexation was completely ignored. It is only fair therefore that the Government should accede to the request of the Jaffa Municipality in annexing these sand dunes to its area" (HA, 105/204, Haganah report, "Yediot me-Yafo," 5/3/44). The Haganah also took an interest in how the residents of Summel and Sheikh Muwannis would react to their incorporation into the

Jewish city. A secret report from 1944 analyzes their reactions as follows: "From conversation with many of the residents of the two villages it is of course clear that they are *happy* (their emphasis) about the annexation" because property values are going up and the improvement in building and in health and education, and only certain leaders who were newspaper owners were against it (HA, ibid.). What is interesting about this analysis is that the Haganah also had a collection of Hebrew and Arabic newspaper clippings on the annexation of the Arab villages from the same file, from which it is clear that there was "joint action" by villagers of the surrounding villages to support the resistance of Sheikh Muwannis to annexation.

113. ISA, M/RG2/564/18, letter to High Commissioner dated 20/3/47. In the letter from the Awqaf Department to the Chief Secretary, they informed him that "Shari'a law prohibits the inclusion of *waqf* land in any town-planning area or scheme since such inclusion would violate the *waqf* deed on the one hand and prejudice the interests of the *waqf* itself on the other." The letter concluded: "The Supreme Moslem Council . . . will be grateful if Your Excellency will be kind enough to prevent the occurrence of this catastrophe so as to avoid the possibility of any troubles in these critical times and safeguard Moslem rights in their *Awqaf* so that such *Awqaf* will continue to be a source of good for the community" (ISA, M/21129/3704, letter dated 14/4/47).

114. ISA, M/21129/3704, ibid.

115. TAMA, Protocols of Va'ad Tel Aviv #35, 1913, p. 312; cf. MHTA, II/A/Neighborhoods for files dealing with the "Merkaz Mal'achah" commercial center, in which a contract was concluded with Tel Aviv's Chief Architect in 1920 that ensured that the quarter was built to the town planning specifications of Tel Aviv.

116. TAMA, Protocols of the Va'ad Tel Aviv, 1920–22.

117. In 1921 the JNF negotiated with the 'Ir Ganim Society to purchase land for them to build five hundred apartments "next to Jaffa in order to expand the urban Jewish *yishuv* there," feeling that this project had "great national importance for the development of our settlement work in Jaffa" (CZA, KKL 3/35, Letter from KKL to 'Ir Ganim Society, 4/7/21, and letter dated 10/6/21).

118. CZA, S25/5936, undated and unsigned letter to District Commissioner, Tel Aviv, clearly from official Jewish representative of Tel Aviv or Jewish Agency, most likely from 1937.

119. CZA S25/5936, letter to the High Commissioner's office dated 5/5/36. Equally important was the issue of "security": "*The fact is that it was not to Jaffa but rather from Jaffa that the refugees of our neighborhoods fled*" (ibid.; original emphasis).

120. CZA, S25/5936, draft of letter to Chief Secretary. Moreover, "the desire [for annexation to Tel Aviv] is not based essentially or even pre-eminently, as would appear to be the view of the Government, on grievances arising from the defective provision of municipal services to these quarters. The demands of the Jewish quarters for a transfer to the jurisdiction of Tel Aviv were raised long before the grievances . . . arose [in 1934]."

121. The Association of House and Land Owners of the Shapira quarter and neighboring lands also wrote to the assistant district commissioner, explaining: "The place of our neighborhood is in Tel Aviv, not in Jaffa. Number 80 Herzl Street belongs to Tel Aviv and the house number 82 is already in Jaffa. . . . Also our business and work interests are tied only to Tel Aviv" (CZA, S25/5936, letter dated 26/11/37).

122. CZA, S25/5936, memo from Shertok to the Jaffa District Commissioner, dated 4/2/38. It continues: "The birth of these quarters has caused the Jaffa Municipality no labour nor has it been particularly solicitous about the needs of their growth, so that I fail to see on what grounds its claim to parentage is upheld. The quarters represent a piece of urban development which is in no way due to the initiative and exertions of the Jaffa Municipality."

123. CZA, S25/5936, letter to the District Commissioner dated 16/2/38, and reply, 9/4/37; 4/10/37 letter from Jaffa Mayor Assem El Said to District Commissioner. The High Commissioner agreed with the views of the district commissioner and Jaffa's mayor (CZA, S25/5936, letter from W. Ormsby Gore to T. Williams, MP, 31/1/38). When the Jewish members of the Jaffa Municipal Council attempted to mediate between the residents of the Shapira, Florentin, Givat Herzl, and nearby quarters and the Jaffa Municipality, the representatives of these quarters wrote a letter to Haim Motro, perhaps the most important Jewish member of the Jaffa Municipality, asking him to resign, saying that "the residents of the Jewish neighborhoods do not recognize the Jewish members of the Jaffa Municipality as representing them. . . . Their participation in the Jaffa Municipality hurts the cause of annexation to Tel Aviv" (CZA, S25/5936, letter dated 23/4/37).

124. CZA, S26/5936, memo from Shertok to the Jaffa district commissioner, 4/ii/38. The allusions to modernity are an important metaphor. Shertok writes that "the birth of these qualities has caused the Jaffa Municipality no labor" (ibid.; emphasis added).

125. CZA S25/5936, meeting 16/5/40. Although the title of the protocol says "Jewish neighborhoods within the borders of *Tel Aviv*," that would seem to be a mistake.

126. Ibid., p. 5. If a local council were constituted, it would have a separate account within Jaffa Municipality, with the money being used for new houses.

127. Ibid., p. 10.

128. To which Moshe Shertok responded, "Are these neighborhoods extraordinary? Aren't there poor neighborhoods in Tel Aviv?" Ben-Ami replied, "Our neighborhoods are special" (ibid., pp. 10–11).

129. Later he added that Jews in Jaffa could boast of their good relations with Mayor Assem Bey (Bek) and that he had in fact been continually persecuted and had to flee from Jaffa precisely because of his good relations with Jews (ibid., p. 33).

130. Ibid., pp. 10–12.

131. Ibid., p. 13. He continued: "To speak about security in this way—I really can't stand it. Who are the keepers of security there, Arab policemen or our youth? How do you [Ben-Ami] dare talk about security? . . . To say . . . after all

the victims . . . that we are secure in Jaffa? In a situation such as this I don't want to be the advocate of annexation" (p. 14).

132. The reason for this was that if they return to the full control of Jaffa Rokach would not be able to keep an inspector there to control the flow of goods and produce into Tel Aviv or to keep their shops closed when shops were closed in Tel Aviv.

133. CZA, S25/5936, memo from Shertok to the Jaffa District Commissioner, dated 4/2/38, p. 15.

134. Ibid., p. 22.

135. Ibid.

136. Yet in the next breath Jerusalem was used as an example of the naïveté in thinking that by getting a few seats on a municipal council Jews would have real power: "There are those that think that we can penetrate into these Arab places and seize and rule over them. . . . Even if Jews got representation in the Jaffa Council, they'd be a minority within a minority" (ibid., p. 18). Also, twenty thousand Jews paying taxes to Jaffa instead of Tel Aviv would hurt Tel Aviv and its economy horribly.

137. Ibid., p. 18 [this paragraph is not in another copy of the same document, which otherwise is identical]. Tel Aviv Deputy Mayor Yitzhak Ben-Tzvi agreed:

> [Jaffa] has become trouble for Tel Aviv. Jaffa wants to bring on the ruin of Tel Aviv, wants to bring ravage and ruin to the Tel Aviv Port. We don't need to strengthen Jaffa but rather to weaken it. And its nice name or historical value won't help it. That's not important. I'm saying that at this moment we have only one function—to strengthen Tel Aviv. We don't have the function of conquering Jaffa—of course, there would be no harm in this—we have the interest now to strengthen Tel Aviv together with the moshavot and neighborhoods around it. I'm not suggesting to declare war on Jaffa, but to do what's in our power to rally our forces and strengthen our power in Tel Aviv. . . . If we cut these neighborhoods, we can plant new ones. At this moment we need to pluck the ripe fruits. . . . In the political and economic meaning the Jaffa [Jews in Jaffa] are connected with Tel Aviv. Because of this I think that our political interests is clear—to strengthen Tel Aviv by joining the neighborhoods that are already mature. There are other neighborhoods that we can't take. They'll remain within Jaffa until their time also comes. (Ibid., pp. 26–27)

138. Ben-Ami similarly commented: "I have an allegorical view that I heard from Motro and from all the residents of the country that came before the last *aliyot* [waves of immigration], that you can't eliminate the land from under our feet in the Arab cities. In fact, I believe that in a political war it's possible to get 4–5 places in Jaffa Municipality" (ibid., p. 33).

139. Ibid., p. 23.

140. Ibid., p. 33. At any rate, he was confident that Jewish merchants would return to Jaffa because there was "no existence for them in Tel Aviv and there [was] a great Jewish upset in Jaffa besides those neighborhoods" (p. 35).

141. Ibid., p. 18.

142. Ibid., p. 24.

143. Ibid., p. 26.

144. Ibid., p. 22. He continued: "We need to consider if there is the possibility of accepting this kind of independence or autonomy in which we won't be bound to Jaffa Municipality. We need to move closer and closer to Tel Aviv. . . . [But] we need to hear a clear decision from the national organizations. If it's your opinion that we should continue the war—with what aim and means can we fight. . . . If you decide we need to continue with negotiations—with what end and means. We are simple people and not politicians. We don't have experience negotiating with governments."

145. One participant claimed that by staying in Jaffa and influencing the Jaffa Municipality the neighborhoods had in fact helped Tel Aviv, but "she didn't even feel it."

146. CZA S25/5936, meeting 16/5/40, p. 32.

147. Ibid., pp. 36–38; my emphasis.

148. Ibid., p. 41.

149. Also, we can see how Remez immediately hedged his description of Allenby Street as a *fortress* within his overall concern for protecting against *breaches* in the Jaffa–Tel Aviv border.

150. CZA, S25/5936, protocol of meeting between Jaffa Mayor and representatives of Jewish Quarters, 6/12/40. There were also legal concerns, such as whether a local council could be established in the land between two municipalities. The representative of the Jewish neighborhoods responded by saying that a local council would not hurt Jaffa in any way.

151. Cf. CZA, S25/5936, letter to Jaffa Municipality from Joint Committee of Jewish Quarters in the Jaffa Area, 14/6/42; protocol of meeting of the Committee of the condition of the question of the Jewish neighborhoods in the region of Jaffa Municipality, 15/7/42.

152. Ibid., protocol of meeting of the Municipal Dept. of the Va'ad Hapo'el, 26/11/45.

153. CZA, S25/5933, protocol of meeting in office of District Commissioner, 2/2/46.

154. For a detailed discussion of the Rutenberg concession, see LeVine, 1999b, chap. 6.

155. al-Jami'a al-Islamiyyah, 14/10/36.

156. ISA, M3C/995/1951, letter dated 15/10/36 to Jaffa Port Manager. He also pointed out that he was still owed £P2 by the Jews for services rendered by him on April 19 (i.e., the first day of the Arab strike) when he transported persons rescued from Jaffa Port to the Tel Aviv foreshore.

157. Ibid.

158. CZA, S25/5936, minutes of meeting between District Commissioner Macpherson and unidentified Zionist official dated 5/2/40.

159. ISA, Protocol of the Meeting of the Provisional Government, 16/6/48, pp. 34–36, Ben-Gurion speaking. Thanks to Benny Morris for bringing this meeting to my attention.

160. What is interesting about the meeting of the Provisional Government cited in the above note is that while Ben-Gurion and other officials were adamant about preventing the return of the Palestinians displaced by the fighting—Minister A. Zisling said, "We ousted them from Eretz Yisrael," while his only worry was "the places where we left them [Palestinians] and didn't have to, because this is dangerous to peace" (ibid., pp. 42, 46)—there was also a sentiment that the Palestinians who remained had to be paid their wages and given the right to vote (p. 34, Ben-Gurion speaking).

161. Castells, 1977, esp. pp. 15–17, 74–76, 89.

162. LeVine, 1995.

163. CZA, A175/96C, undated essay titled "Town Planning of Jewish Settlements in Palestine," by Kauffmann, in his private collection.

164. Smith, 1993, p. 131.

165. Thus if Rutenburg's concessions were neither "indispensable" for development of the Jewish community in Palestine nor quantifiably harmful to the Arab population, they were clearly part of the larger Zionist plan to "conquer Jaffa economically" or become the city's "rulers," as various leaders described it.

166. Stein, 1984, pp. 213–14.

167. According to one member to the Jewish Agency from the Shikun Workmen's Housing Company, in November 1936 Jaffa Municipality began demanding that the government allow it to annex parts of the lands belonging to the villages of Yazur and Salama and the sands south of Jaffa. These included all the Jewish-owned lands in the south of Jaffa that were under "settlement" status, and in fact the percentage of Arab-owned land outside the Salama lands was "very small," and four thousand Jews already lived there (CZA, S25/5936, letter to M. Shertok from Shikun, dated 10/11/36). In January 1937 Shikun again informed the Jewish Agency that Jaffa Municipality was attempting to annex the Jewish neighborhoods south of Jaffa, including Kiryat Avodah, Shchunat Agrobank and adjoining areas, to Jaffa's town planning area (ibid., letter to M. Shertok dated 24/1/37).

In 1944 the Jewish neighborhood of Hatikva, with a population of about six thousand, was faced with annexation to the Jaffa town planning area. Similar to the reaction of the Arab villagers around Tel Aviv, the residents worried that "the neighborhood was under the settlement list under the settlement ordinance." They said, "Now we received a decree and the Government brings us under the jurisdiction of the Jaffa town planning, and who knows if tomorrow or the next day we won't be brought under the control of the Jaffa Municipality and will have to begin to pay taxes to them. Until now we received different rights, help from the Tel Aviv Municipality: education, medical, etc., and now the little help we receive from Tel Aviv will stop and we will be abandoned" (CZA, S25/5936, protocol of meeting in office of the Va'ad Le'umi, 12/3/44). Three thousand residents demonstrated at a public gathering when the annexation to Jaffa's town planning area was announced, and like the Florentin and Shapira neighborhoods, which stopped paying taxes six months before in protest against their annexation to the Jaffa Municipality, they were "ready to withstand ruin to do something."

168. In 1939 the Sheikh Muwannis Local Town Planning Commission debated a new road and development scheme for the village. While there was much objection to the plan, the district commissioner reported to the chief secretary that though "the unofficial minority was strongly opposed to the whole scheme, the official majority supported it on the understanding that the financial aspect would be dealt with by the District Town Planning Commission to whom they referred it" (ISA, Z/183/37, letter dated 6/12/30). That is, the wealthier landowners did not mind having the land expropriated because they knew they would receive adequate compensation, whereas the poorer residents of the village were against any expropriations because they knew they would receive nothing. What is even more interesting is that in this case, while the Beidas family, which was the chief landowner of the village, stood the most to gain, at least two of the objections filed were by members of that family.

CHAPTER 8

1. On the Jewish side, the battle to "liberate" Jaffa was led by fighters from the Revisionist movement, especially the Irgun Tzvai Le'umi, who engaged in fierce, house-to-house fighting and mortar attacks, coupled with psychological warfare that included threatening Arab residents with "another Deir Yassin" if they did not leave (Irgun Museum; interviews with former residents of Jaffa; JA, files on the conquest of Jaffa). On the main display of the Etzel museum in what used to be Manshiyyeh, the words of Menahem Begin to his Etzel fighters before their attack on Jaffa are displayed: "We are going out to conquer Jaffa. This will be one of the most decisive battles of Israel's war of independence. Know who is before you. Remember those you left behind. You are up against a ruthless enemy who intends to wipe us out. Smite the enemy. . . . Show no mercy in battle just as the enemy shows none on our people." Yet a recent oral history by a former Arab resident of Jaffa reveals that more than 240 Arab fighters came to 'Ajami after training in Syria and fought in several battles in 'Ajami before being forced out of Jaffa by the Jewish fighters (Tamari, 2003).

2. Stendel, 1996, p. 54.

3. Quoted in Segev, 1986, p. 75. Cf. ISA, Protocol of the Meeting of the Provisional Government, 16/6/48.

4. Quoted in *Ha'ir*, 2/5/97, p. 24. However, newly arriving immigrants quickly moved into the abandoned houses, and the plan was not carried out.

The five other villages surrounding Tel Aviv, much of whose land had already been incorporated into the town planning area of Tel Aviv in the previous decade, were similarly emptied of their Arab inhabitants and replaced by Jews.

5. As Gideon Levi explained in a recent editorial in *Ha'aretz*, in the eyes of many of the veterans who fought in the battle for Jaffa there was no alternative to emptying the city of its Arab residents: "What would have happened to the Jewish state, if, for example, the residents of Jaffa had remained? How would the first Jewish city be seen that is next door?" he rhetorically asked in the person of one of those veterans ("The Time to Count Has Arrived," *Ha'aretz*, 25/5/97).

6. Amos 9:14.

7. See *Yediot Yafo*, December 1962, p. 11. For an analysis of the name changes, see Andre Mazawi, "The Chosen Street Names in Jaffa Before and After 1948: Ideological Contents and Political Meanings," unpublished article in Rabita Archive [RA], General File ('am). Most side streets in Jaffa still have the numbered names, and the local population does not use them but rather uses local landmarks such as corner stores or mosques or churches to navigate through the city.

Today the Arab community is still greatly concerned about the continued problem of street names in Jaffa: "The street names do not express the character of the area and the names relate to Jewish Rabbis and events without connection to the cultural and historic life of the Arabs of Jaffa," and thus they wanted both Arabic street names and road signage in Arabic (Rabita Archive [RA], General File, "The Society for Jaffa's Arabs, Agenda for meeting with Tel Aviv Mayor Roni Milo" [Hebrew], 18/4/97, pp. 13, 15; cf. 21/2/95 letter from Rabita to Tel Aviv Mayor, included in appendix to Agenda).

8. Golan, 1995, p. 391.

9. Ibid., pp. 393–94.

10. Tel Aviv Municipality, 1974, pp. 5–6.

11. Cf. Tzafrir, 1995.

12. Schnell, 1993, p. 41.

13. A similar process occurred in formerly Arab parts of Haifa; in both cases the Middle Eastern Jewish immigrants who had settled in abandoned Arab quarters gradually moved to better neighborhoods as their socioeconomic situation improved, and Palestinians (almost never the same people who lived there before 1948) returned (Rabinowitz, 1998, p. 77). Jaffa's Arab population receives only 1 percent of the city budget despite constituting 5 percent of its population (Asma Agbarieh, "Housing in Jaffa: Of Class and Ethnos," *Challenge*, July–August 2000, pp. 14–16).

14. Semyonov and Hadas, 1997, p. 195.

15. Position paper drawn up by leading activists, sociologists, and educators for Jaffa Councilman Nassim Shaker to use in the debates over the 1997 budget (summarized in Ali Waqed, "Milo Worries about Jaffa: Here Are Some Examples," *Ha'ir*, 27/12/96, p. 30). The situation is such that (now former) Knesset Speaker Avraham Burg remarked on a visit to Jaffa, "[I was] disappointed to the

depths of my soul. People live like garbage. . . . In Israel should any one live like this?" (quoted in *Ha 'ir*, 3/12/99, p. 24).

16. An earlier and expanded version of the next three sections of this chapter can be found in LeVine, 2001.

17. UNESCO, 2003, pp. 56–61. As I discuss in chapter 6, the report also makes a seemingly ontological separation between "ancient" Jaffa from "modern" Tel Aviv.

18. Lefebvre, 1996, p. 51.

19. *New York Times*, 30/4/98, p. A19. Another report called Tel Aviv "unabashedly sybaritic" (Serge Schmemann, "What's Doing in Tel Aviv," *New York Times*, 21/12/97).

20. Corby Kummer, "Tel Aviv: Secular City, Where Israel Meets the Modern World," *Atlantic Monthly*, December 1995; cf. "Survey of Israel at 50," *Economist*, 25/4/98, p. 18; Serge Schmemann, "What's Doing in Tel Aviv," *New York Times*, 21/12/97. Kummer continues, "If you want to stroll down an Israeli street lined with quirky, forward-looking shops, or sit back and enjoy a relaxed meal in a restaurant that cares about elegance and service, Tel Aviv is the place." Cf. *Economist*, 25/4/98, "Survey of Israel at 50," p. 18; *Le Monde*, 25/4/98.

21. "Survey of Israel at 50," *Economist*, 25/4/98, p. 18.

22. Cf. Gorny, 1984, pp. 19–27.

23. That is, utopia and dysptopia do not have to be experienced by the same people at the same time: for most European Jews, Zionism was utopian; for Palestinians, dystopic (Strath and Kaye, 2000, p. 11).

24. Corby Kummer, *Atlantic Monthly*, December 1995.

25. Including the popular "Jaffa Portraits" crime series, which aired on the "family channel" (Helen Kaye, "A 'Portrait' of Aviva Marks," *Jerusalem Post*, 25/3/97, p. 7). More recently, in a television documentary about Jaffa and its redevelopment called "Things in Their Context" (produced by a European Channel and aired on Israeli TV) the Arab population and history of the city were completely left out (cf. Nir Nader, "Things Out of Context," *Challenge*, July–August 2000, p. 17).

26. Andre Mazawi, "Film Production and Jaffa's Predicament," *Jaffa Diaries*, 9/2/98, at www.jaffacity.com.

27. Official "Tel Aviv-Yafo" guide of the Ministry of Tourism and Tel Aviv Hotel Association, 1997.

28. State of Israel, Ministry of Defense, Museums Unit, *Brochure of the Museum of the I.Z.L*; Eretz Israel Museum, *Guide to Yafo, for Self-Touring*, Tel Aviv, 1988..

29. Ministry of Tourism, *Official Guide to Tel Aviv*, 1997, pp. 23, 32. This theme of the beauty and quaintness of Jaffa at night was already being used in articles in the local Hebrew Jaffa paper, *Yediot Yafo*, as far back as 1963 (see "There's Nothing Like Yafo at Night," *Yediot Yafo*, July 1963, p. 4).

30. Tel Aviv Municipality, 1974, pp. 3, 5–6.

31. *Al-Ayyam*, 19/5/97. Story on the Jaffa Internet Discussion group.

32. *Falastin,* 9/5/46, p. 2.

33. Tamari and Hammami, 1997, p. 73. Tamari, 2003, p. 8.

34. April 1998 meeting sponsored by "Face to Face." Other bourgeois Palestinians with the ability to travel freely in Israel also have told me of their fondness for visiting Tel Aviv.

35. Elie Rekhess reaches a similar conclusion of increased "Palestinianization" of Israeli Arabs in the wake of the Six Day War (Rekness, 1993, p. 84; cf. Schnell, 1994, p. 2).

36. As Yitzhak Schnell writes, "The substance of nationalism is a combination of ethnic identity with the right to territorial sovereignty" (Schell, 1994, p. 26; cf. Bishara, 1993, 1995).

37. During my fieldwork in 1996–98, this demand had won some support among Jewish residents of Jaffa who also see themselves as excluded from the municipality's plans for the neighborhood.

38. RA, public declaration of al-Rabita, 24/6/97, titled "We will not Leave Because We Are Planted Here" *(lan nuraha innna huna manzura'una).*

39. The community has also established ties with the Palestinian National Authority (PNA), corresponding with PNA President Yasser Arafat and hosting visiting PNA ministers. Moreover, several delegations of Jaffans have visited Amman to meet with the local Jaffa Society (many bourgeois Jaffans, especially Christians, fled to Amman in 1948) and put on a music and art festival about Jaffa, at which a senior Rabita member rhapsodized the phrase "Jaffa is Palestine, Jaffa is Palestine," in his speech to the assembled guests. In fact, in internal meetings of Rabita that I attended, the younger members in particular were quite anti-Zionist, and heated discussions took place surrounding the relationship with Tel Aviv Municipality, Arab identity, education, and how much to remain within the Jewish cultural and educational system of Tel Aviv.

40. Talia Margolit, "Cities of the World, Twin Identity," *Ha'aretz,* 2/5/97, p. B6.

41. Nachmias and Menahem, 1993, p. 294; Shachar, 1997, p. 312.

42. *Ha'ir,* 28/2/97, p. 31; 26/9/97, p. 37; 6/6/97, p. 30.

43. For a revealing personal account of the life of African workers in Tel Aviv, see *Ha'ir,* 19/9/97, p. 54.

44. Esther Zandberg, interview with Massimiliano Fuksas, *Ha'aretz,* 14/9/00, Web edition.

45. Most new Israeli apartments, especially luxury models, have special "security rooms" that are bombproof and provisioned in case of chemical attacks.

46. "Yafo Is Disneyland, the North Is a Tragedy" (Hebrew), *Ha'ir,* 12/6/97, p. 24.

47. Ellis, 1996, p. 251.

48. Bilski, 1980. The closest they come is to point out that "it may safely be assumed, for instance, that the political leadership will not approve any national plan that fails to point out how the primary objectives of the Zionist ideology are to be achieved, such as settlement of the country's arid areas." The

deployment of the geography of "arid areas," that is, uninhabited areas, is not by chance, as "making the desert bloom" was from the start a central justification for the Zionist colonization enterprise, while the use of such visually evocative examples elides the reality that hundreds of built-up Arab villages were "emptied" as part of the "settlement" of the country. To take another example, in a chapter titled "Urban and regional Planning in Israel," the discussion begins in the post-1948 period and thereby has a clean slate, since almost all major Arab towns, like Jaffa, no longer had an Arab presence after the war (Hill, 1980, p. 259).

49. Churchman and Alterman, 1997. The best example of this lacuna is the two-volume edited collection by Nachmias and Menahem, *Social Processes and Public Policy in Tel Aviv–Yafo* (1997), specifically Arieh Shachar's "The Planning of Urbanized Areas: A Metropolitan Approach and the Case of the Tel Aviv Region" (Hebrew). Similarly, a 1996 article titled "The Revitalization of Tel Aviv" basically excluded Jaffa—and along with it any hint of the political and national implications of the trend toward "postmodern" architecture and town planning in Tel Aviv—from its analysis (cf. Schnell and Graicer, 1996, esp. pp. 114–15).

50. Bollens describes the Israeli planning system as having a dual strategy: a statutory system hosted by the Ministry of the Interior that is reactive, passive, and regulatory; and a developmental system characterized by organization complexity and pragmatic, proactive, and dynamic strategies (Bollens, 2000, p. 68). While scholars like Yiftachel, Rabinowitz, and Kedar have provided detailed critiques of the larger Israeli planning and land system, their work has not been put in the context of the situation in the Jaffa–Tel Aviv region.

51. Yoscovitz, 1997, pp. 352, 354–56.

52. Geddes, 1925, p. 1.

53. UNESCO, 2003, pp. 56–57, 59.

54. Though the term *frontier* usually refers to sparsely populated national or international border regions, it can also be used felicitously to describe "internal" regions such as minority neighborhoods in cities in which the state attempts to expand its control over territory and inhabitants (Yiftachel, 1995, pp. 494, 496). Ian Lustick has lucidly explained how majority-minority relations in Israel are characterized by "control and exclusion" (Lustick, 1980, pp. 69, 77, 84, 88). More specifically, Lustick details the elaborate system of control (which he states existed at least through the 1970s but which I would argue still exists in a different form today), composed of three mutually reinforcing components—segmentation, co-optation, and dependency—by which the state attempts to achieve the quiescence of Palestinians and the exploitation of their resources to further its goals (cf. Jirvis, 1976).

Similarly, Aziz Haidar points out that "the simultaneous nonrecognition of the status of the Arabs as a national minority, together with unwillingness to absorb them into Israeli society (because of the definition of the boundaries of the society) is . . . contradictory" (Haidar, 1995, p. 4), a complex of attitudes that S. N. Eisenstadt has defined as "semi-colonial paternalism," as opposed to "colonial," because the Arabs have been officially accorded civil rights. Moreover, "since it is the large Arab localities which are potentially more capable of developing a modern economy, their exclusion from top priority development status has denied them the appropriate physical infrastructure on which to base economic projects, deterring potential investors" (Haidar, 1995, p. 32). Haidar was speaking of Arab municipalities, but the same could be said about Jaffa (see Abou Ramadan, 1997).

55. Yiftachel, 1995, p. 498.

56. As local planning committees are appointed by the central government, thereby facilitating land seizure by the state, or land exchange in which Arabs are pushed to lands not slated for Jewish development.

57. Oren Yiftachel has charted the Israeli planning system in such a manner as to demonstrate the interrelationship of official, semigovernmental, and pseudoautonomous planning, supervisory, and ownership organizations (see Yiftachel, 1997, p. 116).

58. An agency that since 1901 has used donations from Jews around the world to purchase land in Palestine/Israel that, once in its possession, can never be sold to non-Jews.

59. *Ha'aretz*, 11/6/98, p. A1.

60. Interview with Oren Yiftachel, November 20, 1998. Yiftachel subsequently added (e-mail comm., 4/6/01) that the plan is still "rak dibburim," that is, "just words," but its impact would seem to be as desired in that the head of the Jaffa department of Tel Aviv Municipality complained about the impact of the various land administrations on the housing situation in Jaffa (Ali Waqed, "Hamishlama, ze 'od lo haya beyafo," *Ha 'ir*, 7/5/99, p. 28).

Haifa University law professor Sandy Kedar adds that "privatization is the 'in' thing today in Israel. . . . [T]he Kibbutzim, Moshavim, and real estate developers all realize that it is no longer as easy to discriminate against Arabs through the state, so they are trying to find new ways to pursue the ideological, economic and psychological goals of continued judaization" (interview with author, 19/11/98).

61. Cf. Tzafrir, 1995.

62. See cover of and articles in *Yediot Tel Aviv*, #8–9, 1954. For a description of the development in Jaffa through 1965, see Tel Aviv Worker's Council, "Development Activities in Jaffa and the Neighborhoods (1960–65)" (Hebrew) (Pe'ulot pituach beyafo ve-hashkhonot [1960–65]), TAMA Library 8–10. Some of the neighborhoods that have received specific attention and planning for renewal are Kfar Shalem (formerly Salama), Neve Eliezar, Hatikva, and Florentin.

63. Cf. the important new study by Segal and Weizman, 2003.

64. Schnell and Graicer, 1996, p. 106. Specifically, Tel Aviv during that time became the center for the management of the large manufacturing enterprises in the country, two-thirds of which manufactured their goods outside the Tel Aviv metropolitan periphery.

65. Ginsberg, 1993, p. 151; Portugali, 1994, p. 312. Yet as Portugali points out, the words *uniform* and *style* represent the very opposite of postmodernism.

66. *Ha'ir*, 30/5/97, pp. 32–33; 6/6/97, p. 32; 4/7/97, p. 30. For a discussion of the opposition to other larger towers in Tel Aviv, see *Ha'ir*, 2/5/97, p. 12.

67. Tel Aviv Municipality, 1974, p. 9.

68. Ellis, 1996, pp. 91–92.

69. Ibid., pp. 65, 91–92. As Scott Lash argues of postmodern architecture, "It simulates humanism without incorporating it. Its humanism is not through incorporation but only through reference. Its humanism is only a simulation. Postmodern spatial forms are thus a matter of 'simulated avant-gardes,' simulated history and simulated humanism" (Lash, 1999, pp. 44–45).

70. Rabinowitz, 1997, p. 15; also see Rabinowitz, 1992.

71. Yiftachel, 1995, pp. 494, 496, 498. For a more detailed analysis of this dynamic in the country at large, see Yiftachel and Meir, 1998.

72. Portugali, 1994, p. 312. This remark was made regarding the Occupied Territories, but it is equally relevant in this context.

73. "Yafo Is Disneyland, the North Is a Tragedy" (Hebrew), *Ha'ir*, 12/6/97, p. 24.

74. *Challenge*, May–June 1998, pp. 12–13, 18.

75. Mazawi, 1988.

76. *Challenge*, May–June 1998, pp. 12–13, 18.

77. *Ha'ir*, 20/6/97, p. 32.

78. Architect Yitzchak Leer, quoted in Mazawi, 1988, p. 4.

79. Mazawi and Machool, 1991, p. 66.

80. "Yafo Is Disneyland, the North Is a Tragedy" (Hebrew), *Ha'ir*, 12/6/97, p. 24.

81. Architect Yosi Tager, quoted in *Ha'ir*, 18/4/97, p. 43.

82. *Ha'ir*, 3/12/99, p. 24.

83. "Regional Descriptive Plan for the Tel Aviv Region" (Hebrew), Interim Report #3, 16/3/98, published by Hebrew University under direction of Prof. Arieh Shachar, pp. 2–4.

84. Quoted in Ali Waqed, "Place for Worry," *Ha'ir*, 20/9/96, p. 1(9?). A public brochure from Tel Aviv Municipality dated November 2000—that is, after the outbreak of the intifada—offered residents homes at low prices but required extensive rebuilding, which few can afford (Hamishlamah Leyafo, "Ila Sukan Medinat Yafa al-Karam").

85. *Ha'ir*, 15/8/97, p. 34. Such marketization of the land and housing situation must also be related to the ironic "lack of money" that is cited as a main obstacle to implementing desired programs in Jaffa (Shagit Lamafrat, Romi Milbaum, "'Eser milyon shekel, shev'im veshalosh pikidim, efes totza'ot," *Ha'ir*, 3/xii/99, p. 24). Even the selling of two-hundred-year-old grave sites is considered part of the "judaization" process in Jaffa (Asma Aghbariya, "Sabab akhar lilkhuf min al-mawt," *Al-Sabar*, 15–26/11/00, p. 11).

86. Shachar, 1997, p. 37. Often, when new building is allowed, it is only on the roofs of existing structures, to keep as much vacant land as possible available for development.

87. *al-Jam'iah al-Islamiyyah*, 18/12/32, p. 7. The phrase was "a fork in the road," ("muftarik fi al-turuq"). Cf. Shachar, 1997.

88. Shachar, 1997; cf. al-Sabar, 24/12/97, p. 8. For more information on the continuing battle between the fishermen and the municipality, see al-Sabar, 7/1/98, p. 4; 12/1/98, p. 9. For another description of the situation, see "The Fishermen Are Furious at the Closure of the Port," al-Sabar, 18/3/97, p. 9.

89. 17/4/97 letter to Schmuel Laskar from Dan Darin of Tel Aviv Planning Commission with attached plan. Copy given to author by local journalist. Also see Ha'ir, 15/8/97, p. 22, for reporting on the plan.

90. Ministry of Tourism, Official Guide to Tel Aviv, 1997, pp. 23, 32. As important, opposition to building a hotel–tourist complex in the port by other officials is being made in the name of "declar[ing] Jaffa Port a national site," which in the eyes of Jaffa's Palestinian residents would still exclude them (cf. comments by Tel Aviv Deputy Mayor Michael Ro'ah in Ha'ir, 13/8/99, p. 33).

91. Lahat was a vocal proponent during his mayoralty of continued "judaization" in Jaffa as well as vigilance against attempts by the local Arab community to gain more control over the neighborhood. For a description of the declared goals of the company, named Ariel Real Estate-Yafo, see their November 1998 publication in Hebrew and Arabic, "Yediot Yafo."

92. For details on this project, see project brochure "Emek Hamelekh" (Hebrew), produced for the Jerusalem 3000 celebration. Also see the English-language "City of David" brochure, whose cover declares: "In 1996 the City of David will be 3000 years old. In 1996 the City of David can be ours again." In his detailed examination of Israeli planning practices in Jerusalem, Scott Bollens describes the strategy as three-part, involving stabilizing the demographic balance, establishing new neighborhoods, and expanding the economic base of the city. The different level of control exercised by the Tel Aviv Municipality over Jaffa, and the total encirclement of 'Ajami and Jebaliyyah by Jewish neighborhoods, has allowed market mechanisms greater power to achieve a larger Jewish demographic presence in the Palestinian neighborhoods.

93. Author's interview with several representatives of Gadish, 13/7/97.

94. Ha'ir, 7/5/99, p. 28. Makom halomi could be translated as "place" or "space," but in the context of the meaning of "place" as related to experiences of its inhabitants I have chosen "space" (cf. Harvey, 1996).

95. Price-Brodie Initiative in Jaffa, Activity Program for the 2000–2001 School Year and 2000 Annual Report, letter by Tel Aviv University Dean of Students Ruth Shalgi.

96. Cf. LeVine, 1998.

97. It should be noted that the Price-Brodie Initiative does have several important programs, especially in the spheres of expanding legal representation for the local community, dental care, and women's issues, which are having a positive impact in the community. Nevertheless, I would argue that the philosophy guiding the program, both by assuming that the Tel Aviv Municipality and Jaffa's Palestinian community share any common interests regarding the quarter's development and by refraining from undertaking any critique of the political economy of the quarter, cannot address the root causes of the many problems it seeks to alleviate.

98. All quotes from Andromeda Hill Web site: www.andromeda.co.il/home.html.

99. GRC is made out of silicon. It is less expensive, lighter, and easier to use. The video shown to prospective customers misleadingly implies that the whole project is being constructed of stone.

100. As the new Arab councilman from Jaffa described it (Ali Waqed and Ronen Zartzki, "I, Rifaʿat Turk," *Haʿir,* 9/5/97, p. 14).

101. For a discussion of the earlier example of this discourse, see LeVine, 1998, 1999a. As of 2004, Andromeda Hill had transformed itself into an apartment hotel to make up for sagging sales.

102. Tom Friedman, *New York Times,* Op-Ed, 8/16/98.

103. Cf. Tamari and Hammami, 1998.

104. A similar architectural and design aesthetic, described as a "neo village, sans mosque or church, with stone walls with electronic access gates," is appearing in Palestinian-controlled areas such as Ramallah, where several new developments for wealthy Diaspora Palestinians are under construction (Esther Hecht, "Homeward Bound," *Jerusalem Post,* 20/11/98).

105. "Andromeda Hill—The New Old Jaffa: Living an Original," 1998 brochure for project.

106. Peres Center for Peace, *Developing Tomorrow's Peace,* 2000–2001 Annual Report.

107. In this capacity, the United Nations asked the Peres Center for Peace to "serve as a global model for peace building around the world" (Tamar Hausman, "Peres Center to be Global Peace Model," *Ha'aretz,* 11/10/00, Web edition).

108. Esther Zandberg, "Simple Sophistication," *Ha'aretz,* 7/9/00. When Shimon Peres first saw the site he exclaimed that the land "would make you want to cry," which coincides in an ironic way with Palestinian views of the fate of their erstwhile hospital, and of Jaffa as a whole (see Esther Zandberg, Interview with Massimiliano Fuksas, *Ha'aretz,* 14/9/00, Web edition).

109. Esther Zandberg, "Simple Sophistication," *Ha'aretz,* 7/9/00. The four-story building, which will tower 16 meters above the street and 26 meters above the seafront, will contain 2,500 meters of floor space. Its prominence on the shoreline seems a fair price to pay, thanks to both its precise appearance and the large, open public space that it leaves surrounding it. The area will be developed as a "dry" garden, as Messer calls it—a park without grass expanses—for gatherings and use by the general public.

110. Here we see that Peter Kook's critique of Jaffa has penetrated the Israeli architectural establishment (see note 80).

111. Interview with senior staff member, December 2000.

112. Interviews with community leaders in Jaffa, December 2000 and fall 2003, including members of al-Rabita, a Palestinian principal of a Jewish-Arab primary school located near the proposed site of the Peres Center for Peace, a Palestinian school teacher, and a Palestinian official of Mishlama.

113. Interview, Peres Center for Peace, 10/12/00.

114. Esther Zandberg, Interview with Massimiliano Fuksas, *Ha'aretz*, 14/9/00, Web edition.

115. Ibid.

116. Ibid.

117. Ibid.

118. Ibid. Fuksas explained that he regards arches as "cheap architectural props. A modern time architectural stepping stone is missing. Architecture is such an impotant thing. It draws together people and is good for the economy."

119. For analyses of 'Ajami's architectural heritage, including International Style, see chap. 6; Tzafrir, 1995.

120. Esther Zandberg, Interview with Massimiliano Fuksas, *Ha'aretz*, 14/9/00, Web edition.

121. I am currently trying to obtain copies of the tours that have been planned to determine whether Jaffa and Tel Aviv are among the destinations, and if so, how they are depicted.

122. Peres, 1993, pp. 83–84.

123. Ibid., p. 35.

124. The choice of Gillon drew strong protests from the Israeli human rights group Btzelem, which accuses him of being responsible for the torture of Palestinians during his tenure at the General Security Services. And indeed, many Palestinian friends in Jaffa have told me over the years that a main reason for the lack of civil protests in the quarter has been the power of the "Shabak education" that so many young people have received, by which is meant the harrassments, arrests, detentions, and sometimes physical abuse at the hands of Israeli security authorities.

125. *Al-Sabar*, 18/10/2000. The headline further reads, "The Solution Is Always Death . . . and in Jaffa the Age of 'Coexistence' Ends." In the article Yefet Street is described as a "ghost street" *(shari'a ashbah)*. One resident interviewed for the story explained, "We are like air to them, we don't exist"— a striking similarity to the view of Jaffa as painted by Suheir Riffi (see fig. 14). Another resident said, "We are prohibited from entering entertainment venues in Tel Aviv, and from buying a house in neighboring Jewish cities. . . . [But] we are not afraid. The whole state needs to be Arab" (Asma Aghbariaya, "Wa fi yafa intiha 'ahad 'al-ta'ayish," *al-Sabar*, 18–30/10/2000, p. 6). I was hearing such "nationalist" language quite openly during my fieldwork in 1996–98.

126. Thus the gentrification that projects like Andromeda Hill symbolize are viewed by residents—symbolized by the plight of the Sawaf family, who have been living in a tent in a public park in Jaffa since being evicted from their home two years ago—as the "ugly side of [an] 'urban renewal'" that demonstrates the relationship between class and ethnicity in Jaffa (Asma Agbarieh, "Housing in Jaffa: Of Class and Ethnos," *Challenge*, July–August 2000, pp. 14–16). That is, "the solution has been elegant: the government need only sell the property to a private person of means, who can then deal with the tenants without having to worry about appearances and covenants. Private property is sacred in the new world order" (Nir Nader, "Things Out of Context," *Challenge*, July–August 2000, p. 17).

127. Asma Agbarieh, "Housing in Jaffa: Of Class and Ethnos," *Challenge*, July–August 2000, pp. 14–16.

128. As interviewed by Batya Feldman, "Mizrah tikhon hadash? Davka be'ajami?" ("The New Midle East? And in Ajami No Less"), *Ha'ir*, 10/9/99, p. 27.

129. Asma Agbarieh, "With Gazan Workers, Six to Nine A.M.," *Challenge*, September–October 2000, pp. 9–11. Also see Yacov Ben Efrat, "Understanding the New Intifada," *Challenge*, November–December 2000, pp. 19–23.

130. Cf. Sasken, 1998.

131. Quoted in Agbarieh, "With Gazan Workers, Six to Nine A.M.," *Challenge*, September–October 2000, pp. 9–11.

132. Peres, 1993, p. 39.

133. As one Jaffan resident explained to me as we drove through 'Ajami in December 2000.

134. Peres, 1993 p. 62.

135. Peres's desire to wage a "war against the desert," and "paint the Middle East green" is also in line with the creation mythology of Tel Aviv as being built on the sands (ibid., p. 74).

136. Herzl, 1943, p. 84.

137. Le Corbusier, 1947, p. 82.

138. Lefebvre, 1991, p. 191.

139. Cf. Slyomovics, 1998, p. 29.

140. Labor Archives, V/329/2, 20/11/85 report by Rabita. In response to the plan as proposed, Rabita suggested the immediate cessation of house demolitions and working to preserve more buildings.

141. al-Rabita was formed in 1979 "to protect the Arab Jaffan essence of the Ajami and Jebaliyya quarters [against] the plans of the authorities whose goal is to transfer us off our land" (RA, General File flyer from Rabita dated 20/1/86).

142. Interview with author, May 1997.

143. Lefebvre, 1996, p. 188.

144. A perfect example of this was the use of the phrase "to live within a picture" *(lagur btokh tziur)*, which spearheaded an ad campaign for the "Jaffa Village" development, as the title for the Arab art festival in Jaffa from which several paintings have been included in this article.

145. For Arabic reporting on the festival, see *al-Sabar*, 25/7 and 8/8/97.

146. In the sense given to it by Lefebvre as "a social practice among others" (1996, p. 189).

147. Interviews with leaders of al-Rabita in 1997 and 1998. See also Ali Waqed, "Politely, Quietly, Jaffa Keeps Its Distance *(Mitraheket)*," *Ha'ir*, 4/4/97, p. 42; Reino Tzaror, "We Are Autonomous, from Today," *Ha'ir*, 9/5/97, p. 19.

148. Interviews with leaders of al-Rabita in 1996 and 1997; cf. Ali Waqed, "Politely, Quietly, Jaffa Keeps Its Distance *(Mitraheket)*," *Ha'ir*, 4/4/97, p. 42, Reino Tzaror, "We Are Autonomous, from Today," *Ha'ir*, 9/5/97, p. 19.

149. Supported by the recent work of Castells, AlSayyad, Rudolph and Piscatori, Bishara, Appadurai, and Yiftachel.

150. That is, where hybridity was a fundamental condition of interaction among parties with varying positions of power who nevertheless had to live together in the same space. For a discussion of the notion of the "third space" and a useful critique of Bhabha's use of the term, see AlSayyad, 2001, p. 8.

151. Roland Barthes describes cities as the "place of our meeting with the other," while Richard Sennett suggests that urban dwellers are always "people in the presence of otherness," and it is precisely these others who have known well the structuring of difference and the importance of identity politics. Public spaces in cities are seen as potentially democratic yet at the same time are places that are "the being together of strangers," or even better, sites structured around the actual, not imagined, "being together of strangers" joined through uneven power relations where "respect for diversity and difference" is an integral part of the "right to the city," which we can extrapolate to the right to the nation (Jacobs and Fincher, 1998, pp. 1, 17).

152. Williams, 1973, pp. 7, 264.

153. Johansen, 1981, p. 147.

154. Ibid., p. 153.

155. Ibid., pp. 64–65.

156. Williams, 1973, p. 280.

157. Ibid., pp. 281, 292. Indeed, the "dramatic extension of the landscape and social relations" in a setting such as late-nineteenth-century London was made possible by increasingly extensive foreign travel and work of the middle class—that is, by dynamics that a century later would be known as globalization.

158. "Andromeda Hill—The New Old Jaffa: Living an Original," 1998 brochure for project.

159. Cf. Holston, 1999.

160. Ibid.

161. Appadurai and Breckenridge, 1995, p. 15.

162. Thus *Falastin* called for the foundation of a society to purchase large plots of lands around the towns before Zionists could purchase them, and at least one notable who had conflicts with Jews over land surrounding Tel Aviv wrote for the paper against land sales to Jews (*Falastin*, 12/7/1913, p. 1; 30/8/1913, pp. 1–2).

163. Cf. Davis, 2002.

164. See *al-Jami'a al-Islamayyah*, 6/9/32, p. 2.

165. The recent work of Yoav Peled, Sarit Helman, Oren Yiftachel, and Sami Shalom Chetrit is interrogating just this issue.

166. Bender, 1988, p. 264.

167. That is, the bourgeois European public sphere excluded more than half the population—that is, women, the poor, and the working class—as participants, while Habermas himself has explained that its functioning has often been hindered by hegemonic political and economic power. Thus the public sphere—which is supposed to be a "free" space where the use of reason as the basis for communicative action is encouraged—has rarely been as "public" as

we would imagine, since so many people are denied "free" entrance, and because the network of economic, political, and cultural powers that control its institutions are usually more opaque than transparent in their workings (and thus not open to "public" scrutiny).

168. Bender, 1988, p. 262.

169. Even if we go farther and recognize that the public culture of the city is "contested terrain[,] . . . a local configuration of power and symbolism" where public meaning is made, inscribed, and deciphered (these three activities constituting the foundation for any synthetic "reading"—or better, performance—of the city; Bender, 1988, p. 263), how are we to decipher the public meaning of a mayor feeling the need to blow up his city's newest market; or closer to the present day, a deputy mayor's blithe assertion that the gentrification of Jaffa could well lead to the disappearance of the Palestinian population within a decade?

These observations can be made vis-à-vis other mixed cities in Israel such as Haifa, Acre, Nazareth, Nazareth 'Illit, and, of course, Jerusalem (for an important discussion of the problems of civil society and the rights and problems of Palestinian citizens of mixed towns, including Jaffa, see the series in *Ha'aretz* titled "Mixed Cities" ("'Irim me'oravot") from November and December 2000, available on-line at http://www.civilsociety.co.il/articles/aarez_arimMeoravot .htm).

170. Bender, 1999, p. 21.

171. See chap. 3, esp. note 9.

172. Cf. Bender, 1999, p. 29.

173. Cited in Bender, 1999, p. 34.

174. Wilson, cited in Bender, 1999, p. 33.

175. Jacobs, 1989, p. 448.

176. Williams, 1973, p. 266. Thus, for example, Nottingham could be said to exist, yet "there *is* no Nottingham," an accusation that can be interpreted as claiming that the modern industrial city has no soul, or that the large processes of colonial, capitalist, nationalist modernity produce spaces that are always something other than their self-perception and presentation.

177. Cf. Holston and Appadurai, 1999, pp. 1–2.

178. Johansen, 1982, p. 141.

179. Although they are not quite dead either, especially in the sense that Mike Davis has recently described nature's reclamation of dead, or posthuman, cities (Davis, 2002).

180. Williams, 1973, pp. 19–20, 188–89.

181. Ibid., p. 289. Holston admonishes us that the most urgent problem in planning and architectural theory today is the need to develop a new "social imaginary," one that is not modernist but that nevertheless reinvents modernism's activist commitments to the invention of society and the construction of the state and thus makes space for an "insurgent citizenship" that is in opposition to dominant modernist state structures (Holston, 1999, p. 137).

182. Lefebvre, 1991, p. 33, 39; 1990a, p. 220.

183. Soja, 1989, pp. 6, 7, 122–23; Lefebvre, 1991, pp. 27–28, 30; Harvey, 1996, chap. 2.

184. Harvey (1989a, p. 219) describes the process as "mental inventions," or spatial discourses that imagine new meanings or possibilities for spatial practices.

185. Lefebvre, 1991, p. 86.

186. Indeed, the relationship between architecture and planning as mechanisms of control of the Palestinian population within Israel is not unique to Jaffa. Recently, a conference was held in the dual Jewish Arab municipality of Ma'alot-Tarshiha, in conjunction with the Israel Architects Association. The Jewish portion of the municipality (Ma'a lot) is the site of an annual sculpture competition whose rapid growth (both in size and as a tourist site) has led its leaders to authorize a competition for a new town plan, and the meeting discussed issues such as the nature of an "Israeli landscape" and "center-periphery relations" as expressed through architecture.

Not surprisingly, no Arabs were invited to join the committee overseeing the expansion of the town, and only one was asked to speak at the conference. While *Ha'aretz* described the difference between the two halves of the town as "the difference between east and west, between a modern, Israeli community and a traditional Arab one, between a planned town and a community that grew and developed 'naturally' over hundreds of years," a local Arab architect from Tarshiha said that what Ma'alot sees as development is viewed by various circles in Tarshiha as an attempt to force "rapid modernization" on them. The one Palestinian Arab speaker at the conference, a town planner, academic, and activist named Dr. Rassam Khameisi, explained to the audience that "Ma'alot's idea of planning is perceived by his community, and the Arab sector in general, as a mechanism of control and a tool with which to continue appropriating and taking control of the land," a criticism that mirrors those of the Arab inhabitants of the Jaffa–Tel Aviv region more than half a century ago when they were fighting the expansion of Tel Aviv onto their lands, which was justified by the same planning and improvement discourses (Esther Zandberg, "Our Fear Is That We Will Be Turned into an Ashkenazi Village," *Ha'aretz*, 5/4/01, Web edition). He continued, "In contrast to the Jews, the Arabs have no sense of security in Israel without maintaining ownership of their lands, and they are developing means of defending themselves."

Bibliography

ARCHIVES/PRIMARY SOURCES

Alliance Israelite Universelle [BAIU], Archive and Library, Paris.
Başbakanlık Arşivleri, [BOA], Istanbul.
Central Zionist Archives [CZA], Jerusalem.
Diplomatic Archives, Ministry of Foreign Affairs, France [DAMFAF], Paris.
Haganah Archive [HA], Tel Aviv.
Israel State Archives [ISA], Jerusalem.*
Jabotinsky Archive [JA], Tel Aviv.
Jaffa Shari'a Court Records [JICR], Haifa University Library.
Keren Kayamet LeYisrael Archives [KKL], Jerusalem.
Labor Archives [LA], Tel Aviv.
Municipal Archives of Tel Aviv [TAMA], Tel Aviv.
Museum of the History of Tel Aviv [MHTA], Tel Aviv.
National Library, Hebrew University of Jerusalem, Jerusalem.
Palestine Exploration Fund [PEF] Archive, London.
Private Papers Collection, Middle East Center, Saint Antony's College [PPCMECSAC], Oxford.
Protocols of the Muslim Association of Jaffa [PMAJ], Jaffa.
Public Records Office [PRO], Kew.
al-Rabita Archive [RA], Jaffa.

*There is potential confusion over the notation system for files at the ISA during the period I was working at the archive, 1996–97. The file numbers on photocopies I made were written by the ISA staff in Hebrew (i.e., from right to left); I switched the order of the components of each file number while keeping the numbers between slashes (/) in the same sequence. Thus, for example, the Hebrew file number "119/D/236/46/M" (to be read right to left) was written by me as "M/46/236/D/119."

NEWSPAPERS AND JOURNALS

al-Ayyam
al-Difa'
al-Jami'a al-Islamiyyah
al-Quds
al-Sabar
Architectural Record
Challenge
Davar
Davar Po'elet
Et-Mol
Falastin
Ha'aretz
Habinyan
Habinyan Bamizrach Hakarov
Ha'ir
Hapo'el Hatza'ir
Haqiqat al-Amr
Hatzofeh
Ittihad al-'Ummal
Journal of the Palestine Oriental Society
Kuntres
Luah Eretz Yisrael
Mischar ve-Taasiya
Palestina, Jahrgang V–VI, 1908–9
Palestina im Umbruch, 1856–82, Stuttgart
Palestine & Near East Economic Magazine
Palestine Post
PEF Quarterly
Yediot Tel Aviv
Yediot Yafo

DISSERTATIONS, MEMOIRS, MONOGRAPHS, AND SECONDARY SOURCES

Aaronsohn, A., and S. Soskin.
  1902. "Die Orangengarten von Jaffa." *Tropenpflanzer Zeitschrift fur Tropische Landwirstschaft: Organ des Kolonial Wirtschaftlichen Komitees*, VI Jahrgang, pp. 341–61.

Abed, George.
  1988. *The Palestinian Economy*. New York: Routledge.

Abou-El-Haj, Rifa'at.
  1991. *Formation of the Modern State: The Ottoman Empire, 16th–18th Centuries*. Albany: State University of New York Press.

Abou Ramadan, Moussa.
1997. "La minorité palestinienne de l'état d'Israel." *L'Observateur des Nations Unies,* 3.

Abu-Bakr, Amin.
1996. *Milkiyya al-'Aradi fi Mutasarrifiyya al-Quds, 1858–1918* (Landownership in the Jerusalem Mutasarrif, 1858–1918). Amman: Abdul-Hamid Shuman Institute.

Abu-Ghazaleh, Adnan.
1973. *Arab Cultural Nationalism in Palestine during the British Mandate.* Beirut: Institute of Palestine Studies.

Abu-Lughod, Ibrahim, ed.
1971. *The Transformation of Palestine.* Evanston, Ill.: Northwestern University Press.

Abu-Lughod, Janet.
1980. *Rabat.* Princeton: Princeton University Press.

Abu-Manneh, Butrus.
1990. "Jerusalem in the Tanzimat Period: The New Ottoman Administration and the Notables." *Die Welt des Islams* 30: 1–44.
1994. "The Islamic Roots of the Gülhane Rescript." *Die Welt des Islams* 34: 173–203.

Agmon, Iris.
1994. "Nashim ve-Hevra: Haisha Hamuslimit, Beit Hadin Hasharai Vehahevra Beyafo Vebechaifa Beshelhei Hashilton Hauthmani (1900–1914)" (Women and Society: Muslim Women, the Shari'a Court and the Society of Jaffa and Haifa under Late Ottoman Rule [1900–1914]). Ph.D. dissertation, Hebrew University of Jerusalem.

Agnon, Shai.
1957. *Tmol Shlishom.* Tel Aviv: Schocken.
1995. "Hill of Sand." In Alan Mintz and Anne Golomb Hoffman, eds., *A Book That Was Lost, and Other Stories.* New York: Schocken. Pp. 87–122.

Alcalay, Ammiel.
1993. *After Jews and Arabs: Remaking Levantine Culture.* Minneapolis: University of Minnesota Press.

AlSayyad, Nezar.
2001. "Hybrid Culture? Hybrid Urbanism: Pandora's Box of the 'Third Place.'" In Nezar AlSayyad, ed., *Hybrid Urbanism: On the Identity Discourse and the Built Environment.* Westport: Praeger. Pp. 1–20.

American Economic Committee for Palestine.
1936. *Palestine Economic Review.*

Amin, Samir.
1989. *Eurocentrism.* New York: Monthly Review Press.

Amit, Irit.
   1991. "The Debate over the Land of Shaykh Muwannis and Its Results" (Hebrew). In Yossi Katz et al., eds., *Research on the Historical Geography of Settlement of Eretz Israel.* Jerusalem: Yad Ben-Zvi.

Anderson, Benedict.
   1992. *Imagined Communities.* London: Verso.

Anzaldúa, Gloria.
   1999. *La Frontera/Borderlands.* San Francisco: Aunt Lute Books.

Appadurai, Arjun.
   1996. *Modernity at Large: Cultural Dimensions of Globalization.* Minneapolis: University of Minnesota Press.

Appadurai, Arjun, and Carol A. Breckenridge.
   1995. "Public Modernity in India." In Carol A. Breckenridge, ed., *Consuming Modernity: Public Culture in a South Asian World.* Minneapolis: University of Minnesota Press, 1995. Pp. 1–22.

Argyrou, Vassos.
   1996. *Tradition and Modernity in the Mediterranean.* Cambridge: Cambridge University Press.
   1999. "Sameness and the Ethnological Will to Meaning." *Current Anthropology* 40, Suppl.: S29–41.
   2002. "Tradition, Modernity and European Hegemony in the Mediterranean." *Mediterranean Studies Journal* 12 (1): 23–42.

Aricha, Yosef.
   1969. *Shishim Shana Leir Tel Aviv* (Sixty Years of the City of Tel Aviv). Tel Aviv: Tel Aviv Municipality, Education Department.

Arlik, Avraham.
   1980. "Reshit ha-Adricalut shel Tel Aviv" (The Beginnings of the Architecture of Tel Aviv). In A. Yaffe, ed., *Eshrim Hashanim Harishonim: Sifrut Vaamanut Betel Aviv Haktana.* Tel Aviv: Keren Tel Aviv Lesifrut va-Laamanut. Pp. 214–34.
   1987a. "Architecture in Tel Aviv" (Hebrew). *Ariel* 48–49: 111–20.
   1987b. "Lack of Style or Mixture of Styles?" *Et-mol,* June 1987, p. 9

Arnason, Johann P.
   2000. "Communism, and Modernity." *Daedalus* (winter): 61–90.

Arraf, Shukri.
   1994. "The Palestinian House and the Nature of Palestine." In Sherif Kanaana, ed., *Folk Heritage of Palestine.* Taybeh: Research Center for Arab Heritage.

Arurui, Naseer, and Edmund Ghareeb, eds.
   1970. *Enemy of the Sun: Poetry of Palestinian Resistance.* Washington, D.C.: Drum and Spear Press.

Asad, Talal.
   1993. *Genealogies of Religion: Discipline and Reasons of Power in Christianity and Islam.* Baltimore: Johns Hopkins University Press.

Atran, Scott.
  1989. "The Surrogate Colonization of Palestine, 1917–1939." *American Ethnologist* 16 (14): 719–44.

al-Audat, Husein, ed.
  1990. *Mawsua al-Mudun al-Filastiniyyah* (The Encyclopedia of Palestinian Cities). Damascus: PLO Press.

Avitzur, Schmuel.
  1965. "First Models for a Regular Port in Jaffa" (Hebrew). In *Shenaton Muze'on Ha'aretz* (Eretz Israel Museum Yearbook), 7.
  1969. "Halomot Jamal Pacha ve-Hayishuv Ha'ivri" (The Dreams of Jamal Pasha and the Hebrew Yishuv). *Keshet*, pp. 171–83.
  1970. "Suggestions for Utilizing the Waters of the Yarkon for the Development of the region of Jaffa in the Days of the First World War" (Hebrew). In *Shenaton Muze'on Ha'aretz* (Eretz Israel Museum Yearbook), 12.
  1972a. *Chai Yom-Yom Beeretz Israel Bemeah Hayud-tet* (Daily Life in Eretz Israel in the Nineteenth Century). Tel Aviv: Am Hasefer Publishing.
  1972b. "The Economic Contributions in the Land and Port of Jaffa" (Hebrew). In *Shenaton Muze'on Ha'aretz* (Eretz Israel Museum Yearbook), 14.
  1972c. *Namal Yafo: Begaoto Vebeshkiato* (Jaffa Port: Its Growth and Decline). Tel Aviv: Milo/Tel Aviv University Publishers.
  1997. *Peirot Yafo, Metaei Pri Heder Baaretz: Hitpatchutam, Gidulam ve-Priyam* (Fruit of Jaffa, Citrus Plantations in the Country: Their Development, Growth, and Crops). Tel Aviv: Histadrut Publishing and Avshalom Institute for Knowledge of the Country.

al-'Awra, Ibrahim.
  [1936] 1989. *Ta'rikh wilayat sulayman basha al-'adil* (History of the Wilayat of Sulayman Basha al-'Adal). Ed. Constantine Pasha al-Mukhalasi. Sidon: Matba'at Dayr al-Mukhalis.

al-Ayyubi, Yusri.
  1990. *Bustan al-Burtuqal* (The Orange Orchard). N.p.: Dar al-Jamhariyya.

Bachelard, Gaston.
  1964. *The Poetics of Space*. Trans. Maria Jolas. Boston: Beacon Press.

Badarna, Muhammad.
  1997. *Yafa: 'Urus al-Bahr* (Jaffa: Bride of the Sea). Jaffa: Rabita Publications.

Baedeker's.
  1876–1904. Tour Guides of the Holy Land, German and English editions.

Baram, Uzi.
  1996. "Material Culture, Commodities, and Consumption in Palestine, 1500–1900." Ph.D. dissertation, University of Massachusetts.

Bardenstein, Carol,
  1997. "The Jaffa Orange in Palestinian and Israeli Discourses of Authenticity." Paper presented at the annual meeting of the Middle East Studies Association, San Francisco, November 24.

Baudelaire, Charles.
   1972. *Selected Writings on Art and Artists.* New York: Penguin.

Bauman, Zygmunt.
   1993. *Modernity and Ambivalence.* London: Blackwell.
   [1989] 2000. *Modernity and the Holocaust.* Ithaca: Cornell University Press.
   2000. "The Duty to Remember—But What?" In James Kaye and Bo Strath, eds., *Enlightenment and Genocide: Contradictions of Modernity.* Philosophy and Politics, 5. Brussels: P.I.E.–Peter Lang. Pp. 31–58.

Beck, Ulrich.
   1992. *Risk Society: Towards a New Modernity.* Trans. Mark Ritter. London: Sage.

Beck, Ulrich, Anthony Giddens, and Scott Lash.
   1994. *Reflexive Modernization: Politics, Tradition and Aesthetics in the Modern Social Order.* Oxford: Polity Press.

Bein, A.
   1976. *History of Jewish Settlement in Israel* (Hebrew). 5th ed. Ramat Gan: Massada Press.

Bender, Thomas.
   1988. "Metropolitan Life and the Making of Public Culture." In John Hull Mollenkopf, ed., *Power, Culture and Place: Essays on New York City.* New York: Russell Sage Foundation. Pp. 261–72.
   1999. "Intellectuals, Cities, and Citizenship in the United States: The 1890s and 1990s." In James Holston, ed., *Cities and Citizenship.* Durham: Duke University Press. Pp. 21–41.

Ben-Gurion, David.
   1931a. *Anachnu Veshcheineinu* (We and Our Neighbors). Tel Aviv: Davar.
   1931b. *Memaamad Leam* (From Class to Nation). Tel Aviv: Davar.
   1932. *Avoda Ivrit* (Hebrew Labor). Tel Aviv: Va'ad Hapo'el.

Benjamin, Walter.
   [1933] 1977. *Erfahrun und Armut, Gesammelte Schriften,* Bd. 2 (1933) Teil 1, Rolf Tiedemann and Hermann Schweppehuser (Hrsg.). Frankfurt am Main: Suhrkamp.

Ben-Porat, Amir.
   1986. *Between Class and Nation: The Formation of the Jewish Working Class in the Period before Israel's Statehood.* New York: Greenwood Press.

Ben-Shachar, Pinhas.
   1990. *Btei Yafo-Tel-Aviv Meseferim: Toldoteiha Shel Hair Haivrit Harishona* (The History of Tel Aviv as Told by Its Houses). Tel Aviv: Ministry of Defense.

Berger, Tamar.
   1998. *Dionysus Basenter* (Dionysus at Dizengoff Center). Tel Aviv: Kibbutz Hameuhad Publishing.

Berkowitz, Michael.
1993. *Zionist Culture and West European Jewry before the First World War.* New York: Cambridge University Press.

Bernstein, Deborah.
1987. *Isha Beeretz Yisrael: Hashaifah Leshivyon Betikufat Hayishuv* (Women in Eretz Israel: The Desire for Equality in the Yishuv Period). Tel Aviv: Kibbutz Hameuhad Publishing.
2000. *Constructing Boundaries: Jewish and Arab Workers in Mandatory Palestine.* Albany: State University of New York Press.

Beverley, John, Michael Aronna, and Jose Oviedo, eds.
1995. *The Postmodernism Debate in Latin America.* Durham: Duke University Press.

Beyer, O., ed.
1967. *Erich Mendelsohn: Letters of an Architect.* London: Abelard Schuman.

Bhabha, Homi.
1994. *The Location of Culture.* New York: Routledge.
1997. "The Other Question." In Padmini Mongia, ed., *Contemporary Postcolonial Theory: A Reader.* London: Arnold. Pp. 37–54.

Biger, Gid'on.
1982. *Crown Colony or National Home?* (Hebrew). Tel Aviv: Yad Ben-Zvi.
1983. "The Industrial Structure of Eretz-Israel in the 1920s" (Hebrew). *Katedra* 29: 79–112.
1984a. "The Development of the Built Region of Tel Aviv" (Hebrew). *Eden* 3: 42–61.
1984b. "European Influence on Town Planning and Town Building in Palestine, 1850–1920." *Urbanism Past and Present* 9: 30–35.
1986. "Urban Planning and the Garden Suburbs of Jerusalem, 1918–25." *Studies in Zionism* 7 (1): 1–9.
1987a. "Arab Farms in the Region of Tel Aviv" (Hebrew). *Ariel* 48–49: 53–56.
1987b. "The Neighborhoods That Became Tel Aviv" (Hebrew). *Ariel* 48–49: 49–52.

Bilski, Raphaella, ed.
1980. *Can Planning Replace Politics? The Israeli Experience.* The Hague: Martinus Nijhoff.

Bishara, Azmi.
1993. "On the Question of the Palestinian Minority in Israel" (Hebrew). *Teoriah Vebikhoret* 3: 7–20.
1995. "The Arab-Israeli: Readings in an Incomplete Political Discourse" (Arabic). *Majelat Dirasat Filastinin* 24: 26–54.
1998. "Israil wa-al-Aulamah: Baad Juanib Jediliyah al- Aulamah Israiliyyan" (Israel and Globalization: Some Aspects of the Israeli Dialectic of Globalization). In Isamah Amin al-Khuli, ed., *al-Arab wa-al-Aulamah: Buhuth*

wa-Munaqashat al-Nadwah al-Fikriyyah Aleti Nathmaha Merkaz Darasat al-Wahdah al-Arabiyyah/al-Said Yassin (The Arabs and Globalization: Research and Discussions of the Intellectual Conference Convended by the Center for the Study of Arab Unity/as-Said Yassin). Beirut: Center for the Study of Arab Unity.

Blaisdell, Donald.
1966. *European Financial Control in the Ottoman Empire.* New York: AMS Press.

Blunt, Alison, and Gillian Rose, eds.
1994. *Writing Women and Space.* New York: Guilford Press.

Bollens, Scott.
2000. *On Narrow Ground: Urban Policy and Ethnic Conflict in Jerusalem and Belfast.* Albany: State University of New York Press.

Boyarin, Jonathan.
1992. *Storm from Paradise.* Minneapolis: University of Minnesota Press.

Bracken, Harry.
1973. "Essence, Accident and Race." *Hermathena* 116 (winter 1973): 81–96.

Braveman, Libbie.
1937. *Children of the Emek.* New York: Furrow Press.

Breytenbach, Breyten.
1998. "Notes from the Middle World." In Heide Ziegler, ed., *The Translatability of Cultures: Proceedings of the Fifth Stuttgart Seminar in Cultural Studies, 3/8–14/8/1998.* Stuttgart: Verlag J. B. Metzler. Pp. 47–64.

Brummett, Palmira.
2000. *Image and Imperialism in the Ottoman Revolutionary Press, 1908–1911.* Albany: State University of New York Press.

Brunner, Jose Joaquin.
1995. "Notes on Modernity and Postmodernity in Latin American Culture." In John Beverley, Michael Aronna, and Jose Oviedo, eds., *The Postmodernism Debate in Latin America.* Durham: Duke University Press. Pp. 34–54.

al-Budayri, Musa.
1981. *Tatawwur al-Harakah al Ummaliyyah al-Arabiyyah fi Filastin: Muqaddama Tarikhiyyah wa-majmua wathaiq* (The Development of the Arab Labor Movement in Palestine). Beirut.

Bunton, Martin.
1997. "The Role of Private Property in the British Administration of Palestine." D.Phil. dissertation, Oxford University.

Calderón, Fernando.
1995. "Latin American Identity and Mixed Temporalities; or, How to be Postmodern and Indian at the Same Time." In John Beverley, Michael Aronna,

and Jose Oviedo, eds., *The Postmodernism Debate in Latin America*. Durham: Duke University Press. Pp. 55–64.

Campos, Michelle.
2001, "Between 'Haviva Otomania' and 'Eretz-Israel': Ottomanism and Zionism among Palestine's Sephardi and Maghrebi Jews, 1908–13." Paper presented at the Second Mediterranean Social and Political Research Meeting, Florence, March 21–25, 2001, Mediterranean Programme, Robert Schuman Centre for Advanced Studies, European University Institute.

Canaan, Taufik.
1927. *Mohammedan Saints and Sanctuaries in Palestine*. London: Luzac & Co.
1933. "The Palestinian Arab House: Its Architecture and Folklore." *Journal of the Palestine Oriental Society* 13 (1–2): 1–83.

Caplan, Neil.
1982. "The Yishuv, Sir Herbert Samuel and the Arab Question in Palestine, 1921–25." In E. Kedourie and S. G. Haim, eds., *Zionism and Arabism in Palestine and Israel*. London: Frank Cass. Pp. 1–51.

Carmiel, Batya.
1987. "The Beginnings of Tel Aviv in the Descriptions of Nahum Gutman" (Hebrew). *Ariel* 48–49: 87–94.

Castells, Manuel.
1977. *The Urban Question*. Trans. Alan Sheridan. Cambridge, Mass: MIT Press.
1983. *The City and the Grass Roots*. Berkeley: University of California Press.
1997. *The Power of Identity*. Oxford: Blackwell.

Celik, Zeynep.
1997. *Urban Forms and Colonial Confrontations: Algiers under French Rule*. Berkeley: University of California Press.

Césaire, Aimé.
1995. *Discourse on Colonialism*. Trans. Joan Pinkham. New York: Monthly Review Press.

Cevat, Ali.
1313h/1895. *Memlik-i Osmaniyenin: Tarih ve Coğertyilugatı* (Historical and Geographical Dictionary of the Ottoman Empire). Istanbul: Dar Saadef.

Chakrabarty, Dipesh.
1999. *Witness to Suffering: Domestic Cruelty and the Birth of the Modern Subject in Bengal*. In Timothy Mitchell, ed., *Questions of Modernity*. Minneapolis: University of Minnesota Press. Pp. 49–86.

Chatterjee, Partha.
1986. *Nationalist Thought and the Colonial World: A Derivative Discourse*. Minneapolis: University of Minnesota Press.

1993. *The Nation and Its Fragments: Colonial and Postcolonial Histories.* Princeton: Princeton University Press.

1999. "Two Poets and Death: On Civil and Political Society in the Non-Christian World." In Timothy Mitchell, ed., *Questions of Modernity.* Minneapolis: University of Minnesota Press. Pp. 35–48.

Cherry, Gordon, ed.
1981. *Pioneers in British Planning.* London: Architectural Press.

Choay, Françoise.
1969. *The Modern City: Planning in the 19th Century.* New York: George Braziller.

Chow, Rey.
1997. "Where Have All the Natives Gone?" In Padmini Mongia, ed., *Contemporary Postcolonial Theory: A Reader.* London: Arnold. Pp. 122–47.

Churchman, Arza, and Rachelle Alterman.
1997. "Conflict Management and Urban Planning in Tel Aviv–Yafo." In David Nachmias and Gila Menahem, eds., *Mechkarei Tel Aviv-Yafo: Tahalikhim Chevratim ve-Mediniot Tzeiburit* (Social Processes and Public Policy in Tel Aviv-Yafo). Tel Aviv: Ramot Publishing House. Vol. 2, pp. 39–64.

Cohen, Amnon.
1973. *Palestine in the Eighteenth Century: Patterns of Government and Administration.* Jerusalem: Magnus Press.

Cohen, E.
1970. *The City in Zionist Ideology.* Jerusalem: Hebrew University of Jerusalem Institute of Urban Studies.
1973. *Integration and Separation in the Planning of a Mixed Jewish-Arab City in Israel.* Jerusalem: Hebrew University Press.

Cohen, Israel.
1912. *The Zionist Movement: Aims and Aspirations.* Berlin: Zionist Central Office.
1941. *Zionist Work in Palestine.* London: Fisher.

Cohen, Mitchell.
1992. *Zion and State.* New York: Columbia University Press.

Coronil, Fernando.
1997. *The Magical State: Nature, Money, and Modernity in Venezuela.* Chicago: University of Chicago Press.

Culture Committee of the Fund for a Free Jaffa.
1990. *Yafa: Haqaiq wa-Maalumat* (Jaffa: Facts and Information). Kuwait: n.p.

Cummings, John Thomas, Hossein Askari, and Ahmad Mustafa.
1980. "Islam and Modern Economic Change." In John Esposito, ed., *Islam and Development: Religion and Sociopolitical Change.* Syracuse: Syracuse University Press. Pp. 25–47.

Dabbagh, Mustafa.
   1972–86. *Biladuna Filastin, Diyar Yafiyyah* (Our Homeland Palestine: Jaffa Volume). Hebron: al-Mawsuah al-Filastiniyah bi-Muhafizat al-Khalil.

al-Dajani, Ahmed Zaki. n.d. *Medinah Yafa wa-Thawrah 1936* (Jaffa and the Revolt of 1936). N.p.

al-Dajani, Sad Yusuf.
   1991. *Kai La Nansa Yafa* (So That We Will Not Forget Jaffa). Amman: Free Arab Jaffa Society.

Dann, Otto.
   1999. "Modernity and the Project of the Modern Nation." In Johannes Müller and Bo Strath, eds., *Nationism and Modernity—An Outdated Relationship?* EUI Working Papers. HEC no. 99/1.

Davis, Mike.
   1990. *City of Quartz: Excavating the Future in Los Angeles.* New York: Verso.
   2002. *Dead Cities and Other Tales.* New York: New Press.

Dear, Michael.
   1997. "Postmodern Bloodlines." In Georges Benko and Ulf Strohmayer, eds., *Space and Social Theory: Interpreting Modernity and Postmodernity.* Oxford: Blackwell. Pp. 49–71.

Deleuze, Gilles, and Félix Guattari.
   [1972] 1983. *Anti-Oedipus: Capitalism and Schizophrenia.* Trans. Robert Hurley, Mark Seem, and Helen R. Lane. Minneapolis: University of Minnesota Press.
   [1980] 1987. *A Thousand Plateaus.* Trans. Brian Massumi. Minneapolis: University of Minnesota Press.

Denoon, Donald.
   1983. *Settler Capitalism.* Oxford: Clarendon Press.

Deringil, Selim.
   1999. *The Well-Protected Domains: Ideology and the Legitimation of Power in the Ottoman Empire, 1876–1909.* London: I. B. Tauris.

Dirbas, Sahrah.
   1993. *Salameh: Ihda al-Qura al-Kabira Qada Yafa* (Salameh: One of the Biggest Villages in the Jaffa District). N.p.

Diyab, Imtiyaz.
   1991. *Yafa: 'Utr Medinah* (Jaffa: Perfume of a City). Beirut: Dar al Fati al-Arabi Publishing.

Dizengoff, Meir.
   1925. "The Future of Tel Aviv, Bright Prospects as Industrial and Trade Center." *Palestine and Near East Economic Magazine*, 2, pp. 69–72.
   1927. *Din Vecheshbon al Hityashvut Ironit* (Report on Urban Colonization). Tel Aviv: n.p.

1931. *Leyedidei Noari* (To the Friends of My Youth). Tel Aviv: n.p.

1932. *Pituach Ha'ir Tel Aviv* (The Development of the City of Tel Aviv). Tel Aviv: n.p.

n.d. *Renaissance of Tel Aviv* (Hebrew). Tel Aviv: Eitan Shashoni Press.

al-Domaniki, A. S. Marmarji.

1928. "Nathra fi Ta'rikh yafa" (A View of the History of Jaffa). *al-Mashriq* 10: 729–35, 833; 11: 826–33.

Donovitz [Dunevich], Nathan.

1959. *Tel Aviv; Holot she hayu likherakh* (Tel Aviv: Sands That Became a Metropolis). Jerusalem: Schocken.

Doumani, Beshara.

1985. "Palestinian Islamic Court Records: A Source for Socioeconomic History." *International Journal of Middle East Studies* (summer).

1995. *Rediscovering Palestine: Merchants and Peasants in Jabal Nablus, 1700–1900*. Berkeley: University of California Press.

Droyanov, A., et al.

1935. *Sefer Tel Aviv* (Tel Aviv Book). Tel Aviv.

Dumper, Michael.

1994. *Muslim Religious Endowments and the Jewish State*. Washington, D.C.: Institute for Palestine Studies.

Dussel, Enrique.

1995a. "Eurocentrism and Modernity (Introduction to the Frankfurt Lectures)." In John Beverley, Michael Aronna, and Jose Oviedo, eds., *The Postmodern Debate in Latin America*. Durham: Duke University Press. Pp. 65–76.

1995b. *The Invention of the Americas*. New York: Continuum.

1996. *The Underside of Modernity: Apel, Ricoeur, Rorty, Taylor and the Philosophy of Liberation*. Trans. E. Mendieta. Atlantic Highlands, N.J.: Humanities Press.

Efrat, Elisha.

1984. *Urbanization in Israel*. London: Croom Helm.

Eisenman, Robert H.

1978. *Islamic Law in Palestine and Israel: A History of the Survival of Tanzimat and Shari'a in the British Mandate and the Jewish State*. Leiden: E. J. Brill.

Eisenstadt, Shmuel.

1999. *Fundamentalism, Sectarianism, and Revolution: The Jacobin Dimension of Modernity*. Cambridge: Cambridge University Press.

2000. "Fundamentalist Movements in the Framework of Multiple Modernities." In Almut Höfert and Armando Salvatore, eds., *Between Europe and Islam: Shaping Modernity in a Transcultural Space*. Brussels: Peter Lang. Pp. 175–96.

Eisenzweig, Uri.
   1981. "An Imaginary Territory: The Problematic of Space in Zionist Discourse." *Dialectical Anthropology* 5 (4): 261–87.

Eisler, Jakob.
   1997. *Der deutsche Beitrag zum Aufstieg Jaffas, 1850–1914: Zur Beschichte Palästinas im 19. Jahrhundert.* Wiesbaden: Harrassowitz.

Elazari-Volkani, Yitzhak.
   1925. "The Transition from Primitive to Modern Agriculture in Palestine." *Palestine Society Economic Bulletin* 2 (June).

Eliav, Mordechai.
   1973. "The Disturbances in Jaffa in Purim, 1908." In Daniel K. Arafi, ed., *Hatzionut: Measaf Letoldot Hatnuah Hatzionut ve-Hayishuv Ha-yehudi be-Eretz Israel* (Zionism: Collection on the History of the Zionist Movement and the Jewish Yishuv in Eretz Israel). Tel Aviv: Kibutz Hameduhad. Pp. 152–97.

Elkayam, Mordekai.
   1990. *Yafo-Neveh-Tzedek: Reshitah Tel Aviv* (Yafo-Neveh-Zedek: The Beginnings of Tel Aviv). Tel Aviv: Ministry of Defense.

Ellis, Nan.
   1996. *Postmodern Urbanism.* London: Blackwell.

Engineers, Architects and Surveyors Union of the Histadrut.
   1940. *Twenty Years of Building* (Hebrew). Tel Aviv.

Ettinger, Jacob.
   1917(?). *Jewish Colonization in Palestine: Methods, Plans and Capital.* Tel Aviv: Jewish National Fund.

Farhi, David.
   1975. "Documents on the Attitude of the Ottoman Government towards the Jewish Settlement in Palestine after the Revolution of the Young Turks (1908–1909)." In Moshe Ma'oz, *Studies on Palestine in the Ottoman Period.* Jerusalem: Hebrew University Press. Pp. 190–210.

Filistin Meselesi—Sionizm Davasi (The Palestine Question–The Zionist Problem). 1334/1915. Istanbul: Matbaa-i Amire.

Filistin Ric'ati (The Retreat of Palestine). 1337/1918. Istanbul: Matbaa-i Askerine.

Filistin Risalesi (The Epistle of Palestine). 1331/1912. Jerusalem: n.p.

Firestone, Yaackov.
   1975a. "Crop-sharing Economies in Mandatory Palestine." *Middle East Studies* 11: 3–23.
   1975b. "Production and Trade in an Islamic Context." *International Journal of Middle East Studies* 6 (April): 185–209, 308–24.

Fishman, Robert.
1994. *Urban Utopias in the Twentieth Century: Ebenezer Howard, Frank Lloyd Wright, and Le Corbusier.* Cambridge, Mass: MIT Press.

Flapan, Simha.
1979. *Zionism and the Palestinians.* London: Croom Helm.

Foucault, Michel.
1984. *The Foucault Reader.* Ed. Paul Rabinow. London: Penguin.
1999. *Religion and Culture: Michel Foucault.* Ed. Jeremy R. Carrette. New York: Routledge.

Frank, Andre Gunder.
1998. *ReOrient: Global Economy in the Asian Age.* Berkeley: University of California Press.

Frankel, Raphael.
1981. "Ideological Motives in the Formation of Kivutza during the Period of the Second Aliya" (Hebrew). *Katedra* 18 (January).

Frankfurter, Felix.
1931. "The Palestine Situation Restated." *Foreign Affairs* (April).

Friese, Heidrun, and Peter Wagner.
2000. "When 'The Light of the Great Culture Problems Moves On': On the Possibility of a Cultural Theory of Modernity." *Thesis Eleven* 61 (May): 25–40.

Frisby, David.
1985. *Fragments of Modernity: Theories of Modernity in the Work of Simmel, Kracauer and Benjamin.* Cambridge: Polity Press.

Fund for a Free Jaffa in Kuwait.
1990. *Jaffa.* Kuwait: Sunduq Yafa al-Khairi fi al-Kuwait.

Galbetz, Shimon.
1940. *Kibbutz 'Ironi* (The Urban Kibbutz). Tel Aviv: n.p.

García Canclini, Néstor.
1995. *Hybrid Cultures: Strategies for Entering and Leaving Modernity.* Minneapolis: University of Minnesota Press.

Gavish, Dov.
1984. "Mivtzah Yafo 1936: Shipur Coloniali shel Pnei 'Ir" (Operation Jaffa 1936: A Colonial Urban Renewal Project). *Tadfis Mtokh Eretz Ysrael: Mehkarim be-Yediot Haaretz Veatikoteha* (Jerusalem) 17: 66–73.

Geddes, Patrick.
1925. *Town Plan for Tel Aviv.* Copies at TAMA and Tel Aviv University Department of Geography Map Room.
1972. *Patrick Geddes, Spokesman for Man and the Environment.* Ed. Marshall Stalley. New Brunswick: Rutgers University Press.

Gelvin, James.
n.d. "Trylon and Perisphere, Tower and Stockade: Zionism and the Representation of Jewish Palestine at the 1939–40 New York World's Fair." Unpublished manuscript.

Gerber, Haim.
1987. *The Social Origins of the Modern Middle East.* Boulder: Lynne Rienner.

Gered, Ronit, and Ephrat Zilberman.
1989. "Exposing an Urban Myth." In *City and Utopia: A Collection of Essays for 80 Years of Tel Aviv,* ed. Chaim Liski. Tel Aviv: Israeli Society for Publishing.

'Gharbiyyah, Izz ad-Din.
1975(?). *Qissat Madinat Yafa* (The Story of the City of Jaffa). Beirut: n.p.

al-Ghouri, Emile.
1972. *Filastin Abara Sittin Amat* (Palestine across Sixty Years). N.p.

Giddens, Anthony.
1971. *Capitalism and Modern Social Theory.* Cambridge, Mass.: Cambridge University Press.
1990. *The Consequences of Modernity.* Cambridge: Polity Press.

Giladi, Garon.
1984. "Jews and Arabs in the Early Days of Tel Aviv" (Hebrew). *Eden* 3: 77–90.

Gilbar, Gad, ed.
1990. *Ottoman Palestine, 1800–1914.* Leiden: E. J. Brill.

Ginsberg, Yona.
1993. "Revitalization of Two Urban Neighborhoods in Tel Aviv: Neve Tzedek and Lev Tel Aviv" (Hebrew). In David Nachmias and Gila Menahem, eds., *Mechkarei Tel Aviv-Yafo: Tahalikhim Chevratim ve-Mediniot Tzeiburit* (Social Processes and Public Policy in Tel Aviv-Yafo). Tel Aviv: Ramot Publishing House. Vol 1, pp. 147–66.

Glass, Joseph B., and Ruth Kark.
1991. *Sephardi Entrepreneurs in Eretz Israel: The Amzalak Family, 1816–1918.* Jerusalem: Magnes Press.

Glavanis, Kathy, and Pandeli Glavanis, eds.
1990. *The Rural Middle East: Peasant Lives and Modes of Production.* London: Zed Books.

Goadby, Frederic, and Moses Doukhan.
1935. *The Land Law of Palestine.* Jerusalem: n.p.

Golan, Arnon.
1995. "The Demarcation of Tel Aviv–Jaffa's Municipal Boundaries following the 1948 War: Political Conflicts and Spatial Outcome." *Planning Perspectives* 10: 383–98.

Gordon, A. D.
　1916. *The Nation and the Work*. N.p.

Gorny, Joseph.
　1984. "Utopian Elements in Zionist Thought." *Studies in Zionism* 5 (1): 19–27.
　1987. *Zionism and the Arabs, 1882–1948*. New York: Oxford University Press.

Graham-Brown, Sarah.
　1982. "The Political Economy of the Jabal Nablus, 1920–48." In Roger Owen, ed., *Studies in the Economic and Social History of Palestine in the Nineteenth and Twentieth Centuries*. Oxford: Oxford University Press. Pp. 88–176.
　1990. "Agriculture and Labor Transformation in Palestine." In Kathy Glavanis and Pandeli Glavanis, eds., *The Rural Middle East: Peasant Lives and Modes of Production*. London: Zed Books. Pp. 53–69.

Graicer, Iris.
　1982. "Workers Neighborhoods: Attempts at Shaping an Urban Landscape through Social Ideologies in Eretz Israel during the Mandate Period" (Hebrew). Ph.D. dissertation, Hebrew University.
　1990. "Social Architecture in Palestine: Conceptions in Working-Class Housing, 1920–1938." In Ruth Kark, ed., *The Land That Became Israel*. New Haven: Yale University Press. Pp. 287–307.

Gran, Peter.
　1996. *Beyond Eurocentrism: A New View of Modern World History*. Syracuse: Syracuse University Press.
　1998. *Islamic Roots of Capitalism: Egypt, 1760–1840*. Syracuse: Syracuse University Press.

Granovsky (Granott), A.
　1930. *Land Settlement in Palestine*. London: Victor Gollancz.
　1940. *Land Policy in Palestine*. New York: Hyperion.

Grant, Linda.
　2000. *When I Lived in Modern Times*. New York: Penguin.

Gregory, David, and John Ury, eds.
　1994. *Social Relations and Spatial Relations*. London: Macmillan.

Gross, Nahum.
　1982. *The Economic Development of Palestine during the British Mandate*. Tel Aviv: Maurice Faulk Institute.

Guerin, M.
　1868. *Description géographique, historique et archéologique de la Palestine*. Paris: L'imprimerie Impériale.

Guha, Ranajit.
　1982. *On Some Aspects of Historiography in Colonial India*. Subaltern Studies, 1. Ed. Ranajit Guha. Delhi: Oxford University Press.

Gutman, Nahum.
1989. *Shvil Klipot Hatapuzim* (The Path of the Orange Peels: Adventures from the First Days of Tel Aviv). Tel Aviv: Yavneh Press.

Habermas, Jürgen.
1985. *The Philosophical Discourse of Modernity.* Trans. Frederick G. Lawrence. Cambridge, Mass.: MIT Press.

Hacohen, Eliyahu.
1985. *Bkhol Zot Yesh Bah Mashehu: Shirei Hazemer Shel Tel Aviv* (The Songs of Tel Aviv, 1909–1984). Tel Aviv: Hevrat Dabir.

Hadani, Aver.
1950. *Sefer Hayuval Shel Aguda Pardes, 1900–1950* (Anniversary Volume for the Pardes Society, 1900–1950). Tel Aviv: n.p.

Haidar, Aziz.
1995. *On the Margins: The Arab Population in the Israeli Economy.* New York: St. Martin's Press.

Hall, Peter.
1988. *Cities of Tomorrow: An Intellectual History of Urban Planning and Design in the Twentieth Century.* New York: Blackwell.

Hamuda, Samih.
1985. *Masjid Hassan Bek* (Arabic). Tayibeh: Center for the Preservation of Arab Culture.

Hanin, R.
1983. "The Kibbutz: Origins of Designs and Principles of Design." M.Sc. thesis, Technion, Haifa.

Haretz, Dalyah, and Ozer Rabin.
1980, 1982. *Shirei Tel Aviv* (Poems and Songs of Tel Aviv). 2 vols. Tel Aviv: Hakibbutz Hameuhad.

Harlaftis, Gelina, and Vassilis Kardasis.
2000. "International Shipping in the Eastern Mediterranean and the Black Sea: Istanbul as a Maritime Centre, 1870–1910." In Şevket Pamuk and Jeffrey Williamson, eds., *The Mediterranean Response to Globalization before 1950.* London: Routledge. Pp. 233–65.

Harlap, Amiram.
1982. *New Israeli Architecture.* London: Associated University Press.

Harvey, David.
1973. *Social Justice and the City.* Baltimore: Johns Hopkins University Press.
1981. "The Urban Process under Capitalism: A Framework for Analysis." In Michael Dear and Allen Scott, eds., *Urbanization and Urban Planning in Capitalist Society.* London: Methuen. Pp. 91–121.
1989a. *The Condition of Postmodernity.* Cambridge: Blackwell.
1989b. *The Urban Experience.* Baltimore: Johns Hopkins University Press.
1996. *Justice, Nature, and the Geography of Difference.* Cambridge, Mass.: Blackwell.

"Hatt-ı Şerif of Gülhane." English translation in J. C. Hurewitz, *The Middle East and North Africa and World Politics: A Documentary Record.* Vol. 1. Pp. 269–71.

Hefner, Robert, ed.
    1998a. *Democratic Civility: The History and Cross-Cultural Possibility of a Modern Political Ideal.* New Brunswick: Transaction Publishers.
    1998b. "Multiple Modernities: Christianity, Islam, and Hinduism in a Globalizing Age." *Annual Review of Anthropology* 27: 83–104.

Heidborn, A.
    1912. *Droit public et administratif de l'empire Ottoman.* Vienna: C. W. Stern.

Herbert, Gilbert, and Silvina Sosnovsky.
    1993. *Bauhaus on the Carmel and the Crossroads of Empire.* Jerusalem: Yad Ben-Zvi.

Herzl, Theodor.
    [1902] 1941. *Old-New Land.* Trans. Lotta Levensohn. New York: Bloch.
    [1896] 1988. *The Jewish State.* Trans. and ed. Jacob Alkow. New York: Dover Books.

Heykal, Yusef.
    1988. *Ayyam al-Sabba* (Days of Juvenility). Amman: Dar al-Galil Press.

Hill, Moshe.
    1980. "Urban and Regional Planning in Israel." In Raphaella Bilski, ed., *Can Planning Replace Politics? The Israeli Experience.* The Hague: Martinus Nijhoff. Pp. 259–82.

Himadeh, Said.
    1938. *The Economic System in Palestine.* Beirut: American University of Beirut.

Hindus, Maurice.
    1949. *In Search of a Future: Persia, Egypt, Iraq and Palestine.* New York: Doubleday.

Hlaileh, S.
    1986. *The Impact of British Mandate Policy and Zionist Settlement on Landownership in Palestine, 1929–39* (Arabic). Birzeit: Birzeit University Press.

Höfert, Almut, and Armando Salvatore, eds.
    2000. *Between Europe and Islam: Shaping Modernity in a Transcultural Space.* Brussels: Peter Lang.

Holiday, C.
    1933. "Town and Country Planning in Palestine." *Palestine and Middle East Economic Magazine* 7–8: 290–92.

Hollier, Denis.
    1993. *Against Architecture: The Writings of Georges Bataille.* Trans. Betsy Wing. Cambridge, Mass.: MIT Press.

Holston, James.
1989. *The Modernist City: An Anthropological Critique of Brasilia.* Chicago: University of Chicago Press.
1999, ed. *Cities and Citizenship.* Durham: Duke University Press.

Holston, James, and Arjun Appadurai.
1999. "Cities and Citizenship." In James Holston, ed., *Cities and Citizenship.* Durham: Duke University Press. Pp. 1–20.

Hope-Simpson, John.
1971. "On the Employment of Arab Labour." In Walid Khalidi, ed., *From Haven to Conquest.* Beirut: Institute for Palestine Studies. Pp. 303–8.

Ichilov, Orit, and Andre Elias Mazawi.
1996. *Between State and Church: Life-History of a French-Catholic School in Jaffa.* Berlin: Peter Lang.

Ingersoll, Richard.
1994. *Munio Gitai Weinraub: Bauhaus Architecture in Eretz Israel.* Milan: Electa.

Islamoglu-Inan, Huri.
1988. *The Ottoman Empire and the World Economy.* Cambridge: Cambridge University Press.

Ishkantana, M. S.
1964. *Israr Sukut Yafa* (Secrets of the Collapse of Yafa). N.p.

Israel Museum, Tel Aviv, ed.
1990. *Tel Aviv Betzilumim: Haishur Harishon, 1909–1918* (Tel Aviv in Photographs: The First Decade, 1909–1918). Tel Aviv.

Israel Yearbook,
1995. Jerusalem: IBRT Publications.

Issawi, Charles,
1995. *The Middle East Economy: Decline and Recovery. Selected Essays.* Princeton: Princeton University Press.

Jacobs, Jane M.
[1961] 1993. *The Death and Life of the Great American Cities.* With a New Foreword by the Author. New York: Vintage Press.

Jacobs, Jane M., and Ruth Fincher.
1998. "Introduction." In Jane M. Jacobs and Ruth Fincher, eds., *Cities of Difference.* New York: Guilford Press. Pp. 1–25.

el-Jader, Adel Hamid.
1976. "The Policies of Granting Concessions to Large-Scale Operations in Palestine during the Mandate" (Arabic). *Shuun Philastiniyyah* 55: 185–205.

Jameson, Fredric.
1994. *Postmodernism, or the Cultural Logic of Late Capitalism.* Durham: Duke University Press.

2002. *A Singular Modernity: Essays on the Ontology of the Present.* New York: Verso.

Jewish Chamber of Commerce and Industry.
1932. *Haifa, City of the Future.* Haifa.

Jirvis, Sabri.
1976. *The Arabs in Israel.* Trans. Inea Bushnaq. New York: Monthly Review Press.

Johansen, Baber.
1981. "The All-Embracing Town and Its Mosques: al-Misr al-Gamiʿ." *Revue de l'Occident Musulman et de la Méditerranée* 32: 139–62.
1999. *Contingency in Sacred Law: Legal and Ethical Norms in the Muslim Fiqh.* Leiden: E. J. Brill.

John Hope Simpson Report.
1930.

al-Junaydi, Salim.
1988. *Al-Harakah al-Ummaliyyah fi Filastin, 1917–1985* (The Arab Labor Movement in Palestine, 1917–1985). Amman: n.p.

Kallner, D. H., and E. Rosenau.
1939. "The Geographical Regions of Palestine." *Geographical Review* 29: 61–80.

Kamen, Charles.
1991. *Little Common Ground: Arab Agriculture and Jewish Settlement in Palestine, 1920–1948.* Pittsburgh: University of Pittsburgh Press.

Kamp-Bandau, Irmel, Pe'era Goldman, and Edina Meyer-Meril.
1994. *Tel Aviv: Modern Architecture, 1930–1939.* Berlin: Ernst Wasmuth Verlag.

Kana'an, Ruba.
1998. "Jaffa and the Waqf of Muhammad Ağā Abū Nabbūt (1799–1831): A Study in the Urban History of an East Mediterranean City." D.Phil. dissertation, Oxford University.
2001a. "Two Ottoman *Sabils* in Jaffa (c. 1810–1815): An Architectural and Epigraphic Analysis." *Levant* 33: 189–204.
2001b. "Waqf, Architecture, and Political Self-Fashioning: The Construction of the Great Mosque of Jaffa by Muhammad Aga Abu Nabbut." *Muqarnas* 18: 120–40.

Kanaana, Sharif, and Lubna 'Abd al-Hadi.
1986. *Salamah.* Birzeit: Markaz al-Wathaiq wa-al-Abhath.

Kark, Ruth.
1988. "Cartographic Sources for the Study of Jaffa: From the Napoleonic Siege to the British Conquest." *Cartographic Journal* 25: 37–49.
1990a. *Jaffa: A City in Evolution, 1799–1917.* Jerusalem: Yad Ben-Zvi.
1990b. *The Land That Became Israel.* New Haven: Yale University Press.

1997. "The Raising and Lowering of the Ottoman Watch Towers in Jerusalem" (Hebrew). Unpublished manuscript.

Kark, Ruth, and Haim Gerber.
1982. "Land Registry Maps in Palestine during the Ottoman Period" (Hebrew). *Katedra* 22: 113–18.

Kark, Ruth, and Shimon Landman.
1980. "The Establishment of Muslim Neighbourhoods in Jerusalem, Outside the Old City, during the Late Ottoman Period." *Journal of the Palestine Exploration Quarterly* (July–December): 113–35.

Karl, Rebecca.
1999. "Exploring the Parameters of State Reform: From Mohammed Ali to the Young Turks in Late-Qing China." Paper presented at the conference "Shared Histories of Modernity," New York University, April 16–17.

Katz, Yossi.
1983. "Attempts to Purchase Sheikh Muwannis on the Eve of World War I" (Hebrew). In David Grossman, ed., *Bein Yarkon Veayalon: Mehkarim al Gush Dan Veemek Lod* (Between Yarkon and Ayalon: Studies on Gush Dan and the Lod Valley). Ramat Gan: Bar Illan University Publishing. Pp. 139–48.
1984a. "The Achuzat Bayit Company, 1906–1909: Founding Suggestions for the Establishment of Tel Aviv" (Hebrew). *Katedra* 33: 160–87.
1984b. "The Diffusion of the Urban Ideal: Tel Aviv Neighborhood as a Model for Planning for the Creation of Modern Suburbs in Eretz Israel at the End of the First Decade of the Century until World War I" (Hebrew). *Ofekim Begeographia* (November–December).
1986. "Ideology and Urban Development: Zionism and the Origins of Tel Aviv, 1906–14." *Journal of Historical Geography* 14 (4): 402–24.
1992. "Zionism and Urban Settlement: The Jewish National Funds Contribution to Urban Settlement prior to World War I." Lecture delivered to the Institute for Research on the History of the JNF, Land and Settlement. May.
1994. *The Business of Settlement: Private Entrepreneurship in the Jewish Settlement of Palestine, 1900–1914.* Jerusalem: Magnes Press.

Kauffmann, Richard.
1925(?). "Town-Planning of Jewish Settlements in Palestine in Accordance with the Plans of Richard Kauffmann." CZA, A175/96C.
1926. "Planning of Jewish Settlements in Palestine." *Town Planning Review* 12 (2): 93–116.
1933. "Workers Housing in Palestine." *Palestine & Middle East Economic Magazine* 7–8: 308–10.

Kayalı, Hasan.
1997. *Arabs and Young Turks: Ottomanism, Arabism, and Islamism in the Ottoman Empire, 1908–1918.* Berkeley: University of California Press.

Kaye, James.
2003. "There's No Place Like Home." In Ron Robin and Bo Strath, eds., *Homelands: Poetic Power and the Politics of Space*. Brussels: Peter Lang. Pp. 333–60.

Kaye, James, and Bo Strath, eds.
2000. *Enlightenment and Genocide: Contradictions of Modernity*. Philosophy and Politics, 5. Brussels: P.I.E.–Peter Lang.

Kayyali, A. W.
1978. *Palestine: A Modern History*. London: Croom Helm.

Kean, Rev. James.
1895. *Among the Holy Places: A Pilgrimage through Palestine*. London: T. Fisher Unwin.

Kedar, B. Z.
[1991] 1995. *Mabat va-ʿod mabat ʿal Erets-Yisraʾel: tatslume-avir mi-yemei milhemet ha-ʿolam ha-rishonah mul tatslumim benei zemanenu* (Looking Twice at the Land of Israel: Aerial Photographs of 1917–1918 and 1987–1991). Jerusalem: Yad Yitshak Ben-Tsvi.

Kellerman, Aharon.
1993. *Society and Settlement*. New York: State University of New York Press.

Khalidi, Raja.
1988. *The Arab Economy in Israel*. New York: Croom Helm.

Khalidi, Rashid.
1997. *Palestinian Identity: The Construction of Modern National Consciousness*. New York: Columbia Unversity Press.

Khalidi, Walid, ed.
1971. *From Haven to Conquest*. Beirut: Institute for Palestine Studies.
1991. *Before Their Diaspora: A Photographic History of the Palestinians, 1876–1948*. Washington, D.C.: Institute for Palestine Studies.
1992, ed. *All That Remains*. Washington, D.C.: Institute for Palestine Studies.

Khoury, Mounah.
1997. *Hasad az-Zakra* (The Harvest of Memory). Ed. and introd. Kaisar A. Afif. Saida: University Publishing Houses.

Kimmerling, Baruch.
1983a. *Zionism and Economics*. Cambridge: Cambridge University Press.
1983b. *Zionism and Territory*. Berkeley: University of California Press.

Kimmerling, Baruch, and Joel Migdal.
1994. *Palestinians: The Making of a People*. Cambridge, Mass.: Harvard University Press.

King, Anthony.
1991. *Urbanism, Colonialism, and the World-Economy*. New York: Routledge.

King, Ross.
  1996. *Emancipating Space: Geography, Architecture, and Urban Design.* New York: Guilford Press.

Kirby, Kathleen.
  1996. *Indifferent Boundaries: Spatial Concepts of Human Subjectivity.* New York: Guilford Press.

Kushner, David, ed.
  1986. *Palestine in the Late Ottoman Period: Political, Social and Economic Transformation.* Jerusalem: Yad Ben-Zvi.
  1995. *Moshel Hayyiti Beyerushalayyim: Ha'ir vehamehuz be'einav shel 'Ali Akram Bey, 1906–1908* (A Governor in Jerusalem: The City and Province in the Eyes of Ali Ekrem Bey, 1906–1908). Jerusalem: Yad Ben-Zvi.

Lane, Barbara Miller.
  1968. *Architecture and Politics in Germany, 1918–1945.* Cambridge, Mass.: Harvard University Press.

Laroui, Abdallah.
  [1967] 1982. *L'idéologie arabe contemporaine: Essai critique.* Paris: Maspero.

Lash, Scott.
  1999. *Another Modernity, a Different Rationality.* Oxford: Blackwell.

Lash, Scott, and John Ury.
  1994. *Economies of Signs and Space.* London: Sage.

Latour, Bruno.
  1988. *The Pasteurization of France.* Trans. Alan Sheridan and John Law. Cambridge, Mass.: Harvard University Press.
  1993. *We Have Never Been Modern.* Trans. Catherine Porter. Cambridge, Mass.: Harvard University Press.

Layish, Aharon.
  1966. "The Muslim Waqf in Israel." *Asian and African Studies* 2: 41–67.
  1975. "The *Sijil* of Jaffa and Nazareth: Sharia Courts as a Source for the Political and Social History of Ottoman Palestine. In Moshe Ma'oz, *Studies on Palestine in the Ottoman Period.* Jerusalem: Hebrew University Press. Pp. 525–32.

Le Corbusier.
  1947. *The City of Tomorrow and Its Planning.* Trans. F. Etchells. London: Architectural Press.

Lefebvre, Henri.
  1991. *The Production of Space.* Trans. Donald Nicholson-Smith. Cambridge: Blackwell.
  1995. *Introduction to Modernity: Twelve Preludes, September 1959–May 1961.* Trans. John Moore. New York: Verso.
  1996. *Writings on Cities.* Ed. and trans. Eleanor Kofman and Elizabeth Lebas. Oxford: Blackwell.

Lesch, Ann.

1979. *Arab Politics in Palestine, 1917–39.* London: Cornell University Press.

Levin, Michael.

1982. "East or West: Architecture in Israel, 1920–33." In Mark Scheps, ed., *The Twenties in Israeli Art.* Tel Aviv: Ariel Press. Pp. 223–40.

1984. *White City: International Style Architecture in Israel.* Tel Aviv: Tel Aviv Museum.

LeVine, Mark.

1993. "At What Cost: A History of the Rhetoric of Security in Zionist and Israeli Political Discourse." M.A. thesis, New York University.

1995. "The Discourse of Development in Mandate Palestine." *Arab Studies Quarterly* (winter): 95–124.

1998. "Conquest through Town-Planning: The Case of Tel Aviv." *Journal of Palestine Studies* 17 (1–2): 36–52.

1999a. "A Nation from the Sands? Architecture, Planning and the Evolution of National Identities in Jaffa and Tel Aviv, 1880–1948." *National Identities,* inaugural issue: 15–38.

1999b. "Overthrowing Geography, Re-Imagining Identity: A History of Jaffa and Tel Aviv, 1880 to the Present." Ph.D. dissertation, New York University.

2001. "The 'New-Old Jaffa': Tourism, Gentrification, and the Battle for Tel Aviv's Arab Neighborhood." In Nezar AlSayyad, ed. *Consuming Tradition, Manufacturing Heritage: Global Norms and Urban Forms in the Age of Tourism.* London: Spon. Pp. 240–72.

2002. "'Overthrowing Geography,' (Mis)Reading Modernity: Jaffa, Tel Aviv and the Struggle for Palestine's History, 1880–1948." *Mediterranean Studies Journal* 12 (1): 81–118.

Lichtblau, Klaus.

1995. "Sociology and the Diagnosis of the Times or: The Reflexivity of Modernity." *Theory, Culture and Society* 12: 25–52.

Light, Henry.

1818. *Travels in Egypt, Nubia, Holy Land, Mount Libanon and Cyprus, in the Year 1814.* London: Rodwell and Martin.

Liski, Chaim, ed.

1989. *City and Utopia: A Collection of Essays for 80 Years of Tel Aviv.* Tel Aviv: Israeli Society for Publishing.

Livingstone, D. N.

1995. "The Spaces of Knowledge: Towards a Historical Geography of Science." *Environment and Planning D: Society and Space* 13: 5–34.

Lockman, Zachary.

1993. "Railway Workers and Relational History: Arabs and Jews in British-Ruled Palestine." *Comparative Studies in Society and History* 35 (3): 601–27.

1996. *Comrades and Enemies: Arab and Jewish Workers in Palestine, 1906–48.* Berkeley: University of California Press.

Lortet, Louis.
1884. *Syrie d'aujourd'hui: Voyages dans la Phénicie, le Liban et la Judée, 1875–1880.* Paris: Librairie Hachette.

Luhmann, N., and Jürgen Habermas.
1971. *Theory of Society or Social Technology: What is Achieved by Systems Research?* Frankfurt: Suhrkamp.

Lustick, Ian.
1980. *Arabs in the Jewish State: Israel's Control of a National Minority.* Austin: University of Texas Press.

Maclean, Donna Landry, and Joseph P. Ward.
1999. *The Country and the City Revisited: England and the Politics of Culture, 1550–1850.* Cambridge: Cambridge University Press.

MacMillan's Guide to Palestine and Syria.
1910. London.

Makdisi, Ussama.
2000. *The Culture of Sectarianism: Community, History and Violence in Nineteenth-Century Ottoman Lebanon.* Berkeley: University of California Press.

Malak, Hana.
1993. *Al-Juzzur al-Yafiyyah* (Roots of Jaffa). Jerusalem: Privately published.
1996. *Zukrayat al-Ailat al-Yafiyyah: Bayna al-Madhi wa-l-Hadar* (Memoirs of Jaffan Families: Between the Past and Present). Jerusalem: Privately published.

Mamdani, Mahmood.
1996. *Citizen and Subject: Contemporary Africa and the Legacy of Late Colonialism.* Princeton: Princeton University Press.

Mandel, Ernest.
1997. *The Long Waves of Capitalist Development: A Marxist Interpretation.* London: Verso.

Mandel, Neville.
1976. *The Arabs and Zionism before World War I.* Berkeley: University of California Press.

Mann, Barbara.
1999. "Framing the Native: Esther Raab's Visual Poetics." *Israel Studies* 4 (1): 234–57.

Ma'oz, Moshe, ed.
1975. *Studies on Palestine in the Ottoman Period.* Jerusalem: Hebrew University Press.

Mardin, Şerif.
1989. *Religion and Social Change in Modern Turkey: The Case of Bediüzzaman Said Nursi*. Albany: State of New York Press.

Marx, Karl.
1967. *Capital: A Critique of Political Economy*. 3 vols. New York: International Publishers. [Vol. 1.]

Mas'ud, Ali Maliji,
1945. *Yafa: Mashrua Takhtit al-Madina* (Jaffa: Planning Scheme for the City). Jaffa.

Mazawi, Andre.
1988. "Spatial Expansion and Building Styles in Jaffa: Past and Present" (Hebrew). In A. Mazawi, ed., *Art and Building in the View of the Paintbrush* (Hebrew). Jaffa: Center for Arabic Culture.

Mazawi, Andre, and Makram Khoury Machool.
1991. "Spatial Policies in Jaffa, 1948–1990" (Hebrew). In Haim Liski, ed., *City and Utopia* (Hebrew). Tel Aviv: Israeli Society for Publishing.

Memmi, Albert.
[1965] 1991. *The Colonizer and the Colonized*. Boston: Beacon Press.

Menahem, Gila.
1994. "Urban Regimes and Neighborhood Mobilization against Urban Development: The Case of an Arab-Jewish Neighborhood in Israel." *Journal of Urban Affairs* 16 (1): 35–50.

Mendelsohn, Erich.
[1940] 1986. "Palestine and the World of Tomorrow." In Ita Hienze-Mühleib, *Erich Mendelsohn, Bauten und Projekte in Palästina (1934–1941)*. Munich: Taschenbuch.

Meroz, Tamar.
1978. *Tel Aviv-Yafo: Sipur Ha-'Ir* (Tel Aviv–Jaffa: A Story of a City). Tel Aviv: Dr. Ben-Zion Kaduri Fund.

Metzer, Jacob.
1998. *The Divided Economy of Mandatory Palestine*. Cambridge: Cambridge University Press.
2000. "Economic Growth and External Trade in Mandatory Palestine: A Special Mediterranean Case." In Şevket Pamuk and Jeffrey Williamson, eds., *The Mediterranean Response to Globalization before 1950*. London: Routledge. Pp. 363–80.

Metzer, Jacob, and Nachum Gross.
1985. "Jointly but Severally: Arab-Jewish Dualism and Economic Growth in Mandatory Palestine." *Journal of Economic History* 215: 327–45.

Migdal, Joel, ed.
1980. *Palestinian Society and Politics*. Princeton: Princeton University Press.

Mignolo, Walter D.
1995. *The Darker Side of the Renaissance*. Ann Arbor: University of Michigan Press.
2000. *Local Histories/Global Designs: Coloniality, Subaltern Knowledges, and Border Thinking*. Princeton: Princeton University Press.

Miller, Ylana.
1980. "Administrative Policy in Rural Palestine: The Impact of British Norms on Arab Community Life, 1920–48." In Joel Migdal, ed., *Palestinian Society and Politics*. Princeton: Princeton University Press. Pp. 124–45.

Mintz, Sidney W.
1995. *Sweetness and Power: The Place of Sugar in Modern History*. New York: Viking Press.

Mitchell, Timothy.
1988. *Colonising Egypt*. Berkeley: University of California Press, 1988.
1998. "Nationalism, Imperialism, Economism: A Comment on Habermas." *Public Culture* 10 (2): 417–24.
1999a. *Questions of Modernity*. Minneapolis: University of Minnesota Press.
1999b. "The Stages of Modernity." In Timothy Mitchell, ed., *Questions of Modernity*. Minneapolis: University of Minnesota Press. Pp. 1–34.

Monk, Daniel.
1997. "Autonomy Agreements: Zionism, Modernism and the Myth of a Bauhaus Vernacular." *AA Files*.
2002. *An Aesthetic Occupation: The Immediacy of Architecture and the Palestine Conflict*. Durham: Duke University Press.

Morgan, D. J.
1980. *The Official History of Colonial Development: The Origins of British Aid Policy, 1924–45*. London: Macmillan.

Müller, Johannes, and Bo Strath, eds.
1999. *Nationism and Modernity—An Outdated Relationship?* EUI Working Papers. HEC no. 99/1.

Mullin, John Robert.
1982a. "Ideology, Planning Theory and the German City in the Inter-War Years, Part I." *Town Planning Review* 53 (2): 115–30.
1982b. "Ideology, Planning Theory and the German City in the Inter-War Years, Part II." *Town Planning Review* 53 (3): 257–72.

Murrays Handbook for Travellers in Syria and Palestine.
1892. London.

Nachmias, David, and Gila Menahem, eds.
1993, 1997. *Mechkarei Tel Aviv-Yafo: Tahalikhim Chevratim ve-Mediniot Tzeiburit* (Social Processes and Public Policy in Tel Aviv–Jaffa). 2 vols. Tel Aviv: Ramot Publishing House.

Najjar, Aida Ali.
1975. "The Arabic Press and Nationalism in Palestine, 1920–1948." Ph.D. dissertation, Syracuse University.

Nandy, Ashis.
1988. *The Intimate Enemy: Loss and Recovery of Self under Colonialism.* Delhi: Oxford University Press.

Nanna, A.
1986. "The Sijjil as Source for the Study of Palestine during the Ottoman Period, with Special Reference to the French Invasion." In David Kushner, ed., *Palestine in the Late Ottoman Period: Political, Social and Economic Transformation.* Jerusalem: Yad Ben-Zvi. Pp. 351–62.

Naor, M., and Y. Ben-Artzi, eds.
1989. *The Development of Haifa, 1918–1948.* Jerusalem: Yad Ben-Zvi.

Newman, David.
1994. "The Functional Presence of an Erased Boundary: The Re-emergence of the Green Line." In Clive Schofild and Richard Schofield, eds., *The Middle East and North Africa: World Boundaries.* New York: Routledge. Vol. 2, pp. 71–98.

Newman, David, and Ghazi Falah.
1995. "The Spatial Manifestation of Threat: Israelis and Palestinians Seek a Good Border." *Political Geography* 14 (8): 689–706.
1998. "Transforming Ethnic Frontiers of Conflict into Political Frontiers of Peace." In Oren Yiftachel and Avinoam Meir, eds., *Ethnic Frontiers and Peripheries: Landscapes of Development and Inequality in Israel.* Boulder: Westview Press. Pp. 17–38.

Nidbah, Yosef.
1978. "The Capture and Sentencing of Hassan Bek" (Hebrew). *Katedra* 12: 175–83.

Nitzan-Shiftan, Alona.
1996. "Contested Zionism—Alternative Modernism: Erich Mendelsohn and the Tel Aviv Chug in Mandate Palestine." *Architectural History* 39: 147–80.

Oppenheimer, Franz.
1908. "Zur Theorie der Kolonisation." *Palestina.* Jahrgang V, 10, pp. 177–78.

Owen, Roger.
1970. "The Attitude of British Officials to the Development of the Egyptian Economy, 1882–1922." In Michael A. Cook, ed., *Studies in the Economic History of the Middle East.* New York: Oxford University Press. Pp. 485–500.
1982. *Studies in the Economic and Social History of Palestine in the Nineteenth and Twentieth Centuries.* Oxford: Oxford University Press.
1991. *The Role of Mushaa (Co-Ownership) in the Politico-Legal History of Mandatory Palestine.* SSRC Workshop on Law, Property and State Power. Buyukada.

Palestine Society Economic Bulletin.
  1922–26.

Pamuk, Şevket.
  1987. *The Ottoman Empire and European Capitalism, 1820–1913.* Cambridge: Cambridge University Press.
  2000a. *İstanbul ve Diğer Kentlerde: 500 yıllık Fiyatlar ve Ücretler, 1469–1998* (500 Years of Prices and Wages in Istanbul and Other Cities). Ankara: State Institute of Statistics.

Pamuk, Şevket, and Jeffrey Williamson, eds.
  2000b. *The Mediterranean Response to Globalization before 1950.* London: Routledge.

Pandolfo, Stefania.
  1999. "The Thin Line of Modernity: Some Moroccan Debates on Subjectivity." In Timothy Mitchell, ed., *Questions of Modernity.* Minneapolis: University of Minnesota Press. Pp. 115–47.

Peled, Yoav.
  2002. "No Arab Jews There: Shas and the Palestinians." Paper presented at Workshop on Socio-Religious Movements and the Transformation of Political Community: Israel, Palestine, and Beyond, University of California, Irvine, October.

Penslar, Derick.
  1990. "Zionism, Colonialism and Technocracy: Otto Warburg and the Committee for the Exploration of Palestine, 1903–7." *Journal of Contemporary History* 25: 143–60.
  1991. *Zionism and Technocracy: The Engineering of Jewish Settlement in Palestine, 1870–1918.* Bloomington: Indiana University Press.

Peres, Shimon.
  1993. *Ha-Mizrah ha-Tikhon he-hadash: misgeret ve-tahalikhim le-'idan ha-shalom.* Bene-Berak: Stimatski.

Phillipp, Thomas.
  2001. *Acre: The Rise and Fall of a Port City, 1730–1831.* New York: Columbia University Press.

Piot, Charles.
  1999. *Remotely Global: Village Modernity in West Africa.* Chicago: University of Chicago Press.

Pollock, Alex.
  1990. "Sharecropping in the North Jordan Valley: Social Relations of Production and Reproduction." In Kathy Glavanis and Pandeli Glavanis, eds. *The Rural Middle East: Peasant Lives and Modes of Production.* London: Zed Books. Pp. 95–141.

Pomeranz, Kenneth.
  2000. *The Great Divergence: China, Europe, and the Making of the Modern World Economy.* Princeton: Princeton University Press.

Pomeranz, Kenneth, and Steven Topik.
  1999. *The World That Trade Created: Society, Culture, and the World Economy, 1400 to the Present.* Armonk, N.Y.: M. E. Sharpe.

Porath, Yehoshua.
  1974. *The Emergence of the Palestinian-Arab National Movement, 1918–29.* London: Frank Cass.

Portugali, Juval.
  1988. "Nationalism, Social Theory and the Israeli/Palestinian Case." In R. J. Johnston, David Knight, and Eleonore Kofman, eds., *Nationalism, Self-Determination and Political Geography.* London: Croom Helm. Pp. 151–65.
  1993. *Implicate Relations: Society and Space in the Israeli-Palestinian Conflict.* Boston: Kluwer.
  1994. "The Taming of the Shrew Environment." *Science in Context* 7 (2): 307–26.

Poulantzas, Nicos.
  2001 *State, Power, Socialism.* Introd. Stuart Hall. Trans. Patrick Camiller. London: Verso.

Prakash, Gyan, ed.
  1995. *After Colonialism.* Princeton: Princeton University Press.

Prochaska, David.
  1990. *Making Algeria French: Colonialism in Bone, 1870–1920.* Cambridge: Cambridge University Press.

Quataert, Donald.
  1994. "The Age of Reforms." in Suraiya Faroqui, Bruce McGowan, Donald Quataert, and Sevket Pamuk, eds., *An Economic and Social History of the Ottoman Empire.* Vol. 2: *1600–1914.* Cambridge: Cambridge University Press. Pp. 759–943.

Quijano, Anibal.
  1992. "Colonialidad y modernidad-racionalidad." In H. Bonilla, ed., *Los Conquistadores.* Bogotá: Tercer Mundo. Pp. 437–47.
  1995. "Modernity, Identity and Utopia in Latin America." In John Beverley, Michael Aronna, and Jose Oviedo, eds., *The Postmodernism Debate in Latin America.* Durham: Duke University Press. Pp. 202–16.
  1998. "The Colonial Nature of Power and Latin America's Cultural Experience." In R. Briceñño-Leon and H. R. Sonntag, eds., *Sociology in Latin America (Social Knowledge: Heritage, Challenges, Perspectives).* Proceedings of the Regional Conference of the International Association of Sociology, Venezuela. Pp. 27–38.

Raafat, Samir.
  1994. *Maadi, 1904–1962: Society and History in a Cairo Suburb.* Cairo: Palm Press.

Rabinow, Paul.
  1989. *French Modern: Norms and Forms of the Social Environment.* Cambridge, Mass.: MIT Press.

Rabinowitz, Dan.

1992. "'An Acre Is an Acre Is an Acre?' Differentiated Attitudes to Social Space and territory on the Jewish-Arab Urban Frontier in Israel." *Urban Anthropology* 21 (1): 67–89.

1997. *Overlooking Nazareth: The Ethnography of Exclusion in Galilee.* Boston: Cambridge University Press.

1999. "The Frontiers of Urban Mix: Palestinians, Israelis, and Settlement Space." In Oren Yiftachel and Avinoam Meir, eds., *Ethnic Frontiers and Peripheries: Landscapes of Development and Inequality in Israel.* Boulder: Westview Press. Pp. 69–85.

Ram, Hana.

1970. "The Sources for the Beginnings of Tel Aviv." *Shenaton Muze'on Ha'aeretz* (Eretz Israel Museum Yearbook). Pp. 79–85.

1978. "The Beginnings of Working the Land by Jewish Hands in the Jaffa Region." *Katedra* 6: 20–37.

1996. *Hayishuv Hayehudi Beyafo Beet Hachadasha: Mekehilah Sefardit Lemarkaz Tzioni* (The Jewish Community in Jaffa: From Sephardic Community to Zionist Center). Tel Aviv: Carmel Publishing.

Ram, Uri.

1993. "The Colonization Perspective in Israeli Sociology: Internal and External Comparisons." *Journal of Historical Sociology* 6 (3): 327–50.

1995. *The Changing Agenda of Israeli Sociology: Theory, Ideology and Identity.* Albany: State University of New York Press.

Ratner, E.

1933. "Architecture in Palestine." *Palestine & Middle East Economic Magazine* 7–8: 293–296.

1950. "Will Israel Have a National Style of Architecture?" *Technion Year Book.* Haifa. Pp. 234–37.

Rekhess, Elie.

1992. *Hamiut Haaravi Beyisrael: Bein Komunizm Leleumiut Aravit* (The Arab Minority in Israel: Between Communism and Arab Nationalism, 1965–1991). Tel Aviv: Kibbutz Hameuhad.

Revusky, Abraham.

1945. *Jews in Palestine.* New York: Bloch.

Ritter, Carl.

1866. *A Comparative Geography of Palestine and the Sinaitic Peninsula.* Trans. Willam Gage. Edinburgh: T. T. Clark.

Rodinson, Maxime.

1973. *Israel: A Colonial-Settler State?* New York: Monad/Pathfinder Press.

Rogan, Eugene.

1999. *Frontiers of the State in the Late Ottoman Empire: Transjordan, 1850–1921.* Cambridge: Cambridge University Press.

Rokah, Yitzchak.

1965. "Pardesim msaprim: Halka (het/lamed/kaf/heh) shel tel-aviv-yafo batoldot hapardasanot" (Orchards Speak: The Plot of Tel Aviv–Yafo in the History of the Orchards). *Shenaton Muze'on Ha'aretz* (Eretz Israel Museum Yearbook) 7: 31–39.

1972. *Vatikim Msaprim* (Tales of the Old Yishuv). Ramat Gan: Massada Press.

Ruppin, Arthur.

1969. "The Foundation of Tel Aviv." In Yosef Aricha, ed., *Shishim Shana Leir Tel Aviv* (Sixty Years of the City of Tel Aviv). Tel Aviv: Tel Aviv Municipality, Education Department. Pp. 37–66.

1971. *Memoirs, Diaries, Letters.* London: Wiedenfeld and Nicolson.

Saba', Shlomo.

1977. *Ho 'Ir, Ho Em* (The Romance of Tel Aviv–Yafo). Tel Aviv: American-Israeli Publishing Society.

Sack, Robert.

1986. *Human Territoriality: Its Theory and History.* Cambridge: Cambridge University Press.

Sa'di, Ahmad, H.

1996. "Minority Resistance to State Control: Towards a Re-analysis of Palestinian Political Activity in Israel." *Social Identities* 2 (3): 395–412.

Said, Edward.

1978. *Orientalism.* New York: Pantheon.

1982. "Yeats and Decolonization." In Barbara Kruger and Phil Mariani, eds., *Remaking History.* Seattle: Bay Press. Pp. 3–29.

1993. *Culture and Imperialism.* New York: Knopf/Random House.

1995. "Secular Interpretation, the Geographical Element, and the Methodology of Imperialism." In Gyan Prakash, ed., *After Colonialism.* Princeton: Princeton University Press. Pp. 22–39.

Salvatore, Armando, and Almut Höfert.

2000. "Beyond the Clash of Civilizations: Transcultural Politics between Europe and Islam." In Almut Höfert and Armando Salvatore, eds., *Between Europe and Islam: Shaping Modernity in a Transcultural Space.* Brussels: Peter Lang. Pp. 13–38.

Samaddar, Ranabir.

1995. "Territory and People: The Disciplining of Historical Memory." In Partha Chatterjee, ed., *Texts of Power: Emerging Disciplines in Colonial Bengal.* Minneapolis: University of Minnesota Press. Pp. 167–200.

Samuel, Maurice, ed. and trans.

1932. *The Plough Woman: Records of the Pioneer Women of Palestine.* New York: Nicholas L. Brown.

Sassen, Saskia.

1998. *Globalization and Its Discontents: Essays on the New Mobility of People and Money.* New York: Norton.

Schiller, Eli.
1981a. "Jaffa in the Nineteenth Century" (Hebrew). *Kardom* 15: 33–39.
1981b. "Orchards and Farms of Jaffa" (Hebrew). *Kardom* 15: 42–47.

Schnell, Yitzhak.
1993. "The Formation of an Urbanite Life Style in Central Tel Aviv" (Hebrew). In David Nachmias and Gila Menahem, eds., *Mechkarei Tel Aviv–Yafo: Tahalikhim Chevratim ve-Mediniot Tzeiburit* (Social Processes and Public Policy in Tel Aviv–Jaffa). Tel Aviv: Ramot Publishing House. Pp. 41–60.
1994. *Perceptions of Israeli Arabs: Territoriality and Identity.* Brookfield: Avebury Press.

Schnell, Yitzhak, and Iris Graicer.
1996. "The Revitalization of Tel Aviv's Inner City." *Israel Affairs* 3 (1): 104–27.

Scholch, Alexander.
1982. "European Penetration and the Economic Development of Palestine, 1856–82." In Roger Owen, ed., *Studies in the Economic and Social History of Palestine in the Nineteenth and Twentieth Centuries.* Oxford: Oxford University Press. Pp. 10–87.
1993. *Palestine in Transformation, 1856–1882: Studies in Social, Economic and Political Development.* Trans. William C. young and Michael C. Gerrity. Washington, D.C.: Institute for Palestine Studies.

Schumpeter, Joseph.
1976. *Capitalism, Socialism and Democracy.* London: Allen and Unwin.

Schwartz, Horacio.
1995. "Tel Aviv: From Patrick Geddes' Utopian Social City to the International City of Late Capititalism." In *ACSA European Conference, 1995 (Lisbon), Geography of Power.* Washington, D.C.: Association of Collegiate Schools of Architecture. Pp. 107–8.

Segal, Rafi, and Eyal Weizman.
2003. *A Civilian Occupation: The Politics of Israeli Architecture.* London: Babel/Verso.

Segev, Tom.
1986. *1949: The First Israelis.* New York: Free Press.

Semyonov, Moshe, Noah Lewin-Epstein, Hadas Mendel.
1997. "The Labor Market Position of Arab Residents of Tel Aviv–Jaffa: A Comparative Perspective" (Hebrew). In David Nachmias and Gila Menahem, eds., *Mechkarei Tel Aviv–Yafo: Tahalikhim Chevratim ve-Mediniot Tzeiburit* (Social Processes and Public Policy in Tel Aviv–Jaffa). Tel Aviv: Ramot Publishing House. Pp. 191–210.

Seyfettin, M.
1971. *Eski Harflere Basilmis Turkçe Eserler Katalögu* (Catalog of Books in Ottoman Script). Istanbul.

Shabtai, Yaakov.
1985. *Past Continuous*. Trans. Dalya Bilu. Philadelphia: Jewish Publication Society.

Shachar, Arieh.
1971. "Jaffa." In *Encyclopaedia Judaica*. Vol. 9. Jerusalem: Keter Publishing House. Pp. 1249–58.
1997. "The Planning of Urbanized Areas: A Metropolitan Approach and the Case of the Tel Aviv Region" (Hebrew). In David Nachmias and Gila Menahem, eds., *Mechkarei Tel Aviv–Yafo: Tahalikhim Chevratim ve-Mediniot Tzeiburit* (Social Processes and Public Policy in Tel Aviv–Jaffa). Tel Aviv: Ramot Publishing House. Pp. 305–20.

Shachar, Nissim.
1997. *Yafa: Fi Muftariq al-Tariq* (Jaffa: At a Fork in the Road). Jaffa: Rabita Publications.

Shafir, Gershon.
1989. *Land, Labor, and the Origins of the Israeli-Palestinian Conflict, 1882–1914*. New York: Cambridge University Press.
1996. *Immigrants and Nationalists: Ethnic Conflict and Accommodation in Catalonia, the Basque Country, Latvia, and Estonia*. Albany: State University of New York Press.

Shamir, Ronen.
1999. "We Have Never Been Colonized: Reflections on the Zionist Experience in Palestine." Paper presented at the conference, The Uncertain State of Palestine: Futures of Research, University of Chicago, February 18–20.

Sharabi, Hisham.
1977(?). *al-Jamr wa-l-Ramad, Zikrayat Muthaqqaf Arabi* (Embers and Ashes: Arabic Cultural Memoirs). Cairo: Ibn Rushd Publishing.
1993. *Suwar al-Madhi: Sirah Zatiyyah* (Pictures of the Past: An Autobiography). Beirut: Beisan Publishing.

Sharon, Arieh.
1976. *Kibbutz + Bauhaus: An Architect's Way in a New Land*. Tel Aviv: Massada Publishing.

Shavit, Ya'akov, and Gid'on Biger.
2001. *Hahistoriah shel Tel-Aviv: Meshchunot le 'ir (1909–1936)* (The History of Tel Aviv. Vol. 1: The Birth of a Town [1909–1936]). Tel Aviv: University of Tel Aviv.

Shavitz, Yosef.
1947. *Haaravim Beeretz Yisrael* (The Arabs in Eretz Israel). Tel Aviv: Workers Library.

Shchori, Ilan.
1990. *Chalom She-Hafakh Lekhrakh: Tel Aviv, Leidah ve-Tzmichah Hair She-Holidah Medinah* (The Dream Turned to a Metropolitan). Tel Aviv: Avivim Press.

n.d. "The Influence of European Architectural Styles on the Built Vision of the Founding of Tel Aviv."Article, TAMA Library.

Shehadeh, Raja.
1982. *The Third Way.* New York: Quartet Books.
2002. *Stranger in the House: Coming of Age in Occupied Palestine.* South Royalton, Vt.: Steerforth Press.

Sherman, A. J.
1997. *Mandate Days: British Lives in Palestine, 1918–1948.* New York: Thames and Hudson.

Shloosh, Yosef Eliahu.
1931. *Parashat Chai, 1870–1930* (Chapters of My Life, 1870–1930). Tel Aviv: n.p.

Shmuelevitz, Aryeh.
1975. "The Archives of Tel Aviv–Jaffa as a Source for the Final Years of the Ottoman Empire in Palestine." In Moshe Ma'oz, ed., *Studies on Palestine in the Ottoman Period.* Jerusalem: Hebrew University Press. Pp. 548–61.

Shohat, Ella.
1994. *Unthinking Eurocentrism: Multiculturalism and the Media.* London: Routledge.

Shorske, Carl E.
1980. *Fin-de-Siècle Vienna: Politics and Culture.* New York: Alfred A. Knopf.

Shure, Natan.
1987. "Reshitah shel Tel Aviv" (The Beginnings of Tel Aviv). *Ariel* 48–49: 63–81.

Sidqi, Najati.
n.d. *al-Akhwat al-Hazinat* (The Sad Sisters). Cairo: Dar al Maarifa Bi-Misr.

Slyomovics, Susan.
1998. *The Object of Memory: Arab and Jew Narrate the Palestinian Village.* Philadelphia: University of Pennsylvania Press.

Smeliansky, W.
1907. "Die Jdische Bevoeklerung in Jaffa." *Palestina.* Jahrgang IV, pp. 22–52.

Smilansky, David,
1981. *'Ir Noledet* (A Town Is Born). Ed. Yosi Katz. Tel Aviv: Defense Ministry Publications.

Smilanksy, Moshe.
1930. *Jewish Colonization and the Fellah: The Effect of Jewish Land Settlement in Palestine on Native Rural Property and Agrarian Development in General.* Tel Aviv: n.p.

Smith, Barbara.
1993. *The Roots of Separatism in Palestine.* Syracuse: Syracuse University Press.

Smith, Pamela Ann.
1984. *Palestine and the Palestinians: 1876–1983*. New York: St. Martin's Press.

Smok, Nitza.
1994. *Batim Min Hachol* (Houses from the Sand). Tel Aviv: Ministry of Defense.

Smooha, Sami.
1979. *Israel: Pluralism and Conflict*. Berkeley: University of California Press.

Soja, Edward W.
1989. *Postmodern Geographies*. New York: Verso.

Stein, Kenneth.
1980. "Legal Protection and Circumvention of Rights of Cultivators in Mandatory Palestine." In Joel Migdal, ed., *Palestinian Society and Politics*. Cambridge: Cambridge University Press. Pp. 233–60.
1984. *The Land Question in Palestine, 1917–39*. Chapel Hill: University of North Carolina Press.

Stein, Rebecca L.
2002. "'First Contact' and Other Israeli Fictions: Tourism, Globalization, and the Middle East Peace Process." *Public Culture* 38: 515–43.

Stendel, Ori.
1996. *The Arabs in Israel*. Brighton: Sussex Academic Press.

Sufian, Sandy.
1999. Healing the Land and the Nation: Malaria and the Zionist Project in Mandatory Palestine, 1920–1947." Ph.D. dissertation, New York University.
Forthcoming. "Anatomy of the 1936–1939 Revolt: Images of the Body in Political Cartoons of Mandatory Palestine." *Journal of Palestine Studies*.

Swedenburg, Ted.
1995. *Memories of Revolt: The 1936–1939 Rebellion and the Palestinian National Past*. Minneapolis: University of Minnesota Press.

Swirsky, Shlomo.
1989. *Israel: The Oriental Majority*. London: Zed Books.

Szakolczai, Arpad.
2000. *Reflexive Historical Sociology*. London: Routledge.

Tamari, Salim.
1982. "Factionalism and Class Formation in Recent Palestinian History." In Roger Owen, ed., *Studies in the Economic and Social History of Palestine in the Nineteenth and Twentieth Centuries*. Carbondale: Southern Illinois University Press. Pp. 177–202.
1990. "From the Fruits of Their Labor: The Persistence of Sharetenancy in the Palestinian Agrarian Economy." In Kathy Glavanis and Pandeli Glavanis,

eds., *The Rural Middle East: Peasant Lives and Modes of Production*. London: Zed Books. Pp. 70–94.

1994. "Problems of Social Science Research in Palestine: An Overview." *Current Sociology* 42 (2): 69–86.

1996a. *Compilation of Reminiscences Collected by Salim Tamari of Various Former Residents of Jaffa*. E-mail to Mark LeVine, August 1996.

1996b. "From Emma Bovary to Hasan al-Banna: The Cultural Dynamics of Small Towns in an Eastern Mediterranean Society." Unpublished manuscript.

2003. "Bourgeois Nostalgia and Exilic Narratives." In Ron Robins and Bo Strath, eds., *Homelands: Poetic Power and the Politics of Space*. Brussels: Peter Lang. Pp. 61–71.

Tamari, Salim, and Rema Hammami.

1997. "The Populist Paradigm in Palestinian Sociology." *Contemporary Sociology* 26 (3): 275–79.

1998. "Virtual Returns to Jaffa." *Journal of Palestine Studies* 27 (4): 64–79.

al-Tamimi, Rafiq, and Muhammad Bahjat.

1979. *Vilayet Beirut* (District of Beirut). Beirut: Dar Lahad Khater.

Taqqu, Rachelle.

1980. "Peasants into Workmen: Migration and the Arab Village Community under the Mandate." In Joel Migdal, ed., *Palestinian Society and Politics*. Cambridge: Cambridge University Press. Pp. 261–86.

al-Tarawnah, Mohammad Salem.

1997. "Qada Yafa fi al-Ahad al-Uthmani, 1281–1333A.H./1864–1914" (Qada Jaffa during the Period 1281–1333A.H./1864–1914). Ph.D. dissertation, University of Jordan.

Tel Aviv Municipality.

1967. *Tel Aviv at Sixty* (Hebrew). Tel Aviv.

1974. *Tel Aviv: People and Their City*. Tel Aviv.

1997. *Statistical Yearbook, 1997*. Tel Aviv.

Teveth, Shabtai.

1985. *Ben-Gurion and the Palestinian Arabs: From Peace to War*. New York: Oxford University Press.

Thalmann, Naftali.

1990. "Introducing Modern Agriculture into Nineteenth-Century Palestine: The German Templars." In Ruth Kark, ed., *The Land That Became Israel*. New Haven: Yale University Press. Pp. 90–104.

Tibi, Bassam.

1995. "Culture and Knowledge: The Politics of Islamization of Knowledge as a Postmodern Project? The Fundamentalist Claim to De-Westernization." *Theory, Culture and Society* 12: 1–24.

Tolkovsky, Samuel.

1924. *The Gateway of Palestine: A History of Jaffa*. London.

1963. The Space of Tel Aviv–Jaffa in Descriptions of European Travelers in the Sixteenth–Nineteenth Centuries (Hebrew). *Teva ve-Aretz* 4: 327–30.

Toprak, Zafer.
1982. *Türkiye'de "Milli iktisat" (1908–18)*. Ankara: Yurt Yayinlar.

Trancik, Roger.
1986. *Finding Lost Space: Theories of Urban Design*. New York: Van Nostrand Reinhold.

Troen, S. Ilan.
1991. "Establishing a Zionist Metropolis: Alternative Approaches to Building Tel Aviv." *Journal of Urban History* 17: 10–36.

Tucker, Judith.
1998. *In the House of the Law: Gender and Islamic Law in Ottoman Syria and Palestine*. Berkeley: University of California Press.

Tuma, Amin.
1973. *Judhur al-qadiyah al-filistaniyah* (The Roots of the Palestinian Problem). Beirut: PLO Research Center.

Turner, Bryan.
1984. *Capitalism and Class in the Middle East: Theories of Social Change and Economic Development*. London: Heineman Educational Books.

Tzafrir, Daron.
1994. *Jaffa between the Second and Third Millennium* (Report of the City Engineer) (Hebrew). Tel Aviv: Office of the City Engineer.
1995. *Yafo: Mavet Leajami* (Jaffa: A Glance at Adjami. An Architectural Profile). Tel Aviv: City Engineers Department.

UNESCO.
2003. Report of 27th Session of ICOMOS, Case no. 1096, March, pp. 56–61.

Vardi, Aharon.
1929. *Tel Aviv: Ir Naflaot* (Tel Aviv: City of Wonders). Tel Aviv: For the Book Publishing.

Vico, Giambattista.
[1774] 1968. *The New Science of Giambattista Vico*. Trans. Thomas Goddard Bergin and Max Harold Fisch. Ithaca: Cornell University Press.

Vilneh, Zeev.
1965. *Tel Aviv–Yafo* (Tel Aviv–Jaffa). Jerusalem: Ahiaver Publishing.

Wagner, Peter.
1999. "The Resistance That Modernity Constantly Provokes: Europe, America and Social Theory." *Thesis Eleven* 58 (August): 35–58
2000. "Plural Interpretations of Modernity: The Social Sciences in the U.S. and in Europe." Paper presented at the 12th International Conference of Europeanists, Council of European Studies, Chicago, March 31.

2001. "Modernity: One or Many?" In Judith Blau, ed., *Blackwell Companion to Sociology*. Oxford: Blackwell. Pp. 30–42.

Watson, Sophie, and Katherine Gibson, eds.
1995. *Postmodern Cities and Spaces*. Cambridge: Blackwell, 1995.

Weiss, Akiva Arieh,.
1967. *Rishotah Shel Tel Aviv* (The Beginning of Tel Aviv). Tel Aviv: Ayanot Press.

Westwood, Sali, and John Williams, eds.
1997. *Imagining Cities, Scripts, Signs, Memory*. New York: Routledge.

Wilkins, Charles.
n.d. "Jaffa in the Early Tanzimate Period, 1840–61." Unpublished manuscript.

Williams, Raymond. 1973. *The Country and the City*. Oxford: Oxford University Press.

Williamson, Jeffrey.
2000. "Real Wages and Relative Factor Prices in the Mediterranean, 1500–1948." In Şevket Pamuk and Jeffrey Williamson, eds., *The Mediterranean Response to Globalization before 1950*. London: Routledge. Pp. 45–75.

Wokler, Robert.
2000. "The Enlightenment Project on the Eve of the Holocaust." In James Kaye and Bo Strath, eds., *Enlightenment and Genocide: Contradictions of Modernity*. Philosophy and Politics, 5. Brussels: P.I.E.–Peter Lang.

Woodiwiss, Anthony.
1997. "Against 'Modernity': A Dissident Rant." *Economy and Society* 26 (1): 1–21.

Wright, Gwendolyn.
1991. *The Politics of Design in French Colonial Urbanism*. Chicago: University of Chicago Press.

Yafeh, A. B.
1980. "Writers and Literature in Little Tel Aviv."In *The First Twenty Years: Literature and Art in Little Tel Aviv, 1909–29* (Hebrew). Tel Aviv: Tel Aviv Fund for Literature and Art. Pp. 11–50.

Yahav, Dan.
1990a. *Komunot Betel Aviv Beshanot Hashloshim Vehaarbaim* (Communes in Tel Aviv in the 1930s and 1940s). Ramat Efal: Yad Tabenkin Press.
1990b. "Komunat-Habiluim Beabu-Kabir (1882–1884)." (The Biluim Commune in Abu Kabir [1882–1884]). *Shedamot*, pp. 9–12.
1994. "Efal—An Urban Kibbutz: 1947–1951." *Kibbutz Trends* 16: 43–48.

Yazbak, Mahmoud.
1998. *Haifa in the late Ottoman Period, 1864–1914: A Muslim Town in Transition*. Leiden: E. J. Brill.

Yehoshua, Ya'acov.

　1969. "Tel Aviv bera'i ha'itonot ha'aravit behamesh hashanim hari'shonot Lavasada (1909–1914)" (Tel Aviv as Seen by the Arabic Press during the First Years of Its Existence (1909–1914). *Hamizrah Hehadash* 19 (3): 218–22.

Yekuti'eli-Cohen, Edna.

　1990. *Tel Aviv Kamakom Besipurim, 1909–1939* (Tel Aviv as a Place in Stories, 1909–1939). Tel Aviv: Bureau of Education and Culture, Tel Aviv Fund for Literature and Art.

Yiftachel, Oren.

　1995a. "The Dark Side of Modernism: Planning as Control of an Ethnic Minority." In Sophie Watson and Katherine Gibson, eds., *Postmodern Cities and Spaces*. Cambridge: Blackwell. Pp. 216–42.

　1995b. "The Internal Frontier: Territorial Control and Ethnic Relations in Israel." *Regional Studies* 30 (5): 493–508.

　1997. "Nation-building or Ethnic Fragmentation? Frontier Settlement and Collective Identities in Israel." *Space and Polity* 1 (2): 149–70

　1997. *Shomrim Al Hakerem* (Watching Over the Vineyard: The Example of Majd el-Krum). Raanana: Institute for Israeli Arab Studies,

　2002. "Between National and Local: Political Mobilization of Mizrahim in Israeli Development Towns." Paper presented at Workshop on Socio-Religious Movements and the Transformation of Political Community: Israel, Palestine, & Beyond, University of California, Irvine, October.

Yiftachel, Oren, and Avinoam Meir, eds.

　1998. *Ethnic Frontiers and Peripheries: Landscapes of Development and Inequality in Israel*. Boulder: Westview Press.

Yoskovitz, Baruch.

　1997. "Urban Planning in Tel Aviv–Yafo: Past, Present, and Future" (Hebrew). In David Nachmias and Gila Menahem, eds., *Mechkarei Tel Aviv–Yafo: Tahalikhim Chevratim ve-Mediniot Tzeiburit* (Social Processes and Public Policy in Tel Aviv–Yafo). Tel Aviv: Ramot Publishing House. Pp. 347–64.

Zaid, Mahmud.

　1974. *Taarikh Filastin Min 1914–1948* (History of Palestine, 1914–1948). Beirut: n.p.

Zalmona, Yigal.

　1998. "To the East?" In Yigal Zalmona and Tamar Manor-Friedman, curators, *To the East—Orientalism in the Arts in Israel*. Jerusalem: Israel Museum. Pp. ix–xv.

Ze'eman, Yehoshua.

　1929. *The Eretz Israeli Economy in Numbers* (Hebrew). Tel Aviv: Davar.

Ziman, Joshua.

　1946. *The Revival of Palestine*. New York: Sharon Books.

Zureik, Elia.

　1979. *The Palestinians in Israel: A Study in Internal Colonialism*. Boston: Routledge.

Index

Italicized page numbers refer to illustrations, maps, and tables.

Reasonable concerns

① Lack of attention/presence yet expectation that I remain attentive and present.

② This is Taiwan.

③ I am scared of Judy.

④ I am too sensitive, Judy says I can't take a joke.

⑤ My childhood trauma and how it affects me.

Text: 10/13 Aldus
Display: Aldus
Indexer: Sharon Sweeney